D0852981

The RAMPAGING HERD

The

RAMPAGING
HERD

*A Bibliography of Books and Pamphlets
on Men and Events in the Cattle Industry*

by RAMON F. ADAMS

NORMAN
UNIVERSITY OF OKLAHOMA PRESS

Books by RAMON F. ADAMS

Cowboy Lingo (Boston, 1936)
Western Words: A Dictionary of the Range, Cow Camp, and Trail (Norman, 1944)
Charles M. Russell, the Cowboy Artist (with Homer E. Britzman) (Pasadena, 1948)
Come an' Get It: The Story of the Old Cowboy Cook (Norman, 1952)
Six-Guns & Saddle Leather: A Bibliography of Books and Pamphlets on Western Outlaws and Gunmen (Norman, 1954)
The Rampaging Herd: A Bibliography of Books and Pamphlets on Men and Events in the Cattle Industry (Norman, 1959)

The publication of this volume has been aided by a grant from the FORD FOUNDATION.

LIBRARY OF CONGRESS CATALOG CARD NUMBER: 59–7957

Dedicated

with high admiration and warm good personal regards to Mr. William A. Blakley, attorney, rancher, businessman, civic developer, and above all, a sincere friend. Without his support and assistance this work would perhaps have never been completed.

Acknowledgments

My ACKNOWLEDGMENTS of help in compiling this work are similar to but more extensive than those recorded in my *Six-Guns and Saddle Leather*: similar because I was collecting material for both works at the same time; more extensive because I made a research trip through the eastern half of the United States after the first bibliography was published.

Taking up my indebtedness in chronological order, I wish to thank Professor Edward Everett Dale, then curator of the Phillips Collection, University of Oklahoma, and Mrs. Elsie D. Hand, librarian of the Oklahoma Historical Society, Oklahoma City, who both rendered valued assistance.

I wish, early in these acknowledgments, to thank Professor Walter Prescott Webb and the Texas State Historical Association for the grant-in-aid from the Rockefeller Foundation which made it possible for me to make my first visits to various states and institutions, as well as a number of private libraries. In Colorado and Wyoming, I wish to thank Miss Ina T. Aulls, then of the Western History Room, Denver Public Library, but now retired; Mrs. Agnes Wright Spring, a friend of long standing, then of the same department, but now of the Colorado Historical Society and State Historian, for digging out many books for me. Also of the Denver Public Library is Mrs. Eulalia Chapman, of the Bibliographical Center, who has my gratitude for her aid in locating certain rare titles. Mr. LeRoy R. Hafen, of the Colorado Historical Society, and his librarian, Miss Frances Shea, were also very helpful. I must also thank my friends Fred A. Rosenstock and Don Bloch, both of Denver, for allowing me to examine their private libraries and for their encouragement. Mr. and Mrs. John J. Lipsey, of Colorado Springs, in whose hospitable home I spent several days, also lent assistance.

My thanks are also extended Miss Mae Cody, of the Wyoming State Library, Cheyenne; in Laramie, at the University of Wyoming, I received much valuable help from Miss Mary E. Marks, librarian, and especially from Miss Lola Homsher, then archivist of the Western Room, and her able assistant, Miss Henryetta Berry. In this library was located the collection of the Wyoming Stock Growers' Association.

In Arizona, I wish to thank Mr. Frederick Cromwell, librarian of the University of Arizona, Tucson, and his assistants for allowing me to search through the bookshelves of this institution; Mr. Mulford Winsor, director of the State Library and Archives of Arizona, Phoenix; and Mrs. Alice B. Good, librarian, for giving me free access to their shelves.

In Austin, Texas, I would like to express my gratitude to Miss Harriett Smithers, archivist, Texas State Library, ever willing to help the researcher; to Mr. E. W. Winkler, University of Texas Library; and to Miss Llerena Friend, of the Texas Collection, for her untiring effort to locate for me new acquisitions not yet catalogued by that institution.

I especially wish to acknowledge my indebtedness to my good friends, Mr. J. Frank Dobie, Mr. Frank Caldwell, and the late Captain R. W. Aldrich of the Texas Rangers, for allowing me the freedom of their private libraries. They all possess outstanding libraries and a willingness to help others.

There are many people to thank for their unlimited help while I was in California. First I wish to give thanks to my friend Jake Zeitlin for his suggestion and help in my securing a grant-in-aid from the Huntington Library, of San Marino, California. My especial thanks, too, to the late Robert Glass Cleland, and Mr. Godfrey Davies of the committee; Mr. John E. Pomfret, director of the library; Mr. Leslie E. Bliss, librarian; Mr. Carey Bliss, assistant curator of rare books; Miss Mary Isabel Fry, reference librarian and registrar; Mrs. Margaret L. Packer, supervisor of the Rare Book Reading Room; and Mr. French Fogel for the many favors extended me during my six weeks' stay.

Aside from the members of the staff of the Huntington Library, my greatest benefactor in California was my friend and an outstanding collector of books, Loring Campbell. He not only went to a great deal of trouble to dig out books for my examination, but cheerfully transported me over wide areas of Los Angeles County to inspect the holdings of rare-book dealers and private libraries. Among these latter was the library of my good friend Robert J. Woods, of Hollywood, in which I spent a most pleasant day and where I found some unusual and rare books.

My friend Paul W. Galleher, of the Arthur H. Clark Book Company, Glendale, was most kind in helping me locate certain books and in allowing me to take his valuable time discussing points of reference in first editions, and I shall ever be in his debt for acting as my cordial host at two dinners given by The Westerners of Los Angeles.

I also wish to thank my friend of long standing, Glen Dawson, of the Dawson Book Shop, Los Angeles, for the many favors extended me and for transportation to places not easily accessible. My gratitude also to Mrs. Ella L. Robinson, librarian of the Southwest Museum Library, Los Angeles, who let me spend the day searching the shelves of that institution. My thanks are also extended to Mrs. Margaret D. Ulridge, University of California Library, Berkeley, and to Mrs. Eleanor A. Bancroft, associate to the director of the Bancroft Library. Thanks are also due my friends Merrill Kitchen, of Stockton, and W. W. Robinson, of Los Angeles.

In my home town of Dallas, Texas, my undying gratitude is extended to that benevolent friend, Mr. William A. Blakley, for financial aid for research in the East. Without his aid this work would never have been finished. Also my gratitude to Mr. Robert A. Wilson, who acted as our ambassador. In Dallas, too, my friend and fellow collector, Dan Ferguson, kindly brought me books from his office to read and examine and allowed me every freedom in examining the contents of his home library.

In Topeka, Kansas, my thanks to Mr. Nyle H. Miller, secretary of the Kansas State Historical Society, whose wonderful library was one of the high spots of my eastern trip. I am also grateful to Mr. Miller for driving me to Kansas City for a meeting of The Westerners Posse of that city, where I, together with Homer Croy, was an honored guest. My thanks also to Miss Alberta Pantle, acting librarian, and Miss Portia Anderson, cataloguer of this same institution. My thanks, too, to Mr. Harry Lose, of the Hotel Jayhawk, Topeka, for inviting me to examine his private library.

Miss Laura Neiswanger, librarian, Kansas Collection, Kansas State University, Lawrence, Kansas, and Miss Sandra Updike, assistant librarian, of the same department, were indeed kind and co-operative.

In Kansas City, Missouri, my good friend Martin E. Ismert, an outstanding collector, allowed me the privilege and freedom of his home for a whole week to examine his most unusual collection. Also in this city I am grateful to Brice J. Mansfield for his hospitality, for allowing me to examine his library, and for transporting me over a goodly portion of Missouri to show me the Jesse James country.

Mrs. Viola A. Perotti, curator of the Snyder Memorial Library, University of Kansas City, gave of her time and knowledge to assist my research in this institution, where I found a few books not seen anywhere else. Mr. Alan W. Farley, of Kansas City, Kansas, was also kind enough to let me spend some time in his private collection, for which I thank him.

My thanks to the entire staff of the Library of Congress, Washington, D. C., where I spent many days, both in the general library and in the rare-book room. My good friend and a well-known book collector, Jeff C. Dykes, of College Park, Maryland, took me to his home as a guest, and not only drove me to points of interest in Washington and its vicinity, but dug out many, many books packed away in cartons in an attic—quite a labor in the heat of the summer, but done with his characteristic enthusiasm—and his courtesies will never be forgotten. In Washington, also, I had the pleasure of examining the private library of Mr. Frederic G. Renner, an opportunity I deeply appreciate.

Continuing north, I spent a week examining the Philip A. Rollins Collection in the Rare Book and Special Collection Department, Princeton University. For a most pleasant and profitable week there I wish to thank Mr. Howard C. Rice, Jr., chief of staff, and his staff assistant, Mr. Lucien Bergeron, Jr., for their many favors in making this one of the most memorable stops of my trip.

In New York, it was a pleasure to receive the willing assistance of Mr. Leon Weidman, first assistant of the American History Room, New York Public Library, and of Miss Shirley L. Spranger, reference assistant in the same department, as well as Mrs. Maude D. Cole, of the Rare Book Department of this excellent library. Also in New York, my thanks to Mr. R. W. G. Vail, director of the New York Historical Society, and Miss Geraldine Beard, a member of his staff, for the trouble she went to in helping my work there to be a success.

Also while in New York I visited such old friends and rare-book dealers as the Eberstadts and Peter Decker, and William F. Kelleher, of Cliffside Park, New Jersey, in whose home I had the pleasure of being a guest. All these dealers have helped me for years in locating rare and valuable additions to my own library.

One of the most enjoyable occasions of this trip was being invited to be a luncheon guest of Mr. Thomas W. Streeter, of Morristown, New Jersey, and being driven there by my artist friend and the illustrator of some of my books, Nick Eggenhofer. We spent some time examining Mr. Streeter's unusual book collection, for he is one of the really great book collectors of America.

At New Haven, Connecticut, I spent a most profitable week working in the Coe Collection at Yale University, and for this privilege I wish to thank its curator, Mr. Archie Hanna, and the assistant librarian, Mrs. Ruth Smith. Mrs. Smith was indeed kind and helpful, and the time I spent with her, both at the library and at our daily luncheons, will always be a bright spot.

Mr. Robert H. Haynes, assistant librarian and curator of the Theodore

Roosevelt Collection, Harvard University, Cambridge, was most kind in helping me locate books in this collection. In Boston, I must thank Mr. Mike J. Walsh, of the Goodspeed Book Shop, for his valuable suggestions as we chatted in his office. In this city, too, I wish to thank Mr. Walter Muir Whitehill, director of the Boston Athenaeum Library, and his assistants, and also the staff of the Boston Public Library.

Mr. Clarence S. Brigham, well-known authority on rare books and director of the American Antiquarian Society Library, of Worcester, Mass., and his assistant, Miss Mary E. Brown, were most gracious and co-operative. I appreciate indeed the interest Mr. Brigham expressed in my work.

Others who have been helpful and who bring back tender memories as close personal friends include the late Walter S. Campbell (Stanley Vestal), of the University of Oklahoma, and the late Floyd B. Streeter, librarian at Fort Hayes Kansas State College. No less appreciated is the help rendered by such good friends as the late Edward N. Wentworth, of Chesterton, Indiana, Don Russell, of Chicago, Carter Taylor, of Fort Worth, Texas, and Fred Cotten, of Weatherford, Texas, all collectors of books of various kinds.

On my journeys from coast to coast I found that librarians and book collectors everywhere were happy and eager to extend every help. This makes the many hours spent in research a pleasant memory, and to express my appreciation in mere words hardly seems adequate. Yet I trust that these words will suffice to make all of these good people realize that my appreciation is sincere and deeply felt. The many new friendships made and the old ones renewed certainly made this work pleasant and worth while, even though it was hard and exacting. So, once more, thanks to all, and may your reward be richly abundant.

RAMON F. ADAMS

Dallas, Texas
October 1, 1959

Contents

Illustrations

[*These pages are reproduced through the courtesy of the Phillips Collection,
University of Oklahoma Libraries.*]

Introduction

FIRST THE INDIAN, then the fur trader, and then the buffalo hunter—all were a part of the early American West. All, too, were destructive forces, yet seemingly necessary to the evolution of a savage land.

It remained for the cattleman to bring some semblance of civilization into this raw country. The extermination of the buffalo helped tame the Indian and preserved the grass for the cowman's cattle. The cowman, in his turn, ever pushed his way westward, softening the savage land for the nester and the settlements which shortly followed. He created his own code of etiquette and laws as he came. Perhaps they were rough, but they were always just, and he respected them more than he did the written laws of the land.

It is not surprising that when he trailed his herds to the end of the railroads in Kansas, his unique character and picturesque calling attracted the attention of the whole nation. Reporters from the East emphasized his wildness, his unique mode of dress, and his colorful occupation. His coming also proved to easterners that his habitat could not be the desert country they had thought it to be.

This brought more and more settlers, and as the railroads extended westward, his cattle trails moved with them, on account of the crowding of farmers and settlements. It was not long until the barbed wire fence and complaints about the Spanish fever left behind by his herds put a stop to his trailing altogether. Yet despite the fact that the day of the open range and the cattle trail ended long ago, the cowboy still, to this day, remains the most picturesque character upon the American scene and a favorite with novelists and other writers of romance.

One cannot realize how many books and pamphlets were written about range cattle and the men who herded them until he delves into the libraries of the nation in search of them. Every Western state and territory, and often each county in a territory, issued pamphlets emphasizing the many attractions of the district for the land-seeker, most often stressing its advantages for cattle raising. Every Western railroad also distributed literature to attract settlers to the new territory served by their rails. Such brochures were published in large editions each year and given to prospective settlers for the asking, yet because of the pulp paper upon which they were printed and their lack of interest and value to the average recipient, few of them have been preserved.

Like all bibliographies, this one is far from complete. Although I did research in many important libraries from coast to coast, I could not, through lack of both time and money, visit them all. I do believe, however, that the items herein listed are representative, some of them being the most important in this field. Many books on cattle, both old and new, have come into my possession since closing the entries in this volume. My regret at the omissions is salved by the thought that others, not yet seen, would take their place, so I am content to realize that neither myself nor anyone else could ever get them all.

I have purposely omitted books on cowboy songs, cowboy poetry, dairying, cattle diseases, breeding, and such subjects (except a representative few of the two latter subjects). These, I feel, do not belong to the range cattle industry, and would only add to the printing cost.

I found in my search many books and pamphlets written by well-educated Englishmen and Scotsmen. Wealthy men and companies of both England and Scotland invested heavily in the cattle business of America in the 1870's and 1880's. They sent men over to manage their interests, many of whom turned out to be good cattlemen. Many of them, too, later wrote books about their experiences, and these became important additions to our literature of the West. Such men as John Clay, William French, Jack Culley, Reginald Aldridge, J. M. Pollock, Peter Wright, and many others have written excellent books which have now become very scarce. Others who came to America and followed the life of a cowboy and whose pamphlets have now become rare collectors' items include Bob Grantham Quickfall and a man who wrote under the pseudonym of "Bunny."

In all humbleness I acknowledge the many unavoidable omissions; yet, in spite of the incompleteness of this volume, if it can be of help to any one librarian, book collector, or antiquarian book dealer, I will feel that my many years of research and hard work has been amply rewarded.

R. F. A.

Table of Abbreviations

adv.	advertisement, advertisements
cm.	centimeters
co.	company
col.	colored
dec.	decorated
diagr., diagrs.	diagram, diagrams
dif.	differs, different
ed.	edition, editor, edited
facsm., facsms.	facsimile, facsimiles
fold.	folding, folded
front.	frontispiece
illus.	illustrated, illustration, illustrations
imt.	imitation
l.	leaf, leaves
ltd.	limited
n.d.	no date
No., Nos.	number, numbers
n.p.	no place
OP.	out of print
p.	page, pages
pict.	pictorial
p.l.	preliminary leaf, leaves
port., ports.	portrait, portraits
prelim.	preliminary
pseud.	pseudonym
pub.	publisher, published
pub. device	publisher's device
t.p.	title page
Vol., Vols.	volume, volumes

The RAMPAGING HERD

A Bibliography of Books and Pamphlets
on Men and Events in the Cattle Industry

1 ABBOTT, E. C. ("TEDDY BLUE"). We pointed them north; recollections of a cowpuncher, by E. C. Abbott ("Teddy Blue") and Helena Huntington Smith. Illustrated with drawings by Ross Santee and photographs. New York, Toronto, Farrar & Rinehart, inc., [1939]. Pict. cloth. OP.
xv p., 1 l., 3–281 p. front. (map), illus., ports., map. 22 cm.
Index, p. 271–281.
Half title; first edition, "F R" in device on copyright p.
Republished in 1955 by the University of Oklahoma Press with new illustrations by Nick Eggenhofer.

This is one of the best books of recent years depicting cowboy life. The hero was a well-known character of his day.

2 ABBOTT, NEWTON CARL. Montana in the making, by N. C. Abbott....
Billings, Montana, Gazette printing company, 1931. Cloth. Scarce.
4 p.l., 3–520 p. front. (map), illus., plates, ports., maps, facsm. 20 cm.
Appendix, p. 504–514; index, p. 515–520.
Map on end papers (dif.).

Although this book went through several editions, it is now difficult to find a copy. Written as a textbook, it contains much material on the Montana cattle industry and has chapters on cattle brands.

3 ABERNATHY, JOHN R. (JACK). "Catch-'em-alive Jack"; the life and adventures of an American pioneer, by John R. Abernathy. New York, Association press, 1936. Cloth. OP.
4 p.l., 9–224 p. front. (port.), plates, ports., 20.8 cm.

This is a reissue, with extensive variations in the text, of the author's *In Camp with Roosevelt*. It is the story of an unusual man who made a business of capturing wolves with his bare hands. It contains several chapters on ranch life.

4 ———. In camp with Roosevelt; or, the life of John R. (Jack) Abernathy, Oklahoma City, John R. (Jack) Abernathy, author. Oklahoma City, published by the Times-Journal publishing co., [1933]. Pict. cloth. Scarce.
2 p.l., [9]–279 p. front. (port.), plates, (1 fold.), ports. 20 cm.

[3]

5 ——. A son of the frontier, by John Abernathy ("Catch-'Em-Alive Jack"). With an introduction by Kermit Roosevelt. ₁New York, Association press₁, 1935. Stiff pict. wrappers. OP.

49 ₁1₁ p. front. (port. verso front wrapper), plate (recto back wrapper). 23 cm.

6 ABNEY, H. A. Life and adventures of L. D. Lafferty; being a true biography of one of the most remarkable men of the great Southwest, from an adventurous boyhood in Arkansas, through a protracted life of almost unparalleled sufferings and hairbreadth escapes upon the frontier of Texas. By H. A. Abney, of Rockport, Texas. New York, H. S. Goodspeed & co., ₁1875₁. Dec. cloth. Scarce.

4 p.l., ₁15₁–219 p. front. (port.), plates, ports. (all with tissues). 19 cm.

This copy seen in the Rollins Collection, Princeton University.

7 ADAIR, CORNELIA. My diary: August 30th to November 5th, 1874. By Cornelia Adair (for private circulation). Bath, Fyson and co., ltd., printers and stationers, 1918. Cloth. Excessively rare.

3 p.l., ₁3₁–125 p. front., 2 ports. 19 cm.

The diary of an English lady who spent part of her life on the famous JA Ranch of Texas, which her husband owned with Charles Goodnight.

8 ADAMS, ANDY. The log of a cowboy; a narrative of the old trail days, by Andy Adams. Illustrated by E. Boyd Smith. . . . Boston and New York, Houghton Mifflin and co., 1903. Pict. cloth.

5 p.l., 387 ₁1₁ p. front. (with tissue), 5 plates, map. 19.2 cm.
Half title; first edition has publication date under imprint on title page.

Reprinted under imprint of Riverside Bookshelf Series in 1927.

6 p.l., 324 p. front. (col.), illus., plates (col.). 22 cm.
Illustrations by R. Farrington Ewell.

Reprinted many times since. Andy Adams wrote six other books, all fiction, and this book is considered fiction by most people, but Adams told Philip A. Rollins that "its only fictional elements are the names of the characters and the ascribing to a single drive occurrences which actually were divided among several." It has become a classic as a picture of trail driving, and no bibliography on cattle would be complete without it.

9 ADAMS, F. G. The homestead guide describing the great homestead region in Kansas and Nebraska and containing the homestead, preemption and timber bounty laws, and a map of the country described. Waterville, Kansas, F. G. Adams, compiler and publisher, 1873. Three-quarter leather. Rare.

5 p.l., ₁13₁–312 p. plates, map, tables. 22.3 cm.
Full page adv. scattered throughout.

Has a chapter on stock raising.

[4]

10 ADAMS, JAMES TRUSLOW. The epic of America, by James Truslow Adams. With illustrations. Boston, Little, Brown and company, 1931. Cloth. OP.

viii p., 2 l., [3]–433 p. illus. 24 cm.
Index, p. [419]–433.
Half title; pub. device; untrimmed.

Has a chapter on cattle.

11 ——. Album of American history. Volume II, 1853–1893. James Truslow Adams, editor-in-chief. R. V. Coleman, managing editor, Atkinson Dymock, art director. New York, Charles Scribner's sons, [1946]. Dec. cloth.

xi, 435 p. illus., plates, facsms. 28.5 cm.

Mostly a picture book, but has some material on cattle, Dodge City, the cattle trails, and Joseph McCoy.

12 ADAMS, RAMON F. Come an' get it; the story of the old cowboy cook, by Ramon F. Adams, with drawings by Nick Eggenhofer. Norman, University of Oklahoma press, [1952]. Cloth.

xi p., 2 l., 5–170 [1] p. illus., 4 full-p. plates. 22.2 cm.
Half title; illus. double t.p.; philosophical sayings at top of each chapter; each chapter preceded by article of rhyming prose by Carter ("Tex") Taylor; "First edition" on copyright p.

The first and only book devoted to this unique and interesting character.

13 ——. Cowboy lingo, [by] Ramon F. Adams. With illustrations [by Nick Eggenhofer]. Boston, Houghton Mifflin company, 1936. Cloth. Scarce.

x p., 1 l., [3]–257 p. front., illus. 19.7 cm.
Index, p. [241]–257.
Half title; pub. device; first edition, "1936" under imprint.

The first book devoted entirely to the language of the cowman.

14 ——. Western words: a dictionary of the range, cow camp, and trail, by Ramon F. Adams. Norman, University of Oklahoma press, 1944. Cloth.

xiv p., 1 l., 3–182 p. 22.2 cm.
Half title; double t.p.; cross indexed; philosophical sayings at head of each alphabetical division.
Double column.

The first and only dictionary of the speech of the cattle country.

15 ——. The best of the American cowboy. Compiled and edited by

[5]

Ramon F. Adams, with drawings by Nick Eggenhofer. Norman, University of Oklahoma Press, [1957]. Cloth.

xiv p., 1 l., 3–289 p. illus. 23.6 cm.
Half title; illus. double t.p.; "First edition" on copyright p.

An anthology of selections from some of the rarer books about cattle.

16 ——, and BRITZMAN, HOMER E. Charles M. Russell, the cowboy artist. A biography by Ramon F. Adams and Homer E. Britzman, with bibliographical check list by Karl Yost. Pasadena, Calif., published by Trail's End publishing co., inc., [1948]. Cloth.

xii p., 3 l., 350 p. front. (col.), 111 plates (12 col.), 37 chapter headings from pen and ink drawings by Charles M. Russell, facsm. 23.6 cm.
Index, p. 327–335; bibliographical check list, p. 339–350.
Col. illus. end papers from Russell's oil painting "Where Great Herds Come to Drink"; "First edition" on copyright p.

Also published in a two-volume collector's edition limited to 600 sets.
Vol. I same as trade edition, except bound in three-quarter leather.
Vol. II, Charles M. Russell, the cowboy artist. A bibliography by Karl Yost, with a note by Homer E. Britzman and Frederic G. Renner. Pasadena, Calif., the Trail's End publishing co., inc., [1948]. Three-quarter leather.

8 p.l., 19–218 p. front. (facsm.), 20 illus. 23.6 cm.
Index, p. 205–218; blank pages at end for notes.
Vol. II also published separately.
Both volumes boxed and issued with envelope of separate sets of colored illustrations.

Also issued in twenty-five sets bound in saddle leather and initialed in metal for recipient and signed by authors.

17 ADAMS, W. L. Oregon as it is; its present and future, by a resident of twenty-five years, being a reply to inquiries. By W. L. Adams. Portland, Oregon, "Bulletin" steam book and job printing room, 1873. Wrappers. Rare.

[3]–62 [2] p. 22.2 cm.
Leaf of errata at end.

Deals with the cattle industry of Oregon.

18 ADAMSON, ARCHIBALD R. North Platte and its associations, by Archibald R. Adamson. . . . North Platte, Nebraska, the Evening Telegraph, [1910]. Cloth. Scarce.

3 p.l., 241 [3] p. front. (port.), plates, ports. 19 cm.
Table of contents last 3 unnumbered pages.

Contains some cattle material of that section and gives a short biographical sketch of John Bratt, a well-known early-day cattleman.

19 ADLER, STAN. Sagebrush strokes; yarns of the Southwestern range, by Stan Adler. Decorations by the author. Bisbee, Arizona, F. A. McKinney, printing, [1936]. Pict. wrappers. OP.

2 p.l., 7–70 [1] p. front., illus., plates, ports. 22.8 cm.
Last page labeled "Index" is the table of contents.

20 AGEE, FRED B., and CUENIN, JOSEPH M. History of Cochetopa National Forest. Compiled by Fred B. Agee, forest supervisor, and Joseph M. Cuenin, forest ranger.... Salida, Colorado, 1924. Wrappers. (Cover title). Scarce.

[44] p. (no pagination). 22.5 cm.
Double column.

Chapters on cattle and grazing in the national forest.

21 AIKMAN, DUNCAN (ED.). The taming of the frontier. El Paso, Ogden, Denver, St. Paul, San Francisco, Portland, Kansas City, Cheyenne, San Antonio, Los Angeles. By ten authors. Edited by Duncan Aikman. New York, Minton, Balch & company, 1925. Cloth. OP.

xv p., 1 l., 3–319 p. front., plates. 21.5 cm.
Half title; pub. device.

The chapter on Cheyenne gives some information on cattle and the Johnson County War.

22 ALDERSON, NANNIE T. A bride goes West, by Nannie T. Alderson and Helena Huntington Smith; drawings by J. O'H. Cosgrave II. New York, Toronto, Farrar & Rinehart, inc., [1942]. Cloth. OP.

vii p., 1 l., 3–273 p. illus., chapter headings. 21 cm.
Half title; first edition, "F R" in device on copyright p.; untrimmed.

23 ALDRIDGE, REGINALD. Life on a ranch; ranch notes in Kansas, Colorado, the Indian Territory, and northern Texas, by Reginald Aldridge. With illustrations. New York, D. Appleton and co., 1884. Stiff wrappers. Scarce.

vi p., 1 l., 227 p. front., 3 plates. 18 cm.
4 p. adv. at end.
(On cover: Appleton's Popular Series). Seldom seen in original wrappers.

London edition, Longmans, Green and co., 1884, has title: "Ranch notes in Kansas, Colorado, the Indian Territory and Northern Texas." Pict. cloth.

3 p.l., 227 [16] p. front. (with tissue), plates. 18.8 cm.
Half title; last 16 p. adv.

This is one of the standard books on cattle. The author was a partner of Benjamin S. Miller in the ranching business in the states and territories mentioned.

24 ALEXANDER, GEORGE S. Nebraska: its resources, prospects and advantages of immigration. . . . ₍By₎ George S. Alexander. . . .₍N. p.₎, published by order of the State Board of Immigration, 1870. Pict. wrappers. Rare.

₍3₎–17 p. tables. 22.5 cm.
Double column.

25 ALLAN, JAMES THOMAS. Central and western Nebraska, and the experiences of its stock growers. Published by the Union Pacific co.'s land department. Omaha, Nebraska, prepared and compiled by J. T. Allan. Omaha Republican printing house, 1883. Pict. wrappers. (Cover title). Scarce.

16 p. 21 cm.

One of the pamphlets issued by the railroads in the early days to induce settlers to move west and go into the cattle business. Most of these are now scarce and have become collector's items.

26 ———. Nebraska and its settlers. What they have done and how they do it. Its crops and people. . . . Prepared and compiled by J. T. Allan. Omaha, Neb., Herald printing house, 1883. Pict. wrappers. Rare.

₍3₎–16 p. map. 22 cm.
Map on verso of front wrapper.

27 ALLDREDGE, EUGENE PERRY. Cowboys and coyotes, by Eugene Perry Alldredge. ₍Nashville, Tenn., Marshall & Bruce co., 1945₎. Cloth. OP.
v, 7–184 p. illus., plates. 23.5 cm.
Illus. chapter headings.

28 ALLEN, JOHN HOUGHTON. San Juan, by Houghton Allen, with 8 illustrations by Harold Bugbee, and a frontispiece by the author. ₍San Antonio, 1945₎. Stiff wrappers. Label pasted on. OP.
3 p.l., 3–53 ₍1₎ p. front., illus. 25.4 cm.
Untrimmed; colophon: "This edition limited to 420 copies, twenty signed by the author and artist . . . ."

29 ———. Southwest, by John Houghton Allen. Illustrated by Paul Laune. Philadelphia and New York, J. B. Lippincott company, ₍1952₎. Pict. cloth.
3 p.l., 9–220 p. front., illus., plates. 20.7 cm.
Half title; illus. chapter headings; "First edition" on copyright p.

30 ALLEN, JOHN TAYLOR. Early pioneer days in Texas, by J. Taylor Allen. ₍Dallas, Texas, printed by Wilkinson printing co., 1918₎. Stiff wrappers. OP.

3 p.l., 267 p. plates, ports. 19 cm.
Leaf of errata tipped in.

A chapter on cowboy life.

31 ALLEN, JULES VERNE. Cowboy lore, by Jules Verne Allen. . . . Illustrated by Ralph J. Pereida. San Antonio, Naylor printing company, 1933. Pict. cloth.

xiii, 1 p., 1 l., 165 [8] p. front., illus., port., facsm., music. 23.8 cm.
Half title; "Biographical sketch of the author," p. viii–ix.
8 p. adv. at end.

Limited edition of 200 preceded trade edition.

32 ALLEN, L. A. Our cattle industry; past, present, and future. Address of Mr. L. A. Allen before the State Board of Agriculture at Topeka, Kansas, January 10th, 1896. Stapled. (Caption title). Rare.

16 p. 22.3 cm.

33 ALLEN, LEWIS FALLEY. American cattle; their history, breeding, and management, by Lewis Falley Allen. New York, O. Judd and co., [1868]. Cloth. OP.

528 p. front., illus. 19.5 cm.

Republished by Taintor bros. and co., 1868; republished in a revised edition and "brought up to date," New York, Orange Judd co., 1884. Cloth.

11 p.l., [21]–528 p. front., illus., plates. 19 cm.

34 ———. History of the short-horn cattle; their origin, progress, and present condition, by Lewis Falley Allen. . . . Buffalo, N. Y., published by the author, 1872. Cloth. OP.

x p., 2 l., [13]–266 p. front., illus., plates. 23.3 cm.
Index, p. 265–266.
Republished in 1878 and 1883.

35 ———. Improvements of native cattle (in U. S. Dept. of Agriculture Report, 1886). Washington, 1867.

p. 294–320. plates XVIII–XXII. 23 cm.

36 ———. The shorthorn breed of cattle considered with reference to the beef and dairy interests of the U. S. (in U. S. Dept. of Agriculture Report of 1875). Washington, 1876.

p. 416–426. plates LVIII–LIX. 23 cm.

37 ALLEY, B. F. Linn County, Oregon, descriptive and resources, its cities and towns, by B. F. Alley. . . . Albany, Oregon, Royce & Hibler electric power print, [1889]. Wrappers. Rare.

2 p.l., [16]–111 p. 22 cm.
Last 36 p. adv.; adv. verso front wrapper; adv. recto and verso back wrapper.

38 ALLEY, JOHN. Memories of roundup days, by John Alley. A souvenir reprint prepared by the University of Oklahoma Association, alumni organization of the University, in response to numerous requests for additional copies of this article, which appeared in *The Sooner Magazine* for January, 1934. ₁Norman, University of Oklahoma press, 1934₁. Wrappers. Scarce.

2 p.l., 5–20 p.   port., map.   18.7 cm.

39 ALLHANDS, J. L. Gringo builders, by J. L. Allhands. . . . ₁Iowa City, Ia.₁, Privately printed, 1931. Cloth. Scarce.

5 p.l., 11–283 ₁13₁ p. illus. 24 cm.
Index, last 13 unnumbered pages.

Contains a chapter on Texas ranches and other cattle material.

40 ALMIRALL, LEON V. From college to cow country, by Leon V. Almirall. Illustrated with photographs. Caldwell, Idaho, the Caxton printers, ltd., 1956. Cloth.

8 p.l., ₁17₁–471 p. front., plates. 21.6 cm.
Half title; pub. device.

41 ALTROCCHI, JULIA COOLEY. Traces in folklore and furrow. The old California Trail, by Julia Cooley Altrocchi. Illustrated from photographs by the author. Caldwell, Idaho, the Caxton printers, ltd., 1945. Cloth.

12 p.l., ₁25₁–327 p. front., plates, ports. 23.5 cm.
Bibliography, p. ₁317₁–320; index, p. ₁321₁–327.
At head of title: "Traces in Folklore and Furrow"; cover and half title: "The Old California Trail"; map on end papers; pub. device.

A chapter on cowboys and Nevada ranches.

42 AMERICAN CATTLE TRUST. Annual statement of the American Cattle Trust for the fiscal year ending December 31st, 1889. New York, ₁Press of the American Bank Note co.₁, 1890. Wrappers. Rare.

45 p. tables, statements. 22.7 cm.

43 AMERICAN GUIDE SERIES. Arizona, a state guide. Compiled by workers of the Writers' Program of the Work Projects Administration in the state of Arizona. Illustrated. . . . New York, Hastings house, publishers, MCMXL. Cloth.

xxv p., 1 l., 3–530 p. illus., ports., maps. 21 cm.
Appendices, p. 499–₁520₁; index, p. 521–530.
Half title; map on end papers.

A section on cattle and the roundup.

44 ———. California. A guide to the golden state. Compiled and written by the Federal Writers' Project of the Works Progress Administration

for the state of California. New York, Hastings house, publishers, MCMXXXIX. Cloth.

xxxi p., 1 l., 3–713 p. plates, ports., maps. 20.2 cm.
Chronology, p. 687–693; selected reading list, p. 694–698; index, p. 699–713.
Half title.

45 ———. Colorado. A guide to the highest state. Compiled by workers of the Writers' Program of the Work Projects Administration in the the state of Colorado. Illustrated. . . . New York, Hastings house, publishers, MCMXLI. Cloth.

xxxiii p., 1 l., 3–511 p. illus., plates, ports., maps. 21 cm.
Appendices, p. 467–[496]; index, p. 497–511.
Half title; map on end papers.

46 ———. Idaho lore, prepared by the Federal Writers' Project of the Work Projects Administration. Vardis Fisher, state director. Caldwell, Idaho, the Caxton printers, ltd., 1939. Cloth.

8 p.l., [13]–256 p. front., illus., plates. 23 cm.
Appendices, p. [217]–245; index, p. [249]–256.
Half title; illus. end papers.

47 ———. Montana, a state guide book. Compiled and written by the Federal Writers' Project of the Work Projects Administration for the state of Montana. Illustrated. . . . New York, the Viking press, MCMXXXIX. Cloth.

xxiii p., 1 l., 3–[442] p. illus., plates, ports., maps, fold. map in pocket at end. 21 cm.
Appendices, p. 413–429; index, p. 430–[442].
Half title; map on end papers; pub. device.

48 ———. Nebraska, a guide to the cornhusker state. Compiled and written by the Federal Writers' Project of the Works Progress Administration for the state of Nebraska. Illustrated. . . . New York, the Viking press, MCMXXXIX. Cloth.

xxiii [3] p., 3–424 p. front., plates, ports., maps, plans, fold. map in pocket at end. 21 cm.
Chronology, p. 401–406; bibliography, p. 407–412; index, p. 413–424.
Half title; map on end papers; pub. device.

49 ———. Nevada, a guide to the silver state. Compiled by workers of the Writers' Program of the Work Projects Administration in the state of Nevada. Illustrated. Portland, Ore., Binfords & Mort, publishers, [1940]. Cloth.

xviii p., 1 l., [3]–315 p. illus., plates, ports., maps (incl. large fold. map in pocket at end). 21 cm.
Appendices, p. 289–304; index, p. 305–315.
Half title.

50 ———. New Mexico, a guide to the colorful state. Compiled by workers of the Writers' Program of the Work Projects Administration in the state of New Mexico. Illustrated. . . . New York, Hastings house, publishers, MCMXL. Cloth.

xxxvii p., 1 l., 3–458 p. illus., plates, ports., maps. 21 cm.
Appendices, p. 423–439; index, p. 441–458.
Half title; map on end papers; vignette.

Republished by the University of New Mexico Press in 1945, with a road map in pocket at end.

51 ———. Oklahoma, a guide to the Sooner state. Compiled by workers of the Writers' Program of the Work Projects Administration in the state of Oklahoma. . . . Illustrated. . . . Norman, University of Oklahoma press, MCMXLI. Cloth.

xxvi p., 1 l., 3–442 p. plates, ports., maps (6 on one folder in pocket at end). 20 cm.
Chronology, p. 415–421; selected reading list, p. 422–426; index, p. 427–442.

52 ———. The Oregon Trail. The Missouri river to the Pacific ocean. Compiled and written by the Federal Writers' Project of the Works Progress Administration. Sponsored by Oregon Trail Memorial Association, inc. . . . New York, Hastings house, publishers, [1939]. Pict. cloth.

xii, 244 p. front., plates. 21 cm.
Appendices, p. 215–227; bibliography, p. 228–230; index, p. 233–244.
Half title.

Some information on cattle raising and the cattle trails.

53 ———. Provo, pioneer Mormon city. Compiled by workers of the Writers' Program of the Work Progress Administration for the state of Utah. . . . Illustrated. . . . Portland, Oregon, Binfords & Mort, publishers, [1942]. Cloth.

8 p.l., [17]–223 p. plates. 20.3 cm.
Notes, p. [190]–201; bibliography, p. [202]–208; index, p. [209]–223.
Half title; map on front end papers; plain on rear end papers; pub. device.

54 ———. Texas, a guide to the Lone Star state. Compiled by workers of the Writers' Program of the Work Projects Administration in the state of Texas. . . . Illustrated. New York, Hastings house, publishers, 1940. Cloth.

xxxiii, [3]–718 p. plates, ports., maps. 20.2 cm.
Glossary, p. 669–670; chronology, p. 671–676; selected reading list, p. 677–682; index, p. 701–718.
Half title; illus. end papers.

55 ———. Tulsa, a guide to the oil capital. Compiled by workers of the Federal Writers' Project of the Works Progress Administration in the

state of Oklahoma. Sponsored by the Tulsa Federation of Women's Clubs. Tulsa, Okla., published by the Mid-West printing co., 1938. Stiff pict. wrappers. Scarce.

3 p.l., 9–79 p. front., plates, plans, map. 21.3 cm.
Bibliography, p. 75; index, p. 76–79.

56 ——. Utah, a guide to the state. Compiled by workers of the Writers' Program of the Work Projects Administration for the state of Utah. . . . Illustrated. . . . New York, Hastings house, publishers, MCMXLI. Cloth.

xxvi p., 1 l., 3–595 p. illus., plates, ports., maps. 21 cm.
Appendices, p. 531–566; index, p. 567–595.
Half title; map on end papers.

57 ——. Wyoming, a guide to its history, highways, and people. Compiled by workers of the Writers' Program of the Work Projects Administration in the state of Wyoming. . . . Illustrated. . . . New York, Oxford University press, [1941]. Cloth.

xxvii p., 1 l., 3–490 p. illus., plates, ports., maps (1 fold. in pocket at end). 21 cm.
Appendices, p. 441–468; index, p. 469–490.
Half title; map on end papers.

58 AMERICAN NATIONAL LIVE STOCK ASSOCIATION. Proceedings of the first annual convention of the American National Live Stock Association, held at Denver, January 30, 31, and February 1, 1906. . . . [Denver, Colo., 1906]. Wrappers.

2 p.l., [5]–105 p. front. 6 ports. (incl. front.). 22.8 cm.

59 ——. Proceedings of the eleventh annual convention of the American National Live Stock Association, held at Denver, Colo., January 21, 22, and 23, 1908. Denver, Colo., and Smith-Brooks press, 1908. Wrappers.

142 p. front., 7 ports. (incl. front.). 22.2 cm.

60 ——. Proceedings of the twelfth annual convention of the American National Live Stock Association held at Los Angeles, California, January 26, 27, and 28, 1909. Denver, Colo., the Smith-Brooks press, 1909. Stiff wrappers.

174 p. front., 9 ports. (incl. front.). 22.5 cm.

61 ——. Proceedings of the thirteenth annual convention of the American National Live Stock Association, held at Denver, Colorado, January 11, 12, and 13, 1910. Denver, Colo., the Smith-Brooks press, 1910. Wrappers.

136 p. front., 6 ports. (incl. front.). 22.2 cm.

62 ——. Proceedings of the seventeenth annual convention of the

American National Live Stock Association, held at Denver, Colorado, January 20, 21, and 22, 1914. Denver, the Smith-Brooks press, ₁1914₁. Stiff wrappers.

156 p. front., 12 ports. (incl. front.). 22.5 cm.

63 ———. Proceedings of the eighteenth annual convention of the American National Live Stock Association, held at San Francisco, California, March 24, 25, and 26, 1915. Denver, the Smith-Brooks press, ₁1915₁. Cloth.

129 p. front., 11 ports. (incl. front.). 23 cm.

64 ———. Proceedings of the nineteenth annual convention of the American National Live Stock Association, held at El Paso, Texas, January 25, 26, and 27, 1916. Denver, the Smith-Brooks press, ₁1916₁. Cloth.

171 p. front., 13 ports. (incl. front.). 23 cm.

65 ———. Proceedings of the twenty-first annual convention of the American National Live Stock Association, January 18, 19, and 20, 1918. ₁Denver, Colo., office of the American National Live Stock association, 1918₁. Stiff wrappers.

202 p. 22.5 cm.

66 ———. Proceedings of the twenty-second annual convention of the American National Live Stock Association, held at Denver, Colorado, January 21, 22, and 23, 1919. ₁Denver, Colo., 1919₁. Stiff wrappers.

188 p. front., 11 ports. (incl. front.). 22.5 cm.

67 ———. Proceedings of the twenty-third annual convention of the American National Live Stock Association, held at Spokane, Washington, January 27, 28, and 29, 1920. ₁Denver, Colo., 1920₁. Wrappers.

191 p. front. (port.). 22.5 cm.

68 ———. Proceedings of the twenty-fourth annual convention of the American National Live Stock Association, held at El Paso, Texas, January 12, 13, and 14, 1921. ₁Denver, Colo., Office of the American National Live Stock association, 1921₁. Stiff wrappers.

222 p. front., 6 ports. (incl. front.), tables. 22.5 cm.

69 ———. Proceedings of the twenty-fifth annual convention of the American National Live Stock Association, held at Colorado Springs, Colorado, Thursday, January 12, 1922. Denver, Colo., Office of the American National Live Stock association, ₁1922₁. Cloth.

190 p. ports. 22.5 cm.

70 ———. Proceedings of the twenty-sixth annual convention of the American National Live Stock Association, held at Los Angeles, Cali-

fornia, January 30, 31, and February 1, 1923. ₁Denver, Colo., Office of the American National Live Stock association, 1923₁. Stiff wrappers.

152 p. front., 7 ports. (incl. front.). 22.5 cm.

71 ———. Proceedings of the twenty-seventh annual convention of the American National Live Stock Association, held at Omaha, Nebraska, January 15, 16, and 17, 1924. ₁Denver, Colo., Office of the American National Live Stock association, 1924₁. Stiff wrappers.

198 p. front., 7 ports. (incl. front.). 22.5 cm.

72 ———. Proceedings of the twenty-eighth annual convention of the American National Live Stock Association, held at Albuquerque, New Mexico, January 14, 15, and 16, 1925. ₁Denver, Colo., Office of the American National Live Stock association, 1925₁. Stiff wrappers.

132 p. front., 8 ports. (incl. front.). 22.5 cm.

73 ———. Proceedings of the twenty-ninth annual convention of the American National Live Stock Association, held at Phoenix, Arizona, January 13, 14, and 15, 1926. ₁Denver, Colo., Office of the American National Live Stock association, 1926₁. Cloth.

150 p. front., 7 ports. (incl. front.). 23.2 cm.

74 ———. Proceedings of the thirtieth annual convention of the American National Live Stock Association, held at Salt Lake, Utah, January 25, 26, and 27, 1927. ₁Denver, Colo., Office of the American National Live Stock association, 1927₁. Stiff wrappers.

195 p. front., 7 ports. (incl. front.). 22.5 cm.

75 ———. Proceedings of the thirty-first annual convention of the American National Live Stock Association, held at El Paso, Texas, January 25, 26, and 27, 1928. ₁Denver, Colo., Office of the American National Live Stock association, 1928₁. Stiff wrappers.

121 p. front., 7 ports. (incl. front.). 22.5 cm.

76 ———. Proceedings of the thirty-second annual convention of the American National Live Stock Association, held at San Francisco, California, February 5, 6, and 7, 1929. ₁Denver, Colo., Office of the American National Live Stock association, 1929₁. Cloth.

159 p. front., 6 ports. (incl. front.). 22.5 cm.

77 ———. Proceedings of the thirty-third annual convention of the American National Live Stock Association, held at Denver, Colorado, January 16, 17, and 18, 1930. ₁Denver, Colo., Office of the American National Live Stock association, 1930₁. Stiff wrappers.

168 p. front., 7 ports. (incl. front.). 22.5 cm.

78 ———. Proceedings of the thirty-fourth annual convention of the American National Live Stock Association, held at Seattle, Washington, January 28, 29, and 30, 1931. ₁Denver, Colo., Office of the American National Live Stock association, 1931₁. Stiff wrappers.

198 p. front., 6 ports. (incl. front.). 22.5 cm.

79 ———. Report of the market committee of the American National Live Stock Association presented January 15, 1918, at the twenty-first annual convention of the American National Live Stock Association, Salt Lake, Utah. Denver, Colorado, Office of the American National Live Stock association, ₁1918₁. Wrappers.

15 p. 22.5 cm.

80 ———. Resolutions adopted at the live stock conference held at Denver, Colorado, August 14 and 15, 1933, together with memberships of committees appointed. Denver, Colo., Office of the American National Live Stock association, ₁1933₁. Pamphlet.

12 p. 20.5 cm.

81 ———. Resolutions adopted at the mid-year meeting of the American National Live Stock Association, held at Salt Lake, Utah, August 26–27, 1921. Denver, Colo., Office of the American National Live Stock association, ₁1921₁. Pamphlet.

12 p. 21.9 cm.

82 ———. Resolutions adopted at the twelfth annual convention of the American National Live Stock Association at Los Angeles, California, January 26, 27, and 28, 1909. ₁Denver, Colo., 1909₁. Pamphlet. (Cover title).

7 p. 23 cm.

83 ———. Resolutions adopted at the thirteenth annual convention of the American National Live Stock Association at Denver, Colorado, July 11, 12, and 13, 1910. ₁Denver, 1910₁. Pamphlet. (Cover title).

8 p. 22.5 cm.

84 ———. Resolutions adopted at the sixteenth annual convention of the American National Live Stock Association at Phoenix, Arizona, January 14 and 15, 1915. ₁Denver, 1913₁. Pamphlet. (Cover title).

8 p. 22.5 cm.

85 ———. Resolutions adopted at the seventeenth annual convention of the American National Live Stock Association at Denver, Colorado, January 20, 21, and 22, 1914. ₁Denver, 1914₁. Pamphlet. (Cover title).

15 p. 22.5 cm.

86 ———. Resolutions adopted at the eighteenth annual convention of the American National Live Stock Association at San Francisco, California, March 24, 25, and 26, 1915. [Denver, 1915]. Pamphlet. (Cover title).

10 p. 22.5 cm.

87 ———. Resolutions adopted at the twentieth annual convention of the American National Live Stock Association at Cheyenne, Wyoming, January 18, 19, and 20, 1917; also report of market committee and list of officers, executive committee, and standing committees. Denver, Colo., Office of the American National Live Stock association, [1919]. Wrappers. (Cover title).

20 [3] p. 22.7 cm.

88 ———. Resolutions adopted at the twenty-third annual convention of the American National Live Stock Association at Spokane, Washington, January 27, 28, and 29, 1920; a list of officers, executive committee, and standing committees. Denver, Colo., Office of the American National Live Stock association, [1920]. Wrappers. (Cover title).

19 [3] p. 22.5 cm.

89 ———. Resolutions adopted at the twenty-fifth annual convention of the American National Live Stock Association held at Colorado Springs, Colorado, January 12, 13, and 14, 1922; a list of officers, executive committee, and standing committees. Denver, Colo., Office of the American National Live Stock association, [1922.] Wrappers. (Cover title).

15 [3] p. 22.5 cm.

90 ———. Resolutions adopted at the twenty-sixth annual convention of the American National Live Stock Association held at Los Angeles, California, January 30, 31, and February 1, 1923; and a list of officers, general council, executive committee, and standing committees. Denver, Colo., Office of the American National Live Stock association, [1923]. Wrappers. (Cover title).

16 [2] p. 22.5 cm.

91 ———. Resolutions adopted at the twenty-eighth annual convention of the American National Live Stock Association held at Albuquerque, New Mexico, January 14, 15, and 16, 1925; and a list of officers, general council, executive committee, and standing committees. Denver, Colo., Office of the American National Live Stock association, [1925]. Wrappers. (Cover title).

13 [2] p. 22.3 cm.

92 ———. Resolutions adopted at the twenty-ninth annual convention of the American Live Stock Association held at Phoenix, Arizona, January 13, 14, and 15, 1926; and a list of officers, general council, executive committee, and standing committees. Denver, Colo., Office of the American National Live Stock association, [1926]. Wrappers. (Cover title).

13 [2] p.   22.5 cm.

93 ———. Resolutions adopted at the thirty-first annual convention of the American National Live Stock Association held at El Paso, Texas, January 25, 26, and 27; and list of officers, general council, executive committee, and standing committees. Denver, Colo., Office of the American National Live Stock association, [1928]. Wrappers. (Cover title).

13 [2] p.   23 cm.

94 ———. Resolutions adopted at the thirty-second annual convention of the American National Live Stock Association held at San Francisco, California, February 5, 6, and 7, 1929; and list of officers, general council, executive committee, and standing committees. Denver, Colo., Office of the American National Live Stock association, [1929]. Wrappers. (Cover title).

11 [3] p.   22.5 cm.

95 ———. Resolutions adopted at the thirty-third annual convention of the American National Live Stock Association held at Denver, Colorado, January 16, 17, and 18, 1930; and list of officers, general council, executive committee, and standing committees. Denver, Colo., Office of the American National Live Stock association, [1930]. Wrappers. (Cover title).

11 [3] p.   23 cm.

96 ———. Resolutions adopted at the thirty-fifth annual convention of the American National Live Stock Association held at San Antonio, Texas, January 27, 28, and 29, 1932; and list of officers and general council. Denver, Colo., Office of the American National Live Stock association, [1932]. Wrappers. (Cover title).

13 [2] p.   22.5 cm.

97 [AN ANNOUNCEMENT of the opening of Ellsworth, Kansas, as a cattle market.] St. Louis, Wm. Sigerson & co., 1869. Folder. Exceedingly rare.

3 p.   map.   25 cm.

98 ANDERSON, ABRAHAM ARCHIBALD. Experiences and impressions; the

autobiography of Colonel A. A. Anderson. New York, the Macmillan company, 1933. Cloth. OP.

xiv p., 1 l., 245 p. front. (port.), illus., plates (2 col.), ports. (1 col.), facsms. 24 cm. Half title; pub. device; untrimmed.

Contains chapters about the Wyoming ranch of this noted American artist.

99 ANDERSON, A. E. Nebraska, then and now. Fifty years progress in agriculture. By A. E. Anderson. . . . Issued by Nebraska State Board of Agriculture, department of publicity, the Capitol, Lincoln, March, 1931. Pict. wrappers.

16 p. plates. 22.3 cm.

100 ANDERSON, AUGUST. Hyphenated; or, the life of S. M. Swensen. By August Anderson. [N. p., 1916]. Cloth. Rare.

3 p.l., [7]–290 p. front., plates. 19 cm.

S. M. Swensen was the founder of the famous SMS Ranch of Texas.

101 [ANDERSON, G. B.] History of New Mexico, its resources and people. Illustrated. Los Angeles, Chicago, New York, Pacific States publishing co., 1907. Three-quarter leather. Pub. in 2 vols. OP.

Vol. I: xxvii, 522 p. plates, ports. (part with tissues). 26 cm.
Vol. II: biographical.

Has some information on cattle as well as the Lincoln County War.

102 ANDERSON, JOHN WESLEY. From the plains to the pulpit, by J. W. Anderson. [Houston], State printing co., 1907. Pict. cloth. OP.

214 p. front. (port.), plates. 18.5 cm.

Also published by J. W. Anderson and sons, Goose Creek, Texas, [1907]. Pict. cloth. OP.

iv, 13–315 p. front. (port.), plates. 17.2 cm.

103 ANDREAS, A. T. History of the state of Nebraska, containing full account of its growth, from an unhabited territory to a wealthy and important state; of its early settlements; its rapid increase in population, and the marvelous development of its great natural resources. . . . Illus. Chicago, the Western Historical company . . . , 1882. Cloth. Scarce.

4 p.l., [32]–1506 p. illus., plates, ports., large fold. map (col.) in front. 30.2 cm.

Has a chapter on cattle and cowboys.

104 ANGELL, GEORGE T. Cattle transportation. An essay by George T. Angell. Boston, [Mass. Society for the Prevention of Cruelty to Animals], 1872. Wrappers. (Cover title). Scarce.

7 p. 25 cm.

105 ———. Cattle transportation. An essay by George T. Angell. . . . Boston, published by the Society ₁for the Prevention of Cruelty to Animals₁, 1874. Wrappers. (Cover title). Scarce.

8 p.   24 cm.
Double column.

106 ANGELO, C. AUBREY. Idaho: a descriptive tour and review of its resources and routes. By C. Aubrey Angelo (Chaos).   San Francisco, H. H. Bancroft & company, 1865.   Wrappers.   Rare.

2 p.l., ₁5₁–52 ₁2₁ p.   18.8 x 11.5 cm.
Last 2 p. adv.

This copy seen in the Rollins Collection, Princeton University.

107 ANSON, LADY CLODAGH. Book: discreet memoirs, by Lady Clodagh Anson. ₁London₁, published by G. Bateman Blackshaw, 1931. Cloth. Rare.

7 p.l., 11–379 p.   front. (port.), plates, ports.   22.5 cm.
Half title.

Has a chapter on ranching in Texas, cowboys, and roundups.

108 APPLEGATE, JESSE. A day with the cow column in 1843, by Jesse Applegate. Recollections of my boyhood, by Jesse Applegate, Oregon pioneer in 1843. Edited, with introduction and notes, by Joseph Schafer. . . . Chicago, printed for the Caxton club, 1934. Pict. cloth. Scarce.

xvii p., 1 l., ₁3₁–207 ₁1₁ p.   19.8 cm.
Appendix, p. ₁195₁–201; index, p. ₁205₁–207.
Untrimmed.
Colophon: "Of this book, designed by William A. Kittredge, three hundred copies have been printed at the Lakeside Press, R. R. Donnelley & Sons Company, in the month of September, 1934, Chicago."

109 ———. Recollections of my boyhood, by Jesse Applegate, Oregon pioneer of 1843.   Roseburg, ₁Oregon₁, Press of Review publishing co., 1914. Pict. wrappers.   Scarce.

99 p.   21 cm.

110 ARAPAHOE LAND AND CATTLE COMPANY. Prospectus and by-laws. Stock non-assessable. Denver, Collier and Cleveland litho. co., printers, 1884. Pict. wrappers.   Rare.

18 p.   front. (map).   22.3 cm.

111 ARIZONA. Arizona, its mineral, farming, and grazing lands, towns and mining camps; its rivers, mountains, plains, and mesas; with a brief summary of its Indian tribes, early history, ancient ruins, climate, etc., a

manual of reliable information concerning the territory. ₁N. p., 1882₁. Wrappers. Rare.

71 p. tables. 22.5 cm.

112 ———. Brands and marks of cattle, horses, sheep, goats, and hogs as they appear of record in the office of the Live Stock Sanitary Board of Arizona at Phoenix, Arizona. . . . Issued by the Live Stock Sanitary Board of Arizona. Phoenix, Press of the McNeil co., 1908. Three-quarter leather. Scarce.

2 p.l., 7–399 p. cattle brands. 24 cm.
Index, p. 309–399.

113 ———. The garden of America; the Salt River Valley, Maricopa County, Arizona. Chicago, 1885. Wrappers. Scarce.

24 p. plates, map. 21.5 cm.

114 ———. A historical and biographical record of the territory of Arizona. . . . Illustrated. Chicago, McFarland & Poole, publishers, 1896. Leather. Scarce.

6 p.l., ₁15₁–612 p. plates, ports. 30.6 cm.

Section on stock raising.

115 ———. History of Arizona Territory showing its resources and advantages; with illustrations descriptive of its scenery, residences, farms, mines, mills. . . . San Francisco, Cal., Wallace W. Elliott & co., publishers, 1884. Three-quarter leather. Scarce.

5 p.l., ₁25₁–322 ₁2₁ p. front. (with tissue), plates (2 double p.), ports., charts (1 col.). 34.7 cm.
Last p. adv.; double column.

Has a long chapter on cattle.

116 ———. Live stock laws of the state of Arizona. Rules and regulations Live Stock Sanitary Board of Arizona. ₁N. p., n. d.₁. Wrappers. Rare.

₁3₁–61 p. 22.4 cm.
Index, p. ₁57₁–61.

117 ———. Live stock laws of Arizona. ₁Issued by the₁ Live Stock Sanitary Board of the territory of Arizona, April 30, 1897. ₁Phoenix, Southwestern Stockman, print, 1897₁. Wrappers. Rare.

3 p.l., 5–93 ₁5₁ p. 20 cm.
5 p. adv. at end and other adv. scattered throughout.

118 ———. Live stock laws of the state of Arizona. Rules and regulations, Livestock Sanitary Board of Arizona. Issued by the Livestock Sanitary

Board and Sheep Sanitary Commission of Arizona. ₍Miami, the Daily Silver Belt, 1923₎. Wrappers. OP.
61 p. 22.5 cm.

119 ――――. Live stock laws of the state of Arizona. Rules and regulations. Livestock Sanitary Board of Arizona, July 1, 1925. Compiled and annotated by Charles T. Francis, sec. Issued by the Livestock Sanitary Board and Sheep Sanitary Commission of Arizona. ₍Phoenix, Arizona printers, 1925₎. Wrappers. OP.
51 ₍4₎ p. 23 cm.

120 ――――. Maricopa County, Arizona. Reliable information on the splendid opportunities it offers to settlers. Phoenix, Maricopa County, Arizona. Prepared and published by the Phoenix Herald office, June 30, 1886 Wrappers. Scarce.
1 p.l., ₍3₎–36 ₍23₎ p. illus., map. 21.5 cm.
Last 23 p. adv.

121 ――――. The new Arizona; a brief review of its resources, development, industries, soil, climate, and especially its advantages for homemaking. San Francisco, Cal., published by the passenger department, Southern Pacific company, 1900. Pict. wrappers. Scarce.
3–40 p. illus., plates, maps (1 double p.). 19.5 cm.

122 ――――. Northern Arizona, its forests, arable and grazing lands. Homes for the million. ₍N. p.₎, Arizona Gazette, 1889. Wrappers. Rare.
32 p. 21.2 cm.

123 ――――. Proceedings of the sixth annual meeting of the Arizona Cattle Growers' Association. Held at Phoenix, Arizona, November 8, 9, and 10, 1911. ₍Phoenix₎, Arizona state press, ₍1911₎. Pict. wrappers. Scarce.
3 p.l., ₍7₎–55 p. 1 illus., 1 diagr. 23 cm.

124 ――――. Proceedings of the seventh annual meeting of the Arizona Cattle Growers' Association at Tucson, Arizona, January 5–6, 1914. Reported by H. C. Nixon, Tucson, Arizona. ₍Phoenix₎, Arizona state press, ₍1914₎. Pict. wrappers.
4 p.l., ₍9₎–77 ₍1₎ p. ports. 23 cm.

125 ――――. Proceedings of the ninth annual meeting of the Arizona Cattle Growers' Association at Prescott, Arizona, January 10–12, 1916. ₍Phoenix₎, Arizona state press, ₍1916₎. Pict. wrappers.
8 p.l., ₍17₎–143 p. front. (port.), illus., plates, ports. 22.5 cm.

126 ――――. Proceedings of the tenth annual convention of the Arizona

Cattle Growers' Association at Globe, Arizona, March 1, 2, 3, 1917. ₁Phoenix₁, Arizona state press, ₁1917₁. Pict. wrappers.
10 p.l., ₁1₁ p., 12–138 p.   front., ports. 23.2 cm.

127 ———. Proceedings of the eleventh annual convention of the Arizona
Cattle Growers' Association at Nogales, Arizona, February 14, 15, 16,
1918. ₁N. p.₁, McNeill printing co., ₁1918₁. Pict. wrappers.
3–57 p. 22.7 cm.

128 ———. Proceedings of the twelfth annual convention of the Arizona
Cattle Growers' Association held at Phoenix, Arizona, February 11, 12,
and 13, 1919. ₁Phoenix, G. G. Morgan printing co., 1919₁ Pict. wrappers.
vii p., 1 l., ₁21₁–152 p. front. (port.). 23 cm.

129 ———. Proceedings of the thirteenth annual convention of the Arizona Cattle Growers' Association held at Tucson, Arizona, February 17,
18, and 19, 1920. ₁N. p.₁, 1920. Pict. wrappers.
xiv, ₁15₁–159 p. 23 cm.

130 ———. Report of the acting Governor of Arizona, made to the Secretary of the Interior for the year 1881. Washington, Government printing office, 1881. Wrappers. Scarce.
25 p. 22.2 cm.

131 ———. Report of the acting Governor of Arizona made to the Secretary of the Interior for the year 1883. Washington, Government printing office, 1883. Wrappers. Scarce.
14 p. 22.2 cm.

132 ———. Report of the acting Governor of Arizona made to the Secretary of the Interior for the year 1884. Washington, Government printing
office, 1884. Wrappers. Scarce.
13 p. 22.2 cm.

133 ———. Report of the acting Governor of Arizona made to the Secretary of the Interior for the year 1885. Washington, Government printing
office, 1885. Wrappers. Scarce.
20 p. 22.2 cm.

134 ———. Report of the acting Governor of Arizona made to the Secretary of the Interior for the year 1887. Washington, Government printing
office, 1887. Wrappers. Scarce.
11 p. 22.2 cm.

135 ———. Report of the acting Governor of Arizona made to the Secre-

tary of the Interior for the year 1888. Washington, Government printing office, 1888. Wrappers. Scarce.

17 p. tables. 22.5 cm.

136 ———. Report of the acting Governor of Arizona made to the Secretary of the Interior for the year 1889. Washington, Government printing office, 1889. Wrappers. Scarce.

24 p. 22.2 cm.

137 ———. Report of the acting Governor of Arizona made to the Secretary of the Interior for the year 1890. Washington, Government printing office, 1890. Wrappers. Scarce.

34 p. 22.2 cm.

138 ———. Report of the acting Governor of Arizona made to the Secretary of the Interior for the year 1891. Washington, Government printing office, 1891. Wrappers. Scarce.

41 p. 22.2 cm.

139 ———. Report of the acting Governor of Arizona made to the Secretary of the Interior for the year 1893. Washington, Government printing office, 1893. Wrappers. Scarce.

v, 3–60 p. tables. 22.5 cm.

140 ———. Report of the acting Governor of Arizona made to the Secretary of the Interior for the year 1894. Washington, Government printing office, 1894. Wrappers. Scarce.

68 p. 22.5 cm.

141 ———. Report of the acting Governor of Arizona made to the Secretary of the Interior for the year 1895. Washington, Government printing office, 1895. Wrappers. Scarce.

119 p. plates, tables, map. 22.5 cm.

142 ———. Report of the acting Governor of Arizona made to the Secretary of the Interior for the year 1896. Washington, Government printing office, 1896. Wrappers. Scarce.

142 p. front., plates, maps (1 fold. at end), tables. 22.5 cm.

143 ———. Report of the acting Governor of Arizona made to the Secretary of the Interior for the year 1897. Washington, Government printing office, 1897. Wrappers. Scarce.

152 p. plates, fold. map at end, tables. 22.5 cm.

144 ———. Report of the acting Governor of Arizona made to the Secre-

tary of the Interior for the fiscal year ended June 30, 1898. Washington, Government printing office, 1898. Wrappers. Scarce.

179 p. tables. 22.5 cm.

145 ———. Report of the acting Governor of Arizona made to the Secretary of the Interior, 1899. Washington, Government printing office, 1899. Wrappers. Scarce.

255 p. plates, ports., fold. map at end, tables. 22.5 cm.

146 ———. Report of the acting Governor of Arizona to the Secretary of the Interior, 1900. Washington, Government printing office, 1900. Wrappers. Scarce.

64 p. front., tables. 22.5 cm.

147 ———. Report of the Governor of Arizona to the Secretary of the Interior. Washington, Government printing office, 1901. Wrappers. Scarce.

144 p. front., plates, fold. map at end, tables. 22.5 cm.

148 ———. Report of the Governor of Arizona to the Secretary of the Interior for the year ended June 30, 1902. Washington, Government printing office, 1902. Wrappers. Scarce.

126 p. fold. map at end, tables. 22.5 cm.

149 ———. Report of the Governor of Arizona to the Secretary of the Interior for the year ended June 30, 1903. Washington, Government printing office, 1903. Wrappers. Scarce.

264 p. front., plates, 2 fold. scenes, 1 fold. map at end, tables. 22.5 cm.

150 ———. Report of the Governor of Arizona to the Secretary of the Interior for the year ended June 30, 1904. Washington, Government printing office, 1904. Wrappers. Scarce.

157 p. 2 fold. maps (1 at end), tables. 22.5 cm.

151 ———. Report of the Governor of Arizona to the Secretary of the Interior, 1905. Washington, Government printing office, 1905. Wrappers. Scarce.

91 p. fold. map at end, tables. 22.5 cm.

152 ———. Report of the Governor of Arizona to the Secretary of the Interior, 1906. Washington, Government printing office, 1906. Wrappers. Scarce.

32 p. fold. map at end, tables. 22.5 cm.

153 ———. Report of the Governor of Arizona to the Secretary of the In-

terior, 1907. Washington, Government printing office, 1907. Wrappers. Scarce.

38 p. fold. map at end, tables. 22.5 cm.

154 ———. Report of the Governor of Arizona to the Secretary of the Interior for the fiscal year ended June 30, 1908. Washington, Government printing office, 1908. Wrappers. Scarce.

17 p. fold. map at end, tables. 22.5 cm.

155 ———. Report of the Governor of Arizona to the Secretary of the Interior for the fiscal year ended June 30, 1909. Washington, Government printing office, 1909. Wrappers. Scarce.

30 p. fold. map at end, tables. 22.5 cm.

156 ———. Report of the Governor of Arizona to the Secretary of the Interior for the fiscal year ended June 30, 1910. Washington, Government printing office, 1910. Wrappers. Scarce.

34 p. fold. map at end, tables. 22.5 cm.

157 ———. Report of the Governor of Arizona to the Secretary of the Interior for the fiscal year ended June 30, 1911. Washington, Government printing office, 1911. Wrappers. Scarce.

42 p. fold. map at end, tables. 22.5 cm.

158 ———. The resources of Arizona; its mineral, farming, and grazing lands, towns and mining camps; its rivers, mountains, plains, and mesas; with a brief summary of its Indian tribes, early history. . . . A manual of reliable information concerning the territory. Wrappers. Scarce.

71 p. 22.5 cm.

This booklet bears no imprint, but the text shows date to be 1881 and the place of publication is probably Florence.

159 ———. Resources of Arizona Territory, with a description of the Indian tribes; ancient ruins; Cochise, Apache chief; Antonio, Pima chief; stage and wagon roads; trade and commerce, etc., by authority of the Legislature. San Francisco, Francis & Valentine, steam printers and engravers, 1871. Wrappers. Scarce.

[3]-30 [1] p. 22.7 cm.

160 ———. Resources of Salt River Valley, Maricopa County, Arizona. Phoenix, Arizona, published by the Phoenix Chamber of Commerce, August, 1891. Stiff wrappers. Scarce.

2 p.l., 5-48 p. plates, fold. map at end. 17.7 x 22.2 cm.

161 ———. Southeastern Arizona, its varied climate and wonderful re-

sources. Inducements for emigrants. Phoenix, Arizona, Gazette print, 1889. Wrappers. Scarce.

47 p. 19.5 cm.

Sketches of the history of Pima, Cochise, and Graham counties, giving, among other things, information on stock raising.

162 ———. Territory of Arizona and summary of the territory's acquisition, organization, and mineral, agricultural, and grazing resources. . . . By authority of the Legislature. Tucson, printed at the Citizen office, 1874. Wrappers. (Cover title). Rare.

2 p.l., ₁3₁–38 p. tables. 22.6 cm.

163 ———. What the Salt River Valley offers to the immigrant, capitalist, and invalid. A land of homes, for health, for investments. Published by the Maricopa County Immigration Union, Phoenix, Arizona. Chicago, Rand, McNally and co., printers and engravers, 1887. Pict. wrappers. Scarce.

3–48 p. illus., large fold. map at end, tables. 21.8 cm.

164 ———. The United States Land and Cattle Co., of Arizona. Incorporated under the laws of Arizona. Capital $3,000,000 to be represented by 30,000 shares at $100 each. Washington, Gibson brothers, printers, 1884. Wrappers. (Cover title). Rare.

16 p. 22.7 cm.

165 ———. Brand book of the Yavapai Co. Stock Growers' Association, prepared May 1, 1885. . . . Headquarters, Prescott, Arizona. Kansas City, Mo., Isaac P. Moore, printer and binder, 1885. Sheep. Very rare.

iv, ₁3₁–44 p. cattle brands. 16.7 cm.

Seen in the library of Thomas W. Streeter, Morristown, N. J.

166 ARMOUR, JONATHAN OGDEN. The livestock producer and Armour. . . . Chicago, Armour and co., 1919. Wrappers. OP.

24 p. illus. (part col., incl. front.), diagr. 24 cm.

167 ———. The packers, the private car lines, and the people. By J. Ogden Armour. Illustrated. Philadelphia, Henry Altemus company, ₁1906₁. Pict. cloth. OP.

xi p., 1 l., 15–380 p. front. (port. with tissue), 7 plates. 19.7 cm.
Half title.

Also published in London in the same year by T. W. Laurie.

168 ARNOLD, GEORGE. Woonsocket, the gem of the prairie. Sanborn Coun-

ty, the husbandman's paradise. . . . Woonsocket, Dakota, News job printing house, ₁1885₁. Wrappers. (Cover title). Rare.

₁28₁ p. (no pagination). fold. map at end. 19.6 cm.

Contains a business directory and material on stock raising.

169 ARNOLD, OREN. Sun in your eyes, by Oren Arnold. Illustrations by
Lloyd Lozes Goff. Albuquerque, University of New Mexico press,
₁1947₁. Pict. cloth.

5 p.l., ₁3₁–253 p. illus. 19 cm.
Bibliography, p. ₁242₁–253.
Half title; illus. double t.p.; Indian pictographs on end papers; "First edition" on
copyright p.

170 ———. Thunder in the Southwest. Echoes from the wild frontier, by
Oren Arnold, with drawings by Nick Eggenhofer. Norman, University
of Oklahoma press, ₁1952₁. Cloth.

ix p., 1 l., 3–237 p. illus. 21.9 cm.
Half title; "First edition" on copyright p.

171 ———. Wonders of the West. A book for young people, and all others
who would know western America, by Oren Arnold. With frontispiece
by George Elbert Burr. Seven full-color plates by Lillian Wilhelm Smith.
Thirty-two full-page camera studies and numerous informal sketches by
Reg Manning. Dallas, Banks, Upshaw and co., ₁1936₁. Cloth. OP.

3 p.l., ₁ix₁–xiii p., 3 l., ₁5₁–229 p. front. (col.), plates (part col.), ports., drawings. 22.7 cm.
Illus. end papers.

172 ——— (ED.). The roundup. A collection of western stories, poems,
and articles for young people, edited by Oren Arnold. . . . Illustrated by
Creston F. Baumgartner. Dallas, B. Upshaw and company, ₁1937₁.
Cloth. OP.

xvii, 301 p. front., illus. 23 cm.
Glossary, p. 299–301.
Illus. end papers; "First edition" on copyright p.

173 ———, and JOHN P. HALE. Hot irons; heraldry of the range, by
Oren Arnold and John P. Hale. New York, the Macmillan company,
1940. Cloth. OP.

viii p., 2 l., 242 p. illus., cattle brands. 21.7 cm.
Half title; cattle brands on end papers.

174 ARNY, WILLIAM FREDERICK MILTON. Interesting items regarding New
Mexico. Its agricultural, pastoral, and mineral resources, peoples, climate, soil, scenery, etc., by W. F. M. Arny, acting governor of New

Mexico. Santa Fe, N. M., Manderfield & Tucker, printers, 1873. Wrappers. Rare.

2 p.l., ₁5₁–112 p. 21.3 cm.

175 ARTRIP, LOUISE and FULLEN. Memoirs of Daniel Fore (Jim) Chisholm and the Chisholm Trail, by Louise and Fullen Artrip. ₁Boonville, Ark., published by Artrip publications, 1949₁. Stiff wrappers. OP.

4 p.l., 11–89 p. front., plates, ports. 19.6 cm.

The authors here erroneously claim that Daniel Chisholm bossed the first herd of cattle to leave Texas, and that the Chisholm Trail was named after him. They also state that this trail led through Vernon, Texas, and crossed Red River at Doan's Crossing. This was not the original Chisholm Trail, but the Western Trail, a later route pushed farther west by the settlements.

176 [ASH, GEORGE]. Captain George Ash. His adventures and life story as cowboy, ranger, and soldier. . . . Eastleigh ₁England₁, Eastleigh printing works . . . , ₁n. d.₁. Pict. boards. OP.

6 p.l., 17–180 p. plates, ports. 18.8 cm.

Another edition was printed in England (London, 1923), with 234 p.

177 [ATCHISON, TOPEKA AND SANTA FE RAILWAY COMPANY]. Cattle raising in south-central and south-west Kansas. Topeka, Sexton, printer, ₁n. d., c.1881₁. Sewn. (Cover title). Rare.

₁3₁–23 p. 23 cm.

Also published in Leavenworth by the Times Printing House with same collation.

178 ———. Impartial testimony as to the profits of sheep and cattle raising in south west Kansas. Topeka, Hamilton, 1884. Wrappers. Rare.

39 p. 23 cm.

179 ATEN, IRA. Six and one-half years in the Ranger service. The memoirs of Ira Aten, sergeant Company D, Texas Rangers. Bandera, Texas, published by Frontier Times, 1945. Pict. wrappers. (Cover title). Scarce.

64 p. front., (port.), plates. 26.7 cm.
Double column.

180 ATHEARN, ROBERT G. Westward the Briton, by Robert G. Athearn. New York, Charles Scribner's sons, 1953. Cloth.

xiv p., 1 l., 208 p. illus., plates (all in one section). 24.2 cm.
Notes, p. 165–181; bibliography, p. ₁185₁–202; index, p. 203–208.
Half title; headpieces.

Many English men and women came to America's West and wrote books about their experiences. Mr. Athearn deals largely with their reactions.

181 ATKINSON, S. W. Oklahoma Bill, hunter and trapper. New York, Dick's publishing house, ₍n. d.₎. Pict. wrappers. Exceedingly rare.
₍16₎ p. (no pagination). 17.2 cm.

Gives some information on how to become a cowboy, what to wear, etc., but the author appears to know little about his subject.

182 [ATLANTIC AND PACIFIC RAILWAY Co.]. The far West. Items of general information for travelers and seekers after new homes in the western states and territories. Issued by the Atlantic & Pacific and Missouri Pacific R. R.'s St. Louis, 1875. Wrappers. Rare.
₍3₎-31 p. large fold. map in front. 16 cm.

Has information on stock raising in Texas. Copy seen in the Coe Collection, Yale University.

183 ATWOOD, WALLACE W. The Rocky Mountains, by Wallace W. Atwood. Third volume in the American Mountain Series, edited by Roderick Peattie. New York, the Vanguard press, ₍1945₎. Pict. cloth. OP.
8 p.l., 17–324 p. illus., plates, ports., maps (1 fold.). 23.5 cm.
Bibliography, p. 311–315; index, p. 317–324.
Half title; illus. double t.p.; tailpieces.

184 AUSTIN, MARY. The road to Mammon, by Mary Austin. New York, Pegasus publishing co., ₍1938₎. Boards, label pasted on. Scarce.
4 p.l., 9–48 p. 20.6 cm.
Vignette; "First edition" on copyright p.

185 AUZIAS, TURENNE. Cow-boy. ₍By Turenne Auzias₎. Paris, Calmann Levy, editeur, 1896. Wrappers. Scarce.
318 p. 18.5 cm.

A book written in French about the American cowboy.

186 AVERY, A. Hand-book and travelers' guide of New Mexico, by A. Avery. For tourists, miners, capitalists, and emigrants. Denver, E. Price and co., printers, 1881. Pict. wrappers. Exceedingly rare.
106 p. illus. 14.8 cm.
12 p. adv. at end.

187 AVERY, W. C. Cattle raising in South Dakota. The most profitable field in the West and why. The best and cheapest lands and the healthiest climate. Forest City and Gettysburg R. R. co., write to W. C. Avery, land commissioner, Forest City, South Dakota, ₍n. d.₎ Wrappers. Rare.
₍3₎-31 ₍1₎ p. plates, map, tables. 23.2 cm.
Last p. adv.

One of those rare promotional booklets issued in the early days by the various railroads.

188   AYER, I. WINSLOW. Life in the wilds of America, and wonders of the West in and beyond the bounds of civilization. Illustrated. . . . By I. Winslow Ayer. . . . Grand Rapids, Michigan, published by the Central publishing company, 1880. Cloth.

5 p.l., [13]–528 p.   front., illus., plates.   22 cm.
Vignette.

189   AYERS, NATHANIEL M. Building a new empire, by Nathaniel M. Ayers. A historical story of the settlement of the wild West. Taking up the wild scenes incident to the settlement of a country inhabited by buffalo and hostile Indians. . . .   New York, Broadway publishing co. . . . , [1910]. Cloth. Scarce.

3 p.l., 7–221 p.   front. (port. with tissue), plates, ports.   20 cm.
Untrimmed.

190   BABER, DAISY F. Injun summer. An old cowhand rides the ghost trails, by Daisy F. Baber as told by Bill Walker. Illustrated with photographs. Caldwell, Idaho, the Caxton printers, ltd., 1952. Cloth.

9 p.l., [19]–223 p.   front., plates, ports.   23.5 cm.
Half title; headpieces; vignette; pub. device.

191   ———. The longest rope; the truth about the Johnson County cattle war, by D. F. Baber as told by Bill Walker. Illustrated by R. H. Hall. Caldwell, Idaho, the Caxton printers, ltd., 1940. Pict. cloth.

9 p.l., [19]–320 p.   illus., plates.   23.5 cm.
Appendix, p. [297]–320 (George Dunning's confession).
Half title; map on end papers; illus. double t.p. in red; headpieces.

192   BACA, FABIOLA CABEZA DE (pseud. of Fabiola Gilbert). We fed them cactus, by Fabiola Cabeza de Baca. With drawings by Dorothy L. Peters. [Albuquerque], the University of New Mexico press, [1954]. Pict. cloth.

x p., 1 l., 186 p.   illus.   21.5 cm.
Glossary, p. 179–180; index, p. 181–186.
Half title.

193   BAILEY, HARRY H. When New Mexico was young, by Harry H. Bailey. His autobiography. Edited by Homer E. Gruver. [Las Cruces, N. M., published by the Las Cruces Citizen, 1948]. Pict. wrappers. (Copyright 1946).

202 [1] p.   illus., ports.   22.8 cm.
Double column; port. of author on cover; foreword on verso of title page; copyright notice on verso of flyleaf preceding t.p.

This is a separate reprint from a series which ran in the *Las Cruces Citizen* from 1946 to 1948, which accounts for the fact that copyright antedates the book by two years.

[31]

194 BAILLIE-GROHMAN, WILLIAM A. Camps in the Rockies. Being a narrative of life on the frontier, and sport in the Rocky Mountains, with an account of the cattle ranches of the West, by Wm. A. Baillie-Grohman. With illustrations and an original map based on the most recent U. S. government survey. London, Sampson Low, Marston, Searle & Rivington, 1882. Cloth. OP.

viii, 438 [4] p. front., fold. map in front. 19 cm.
Appendix, p. [397]–431; list of authors consulted, p. 432; index, p. [433]–438. Half title; 4 p. adv. at end.
American edition, New York, C. Scribner's sons, 1882, same collation. There were several later editions, both English and American.

195 BAKER, C. W. Proceedings of the National Live Stock Association at Ft. Worth, Texas, 1896. Together with a roster of officers and the rules and by-laws. By C. W. Baker. Chicago, 1896. Wrappers. Scarce.

96 p. 20 cm.

196 BAKER, INEZ. Yesterday in Hall County, Texas, by Inez Baker. Memphis, Texas, [privately printed], 1940. Cloth. OP.

5 p.l., 219 p. illus., plates, ports. 23.4 cm.

Much on cattle, cowboys and ranch life.

197 BAKER, JAMES H. (ED.). History of Colorado, prepared under the supervision of the State Historical and Natural History Society of Colorado. James H. Baker, editor . . . LeRoy Hafen, associate editor. . . . Denver, Linderman co., inc., 1927. Cloth. OP. Pub. in 5 vols.

Vols. I–III: front., ports., maps. 23.5 cm. Paged continuously.
Vols. IV–V: biographical.

198 BAKER, VALENTINE. Valentine Baker real estate, loan, and livestock broker. Cheyenne, Wyo., Daily Sun printing house, [n. d.]. Wrappers. Rare.

32 p. 21.4 cm.

Advertisements and business cards scattered throughout. Gives some information on ranching in Wyoming.

199 BALLINGER, R. H. Does it pay? A book on the stock industry of southwestern Kansas. By R. H. Ballinger. . . . [Larned, Kansas], Chronoscope job print, 1883. Wrappers. Rare.

48 p. 16 cm.
First 16 p. and last 13 p. adv.; adv. verso of both front and back wrappers.

200 BALLOU, ROBERT. Early Klickitat Valley days, by Robert Ballou. . . . [Goldendale, Washington, printed by the Goldendale Sentinel, 1938]. Cloth. OP.

3 p.l., 7–496 p. illus., plates, ports. 23.6 cm.
Errata on last p.; double column.

201 BANCROFT, HUBERT HOWE. Works of Hubert Howe Bancroft. Vol. III. Chronicles of the builders of the commonwealth. Historical character study. By Hubert Howe Bancroft. San Francisco, the History co., publishers, 1892. Sheep. OP.

ix, 620 p. 24 steel-plate ports. (incl. front.). 23.4 cm.

Chapters on Henry Miller and other prominent ranchmen; cattle raising and stock associations.

202 ———. Works of Hubert Howe Bancroft. Vol. XVII. History of Arizona and New Mexico, 1530–1888. San Francisco, the History co., publishers, 1889. Sheep. OP.

xxxvii, 829 p. maps (1 fold.). 23.6 cm.
Index, p. 802–829.

203 ———. Works of Hubert Howe Bancroft. Vol. XXV. History of Nevada, Colorado, and Wyoming, 1540–1889. San Francisco, the History co., publishers, 1890. Sheep. OP.

xxxii, 828 p. illus. 23.6 cm.
Index, p. 802–828.
Half title.

204 BARDE, FREDERICK S. Life and adventures of "Billy Dixon" of Adobe Walls, Texas Panhandle. A narrative in which he describes many things relating to the early Southwest. . . . Compiled by Frederick S. Barde. Guthrie, Okla., ₁Co-Operative publishing co., 1914₁. Cloth. Scarce.

320 p. front., ports. 20 cm.
Republished in Dallas, Texas, by Turner publishing co., in 1927.

205 BARKER, ELLIOTT S. When the dogs bark "treed." A year on the trail of the longtails, by Elliott S. Barker. ₁Illustrated with drawings and photographs₁. Albuquerque, the University of New Mexico press, 1946. Cloth.

xviii, 209 p., 1 l. front., plates, ports. 23.5 cm.
Half title; map on end papers; illus. double t.p.

206 BARLER, MILES. "Early days in Llano," by Miles Barler. Personal reminiscences. ₁Llano, c.1898₁. Stiff wrappers. Rare.

68 p. 14.6 cm.
Later reprinted in small edition with 76 p. (c.1905).

207 BARNARD, EVAN G. A rider of the Cherokee Strip, ₁by₁ Evan G. Barnard. With illustrations. Boston, New York, Houghton Mifflin company, 1936. Cloth.

xviii p., 1 l., 233 p. front., plates, ports. 21.3 cm.
Appendix, p. ₁225₁–227; index, p. ₁229₁–233.
Half title; map on end papers; pub. device; untrimmed; first edition, "1936" under imprint.

208 BARNES, WILLIAM CROFT. Apaches & longhorns; the reminiscences of Will C. Barnes, edited and with an introduction by Frank C. Lockwood. . . . With a decoration by Cas Duchow. Los Angeles, the Ward Ritchie press, MCMXLI. Pict. cloth. OP.

xxiii p., 1 l., 3–210 p. front. (port.), plates, ports., plan. 21.5 cm.
Half title; vignette.

209 ———. Stock-watering places on western grazing grounds, by Will C. Barnes. . . . ₁Washington, D. C.₁, 1914. Stapled. (Caption title).

27 p. plates, map. 23.2 cm.
U. S. Dept. of Agriculture *Farmer's Bulletin 592.*

210 ———. The story of the range, by Will C. Barnes. . . . An account of the occupation of the public domain ranges by the pioneer stockman, the effect on the forage and the land of unrestricted grazing, and the attempts that have been made to regulate grazing practice and perpetuate the great natural forage resources of the open ranges. . . . Washington, Government printing office, 1926. Wrappers. Scarce.

iii, 60 p. plates, ports., maps. 23.2 cm.
"Literature cited," p. 60.

211 ———. Tales from the X–Bar horse camp; the blue-roan "outlaw" and other stories, by Will C. Barnes. . . . Chicago, Illinois, published by the Breeder's Gazette, 1920. Boards and cloth. Scarce.

6 p.l., 217 p., 1 l. illus., plates. 20 cm.
Half title.

A scarce collection of true stories, first printed in various magazines, dealing with the rough life of the cowman and peace officers of northern Arizona.

212 ———. Western grazing grounds, and forest ranges; a history of the live-stock industry as conducted on the open ranges of the arid west, with particular reference to the use now being made of the ranges in the national forests, by Will C. Barnes. . . . Chicago, the Breeder's Gazette, 1913. Cloth. Scarce.

10 p.l., 21–390 p. front. (col.), illus., col. plates. 20 cm.
"List of books consulted," p. 20; appendix, p. 377–384; index, p. 385–390.
Half title.

213 BARNES, WILLIAM CROFT, and JAMES T. JARDINE. Live stock production in the eleven far western range states, based on reports from stockmen and country correspondents, by Will C. Barnes . . . and James T. Jardine. . . . Washington, Government printing office, 1916. Wrappers. Scarce.

2 p.l., 5–100 p. plates, fold. map, tables. 21 cm.
U. S. Dept. of Agriculture *Report No. 110.*

214 BARRETT, MAJOR GENERAL CHARLES F. Oklahoma after fifty years. A history of the Sooner State and its people, 1889–1939. . . . Hopkinsville, Kentucky, Oklahoma City, Oklahoma, the Historical Record association, 1941. Raised leather. Pub. in 4 vols.

Vol. I: 11 p.l., ₍11₎–366 p. front. (port.), plates, ports. 26.8 cm.
Half title.
Vols. II, III, and IV: biographical. Paged continuously.
Index, p. ₍1498₎–1538 (end of Vol. IV).

215 BARROWS, JOHN RUMSEY. Ubet, by John R. Barrows. Caldwell, Idaho, the Caxton printers, ltd., 1934. Cloth. Op.

3 p.l., 7–278 p. illus. 19.5 cm.
Half title; illus. end papers; illus. double t.p.; pub. device.

216 ———. A Wisconsin youth in Montana, 1880–1882, by John R. Barrows. . . . Missoula, State University of Montana, 1932. Wrappers. (Cover title).

3–15 p. 24.2 cm.
Double column.
(Historical reprints . . . *Sources of Northwest History No. 1*). "Reprinted from the historical section of the *Frontier,* a magazine of the Northwest . . . Vol. VIII, No. 1, Nov. 1927. Reprinted in March, 1932."

217 BARTLETT, I. S. (ED.). History of Wyoming. I. S. Bartlett, editor. Chicago, the S. J. Clarke publishing company, 1918. Pict. cloth. Pub. in 3 vols.

Vol. I: 8 p.l., 17–667 p. front. (col. flag), plates, ports. 27.2 cm.
Vols. II and III: biographical.

Vol. I has a chapter on the cattle industry and one on the Johnson County War.

218 BARTLETT, WILLIAM SYLVESTER. My foot's in the stirrup. ₍By₎ W. S. Bartlett. Edited by Mabel Majors and Rebecca Smith. Illustrations by Hortense Lindenfield. Dallas, Texas, Dealy and Lowe, 1937. Cloth. OP.

6 p.l., 202 ₍1₎ p. front. 21.6 cm.
Illus. front end papers; map on rear end papers.

219 BATCHELDER, GEORGE ALEXANDER. A sketch of the history and resources of Dakota Territory. By George Alexander Batchelder. . . . Yankton, Press steam power printing co., 1870. Wrappers. Very rare.

2 p.l., ₍3₎–56 p. front. (col. map). 22.5 cm.
Reprinted in 1928 by Hipple printing co., of Pierre, South Dakota.
3–71 p. 22.9 cm.

Contains a chapter on the possibilities of cattle raising in the Dakotas.

220 BATEMAN, ED, SR. Horse breaker, by Ed Bateman, Sr. Photographic

series produced commercially by Tommy Thompson under editorial direction of the author. Seattle, Carl K. Wilson company, 1947. Cloth. OP.
2 p.l., 3–110 p. front., 44 plates, ports. 24.2 cm.
"First edition" on last page.

221 ———. Rawhide bound, by Ed Bateman, Sr. Incidental western silhouettes by Ace Reid, Jr. Seattle, Washington, Carl K. Wilson company exclusive distributors, [1950]. [Printed by Moss publishing company, San Angelo, Texas]. Cloth. OP.
4 p.l., 11–100 p. illus. (5 full-p. silhouettes). 23.5 cm.
Half title; "First edition" on copyright p.

222 BATES, EDMOND FRANKLIN. History and reminiscences of Denton County, by Ed F. Bates. . . . Denton, Texas, McNitzky printing company, [1918]. Cloth. Scarce.
xi p., 2 l., 412 p. front. (port.), plates, ports., 2 fold. photographic scenes. 23.5 cm.
Index, p. 408–412.
Half title.

The author gives some erroneous information about the Chisholm Trail.

223 BAUER, HELEN. California rancho days, by Helen Bauer. Garden City, N.Y., Doubleday & company, inc., [1953]. Pict. cloth.
2 p.l., 5–128 p. plates, maps, cattle brands. 21.5 cm.
Illus. t.p.

224 BAUGHMAN, THEODORE. Baughman, the Oklahoma scout. Personal reminiscences by Theodore Baughman. . . . Chicago and New York, Belford, Clarke & co., 1886. Dec. cloth. Scarce.
3 p.l., 9–216 p. front. (port.), plates. 18.2 cm.

In a later edition published by the Homewood Publishing Co., Chicago, the word "Baughman" was dropped and the title reads simply, *The Oklahoma Scout.*

225 BAUMANN, JOHN. Old man Crow's boy. Adventures in early Idaho, by John Baumann. New York, William Morrow & company, 1948. Cloth. OP.
4 p.l., 3–278 p. 22 cm.
Half title; map on end papers.

226 BEACH, MRS. ALFRED H. (CORA M.). Women of Wyoming, including a short history of some of the early activities of women in our state. . . . Compiled and edited by Mrs. Alfred H. (Cora M.) Beach. Casper, Wyoming, [S. E. Boyer & Company, 1927]. Cloth. OP.
viii p., 1 l., 582 p. plates, ports. 23.7 cm.
Index, p. 580–582.

Contains material on the wives of the ranchers of the state.

227 BEAL, M. D. A history of southeastern Idaho. An intimate narrative of peaceful conquest of empire builders. The fruits of their labors along tortuous rivers and valleys now sparkle like pearls in the diadem that is Idaho, the gem of the mountains. By M. D. Beal. . . . Illustrated with photographs. Caldwell, Idaho, the Caxton printers, ltd., 1942. Cloth. OP.

11 p.l., ₍23₎–443 p. front., plates, ports., map. 19.7 cm.
Bibliography, p. ₍385₎–392; notes, p. ₍395₎–432; index, p. ₍433₎–443.
Half title; pub. device.

228 BEALS, CARLETON. American earth. The biography of a nation. ₍By₎ Carleton Beals. Philadelphia, New York, Toronto, J. B. Lippincott company, ₍1939₎. Cloth. OP.

4 p.l., 9–500 p. 21.8 cm.
Bibliography, p. ₍471₎–475; index, p. 477–500.
Half title; vignette; untrimmed.
At head of title: Carleton Beals.

Has a chapter on the Johnson County War.

229 BEAUGRAND, HONORÉ. Six mois dans les Montagnes-Rocheuses Colo-rado—Utah—Nouveau-Méxique, par H. Beaugrand. Ouvrage accom-pagné d'une carte-itinéraire et orné de nombreuses illustrations hors texte. Avec une préface de Louis Fréchette. Montreal, Granger frères, 1890. Wrappers. Scarce.

6 p.l., ₍18₎–323 ₍1₎ p. front., plates, fold. map. 23cm.
Tables des matières, p. ₍324₎.

230 BECHDOLT, FREDERICK RITCHIE. Tales of the old-timers, by Frederick Bechdolt. . . . New York and London, the Century co., ₍1924₎. Pict. cloth. OP.

6 p.l., 3–367 p. front. 19.5 cm.
Half title; device.

231 ———. When the West was young, by Frederick Bechdolt. . . . New York, the Century co., 1922. Cloth. OP.

6 p.l., 3–309 p. front. 19.4 cm.
Half title.

232 BECKER, MAY LAMBERTON (ED.). Golden tales of the far West. Selected with an introduction by May Lamberton Becker. Decorations by Lois Lenski. New York, Dodd, Mead & company, 1935. Cloth. OP.

xiii, 304 p. illus. 20.2 cm.
Half title; untrimmed.

233 ———. Golden tales of the Southwest. Selected, with an introduc-

tion, by May Lamberton Becker. Decorations by Lois Lenski. New York, Dodd, Mead & company, 1939. Cloth. OP.

xiii, 265 p. illus. 20.2 cm.
Half title; illus. end papers.

Stories by J. Frank Dobie, Ross Santee, Charles M. Russell, Andy Adams, Alfred Henry Lewis, and others.

234 BEEBE, LUCIUS, and CHARLES CLEGG. The American west, the pictorial epic of a continent. [By] Lucius Beebe and Charles Clegg, with title page in color by E. S. Mammack. New York, E. P. Dutton & co., inc., publisher, 1955. Cloth.

5 p.l., 11–511 [1] p. illus., plates, map, facsms. 28.6 cm.
Bibliography, p. 508–511.
Half title; illus. end papers; illus. double t.p. (col.); "First edition" on copyright p.

Chapter XVIII deals with the cattle industry and the cattle trails.

235 BELL, JAMES G. A log of Texas-California cattle trail, 1854, [by] James G. Bell. Edited by J. Evetts Haley. [Austin, Texas, 1932]. Stiff wrappers. Scarce.

3 p.l., [7]–78 [1] p. 24 cm.
Index, p. [79].
"Reprinted from the *Southwestern Historical Quarterly,* 1932."

236 BELL, JOHN C. The pilgrim and the pioneer. The social and material developments in the Rocky Mountains, by John C. Bell. . . . Lincoln, Nebraska, printed by the International publishing ass'n., [1906]. Cloth. Scarce.

xii, 13–531 p. front., plates. 20.8 cm.

237 BELL, JOHN T. History of Washington County, Nebraska. Its early settlement and present status, resources, advantages, and future prospects. [By] John T. Bell. . . . Omaha, Neb., printed at the Herald steam book and job printing house, July, 1876. Wrappers. Rare.

[3]–64 [6] p. 21.6 cm.
Last 6 p. adv.

238 BENEDICT, CARL PETERS. A tenderfoot kid on gyp water, by Carl Peters Benedict. Illustrated. Introduction by J. Frank Dobie. [Austin, Texas], published by the Texas Folklore Society, Austin, Texas, and the University press in Dallas [printed by Carl Hertzog, El Paso, Texas], 1943. Pict. cloth. OP.

xviii, 115 p. front., plates, ports. 22.2 cm.
Half title: "Range Life Series under the general editorship of J. Frank Dobie."
Colophon: "550 copies of this book have been printed and the type melted."

239 BENEDICT, HARRY YANDELL, and JOHN A. LOMAX. The book of Texas, by H. Y. Benedict and John A. Lomax. . . . Fully illustrated. Garden City, New York, Doubleday, Page & company, 1916. Cloth. OP.

xxiii p., 1 l., 3–448 p., 1 l., front., illus., plates, ports., diagrs., maps. 24.7 cm. Device.

240 BENEDICT, JOHN D. Muskogee and northeastern Oklahoma, including the counties of Muskogee, McIntosh, Wagoner, Cherokee, Sequoyah, Adair, Delaware, Mayes, Rogers, Washington, Nowater, Craig, and Ottawa. By John D. Benedict. Chicago, S. J. Clarke company, 1922. Cloth. Pub. in 3 vols. Scarce.

Vol. I: 9 p.l., 19–693 p. plates, ports. 27.6 cm.
Vols. II and III: biographical.

Vol. I contains some information on cattle raising in these counties.

241 BENEFIELD, HATTIE STONE. For the good of the country. "Por el bien del Pais," by Hattie Stone Benefield. Illustrations by Patricia Benefield Williams. Los Angeles, Lorrin L. Morrison, publisher, 1951. Pict. cloth.

6 p.l., 138 p. front. (port.), illus., plates, ports., maps. 28 cm.
Foxen family tree, p. [87]–135; index, p. 136–138.
Half title; illus. end papers; double t.p. with map; colophon: "'For the Good of the Country' is printed in a limited edition of 600 copies, 500 copies of which are numbered. This copy being number —." (Signed).

242 [BENNETT, M. H.]. Cherokee Strip brand book authorized by stockmen's convention held at Caldwell, Kan., March 16th, 1881. This strip lies west of the Arkansas River, north of Cimaron [*sic*], and south of Kansas line. Kansas City, Mo., Sam I. C. Rhodes, printer, 1881. Sheep. Rare.

66 p. cattle brands. 14.9 cm.
Last 9 p. adv., also back and front covers, and adv. scattered throughout.

243 BENNETT, RUSSELL H. The compleat rancher, [by] Russell H. Bennett. With drawings by Ross Santee. New York, Toronto, Rinehart & company, incorporated, [1946]. Cloth. OP.

ix p., 1 l., 3–246 p. 21.2 cm.
Bibliography, p. 245–246.
Half title; illus. chapter headings; first edition, letter "R" in circle on copyright p.

A treatise on how to run a cattle ranch.

244 BENSCHOTER, GEORGE E. Book of facts concerning the early settlement of Sherman County, descriptive of its present business and agricultural developments and natural advantages. By Geo. E. Benschoter. Loup City, Nebraska, Loup City Northwestern print, [n. d., c.1897]. Wrappers. Rare.

2 p.l., 76 p. 18.4 cm.

[39]

245 BENT, SILAS. Meteorology of the mountains and plains of North America as affecting the cattle-growing industries of the United States. An address delivered before the cattle growers' convention, by Silas Bent, St. Louis, November 18th, 1884. St. Louis, Mo., R. F. Studley & co., printers and general stationers, 1885. Pamphlet. (Cover title). Rare.

7 p., 1 l. 21.6 cm.
5 p. addendum on pink paper at end.

A rare pamphlet dealing with the effect of rainfall upon the cattle ranges.

246 BENTLEY, HENRY LEWIS. Cattle ranges of the Southwest. A history of the exhaustion of the pasturage and suggestions for its restoration. By H. L. Bentley. . . . Washington, Government printing office, 1898. Stapled.

5–32 p. illus. 23.3 cm.
U. S. Dept. of Agriculture *Farmer's Bulletin No. 72.*

247 ———. Experiments in range improvements in central Texas, by H. L. Bentley. . . . Washington, Government printing office, 1902. Stiff wrappers.

3 p.l., 7–72 p. illus., plates. 22.5 cm.
U. S. Dept. of Agriculture, Bureau of Plant Industry, *Bulletin No. 13.*

248 BENTLEY, O. H. (ED.). History of Wichita and Sedgwick County, Kansas, past and present, including an account of the cities, towns, and villages of the county. Editor-in-chief Hon. O. H. Bentley. Illustrated. Chicago, C. F. Cooper & co., 1910. Cloth. Scarce. Pub. in 2 vols.

Vol. I: xv, 454 p. front. (with tissue), plates, ports. (with tissues). 25.3 cm.
Vol. II: 455–933 p. front. (with tissue), plates. 25.3 cm.
Index, p. 925–933.
Paged continuously.

Has some material on cattle trails, cow towns, and Jesse Chisholm.

249 BENTON, FRANK. Cowboy life on the sidetrack; being an extremely humorous and sarcastic story of the trials and tribulations endured by a party of stockmen making a shipment from the West to the East. By Frank Benton. . . . Illustrated by E. A. Filleau. . . . Denver, Colo., the Western Stories syndicate, [1903]. Pict. cloth. Scarce.

4 p.l., 11–207 [3] p. plates, ports. 19.7 cm.
Last 3 p. adv.

A humorous dig at the railroad companies for the way they handled stock shipments.

250 ———. Land leasing. Speech of Frank Benton of Wyoming delivered before the American National Cattle Growers' Association at Denver,

Colorado, March 5, 1902. In support of a resolution indorsing the bill to lease the arid lands for grazing. . . . Denver, Colo., the Smith-Brooks printing co., [1902]. Pamphlet. (Cover title). Rare.

7 p. 22.7 cm.

251 BENTON, JESSE JAMES. Cow by the tail, by Jesse James Benton, with an introduction by Richard Summers. Boston, Houghton Mifflin company, 1943. Cloth. OP.

xii p., 1 l., 225 p. 20.4 cm.
Half title; illus. double t.p.; signature in facsm. at end; headpieces; first edition, "1943" over imprint on t.p.

252 BERRY, GERALD, L. The Whoop-up Trail (Alberta-Montana relationships), by Gerald L. Berry. . . . Edmonton, Alberta, published by Applied Arts Products, ltd., 1953. Cloth.

3 p.l., 7–143 p. plates, ports., plan, maps. 23.3 cm.
Appendices, p. 133–136 (Appendix B before Appendix A); bibliography, p. 137–139; index, p. 140–143.

Contains a chapter on the cattlemen of Alberta and of Montana.

253 BERRYMAN, OPAL LEIGH. Pioneer preacher, [by] Opal Leigh Berryman. New York, Thomas Y. Crowell company, [1948]. Cloth. OP.

vi p. 1 l., 248 p. 21 cm.
Half title; untrimmed.

Life among the cowboys of West Texas.

254 BERTON, ALVA H., and HAROLD E. SEIELSTAD. Co-operative marketing of livestock in North Dakota, by Alva H. Berton and Harold E. Seielstad. Fargo, North Dakota, Agricultural Experiment Station, North Dakota Agricultural College, 1927. Wrappers. OP.

2 p.l., [5]–63 p. illus., maps, tables. 21.6 cm.

255 BESHOAR, M. All about Trinidad and Las Animas County, Colorado. Their history, industries, resources, etc. By M. Beshoar. Denver, Colo., Times steam printing house and blank book manufactory, 1882. Wrappers. Rare.

iv, [5]–118 [9] p. 19.3 cm.
Last 9 p. adv.

256 "BESOM," A. (PSEUD.). A guide to south eastern Nebraska, with a new map of the wonderful Nemaha Valley. . . . By A. "Besom," . . . [Lincoln, Neb.], South Eastern Nebraska Immigration Union, Atchison, Kansas, 1878. Wrappers. (Cover title). Rare.

20 [2] p. fold. map. 26.2 cm.
Double column; business cards scattered throughout.

257 BEVERLY, ROBERT (BOB). Hobo in rangeland, by Bob Beverly. Lovington, New Mexico, ₁Leader publishing co., n. d.₁. Pict. wrappers. Scarce.

3 p.l., 5–87 ₁1₁ p. plates. 23.4 cm.

True stories as told by an old-time cowboy.

258 BIGGERS, DON H. From cattle range to cotton patch. A series of historical sketches dealing with the industrial, social, and commercial evolutions that have taken place in western Texas from the beginning of the buffalo slaughter to the present. First published in the Dallas-Galveston News. By Don H. Biggers. Abilene, Texas, Press of the Abilene printing co., ₁n. d., c.1908₁. Stiff wrappers. Very rare.

2 p.l., 156 p. front., plates. 22 cm.
Errata slip tipped in at p. 83.

Reprinted by the Frontier Times, Bandera, Texas, in 1944.

80 p. 26.5 cm.
Double column.

259 ——. German pioneers in Texas. A brief history of their hardships, struggles, and achievements. Compiled for the Fredericksburger Wochenblatt and Frederick Standard. By Don H. Biggers. ₁Fredericksburg₁, Press of the Fredericksburg publishing co., 1925. Cloth. OP.

4 p.l., ₁3₁–230 p. plates, ports. 22.2 cm.

260 ——. Shackleford County sketches. ₁By₁ Don H. Biggers. Done into a book in the Albany News office, October, 1908. Boards. Very rare.

₁71₁ p. (no pagination). front. 26.7 cm.
Appendix, (articles first published in the *Dallas News*) last 35 pages.

261 BILES, J. HUGH. The early history of Ada. By J. Hugh Biles. Ada, Oklahoma, published by the Oklahoma State Bank of Ada, Oklahoma, in commemoration of its fiftieth anniversary, 1954. Cloth.

xv p., 2 l., 5–160 p. plates, ports. 23.5 cm.
Half title; device; "First edition" on copyright p.

262 BILLINGTON, RAY ALLEN. Westward expansion. A history of the American frontier, by Ray Allen Billington. . . . With the collaboration of James Blaine Hedges. . . . New York, the Macmillan company, 1949. Cloth.

xiii, 873 p. maps. 24.3 cm.
Bibliographical notes, p. 757–834; index, p. 835–873.
Half title; map on end papers.

263 BIRD, ISABELLA LUCY. A lady's life in the Rocky Mountains. By Isabella L. Bird, with illustrations. London, John Murray, 1879. Cloth. Scarce.

xii, 296 p. front., plates. 19.3 cm.
"Previously published in *Leisure Hour,* 1878"—cf. prefatory note.
American edition, New York, G. P. Putnam's sons, 1879, 1880, 1888, and 1894.

An Englishwoman's impressions of ranch life in Montana as told to friends in England through letters.

264 [BISHOP, C. C.]. Frontier stories of the Lone Star state, [by C. C. Bishop]. [N. p.], 1936. Wrappers. OP.
52 p. 22 cm.

Some material on cowboys and cattle brands.

265 BISHOP, CURTIS. Lots of land. From material compiled under the direction of the commissioner of the General Land Office of Texas, Bascom Giles. Written by Curtis Bishop. Decorations by Warren Hunter. Austin, the Steck company, [1949]. Pict. cloth.
x, 307 p. illus., port. 22.2 cm.
Bibliography, p. 303–307.
Half title; illus. t.p.

Chapter V deals with the cowboy and the Texas cattle industry.

266 BIXBY-SMITH, SARAH. Adobe days, being the truthful narrative of the events in the life of a California girl on a sheep ranch and in El Pueblo de Nuestra Señora de los Angeles while it was yet a small and humble town. . . . By Sarah Bixby-Smith. Cedar Rapids, Iowa, the Torch press, 1925. Cloth and boards. OP.
5 p.l., 11–208 p. 19 cm.
Half title; device.
Republished in 1926 with 217 pages.

267 BLACK, A. P. (OTT). The end of the long horn trail, by A. P. (Ott) Black. Selfridge, N. D., published by the Selfridge Journal, [n. d., c.1936]. Stiff wrappers. (Cover title). OP.
4–59 p. front., illus., plates. 22.5 cm.
Blank leaf following each of the first three chapters.

268 BLACK, JOHN A. Arizona, the land of sunshine and silver, health and prosperity, the place of ideal homes, by John A. Black, commissioner of immigration. Phoenix, Arizona, Republican book and job print, [1890]. Wrappers. Scarce.
1 p.l., [5]–146 p. tables. 21 cm.

Also published at Tucson, Arizona, same year.
143 p. 21.6 cm.

269 BLACK, WILLIAM HENRY, A. T. SEMPLE, and J. L. LUSH. Beef produc-

tion and quality as influenced by crossing Brahma with Herefords and
shorthorn cattle. By W. H. Black . . . and A. T. Semple . . . and J. L. Lush.
. . . Washington, [Government printing office], 1934. Wrappers. (Cover
title).

54 p. illus., diagrs. 23 cm.
"Literature cited," p. 53.
U. S. Dept. of Agriculture *Technical Bulletin No. 417*. Contribution from the
Bureau of Animal Industry.

270 BLACK, WILLIAM HENRY, and V. V. PARR. Dehorning, castrating,
branding, and marking beef cattle. [By W. H. Black and V. V. Parr.
Washington, U. S. Government printing office, 1929]. Wrappers. OP.

ii, 12 p. illus., diagrs. 23.5 cm.
U. S. Dept. of Agriculture *Farmer's Bulletin No. 1600*. Contribution from Bureau of
Animal Industry.

A revision of and superseding *Farmer's Bulletin 949*, "Dehorning and Castrating
Cattle," by F. W. Farley.

271 BLACKBURN, W. D. Nemaha land district in southern Nebraska. Its
resources and capabilities, and advantages it offers to immigration. . . .
Compiled and written by W. D. Blackburn. . . . [Omaha, Omaha Daily
and Weekly Republican steam printing house], 1870. Wrappers. Rare.

2 p.l., [5]-104 p. 21.3 cm.
Last 12 p. adv.; adv. on verso of most pages of text.

272 BLACKMORE, WILLIAM. Colorado: its resources, parks, and prospects
as a new field for emigration; with an account of the Trenchara and Cas-
tilla estates in the San Luis Park. By William Blackmore. London,
Sampson Low, Son and Marston . . . , 1869. Cloth. Rare.

8 p.l., [15]-217 p. front. (port. pasted in), 2 large fold. maps in front. 28.2 cm.

273 BLAKE, FORRESTER. Riding the mustang trail, by Forrester Blake. New
York, Charles Scribner's sons, 1935. Cloth. OP.

5 p.l., 261 p. front., plates, ports. 22.2 cm.
Half title; untrimmed.

274 BLAKE, WILLIAM P. Description of the Piedmont stock range in Maricopa, Yavapai, and Yuma counties, Arizona Territory, with observations
upon the advantages of Arizona as a stock-raising region. By William
P. Blake. New Haven, Tuttle, Morehouse & Taylor, printers, 1886.
Cloth. Rare.

1 p.l., [3]-20 p. 17.7 cm.

275 BLANCHARD, LEOLA HOWARD. Conquest of southwest Kansas, by Leola
Howard Blanchard. A history and thrilling stories of frontier life in the

state of Kansas. ₁Wichita, printed and bound by the Wichita Eagle press, 1931₁. Pict. cloth. OP.

3 p.l., 7–355 p. illus., plates, ports. 20.3 cm.
Vignette; copyright notice on verso of flyleaf.

276 BLUMENFELD, RALPH D. Home town: story of a dream that came true, by Ralph D. Blumenfeld. London, New York, Melbourne, Hutchinson & co., (publishers), ltd., ₁n. d.₁. Cloth. OP.

3 p.l., 7–116 p. 21.8 cm.
Half title.

Among other things, the author tells of some of his experiences in Kansas City and Dodge City among the cowboys.

277 BOATRIGHT, MODY COGGIN. Tall tales from Texas, by Mody C. Boatright; illustrated by Elizabeth E. Keefer; foreword by J. Frank Dobie. Dallas, Texas, the Southwest press . . . , ₁1934₁. Cloth and boards. OP.

xxiv, 100 p. illus. 19.7 cm.
Vignette; title label pasted on.

278 ——, and DONALD DAY (EDS.). Backwoods to border, Mody C. Boatright, Donald Day, editors. Texas Folklore society, Austin, and University press in Dallas, 1943. Cloth. OP.

xv, 235 p. illus., music. 23.5 cm.
Bibliographical footnotes; "Proceedings of the Texas Folklore Society, 1942," p. ₁218₁–220; index, p. ₁225₁–235.
Half title.
Texas Folklore Society Publications No. XVIII.

279 ——, and DONALD DAY (EDS.). From hell to breakfast; Mody C. Boatright, Donald Day, editors. Austin, Texas, Texas Folk-lore society. Dallas, University press, Southern Methodist university, 1944. Cloth.

x, 215 p. illus., 23.5 cm.
Index, p. ₁206₁–215.
Half title.
Texas Folk-lore Society Publication Number XIX, J. Frank Dobie, general editor.

280 ——, WILSON M. HUDSON, and ALLEN MAXWELL (EDS.). Mesquite and willow, edited by Mody C. Boatright, Wilson M. Hudson, Allen Maxwell. Dallas, Texas, Southern Methodist University press, ₁1957₁. Pict. cloth.

viii p., 1 l., 3–203 p. map, fold. table. 23.3 cm.

281 BOBBITT, GEORGE G. The three harvests and supplement . . . ₁by George G. Bobbitt₁. Panhandle, Texas, ₁Panhandle Herald, distributor, n. d., c.1947₁. Stiff wrappers.

2 p.l., 5–142 p. illus., plates, ports., map. 22.2 cm.
Supplement, "Born and Raised in the Longhorn Country. Memoirs of Charlie Wright," p. ₁107₁–142.

282 BODINE, L. T. Kansas illustrated. An accurate and reliable description of this marvelous state for the information of persons seeking homes
in the great West. By L. T. Bodine. Kansas City, Mo., Ramsey, Millett
& Hudson, 1879. Wrappers. Rare.

[3]–40 [8] p. illus. 22.8 cm.
Last 8 p. adv.

283 BOETHEL, PAUL C. The history of Lavaca County, by Paul C. Boethel.
San Antonio, Texas, the Naylor co., 1936. Pict. cloth. OP.

5 p.l., 151 p. 23.5 cm.
Half title.

284 BOLIN, WILLIAM J. The universal stock register of eastern Oregon
brands, together with the laws of the state of Oregon, relating to the
branding and marking of stock. By William J. Bolin. . . . Union, Oregon,
published by L. J. & M. F. Davis, 1890. Cloth. Rare.

2 p.l., [5]–212 [12] p. cattle brands. 16.5 cm.
Last 10 p. adv.

285 BOLLING, RUTH J. Tale of a Texas ranch, by Ruth J. Bolling. San
Antonio, Texas, the Naylor company, publishers of the southwest, [1957].
Pict. fabricoid.

ix, 96 p. 20 cm.
Half title.

286 BOLTON, HERBERT EUGENE. Cross swords & gold pan. A group of
notable full-cover paintings depicting outstanding episodes in the exploration and settlement of the West. By Carl Oscar Borg and Millard
Sheets, with interpretive historical essays by Herbert Eugene Bolton,
and a ballad by John R. McCarthy. Los Angeles, the Premavere press,
[1936]. Boards. Scarce.

[31] p. (no pagination). 14 full-p. col. plates (1 double p.). 32.5 cm.

Has a chapter on the "Coming of Cattle."

287 BORDERS, MICHAEL WASHINGTON. Evils of direct marketing, [by] M. W.
Borders. [Wichita, 1928]. Stiff wrappers. Scarce.

31 p. 22.7 cm.
Cover title: "Annual meeting of Kansas Live Stock Association, Wichita, Kansas,
March 8, 1928."

288 ———. The marketing of livestock. Address delivered before Texas
Bankers' Association, Galveston, Texas, May 14, 1929. By M. W. Borders.
[N. p., n. d., c.1929]. Stiff wrappers. (Cover title). OP.

32 p. 23 cm.

289 BOTKIN, B. A. (ED.). A treasury of American folklore. Stories, ballads,

and traditions of the people. Edited by B. A. Botkin . . . , with a foreword by Carl Sandburg. New York, Crown publishers, ₁1944₁. Cloth.

xxvii ₁2₁, 2–932 p. music. 22 cm.
Index, p. 919–932.
Half title.

290 ———. A treasury of western folklore, edited by B. A. Botkin. Foreword by Bernard DeVoto. . . . New York, Crown publishers, inc., ₁1951₁. Pict. cloth.

xxvi, 806 p. music 21.8 cm.
Index, p. 793–806.
Illus. t.p.

Issued in special Southwest, Rocky Mountain, and West Coast editions, each with a foreword by a different author.

291 BOUGHTON, J. S. The Kansas handbook, containing a general description of the state . . . , the public lands and how to obtain them. . . . Published by J. S. Houghton. Lawrence, Kansas, Daily Journal steam printing press, 1878. Wrappers. Rare.

₁3₁–112 p. tables 16.2 cm.
Calls for map but none found; adv. scattered throughout.

292 BOWERS, D. N. Seventy years in Norton County, Kansas, 1872–1942. By D. N. Bowers . . . , written and compiled from the records, newspaper files, and personal interviews. Special articles contributed by local writers. Norton, Kansas, the Norton County Champion, 1942. Cloth. OP.

xiv p., 1 l., 238 p. front., plates. 19 cm.
Appendix, p. 235–238.

293 BOWMAN, JAMES CLOYD. Pecos Bill, the greatest cowboy of all time, by James C. Bowman . . . pictures by Laura Bannon. . . . Chicago, Albert Whitman & co., 1937. Pict. cloth. OP.

10 p.l., 29–296 p. front. (col.), illus., plates (part col.). 23 cm.
Half title; illus. end papers (col.).
"Junior Press books."

294 BOYCE, JAMES RICHARD, SR. Facts about Montana Territory, and the way to get there. Contributed to the Rocky Mountain Gazette, by J. R. Boyce, Sr. ₁Helena, Mont., 1872₁. Wrappers. (Cover title). Rare.

₁2₁–24 p. 23.5 cm.

Has a section on stock raising.

295 BOYCE, ANNIE M. Tall tales from a ranch, by Annie M. Boyce. Illustrated by Walter A. McKinney. ₁San Antonio, Texas₁, the Naylor company, ₁1957₁. Pict. cloth.

xiii, 97 p. illus. 21.7 cm.
Half title; illus. t.p.

296 BOYD, DAVID. A history; Greeley and the Union colony of Colorado, by David Boyd. Greeley, Colo., the Greeley Tribune press, 1890. Cloth. Scarce.

x, ₁11₁–448 p. front., plates, ports., facsm. 23 cm.
Leaf of errata.

Chapter on cattle and fence troubles.

297 BOYLE, LOUIS M. Out West. Growing cymbidium orchids and other flowers. By Louis M. Boyle. The story of El Rancho Rinconana. ₁Los Angeles, printed by Times-Mirror press, 1952₁. Pict. Cloth.

4 p.l., 11–526 p. illus. (part col.), plates, ports. 24.8 cm.
Index p. 503–519.
Illus. end papers.

Has some material on California ranches.

298 BRACKE, WILLIAM B. Wheat country, by William B. Bracke. Edited by Erskine Caldwell. New York, Duell, Sloan & Pearce, ₁1950₁. Cloth. OP.

viii p., 1 l., 3–309 p. 22 cm.
Index, p. 299–309.
Half title; map on end papers.

299 BRACKENBURY, RICHARD. Western sketches and war poems. By Richard Brackenbury. ₁La Jolla, California, 1945₁. Pict. cloth. OP.

2 p.l., 1 p., 6–129 p. front. (port.). 20.5 cm.
8 blank l. at end.

Some true experiences of the author as a cowboy.

300 BRACKETT, R. W. A history of the ranchos. The Spanish, Mexican, and American occupation of San Diego County, and the story of ownership of the land grants therein, by R. W. Brackett. . . . San Diego, Calif., published by Union Title Insurance and Trust company, 1939. Wrappers.

4 p.l., 86 p. illus., cattle brands, map. 23 cm.
Bibliography, p. 85–86.
Half title; t.p. on verso of half title.

301 BRADFORD, HARRY ELWYN, and GEORGE ALBERT SPIDEL. Nebraska, its geography and agriculture. By Harry Elwyn Bradford and George Albert Spidel. . . . New York, the Macmillan company, 1931. Pict. cloth. OP.

ix ₁1₁ p., 1 l., 355 p. front., illus., plates, charts, maps, tables. 20.2 cm.
Appendices, p. 333–346; index, p. 347–355.
Half title; seal of state on cover.

302 [BRADY, BUCKSKIN]. Stories and sermons. By Buckskin Brady. . . . Toronto, William Briggs, 1905. Cloth. Port. label pasted on. Scarce.

4 p.l., 7–135 p. front., plates, ports. 19.8 cm.

303 BRADY, WILLIAM. Glimpses of Texas, its divisions, resources, development, and prospects. By Wm. Brady. Houston, Texas, 1871. Stiff wrappers. Rare.

[3]-104 p. fold. map in front. 18 cm.
Last 19 p. adv.

Chapter on stock raising.

304 BRAKE, HEZEKIAH. On two continents. A long life's experience. By Hezekiah Brake. Published by the author. Topeka, Kansas, Crane & Company, printers, 1896. Cloth. Scarce.

5 p.l., 11-240 p. 2 ports. (incl. front.). 19.6 cm.

A chapter on ranching in New Mexico.

305 BRAMAN, D. E. E. Information about Texas, carefully prepared by D. E. E. Braman. Philadelphia, J. B. Lippincott and co., 1857. Cloth. Rare.

viii, 9-192 p. 18.8 cm.
Reprinted in 1858.

A chapter on stock raising in Texas.

306 BRANCH, E. DOUGLAS. The cowboy and his interpreters, [by] Douglas Branch; illustrations by Will James, Joe DeYong, Charles M. Russell. New York, London, D. Appleton and company, 1926. Dec. cloth. OP.

ix [1] p., 1 l., 277 [1] p. front., illus. 21.3 cm.
Bibliography, p. 271-[278].
Half title; illus. end papers; pub. device; untrimmed; first edition, figure "(1)" at end of bibliography.

307 ———. Westward. The romance of the American frontier. By E. Douglas Branch. Woodcuts by Lucinda Smith Wakefield. New York and London, D. Appleton and company, 1930. Cloth. OP.

ix [1] p., 2 l., 3-626 [1] p. illus., maps (1 double p.). 22.2 cm.
Notes on material, p. 598-[609]; index, p. 611-[627].
Half title; map on end papers; illus. chapter headings; vignette; untrimmed; first edition, figure "(1)" at end of index.

Chapter XXXI, on the open range, deals with the cattle industry.

308 [BRANDS]. Brand book, Jackson County Stockmen's Association. [Medford], Medford Mail print, 1904. Leather. Rare.

[59] p. (no pagination). cattle brands. 14 cm.

Seen in the Rollins Collection, Princeton University.

309 ———. The history of cattle brands and how to read them. [N. p.], Carter Oil company, [1955]. Pict. wrappers.

14 p. illus., cattle brands. 15.7 cm.

310 BRATT, JOHN. Trails of yesterday, by John Bratt. Lincoln, Chicago, Dallas, the University publishing company, 1921. Pict. cloth. OP.

xi p., 1 l., 302 p. front. (port. with tissue), illus., plates, ports. 23.5 cm.
Vignette; untrimmed; dedication at end of text.

Mr. Bratt was a well-known cattleman in the early days. This autobiography was published by his widow and four daughters.

311 BRAY, CHARLES ISEARD. Financing the western cattleman, by Charles I. Bray. Fort Collins Experiment Station, Colorado Agricultural College, December, 1928. Pict. wrappers. OP.

2 p.l., [5]–87 p. illus., ports., maps, diagrs., tables. 23 cm.
"Literature cited," p. 83–87.
Thesis (Ph. D.), University of Illinois, 1926.
"Reprinted from Colorado Experiment Station, *Bulletin 338,* December, 1928."
Illus. t.p.

312 BRAYER, HERBERT OLIVER. The L 7 ranches. An incident in the economic development of the western cattle industry, by Herbert O. Brayer. Reprinted from the *Annals of Wyoming,* Vol. XV, No. 1 (January, 1943). Cheyenne, Wyoming Historical department, [1943]. Stiff pict. wrappers. (Cover title). OP.

34 p. front., diagrs., tables. 22.8 cm.

313 ———. Ranchero. [By] Herbert O. Brayer. Reprinted from the *Pacific Historical Review,* Vol. XII, No. 2 (June, 1943). Pamphlet. (Cover title). OP.

p. 181–195. 25.4 cm.

314 BRAYER, GARNET M. and HERBERT OLIVER. American cattle trails, 1540–1900, by Garnett M. and Herbert O. Brayer. Illustrations by Edward Borein, Joseph Easly, George Froid, Herman Palmer, Herbert M. Stoops. Ruth T. Glen, cartographer. Bayside, New York, Western Range Cattle Industry study in co-operation with the American Pioneer Trails association, 1952. Cloth.

3 p.l., 7–128 p. illus., plates, 3 maps, facsm. 21 cm.
Also issued in pict. wrappers, same illustrations and number of pages, but 17.8 cm. in height.

315 BREAKENRIDGE, WILLIAM M. Helldorado. Bringing the law to the mesquite, by William M. Breakenridge. With illustrations. Boston and New York, Houghton Mifflin company, 1928. Cloth. OP.

xix, 256 p. front. (port.), plates, ports. 23.2 cm.
Half title; pub. device; first edition, "1928" under imprint.

316 BRENNEN, C. A. The main reasons why range cattle ranchers succeed

or fail. Cattle production costs per head and pound, 1928 to 1932 figures and long-time averages. By C. A. Brennen. . . . Reno, Nevada, published by the University of Nevada, 1933. Pict. wrappers. OP.

[5]-22 p. plates. 21.8 cm.
Agricultural Experiment Station *Bulletin No. 133,* September, 1933.

317 ———. The public range and the livestock industry in Nevada. By C. A. Brennen. . . . Reno, Nevada, published by the University of Nevada, 1935. Pict. wrappers. OP.

[3]-19 p. plates. 21.8 cm.
Agricultural Experiment Station *Bulletin No. 139,* March, 1935.

318 BREVOORT, ELIAS. New Mexico. Her natural resources and attractions, being a collection of facts, mainly concerning her geography, climate, population, schools, mines, and minerals . . . Spanish and Mexican land grants. By Elias Brevoort. . . . Santa Fe, printed and published by Elias Brevoort, 1874. Wrappers. Scarce.

x, [11]-176 [3] p. tables. 22.8 cm.
Leaf of errata at end (seldom found, and it is presumed these leaves have been lost through the years); 2 p. adv. at end.

319 BRIGGS, HAROLD E. Frontiers of the Northwest. A history of the upper Missouri Valley, by Harold E. Briggs. . . . Illustrated. New York, London, D. Appleton-Century company, incorporated, 1940. Cloth. OP.

xiv p. 1 l., 3-629 p. front., plates (4 ports. on 1 plate), maps. 22.8 cm.
Bibliography, p. 595-612; index, p. 613-629.
Half title; map on end papers; pub. device; first edition, figure "(1)" at end of index.

Contains a long section of twenty-four chapters on the cattle industry.

320 BRIMLOW, GEORGE FRANCIS. Harney County, Oregon, and its range land, by George Francis Brimlow, under sponsorship of the Harney County Historical Society, Burns, Oregon. Portland, Oregon, Binfords & Mort, publishers, [1951]. Cloth.

8 p.l., 316 p. plates, ports. 23.8 cm.
Appendix, p. 285; sources, p. [286]-304; index, p. 305-316.
Half title; pub. device.

321 BRINLEY, GORDON. Away to the Canadian Rockies and British Columbia, by Gordon Brinley. . . . Illustrated, by D. Putnam Brinley. New York, Dodd, Mead & company, 1938. Cloth. OP.

x p., 1 l., 301 [7] p. front. (col.), illus., plates (col.). 22.3 cm.
Supplement, p. 267-301.
Half title; map on end papers; vignette; untrimmed; last 7 p. blank for memoranda.

Has chapters on the rodeo.

322 BRISBIN, JAMES SANKS. The beef bonanza; or, how to get rich on the plains. Being a description of cattle-growing, sheep-farming, horse-raising, and dairying in the West. By Gen. James S. Brisbin. With illustrations. Philadelphia, J. B. Lippincott & co., 1881. Pict. cloth. Scarce.

11 p.l., 23–222 ₍6₎ p.   front., 7 plates.   19 cm.
Last 6 p. adv.
Index, p. 219–222.
Reprinted 1959 by the University of Oklahoma press.

A treatise on cattle as an investment and one of the books which caused a boom in the cattle industry through foreign investments.

323 ———. The great Yellowstone Valley, described by Gen. James S. Brisbin. St. Louis, Mo., Commercial printing co., printers and engravers, 1882. Leather. Rare.

3 p.l., 7–84 ₍1₎ p.   front., illus.   19.3 cm.

These little books were given away with the compliments of the author and Henry Villard, president of the Union Pacific Railroad.

324 BRITTON, SARAH ANN. The early history of Baylor County, by Sarah Ann Britton. Dallas, Texas, the Story Book press, ₍1955₎. Cloth.

6 p.l., 13–185 p.   plates.   19.7 cm.

Published in an edition of 400 copies, but when the first 100 copies had been bound, the company went bankrupt and it became necessary to get another company to bind the remaining 300. These have a different binding from the first 100. There is a chapter on cattle ranching and some corrections made by the author in ink.

325 BROCK, CHARLES E. M. Let the world judge. A romance of the Pacific, by Charles E. M. Brock. Illustrated. New York, Broadway publishing co., 1904. Dec. cloth. OP.

x p., 2 l., 195 p.   front. (port. with tissue), plates.   19.6 cm.
Pub. device; untrimmed.

326 BROCKETT, LINUS PIERPONT. Our western empire; or, the new West beyond the Mississippi; the latest and most comprehensive work on the states and territories west of the Mississippi. . . . By L. P. Brockett. With illustrations and maps by the most distinguished artists. Philadelphia, Bradley and co., 1881. Cloth. Scarce.

1,312 p.   front., illus., plates, maps (part double p.).   25 cm.
Reprinted in 1882 with same imprint and collation.

327 BROMFIELD, LOUIS, and others. Flat Top Ranch. The story of a grassland venture. By Louis Bromfield, C. C. Booth, B. W. Allred, Martine Emert, J. C. Dykes, G. O. Hedrick, W. B. Roberts, Charles Pettit, W. R.

THE BEEF BONANZA;

OR,

HOW TO GET RICH ON THE PLAINS.

BEING A DESCRIPTION OF

CATTLE-GROWING, SHEEP-FARMING, HORSE-RAISING,
AND DAIRYING

IN THE WEST.

BY

GEN. JAMES S. BRISBIN, U.S.A.,

AUTHOR OF "BELDEN, THE WHITE CHIEF," "LIFE OF GENERAL GRANT,"
"LIFE OF J. A. GARFIELD," "LIFE OF GEN. W. S. HANCOCK."

WITH ILLUSTRATIONS.

PHILADELPHIA:
J. B. LIPPINCOTT & CO.
LONDON: 16 SOUTHAMPTON ST., COVENT GARDEN.
1881.

Van Dersal, and Frank Reeves. Edited by B. W. Allred and J. C. Dykes. Norman, University of Oklahoma press, [1957]. Cloth.

xxiv p., 1 l., 3–232 p. plates. 21.7 cm.
Appendix, p. 207–221; index, p. 223–232.
Half title; illus. double t.p.; "First edition" on copyright p.

328 BRONSON, EDGAR BEECHER. Cowboy life on the western plains; reminiscences of a ranchman, by Edgar Beecher Bronson. . . . New York, George H. Doran company, [1910]. Cloth with col. illus. label pasted on. OP.

6 p.l., 3–369 [1] p. front., plates. 19.5 cm.
Appendix, p. 361–[370].
Half title.

This is a reprint of the author's *Reminiscences of a Ranchman*. See Item 330.

329 ———. Red blooded, by Edgar Beecher Bronson. Chicago, A. C. McClurg and co., 1910. Pict. cloth. OP.

5 p.l., 3–342 p. front., plates. 21 cm.
Partly reprinted from various periodicals. Later reprinted by George H. Doran co., with some changes in the title page.

330 ———. Reminiscences of a ranchman, by Edgar Beecher Bronson. New York, the McClure company, MCMVIII. Cloth. OP.

4 p.l., 3–314 p. 19.8 cm.
Half title; pub. device.

Reprinted in revised edition, Chicago, 1910, with 369 p.; also same year by Doran and Co., under the title *Cowboy Life on the Western Plains* (see item 329). Revised with some new material added in 1920.

331 ———. The vanguard, by Edgar Beecher Bronson. . . . New York, George H. Doran company, [1914]. Pict. cloth. OP.

5 p.l., 9–316 p. 19.6 cm.
Half title; illus. end papers (col.).

332 BROOKS, BRYANT BUTLER. Memoirs of Bryant B. Brooks, cowboy, trapper, lumberman, stockman, oilman, banker, and governor of Wyoming. Glendale, California, privately printed in a limited edition by the author, [printed by] the Arthur H. Clark company, 1939. Cloth. Scarce.

9 p.l., [21]–370 p. front. (port. with tissue), plates, ports. (all with tissues), coat of arms (col.). 24.5 cm.
Index, p. [359]–370.
Half title: "Genealogical chart[s]" on end papers.

Because the edition was limited to 150 copies, this book is very scarce.

333 ———. The state of Wyoming. A book of reliable information published by authority of the Eighth Legislature. Edited and published under

[54]

the direction of Bryant B. Brooks, governor, 1905. Sheridan, Wyo., Sheridan Post co., printers, 1905. Stiff wrappers. OP.

5 p.l., ₁9₁–144 ₁1₁ p. plates, tables. 22.5 cm.
Col. map on back wrapper.

334 BROOKS, SARAH WARNER. Alamo ranch; a story of New Mexico, by Sarah Warner Brooks. . . . Cambridge, ₁Mass.₁, privately printed, MCMIII. Boards. Scarce.

3 p.l., 148 p. front. 22.2 cm.
Half title.
Colophon: "This edition is limited to two hundred and fifty numbered copies of which this is number —."

335 BROPHY, FRANK CULLEN. Arizona sketch book. Fifty historical sketches, by Frank Cullen Brophy. ₁Phoenix, Arizona, printed by Ampco Press, Arizona-Messenger printing co., 1952₁. Cloth.

xi, 310 p. plates. 21 cm.
Bibliography, p. 297–301; index, p. 303–310.
Half title; map on end papers.

336 BROSNAN, CORNELIUS JAMES. History of the state of Idaho, by C. J. Brosnan. . . . New York, Chicago, Boston, Charles Scribner's sons, ₁1918₁. Cloth. Scarce.

xiii p., 2 l., 237 p. front. (port.), illus., plates, ports., maps (1 double p. col.). 20 cm.
Supplements, p. 213–231; index, p. 233–237.
Republished in 1926 and 1935.

337 BROTHERS, MARY HUDSON. A Pecos pioneer, by Mary Hudson Brothers. Albuquerque, published by the University of New Mexico press, 1943. Cloth.

vii p., 1 l., 169 p. front. (group port.). 23.5 cm.
Half title; device.

338 BROWN, BELLE SCOTT. Grandmother Belle remembers, by Belle Scott Brown. Illustrations by Caroline Keller Lewis. San Antonio, the Naylor company, publishers, 1941. Cloth.

ix, 119 p. illus. 21 cm.
Half title.

A Texas ranch woman's memories of her family and ranch life.

339 BROWN, C. E. (ED.). Cowboy tales. Pecos Bill, tall yarns of the mighty hero of the American cattle trails and ranches. Other cowboy stuff. ₁Edited by₁ C. E. Brown. . . . Madison, Wisconsin, C. E. Brown, 1929. Pict. wrappers. OP.

5–16 p. 22.9 x 10 cm.
"First edition" on t.p.

340 BROWN, DEE, and MARTIN F. SCHMITT. Trail driving days. Text by Dee Brown, picture research by Martin F. Schmitt. New York, Charles Scribner's sons; London, Charles Scribner's sons, ltd., 1952. Pict. cloth.

xxii p., 1 l., 264 p. plates, ports., cattle brands, facsms. 30.5 cm.
Bibliography, p. 255–264.
Half title; errata leaf tipped in; vignette; first edition, letter "A" on copyright p.

341 BROWN, GEORGE L. The state of Nebraska as a home for emigrants. Prepared and published by George L. Brown. . . . Omaha, Neb., Republican printing company, 1875. Wrappers. Rare.

[3]–32 [1] p. 22.3 cm.
Errata recto back wrapper; illus. t.p.

342 BROWN, JESSE, and A. M. WILLARD. The Black Hills trails. A history of the struggles of the pioneers in the winning of the Black Hills, by Jesse Brown and A. M. Willard. Edited by John T. Milek. Rapid City, South Dakota, Rapid City Journal company, 1924. Cloth. Scarce.

6 p.l., [17]–572 p. front., illus., plates, ports. 23.7 cm.

Has section on "The Language of the Roundup."

343 BROWN, JOHN. Twenty-five years a parson in the wild West; being the experience of Parson Ralph Riley, by Rev. John Brown. . . . Fall River, Mass., printed for the author, 1896. Cloth. Scarce.

4 p.l., 9–215 p. front. (port.). 18.7 cm.

Experiences principally in Nevada and Texas; ranch and cowboy life.

344 BROWN, JOHN EARL. Yesteryears of Texas, by John Earl Brown. San Antonio, Texas, the Naylor company, 1936. Cloth.

x, 157 p. front., plates. 23.3 cm.
Half title; device.

345 BROWN, LONDON. An old time cowboy, by London Brown. [N. p., n. d.]. Pict. wrappers. (Cover title). Rare.

82 [1] p. 14.5 cm.

A very rare, crudely printed little book on cowboy life.

346 BROWN, MARK H., and W. R. FELTON. Before barbed wire, by Mark H. Brown and W. R. Felton. L. A. Huffman, photographer on horseback. Illustrated with photographs. New York, Henry Holt and company, [1956]. Cloth.

6 p.l., 13–256 p. plates, ports. 28.6 cm.
Notes, p. 225–236; bibliography, p. 237–240; acknowledgments, p. 241–243; index, p. 245–254; key to symbols on end-paper map, p. 256.
Half title; map on end papers.

347 ———. The frontier years, by Mark H. Brown and W. R. Felton. L. A. Huffman, photographer of the plains. New York, Henry Holt and company, [1955]. Cloth.

6 p.l., 13–272 p. front. (port.), plates, ports., facsm. 28.5 cm.
Notes, p. 237–257; bibliography, p. 259–261; acknowledgments, p. 263–266; index, p. 267–272.
Half title; maps on end papers (dif.).

348 BROWN, RALPH H. Historical geography of the United States. By Ralph H. Brown . . . under the editorship of J. Russell Whitaker. New York, Harcourt, Brace and company, [1948]. Cloth. OP.

viii p., 1 l., [3]–596 p. illus., maps. 24 cm.
Bibliography, p. [539]–571; biographical index, p. [574]–576; subject index, p. [577]–596.

A chapter on the Texas cattle industry and the cattle trails.

349 BRUCE, ISABELLA. The history of the Aberdenshire shorthorns. By Isabella Bruce. . . . Aberdeen, Aberdeen Press and Journal, 1923. Cloth.

xii, 655 p. front. (port.), plates, ports., tables. 22 cm.
Index, p. [629]–655.

350 BRUSH, W. PROVISO. 1882 brand book containing the brands of the Cherokee Strip authorized by stockmen's convention held at Caldwell, Kan., March 1 and 2, 1882. Also the brands of the Southwestern Cattle-Growers' Association, organized at Medicine Lodge, Kan., March 17 & 18, 1882. W. Proviso Brush compiler and publisher. Kansas City, Mo., Isaac P. Moore, printer and binder, 1882. Wrappers. Rare.

3 p.l., 56 [2] p. cattle brands. 17 x 9.2 cm.
Last 2 p. adv.

351 BRYSON, JOHN. The cowboy. Photographs by Leonard McCombe. Material for text and captions by John Bryson. A Picture Press book distributed by Garden City Books, Garden City, N. Y., 1951. Stiff pict. wrappers.

1 l., 3–78 [2] p. front., plates, ports., map (verso front wrapper). 27.9 x 21.7 cm.

352 BUECHEL, F. A. Eight years of livestock shipments in Texas, 1925–1932. . . . Cattle and calves. Monthly shipments and receipts from and to Texas classified by points or origin and destination on a distinct basis. By F. A. Buechel, Bureau of Business Research, monograph No. 10. Austin, University of Texas, [1933]. Wrappers. OP.

3 p.l., [7]–131 p. maps, tables, charts. 20.3 cm.
Head of title, "The University of Texas *Bulletin No. 3311*, March 15, 1933."

353 BUNNY (no other name given). Two years a cowboy, and life on the

[57]

prairie among the Indians and backwoods of America, by Bunny. London, London Literary society, 1887. Pict. wrappers. Very rare.

3 p.l., ₍7₎–128 p. 18.5 cm.
Adv. verso front wrapper; adv. recto and verso back wrapper.

An extremely rare and unusual item on the American cowboy by an Englishman.

354 BUNTON, MARY TAYLOR. A bride on the old Chisholm Trail in 1886, by Mary Taylor Bunton. San Antonio, Texas, the Naylor company, 1939. Pict. cloth. OP.

ix, 77 p. front. (port., signed in facsm.), illus. 2 ports. (incl. front.). 19.7 cm.
Addenda, p. 75–77.
Half title.

355 BURCH, LAWRENCE D. Kansas as it is. A complete review of the resources, advantages, and drawbacks of the great central state. By L. D. Burch. Chicago, Ill., C. S. Burch and co., 1878. Pict. wrappers. Scarce.

4 p.l., ₍9₎–142 p. illus., fold. map in front, tables. 22.6 cm.
Illus. t.p.; 2 p. adv. in front; 12 p. adv. at end.

356 ———. Nebraska as it is. A comprehensive summary of the resources, advantages, and drawbacks of the great prairie state. By L. D. Burch. . . . Chicago, C. S. Burch and co., 1878. Pict. wrappers. Scarce.

164 ₍20₎ p. front. (fold. map), illus. 24 cm.

357 BURCHAM, L. T. California range land. An historical-ecological study of the range resource of California, ₍by₎ L. T. Burcham. . . . Sacramento, published by Division of Natural Resources, state of California, 1957. Pict. cloth.

3 p.l., 7–261 p. plates, maps, graphs, facsms., tables, 2 fold. maps in pocket at end. 23.7 cm.
Bibliography, p. 236–247; appendices, p. 250–261.
State seal on t.p.

358 BURDICK, USHER LLOYD. William Smith Davidson, pioneer, ₍by Usher L. Burdick₎. ₍N.p., n.d., c.1955₎. Stiff pict. wrappers.

₍3₎–12 p. front. (port.), plates (1 double p.). 22.8 cm.

359 ———. Jim Johnson, pioneer. A brief history of the Mouse River Loop country, by Usher L. Burdick. ₍Williston, N. D., privately printed, 1941₎. Wrappers. OP.

2 p.l., 7–32 ₍1₎ p. front. (port.), plates. 22.8 cm.
On cover: "First printing. This edition is limited to 300 copies of which this book is number —."

360 ———. Life and exploits of John Goodall, by Usher L. Burdick. . . .

Watford City, North Dakota, published by the McKenzie County Farmer, 1931. Wrappers. OP.

3 p.l., [7]–29 p. plate, port. 22.7 cm.
Copyright notice and "First edition" on t.p.

John Goodall was Teddy Roosevelt's ranch foreman.

361 ———. Marquis de Mores at war in the Bad Lands, by Usher L. Burdick. . . . Fargo, North Dakota, 1929. Wrappers. OP.

3 p.l., [7]–24 p. front. (port.). 22.8 cm.
A second edition contains 27 pages.

362 ———. Recollections and reminiscences of Graham's Island, by Usher L. Burdick. Reprinted from *North Dakota History,* Vol. XVI, Nos. 1, 2, and 3 (January, April, July, 1949). Bismarck, North Dakota, published by the State Historical Society of North Dakota, 1949. Stiff wrappers. (Cover title).

84 [2] p. front., plates, ports., map (double p.). 22.7 cm.

363 ———. Some of the old-time cow men of the great West, by Usher L. Burdick. Baltimore, Md., Wirth brothers, 1957. Cloth.

vii, [9]–175 p. front., plates, port. 22.2 cm.
Vignette.

364 ———. Tales from buffalo land. The story of George "W." Newton (old time buffalo hunter of Dakota and Montana), by Usher L. Burdick. Baltimore, Wirth brothers, 1939. Wrappers. OP.

3 p.l., 9–27 p. front. (port.), plates. 22.8 cm.
Vignette.
Reprinted same year.

365 ———. Tales from buffalo land. The story of Fort Buford, by Usher L. Burdick. Baltimore, Wirth brothers, 1940. Cloth. OP.

3 p.l., [7]–215 p. front. (port.), plates, ports., fold. letter in facsm. 20.6 cm.
Untrimmed.

366 BURKE, E. L. Some features of concentration. Address of E. L. Burke, of Omaha, Nebraska, at Denver, Colorado, at the seventeenth annual convention of the American National Live Stock Association at the Broadway Theatre, Denver, Colorado, January 21, 1914. Denver, Colo., published by American National Live Stock Association, [1914]. Pamphlet. (Cover title). Rare.

8 p., 22.5 cm.

367 BURKHART, C. G. Settler's guide to homes in the Willamette Valley,

Oregon. For use and information of immigrants. Published by C. G. Burkhart. . . . Albany, Or., ₁1887₁. Wrappers. Rare.

4 p.l., ₁9₁–75 ₁21₁ p. front. 19.7 cm.
Last 21 p., adv.; 5 p. adv. in front; adv. verso front wrapper; adv. recto and verso back wrapper.

368 BURKLEY, FRANK J. The faded frontier, by Frank J. Burkley. . . . Omaha, Nebraska, Burkley envelope and printing co., 1935. Cloth. OP.

2 p.l., 5–436 ₁6₁ p. illus., plates, ports., maps. 23.4 cm.
Last 6 p. index.

A chapter on "Cattle of the Plains."

369 BURLINGAME, MERRILL G. The Montana frontier, by Merrill G. Burlingame. . . . End plates and maps by George A. Balzhiser. Helena, Mont., State publishing co., ₁1942₁. Cloth. OP.

xiii p., 1 l., 418 p. front. (relief map), illus., plates, ports., maps, diagr., tables. 22.2 cm.
Footnotes, p. 357–381; appendix (chronological outline), p. 385–390; bibliography, p. 391–397; index, p. 399–418.
Map of Montana, 1863 (front end papers); map of Montana, 1890 (back end papers); vignette.

370 [BURLINGTON & MISSOURI RIVER RAILWAY]. Views and descriptions of Burlington & Missouri River Railroad lands with important information concerning where and how to select and purchase farms in Iowa and Nebraska on ten years' credit. Burlington, Iowa, and Lincoln, Neb., issued by the land department of the Burlington & Mo. River Railroad co., ₁n. d.₁. Wrappers. (Cover title). Rare.

₁80₁ p. (no pagination), plates, map at end. 24.2 cm.

Seen in Rollins Collection, Princeton University.

371 BURMAN, BEN LUCIEN. It's a big country. America off the highways, ₁by₁ Ben Lucien Burman. Drawings by Alice Caddy. New York, Reynal & company, ₁1956₁. Boards.

9 p.l., 9–277 ₁1₁ p. illus., plates. 21.8 cm.
Half title; vignette.
Colophon: "192 copies from the first edition have been specially bound and autographed for the friends of the author and his publishers. Of this edition each copy is numbered."

Has a chapter on the cowboys of the brush country.

372 BURNETT, H. C. (ED.). 1889. New Mexico. Winter edition. Publication of the Bureau of Immigration, Santa Fe, New Mexico. Edited by H. C. Burnett, secretary. Las Vegas, J. A. Carruth, printer, binder and blank book manufacturer, 1889. Pict. wrappers. (Cover title). Rare.

48 p. 21.5 cm.

373 BURNHAM, FREDERICK RUSSELL. Scouting on two continents, by Major Frederick Russell Burnham . . . elicited and arranged by Mary Nixon Everett. Garden City, N. Y., Doubleday, Page & co., 1926. Cloth. OP.

xxii p., 1 l., 370 p. front. (port.), illus., plates, ports., maps, facsms. 23.5 cm.
Half title; t.p. in red and black; device.
Reprinted in 1927.

374 BURNS, JAMES N. Debate of Hon. James N. Burns, of Missouri, and others in the House of Representatives, January 21, 1885, on the Oklahoma country. Washington, 1885. Sewn. Scarce.

[3]-12 p. 21.7 cm.

A debate over the policy of letting cattle enter the Territory and keeping settlers out.

375 BURNS, JOHN C. Facts about Mill Iron ranches and cattle, [by] John C. Burns. [N.p., n.d.]. Pict. boards.

6-13 p. front. (port.). 16.3 cm.

376 BURNS, JOHN H. Memoirs of a cow pony, as told by himself. Illustrated. By John H. Burns. Boston, Eastern publishing co., [1906]. Pict, cloth. Scarce.

3 p.l., 7-178 p. front. (port. with tissue), illus., plates, ports. 18.7 cm.
Headpieces.

377 BURNS, ROBERT HOMER, ANDREW SPRINGS GILLESPIE, and WILLING GAY RICHARDSON. Wyoming's pioneer ranches, by three native sons of the Laramie plains, Robert Homer Burns, Andrew Springs Gillespie, Willing Gay Richardson. Laramie, Wyoming, Top-of-the-World press, printed by Mountain states litho co., bound by Laramie printers, inc., 1955 . . . . Cloth.

vii p., 1 l., 3-752 p. plates, ports., cattle brands, maps (3 double p.), facsms., tables. 26 cm.
Selected bibliography, p. 705-715; index to text, p. 716-740; index to pictures, p. 741-746; addenda (errata), p. 747-752.
Vignette; double column.

378 BURROUGHS, JOHN. Camping with President Roosevelt, by John Burroughs. [Boston], Houghton Mifflin co., [1906]. Wrappers. OP.

45 [1] p. front., 6 plates (incl. front.). 18.6 cm.
"Reprinted from the *Atlantic Monthly,* May, 1906."

379 ———. Camping and tramping with President Roosevelt, by John Burroughs. Boston and New York, Houghton Mifflin co., 1907. Stiff wrappers. OP.

xiv p., 2 l., 3-110 [2] p. front. 11 plates. 19.5 cm.

380 BURT, MAXWELL STRUTHERS. The diary of a dude-wrangler, by Struthers Burt. New York, London, Charles Scribner's sons, 1924. Pict. cloth. OP.

viii p., 2 l., 3–331 p. front. (with tissue). 21 cm.
Half title; vignette; untrimmed.
Reprinted in 1938 with "List of Ranches," p. 333–343.

381 ———. Powder River; let 'er buck, by Struthers Burt. Illustrated by Ross Santee. New York, Toronto, Farrar & Rinehart, incorporated, [1938]. Cloth. OP.

xi p., 1 l., 3–389 [13] p. illus., map. 20.8 cm.
Bibliography, p. 377–380; index, p. 281–289.
Half title; t.p. in red and black; vignette; first edition, "FR" in device on copyright p.
Last 13 p., "Rivers and American Folk," by Constance L. Skinner.

382 BURTON, HARLEY TRUE. A history of the JA Ranch, by Harley True Burton. A thesis presented to the faculty of the graduate school of the University of Texas in partial fulfillment of the requirements for the degree of Master of Arts, June, 1927. Austin, Texas, Press of von Boeckman-Jones co., 1928. Cloth. Scarce.

vii p., 1 l., 147 p. front. (port.), illus., map, plates. 23.6 cm.
Bibliography, p. 138–141; index, p. [143]–147.

383 BUSH, I. J. Gringo doctor, by Dr. I. J. Bush. Foreword by Eugene Cunningham. Illustrated by James Wallis. Caldwell, Idaho, the Caxton printers, ltd., 1939. Pict. cloth.

8 p.l., [17]–261 p. front., illus. 23.6 cm.
Half title; illus. end papers; pub. device.

384 BUSHICK, FRANK H. Glamorous days, by Frank H. Bushick. San Antonio, Texas, the Naylor company, 1934. Cloth. OP.

vi, 308 p. front. (port.), plates, ports. 23.8 cm.
Appendix, p. 305–308.
Half title; device; "First edition" on t.p.

385 BUTCHER, SOLOMON D. S. D. Butcher's pioneer history of Custer County and short sketches of early days in Nebraska. Broken Bow, Nebraska, [privately printed at Denver, by the Merchants publishing co.], 1901. Cloth. Scarce.

4 p.l., [7]–403 [5] p. plates, ports. (1 with tissue and signature in facsm.). 24 cm.
5 p. adv. at end; leaf of errata.

386 BUTLER, PROF. JAMES D. Nebraska, its characteristics and prospects, by Prof. J. D. Butler. [N.p., c.1873]. Wrappers. (Cover title). Scarce.

[3]–36 [2] p. front., illus., plates. 19.8 cm.
Last 2 p., "contents."

Seen in the Rollins Collection, Princeton University.

387 ——. A September scamper, by Prof. J. D. Butler. [N. p., c.1877].
Wrappers. (Cover title). Rare.

[3]–30 p. plates. 18.8 cm.

Seen in the Rollins Collection, Princeton University.

388 BYE, JOHN O. Back trailing in the heart of the short-grass country,
by John O. Bye. Illustrated by John G. McCormack. [Everett, Washington, privately printed, 1956]. Pict. cloth.

ix [1] p., 2 l. 392 p. illus., plates, ports., cattle brands, 2 large fold. maps laid
in. 25.8 cm.
Lithoprinted; illus. t.p.

389 BYERS, CHESTER. Roping; trick and fancy rope spinning, by Chester
Byers, with contributions by Fred Stone, Will Rogers, and Elsie Janis.
Illustrated. New York, London, G. P. Putnam's sons, 1928. Cloth.
Scarce.

xix p., 1 l., 105 p. front., plates, ports. 19.2 cm.
Vignette.

390 BYNUM, LINDLEY (ED.). The record book, Rancho Santa Ana del
Chino. Transcribed and edited by Lindley Bynum. Los Angeles, printed
and bound by Vocational Printing Class of John C. Fremont High School,
1935. Stiff wrappers. Three-hole tie. Scarce.

55 p. front. (facsm. of original record book in Spanish pasted in). 25.4 cm.

391 CADY, JOHN HENRY. Arizona's yesterdays, being the narrative of John
H. Cady, pioneer. Rewritten and revised by Basil Dillon Woon, 1915.
[Los Angeles, Times-Mirror printing and binding house, 1916]. Stiff
pict. wrappers. Scarce.

6 p.l., [13]–127 p. front., plates. 18.5 cm.
Untrimmed.

392 [CALDERHEAD, J. H.]. "The treasure state." Montana and its magnificent resources. Extra edition of the Sixth Annual Report of the Bureau
of Agriculture, Labor, and Industry of the state of Montana, 1898. . . .
Helena, Montana, Independent publishing co., State printers and binders,
1899. Wrappers. Rare.

[4]–120 [25] p. maps (1 fold.), tables. 24.3 cm.
Last 25 p. maps (1 fold.).

393 CALHOUN, S. H., JR. (COMPILER). Texas stock laws, containing all the
laws of the state of Texas which apply to or in any manner affect the stock
interests. Federal laws relative to the responsibility of common carriers;
state inspectors. Also the officers and by-laws of the Cattle Raisers' Asso-

ciation of Texas. S. H. Calhoun, Jr., compiler. Denver, Colo., [Daily Livestock Record print], Nov. 20, 1893. Wrappers. Scarce.

[3]–40 p. 19.5 cm.

Advertisements scattered throughout.

394 CALIFORNIA. Laws concerning rodeos, and defining the duties of judges of the plains. [Los Angeles, printed at the office of the Los Angeles Star, n. d., c.1858]. Wrappers. (Caption title). Excessively rare.

8 p. 19.5 cm.

The word "rodeo" in this sense is used to mean "roundup," from the Spanish. This little pamphlet is a copy of the early laws of the California roundup. The only copy, to my knowledge, is in the Huntington Library.

395 ———. Report of the subcommittee on hide and brand laws of the joint interim committee on agriculture and livestock problems. [Sacramento], published by the Senate of the state of California, [1947]. Stiff wrappers. OP.

3–328 p. cattle brands, map. 23 cm.

396 ———. State of California protection board, cattle brands and licensed slaughterers, 1918 . . . . Issued by the Cattle Protection Board of California . . . . San Francisco, Cattle Protection board, 1918. Cloth. OP.

vii, 355 [1] p. 20 cm.

397 CALKINS, FRANK W. Frontier sketches, by Frank W. Calkins. Chicago, Donohue, Henneberry and co., [1893]. Pict. cloth. Scarce.

3 p.l., 5–134 p. front. (port.), illus. 20 cm.

398 CALLISON, JOHN J. Bill Jones of Paradise Valley, Oklahoma. His life and adventures for over forty years in the great Southwest. He was a pioneer in the days of the buffalo, the wild Indian, the Oklahoma boomer, the cowboy and the outlaw. Copiously illustrated from photographs and drawings from real life, by John J. Callison . . . . [Chicago, printed by M. A. Donohue & co., 1914]. Cloth. Scarce.

6 p.l., 13–328 p. front., illus. 19.5 cm.

399 CALVIN, ROSS. River of the sun. Stories of the storied Gila, by Ross Calvin. Albuquerque, University of New Mexico press, 1946. Cloth.

xix p., 1 l., 153 p. plates, ports. 23.8 cm.

Half title; Indian designs on end papers; double t.p. with map at heading.

Chapter VIII, "Thomas, the Lion, Cattle Baron," deals with the cattle industry.

400 ———. Sky determines. An interpretation of the Southwest, by Ross Calvin. New York, the Macmillan company, 1934. Dec. cloth.

xii p., 1 l., 354 p. front., plates. 20.2 cm.

Bibliography, p. 343–346; index, p. 347–354.
Half title; untrimmed.

Republished in a revised and enlarged edition in 1948 by the University of New Mexico press, Albuquerque.

401 CAMP, CHARLES. Muggins, the cow horse, by Charles Camp. ₍Denver, Colorado, the Welsh-Haffner printing co., 1928₎. Stiff wrappers. Label pasted on. Scarce.

2 p.l., 5–110 p., 1 l. illus. (incl. marginal), ports. 26 cm.

The story of an unusual cow horse.

402 CAMPBELL, Gov. J. A. Message of Governor Campbell to the Third Legislative Assembly of Wyoming Territory, convened at Cheyenne, November 4th, 1873. Cheyenne, Wyoming Territory, H. Glafcke, printer, Daily Leader office, 1873. Wrappers. Rare.

₍3₎–17 p. 21.4 cm.

403 CAMPBELL, J. L. The great agricultural and mineral West. A hand book and guide for the emigrant. To the most inviting agricultural fields of the West; to the richest gold and silver regions of the Rocky Mountains and the Pacific Slope. . . . By J. L. Campbell. Chicago, Church, Goodman & Donnelly, steam book and job printers, 1866. Pict. wrappers. Rare.

2 p.l., ₍15₎–77 ₍23₎ p. illus., fold. map. 22 cm.
Last 23 p. adv.; 22 p. adv. in front and verso front wrapper; adv. recto and verso back wrapper.

A section on livestock in Nebraska.

404 CAMPBELL, MARJORIE WILKINS. The Saskatchewan. ₍By₎ Marjorie Wilkins Campbell. Illustrated by Illingworth H. Kerr. New York, Toronto, Rinehart and co., inc., ₍1950₎. Cloth.

8 p.l., 5–400 p. front. (double-p. map), plates. 21 cm.
Acknowledgments, p. 371–373; bibliography, p. 375–380; index, p. 381–400.
Half title; illus. end papers; headpieces.
Added title: "Rivers of America."

405 CAMPBELL, WALTER S. (Stanley Vestal). The book lover's Southwest. A guide to good reading, by Walter S. Campbell (Stanley Vestal). Norman, University of Oklahoma Press, ₍1955₎. Cloth.

xii p., 1 l., 3–287 ₍1₎ p. 23.6 cm.
Bibliography, p. 269–272; index to authors and editors, p. 273–287.
Half title; pub. device; "First edition" on copyright p.

406 CAMPBELL, WILLIAM CAREY. A Colorado colonel and other sketches,

by William Carey Campbell. Topeka, Kansas, Crane & company, publishers, 1901. Pict. cloth. OP.

3 p.l., 7–402 p. front., illus. 19.9 cm.

407 CANADA, J. W. Life at eighty, by J. W. Canada, A. B. Memories and comments by a tarheel in Texas. . . . ₁La Porte, Texas, published by the author, 1952₁. Cloth.

4 p.l., ₁1₁ p., 10–198 p. 22.4 cm.

There are six leaves bradded together, with printed instructions that "These pages should be pasted in the book following page 196 . . . ." They contain some information for an additional two years after the eighty discussed in the original text. The latter part of the book deals with the various breeds of cattle.

408 CANNON, MILES. Toward the setting sun, by Miles Cannon. Portland, Oregon. Printed by Columbian press, inc., ₁1953₁. Stiff wrappers.

3 p.l., 6–157 p. 1 port. 22.8 cm.

409 CANTON, FRANK M. Frontier trails. The autobiography of Frank M. Canton. Edited by Edward Everett Dale. With illustrations. Boston and New York, Houghton Mifflin company, 1930. Cloth. Scarce.

xvii p., 1 l., ₁3₁–236 ₁1₁ p. front., ports. 21.3 cm.
Half title; pub. device; first edition, "1930" under imprint.

This autobiography of Frank Canton, written shortly before his death and edited from the manuscript he left, tells of his experiences during the Johnson County War in Wyoming and some of his later life in Oklahoma. He failed, however, to tell his real name, which was Joe Horner, or at least this was the name he went by in Texas before he took the name of Canton. The group picture following page 110 is erroneously labeled "The Dalton brothers and their sister." It is a picture of the Younger brothers and their sister.

410 CANTONWINE, ALEXANDER. Star forty-six, Oklahoma. ₁Oklahoma City, printed by Pythian Times publishing co.₁, 1911. Cloth. Scarce.

334 p. front. (port.), illus. 24 cm.

411 CARDWELL, LAWRENCE. Mountain medicine, by Lawrence Cardwell. Illustrated with photographs. Caldwell, Idaho, the Caxton printers, ltd., 1941. Pict. cloth. OP.

6 p.l., ₁13₁–232 p. front., 26 plates (incl. front.). 23.4 cm.
Half title; illus. t.p.; headpieces.

412 CAREY, FRED. Mayor Jim, by Fred Carey. Omaha, Neb., Omaha printing co., 1930. Stiff pict. wrappers. Scarce.

2 p.l., ₁7₁–175 ₁1₁ p. illus., plates, ports., map. 22.2 cm.
Lettered on cover: "An Epic of the West."
Running title: "Life of James C. Dahlman."

413 CAREY, HENRY L. (ED.). The thrilling story of famous Boot Hill and modern Dodge City . . . edited by Henry L. Carey, publisher. Dodge City, Herbert Etrick, printers, 1937. Pict. wrappers. OP.

[24] p. (no pagination). illus., plates, ports. 19.5 cm.
8 p. adv. at end.

414 [CAREY, JOSEPH M.]. Stockmen should study both sides of the question. (A letter by former Senator Carey on a proposed land lease). [Cheyenne, Wyo.], the Tribune, 1908. Pamphlet. Scarce.

[4] p. (no pagination). double column. 22.7 cm.

415 CARHART, ARTHUR. Hi, stranger! The complete guide to dude ranches, by Arthur Carhart. Chicago, New York, Ziff-Davis publishing company, [1949]. Pict. cloth.

ix p., 2 l., 222 p. front., plates. 20.8 cm.
Half title; vignette.

416 CARLYSLE, W. L. Bulletin of beef production in Colorado, prepared by W. L. Carlysle, dean of agriculture. Published by the Denver Chamber of Commerce and Board of Trade. Denver, [n. d.]. Wrappers. (Cover title). Scarce.

[7] p. (no pagination). 15.7 x 8.6 cm.

417 CARPENTER, FRANK G. Canada and Newfoundland, by Frank G. Carpenter . . . . With 116 illustrations from original photographs. Garden City, New York, Doubleday, Page & Company, 1924. Pict. cloth. OP.

xiv p., 1 l., 311 p. front., plates. 23.5 cm.
Index, p. 303–311.
Half title, "Carpenter's World Travels"; map on end papers; pub. device; t.p. in red and black; "First edition" on copyright p.

Chapter XXVII, entitled "The Passing of the Cattle Range," deals with the cattle industry of later days.

418 CARPENTER, WILL TOM. Lucky 7. A cowman's autobiography, by Will Tom Carpenter. Edited with an introduction and notes by Elton Miles. Illustrated by Lee Hart. Austin, University of Texas press, [1957]. Cloth.

xxii p., 1 l., 3–119 [1] p. front., illus. 21.9 cm.
Half title; device.

419 CARR, HARRY. The West is still wild. Romance of the present and the past, by Harry Carr. With illustrations by Charles H. Owens. Boston and New York, Houghton Mifflin company, 1932. Cloth. Title label pasted on. OP.

iv p., 1 l., ₍3₎–257 p. front., illus., map. 21.2 cm.
Vignette; map on end papers; illus. chapter headings; "First edition 1932" under imprint.

Has a chapter on a California cattle ranch.

420 CARREL, FRANK. Canada's west and farther west, by Frank Carrel, journalist. Latest book on the land of golden opportunities. Quebec, published and printed by the Telegraph printing company, 1911. Cloth. Picture pasted on. OP.
xvi, 258 p. plates. 20.5 cm.
Half title.

421 CARRIZIZO CATTLE RANCH CO., LTD. Memorandum of association and articles of association. London, Ingledew, Ince and Colt, ₍n. d.₎. Wrappers. Scarce.
59 p. 23 x 15.5 cm.

422 CARSON, THOMAS. Ranching, sport, and travel, by Thomas Carson. With sixteen illustrations. London, Leipsic, T. Fisher Unwin, 1911. Pict. cloth. OP.
5 p.l., 13–319 p. front. (with tissue), plates. 23 cm.
Half title; pub. device; untrimmed.
The American edition by Charles Scribner's sons the following year with same collation.

"The main portion of the volume is devoted to cattle ranching in Arizona, New Mexico, and Texas."

423 CARTER, CAPTAIN ROBERT GOLDTHWAITE. Massacre of Salt Creek Prairie and the cowboy's verdict. By Captain Robert Goldthwaite Carter, U. S. Army. Washington, D. C., Gibson bros., printers, 1919. Wrappers. Scarce.
₍3₎–48 p. 22.8 cm.

424 CARTER, WILLIAM GILES HARDING. The horses of the world; the development of man's companion in war camp, on farm, in the marts of trade, and in the field of sports, by Major General William Harding Carter, U. S. A.; paintings by Herbert Miner. With 95 illustrations, including 24 pages in color. Washington, the National Geographic society, 1923. Cloth. Scarce.
3 p.l., 118 p. front. illus. (part col.), plates, ports. 25 cm.

A separate publication of this article from *The National Geographic* magazine.

425 CASE, THEODORE S. (ED.). History of Kansas City, Missouri, with illustrations and biographical sketches of some of its prominent men and

pioneers. Edited by Theodore S. Case. Syracuse, N. Y., Mason & co., publishers, 1880. Leather. Rare.

5 p.l., ₁13₁–726 p. front., ports. (all with tissues, incl. front.). 26 cm.

426 CASEMENT, DAN DILLON. The address of Mr. Dan D. Casement at the Thirtieth Annual Meeting of the Panhandle Plains Historical Society at Canyon, Texas, May 11, 1951. Wrappers. (Cover title).

₁8₁ p. (no pagination). 23.8 cm.

427 ———. Dan Dillon Casement, the abbreviated autobiography of a joyous pagan. Manhattan, Kan. ₁privately printed₁, 1944. Wrappers. (Cover title). Rare.

3 p.l., 74 p. front. (col.), plates, ports. 18.7 cm.

The story of a successful cattleman.

428 ———. Random recollections. The life and times—and something of the personal philosophy—of a 20th century cowman. An autobiographical account, by Dan D. Casement. Kansas City, Walker publications, inc., 1955. Cloth.

8 p.l., 17–111 p. 1 port. 23.6 cm.
Half title; text double column.

429 CASEY, ROBERT J. The Texas border and some borderliners. A chronicle and a guide, by Robert J. Casey. Indianapolis, New York, the Bobbs-Merrill company, inc., publishers, ₁1950₁. Cloth.

6 p.l., 13–440 p. front., plates., ports., guide in pocket at end. 22 cm.
Appendix, p. 397–417; bibliography, p. 418–425; index, p. 427–440.
Half title; map on end papers; untrimmed; "First edition" on copyright p.

Published also in a special "Lone Star Edition" signed and tipped in.

430 CASNER, MABEL B., and RALPH HENRY GABRIEL. The story of American democracy. ₁By₁ Mabel B. Casner ₁and₁ Ralph H. Gabriel . . . . New York, Chicago, Harcourt, Brace and company, 1942. Pict. cloth. OP.

xvi p., 2 l., ₁5₁–632 p. illus., plates (part col.), ports., maps. 24 cm.
Index, p. ₁613₁–632.
Half title; double column; class quizz at end of each chapter.

431 CATES, CLIFF D. Pioneer history of Wise County. From red men to railroads. Twenty years of intrepid history, by Cliff D. Cates. Compiled under the auspices of the Wise County Old-settlers' Association. Decatur, Texas, 1907. Stiff wrappers. Rare.

12 p.l., 25–471 p. front. (port.), plates, ports. 23 cm.
Advertisements scattered throughout.

432 CATTLE CLAIMS. Cattle claims for 1848 and 1849 in the American and

Mexican joint commission. Brief upon additional evidence in defense of the U. S. ₍N. p., n. d.). Wrappers. Rare.

25 p. fold. table. 21.8 cm.

433 ———. Cattle claims for 1848 and 1849 in the American and Mexican joint commission. The heirs of Vicente Hinojosa, No. 506, and others against the U. S. Argument and evidence in defense of the U. S. ₍N. p., n. d.₎. Wrappers. Rare.

11 p. 21.8 cm.

434 ———. Cattle claims for 1848 and 1849, and for 1863, 1864, and 1865. In the American and Mexican joint commission. Additional evidence in defense of the U. S. ₍N. p., n.d.₎. Wrappers. Rare.

109 p. 21.8 cm.

435 ———. Cattle claims for 1863, 1864, and 1865 in the American and Mexican joint commission in the matter of the claims of the heirs of Pedro de la Garza, No. 736, and other claims against the U. S. Defense evidence on the part of the U. S. ₍N. p., n. d.₎. Wrappers. Rare.

59 p. 21.8 cm.

436 ———. Cattle claims for 1863, '64, '65. In the American and Mexican joint commission in the matter of the claims of the heirs of Pedro Jose de la Garza, and the forty-five other similar claims against the United States. Exceptions of raising questions of law and argument thereon. General argument for the U. S. on the facts applicable thereon. General argument for the U. S. on the facts applicable to all the claims. ₍N. p., n. d.₎. Wrappers. Rare.

14 p. 21.8 cm.

437 ———. Cattle claims for 1863, '64, '65 in the American and Mexican joint commission. In the matter of the claim of the heirs of Pedro de la Garcia, No. 736, and fifty-one other claims against the U. S. Argument on the law and the facts of the case. J. Hubley Ashton, counsel for the U. S. ₍N. p., n.d.₎. Wrappers. Rare.

138 p. 21.8 cm.

438 CATTLE PURCHASES. By Agricultural Adjustment Administration from drought areas June, 1934, to February, 1935. A report to G. B. Thorne, director, division of livestock and feed grains, by Harry Petrie. Chief cattle and sheep section (A.A.A.). ₍N. p., n. d.₎. Stiff wrappers. Rare.

129 p. plates, forms (tipped in), tables (5 fold.). 28.8 cm.
Lithoprinted on one side of paper only.

439 CATTLE RANCHES. Cattle ranches and cattle raising on the plains.

Boston, Mass., published by Henry W. Brooks & co., [c.1881]. Pict. wrappers. Rare.

2 p.l., [5]–42 [1] p. 14.8 cm.

Deals with stock raising in various states of the West.

440 CAULEY, TROY JESSE. Early business methods in Texas cattle industry, by T. J. Cauley. Cambridge, Harvard University press, 1932. Cloth. (Cover title). OP.

p. [416]–486.
Thesis (Ph. D.), University of Wisconsin, 1931.
Reprinted from the *Journal of Economic and Business History,* Vol. IV, No. 3 (May, 1932).

441 ———. Early meat packing plants in Texas. By T. J. Cauley . . . . Austin, Texas, reprinted from the *Southwestern Political and Social Science Quarterly,* Vol. IX, No. 4 (March, 1929). Wrappers. (Cover title). OP.

15 p. 25.4 cm.

442 CAVE-BROWN-CAVE, REV. SIR GENILLE. From cowboy to pulpit, by Rev. Sir Genille Cave-Brown-Cave. London, Herbert Jenkins, limited . . . , MCMXXVI. Cloth. OP.

ix p., 1 l., 13–312 [8]p. plates. 21.8 cm.

Chapters on ranching and punching cows. Experiences of an Englishman who came to America and eventually became a minister.

443 CHAFFIN, LORAH B. Sons of the West; biographical account of early-day Wyoming, [by] Lorah B. Chaffin. Illustrated with photographs. Caldwell, Idaho, the Caxton printers, ltd., 1941. Pict. cloth.

10 p.l., [21]–284 p. plates, ports. 23.5 cm.
Bibliography, p. [277]–279; appendix, p. [280]–284.
Half title; pub. device; vignette.

Chapters on the cattle industry of Wyoming and touches upon the Johnson County War.

444 CHALFANT, WILLIE ARTHUR. The story of Inyo, by W. A. Chalfant. [Chicago, W. B. Conkey co.], published by the author, 1922. Cloth. OP.

xviii, 358 p. front. (fold. map). 19.6 cm.
Leaf of errata pasted on inside back cover.

Republished [Los Angeles, Citizen's print shop, inc., 1933].

6 p.l., 13–430, vii p. front. (map). 23.4 cm.

Has a chapter on "The Coming of the Stockmen."

445 CHAMBERS, HOMER S. The enduring rock. History and reminiscences

of Blackwell, Okla., and the Cherokee Strip . . . . By Homer S. Chambers . . . . Blackwell, Oklahoma, Blackwell publications, inc., publisher, 1954. Cloth.

3 p.l., 120 p. front., illus., plates, ports. 23.5 cm.
Double column.

446 CHANDLER, ELEANOR TAYLOR. Western memories, by Eleanor Taylor Chandler. Philadelphia, the John C. Winston company, 1914. Cloth. Scarce.

6 p.l., 13–91 p. 20 cm.
Half title; untrimmed.

Ranching in Wyoming.

447 CHAPMAN, ARTHUR. The story of Colorado out where the West begins, by Arthur Chapman, with three illustrations by Will Crawford, three maps and seventy-five half-tone reproductions from photographs and prints. Chicago, New York, Rand, McNally and co., [1924]. Dec. cloth. OP.

6 p.l., 13–270 p. front. (col.), illus., plates, facsm., maps. 20.4 cm.
Half title.
Republished in 1925.

448 CHAPMAN, BERLIN BASIL. The founding of Stillwater. A case study in Oklahoma history, by Berlin Basil Chapman . . . . [Oklahoma City, Oklahoma, published by the Times Journal publishing co., 1948]. Cloth. Scarce.

xii, 245 p. plates, ports., maps, facsms., plans. 23.8 cm.
Appendices, p. 160–230; bibliography, p. 231–233; index, p. 234–245.

449 CHAPMAN, MANVILLE. Blazed trails. A series of Colfax County historical narratives based on the mural paintings in the Shuler Auditorium of Raton, N. M., done under P.W.A. project and written by the artist Manville Chapman. [N. p.], 1935. Pamphlet. Scarce.

[15] p. (no pagination). illus. 15.2 x 22.8 cm.
Triple column.

450 CHASE, CHARLES MONROE. The editor's run in New Mexico and Colorado, embracing twenty-eight letters on stock raising, agriculture, etc. . . . . By C. M. Chase, editor of the *Vermont Union,* Lyndon, Vermont. [Montpelier, printed at the Argus and Patriot steam book and job printing house, 1882]. Pict. wrappers. Scarce.

2 p.l., [5]–233 [3] p. front., illus. 22.5 cm.
3 p. adv. at end; adv. verso front wrapper, recto and verso back wrapper.

451 CHATTERTON, FENIMORE (ED.). The state of Wyoming. An official

publication containing valuable information concerning the resources of the state. Originally compiled by Hon. C. W. Burdick, secretary of state, 1898. Revised, re-edited, and published by Fenimore Chatterton, secretary of state, 1899. Cheyenne, Wyo., the S. A. Bristol company, printers and bookbinders, 1899. Wrappers. Scarce.

2 p.l., ₁7₁–104 p. plates, col. map on back wrapper. 22.8 cm.

Republished in 1901 with same imprint but in an edition of 148 p. and with fold. map. Published again in 1904 under the imprint of Chaplin, Spofford and Mathison, Laramie, Wyoming, in an edition of 144 pages.

452 CHATTERTON, FENIMORE C. Yesterday's Wyoming. The intimate memoirs of Fenimore Chatterton, territorial citizen, governor and statesman. An autobiography. ₁Aurora, Colorado₁, published by Powder River publishers & booksellers, 1957. Cloth.

6 p.l., ₁13₁–133 p. plates, ports. (1 tipped in). 23.6 cm.
Index, p. ₁126₁–133.
Half title.
Colophon: "Edition limited to 100 copies of which this is No. —."

Has some material on the Wyoming cattle industry and the Johnson County War.

453 CHEEVER, LAWRENCE OAKLEY. The house of Morrell, by Lawrence Oakley Cheever. With a foreword by William J. Petersen and illustrations by Elmer Jacobs. Cedar Rapids, Iowa, the Torch press, 1948. Cloth. Scarce.

xi p., 1 l., 3–303 p. illus., plates (part col.), ports. (part col.), facsm. (col.), map. 26.2 cm.
Index, p. 285–301.
Half title; vignette; head and tail pieces.

A history of the Morrell packers.

454 CHEROKEE STRIP. Cherokee Strip brand book, authorized by stockmen's convention held at Caldwell, Kan., March 16, 1881. This strip lies west of the Arkansas River, north of Cimarron and south of Kansas line. Kansas City, Sam L. C. Rhodes, printer, 1881. Sheep. Rare.

66 p. (incl. adv.). cattle brands. 14.8 cm.

Contains an account of the convention at Caldwell when a discussion was held regarding the establishment of a "trail from Red River to some point on the Salt Fork within the quarantine grounds laid out by the convention." This rare book examined in the library of Thomas W. Streeter.

455 ——. Cherokee Strip brand book containing the marks and brands of the members of the Cherokee Strip Live Stock Association for the

round-up of 1886 .... Caldwell, Kansas, Journal company, job printers, 1886. Leather. Rare.

₍3₎–48 p. cattle brands. 15.5 cm.

456 CHEROKEE STRIP COW PUNCHERS ASSOCIATION. Roster, Cherokee Strip Cow Punchers' Association. Report of 10th annual reunion C.S.C.P.A., September, 1930. ₍N. p.₎, Crescent publishing co., 1930. Wrappers. (Cover title). Scarce.

₍25₎ p. (no pagination). 15 cm.

457 ——. Roster Cherokee Strip Cow Punchers' Association. Report of 17th annual reunion C.S.C.P.A. ₍Guthrie, Logan County News print₎, September, 1938. Stiff wrappers. (Cover title). Scarce.

₍27₎ p. (no pagination). 16 cm.

458 ——. Roster Cherokee Strip Cow Punchers' Association. Report of 19th annual reunion C.S.C.P.A. ₍N. p.₎, September, 1940. Stiff wrappers. (Cover title). Scarce.

₍24₎ p. (no pagination). 12.4 cm.

459 CHEROKEE STRIP LIVE STOCK ASSOCIATION. A memorial to the President of the United States from the members of the Cherokee Strip Live Stock Association. Kansas City, Mo., Lawton, Havens & Burnap, printers and stationers, 1889. Wrappers. Rare.

₍3₎–16 p. 21.5 cm.

This is a petition addressed to President Harrison protesting the closing of the Indian lands to the cattlemen, drawn up by the committee appointed by the Cherokee Strip Live Stock Association's president, composed of John L. McAtee, Eli Titus, Andrew Drumm, E. C. Moderwell, and Oliver P. Ewell.

460 CHILD, FRANK S. South Dakota: resources, people, statehood. The gleanings of a journey through the territory. By Frank S. Child. New York, the Baker & Taylor company, MDCCCLXXXVIII. Wrappers. Rare.

2 p.l., ₍5₎–67 p. 19.7 cm.

Examined in the Coe Collection, Yale University.

461 CHOHLIS, JOHN. Prime, choice, and baloney, by John Chohlis. Illustrated by Charlie Plumb. ₍Hollywood, Calif., Oxford press, 1955₎. Pict. cloth.

7 p.l., 17–210 p. illus., plates, ports. 21 cm.
Half title; illus. t.p.

462 CHRISTIE, GEORGE IRVING. Livestock in the Southwest, by G. I. Christie

. . . . Los Angeles, published by the Los Angeles corp. . . . , 1923. Wrappers. Scarce.

3 p.l., 7–54 p. front. (port.), illus., plates. 24.2 cm.
Double column.

463 CLANCY, "FOG HORN." My fifty years in rodeo, living with cowboys, horses, and danger, by Foghorn Clancy. Drawings by Olaf Wieghorst. San Antonio, Texas, the Naylor company, [1952]. Cloth.

ix p., 6 l., 285 p. illus., plates, ports. 21.6 cm.
Index, p. 273–285.
Half title; illus. t.p.

464 CLARK, BADGER. When Hot Springs was a pup. By Badger Clark. Foreword by Kenneth Harris. Hot Springs, published by Hot Springs Kiwanis Club, Star print, [1927]. Stiff pict. wrappers. OP.

2 p.l., 52 [1] p. front. (port.), plates, ports. 24 cm.

Has a chapter on cowboys.

465 CLARK, CARROLL, and ROY L. ROBERTS. People of Kansas. A demographic and sociological study by Carroll D. Clark . . . and Roy L. Roberts . . . , with a foreword by William Allen White. Topeka, Kansas, a publication of the Kansas State Planning board, [1936]. Cloth. OP.

ix, 272 p. maps, graphs, tables. 23.5 cm.
Appendix, p. 208–261; index, p. 263–272.

Some information on cattle and cattle trails.

466 CLARK, DAN ELBERT. The West in American history, by Dan Elbert Clark . . . . New York, Thomas Y. Crowell company, publishers, [1937]. Pict. cloth. OP.

xi p., 1 l., 3–682 p. maps. 22.2 cm.
Bibliographical notes, p. 629–654; index, p. 655–682.
Half title; vignette.

467 CLARK, FRANK H. Over blazed trails and country highways. The story of a midsummer journey, by Frank H. Clark. Lisle, N. Y., 1919. Wrappers. OP.

3 p.l., 9–146 p. 19 cm.

468 CLARK, IRA G. Then came the railroads. The century from steam to diesel in the Southwest, by Ira G. Clark. Norman, University of Oklahoma press, [1958]. Cloth.

xv p., 1 l., 3–336 p. plates, ports., maps (1 double p.). 23.6 cm.
Bibliography, p. 318–324; index, p. 325–336.
Half title; double t.p.; "First edition" on copyright p.

469 CLARKE, DONALD HENDERSON. The autobiography of Frank Tarbeaux,

as told to Donald Henderson Clarke . . . . New York, the Vanguard press, MCMXXX. Boards and cloth. Scarce.

ix [1] p., 3 l., 3–386 [1] p. 21.3 cm.
Half title; illus. end papers; pub. device; untrimmed.

The author claims (but it is untrue) that he and his father opened the Chisholm Trail in 1863. He states that they bought 10,000 yearlings and 5,000 two-year-olds in Texas and drove them up this trail, leaving the impression that these were driven in one herd—an impossible task.

470 CLARKE, MARY WHATLEY. The Palo Pinto story, by Mary Whatley Clarke. Fort Worth, Texas, printed and bound by the Manney company . . . , [1956]. Cloth.

x, 172 p. plates, ports. 22 cm.
Index, p. 171–172.
Half title.

471 CLARY, ANNIE VAUGHAN. The pioneer life, by Annie Vaughan Clary. Dallas, Texas, American Guild press, [1956]. Cloth.

4 p.l., 11–264 p. front. (port.), plates. 20.2 cm.

Cowboys, ranches, and cowboy reunions.

472 CLAUSSEN, W. EDMUNDS. Cimarron—"Last of the frontier." Pictures and story by W. Edmunds Claussen . . . . [N. p.], 1948. Pict. wrappers. OP.

[24] p. (no pagination). plates. 22.6 cm.

473 CLAWSON, MARION. Range lands of northeastern Nevada, their proper and profitable use (a progress report). By Marion Clawson . . . . Washington, D. C., June, 1938. Wrappers.

63 p. charts, maps, tables. 26.4 cm.
U. S. Dept. of Agriculture.
Photo-offset.

474 ———. The western range livestock industry. By Marion Clawson . . . . New York, Toronto, McGraw-Hill book company, inc., 1950. Cloth.

xiii, 401 p. plates, charts, maps. 23.6 cm.
Index, p. 387–401.
Half title; "First edition" on t.p.

475 CLAY, JOHN. My life on the range, by John Clay. Chicago, privately printed, [1924]. Cloth. Scarce.

4 p.l., 365 [1] p. front. (port., signature in facsm.), plates, ports. 23.5 cm.
Half title; device; gilt top; untrimmed.

This well-written book about the author's ranch experiences has become very scarce and is one of the most sought after cattle books. It is said that the author kept copies on his desk and his many friends helped themselves until

My Life
On the Range

BY

JOHN CLAY

Privately Printed

CHICAGO

the supply became exhausted. He was one of the better-known ranch owners of the Northwest and a well-educated Scotsman. His picture of ranch life is interesting and authentic.

476 ———. My recollections of Ontario, by John Clay. Chicago, ¡privately printed₁, 1918. Cloth. Scarce.
3 p.l., 7–60 p. front., (port. with tissue), plates (1 fold., 2 col.), ports. 23.5 cm.
Half title; t.p. in red and black.

477 ———. New world notes; being an account of journeyings and so-journings in America and Canada, by John Clay, Jr. Kelso, ₁Scotland₁, J. and H. Rutherford, 1875. Cloth. Scarce.
4 p.l., 200 p. 17.5 cm.

478 ———. A review of the international Live Stock Exposition . . . . A great movement to improvement of the domestic animals of the United States, Nov. 29 to Dec. 6, 1924. Chicago, Union Stock Yards, 1924. Cloth.
3 p.l., ₁7₁–351 ₁1₁ p. front. (double p.), plates, ports. 14.6 x 20.7 cm.
Last 12 p. adv.

479 ———. Short review of the live stock trade of America for 1889. By Clay, Robinson and company, with copy of an article on American cattle markets and the dressed beef trade, contributed by John Clay, member of the above firm, to the Journal of the Royal Agricultural Society of England, in April, 1889. ₁Chicago, C. H. Blakely and co., printers₁, 1889. Wrappers. (Cover title). Scarce.
42 p. illus., 1 plate, tables. 21.6 cm.

480 ———. The silence of Sybille. Written for the Christmas number of *The Breeder's Gazette.* . . . By John Clay. Chicago, the Henry O. Shepherd co., printers and binders, 1901. White cloth, decorated in gold. Rare.
3–32 p. plates. 23.5 cm.
Published with "Soo-Killing in southern Scotland" and "Under Shadow of the Cotswolds."

This copy examined in the Rollins Collection, Princeton University.

481 ———. The tragedy of Squaw Mountain, by John Clay. ₁Chicago, designed and printed by Maders printing co., n. d.₁. Stiff wrappers. Rare.
19 ₁1₁ p. illus., ports. 21 cm.
Top of each page decorated with colored drawings.

482 ———. Work of the breeder in improving live stock, by John Clay. (U. S. Dept. of Agriculture Year Book, 1890). Washington, 1890.
p. 627–642. 23 cm.

483 CLEAVELAND, AGNES MORLEY. No life for a lady, by Agnes Morley Cleaveland. Illustrations by Edward Borein. Boston, Houghton Mifflin company, 1941. Cloth.

ix p., 1 l., ₃₃₁–356 p. illus. 23.5 cm.
Half title; map on end papers; illus. chapter headings; device; first edition, "1941" under imprint.
Life in America Series; reprinted several times.

484 ———. Satan's paradise, from Lucien Maxwell to Fred Lambert, by Agnes Morley Cleaveland. With decorations by Fred Lambert. Boston, Houghton Mifflin co., 1952. Cloth.

viii p., 1 l., 274 p. 21.4 cm.
Half title; tailpieces; vignette; first edition, "1952" under imprint.

485 CLELAND, ROBERT GLASS. The cattle on a thousand hills; southern California, 1850–1870, by Robert Glass Cleland. San Marino, California, the Huntington library, 1941. Cloth. OP.

xiv p. 1 l., ₃₃₁–327 p. cattle brands, facsm., map. 23.3 cm.
Appendix, p. ₂₇₇₁–315; index, p. ₃₁₉₁–327.
Half title, "Huntington Library Publications"; vignette.

Republished with additions in 1951.

xvi p., 1 l., 13–365 p. plates, ports., map, facsm. 23.3 cm.
Appendices, p. 235–279; notes, p. 281–338; bibliography, p. 339–349; index, p. 351–365.
Half title, "Huntington Library Publications"; vignette.

486 ———. A history of California: the American period, by Robert Glass Cleland. New York, the Macmillan co., 1922. Cloth. OP.

xiii p., 1 l., 512 p. front. (fold. map), plates, map, facsm. 22.6 cm.
Appendices, p. 469–502; index, p. 503–512.
Half title.

487 ———. The Irvine ranch of Orange County, 1810–1950, by Robert Glass Cleland. San Marino, California, the Huntington Library, 1952. Cloth.

vii p., 1 l., 3–163 p. plates, ports., map. 23.5 cm.
Index, p. 155–163.
Half title.

488 ———. The place called Sespe; the history of a California ranch, by Robert Glass Cleland . . . . ₍Chicago, privately printed₁, 1940. Cloth. Scarce.

vi p., 1 l., 3–120 p., 1 l. front. (fold. map with tissue). 22 cm.
Half title.

This first edition was privately printed at the Lakeside Press for the owners of the ranch, Mr. and Mrs. Keith Spalding, in a small edition and has become very scarce, but was reprinted in 1953 by photo-lithographic process.

489 CLEMENT, RUDOLPH ALEXANDER. The American livestock and meat industry, by Rudolph Alexander Clement. New York, the Ronald press co., 1923. Cloth. Scarce.

ix, 827 p. front., illus., plates, ports., diagrs. 22 cm.
Bibliography, p. 811–841.

The author's doctoral dissertation, Harvard University, but not published as a thesis.

490 ———. Cattle trails as a factor in development of livestock marketing. By Rudolph A. Clement . . . . [N. p.], 1926. Wrappers. (Caption title). Scarce.

p. 427–442. map. 23 cm.
Reprinted from the October, 1926, *Journal of Farm Economics.*

491 CLEVER, CHARLES P. New Mexico; her resources, her necessities for railroad communication with the Atlantic and Pacific states; her great future. By Charles P. Clever . . . . Washington, D. C., McGill & Witherow, printers and stereotypers. 1868. Wrappers. Rare.

[3]–47 p. 23.2 cm.

492 CLIFTON, FRED A. Practical hints to strangers about to commence ranching in Colorado, by Fred A. Chilton . . . . Denver, Woodbury and Walker printers, Tribune office, 1871. Wrappers. Rare.

8 p. 19.9 cm.

A series of five short letters, originally appearing in the *Rocky Mountain News,* beginning with the issue of August 21, 1870.

493 CLOVER, SAMUEL TRAVERS. On special assignment; being the further adventures of Paul Travers; showing how he succeeded as a newspaper reporter, by Samuel Travers Clover. . . . Illustrated by H. G. Laskey. Boston, Lothrop publishing company, [1903]. Pict. cloth. Very scarce.

5 p.l., 11–307 [4] p. front., illus. 18.3 cm.
4 p. adv. at end; device.

The author was a reporter sent out by a Chicago newspaper to cover the Johnson County War. Although written in the form of fiction, this book calls actual names and relates factual events as the author witnessed them.

494 COAN, CHARLES FLORUS. A history of New Mexico, by Charles F. Coan . . . assisted by a board of advisory editors . . . . Chicago, and New York, the American Historical Society, inc., 1925. Leather. Pub. in 3 vols.

Vol. I: xlviii, 586 p. front., illus., plates, ports., maps, tables. 26.7 cm.
Vols. II and III: biographical; bibliography at end of some chapters in Vol. I.

Volume I contains a chapter on the livestock industry with an account of the Lincoln County War.

495 COBURN, WALT. Stirrup high, by Walt Coburn. Decorations by Ross Santee. Foreword by Fred Gipson. New York, Julian Messner, inc., [1957]. Cloth.

4 p.l., 9–190 p. front., illus. 21.5 cm.
Half title; illus. t.p.

A story of the author's boyhood days on his father's Montana ranch.

496 CODMAN, JOHN. The round trip by way of Panama, through California, Oregon, Nevada, Utah, Idaho, and Colorado, with notes on railroads, commerce, agriculture, mining, scenery, and people. By John Codman. New York, G. P. Putnam's sons, 1879. Pict. cloth. Scarce.

xiii, 331 [4] p. 19.7 cm.

Has a chapter on ranching.

497 COE CHARLES H. Juggling a rope; lariat roping and spinning, knots and splices; also the truth about Tom Horn, "King of the Cowboys," by Charles H. Cow .... Pendleton, Oregon, Hamley & company, 1927. Cloth. Scarce.

4 p.l., 9–114 p. front., plates, ports. 19.7 cm.
Index, third prelim. leaf.

498 COE, GEORGE WASHINGTON. Frontier fighter. The autobiography of George W. Coe, who fought and rode with Billy the Kid, as related to Nan Hillary Harrison. Boston and New York, Houghton Mifflin company, 1934. Pict. cloth. OP.

xiv p., 1 l., 220 p. front. (port.), plates, ports., facsms. 21.2 cm.
Half title; pub. device; first edition, "1934" under imprint.

499 COLBERT, WALTER. The cattle industry, what it is now and what it was 65 to 70 years ago, by Walter Colbert. Ardmore, Oklahoma, 1941. Wrappers. (Cover title). OP.

4 p. 28 cm.
Mimeographed on one side of paper only.

500 COLEMAN, MAX M. From mustanger to lawyer, by Max Coleman .... Book One, Part A, from 1890 to 1910 .... [San Antonio, Texas, printed ... by the Carleton printing co., 1952]. Cloth.

13 p.l., [29]–156 p. illus., plates, ports. 23.6 cm.
Colophon (verso third prelim. leaf): "This limited first edition of Part A From Mustanger To Lawyer consists of 500 copies signed by the author of which this is number —."

501 ———. From mustanger to lawyer, by Max Coleman .... Book One,

Part B, from 1890 to 1910 . . . . ₗSan Antonio, Texas, printed and bound
. . . by the Carleton printing co., 1953₎. Cloth.

7 p.l., ₗ17₎–207 p.   plates, ports., cattle brands.   23.6 cm.
Colophon: "This restricted first edition of Part B From Mustanger to Lawyer consists of 500 copies signed by the author of which this is number —."

502 COLEMAN, NORMAN J.   Addresses by the Honorable Norman J. Coleman, U. S. commissioner of agriculture, and Dr. D. E. Salmon, chief of
the Bureau of Animal Industry, before the third national convention of
stockmen, held at Chicago, Ill., November 17th and 18th, 1885.   Washington, Government printing office, 1885.   Wrappers.   Scarce.

29 p.   23 cm.

Speeches on the American beef supply and the legislation for the contagious
diseases of animals.

503 COLLINGS, ELLSWORTH.   Adventures on a dude ranch, ₗby₎ Ellsworth
Collings.   Indianapolis, New York, the Bobbs-Merrill company, ₗ1940₎.
Cloth.   OP.

v, 250 p.   plates, cattle brands.   26 cm.

504 ———.   The 101 Ranch, by Ellsworth Collings, in collaboration with
Alma Miller England, daughter of the founder of the 101 Ranch.   Norman, University of Oklahoma press, 1937.   Cloth.   OP.

xiv p., 1 l., 3–249 ₗ1₎ p.   front., plates, ports.   23.5 cm.
Half title; illus. map on end papers; "First edition" on copyright p.

505 COLLINS, DENNIS.   The Indians' last fight; or, the Dull Knife raid, by
Dennis Collins.   ₗGirard, Kansas, Press of the Appeal to Reason, 1915₎.
Cloth.   Scarce.

3 p.l., ₗ9₎–326 p.   front. (port.), plates, ports.   23.7 cm.

506 COLLINS, HUBERT EDWIN.   Warpath & cattle trail, by Hubert E. Collins;
with a foreword by Hamlin Garland. Illustrated by Paul Brown.   New
York, William Morrow & company, 1928.   Cloth.   OP.

xix p., 1 l., 296 p.   front., illus., plates.   24 cm.
Notes, p. 289–296.
Half title; illus. front end papers; map on rear end papers; vignette; untrimmed.
Reprinted in 1933.

507 [COLLINS, MARY].   Pioneering in the Rockies. ₗBy Mary Collins . . . ,
N.p., n.d., c.1909₎.   Cloth.   Scarce.

4 p.l., 11–98 ₗ1₎ p.   22.9 cm.
Half title only.

Chapters on cattle and cowboy life.

508 COLLISON, JOHN, and W. A. BELL. The Maxwell land grant, situated in Colorado and New Mexico, United States of America. By John Collison ... and W. A. Bell .... London, printed by Taylor and co. ..., 1870. Wrappers. Rare.

[3]–32 p. large fold. map in front. 21.5 cm.

A promotional booklet for foreign consumption in an effort to sell the land of the Maxwell Land Grant. This copy examined in the Coe Collection, Yale University.

509 COLLISON, THOMAS F. El Diario del Viaje de los Rancheros Visitadores. (The log of the R. V.), 1935. By Thomas F. Collison. [Santa Barbara, California, News-Print, 1935]. Stiff wrappers. OP.

3 p.l., [7]–154 [5] p. illus., plates, (1 double p.), ports. 20.7 cm.

510 COLORADO. Brand book containing the brands of the Bent County Cattle and Horse Growers' Association for the year of 1885. West Las Animas, Colo., printed at the Leader office, 1885. Leather. Rare.

3–78 p. cattle brands. 14.7 cm.

p. 56–66 adv.; p. 67–78 blank for memoranda.

511 ———. Colorado brand book and stock growers' and breeders' ready reference, with index of brands of owners, containing all stock brands on record in the office of the secretary of state of Colorado. Denver, Colo., S. H. Standart, publisher and proprietor, [1887]. Leather. Scarce.

v [1] p., 313 [9] p. cattle brands. 19 cm.

Last 3 p. adv.

512 ———. Bureau of information upon the resources of southeastern Colorado and opening of the Ute reservation. Carefully compiled by Harry Schiffer, O. F. Boyle, Chas. Newman, committee. Durango, Colorado, [n. d.]. Wrappers. 2-hole tie. Rare.

[16] p. (no pagination). illus. (verso front wrapper, recto and verso back wrapper). 15 x 23.6 cm.

513 ———. Cattle Raising Company, ltd., of Colorado and New Mexico. [N. p., n. d.]. Boards. Rare.

32 p. fold. map at end. 17.4 cm.

514 ———. Certificate of incorporation and by-laws of the Wendling Cattle and Land company of Colorado and New Mexico .... Denver, Republican publishing co., 1887. Wrappers. Rare.

2 p.l., [3]–15 p. fold. map. 21.6 cm.

515 ———. Colorado, its resources and attractions. [Omaha, 1901]. Wrappers. Scarce.

4 p.l., [9]–114 p. map (verso front wrapper), tables. 20.8 cm.

516 ——. Colorado round-ups for the year 1888. Issued by the Colorado Cattle Growers' association, [Denver, Colo., 1888]. Folder. Very rare.

8 p. 14.2 x 8.4 cm.

These little publications are practically impossible to come by. This copy seen in the library of Thomas W. Streeter.

517 ——. Colorado stock brands and live stock statutes, 1914. This book contains a complete transcript of the live stock brands and marks on record in the office of the Colorado State Board of Stock Inspection Commissioners at Denver August 15, 1914 . . . . Denver, Colo., published and for sale by the Denver Record-Stockman . . . , [1914]. Thin cloth. Scarce.

695 p. cattle brands. 19.7 x 11 cm.
Brand index, p. 539–656; Colorado stock laws, p. 657–694; index to live stock laws, p. 695–697.

518 ——. Colorado stock laws. Compiled and collated in pursuance of the provisions of "an act to provide for the compilation and collation, printing and distribution of all acts and parts of acts relating to stock." Approved Feb. 12, 1883. Denver, Colo., Tribune publishing co., 1883. Wrappers. Scarce.

2 p.l., [5]–43 [i–iv] p. 22.2 cm.
Index, p. [i]–iv at end.

519 ——. Colorado stock laws containing all the laws of the state of Colorado which apply to or in any way affect the stock interests; the roundup and inspection division; state inspectors; quarantine boundaries and the federal laws relative to the responsibility of common carriers and other items of importance. Also the by-laws, constitution, and directory of the Colorado Cattle Growers' Association. Compiled and published by S. H. Calhoun, Sr., Denver, Daily Live Stock Record print, 1892. Wrappers. Scarce.

80 p. 16.3 cm.
Adv. scattered throughout.

520 ——. Colorado stock laws containing all the laws of the state of Colorado which apply to or in any manner affect the live stock interests. The roundup and inspection divisions; state inspectors; the federal laws relative to the responsibility of common carriers. The by-laws, constitution, and directory of the Colorado Cattle Growers' Association. . . . Compiled and published by S. H. Calhoun, Jr., 1896. Wrappers. Scarce.

40 p. 19.5 cm.
Adv. scattered throughout.

521 ———. Fremont County at the grand national, mining, and industrial exposition at Denver, Colorado, 1882. ₍Cañon City, Colo., Gazette-Express print, 1882₎. Wrappers. Scarce.

30 ₍3₎ p. 24.8 cm.

Tells of the cattle-raising possibilities of this county.

522 ———. The great divide, natural farming lands in Colorado. ₍Colorado Springs₎, published by the Divide Board of Trade, 1889. Wrappers. Rare.

31 p. front. (double p. col.). 13 cm.
Leaf of errata tipped in.

523 ———. Gunnison County, Colorado, the majestic empire of the western slope . . . . Pitkin, Gunnison County, Colorado, published by A. P. Nelson, ₍1916₎. Wrappers. Scarce.

10 p.l., ₍21₎–81 ₍13₎ p. plates, ports., map (1 fold.). 26.8 cm.
Double column.
14 p. adv. in front; 9 p. adv. at end.

524 ———. Hand-book of Colorado containing a directory of places and routes, statistics of population, and facts about climate, colonization, mining, farming, stock raising, together with a business index, railroad and stage guide etc. Denver, J. A. Blake, publisher, 1871. Cloth. Rare.

2 p.l., ₍3₎–138 p. 15 cm.
Adv. scattered throughout.

Copy seen in the Rollins Collection, Princeton University.

525 ———. Hand book of Colorado's essential stock laws abstracted and assembled by B. F. Davis, secretary Colorado Stock Growers' and Feeders' Association, 1867–1940 . . . . Denver, Colo., Stock Growers' and Feeders' association, ₍1940₎. Stiff wrappers. OP.

49 p. 20.5 cm.

526 ———. Historical sketches of early Gunnison. ₍By₎ Class of Nineteen Hundred Sixteen, the Colorado State Norman School, ₍1916₎. Wrappers.

2 p.l., ₍5₎–59 p. front. (port.), plates, ports. 25.8 cm.
Bulletin of Colorado State Normal School, Vol. V, No. 3 (June 1, 1916).

Has a chapter on ranching in the pioneer days.

527 ———. History of the Arkansas Valley, Colorado. Illustrated. Chicago, O. L. Baskin & co., historical publishers, 1881. Three-quarter leather. Scarce.

vii ₍1₎ p., 3 l., ₍17₎–889 p. front., plates, ports. 25.5 cm.
Double column; gilt edges.

528 ——. History of Clear Creek and Boulder valleys, Colorado. Containing a brief history of the state of Colorado, from its earliest settlement to the present time. . . . Illustrated. Chicago, O. L. Baskin & co., historical publishers, 1880. Three-quarter leather. Scarce.

6 p.l., [17]–713 p. plates, ports. 25.4 cm.

529 ——. Its resources and attractions. [Omaha, Neb., 1901]. Wrappers. Scarce.

4 p.l.., [9]–114 p. 20.8 cm.
Map on verso front wrapper.

530 ——. La Junta Tribune brand book and map. La Junta, Colorado, published by Geo. D. Phillips, [1886]. Calf. Very rare.

2 p.l., 5–88 p. cattle brands, leaf of errata, large fold. map in front. 16.8 cm.

The map indicates the ranches by their brands. The area covered extends as far south as the Canadian River in the Texas Panhandle on the east and goes a little west of Las Vegas, New Mexico, on the west. The northern limits are Bent and Pueblo counties in Colorado. A copy of this rare item is in the Thomas W. Streeter Collection.

531 ——. The land of sunshine and bountiful harvests, Montrose County. Its climate, agricultural, pastoral, and mineral productions. [Denver, Republican publishing company, c.1887]. Wrappers. Rare.

2 p.l., [5]–22 [2] p. illus., large fold. map in front. 22.2 cm.
2 p. adv. in front; 2 p. adv. at end; adv. verso front wrapper; adv. recto and verso back wrapper.

532 ——. The leading industries of the West. The object of this industrial publication is to place before the public reliable information concerning the industries of the west, its prospects and future, and to establish a better understanding between eastern capitalists and those who by their enterprise are building up western industries . . . . Chicago, Illinois, Lincoln, Neb., H. S. Reed & company, 1884. Wrappers. Rare.

2 p.l., [5]–95 [1] p. 1 illus., maps on last p., and back wrapper. 22.8 cm.

533 ——. Natural resources and industrial development and condition of Colorado. Published by authority of the state by the Bureau of Immigration and Statistics. Denver, Colo., 1889. Wrappers. Rare.

2 p.l., [5]–120 p. tables. 22.8 cm.

534 ——. Official information. Colorado. A statement of facts prepared and published by authority of the Territorial Board of Immigration . . . . Denver, Colo., Rocky Mountain News steam printing house, 1872. Wrappers. Rare.

2 p.l., [5]–35 p. 22.2 cm.

535 ———. Official state brand book of Colorado. Containing all the brands filed with the secretary of state of the state of Colorado to January 1st, 1894; together with a digest of laws concerning stock growers. Printed in English and in Spanish . . . . Denver, Colorado, compiled by the State Brand Book publishing company under the auspices of the State Cattle Growers' Ass'n. Denver, Colorado, the Merchants publishing co., printers, 1894. Wrappers. Scarce.
3 p.l., 3–366 p. cattle brands. 22.9 cm.

536 ———. The official state brand book of Colorado, containing all the brands filed with the secretary of state of the state of Colorado, to October 1st, 1898; together with laws of Colorado appertaining to live stock interests. . . . Denver, Colo., compiled by the Merchants publishing company, 1898. Cloth. Scarce.
3–466 p. cattle brands. 23 cm.
Adv. scattered throughout.

537 ———. Official stockmen's green book issued by authority of the State Board of Stock Inspection Commissioners and the Colorado Cattle and Horse Growers' Association. Containing the stock laws of Colorado, quarantine regulations. Constitution of the Colorado Cattle and Horse Growers' Association. Denver, published by the Record Stockman publishing co., 1903. Stiff wrappers. Scarce.
93 p. 23 x 7.9 cm.

538 ———. Organization [of] National Live Stock Association of the United States and facts concerning Denver, Colorado. [N. p., n. d.]. Wrappers. (Cover title). Scarce.
359 [1] p. ports., tables. 22.5 cm.

539 ———. The pasture lands of the New York and Boston Cattle Company. The range in Las Animas County, Colorado. Report made for the New York and Boston Cattle Company, by H. M. Taylor, of Houston, Texas, live stock agent for the Galveston, Harrisburg and San Antonio Railway system and Morgan's Louisiana and Texas Railroad. [New York, c.1884]. Wrappers. (Caption title). Rare.
5–47 p. 21.8 cm..

540 ———. Proceedings of the Colorado Stock Growers' Association held in Denver, Friday, January 31, and Saturday, February 1, 1873. Denver, 1873. Wrappers. Rare.
32 p. 19.9 cm.
Double column.

541 ———. Radio reports on Rocky Mountain industrial resources. Ex-

cerpts from the Saturday Stock Show. Written and produced by the Rocky Mountain Radio Council. Broadcast by Station KOA. Denver, Colo., ₁1944₁. Pamphlet. Wrappers. Scarce.

28 p. 22.5 cm.

542 ———. Regulations governing the admission of southern cattle into Colorado, Wyoming, and Montana for 1889. ₁N. p., n. d.₁. Large folder. Rare.

4 p. 27.7 x 21.6 cm.

"Map of Texas ₁and the Northwest₁ and quarantine lines."

543 ———. Regulation governing the admission of southern cattle into Colorado, Wyoming, Montana, Nebraska, Kansas, and New Mexico, together with a map showing the location of the quarantine lines of these states and territories and also the government fever lines as fixed by the Department of Agriculture. ₁N. p.₁, published by the Union Pacific Railway system, ₁n. d.₁. Pamphlet. (Cover title). Rare.

₁6₁ p. (no pagination). map on verso last p. 27 cm.

544 ———. Resources and advantages of Colorado. Prepared and published by authority of the Territorial Board of Immigration. Denver, Colo., 1873. Wrappers. (Cover title). Rare.

2 p.l., ₁5₁–47 p. tables. 22.5 cm.

545 ———. The resources and attractions of Colorado for the home seeker, capitalist, and tourist. Facts on climate, soil, farming, stock raising, ₁etc.₁ .... Chicago, Rand, McNally & co., printers, 1889. Wrappers. Scarce.

91 p. map on verso front wrapper, tables. 21.2 cm.

546 ———. The resources and attractions of Colorado for the homeseeker, capitalist, and tourist. Facts on climate, soil, farming, stock raising .... Battle Creek, Mich., Wm. C. Gage & son, printers, 1890. Wrappers. Rare.

₁7₁–152 p. map (verso front wrapper), tables. 21 cm.

Reprinted many times.

547 ———. Resources, population, industries, opportunities, and climate. Revised in August, 1909. ₁Omaha, Union Pacific Railway, 1909₁. Wrappers. Rare.

128 p., 2 l. tables. 20 cm.

548 ———. Resources, wealth, and industrial development of Colorado. Published by the Agricultural Department, Colorado Exhibit at the World's Columbian Exposition, June 1, 1893. ₁Denver₁, Press of G. M. Collier, 1893. Wrappers. Scarce.

196 p. tables. 22.8 cm.

549 ———. San Juan, its past and present, ways of getting there, developments and prospects, gold and silver mines, water power, timber and agricultural lands . . . . Denver, Colorado, published by C. A. Warner & co.,
1876. Wrappers. Rare.

[3]–90 [1] p. 15.6 cm.
Last 21 p. adv.

550 ———. See-Bar-See Land and Cattle Company, incorporated under
the laws of Colorado. Owning and controlling 400,000 acres of land in
Colorado . . . . Washington, Gibson brothers, printers and book binders,
1886. Pict. wrappers. Rare.

[3]–14 p. 17.2 cm.

551 ———. Southern Colorado Cattle Growers' Association. [Leasing public domain]. Promulgated by the Southern Colorado Cattlegrowers' Protective Association. Pueblo, Colorado, Daily Chieftain steam printing
house, 1885. Wrappers. Very rare.

8 p. 22.4 cm.
"Leasing Public Domain" appears on the front wrapper and at the head of p. [3],
but not on title page.

This pamphlet draws a distinction between "Corporations and Massed Capital" and individual owners of small ranches who ask the right "to fence their
small ranges, in order that they may not be overrun by the numberless herds
of the rich and powerful of both continents." Seen in the library of Thomas W.
Streeter.

552 ———. Southern Colorado. Historical and descriptive treatise of Fremont and Custer counties with their principal towns, Cañon City and
other towns, Fremont County, Rosite, Silver Cliff, Ula, and Wet Mountain Valley, Custer County . . . . Illustrated. Cañon City, by Binkley &
Hartwell, 1879. Boards. Rare.

2 p.l., 5–136 p. front., plates. 23.5 cm.
Last 16 p. adv.; adv. on end papers.

553 ———. State brand book of Colorado. Supplement. Containing all
stock brands filed in the office of the secretary of state from April 1, 1897,
to July 1, 1897. Published by C. H. S. Whipple, secretary of state, by
authority of the Eighth General Assembly of the State of Colorado.
Denver, Colo., the Merchants publishing co., 1897. Stiff wrappers.
Scarce.

3–49 p. cattle brands. 25.3 cm.

554 ———. Summering in Colorado. Denver, Richards and co., publishers, 1874. Cloth. Scarce.

4 p., [9]–158 p. 4 plates (pasted in). 18.2 cm.
1 p. adv. in front; 4 p. adv. at end.

555 ———. Supplement No. 1 to the Colorado Stock Brand Book of 1928. This book contains a complete transcript of the live stock brands and marks on record in the office of the Colorado State Board of Stock Inspection Commissioners at Denver, from May 15, 1928 to May 15, 1931. Denver, published and for sale by the Colorado State Board of Stock Inspection Commissioners, [1931]. Cloth. OP.

178 p. cattle brands. 20.8 cm.

556 ———. 3,000,000 acres of choice farming, grazing, coal, and timber land in Colorado along the Kansas Pacific and Denver railways, for sale at low prices, upon long time with nominal rate of interest . . . . Denver, Colo., Rocky Mountain News steam printing house, 1873. Wrappers. (Cover title). Rare.

24 p. front. (map), map on back wrapper. 22.8 cm.

Like nearly all these little books issued by the western railroads, this one has a section on stock raising. This book was examined in the Rollins Collection, Princeton University.

557 ———. Western Colorado and her resources. Mineral, agricultural, horticultural, stock raising . . . . Report made to the Western Colorado Congress held in Aspen, December 15, 16, and 17, 1891. Aspen, Aspen Times print, 1891. Wrappers. Scarce.

[4]–73 [7] p. large fold. map at end. 23 cm.
Last 7 p. adv.

558 COMMITTEE OF INVESTIGATION. Reports of the Committee of Investigation. Sent in 1873 by the Mexican government to the frontier of Texas. Translated from the official edition made in Mexico. New York, Barker and Godwin, printers, 1875. Leather. Rare.

viii, 443 p. 2 maps (col.). 23.3 cm.

The northern frontier question and cattle and horse stealing.

559 CONDRA, GEORGE EVERT. Geography, agriculture, industries of Nebraska. By George Evert Condra . . . . Lincoln, Chicago, Dallas, New York, the University publishing company, 1934. Pict. cloth. OP.

x, 307 p. front. (double-p. col. map), illus., plates, maps. 19.6 cm.
Index, p. 303–307.

560 ———, JAMES OLSON, and ROYCE KNAPP. The Nebraska story, by George E. Condra, James Olson, and Royce Knapp. Illustrated by Terry Townsend and Stanley Sohl. Lincoln, New York, Dallas, Kansas City, the University publishing company, [1951]. Pict. cloth.

14 p.l., 13–296 p. illus., (1 double-p. col.), plates, ports., maps (1 double-p. col.). 26 cm.

[90]

Index, p. 289–296.
Double column; seal on t.p.

561 CONKLIN, EMMA BURKE. A brief history of Logan County, Colorado, with reminiscences by pioneers. Compiled and arranged for Elfridge Gerry Chapter, Daughters of the American Revolution, by Emma Burke Conklin . . . . [Denver, Colorado, printed by Welch-Haffner printing company, 1928]. Dec. cloth. OP.

4 p.l., 11–354 p. plates, ports. 23.5 cm.

562 CONN, WILLIAM. Cow-boys and colonels. Narrative of a journey across the prairie and over the Black Hills of Dakota. From *Dans les Montagnes Rocheuses* of Baron E. de Mandat-Grancey, with additional notes not contained in the original edition, by William Conn. London, Griffith, Farran, Okeden & Welsh, 1887. Cloth. Scarce.

xi, 352 p. front., illus., plates. 22 cm.
Half title; pub. device.

Another edition of 264 pages published in 1888. The first American edition published in New York in 1887. It also has 364 pages.

A narrative of travels in the Black Hills country and experiences with cowboys and cattle ranches, with some information on the Marquis de Mores.

563 CONNELL, ROBERT, SR. Arkansas, by Robert Connell, Sr. New York, The Paebar company, publishers, 1947. Cloth. OP.

ix, 9–128 [2] p. front., plates, ports. 21 cm.

564 CONNER, PALMER. The romance of the ranchos, by Palmer Conner; with illustrations by Charles H. Owens. Los Angeles, Title Insurance and Trust company, 1941. Stiff pict. wrappers. OP.

44 p. illus., fold. map (col.) at end. 22.8 cm.

565 CONOVER, GEORGE W. Sixty years in southwest Oklahoma; or, the autobiography of George W. Conover, with some thrilling incidents in Indian life in Oklahoma and Texas . . . . Anadarko, Oklahoma, N. T. Plummer book and job printer, 1927. Cloth. OP.

iii, 129 p. plates, ports. 20 cm.

The author denies that there ever was such a thing as the Chisholm Trail, and claims the Indian Red Blanket drove the first cattle over the trail.

566 CONWAY, JAY T. A brief community history of Raton, New Mexico, 1880–1930. . . . By Jay T. Conway. . . . [Raton, Gazette print, 1930]. Wrappers. Scarce.

[17] p. (no pagination). 23.2 cm.

567 COOK, FRANCIS H. The territory of Washington, as described by an

impartial pen, in the hand of Francis H. Cook, who is perfectly familiar with the country of which he has attempted to draw a plain pen picture. Edited, with an introduction, by J. Orin Oliphant. Cheney, Washington, State Normal School, 1925. Wrappers. Scarce.

2 p.l., 5–38 [1] p. front. (port.). 21.5 cm.
Half title.

568 Cook, H. G. ("Teen"). Boomer-Sooner, a life story. Norman, Okla., Co-operative Books, 1939. Stiff wrappers. OP.

3–53 [3] p. 21 cm.
3 p. adv. at end.

569 Cook, James Henry. Fifty years on the old frontier, as cowboy, hunter, guide, scout, and ranchman, by James H. Cook; with an introduction by Brigadier-General Charles King, U. S. V. . . . New Haven, Yale University press . . . , MDCCCCXXIII. Cloth. OP.

xix p., 1 l., 3–291 p. front., plates (1 col., 2 fold.), ports. 24 cm.
Index, p. 283–291.
Half title; pub. device.

Reprinted in several editions, one by the Lakeside press of Chicago, and the last by University of Oklahoma press in 1957, with a foreword by J. Frank Dobie.

xxiv p., 2 l., 3–253 p. plates, ports. 23.6 cm.
Index, p. 243–253.
Half title.

570 ——. Longhorn cowboy, by James H. Cook. Edited and with an introduction by Howard H. Driggs, and with drawings by Herbert Stoops. New York, G. P. Putnam's sons, [1942]. Pict. cloth. OP.

xi p., 1 l., 241 p. front., illus. (double p.). 20.5 cm.
Half title; illus. end papers; headpieces.

This book is founded upon the original edition of the preceding book and arranged for younger readers.

571 ——. Wild horses of the plains, by James H. Cook. Stapled.

p. 104–110. 24 cm.
Double column.
Reprinted from *Natural History*, Vol. XIX, No. 1 (1919).

572 Cook, Jim (Lane). Lane of the Llano, being the story of Jim (Lane) Cook as told to T. M. Pearce; illustrated by Walter J. Heffron. Boston, Little, Brown and company, 1936. Pict. cloth. OP.

xiv p., 1 l., [3]–269 p. front., illus. 21.3 cm.
Half title; pict. map on end papers; vignette; untrimmed.

573 COOLIDGE, DANE. Arizona cowboys, by Dane Coolidge, with photographs by the author. New York, E. P. Dutton and co., inc., 1938. Pict. cloth. OP.

5 p.l., 13–160 p. front., plates. 20.8 cm.
Half title; "First edition" on copyright p.; untrimmed.

574 ———. Fighting men of the West, by Dane Coolidge, with an introduction by the author. Illustrated with halftones. New York, E. P. Dutton & co., inc., publishers, [1932]. Cloth. OP.

6 p.l., 13–343 p. front., plates, ports. 22.3 cm.
Index, p. 339–343.
Half title; vignette; "First edition" on copyright p.; untrimmed.

575 ———. Old California cowboys, by Dane Coolidge; with photographs by the author. New York, E. P. Dutton and co., inc., 1939. Pict. cloth. OP.

5 p.l., 11–158 p. front., plates. 21 cm.
Half title; "First edition" on copyright p.; untrimmed.

576 ———. Texas cowboys, by Dane Coolidge; with photographs by the author. New York, E. P. Dutton & co., inc., [1937]. Pict. cloth. OP.

4 p.l., 11–162 p. front., plates, ports. 21 cm.
Half title; "First edition" on copyright p.; device; untrimmed.
At head of title: "By Dane Coolidge."

577 COOMBES, CHARLES E. Moods, meditations, and memories, [by Charles E. Coombes]. Stamford, Texas, Chas. E. Coombes, [1939]. Stiff wrappers. Scarce.

3–38 p. 18.7 cm.
Vignette.

Has a chapter on the Texas cowboy.

578 ———. The prairie dog lawyer, by Charles E. Coombes. Foreword by Amon Carter. [Dallas], Texas Folklore society and University press in Dallas, 1945. Pict. cloth. OP.

xv, 286 [1] p. 22.2 cm.
Index, p. 277–[287].
Half title: "Range Life Series."

579 COOPER, COURTNEY RYLEY. High country, the Rockies yesterday and today, by Courtney Ryley Cooper. Illustrated. Boston, Little, Brown and company, 1926. Pict. cloth. OP.

6 p.l., [3]–294 p. front., plates. 21.2 cm.
Half title; device.

580 COPE, GEORGE F. (COMPILER). Statistical and descriptive report upon

the mines, farms, and ranges of Madison County, Montana. George F. Cope, compiler. Virginia City, Madison County, Montana, September, 1888. Pink wrappers. Scarce.

[3]–63 p. 23 cm.

581 COPLEY, JOSIAH. Kansas and the country beyond on the line of the Union Pacific Railway, eastern division, from the Missouri to the Pacific Ocean . . . . By Josiah Copley, with a map. Philadelphia, J. B. Lippincott & co., 1867. Wrappers. Rare.

2 p.l., 5–96 p. large fold. map in front. 23.2 cm.
Last 8 p. adv.

Originally written as a series of letters to the *Pittsburgh Gazette*. This copy seen in the Rollins Collection, Princeton University.

582 CORLE, EDWIN. Desert country, by Edwin Corle. Edited by Erskine Caldwell. New York, Duell, Sloan & Pearce, [1941]. Cloth. OP.

viii p., 1 l., 3–357 p., 22.2 cm.
Index, p. 349–357.
Half title; map on end papers; "First edition" on copyright p. "American Folkways Series."

583 ——. The Gila River of the Southwest, by Edwin Corle. Illustrated by Ross Santee. New York, Toronto, Rinehart & company, inc., [1951]. Cloth. OP.

9 p.l., 5–402 p. front. (double-p. map), illus. 21 cm.
Bibliography, p. 377–386; index, p. 387–402.
Half title; illus. t.p.; first edition, letter "R" in device on copyright p. "Rivers of America Series."

584 [CORPUS CHRISTI]. Corpus Christie, 100 years. Illustrated. [Corpus Christi, Texas], sponsored and published by the Corpus Christi Caller-Times, 1952. Cloth.

10 p.l., 11–148 p. plates, ports. 21 cm.

Contains a chapter on the King Ranch and its cattle.

585 CORY, V. L. Activities of livestock on the range, [by V. L. Cory]. College Station, Texas, Texas Agricultural Experiment Station, 1927. Wrappers.

[5]–47 p. plates, tables. 20.8 cm.

586 COTTEN, KATHRYN. Saga of Scurry, by Kathryn Cotten. San Antonio, Texas, the Naylor company . . . , [1957]. Pict. cloth.

vii p., 7 l., 3–165 p. plates. 21.6 cm.
Half title.

History of various ranches of Scurry County, Texas.

587   COTTON, J. S.   A report on the range condition of central Washington, by J. S. Cotton . . . . Pullman, Washington, 1904. Wrappers. Scarce.
[3]–45 p. illus. 21.6 cm.
Bulletin No. 60, Dept. of Agriculture, Washington State Agricultural College and School of Science. Experiment Station Dept. of Agriculture.

588   COWAN, ROBERT ELLSWORTH (BUD).   Range rider, by Bud Cowan; an introduction by B. M. Bower; illustrations by Ross Santee.   Garden City, N. Y., Doubleday, Doran & company, inc., 1930.   Pict. cloth.   OP.
x p., 1 l., 289 p. front., plates. 21.3 cm.
Half title; device; untrimmed.

589   COWAN, SAM H.   Effect on the cattle industry of empowering the Interstate Commission to fix rates, by Sam H. Cowan. Address before the annual convention of the Cattle Raisers' Association of Texas, Ft. Worth, March 22, 1905 . . . . Ft. Worth, A. B. Moore printing house, 1905. Wrappers. (Cover title). Rare.
29 p. 24.5 cm.

590   ———.   Legislature need by livestock industry. An address delivered by Sam H. Cowan at Denver, Colorado, May 10, 1905. Denver, Colo., published by American Stock Growers' association, 1905. Wrappers. Scarce.
[14] p. (no pagination). 23 cm.

591   COWIE, JAMES.   Colorado brand book. [Denver, 1906]. Cloth. Scarce.
115 p. cattle brands. 19.6 cm.

592   COWLING, MARY JO.   Geography of Denton County, by Mary Jo Cowling . . . . Dallas, Banks Upshaw and company, 1936. Cloth. OP.
xii, 132 p. front. (cattle brands), plates, ports., map, tables. 22.3 cm.
Bibliography, p. 126–130; index, p. [131]–132.
Map on end papers; vignette.

593   COX, JAMES.   Historical and biographical record of the cattle industry and the cattlemen of Texas and adjacent territory, by James Cox.   Saint Louis, published by Woodward & Tiernan printing co., 1895. Dec. leather. Very rare.
4 p.l., 9–743 p. front. (col. with tissue), plates, ports. 31.7 cm.
Index, p. 735–743.

One of the "big four" cattle books. An important book on the history of the cattle industry, and no collector's library would be complete without it. It is rarely found with the frontispiece, and since it is an unusually heavy book and the leather has deteriorated with age, its back strip is usually missing or in bad condition. It is said that the scarcity of this book is due to the fact that nearly all the edition was lost in a warehouse fire. Republished in two vols. (boxed) in 1959 by Antiquarian Press with introduction by J. Frank Dobie.

594 Cox, James. My native land. The United States; its wonders, its beauties, and its people; with descriptive notes, character sketches, folk lore, traditions, legends, and history, for the amusement of the old and the instruction of the young, by James Cox . . . . Profusely illustrated. Philadelphia, published by the Blair publishing co., 1895. Cloth. OP.

6 p.l., 13–400 p. front., illus., plates. 21.5 cm.

595 Cox, Mary L. History of Hale County, Texas, by Mary L. Cox. Plainview, Texas, ₁privately printed₁, 1937. Cloth. OP.

xi, 230 p. front., plates, 2 ports. on 1 plate, tables. 23.3 cm.

596 Cox, S. W. Pioneer sketches. Some interesting incidents of the pioneer days of Montague County. By S. W. Cox. ₁N. p., n. d.₁. Wrappers. Port. on wrapper. Rare.

44 p. 20.8 cm.
Double column.

597 Coze, Paul. Rodeos de cow-boys et les jeux du lasso; croquis originaux et textes de Paul Coze. Paris, Société française de librairie et d'éditions, 1934. Cloth. Scarce.

5 p.l., 13–190 ₁2₁ p. illus., 4 plates on 2 l., 27 cm.
"Lexique d'expressions cow-boys", p. ₁185₁–190; tables des illustrations, p. ₁191₁–₁192₁.
Half title; vignette.

Also bound in French wrappers.

598 Craig, John Roderick. Ranching with Lords and Commons; or, twenty years on the range, being a record of actual facts and conditions relating to the cattle industry of the Northwest territories and Canada; and comprising the extraordinary story of the formation and career of a great cattle company, by John R. Craig. Illustrated, Toronto, printed for the author by William Briggs, ₁1903₁. Pict. cloth. Scarce.

vi p., 1 l., 9–293 p. front. (port. with tissue), plates, ports. 19.5 cm.

The inside story of the great Oxley Ranch. For an opposite picture see Alexander Hill's *From Home to Home* (item No. 1033 below).

599 Craighead, Barclay. Facts about Montana. Published by the Department of Agriculture, Labor, and Industry, Division of Publicity . . . . ₁Great Falls, the Tribune printing co., n. d.₁. Wrappers. Scarce.

₁32₁ p. (no pagination). 12.6 x 15.2 cm.
State seal on t.p. and front wrapper.

600 ———. Montana. Resources and opportunities edition . . . . Helena, Montana, August, 1928. Wrappers. OP.

[3]–320 p. front., plates (4 fold., all col.), maps (1 fold. at end). 22.8 cm.
State seal on t.p. and front wrapper.

601 [CRALL, LEANDER H.]. The great north-west. A brief description of the resources, the agricultural products, the manufacturers, the trade and general prosperity of the north western states. Illustrated with diagrams . . . . New York City, Leander H. Crall, [n. d.]. Wrappers. Rare.

v, 30 p. diagrs. 21.3 cm.
Adv. verso front wrapper; adv. recto and verso back wrapper.

602 CRANE, CHARLES JUDSON. The experiences of a colonel of infantry. By Charles Judson Crane, colonel U. S. Army (retired). New York, the Knickerbocker press, 1923. Cloth. Scarce.

xi p., 1 l., 3–578 p. plates, ports. 19.2 cm.

Some of his experiences were with cattle.

603 CRANFILL, J. B. Dr. J. B. Cranfill's chronicle. A story of life in Texas, written by himself about himself. New York, Chicago, Toronto, London, Edinburgh, Fleming H. Revell company, [1916]. Cloth. Scarce.

xi [1] p., 1 l., 496 p. front. (port.), illus., plates, ports. 21 cm.
Half title.

604 CRAWFORD, LEWIS FERANDUS. Badlands and broncho trails, by Lewis F. Crawford. Bismarck, N. D., Capital book co., [1922]. Cloth. Scarce.

3 p.l., 7–114 p., 1 l. front., plates. 20 cm.
Also published in wrappers. Republished in 1926 in boards.

605 ———. History of North Dakota, by Lewis F. Crawford. North Dakota biography by a separate staff of special writers. Issued in three volumes . . . . Illustrated. Chicago and New York, the American Historical society, inc., 1931. Leather. Scarce.

Vol. I: xxxix, 641 p. front. (port.), plates, ports., fold. map, facsms. 26.5 cm.
Appendix, p. 521–641.
Vols. II and III: biographical.

606 ———. Ranching days in Dakota, and Custer's Black Hills Expedition of 1874, by Lewis F. Crawford. Introduction by Usher L. Burdick. Baltimore, Wirth brothers, 1950. Cloth.

4 p.l., 9–110 [1] p. front., plates. 21.8 cm.

607 ———. Rekindling camp fires. The exploits of Ben Arnold (Conner) (Wa-si-cu-Tam-a-he-ca). An authentic narrative of sixty years in the old west as Indian fighter, gold miner, cowboy, hunter, and army scout. Map,

illustrations, bibliography, index, and notes by Lewis F. Crawford . . . .
Bismarck, N. Dakota, Capital book co., [1926]. Cloth. OP.

8 p.l., 15–324 p. front. (port.), plates, map. 22.4 cm.
Bibliography, p. 311–313; index, p. 315–324.
Illus. half title; untrimmed.
Also published in a de luxe edition of one hundred signed and numbered copies, three-quarter leather and boxed.
Colophon: "This edition is limited to one hundred copies of which this is No. —."

608 CRAWFORD, SAMUEL J. The state of Kansas. A home for immigrants. Agricultural, mineral, and commercial resources of the state. Great inducements offered to persons desiring homes in a new country. The homestead law. Topeka, Kansas, MacDonald & Baker, printers, 1865. Wrappers. Rare.

[3]–24 p. 21.3 cm.

609 CRESCENT LIVE STOCK COMPANY. Articles and by-laws of the Crescent Live Stock Company, incorporated under the laws of the state of Minnesota. Minneapolis, Geesaman and Murphy, printers, 1884. Wrappers. Rare.

7 p. 14.8 x 10 cm.

610 CRIMMINS, MARTIN LALORY. Texas brands. [By Martin Lalory Crimmins. San Antonio, 1928]. Pict. wrappers. (Cover title). Rare.

[7] p. (no pagination). 17.7 cm.

611 CRISSEY, FORREST. Alexander Legge, 1866–1933. The life of a truly great American who loved and served his country well, who achieved world-wide distinction as an industrial leader, as a patriotic public servant, and as the devoted friend and champion of all who till the soil. By Forrest Crissey. Chicago, Illinois, privately printed by the Alexander Legge Memorial Committee, 1936. Cloth. OP.

xiv, 232 p., 1 l., front. (port. col.), plates, ports. 24.2 cm.
Half title; vignette; untrimmed.

Has a chapter on ranch life in Nebraska and "Big Sandy," Wyoming cowboy.

612 CRISSMAN, GEORGE R. A history of Woods County, Oklahoma, by George R. Crissman . . . Ruth Davies, co-operator . . . . [N. p., n. d.]. Stiff wrappers. Scarce.

2 p.l., 1 p., 8–119 p. front., plates, ports., maps. 18.5 cm.

Chapters on the cattle trails, the Cherokee Strip Cattle Association, and cowboys.

613 CRITES, ARTHUR S. Pioneer days in Kern County, by Arthur S. Crites. Los Angeles, the Ward Ritchie press, 1951. Pict. cloth.

viii p., 1 l., 3–279 p.   plates, ports., maps, legend.   23.6 cm.
Half title; vignette.

614   [CROSBY, GOV. JOHN SCHUYLER].   Report of the Governor of Montana made to the Secretary of the Interior, 1883.   Washington, Government printing office, 1883.   Wrappers.   Rare.
[3]–12 p.   21.4 cm.
3 leaves of errata tipped in.

615   ———.   Report of the Governor of Montana to the Secretary of the Interior, 1884.   Washington, Government printing office, 1884.   Wrappers.   Rare.
3–11 p.   23 cm.

616   CROSS, FRED J.   Dakota territory as it is. By Fred J. Cross.   Sioux Falls, Dakota, M'Donald & Sherman, printers, Sioux Falls Independence office, 1875.   Pict. wrappers.   Rare.
[3]–45 [1] p.   20.5 cm.
Illus. t.p.

617   ———.   The free lands of Dakota; a description of the country; the climate, the beautiful valleys and ocean like prairies; the crops; the land laws, and the inducement offered to immigrants. By Fred Cross, territorial superintendent of immigration. Published by order of the Board of Immigration.   Yankton, Dakota, Bowen & Kingsbury, prs., Press and Dakotain office, 1876.   Wrappers.   Rare.
2 p.l., [5]–31 p.   21 cm.

618   CROSS, JOE.   Cattle clatter; a history of cattle from the creation to the Texas Centennial in 1936, [by] Joe Cross.   [Kansas City, Missouri, Walker publications, inc., 1938].   Pict. cloth.   Scarce.
5 p.l., 13–166 p.   front. (port.), illus., plates, ports.   23.5 cm.
"First published in installments in the American Hereford Journal" . . .

619   CROUCH, CARRIE J.   A history of Young County, Texas, by Carrie J. Crouch.   Austin, Texas, Texas State Historical association, 1956.   Pict. cloth.
xiv p., 1 l., 3–326 p.   plates, ports., cattle brands.   24 cm.
Bibliography, p. 295; index, p. 297–326.
Half title; map on end papers; device.
Volume II of Texas County and Local History Series.

620   ———.   Young County, history and biography, by Carrie J. Crouch.   Dallas, Texas, Dealey and Lowe, 1937.   Fabricoid.   OP.
7 p.l., 339 [3] p.   front., plates, ports., cattle brands, diagr.   22.3 cm.
Bibliography and index on unnumbered pages at end.
Map on end papers; pub. device; "First edition" on copyright p.

621 CROWE, EARLE. Men of el Tejon. Empire in the Tehachapis, by Earle Crowe. Los Angeles, the Ward Ritchie Press, 1957. Cloth.

xiii p., 1 l., 3–165 p. front., plates, ports. 23 cm.
Notes, p. 147–150; bibliography and references, p. 151–153; appendix, p. 154–157; index, p. 159–165.
Half title; map on end papers; cattle brands on t.p.

622 CRUMBINE, SAMUEL J. Frontier doctor, by Samuel J. Crumbine, M. D. The autobiography of a pioneer on the frontier of public health. Philadelphia, Dorrance & company, [1948]. Cloth.

ix, 11–284 p. 20.5 cm.
Pub. device.

623 CULLEY, JOHN HENRY (JACK). Cattle, horses & men of the western range, by John H. (Jack) Culley. Illustrations by Katherine Field. Los Angeles, California, the Ward Ritchie press, [1940]. Cloth. OP.

xvi p., 1 l., [3]–337 p. front. (port.), illus. plates. 23.3 cm.
Index, p. [333]–337.
Half title; illus. t.p.

This excellent book was written by a well-educated Englishman who came to America and became manager of the large Bell Ranch of New Mexico, and he devotes some space to the history of this ranch.

624 CULLEY, MATTHEW JAMES. An economic study of the cattle business on a southwestern semi-desert range, by Matt Culley . . . . Washington, D. C., U. S. Department of Agriculture, 1937. Stapled. (Caption title).

24 p. 2 plates, tables. 23.2 cm.
Circular No. 448.

625 CURLEY, EDWIN A. Nebraska, its advantages, resources, and drawbacks. Illustrated. By Edwin A. Curley . . . . London, Sampson Low, Marston, Low and Searle . . . , [1875]. Pict. cloth. Scarce.

12 p.l., 433 [18] p. front., illus., plates, 1 fold. panoramic scene, maps (5 double p., 1 fold.). 23.4 cm.
Index, p. 431–433.
Half title; 4 p. adv. in front; last 18 p. adv.

American edition same except all advertisements placed at end. New York, the American News company, 1876.

626 CURTIS, GEORGE W. Horses, cattle, sheep, and swine. Origin, history, improvement, description, characteristics, merits, objections, adaptability . . . , of each of the different breeds, with hints in selection, care and management . . . Illustrated. By Geo. W. Curtis . . . . College Station . . . , Texas, published by the author, 1888. Cloth. Scarce.

3 p.l., [1] p., 8–269 [3] p. plates. 27 cm.
Index, p. [263]–269.
Errata, p. [270].

627 CUTBIRTH, RUBY NICHOLS. Ed Nichols rode a horse, as told to Ruby Nichols Cutbirth. Frontispiece by Jerry Bywaters. ₁Dallas₁, Texas Folklore society and University press in Dallas, 1943. Pict. cloth. OP.

x, 134 p. front. 22 cm.
Vignette.
"Range Life Series."

628 DAKIN, SUSANNA BRYANT. The lives of William Hartnell, by Susanna Bryant Dakin. Stanford, California, Stanford University press, ₁1949₁. Pict. cloth.

6 p.l., 308 p. front. (port.), plates. 23.5 cm.
Bibliography, p. 292–302; index, p. 303–308.
Half title; illus. end papers.

Has a chapter on ranching.

629 DALE, EDWARD EVERETT. The Cheyenne-Arapaho country, by Edward Everett Dale . . . . Reprinted from the *Chronicles of Oklahoma,* December, 1942. ₁Oklahoma City₁, 1942. Wrappers. (Cover title). OP.

12 p. 22 cm.

630 ———. The Cherokee Strip Live Stock Association, by Edward Everett Dale. Reprinted from proceedings of Fifth Annual Convention of the Southwestern Political and Social Science Association, Ft. Worth, Texas, Southwestern Political and Social Science Association, March 24–26, 1924. Wrappers. (Cover title). OP.

19 p. 23.2 cm.

631 ———. The Cherokee Strip Live Stock Association, by Edward Everett Dale . . . and charter and by-laws of the Cherokee Strip Live Stock Association. Wichita, Kansas, facsimile reprints by First National Bank of Wichita, 1951. Wrappers. Scarce.

19 ₁3₁ p. 22.8 cm.
Facsimile of charter and by-laws at end.

632 ———. Cow country, by Edward Everett Dale. Norman, University of Oklahoma press, 1942. Cloth. OP.

ix p., 2 l., ₁3₁–265 p. illus. 21 cm.
Index, p. ₁259₁–265.
Half title; headpieces; vignette; "First edition" on copyright p.

"A collection of essays which have been published in various periodicals during the past quarter of a century"—cf. preface.

633 ———. The cow country in transition, by Edward Everett Dale. Reprinted from the *Mississippi Valley Historical Review,* Vol. XXIV, No.

1 (June, 1937). ₁Cedar Rapids, the Torch press, 1937₁. Wrappers. (Cover title). OP.

3–20 p. 25.3 cm.

634 ———. Cowboy cookery. Its pillars: flour, beef, bacon, beans, coffee, syrup, and dried fruit, by Edward Everett Dale. ₁Kansas City, Reprint from January 1, 1946 issue of the *Hereford Journal*₁. Wrappers. (Cover title). Scarce.

₁7₁ p. (no pagination). illus., full-p. plates. 29 cm.
Triple column.

635 ———. The history of the ranch cattle industry in Oklahoma, by Edward Everett Dale. Reprinted from the Annual Report of the American Historical Association for 1920. . . . Washington, Government printing office, 1925. Wrappers. OP.

2 p.l., p. 307–322. 24.2 cm.

636 ———. The humor of the cowboy, by E. E. Dale. Reprinted from *The Cattleman,* January, 1936. Pamphlet. (Cover title). OP.

₁3₁ p. (no pagination). 20.5 cm.
Triple column.

637 ———. Old Navajoe, by Edward Everett Dale. Reprinted from the *Chronicles of Oklahoma,* Vol. XXIV, No. 2 (Summer, 1946). Stiff pict. wrappers. (Cover title). Scarce.

p. 128–145. illus., plates, facsms. 23 cm.

638 ———. Ranching on the Cheyenne-Arapaho Reservation, 1880–1885. ₁By₁ Edward Everett Dale. ₁N. p., n. d.₁. Wrappers. (Cover title).

24 p. 24.2 cm.

639 ———. The range cattle industry, by Edward Everett Dale. Norman, University of Oklahoma press, 1930. Cloth. Rare.

xvii p., 1 l., ₁21₁–216 p. front., illus., plates, maps. 27.5 cm.
Bibliography, p. ₁197₁–208; index, p. ₁211₁–216.
Half title; map on t.p.

640 ———. The speech of the frontier, by Edward Everett Dale. . . . Reprinted from the *Quarterly Journal of Speech,* October, 1941. ₁Oklahoma City₁. Wrappers. (Cover title). OP.

p. ₁352₁–363. 25.3 cm.

641 ———. Those Kansas Jayhawkers. A study in sectionalism, by Edward Everett Dale. Reprinted from *Agricultural History,* Vol. II, No. 4 (October, 1928). ₁N. p., c.1928₁. Wrappers. (Cover title). OP.

p. 167–184. 25.4 cm.

642 DANA, RICHARD HENRY. Two years before the mast. A personal narrative of life at sea.... [By Richard Dana].... New York, Harper & brothers ..., 1840. Cloth. Exceedingly rare.

1 p.l., 483 p. 15.8 cm.

The first state has a listing of books on the back cover which ends with the number 105. It is designated as "Family Library CVI" and does not bear the author's name. The second issue is the same except it has more books listed in back. The third issue has still more books listed and is bound in gray or black cloth and also has damaged type in the copyright notice on page 9. A new edition was issued in 1869 which included the author's California visit of 1859. This edition contains 470 pages. An English edition was published in 1841 with 124 pages. The book contains much material on the hide and tallow industry of California, which was the reason for the cattle industry of that state in its early years. Reprinted since many times, but the first state is very difficult to come by.

643 DANNER, MRS. J. M. (COMPILER). Sayre of Red River Valley. A collection of historical data concerning the origin and growth of the city of Sayre. Assembled by Mrs. J. M. Danner. [Sayre, the Sayre Sun printery, 1939]. Stiff wrappers. OP.

101 [3] p. 25 cm.

644 DARROW, ROBERT A. Arizona range resources and their utilization in Cochise County. By Robert A. Darrow. Tucson, Ariz., published by the University of Arizona, 1944. Stiff wrappers. (Cover title). OP.

1 p.l., 311–366 p. illus., maps (1 fold. at end). 23 cm.
Technical Bulletin No. 103.

645 DAVENPORT, B. M. Resources of Nebraska. A brief account of its soil, agricultural and mineral products, wonderful increase in wealth and population, and other important information to immigrants and others who design locating in the West. By B. M. Davenport.... Nebraska City, Nebraska, Nebraska Press printing office, 1869. Wrappers. Rare.

[3]–20 [4] p. 22.2 cm.
Last 3 p. adv.; adv. verso front wrapper; adv. recto and verso back wrapper.

646 DAVID, ROBERT BEEBE. Finn Burnett, frontiersman; the life and adventures of an Indian fighter, mail coach driver, miner, pioneer cattleman, participant in the Powder River expedition, survivor of the Hay Field fight, associate of Jim Bridger and Chief Washakie, by Robert Beebe David. Glendale, Calif., the Arthur H. Clark company, 1937. Cloth.

7 p.l., [17]–378 p. front. (port. with tissue), plates, ports., diagr. 24.6 cm.
Index, p. [369]–378.
Half title; untrimmed; gilt top.

647 ———. Malcolm Campbell, sheriff, by Robert B. David. The rem-

iniscences of the greatest frontier sheriff in the history of the Platte Valley, and the famous Johnson County invasion of 1892. Casper, Wyoming, Wyomingana, inc., [1932]. Cloth. Scarce.

4 p.l., [7]–361 [5] p. front. (port.), plates, ports., maps, facsms., plan. 20.2 cm.
Chronological table of contents, last 5 p.
Half title.

648 DAVIDSON, GRACE L.   The gates of memory. Recollections of early Santa Ynez Valley. By Grace L. Davidson.   [Solvang, California, published by the Santa Ynez Valley News, 1955]. Pict. cloth.

4 p.l., 101 [1] p. plates. 20.8 cm.
Half title; vignette.

649 DAVIDSON, LEVETTE J., and FORRESTER BLAKE (EDS.).   Rocky Mountain tales.   Edited by Levette J. Davidson and Forrester Blake, with drawings by Skelly.   Norman, University of Oklahoma press, 1947.   Cloth.

xiv p., 1 l., 3–302 p. illus. 22 cm.
Index, p. 293–302.
Half title.

650 DAVIE, JOHN L.   My own story, by John L. Davie, mayor emeritus of the city of Oakland, California.   Oakland, the Post-Enquirer publishing co., 1931.   Stiff wrappers. Scarce.

5 p.l., 1 p., [14]–174 p. front. (port.), plates. 23.3 cm.
Double column.

651 DAVIS, B. F.   Hand book of Colorado's essential stock laws. Abstracted and assembled by B. F. Davis, secretary Colorado Stock Growers' and Feeders' Association. . . . Denver, Colorado Stock Growers' and Feeders' association, [1940]. Stiff wrappers. OP.

49 p. 20.5 cm.

652 DAVIS, CLYDE BRION.   The Arkansas, by Clyde Brion Davis; illustrated by Donald McKay.   New York, Toronto, Farrar & Rinehart, incorporated, [1940].   Cloth.

x p., 1 l., 3–340 p. illus., map. 20.9 cm.
Acknowledgments, p. 328–330; index, p. 331–340.
Half title; illus. end papers; illus. t.p.; first edition; "F R" in device on copyright p.
Rivers of America Series.

653 DAVIS, DUKE.   Flashlights from mountain and plain, by Duke Davis. Bound Brook, N. J., published by the Pentecostal Union, 1911. Pict. cloth. Scarce.

4 p.l., [13]–266 [3] p. front. (port.), plates (part col.), ports. 20 cm.
Last 3 p. adv.

654 DAVIS, EVELYN, and THOMAS CLEMENT DAVIS. Spirit of the Big Bend, by Evelyn Davis and Thomas Clement Davis. Chronology of Presidio's outstanding dates. San Antonio, Texas, the Naylor company, ₁1948₁. Stiff pict. wrappers. OP.

2 p.l., 59 p. illus., maps. 19.3 cm.

655 DAVIS, LUTE L. Blankets in the sand. By Lute L. Davis. ₁Wichita Falls, Texas, printed by Terry brothers, printers, 1948₁. Stiff wrappers.

4 p.l., 72 ₁1₁ p. plates, ports. 19.7 cm.
Illus. t.p. (port. of author).

656 DAVIS, RICHARD HARDING. The West from a car-window, by Richard Harding Davis. Illustrated. New York, Harper & brothers . . . , 1892. Pict. cloth. OP.

5 p.l., 3–242 ₁1₁ p. front., illus., plates. 19 cm.
Pub. device.

A chapter on Texas ranch life, mostly on the King Ranch.

657 DAVIS, ROBERT H., and ARTHUR B. MAURICE. The Caliph of Bagdad. Being Arabian nights flashes of the life, letters, and work of O. Henry, William Sydney Porter. ₁By₁ Robert H. Davis and Arthur B. Maurice. New York, London, D. Appleton and company, MCMXXXI. Cloth. OP.

xi p., 1 l., 3–411 p. front. (port.), illus. (1 col.), plates, ports., facsms. 22.5 cm.
Index, p. 403–411.
Half title; pub. device; untrimmed.

Has a chapter on O. Henry's ranch days in Texas.

658 DAVIS, SAM P. (ED.). The history of Nevada. Edited by Sam P. Davis. . . . Illustrated. Reno, Nev., Los Angeles, Cal., published by the Elms publishing co., 1913. Cloth. Pub. in 2 vols.

Vol. I: 3 p.l., ₁11₁–646 p. front. (port. with tissue), plates, ports. (part with tissues). 24.3 cm.
Vol. II: 647–1279, i–xxiii p. front. (with tissue), plates, ports. (part with tissues). 24.3 cm.
Index: (vol. II), p. i–xxiii.

659 DAVIS, WILLIAM HEATH. Sixty years in California. A history of events and life in California; personal, political, and military, under the Mexican regime; during the quasi-military government of the territory by the United States and after admission of the state into the Union, being a compilation by a witness of the events described, by William Heath Davis. San Francisco, A. J. Learly, publisher, 1889. Cloth. OP.

xxii, 639 p. 22.5 cm.

A scarce book with chapters on the cattle industry of California.

660 DAVY, JOSEPH BURTT. Stock ranges of northwestern California; notes on grasses and forage plants and range conditions, by Joseph Burtt Davy. . . . Washington, Government printing office, 1902. Wrappers. OP.

5 p.l., 11–81 p. illus., plates, maps. 25 cm.
Index, p. 79–81.

U. S. Dept. Agriculture, Bureau of Plant Industry, *Bulletin No. 12.*

661 DAWSON, NICHOLAS ("CHEYENNE"). Narrative of Nicholas Dawson; California in '41, Texas in '51. Memoirs, by Nicholas Dawson. [Austin, Texas, c.1904]. Wrappers. Rare.

2 p.l., [5]–119 p. front. (port.). 16.5 cm.
"Narrative was commenced March 1, 1894"—cf. preface.

Reprinted in 1933 by the Grabhorn press as No. 7 of the Rare Americana Series. Pict. boards. Scarce.

6 p.l., 100 [7] p. 25.5 cm.
Illus. chapter headings (col.); illus. t.p. (col.); last 7 p. no pagination; untrimmed.
Introduction by Charles L. Camp; notes on the Emigrant party of 1841, by Charles L. Camp last 7 p.

The author, familiarly called "Cheyenne" Dawson, was in the first company to cross the Rocky Mountains in 1841. The first issue is practically unprocurable and the reprint is now very scarce. Some scattered information on cattle of California and Texas.

662 DAY, B. F. Gene Rhodes, cowboy (Eugene Manlove Rhodes), by B. F. Day. Illustrated by Lorence F. Bjorklund. New York, Julian Messner, inc., [1954]. Cloth.

6 p.l., 13–192 p. illus. 21.5 cm.
Books [and other writings] by Rhodes, p. 185–187; index, p. 189–192.
Half title; illus. t.p.; illus. chapter headings.

663 DAY, DONALD. Big country: Texas, by Donald Day. New York, Duell, Sloan & Pearce, [1947]. Cloth. OP.

x p., 1 l., 3–6 p., 1 l., 9–326 p. 21.7 cm.
Index, p. 316–326.
Half title; map on end papers.
American Folkways Series, ed. by Erskine Caldwell.

664 ———. (ED.). The hunting and exploring adventures of Theodore Roosevelt. Told in his own words and edited by Donald Day. Introduction by Elting E. Morrison. New York, the Dial press, 1955. Boards and cloth.

xvi p., 1 l., 3–431 p. 21 cm.
Half title; pub. device; untrimmed.

Contains several chapters on Roosevelt's ranching experiences.

665 DAYTON, EDSON CARR. Dakota days, May, 1886–August, 1898, by Ed-

son C. Dayton.   Privately printed. ₍Hartford, Case, Lockwood and Brain-
ard Co.₎, 1937.   Cloth.   Scarce.

5 p.l., 128 p.   front. (map), plates.   23.5 cm.
Index, p. 127–128.
Half title.
"300 copies printed."

666   DEARING, J. S.   A drummer's experience, by J. S. Dearing, 103 half-
tone illustrations representing beauty spots and noted scenes of the North
American continent.   Colorado Springs, Colorado, Pike's Peak publishing company, ₍1913₎.   Tooled leather.   Scarce.

5 p.l., ₍11₎–567 p.   plates.   19 cm.
Half title.

Has a chapter on cowboys.

667   DEBO, ANGIE.   Oklahoma, foot-loose and fancy-free, by Angie Debo.
Norman, University of Oklahoma press, 1949.   Cloth.   OP.

xi p., 1 l., 3–258 p.   plates, ports., map.   22.2 cm.
Index, p. 245–258.
Half title.

668   ——.   Prairie city, the story of an American community. By Angie
Debo.   New York, Alfred A. Knopf, 1944.   Cloth.

xiv p., 1 l., 3–245, i–viii p.   plates.   21.8 cm.
Index, p. i–viii.
Half title; vignette; "First edition" on copyright p.; untrimmed.

669   ——.   Tulsa: from creek town to oil capital. By Angie Debo.   Norman, University of Oklahoma press, MCMXLIII.   Cloth.   OP.

xii p., 1 l., 3–123 p.   plates, ports., map.   20.4 cm.
Index, p. 119–123.
Half title.

670   —— (ED.).   The cowman's Southwest, being the reminiscences of
Oliver Nelson, freighter, camp cook, cowboy, frontiersman in Kansas,
Indian Territory, Texas, and Oklahoma, 1878–1893. Edited by Angie
Debo. . . .   Glendale, California, the Arthur H. Clark company, 1953.
Cloth.

9 p.l., ₍19₎–343 p.   front. (map), plates, cattle brands, maps.   24 cm.
Index, p. ₍333₎–343.
Half title: "Western Frontiersman Series No. IV"; pub. device; untrimmed.

671   DEWEES, W. B.   Letters from an early settler of Texas, by W. B.
Dewees. Compiled by Clara Cordelle.   Louisville, Ky., Morton & Griswold, 1852.   Cloth.   Scarce.

viii, ₍9₎–312 ₍8₎ p.   19.8 cm.
Last 8 p. adv.

672 DELARUE-MARDRUS, LUCIE. Le Far-West d'aujourd'hui. Illustré de planches hors texte. ₍By₎ Lucie Delarue-Mardrus. Paris, Fasquelle éditeurs, ₍1932₎. Pict. wrappers. OP.

8 p.l., ₍17₎–201 ₍3₎ p. front., plates, ports., map. 19.5 cm.
Half title; untrimmed.

A Frenchwoman's views on travel in New Mexico, Colorado, and Wyoming, with material on cowboys.

673 DE LOACH, ROBERT JOHN HENDERSON. Live stock as a business, by R. J. H. De Loach. Chicago, 1918. Wrappers. Scarce.

₍14₎ p. (no pagination). 12.6 x 8.8 cm.
Reprinted from *"Florida Farmer and Stockman,* March 16, 1918."

674 DEMING, WILLIAM CHAPLIN. Roosevelt in the bunk house and other sketches. Visits of the great Rough Rider to Wyoming in 1900, 1903, and 1910, by William Chaplin Deming. Laramie, the Laramie printing company, ₍1927₎. Cloth. Scarce.

4 p.l., 5–80 p. front. (port.), plates, ports. 23.5 cm.

675 DENHARDT, ROBERT MOORMAN. The horse of the Americas, ₍by₎ Robert Moorman Denhardt. Norman, University of Oklahoma press, 1947. Cloth. OP.

xvii p., 2 l., 5–286 p. plates, ports. 23 cm.
Appendices, p. 231–271; bibliographical sketch, p. 273–280; index, p. 281–286.
Half title; double illus. t.p.

676 ———. The quarter horse; a varied assortment of historical sketches, equine biographies, sketches of horsemen, and other lore, all pertaining to the quarter horse. Penned up by Bob Denhardt. Ft. Worth, Texas, published by the American Quarter Horse association, 1941. Cloth. OP.

xxvi p., 1 l., 229 p. front., plates, ports. 23.5 cm.
Colophon: "Of this limited edition one hundred and twenty-five copies have been printed and numbered . . . ."
Also published in a trade edition.

677 ———. The quarter horse. Vol. two. A varied assortment of historical articles, equine biographies and characteristics, sketches of horsemen, and other lore, all pertaining to the quarter horse, collected by Bob Denhardt and Helen Michaelis. Eagle Pass, Texas, published by the American Quarter Horse association, 1945. Cloth. OP.

xi, 3–217 p. front., plates. 23.6 cm.
Author index, p. 213–216; general index, p. 217.
Illus. end papers.

678 DENTON, B. E. "CYCLONE." A two-gun cyclone. A true story, by B. E.

"Cyclone" Denton. Illustrated by Jack Patton. Dallas, Texas, B. E. Denton, publisher . . . , ₁1927₁. Pict. cloth.

viii p., 2 l., 145 p. front. (port.), plates (1 col.). 19.4 cm.
Half title.

A little book of reminiscences written by an old-time cowboy after he had reached his seventies. He was a typical old-time Texas cowboy, uneducated and big hearted. I knew him well, and he could have written a much better story if he had recorded some of the stories he told me during our association.

679 DeRicqles, A. E. Live stock policy for Washington. Address of Mr. A. E. DeRicqles, president of the American Live Stock Loan company of Denver, Colorado. ₁Held at the convention of the American National Live Stock association at Salt Lake, Utah, January 14, 15, 16, 1918₁. Wrappers. Scarce.

14 p. 22.5 cm.

680 ———. Railway rates and service. Address delivered by A. E. DeRicqles, general manager of the American Live Stock and Loan company, Denver, Colorado, at the seventeenth annual convention of the American National Live Stock Association at the Broadway Theatre, Denver, Colorado, January 21, 1914. Denver, Colo., published by American National Live Stock Association, ₁1914₁. Wrappers. Scarce.

7 p. 22.5 cm.

681 DeRousiers, Paul. American life. Translated from the French by A. J. Herbertson. Paris and New York, Firmin-Didot and co., 1892. Cloth. Scarce.

8 p.l., ₁19₁–437 p. 25.8 cm.

682 Devine, Edward James. Across widest America. Newfoundland to Alaska, with impressions of two years' sojourn on the Bering coast. Profusely illustrated. By Edward J. Devine. . . . Montreal, the Canadian Messenger, publisher, 1905. Pict. cloth. OP.

5 p.l., 307 p. front. (port., signature in facsm.), plates, ports., fold. map. 20.5 cm.
Half title.

Chapter III deals with cattle and cowboys of the Canadian Northwest.

683 DeWolf, J. H. Pawnee Bill (Major Gordon W. Lillie), his experiences and adventures on the western plains; or, from the saddle of a "cowboy and ranger" to the chair of a "bank president," by J. H. DeWolf. ₁N. p.₁, published by Pawnee Bill's Historic Wild West co., 1902. Col. pict. boards. Scarce.

4 p.l., 13–108 p. front., illus., plates, ports. 23.7 cm.

684 Dick, Everett Newton. The long drive, by Everett Dick. Reprinted

from Collections of the Kansas State Historical Society, 1926–1928, Vol. XVII. Stapled. (Caption title). OP.

71 p. illus. 22.9 cm.

A thesis presented to the faculty of the Graduate College of the University of Nebraska in partial fulfillment of requirements for the degree of Master of Arts, Department of History, Lincoln, Neb., June, 1925. Much on the Chisholm Trail.

685 ———. The sod-house frontier, 1854–1890. A social history of the northern plains from the creation of Kansas and Nebraska to the admission of the Dakotas, by Everett Dick. . . . Illustrated. New York, London, D. Appleton-Century company, incorporated, 1937. Pict. cloth. OP.

xviii p., 1 l., 550 p. illus., plates. 22.8 cm.
Bibliography, p. 519–528; index, p. 529–550.
Half title; map on end papers; pub. device; untrimmed; first edition: figure "(1)" at end of index.

Reprinted in 1938 with same imprint, and again fifteen years later (1953) by Johnson publishing co., of Lincoln, Nebraska.

686 ———. Vanguards of the frontier. A social history of the northern plains and Rocky Mountains from the earliest white contacts to the coming of the homemaker, by Everett Dick. . . . Illustrated. New York, London, D. Appleton-Century company, incorporated, 1941. Pict. cloth. OP.

xvi p., 1 l., 574 p. front., plates. 23 cm.
Bibliography, p. 519–545; index, p. 547–574.
Half title; map on end papers; pub. device; untrimmed; first edition: figure "(1)" at end of index.

687 DIEKER, LEO E. A brief historical sketch, Hollenberg ranch, Pony Express station, Hanover, Kansas, by Leo E. Dieker. . . . [Hanover], the Hanover News, publisher . . . , [n.d.]. Stiff wrappers.

[7] p. (no pagination). 1 plate at end. 21.2 cm.

688 DILLS, LUCIUS. Roswell, some facts and observations relative to its settlement and early growth. [By] Lucius Dills. [Roswell, New Mexico, 1933]. Wrappers. (Cover title). Scarce.

[26] p. (no pagination). front., plates, ports. 22.5 cm.

689 DISBROW, EDWARD DELAVAN. The man without a gun. [By] Edward Delavan Disbrow. Boston, Chapman & Grimes, [1936]. Cloth. OP.

4 p.l., 9–96 p. front. 20.7 cm.
Half title; device; untrimmed.

690 DOBIE, J. FRANK. The first cattle in Texas and the southwest pro-

genitors of the longhorns, by J. Frank Dobie. ₁Austin, 1939₁. Wrappers. (Cover title). OP.

₁3₁–29 p. 22.8 cm.

Reprinted from the *Southwestern Historical Quarterly,* Vol. XLII, No. 3 (January, 1939).

691 ——. The flavor of Texas, by J. Frank Dobie, with illustrations by Alexander Hogue. Dallas, Texas, Dealey and Lowe, 1936. Cloth. OP.

6 p.l., 287 p. front., illus. 22.4 cm.
Index, p. ₁285₁–287.

692 ——. Guide to life and literature of the Southwest, with a few observations. By J. Frank Dobie. Illustrated. Austin, published by the University of Texas press; specially printed for University press in Dallas, Southern Methodist University, 1943. Pict. cloth.

2 p.l., ₁7₁–111 p. illus. 23.5 cm.
Also published in wrappers.

693 ——. Guide to life and literature of the Southwest. Revised and enlarged in both knowledge and wisdom. ₁By₁ J. Frank Dobie. Dallas, Southern Methodist University press, 1952. Cloth.

viii, 222 p. illus., music. 23.5 cm.
Index, p. 197–222.
Half title; double t.p.; facsimile of signature on cover.

694 ——. The longhorns, by J. Frank Dobie; illustrated by Tom Lea. Boston, Little, Brown and company, 1941. Cloth.

xxiii p., 1 l., 3–388 p. illus., plates. 22.6 cm.
Notes, p. 347–379; index, p. 381–388.
Half title; double t.p. illus. in color. (The picture is "The Stampede," the original of which is a mural in the U. S. Post Office, Odessa, Texas); each chapter has separate dedication; untrimmed.

Also published in a de luxe edition of 265 copies, bound in saddle leather, boxed in illus. cloth.

Colophon: "265 numbered copies of this rawhide edition have been printed, roped and tallied. They have been branded by the author and the artist. This is number —."

695 ——. The Mexican vaquero of the Texas border, by J. Frank Dobie. Austin, Texas, ₁n. d.₁. Wrappers. (Cover title). Scarce.

12 p. 25.7 cm.

Reprinted from *Southwestern Political and Social Science Quarterly,* Vol. VIII, No. 1 (June, 1927).

696 ——. The mustangs by J. Frank Dobie. Illustrated by Charles Banks Wilson. Boston, Little, Brown and company, ₁1952₁. Pict. two-tone cloth.

xvii p., 1 l., 3–376 p. front. (col.), 1 illus., plates. 22 cm.
Notes, p. 333–364; index, p. 367–376.
Half title; vignette; illus. end papers; illus. chapter headings.
Also published in a de luxe edition, bound in horsehide with the hair left on, and boxed.

697 ———. My salute to Gene Rhodes, by J. Frank Dobie. A Christmas remembrance from Bertha and Frank Dobie. ₁El Paso, Carl Hertzog, printer₁, 1947. Wrappers.

12 ₁1₁ p. 24 cm.
Issued as a Christmas booklet and given to friends.

698 ———. On the open range, by J. Frank Dobie. . . . Illustrated by Ben Carleton Mead. Dallas, Texas, the Southwest press, ₁1931₁. Pict. cloth.
xii, 312 p. front. (col.), illus., plates (part col.), cattle brands. 19.5 cm.
"Suggested readings," p. 297–302; "words, names, and phrases peculiar to the open range country," p. 303–312.
Illus. end papers.

699 ———. Pitching horses and panthers, by J. Frank Dobie. ₁Austin, Texas, Texas Folklore society, 1940₁. Stiff wrappers. OP.
3–15 p. 1 illus. 22.8 cm.
Reprinted from *Mustangs and Cow Horses,* published by the Texas Folk-lore society, Austin, Texas, 1940.

700 ———. Tales of the mustang, by J. Frank Dobie; illustrations by Jerry Bywaters. Dallas, the Book Club of Texas, 1936. Boards. Rare.
4 p.l., ₁13₁–89 ₁1₁ p. illus. 23 cm.
Half title; vignette; illus. chapter headings; untrimmed.
Colophon: "Of this edition three hundred copies have been printed by the Rein Company for the Book Club of Texas."

701 ———. Tales of old-time Texas ₁by₁ J. Frank Dobie. Illustrated by Barbara Latham. Boston, Toronto, Little, Brown and company, ₁1955₁. Boards and cloth.
xvi p., 1 l., ₁3₁–336 p. front., illus. 22 cm.
Notes and credits, p. ₁313₁–327; index, p. ₁329₁–336.
Half title; pub. device.

702 ———. A vaquero of the brush country, by J. Frank Dobie, partly from the reminiscences of John Young. Illustrated by Justin C. Gruelle. Dallas, Texas, the Southwest press, 1929. Cloth and boards.
xv, 314 p. front. (col.), illus., plates, facsm. 24 cm.
Appendix, p. 299–303; index, p. 305–314.
Map on end papers; pub. device; untrimmed.

The first edition may be identified by the word "river" after "Rio Grande" on the map of the end papers. The author told me: "I have always had a particular dislike for the redundance of 'river' in conjunction with 'Rio.' When I found this idiotic redundancy in my own book, I was not happy. I had not seen the proof of these end papers. I immediately had 'river' taken out and also made other corrections."

The plates of the original book were destroyed, and when the Southwest Press went bankrupt, they turned the copyright back to the author. Grossett and Dunlap then reset the book in 1934, but later quit printing it and turned the plates back to the author. He then let Little, Brown and Company have them, and they have since kept the book in print.

703 ———. The voice of the coyote, by J. Frank Dobie. Illustrated by Olaus J. Murie. Boston, Little, Brown and Company, 1949. Cloth.

xx p., 1 l., 3–386 p. front., illus., plates. 22.3 cm.
Notes, p. 353–368; [acknowledgments], p. 369–376; index, p. 379–386.
Half title; illus. chapter headings; t.p. and front. in color.

704 ———. (ED.). Coffee in the gourd, edited by J. Frank Dobie. Publications of the Texas Folk-lore Society Number II, 1923. Austin, Texas, published by Texas Folk-lore society, 1923. Cloth. OP.

3 p.l., 110 [1] p. illus. 23.3 cm.
Index, p. [103]–110.

705 ———. Mody C. Boatright, and Harry H. Ransom (EDS.). Mustangs and cow horses. Edited by J. Frank Dobie, Mody C. Boatright, and Harry H. Ransom. Illustrated. Austin, Texas, Folk-lore society, 1940. Cloth.

xi p., 1 l., 3–429 p. illus., map, music. 23.2 cm.
Contributors, p. 419–423; index, p. 425–429.
Half title; illus. end papers.
Publication of the Texas Folk-lore Society, No. XVI.

706 Dobie J. Frank (ED.). Southwestern lore, edited by J. Frank Dobie. Publications of the Texas Folk-lore Society, Number IX, 1931. . . . Dallas, the Southwest press, [1931]. Cloth.

v, 199 p. illus., music. 23.4 cm.

707 ———, Mody C. Boatright, and Harry H. Ransom (EDS.). Texian stomping ground. Texas Folk-lore Society, Publication Number XVII. Edited by J. Frank Dobie, Mody C. Boatright, Harry H. Ransom. Austin, Texas, Texas Folk-lore society, 1941. Cloth.

4 p.l., 162 [1] p. illus., music, diagrs. 23.5 cm.
Index, p. [159]–162.
Half title.

708 [Dodd, C. H.]. Oregon as it is. Solid facts and actual results. For the use and information of immigrants. Issued by the Oregon Immigration

board. Portland, Or., D. C. Ireland & co., [1885]. Wrappers. (Cover title). Rare.

[3]–56 p. large fold. map in front. 20.7 cm.

709 DODGE, ORVIL. Pioneer history of Coos and Curry counties, Or., heroic deeds and thrilling adventures of the early settlers. . . . Orvil Dodge, historian. Salem, Oregon, Capital printing co., 1898. Cloth. Scarce.

4 p.l., [6]–468, 103 p. front. (port.), plates, ports. 21.8 cm.
Appendix, p. [1]–103 (at end).
Double column.

710 DODGE, THEODORE AYRULT. Riders of many lands, by Theodore Ayrult Dodge. . . . Illustrated with numerous drawings by Frederic Remington and from photographs of oriental subjects. New York, Harper & brothers, publishers, 1894. Pict. cloth. OP.

viii, 486 [2] p. front., illus., plates. 23.5 cm.
Pub. device; untrimmed; 2 p. adv. at end.

Chapters on the cowboy and horse breaking.

711 DONAGHEY, GEORGE WASHINGTON. Autobiographical sketch of George W. Donaghey. The first three stages of life. . . . [By George W. Donaghey, n. p., 1924]. Pict. wrappers. (Cover title). Scarce.

[5]–31 [1] p. front. (port.). 26 cm.
Double column.

Some material on the author's cowboy days and experiences up the trail before he became governor of Arkansas.

712 ———. Building a state capitol. [By George W. Donaghey, governor of Arkansas, 1909–1913 . . .]. Little Rock, Arkansas, Parke-Harper company, 1937. Pict. cloth. Scarce.

xv p., 12 l., [3]–376 [1] p. plates, ports. 24 cm.

Some material on cowboys.

713 DONAN, P. The Columbia River empire. A land of promise for the homeseeker and homemaker. By P. Donan. Portland, Oregon, published by the passenger department of the Oregon Railroad and Navigation company, 1902. Pict. wrappers. Scarce.

[3]–72 p. illus., plates, large fold. map at end. 23.3 cm.
Illus. t.p.

714 ———. The heart of the continent; an historical and descriptive treatise for business men, homeseekers, and tourists, of the advantages, resources, and scenery of the great West. Published by the passenger department,

Chicago, Burlington & Quincy Railroad. Chicago, Ill., 1882. Pict. wrappers. Rare.

[3]–63 [1] p.   illus., map at end.   16.8 cm.

715 DONNELLY, THOMAS C. (ED.).   Rocky Mountain politics. Edited by Thomas C. Donnelly . . . with a foreword by Arthur N. Holcombe. . . . Albuquerque, the University of New Mexico press, [1940]. Cloth. OP.

vi p., 6 l., 11–304 p.   9 maps (inc. front.).   23.5 cm.
Bibliography, p. 292–295; contributors, p. 296–297; index, p. 299–304.
Half title.

716 DONOHO, MILFORD HILL.   Circle-dot, a true story of cowboy life forty years ago, by M. H. Donoho.   Topeka, monotyped and printed by Crane & company, 1907. Cloth. Scarce.

3 p.l., 7–256 p.   front., 20 cm.

717 DOUBLEDAY, RUSSELL.   Cattle-ranch to college, the true tale of a boy's adventure in the Far West, by Russell Doubleday. . . . New York, Doubleday & McClure co., MDCCCXCIX. Pict. cloth. Scarce.

xii p., 2 l., 347 p.   front., illus., 23 plates.   21 cm.
Half title; marginal illus.

718 DOUGHITT, KATHERINE CHRISTIAN (MRS. J. W.).   Romance and dim trails. A history of Clay County [Texas], Katherine Christian, Mrs. J. W. Doughitt, editor-in-chief. Dallas, Texas, William T. Tardy, publisher, 1938. Imt. leather. Scarce.

7 p.l., 280 p.   front., plates, ports., cattle brands.   23.3 cm.
Cattle brands, p. 269–280.
Map on end papers; leaf of errata tipped in; device.

719 DOUGLAS, CLAUD LEROY.   Cattle kings of Texas, by C. L. Douglas. Dallas, Texas, published by Cecil Baugh, [1939]. Cloth. OP.

xiv, 376 p.   front., illus., plates, ports., cattle brands.   22.5 cm.
Half title; illus. end papers; pub. device.

First appeared serially in *The Cattleman* magazine. Some copies were bound in cowhide with the hair left on. It contains short histories of some of the famous Texas ranches and their owners.

720 DOUGLAS, FORD.   The cattle rustlers of Wyoming; or, Thorpe of the Hole-In-the-Wall country. A story of Wyoming and the cattle country, written around one of the most thrilling and dramatic incidents in the history of the West—the "Rustlers War" of 1892. By Ford Douglas, New York, J. S. Ogilvie publishing company, 1916. Stiff pict. col. wrappers. Scarce.

3–190 p.   18.8 cm.
Published with "The Secret Service Stories" of 56 pages, 12 p. adv. at end.

721 Dow, J. L.   The Australian in America, being letters of J. L. Dow. . . .
Melbourne, the "Leader" office, 1884. Wrappers. Scarce.

xvi, [9]–176, i–xx p.   21.3 cm.
8 p. adv. in front; i–xx adv. at end.

Seen in the Rollins Collection, Princeton University.

722 DOWELL, AUSTIN ALLYN.   Livestock marketing, by Austin Allyn
Dowell . . . and Knure Bjorka. . . . First edition. New York and London, McGraw-Hill book co., inc., 1941. Cloth. OP.

x, 534 p.   illus., maps, tables, diagrs.   23.5 cm.
Bibliographical footnotes; "selected readings" at end of each chapter except the last.

723 [DOWNEY, S. W.].   Prospectus of the Wyoming Central Land and Improvement Company. Including a statement of the business interests of
the country, and a description of the lands and prospects of development.
St. Louis, 1884. Wrappers. Rare.

20 p.   18.5 cm.

Written primarily to induce cattle interests to the state, especially to Albany
and Carbon counties.

724 DOWSE, THOMAS.   The new northwest, Montana. Fort Benson, its past,
present, and future. By Thomas Dowse.   St. Paul, Minnesota, 1879. Pict.
wrappers. (Cover title). Rare.

22 p.   illus.   26.6 cm.
Triple column.

725 DRIGGS, BENJAMIN WOODBURY.   History of Teton Valley, Idaho, by
B. W. Driggs.   Caldwell, Idaho, the Caxton printers, ltd., MCMXXVI.
Boards. Scarce.

6 p.l., [13]–227 p.   front., plates.   23.5 cm.

726 DRIGGS, HOWARD ROSCOE.   The old West speaks, by Howard R. Driggs.
Water-color paintings by William Henry Jackson. Englewood Cliffs,
N. J., Prentice-Hall, inc., [1956]. Cloth.

9 p.l., 19–220 p.   plates (37 col.).   28 cm.
Bibliography, p. 203–205; index, p. 207–220.
Half title; double t.p.

727 ———.   Westward America, by Howard R. Driggs. With reproductions of forty water color paintings by William H. Jackson. Trails edition.
New York, G. P. Putnam's sons, [1942]. Cloth. OP.

x p., 1 l., 312 p.   40 col. plates (incl. front.).   29.3 cm.
Bibliography, p. 301–302; index, p. 305–312.
Half title.
Also published in a trade edition.

728 DRISCOLL, R. E. Seventy years of banking in the Black Hills, by R. E. Driscoll. First National Bank of the Black Hills, 1876–1946. [Rapid City, S. D., the Gate City Guide, publishers, 1948]. Stiff pict. wrappers.

4 p.l., 11–87 p. port. 23 cm.

A chapter on livestock in the Black Hills.

729 DROULERS, CHARLES. Le Marquis de Mores, 1858–1896. Avec 7 gravures et une carte hors texte. Paris, Librairie Plon, les Petits-Fils de Plon et Nourrit . . . , [1932]. Wrappers. Scarce.

2 p.l., 254 [1] p. front., plates, port., map, facsm. 18.8 cm.
Half title; untrimmed.

730 DRUMHELLER, DANIEL. "Uncle Dan" Drumheller tells thrills of western trails in 1854, by "Uncle Dan" Drumheller. Spokane, Washington, Inland-American printing company, 1925. Raised leather. Scarce.

xi, 131 p. 2 ports. (incl. front. with tissues). 19.5 cm.
Half title; chapter headings and divisions printed in red.

731 DUN, JOHN. Eleven stories inspired by Arizona sunshine . . . , by John Dun. [East Aurora, N. Y., printed and bound by the Roycrofters, 1938]. Cloth. Pict. label pasted on. OP.

4 p.l., 11–175 p. illus. 21 cm.
Map on end papers; table of contents on t.p.; head and tail pieces; cover title, "No New Frontiers."

732 DUNN, JOHN BEAUMOND. Perilous trails of Texas, by J. B. (Red) John Dunn (edited by Lilith Lorraine). Dallas, Texas, published for the author by the Southwest press, publishers, [1932]. Cloth. OP.

ix, 163 p. front. (port.), plates, ports. 21.6 cm.
"Official trail names adopted," p. 155–163.
Untrimmed.

733 DUNN, J. E. Indian Territory, a pre-commonwealth. By J. E. Dunn. . . . Illustrations by courtesy of the *Twin Territories Magazine*. Indianapolis press of American printing company, inc., 1904. Pict. cloth. Scarce.

10 p.l., 28–250 p. front. (port.), illus., plates, ports., map. 20 cm.

734 DUNHAM, HAROLD HATHAWAY. Government handout. A study in the administration of the public lands 1875–1891. Submitted in partial fulfillment of the requirements for the degree of Doctor of Philosophy, in the faculty of political science, Columbia University, N. Y., 1941. Multilitho offset. Stiff wrappers. OP.

vii, 364 [1] p. 22.8 cm.
Bibliography, p. 345–351; index, p. 353–364.

735 DYER, T. J. Old Kiowa in history and romance. A partial history of
the old town, established in 1874, now known as Old Kiowa. By T. J.
Dyer. ₁N.p.₁, 1934. Stiff wrappers. (Cover title). Scarce.
2 p.l., ₁5₁–25 p. front. (port.). 19.5 cm.

736 DYKSTERHUIS, E. J. Some notes and quotes: on range education, ₁by₁
E. J. Dyksterhuis. . . . ₁Baltimore, Md.₁, 1953. Folder.
p. 295–298. 25.3 cm.
Double column.
Reprinted from *Journal of Range Management,* Vol. VI, No. 5 (September, 1953).

737 EARLE, J. P. History of Clay County and northwest Texas, by J. P.
Earle. ₁Henrietta, Texas, 1900₁. Wrappers. Rare.
64 p. front., ports. 22.4 cm.

738 EATON, FRANK. Pistol Pete, veteran of the old West, by Frank Eaton.
With illustrations. Boston, Little, Brown and company, 1952. Cloth.
x p., 1 l., ₁3₁–278 p. plates, ports. 21 cm.
Half title; pub. device; signature in facsm. at end; "First edition" on copyright p.

One of the wildest tales on record of a man's experiences in the cattle country.

739 EATON, JEANETTE. Bucky O'Neill of Arizona, by Jeanette Eaton. Illustrated by Edward Shenton. New York, William Morrow and company,
1949. Pict. cloth.
6 p.l., 13–219 p. illus., plate (double p.). 20.8 cm.
Half title; illus. double t.p.; chapter headings.

740 EAVES, CHARLES DUDLEY, and C. A. HUTCHINSON. Post City, Texas.
C. W. Post's colonizing activities in West Texas. ₁By₁ Charles Dudley
Eaves and C. A. Hutchinson. Austin, the Texas State Historical association, 1952. Pict. cloth.
xiii p., 1 l., 3–171 p. front. (port.), plates, ports., maps. 24.2 cm.

741 EBBUTT, PERCY G. Emigrant life in Kansas. By Percy G. Ebbutt. London, Swan Sonneschein and co., 1886. Pict. cloth. Scarce.
viii, 237 p. front. (with tissue), illus. 22.6 cm.
Vignette; untrimmed.

742 EDDINS, ROY (ED.). History of Falls County, Texas. . . . Compiled by
Old Settlers and Veterans Association of Falls County, Texas. Roy Eddins,
editor. ₁N. p., 1947₁. Cloth.
viii p., 2 l., ₁5₁–312 p. illus., ports., cattle brands. 23.6 cm.
Index, p. ₁303₁–312.
Illus. t.p.

743 [EDINBURGH LADY, AN]. A rapid run to the wild West, by an Edin-

burgh lady. Edinburgh, privately printed, by R. & R. Clark, 1884. Stiff wrappers. Rare.

2 p.l., ₍5₎–35 p. 17.5 cm.
Half title; untrimmed.

Quite a bit about cowboys. Seen in the Rollins Collection, Princeton University.

744 EDMINISTER, LYNN RAMSAY. The cattle industry and the tariff. By Lynn R. Edminister.... New York, the Macmillan co., 1926. Cloth. OP.

xv, 331 p. graphs, tables. 19 cm.
Bibliography, p. 317–326; index, p. 327–331.
Head of half title: "The Institute of Economic Investigations in International Commercial Policies."

745 EDWARDS, JOHN A. In the western tongue; a collection of speeches and letters by John A. Edwards. . . . Wichita, Kansas, published by the McCormick-Armstrong press, ₍1920₎. Stiff pict. wrappers. Scarce.

4 p.l., ₍9₎–136 p. front. (port.), illus. 19.7 cm.
Half title.

746 EDWARDS, J. B. Early days in Abilene, by J. B. Edwards. Edited and published by C. W. Wheeler, printed in the Abilene Chronicle 1896, reprinted in the Abilene Daily Chronicle, 1938, with added material from the papers of J. B. Edwards. ₍N. p., n. d.₎. Pict. wrappers. (Caption title). Scarce.

16 p. illus., plates, ports. 30.5 x 23.4 cm.
Triple column.

The author relates some events in early Abilene. He lived there from its founding and knew its history firsthand when it was a cowtown.

747 EDWARDS, PHILIP LEGET. California in 1837. Diary of Col. Philip L. Edwards, containing an account of a trip to the Pacific coast . . . , Sacramento, A. J. Johnston & co., printers, 1890. Wrappers. Rare.

1 p. ₍3₎–47 p. 16.6 cm.

First published serially in *Themis* magazine in the 1860's by authority of the board of State Library Trustees of the state of California. This rare little booklet is written in the form of a diary and contains details of the earliest cattle drive.

748 ———. The diary of Philip Leget Edwards; the great cattle drive from California to Oregon in 1837. San Francisco, Grabhorn press, 1932. Dec. boards. Scarce.

3 p.l., 47 p. front. (col.). 25.7 cm.
Headpieces; untrimmed.
Rare Americana Series No. 4.
"Introduction to the Diary of Phil Leget Edwards, by Douglas S. Watson," 2d–3d prelim. leaves.

A reprint of the preceding item.

749 EICKEMEYER, CARL. Over the great Navajo Trail, by Carl Eickemeyer.
... Illustrated with photographs taken by the author. New York [Press
of J. J. Little & co.], 1900. Pict. cloth. Scarce.
9 p.l., 21–270 p. front. (port. with tissue), plates (1 col., with tissue). 21.5 cm.

750 EICKEMEYER, RUDOLF. Letters from the South-West, by Rudolf Eickemeyer.... Illustrated by E. W. Deming. [New York, Press of J. J. Little
and co.], 1894. Cloth. Scarce.
2 p.l., [5]–111 p. front. (with tissue), illus. 24.3 cm.

Letters written by an educated New Yorker seeking health in the Southwest,
in which he gives some information on the cowboy.

751 [ELBERT, S. H.]. Biennial message of Governor S. H. Elbert to the
Tenth Legislature of Colorado, delivered January 6, 1874. Printed by authority. Central City, Register printing house, 1874. Wrappers. Scarce.
[3]–34 p. tables. 22.9 cm.

752 EL COMANCHO (Pseud. of Walter Shalley Phillips). The old timer's
tale, by El Comancho. Chicago, the Canterbury press, 1929. Pict. boards.
Scarce.
5 p.l., 114 p. front. (port.), plates. 20.3 cm.
Half title; pub. device.
Two errata slips inserted, the first reading, "Page 15, line 7 should be line 6"; the
second reading: "Page 47, line 5 should follow line 24."

753 ELKINS, HON. STEPHEN B. Admission of New Mexico as a state—her
resources and future. Speech of Hon. Stephen B. Elkins, delegate from
New Mexico in the House of Representatives, May 21, 1874.... Washington, Government printing office, 1874. Sewn. Rare.
[3]–33 p. 21.5 cm.

754 ELIOTT, HOWARD. Montana. An address by Howard Elliott, president
of the Northern Pacific Railway Company, delivered at the Inter-State
Fair, Bozeman, Mont., September 1, 1910. [N.p., c.1910]. Wrappers.
Scarce.
[14] p. (no pagination). 22.5 cm.

755 ELLIOTT, JOHN F. All about Texas. A hand book of information for
the home seeker, the capitalist, the prospector, the tourist, the health
hunter. ... By John F. Elliott. ... Austin, Texas, Hutchins printing
house, 1888. Stiff pict. col. wrappers. Rare.
2 p.l., [3]–47 [21] p. 22.8 cm.
Last 21 p. adv.; adv. verso front cover; adv. recto back wrapper.

756 [ELLIOTT, R. S.]. Industrial resources of western Kansas and eastern

Colorado. Kansas Pacific Railway. Saint Louis, Levison & Blithe, stationers ..., 1871. Wrappers. Rare.

[3]–32 p.   22 cm.

757 ELLIOT, W. J.   The Spurs, by W. J. Elliot. [Spur, Texas], the Texas Spur, publishers, 1939. Cloth. Scarce.

6 p.l., 274 p.   front. (port.), plates, ports., map.   18.4 cm.
Half title; illus. on green paper.

A history of this famous ranch by one connected with it. Privately printed and now quite difficult to come by.

758 ELLIS, ANNE.   "Plain" Anne Ellis. More about the life of an ordinary woman, by Anne Ellis.   Boston and New York, Houghton Mifflin company, 1931. Cloth. OP.

3 p.l., 264 [1] p.   front.   21 cm.
Untrimmed; first edition, "1931" under imprint.

A story of life in the cattle country.

759 ELLISON, EDITH NICHOLL.   The desert and the rose, by Edith Nicholl Ellison....   Boston, the Cornhill company, [1921]. Cloth. Scarce.

8 p.l., [9]–215 p.   front., plates.   19.2 cm.
Half title; pub. device.

Much on ranching in New Mexico.

760 ELMHIRST, CAPTAIN PENNELL.   Fox-hound, forest, and prairie. By Captain Pennell Elmhirst.... Illustrated by J. Sturgess and J. Marshman.... London, George Routledge and sons, limited ..., 1892. Pict. cloth. Scarce.

xv [1], 584 p.   front. (col., with tissue), illus., plates, map.   23 cm.
Half title; 2 p. adv. in front; illus. t.p.

This book was written by an English sportsman who visited this country in the early 1890's. It has a chapter on "Western cattle lands" dealing with ranching and cowboys.

761 ELSENSOHN, SISTER M. ALFREDA (ED.).   Pioneer days in Idaho County, Vol. I. By Sister M. Alfreda Elsensohn ... (ed.)....   Caldwell, Idaho, the Caxton printers, ltd., 1947. Pict. cloth.

xx p., 1 l., 527 p.   front., plates, ports., facsm.   23.6 cm.
Bibliography, p. 503–512; index, p. [513]–527.
Half title; map on end papers; footnotes at end of each chapter.

Vol. II published several years later.

762 ELY, BURNHAM, and BARTLETT.   Proceedings and debates of the American convention of cattle commissioners held at Springfield, Illinois, De-

cember 1st, 2nd, and 3d, 1868. ₁By₁ Ely, Burnham, and Bartlett, official reporters. Springfield, Illinois Journal printing office, 1869. Wrappers. Rare.

₁3₁–163 p.   21 cm.

A rare record of the proceedings of the meeting of cattle commissioners from the various states interested in the raising, sale, and purchase of cattle. Deals with the drafting of laws to regulate the cattle trade and the establishment of the industry upon a basis of mutual protection.

763 ELZNER, JONNIE ROSS. Lamplights of Lampasas County, Texas, by Jonnie Elzner.   Austin, Texas, Firm Foundation publishing house, ₁1951₁. Pict. cloth. OP.

ii, ₁5₁–219 p.   plates, maps, diagr.   23.6 cm.
Appendices, p. 187–219.

Has chapters on cattle and the cowboy.

764 EMMETT, CHRIS. Shanghai Pierce, a fair likeness, by Chris Emmett, with drawings by Nick Eggenhofer.   Norman, University of Oklahoma Press, ₁1953₁. Cloth.

xiii p., 1 l., 3–326 p.   illus., plates, ports., maps.   24 cm.
Bibliography, p. 313–319; index, p. 321–326.
Half title; illus. double t.p.; illus. chapter headings; "First edition" on copyright p.

765 EMRICH, DUNCAN. The cowboy's own brand book. ₁By₁ Duncan Emrich. Illustrated by Ava Morgan.   New York, Thomas Y. Crowell company, ₁1954₁. Cloth.

xiii, 69 ₁13₁ p.   cattle brands.   11.5 x 15.5 cm.
Half title; "First edition" on copyright p.

766 ———. It's an old wild West custom. ₁By₁ Duncan Emrich. New York, the Vanguard press, inc., ₁1949₁. Pict. cloth.

xiv p. 1 l., 3–313 p.   illus., cattle brands.   21.3 cm.
Half title; illus. t.p.; illus. chapter headings; untrimmed.

767 ENFIELD, DR. J. E. The man from Packsaddle. By Dr. J. E. Enfield. Hollywood, House-Warven, publishers, 1952. Cloth.

3 p.l., 5–186 p.   23.5 cm.
Device.

768 EPPERSON, HARRY A. Colorado as I saw it, by Harry A. Epperson. ₁Kaysville, Utah, Inland printing co., 1943₁. Morocco. OP.
3 p.l., 137 p.   illus., plates, ports.   23.6 cm.

769 ERSKINE, MRS. GLADYS (SHAW). Broncho Charlie; a saga of the saddle, by Gladys Shaw Erskine. The life story of Broncho Charlie Miller, the

last of the pony express riders. New York, Thomas Y. Crowell company, publishers, ₁1934₁. Cloth. OP.

xiv p., 1 l., 316 p. plates, ports., maps (1 fold.), facsm. 22.5 cm.
Half title; map on end papers; vignette; untrimmed.

770 Esor (no other name found). Eighty-eight days in America, by Esor. London, printed by Strangeways and sons, 1884. Boards. Rare.

iv, 129 ₁2₁ p. 17.4 cm.
Last 2 p., "Table of Route."

Some information on ranching in Dakota and on the Marquis de Mores. This copy seen in the Rollins Collection, Princeton University.

771 Eustis, P. S. South-western Nebraska and north-western Kansas. A brief description of the country, its products and resources, together with a synopsis of the homestead, pre-emption, and timber culture laws. . . . Omaha, Nebraska, State printers, 1887. Wrappers. Rare.

₁2₁–16 p. large fold. map at end. 22.4 cm.

772 Evans, Charles. Lights on Oklahoma history, by Charles Evans. Oklahoma City, Harlow publishing company, 1926. Pict. cloth. OP.

3 p.l., 183 p. 19.5 cm.

773 Evans, George S. Wylackie Jake of Colevo. By George S. Evans. San Francisco, Press of the Hicks-Judd co., ₁1904₁. Pict. cloth. Scarce.

3 p.l., 107 p. front. (port.). 20.2 cm.

774 Evans, Joe M. A corral full of stories, rounded up by Joe Evans. . . . ₁El Paso, Texas, the McMath company, inc., 1939₁. Pict. French wrappers. OP.

x p., 1 l., ₁3₁–66 p. front., illus., ports. 21 cm.
Half title; vignette; untrimmed.

775 ———. The cow, by Joe M. Evans. About all I know I learned from a cow. ₁El Paso, Texas, printed by Guynes printing co., 1944₁. Stiff pict. wrappers. (Cover title). OP.

3 p.l., ₁7₁–71 p. front., illus., plates, ports., cattle brands. 19.8 cm.
Half title.

776 ———. Cowboy's hitchin' post, by Joe M. Evans. El Paso, ₁privately printed, n. d., c.1947₁. Stiff pict. wrappers. (Cover title). OP.
2 p.l., 5–105 p. plates (1 double p.), 21 cm.

The Bloys cowboy camp meeting and other cowboy religious meetings.

777 Evans, William Franklin. Border skylines; fifty years of "tallying out" on the Bloys round-up ground, by Will F. Evans. Dallas, Texas,

published for the Bloys Camp Meeting association by Cecil Baugh, [1940].
Pict. cloth. OP.

xiv p., 3 l., 587 [1] p. front. (port.), illus., plates, ports. 23.4 cm.
Half title; illus. end papers (col.).

Much on cowboys and the Bloys cowboy camp meetings.

778 ———. Hunting grisslys, black bear, and lions "Big Time" on the old
ranches, by Will F. Evans. [El Paso, Texas, printed by the McMath
company, inc., 1950]. Stiff pict. wrappers. OP.

v, 6–109 p. front., illus. 23 cm.
Table of contents labeled "Index" at end.

779 EWELL, THOMAS T. A history of Hood County, Texas, from its earliest
settlement to the present, together with biographical sketches of many
leading men and women among the early settlers, as well as many incidents in the adjoining territory. Also a sketch of the history of Somervell County. Written by Thomas T. Ewell. Grandbury, Texas, published by the Grandbury News, 1895. Cloth. Rare.

2 p.l., 2 l. (adv. on pink paper), 160 [8] p. 22.3 cm.
Last 8 p. adv. and history of Somervell County; adv. scattered throughout.

780 EXTRACTS from the speeches of Messrs. Eaton, of Connecticut, Reagan,
of Texas, and Cox, of New York, upon the constitutional powers of Congress to legislate upon the subject of suppressing pleuro-pneumonia in
cattle and the replies thereto of Hons. J. A. Anderson, S. R. Peters, and
B. W. Perkins, of Kansas, in the House of Representatives, February 6,
1884. Washington, 1884. Rare.

[3]–12 p. 21.7 cm.

781 FAETH, MARY LILLIAN. Kansas in the 80s, being some recollections of
life on its western frontier. By Mary Lillian Faeth. New York, the Pro-
cyon press, publishers, [1947]. Cloth. Label pasted on. OP.

5 p.l., [11]–32 [4] p. 20.5 cm.
Last 4 p. facsms.

782 FAIRFIELD, ASA MERRILL. Fairfield's pioneer history of Lassen County,
California, containing everything that can be learned about it from the
beginning of the world to the year of our Lord, 1870. The chronicles of a
border county settled without law, harassed by savages, and infested by
outlaws. . . . By Asa Merrill Fairfield. San Francisco, published for the
author by H. S. Crocker co., [1916]. Pict. cloth. Scarce.

4 p.l., ix–xxii p., 1 l., 3–506 [1] p. front. (port., signature in facsm.), plates, fold.
map. 22.5 cm.
Half title.

783 FARBER, JAMES. Those Texans, by James Farber. Illustrations by John H. McClelland. San Antonio, Texas, the Naylor company, [1945]. Cloth.
xi p., 1 l., 3–171 p. front., illus. 21 cm.
Index, p. 167–171.
Half title.

Has a chapter on the cowboy, but the author knows little of what he writes about.

784 FARLEY, FRANK WEBSTER. Dehorning and castrating cattle. [By] Frank W. Farley. Washington, Government printing office, 1918. Wrappers. OP.
14 p. illus. 23 cm.
U. S. Dept. of Agriculture *Farmer's Bulletin 949.* A contribution from the Bureau of Animal Industry.

785 ———. Hereford husbandry, by Frank W. Farley. Kansas City, published by Walker publications, inc., 1941. Leather. OP.
6 p.l., [13]–431 p. plates, plan, tables. 23.5 cm.
Index, p. [422]–431.

786 ———. Raising beef cattle on farm and range, by Frank W. Farley. ... Edited by John M. Hazelton. ... Kansas City, Walker publications, inc., [1931]. Wrappers. OP.
4 p.l., [11]–179 [5] p. illus. 21.4 cm.

787 FARMER, E. J. The resources of the Rocky Mountains, being a brief description of the mineral, grazing, agricultural, and timber resources of Colorado, Utah, Arizona, New Mexico, Wyoming, Idaho, Montana, and Dakota. By E. J. Farmer. ... Cleveland, Ohio, Leader printing company, 1883. Limber cloth. Scarce.
4 p.l., 9–196 p. front., illus., tables. 19.8 cm.

788 FARRELL, NED E. Colorado, the Rocky Mountain gem, as it is in 1868. Gazetteer and handbook, containing a description of every county, her mineral and agricultural resources. ... Chicago, published by the Western News company, 1868. Pict. wrappers. Rare.
4 p.l., [9]–72 p. 2 fold. maps. 19.2 cm.

This is doubtless the first Colorado history on the county-by-county basis, and, among other things, it gives valuable information about the beginning of the cattle industry in that state. One of the maps shows Wyoming as a part of Nebraska.

789 FARRISH, T. E. Central and southwestern Arizona, the garden of

America. By T. E. Farrish, commissioner of immigration. ₁Tucson₁, Tucson Citizen print, 1889. Wrappers. Scarce.

39 ₁1₁ p. 21.4 cm.

Another edition same year:

48 p. plates. 19.3 cm.

790 ———. Northern Arizona, its forests, arable and grazing lands. Homes for the millions. ₁N.p.₁, Arizona Gazette, 1889. Wrappers. Scarce.

32 p. 21.5 cm.

791 ———. Southeastern Arizona, its varied and wonderful resources, by T. E. Farrish, commissioner of immigration. ₁N.p.₁, Arizona Gazette, 1889. Wrappers. Scarce.

119 p. 22 cm.

792 ———. Southwestern Arizona, its varied climate and wonderful re-sources. By T. E. Farrish, commissioner of immigration. ₁Phoenix₁, Arizona Gazette, 1889. Wrappers. Scarce.

47 p. 20.6 cm.

793 FAST, HOWARD MELVIN. The last frontier, ₁by₁ Howard Fast. . . . New York, Duell, Sloan and Pearce, ₁1941₁. Cloth. OP.

xii p., 1 l., 3–307 p. 22 cm.
Half title; map and illus. on end papers; "First edition" on copyright p.

794 FAULKNER, VIRGINIA (ED.). Roundup: a Nebraska reader, compiled and edited by Virginia Faulkner. Line drawings by Elmer Jacobs. Lincoln, University of Nebraska press, 1957. Pict. cloth.

xv p., 1 l., 493 p. illus. (col.). 23.7 cm.
Sources, p. 491–493.
Half title; map on end papers; illus. double t.p.

795 FEAGLES, ELIZABETH. Talk like a cowboy. A dictionary of real western lingo for young cowboys and cowgirls. By Elizabeth Feagles. San Antonio, Texas, the Naylor company, ₁1955₁. Cloth.

ix, 82 p. illus. (col.). 19.7 cm.
Index and key to pronunciation, p. 79–82.
Half title; illus. t.p. (col.).

796 FEATHERSTON, EDWARD BAXTER. A pioneer speaks, by Edward Baxter Featherston. Edited and compiled by Vera Featherston Bach. Dallas, Texas, published by Cecil Baugh and company, ₁1940₁. Pict. cloth. OP.

xvii, 239 p. front., illus., plates, ports. 22.5 cm.
Half title.

797 FELTON, HAROLD W. Pecos Bill, Texas cowpuncher, by Harold W. Felton. Illustrations by Aldren Auld Watson. New York, Alfred A. Knopf, 1949   Pict. cloth. OP.

vii p., 2 l., 3–177 p., 1 l.   illus. (col.).   21.9 cm.
Bibliography, p. 169–177.
Half title; illus. t.p.; illus. chapter headings (col.); untrimmed.

798 FENLEY, FLORENCE. Grandad and I. A story of a grand old man and other pioneers in Texas and the Dakotas, as told by John Leakey to Florence Fenley. ₁Leakey, Texas, John Leakey, publisher, 1951₁. Cloth. OP.

4 p.l., 9–179 p.   plates, ports.   21.3 cm.
Last 18 p. plates and ports.; "First printing" on copyright p.

799 ———. Old timers, their own stories, by Florence Fenley. Uvalde, Texas, the Hornsby press, 1939. Cloth. Scarce.

3 p.l., 254 p.   front. (map), plates, ports.   22.5 cm.
Port. on t.p.

True stories of real cattlemen. Privately printed in a small edition and now becoming scarce.

800 FENTON, H. W. The territory of Washington. A sketch of its history, geography, climate, soil, and productions, with particular reference to King County, and the city of Seattle. Specially compiled by H. W. Fenton, for Cook & Moore. . . . Seattle, Wash., 1888. Wrappers. Scarce.

₁3₁–40 ₁1₁ p.   tables.   20.3 x 11.6 cm.

A section on stock raising.

801 FERGUSSON, ERNA. New Mexico. A pageant of three peoples. ₁By₁ Erna Fergusson.   New York, Alfred A. Knopf, 1951.   Pict. cloth.

xii p., 2 l., 3–408 p.   front. (relief map), plates, ports., maps.   21.7 cm.
Further readings, p. 395–404; glossary, p. 405–408; index, p. i–vi ₁1₁ p. (at end).

802 ———. Our Southwest, by Erna Fergusson; photographs by Ruth Frank and others. New York and London, Alfred A. Knopf, 1940. Cloth. OP.

7 p.l., 3–376, i–vi p.   front., plates, 2 fold. maps, 1 double-p. map (col.).   22.5 cm.
Index, p. i–vi (at end).
Half title; map on end papers; pub. device; untrimmed; "First edition" on copyright p.

803 FERGUSSON, HARVEY. Rio Grande, by Harvey Fergusson. New York, Alfred A. Knopf, 1933. Pict. cloth. OP.

x p., 1 l., 3–296, i–viii p., 1 l., 15 plates at end.   22.4 cm.
Bibliography, p. 293–296; index, p. i–viii (at end).
Half title; pub. device; untrimmed; "First edition" on copyright p.

804 FIELDING, LORAINE HORNADAY. French heels to spurs, by Loraine Hornaday Fielding; with an introduction by Will James. Illustrated by Eve Ganson. . . . New York, London, the Century co., [1930]. Pict. cloth. OP.

viii p., 2 l., 3–203 p. illus. 19.3 cm.
Half title; illus. t.p.; "First printing" on copyright p.

805 FISHER, O. C. It occurred in Kimball County, by O. C. Fisher; illustrations by Lonnie Rees, cover design by Hal Jones. Houston, Texas, the Anson Jones press, MCMXXXVII. Pict. cloth. OP.

13 p.l., [29]–237 [3] p. front., illus., ports. 23.6 cm.
"Printed sources consulted," p. [239].
Half title; on cover, "The Story of a Texas County."
Colophon: "Of this first edition . . . 500 copies have been printed of which this is —."

806 FISHWICK, MARSHALL W. American heroes, myth and reality, by Marshall W. Fishwick. Introduction by Carl Cramer. Washington, D. C., Public Affairs press, [1954]. Cloth.

viii p., 3 l., 3–242 p. 23.5 cm.
Sources, p. 234–238; bibliographical notes p. 239; index, p. 240–242.
Half title.

807 FITCH, MICHAEL HENDRICK. Ranch life and other sketches, by Michael Hendrick Fitch . . . . Pueblo, the Franklin press company, 1914. Cloth. Scarce.

3 p.l., [9]–309 [2] p. 20.6 cm.
Untrimmed.

Most of this book is comprised of patriotic speeches and miscellaneous writings, but it contains a good chapter on ranch life in Colorado. Privately printed in an edition of 150 copies, 50 of which were given away by the author, hence its scarcity.

808 FITZGERALD, D. A. Livestock under the A.A.A. by D. A. FitzGerald. Washington, the Brookings institute, 1935. Cloth. OP.

xiii, 384 [4] p. maps, graphs, tables. 21.2 cm.

809 FITZPATRICK, GEORGE (ED.). This is New Mexico. Edited by George Fitzpatrick. Sketches by Wilfred Stedman. Santa Fe, the Rydal press, [1948]. Cloth.

x p., 2 l., 3–328 p. 23.5 cm.
Half title; map on end papers; vignette.

A collection of stories from the *New Mexico Magazine,* among which are some about cowboys.

810 FLETCHER, ROBERT S. That hard winter in Montana. By Robert S.

Fletcher . . . . Reprinted from *Agricultural History,* Vol. IV, No. 4 (October, 1930). Stiff wrappers. (Cover title). Scarce.
p. 123–130. 25.5 cm.

811 ——. The end of the open range in eastern Montana. By Robert S. Fletcher. Reprinted from the *Mississippi Valley Historical Review,* Vol. XVI, No. 2 (September, 1929). Stiff wrappers. (Cover title). Scarce.
p. 188–211. 25.5 cm.
Half title.

812 ——. Organization of the range cattle business in eastern Montana, by Robert S. Fletcher . . . . Bozeman, Montana, Montana State College Agricultural Experiment Station, 1932. Wrappers. (Cover title).
[3]–63 p. map, facsms. 22.2 cm.
Literature cited, p. 54–63.
Bulletin No. 265.

813 FLETCHER, SYDNEY E. The cowboy and his horse. By Sydney E. Fletcher, with an introduction by Joseph Henry Jackson. New York, Grossett & Dunlap, publishers, [1951]. Cloth.
x p., 1 l., 13–159 [1] p. front., illus., cattle brands, music, map. 28.5 cm.
Glossary, p. 150–154; bibliography, p. 155–156; index, p. 157–159.
Half title; illus. end papers with map; illus. t.p.

Grossett and Dunlap as publisher usually means a reprint, but this book was originally published by them. It is an excellent example of western art illustrating some of the technical points of the cowboy's life.

814 FLORY, JACOB STONER. Thrilling echoes from the wild frontier. Interesting personal reminiscences of the author. By J. S. Flory . . . . Chicago, Rhodes & McClure publishing company, 1893. Cloth. Scarce.
3 p.l., 17–248 [2] p. front., illus. 19.8 cm.
Last 2 p. adv.

815 FOGARTY, KATE HAMMOND. The story of Montana, by Kate Hammond Fogarty. New York and Chicago, the A. S. Barnes company, [1916]. Pict. cloth. Scarce.
x, 302 p. front., plates, map. 19 cm.
Index, p. [293]–302.

816 FOGHT, HAROLD WALDSTEIN. The trail of the Loup; being a history of the Loup River region, with some chapters on the state, [by] H. W. Foght. [Ord, Nebr.], 1906. Cloth. Scarce.
8 p.l., [17]–296 p. front. (port.), illus., plates (1 fold.), ports., maps, plans. 26 cm.

817 FOLEY, THADDEUS J. Memories of the old West, by Thaddeus J. Foley. [N. p., n.d., c.1928]. Wrappers. Scarce.
2 p.l., 5–54 p. 17.2 cm.

A chapter on the cattle industry in Nebraska.

818 FORD, GUS L. (ED.). Texas cattle brands. A catalogue of the Texas Centennial Exhibit, 1936. Edited by Gus L. Ford, historical supervisor. Dallas, Texas, published by Clyde C. Cockrell company, [1936]. Pict. cloth. OP.

xx, 240 p. maps, cattle brands on margins. 20 cm.
Map on end papers.
Republished by the author's widow in 1958.

819 FORD, TIREY L. Dawn and the dons. The romance of Monterey. By Tirey L. Ford. With vignettes and sketches by Jo Mora. San Francisco, A. M. Robertson, MCMXXVI. Pict. cloth. OP.

xii p., 1 l., 236 p. illus., plates. 23.6 cm.
Index, p. 233–236.
Vignette; map on end papers.

Contains a chapter on cattle raising in California.

820 FOREMAN, GRANT. Muskogee, the biography of an Oklahoma town. By Grant Foreman. Norman, University of Oklahoma press, MCMXLIII. Cloth. OP.

xi p., 2 l., 3–169 p. front., plates, ports., fold. map. 19.5 cm.
Index, p. 156–169.

Enlarged and privately printed by the author in a later edition. Contains some material on the cattle trails and cattle traffic through Oklahoma.

821 FORGAN, DAVID ROBERTSON. Proposed currency legislation. An address by Hon. David R. Forgan, president National City Bank, Chicago, delivered at the fifteenth annual convention of the American National Live Stock Association at Denver, Colorado, December 13, 1911. Denver, Colo., Published by American National Live Stock association, [1911]. Pamphlet. (Cover title). Rare.

1 p.l., 10 p. 22.5 cm.

822 FORNEY, JOHN W. What I saw in Texas, by John W. Forney. Philadelphia, Ringwalt & Brown prs., [1872]. Pict. wrappers. (Cover title). Rare.

5–92 p. front. (map), illus. 23.6 cm.

823 FORREST, EARLE ROBERT. Arizona's dark and bloody ground, by Earle R. Forrest; with introduction by William MacLeod Raine. Caldwell, Idaho, the Caxton printers, ltd., 1936. Cloth.

10 p.l., [21]–370 p. illus., plates, ports. 19.5 cm.
Notes, p. [310]–339; acknowledgments, p. [340]–341; bibliography, p. [342]–343; principal characters, p. [344]–352; index, p. [353]–370.
Half title; map on end papers; pub. device.
Reprinted in 1948 with additions and changes.

824 FORT BASCOM CATTLE COMPANY. The Fort Bascom Cattle Raising Company of Connecticut. . . . [N.p., n.d., c.1878]. Cloth. Rare.

[3]–21 p. large fold. map at end (2 maps and 3 illus. on 1 sheet). 17.4 cm. "For private circulation only."

One map shows property of the company in San Miguel County, Territory of New Mexico, the other shows Fort Bascom and its connections with the cattle markets of the United States. Contains the by-laws of the company. The first part of the book gives extracts from various articles on cattle raising in the West, the latest one being dated January 19, 1878.

825 ———. First annual report of the directors, secretary and treasurer, June 29, 1885. New Haven, D. S. Thomas print, [1885]. Wrappers, Rare.

12 p. 18.5 cm.

826 FOSSET, FRANK. Colorado: a historical, descriptive, and statistical work. By Frank Fossett. Denver, 1876. Cloth. Rare.

470 p. front., plates, maps. 19.6 cm.

827 ———. Colorado: its gold and silver mines, farms and stock ranges, and health and pleasure resorts. Tourist's guide to the Rocky Mountains. By Frank Fossett. New York, C. G. Crawford, printer and stationer, 1879. Dec. cloth. OP.

vii, 540 p. front., illus., fold. plates, maps (part fold.), fold. plan. 19.6 cm.

This is a rewrite, with changes and additions, of his first book and has a chapter on stock raising. It was reprinted in 1880.

828 FOSTER-HARRIS. The look of the old west, by Foster-Harris, with illustrations by Evelyn Curro. New York, the Viking press, 1955. Pict. cloth and boards.

x p., 1 l., [3]–316 p. illus., maps (1 double p.). 27.8 cm. Bibliography, p. [303]–305; index, p. [307]–316. Half title; illus. t.p.

829 FOSTER, JAMES S. Outlines of history of the territory of Dakota, and emigrant's guide to the free lands of the northwest . . . . Accompanied with a new sectional map. By James S. Foster . . . . Yankton, Dakota Territory, M'Intyre & Foster, Union and Dakotaian office, 1870. Pict. wrappers. Rare.

2 l., [1] p., [6]–127 p. large fold. map in front. 22.6 cm. 20 p. adv. at end.

830 FOUNTAIN, ALBERT J. Bureau of Immigration of the territory of New Mexico. Report of Doña Ana County. By Albert J. Fountain, commissioner. Santa Fe, New Mexican print, 1882. Wrappers. Scarce.

[3]–34 p. 22 cm. Leaf of errata tipped in at end.

831 FOUNTAIN, PAUL. The great deserts and forests of North America, by Paul Fountain, with a preface by W. H. Hudson. New York and Bombay, Longmans, Green and Co., 1901. Cloth. OP.

ix, 295 p. 23 cm.

A chapter on cowboys.

832 FOWLER, GENE. Timber line. A story of Bonfils and Tammen, by Gene Fowler. New York, Covici Friede, publishers, MCMXXXIII. Cloth. Scarce.

6 p.l., 13–480 p. 2 ports. 21.8 cm.
Half title; t.p. in green and black; untrimmed.

Has a chapter on Tom Horn and the Johnson County War.

833 FOX, R. L., and C. G. RANDELL. Decentralized marketing by Producers Livestock Co-operative Association, Columbus, Ohio. By R. L. Fox and C. G. Randell . . . . Washington, D. C., Co-operative Research of Agriculture . . . , May, 1951. Wrappers.

vii, 152 p. illus., graphs, maps, tables. 22.5 cm.
U. S. Dept. Agriculture *Bulletin No. 65.*

834 FRACKLETON, WILL. Sagebrush dentist, as told by Dr. Will Frackleton to Herman Gastrell Seely. Chicago, A. C. McClurg & co., [1941]. Cloth. OP.

3 p.l., 9–246 p. 22.3 cm.
Half title.

Republished with additional material (publisher's preface, introduction, and a chapter on Buffalo Bill's divorce suit) in 1947, by Trail's End publishing co., Pasadena, Calif.

6 p.l., 13–258 p. port. 22 cm.
Half title; pub. device.

835 FRANCE, GEORGE W. The struggles for life and home in the North-West. By a pioneer homebuilder. Life, 1865–1889. [By] Geo. W. France. New York, I. Goldmann, steam printer, 1890. Cloth. Rare.

11 p., 23–607 p. front. (port.), plates, facsms. 24 cm.

Has a chapter on "Ranch Life in the West." This copy seen in the Rollins Collection, Princeton University.

836 FRANCIS, FRANCIS, JR. Saddle and moccasin, by Francis Francis, Jr. London, Chapman and Hall, limited, 1887. Cloth. Scarce.

xi, 322 p. 20.3 cm.

Some information on ranching in the Animas Valley.

837 FRANKLIN, BENJAMIN J. Biennial message of Benjamin J. Franklin, governor of Arizona Territory. Delivered to the Nineteenth Legislative Assembly in joint session, January 28, 1897. Phoenix, Wood and Irvine book and job print, 1897. Wrappers. Rare.

45 p. 21.6 cm.

838 FRANKLIN, GEORGE CORY. Wild horses of the Rio Grande, by George Cory Franklin. Illustrated by William Moyers. Boston, Houghton Mifflin company, 1951. Pict. cloth.

viii p., 1 l., 181 p. illus., plates (8 col.). 23.5 cm.
Half title; illus. double t.p.; illus. end papers (col.); first edition, "1951" under imprint.

839 FRANKS, J. M. Seventy years in Texas; memories of the pioneer days, Indian depredations, and the northwest cattle trail, by J. M. Franks, Gatesville, Texas, 1924. Wrappers. Scarce.

2 p.l., [5]–133 [1] p. port. 23.5 cm.

840 FRANTZ, JOE B., and JULIAN ERNEST CHOATE, JR. The American cowboy, the myth & the reality, [by] Joe B. Frantz and Julian Ernest Choate, Jr. Norman, University of Oklahoma press, [1955]. Cloth.

xiii [1] p., 1 l., 3–232 p. plates. 22 cm.
Bibliography, p. 203–222; index, p. 223–232.
Half title; pub. device; "First edition" on copyright p.

841 [FRAZAN, THOMAS]. Oregon, its resources, soil, climate, and productions. Containing some facts for the consideration of emigrants. Issued by the Board of Statistics, Immigration and Labor Exchange. Portland, Oregon, Albert G. Walling, book and job printer, December 1869. Wrappers. Rare.

[3]–12 p. 21 cm.

842 FRAZER, MARIE MILLIGAN. On the old trails to Wyoming. A history of Wyoming for the elementary schools, grades 3–8. [By] Marie M. Frazer. Laramie, published by Wyoming State School Supply, 1928. Pict. cloth.

3 p.l., [6]–186 p. plates, ports., maps. 23.3 cm.
Index, p. 184–186.
"Help for pupils" at end of each chapter.

843 FREEMAN, GEORGE D. Midnight and noonday; or, dark deeds unraveled. Giving twenty years experience on the frontier; also the murder of Pat Hennesey [*sic*], and the hanging of Tom Smith, at Ryland's Ford, and facts concerning the Talbert raid on Caldwell. Also the death dealing career of McCarty and incidents happening in and around Caldwell,

Kansas, from 1871 to 1890, by G. D. Freeman. Caldwell, Kansas, [the author], 1890. Boards. Exceedingly rare.

4 p.l., 9–405 p., front. (port.), 20 cm.

Reprinted in 1892 bound in cloth and with the same collation, but in the second printing there is appended on page 106 a certificate signed by seven old-time pioneers attesting to the truth of the narrative. They, in turn, are vouched for by the editor of the *Caldwell News*. The second printing is bound in red cloth, and the first edition is so scarce that some collectors think the 1892 edition the only one published.

844 FREEMAN, JAMES W. (ED.). Prose and poetry of the live stock industry of the United States, with outlines of the origin and ancient history of our live stock animals. Volume I. Issued in three volumes. Illustrated. Prepared by authority of the National Live Stock Association. Denver and Kansas City, published by the National Live Stock Historical association [Franklin Hudson publishing co., 1905]. Dec. leather. Exceedingly rare.

11 p.l., 25–757 p. illus., plates, ports. (all with tissues), map. 27.8 cm.
Double column; gilt top.

Republished in 1959 by the Antiquarian Press with a new introduction by Ramon F. Adams. Boxed.

One of the most important and most sought-after books on the cattle industry. In all my years of book collecting, I have never seen this book listed in a dealer's catalog. When a dealer finds a copy, he always has a waiting list. All copies of this exceedingly rare book were issued to members of the National Live Stock Association, each with the name of the individual member stamped in gold on the cover and a certificate with seal bound in. It is said that the publication of this one volume broke one printing company and almost broke the association. Originally three volumes were planned, but, after the expense of the first volume, the project was abandoned.

845 FRENCH, CHAUNCEY DEL. Railroadman, by Chauncey Del French. New York, the Macmillan company, 1938. Cloth. OP.

vi p., 2 l., 292 p. plates, ports., facsm. 22 cm.
Half title.

The cattle trails and cow towns as seen by a railroad man in the 1870's.

846 FRENCH, GEORGE H. (ED.). Indianola scrap book. Fiftieth anniversary of the storm of August 20, 1886. History of a city that once was the gateway of commerce for this entire section. Victoria, Texas, compiled and published by the Victoria Advocate, 1936. Cloth. OP.

3–198 p. plates, ports., facsm., map. 23.6 cm.

847 FRENCH, WILLIAM. Some recollections of a western ranchman; New

Mexico, 1883–1889, by the Hon. William French. London, Methuen & Co., ltd., [1927]. Cloth. Scarce.

vi p., 1 l., 283 [8] p.   22.5 cm.
Half title.
Last 8 p. lists other books of the publishers.
Republished with same imprint, but without date. American edition published by Frederick A. Stokes Co., [1928], with same collation, but without the book list at the end.

This is one of the really good but little-known books on ranch life.

848   FRENCH, W. J.   Wild Jim, the Texas cowboy and saddle king. By Capt. W. J. French. Illustrated. Antioch, Lake co., Capt. W. J. French, publishers, 1890. Pict. wrappers. Very rare.

76 p.   front. (port.), illus.   23.2 cm.

849   FREWEN, MORETON.   American competition. By Moreton Frewen. London, Chapman and Hall, ltd., 1885. Wrappers. (Cover title). Rare.

60 p.   fold. map in front.   21.5 cm.

A paper read before the Newcastle Farmer's Club, April 11, 1885.

850 ———.   Melton Mobray, and other memories, by Moreton Frewen. London, Herbert Jenkins, limited, MCMXXIV. Cloth. Scarce.

viii p., 2 l., 311 p.   front. (port.), plates, ports.   21.7 cm.
Index, p. 305–311.
Half title.

About ten chapters on cattle ranching, plus reminiscences of an Englishman who tried his hand, unsuccessfully, at ranching on the Powder River in Wyoming.

851   [FRIDGE, IKE].   History of the Chisum War; or, life of Ike Fridge. Stirring events of cowboy life on the frontier [as told to Jodie D. Smith]. [Electra, Texas, J. D. Smith, 1927]. Stiff pict. wrappers. Scarce.

70 [1] p.   port., illus.   22 cm.

For some years this little book was so scarce that J. Frank Dobie, in the introduction of his *Life and Literature of the Southwest* (1943 edition), said that it was unprocurable. As a book collector, I found my interest aroused by this statement, and after much diligent search finally located and bought the small remainder which had been stored in a small-town print shop. Since then I have scattered a few copies among fellow collectors and dealers, and the book has become better known, although it is still considered comparatively rare and the remainder is now exhausted.

   Like most of the old-timers who have written books, Fridge seems to have had a bad memory and little knowledge of his characters before his association with them. Many of his statements are most unreliable. This book was eventually the cause of the author's death. After it was printed for him by

Jodie D. Smith at Electra, Texas, the author, an old man, started with two large suitcases full of books to sell his friends down in Seymour, Texas. He had to change trains at Wichita Falls, carrying the two heavy cases from one train to another. Their weight was too much for him—some adhesions from an old bullet wound in his abdomen tore loose while he was carrying the suitcases. He died a few days later in a Wichita Falls hospital.

852 FRINK, MAURICE. Cow country cavalcade. Eighty years of the Wyoming Stock Growers' Association. By Maurice Frink. Denver, Colo., the Old West publishing co., Fred A. Rosenstock, 1954. Cloth.

xvi p., 1 l., 3–243 p. plates, ports., facsms., maps, earmarks, cattle brands. 23.5 cm. Appendix, p. 237–238; sources, p. 239–240; index, p. 241–243. Half title.

This is the most recent of a series of histories which have been written on the Wyoming Stock Growers' Association every ten years for the past thirty years.

853 ——, W. TURRENTINE JACKSON, and AGNES WRIGHT SPRING. When grass was king. Contributions to the western range cattle industry study. [By] Maurice Frink ... W. Turrentine Jackson ... Agnes Wright Spring. Boulder, University of Colorado press, 1956. Cloth.

xv p., 2 l., 5–465 [1] p. illus., plates, ports., facsm., tables. 23.7 cm. Bibliography after each section; index, p. 452–465. Half title; map on end papers; illus. double t.p.

854 FRITZ, PERCY STANLEY. Colorado, the centennial state, by Percy Stanley Fritz. New York, Prentice-Hall, inc., 1941. Cloth. OP.

xii p., 2 l., 3–518 p. front. (double-p. map), illus., plates, facsms., maps. 23.5 cm. Appendix, p. 493–495; index, p. 497–518. Half title; selected bibliography after each chapter.

855 FROST, MAX. Compilation of facts concerning the Pecos Valley. Résumé of the improvements being made in southeastern New Mexico. Santa Fe, 1891. Wrappers. Scarce.

20 p. plates. 22 cm.

856 ——. Ho! To the land of sunshine. A guide to New Mexico for the settler and the emigrant. The public lands and the laws under which they can be obtained—general information for the homeseeker. Published by the Bureau of Immigration of the territory of New Mexico, Max Frost, secretary. Fourth revised edition. [Santa Fe], 1916. Wrappers. Scarce.

[3]–52 p. 20.4 x 9 cm.

857 FROST, MAX (ED.). New Mexico, its recources, climate, geography, and geological condition. Official publication of the Bureau of Immigration.

Edited by Max Frost. . . . Santa Fe, New Mexican printing co., 1890. Col. pict. wrappers. Scarce.

₍3₎–216 p. 2 large fold. maps. 23.3 cm.
Vignette.
Reprinted in 1894 with 343 ₍1₎ p., with large fold. map at end.

858 ———, and PAUL A. F. WALTERS. The land of sunshine. A handbook of the resources, products, industries and climate of New Mexico. Published under and by authority of the New Mexico Board of Managers of the Louisiana Purchase Exposition. Compiled and edited by Max Frost and Paul A. F. Walters. Santa Fe, N. M., New Mexican printing company, 1904. Pict. wrappers. Scarce.

xv, 299 ₍3₎ p. front., plates, ports. 22.7 cm.
Table of contents, p. ₍301₎.
Leaf of errata tipped in; device.

Republished with additions in 1906.

445 ₍1₎ p. front., plates. 24 cm.
Appendix, p. ₍403₎–433; table of contents, p. 435–445.

859 ———. Santa Fe County. The heart of New Mexico, rich in history and resources. Written by Max Frost and Paul A. F. Walters. Published by authority of the Bureau of Immigration of New Mexico. ₍N. p.₎, 1906. Wrappers. Scarce.

₍3₎–145 ₍5₎ p. front., plates, ports. 23.6 cm.

860 FUCHS, JAMES R. History of Williams, Arizona, 1876–1951. By James R. Fuchs. Tucson, Arizona, published by University of Arizona, 1955. Wrappers.

3 p.l., 7–168 p. plates, ports. 23 cm.
Appendices, p. 158–163; bibliography, p. 164–168.
University of Arizona *Bulletin No. 23,* Vol. XXIV, No. 5 (November, 1953).

861 FULLER, E. O. Cheyenne looking north, by E. O. Fuller. Reprinted from *Annals of Wyoming,* courtesy of Wyoming State Historical Department. ₍Lusk, Wyo., the Herald₎, 1951. Wrappers. OP.

₍3₎–59 p. 1 plate, 2 maps, tables. 23 cm.
Index, p. ₍52₎–59.

Edition limited to 200 copies and not placed on sale.

862 FULLER, GEORGE W. A history of the Pacific Northwest, by George W. Fuller . . . . New York, Alfred A. Knopf, 1931. Dec. cloth. OP.

xvi p., 1 l., ₍3₎–383 ₍15₎ p. front., plates, ports., maps, (1 fold.). 24.2 cm.
Notes, p. ₍341₎–383; index, p. ₍385₎–399₎.

863 FULLER, ROBERT P. (ED.). Wonderful Wyoming, the undeveloped em-

pire. Compiled and edited by Robert P. Fuller. ₁Cheyenne, Wyo., n. d.₁.
Stiff wrappers. Rare.

128 p. illus., plates. 19.3 cm.

Introduction on verso front wrapper; some condensed facts on recto of back
wrapper; issued by the Wyoming State Board of Immigration and has a chapter on stock raising.

864 FULLERTON, JAMES. Autobiography of Roosevelt's adversary, by James
Fullerton. Boston, the Roxburgh publishing company, inc., ₁1912₁.
Cloth. OP.

2 p.l., ₁5₁–162 p. front. (with tissue), plates. 20.2 cm.

865 FULTON, MAURICE GARLAND, and PAUL HORGAN (EDS.). New Mexico's
own chronicle. Three races in the writings of four hundred years. Adapted
and edited by Maurice Garland Fulton, and Paul Horgan. Dallas, Banks
Upshaw and company, ₁1937₁. Cloth. Scarce.

xviii p. 1 l., 3–155 p., i–xxiv ₁2₁, 159–372 p. illus., ports., maps (1 double p.),
facsm. 23 cm.
Notes, p. 351–364; index, p. 367–372.
Half title; t.p. in brown and black.

Consists of excerpts from books on New Mexico history, some of which concern cattle.

866 FURLONG, CHARLES WELLINGTON. Let 'er buck. A story of the passing
of the old West, by Charles Wellington Furlong . . . . with fifty illustrations taken from life by the author and others. New York and London,
G. P. Putnam's sons, 1921. Cloth. Illus. pasted on. OP.

xxxviii p., 2 l., 5–242 ₁4₁ p. illus., plates. 21 cm.
Half title; illus. t.p.; 4 p. adv. at end; untrimmed; plates, with one exception,
printed on both sides.

867 FURNAS, ROBERT W. Nebraska, her resources, advantages, advancement, and promise. Prepared and compiled by Robert W. Furnas. Also
the school land laws . . . . Lincoln, Neb., Journal company, state printers,
1885. Wrappers. Rare.

₁5₁–48 p. 21.8 cm.

868 Future of the Great Plains, The. Report of the Great Plains Committee. Washington, D. C., United States Government printing office, December, 1936. Stiff wrappers.

17 p.l., 23–194 p. front., plates, graphs, charts, maps, tables. 25.4 cm.
Appendices, p. 131–194.
Double column.

869 GAFF. Rambles through the great Kansas Valley and in eastern Colo-

rado. By Gaff. With illustrations. Kansas City, Mo., Press of Ramsey, Millett & Hudson, 1878. Wrappers. Rare.

2 p.l., ₍3₎–84 ₍22₎ p.   illus.   23 cm.
Last 22 p. adv.

870 GANN, WALTER. Tread of the longhorn, by Walter Gann. Illustrations by R. L. McCollister. San Antonio, Texas, the Naylor company, ₍1949₎. Cloth.

ix, 188 p.   21.5 cm.
Index, p. 187–188.
Half title; illus. chapter headings.

871 GANNETT, HENRY. On the arable and pasture lands of Colorado. By Henry Gannett. [Extracted from the Tenth Annual Report of the Survey, for the year 1876]. Washington, Government printing office, 1878. Sewn. (Cover title). Rare.

₍313₎–347 p.   tables.   23 cm.
At head of title, "Department of Interior, United States Geological Survey. F. V. Hayden, U. S. Geologist-in-charge."

872 GANZHORN, JACK. I've killed men, by Jack Ganzhorn. Illustrated. London, Robert Hale, ltd., ₍1940₎. Cloth. Scarce.

ix, 11–288 p.   front. (port.), plates, ports.   22 cm.
Half title.

An excellent and little-known book with some material on the cowboys of Arizona.

873 GARD, ROBERT EDWARD. Midnight, rodeo champion, by Robert E. Gard. Illustrated by C. W. Anderson. New York, Duell, Sloan and Pearce, ₍1951₎. Cloth.

5 p.l., 11–159 p.   plates.   22 cm.
Half title.

A history of one of the most famous rodeo bucking horses.

874 GARD, WAYNE. Cattle brands of Texas. ₍Dallas, Texas, First National Bank . . . , 1956₎. Stiff wrappers.

₍34₎ p. (no pagination).   plates (2 col.), 1 port., cattle brands.   12.7 x 22.3 cm.

Cattle brands taken from "Texas Cattle Brands" edited by Gus Ford (1936).

875 ——. The Chisholm Trail. By Wayne Gard, with drawings by Nick Eggenhofer. Norman, University of Oklahoma press, ₍1954₎. Cloth.

xi p., 1 l., 3–296 p.   illus., plates, ports., maps.   24 cm.
Bibliography, p. 265–280; index, p. 281–296.
Half title; illus. double t.p.; illus. chapter headings.

Not the first history of this famous cattle trail, but one of the best.

876 ———. The fence cutters, [by] Wayne Gard. Reprinted from the *Southwestern Historical Quarterly,* Vol. LI, No. 1 (July, 1947). Wrappers. (Cover title). OP.

15 p. 24 cm.

A chapter from the author's *Frontier Justice* read before the Southwestern Historical Society.

877 ———. Frontier justice, by Wayne Gard. Norman, University of Oklahoma press, 1949. Cloth.

xi p., 1 l., 3–324 p. plates, ports., map, facsm. 21 cm.
Bibliography, p. 291–308; index, p. 309–324.
Half title; vignette; "First edition" on copyright p.

878 ———. Retracing the Chisholm Trail, [by] Wayne Gard. Austin, Texas, published by the Texas State Historical association, 1956. Wrappers. (Cover title). OP.

3 p.l., 7–24 [8] p. port., map. 24 cm.

Published as an extra number of the *Southwestern Historical Quarterly,* May 1, 1956, in commemoration of a trek of the Chisholm Trail Committee from San Antonio, Texas, to Monument Hill, Oklahoma, May 1–3, 1956.

879 GARDINER, CHARLES Fox. Doctor at Timberline, by Charles Fox Gardiner. Illustrations by R. H. Hall. Caldwell, Idaho, the Caxton printers, ltd., 1938. Cloth.

8 p.l., [17]–315 p. front. (col.), illus., plates. 23.5 cm.
Half title.

Reminiscences of frontier days in Colorado; cattle ranches and cow towns.

880 GARDNER, KELSEY BEELER. A business analysis of the Producers Live Stock Commission of the National Stock Yards, Illinois. By Kelsey B. Gardner . . . . Washington, [Government printing office], 1929. Wrappers. OP.

45 p. diagrs. 23.4 cm.
U. S. Dept. of Agriculture *Circular No. 86.*

881 GARNEAU, JOSEPH, JR. Nebraska, her resources, advantages, and development. Prepared and compiled by Jos. Garneau, Jr., commissioner general, Nebraska Columbian Exhibit, 1893. Omaha, Rees printing co., 1893. Wrappers. (Cover title). Rare.

[3]–24 p. 17.8 x 10 cm.

882 GARRETSON, MARTIN S. The American bison. The story of its extermination as a wild species and its restoration under federal protection, by Martin S. Garretson. New York, New York, Zoological society, [1938]. Cloth. OP.

xii p., 1 l., 254 p.   front., plates, ports.   22 cm.
Illus. end papers.

883   GARRISON, MYRTLE.   Romance and history of California ranchos, by
Myrtle Garrison.   Illustrations by William Johnson Goodacre . . . .   San
Francisco, California, Harr Wagner publishing company, ₁1935₁.   Cloth.
OP.

xii p., 1 l., 206 p.   illus., plates.   23.5 cm.
Bibliography, p. 191; index, p. 193–206.
Vignette.

884   GARST, DORIS SHANNON.   The story of Wyoming and its constitution
and government, by Doris Shannon Garst.   ₁Douglas, Wyo.₁, printed
by Douglas Enterprise, ₁1938₁.   Cloth.   OP.

3 p.l., 179 p.   front. (col. flag), ports., map.   19 cm.
Index, p. 173–179; questions and references after each chapter.

885   ———.   When the West was young, by Shannon Garst.   Drawings by
F. G. Reed.   Douglas, Wyoming, Enterprise publishing company, 1942.
Cloth.   OP.

5 p.l., ₁13₁–248 p.   front., illus.   23.4 cm.
Illus. half title; illus. end papers.

886   GAUTIER, GEORGE R.   Harder than death. The life of George R. Gautier,
an old Texan, living at the Confederate Home, Austin, Texas.   Written
by himself.   ₁N. p.₁, 1902.   Wrappers.   Very rare.
62 p.   3 plates, 1 port.   21.3 cm.

Tells of some early cattle driving.

887   GAY, BEATRICE GRADY.   "Into the setting sun." A history of Coleman
County, by Beatrice Grady Gay.   Drawings by Mollie Grady Kelley . . . .
₁N. p., n. d.₁.   Pict. cloth.   Scarce.

x, 193 p.   illus., plates, ports., map.   20.4 cm.

888   GAY, CARL WARREN (ED.).   Breeds of livestock by livestock breeders,
revised and arranged by Carl W. Gay.   New York, the Macmillan co.,
1916.   Cloth.   OP.

xviii p., 1 l., 483 p.   front., illus., plates.   19.5 cm.
Half title: The Rural Text Book Series, ed. by L. H. Bailey.

"The original material of which this book is composed was prepared by the
Cyclopedia of American Agriculture, Vol. III."

889   GEFFS, MARY L.   Under ten flags; a history of Weld County, Colorado,
by Mary L. Geffs.   Greeley, Colo., ₁published by the McVey printery₁,
1938.   Cloth.

3 p.l., 7–318 p.   maps.   22.2 cm.

890 [GELTZ, JACOB]. Uncle Sam's life in Montana. [Butte City, Montana, 1905]. Stiff wrappers. Scarce.

[3]–118 [2] p. front. 19.2 cm.

891 GIBSON, J. W. (WATT). Recollections of a pioneer, by J. W. (Watt) Gibson. [St. Joseph, Mo., Press of Nelson-Hanne printing co., 1912]. Cloth. Scarce.

2 p.l., [5]–216 p. front. (port.). 19.8 cm.

Chapters on driving cattle across the plains.

892 GILDAY, JOHN P., and MARK H. SALT (EDS.). Oklahoma history south of the Canadian. Historical and biographical. John P. Gilday and Mark H. Salt, editors. Compiled under supervision of Roy M. Johnson. Illustrated . . . . Chicago, Ill., the S. J. Clarke publishing co., 1925. Cloth. Pub. in 3 vols. Rare.

Vol. I: 8 p.l., 19–505 p. front. (port with tissue), plates, map (double p.). 27.5 cm.
Vol. II: 509–957 p. plates, ports. (part with tissues). 27.5 cm.
Vol. III: 963–1435 p. front., ports. (incl. front., part with tissues). 27.5 cm.
Paged continuously. Vol. II, partly biographical; Vol. III, all biographical.

893 GILFILLAN, ARCHER BUTLER. Sheep, by Archer B. Gilfillan. Illustrations by KURT WIESE. Boston, Little, Brown and company, 1929. Pict. cloth. Scarce.

xix p., 2 l., [3]–272 p. front., illus. 21.2 cm.
Half title; pub. device; headpieces.
Reprinted in 1930 and 1936.

A chapter on the sheepherder and the cowboy.

894 GILLESPIE, A. S. ("BUD"), and R. H. ("BOB") BURNS. Steamboat—symbol of Wyoming. By A. S. "Bud" Gillespie and R. H. "Bob" Burns. [Laramie], University of Wyoming, [n.d.]. Pict. wrappers.

20 p. illus. 20.5 cm.
Illus. t.p.; double column.

About another famous bucking horse.

895 GILLETT, ELD. C. E. Pioneering, by Eld. C. E. Gillett. Elgin, Ill., published for the author by the Brethern publishing house, 1929. Cloth. Scarce.

5 p.l., 11–218 p. front., ports. 19 cm.

896 GILMAN, BRADLEY. Roosevelt, the happy warrior, by Bradley Gilman, with illustrations from photographs . . . . Boston, Little, Brown and company, 1923. Cloth. OP.

x p., 2 l., 376 p. front. (port. with tissue), plates, ports., facsm. 23 cm.

Index, p. 363–376.
Half title; pub. device.

Chapter VI deals with Theodore Roosevelt's experiences as a rancher in Dakota.

897 GIPSON, FRED. Cowhand; the story of a working cowboy. By Fred Gipson. New York, Harper & brothers, publishers, [1953]. Cloth.
vi p., 1 l., 216 p. 21.2 cm.
Half title; pub. device; untrimmed; "First edition" on copyright p.

898 ———. Fabulous empire; Colonel Zack Miller's story, by Fred Gipson, with an introduction by Donald Day. Boston, Houghton Mifflin company, 1946. Cloth. OP.
ix p., 1 l., 411 p. 21 cm.
Half title; first edition, "1946" under imprint.

A history of the famous 101 Ranch of Oklahoma.

899 GLASSOCK, C. B. Then came oil. The story of the last frontier, by C. B. Glasscock. Indianapolis, New York, the Bobbs-Merrill company, publishers, [1938]. Cloth. OP.
5 p.l., 11–349 p. front., plates, ports. 22.3 cm.
Bibliography, p. 327–329; index, p. 333–349.
Half title; map on end papers; untrimmed; "First edition" on copyright p.

Has a chapter on the cattle trails.

900 GLEED, CHARLES S. (ED.). From river to sea; a tourist's and miner's guide from the Missouri River to the Pacific Ocean via Kansas, Colorado, New Mexico, Arizona, and California. [Edited by] Charles S. Gleed. Chicago, Rand, McNally and co., 1882. Cloth. Scarce.
240 p. illus. 20.4 cm.
16 p. adv. at end.

Contains the stock laws of Colorado.

901 GODING, HARRY and A. JOSEPH RAUB. The 28 hour law regulating the interstate transportation of live stock; its purpose, requirements and enforcements. By Harry Goding and A. Joseph Raub .... Washington, D.C., 1918. Wrappers. (Caption title). OP.
19 [1] p. plates, plans. 22.7 cm.
U. S. Dept. of Agriculture *Bulletin No. 589.*

902 GOOD, MILTON. Twelve years in a Texas prison, by Milt Good, as told to W. E. Lockhart. (Illustrations drawn by Isabel Robinson) .... Amarillo, Texas, printed by Russell stationery company, 1935. Stiff pict. wrappers. Scarce.
3 p.l., 7–88 p. front. (port.), illus., ports. 24 cm.

The story of a cowboy gone wrong.

903 GOODNIGHT, CHARLES, and others. Pioneer days in the Southwest from 1850 to 1879. Thrilling descriptions of buffalo hunting, Indian fighting and massacres, cowboy life, and home building. Contributions by Charles Goodnight, Emanuel Dubbs, John A. Hart, and others. Guthrie, Okla., the State Capital company, 1909. Pict. cloth. Scarce.

v p., [7]–320 p. front. (col.), plates, ports. 19.6 cm.
Table of contents, labeled "Index," p. [319]–320.
"Second edition" on t.p.

An enlarged reprint with the additions of *History of Pioneer Days*, by John A. Hart, and thus considered a second edition.

904 GOODSPEED, THOMAS W. Gustavus Franklin Swift, 1839–1903. By James W. Goodspeed . . . . Reprinted from the University of Chicago Biographical Sketches, Vol. I. [N. p., n. d.]. Stiff wrappers. Scarce.

p. 171–197. front. (port.). 22.8 cm.

905 GOODWYN, FRANK. Life on the King ranch, by Frank Goodwyn. Photographs by Toni Frissell, drawings by Bruce Marchin. New York, Thomas Y. Crowell company, [1951]. Cloth.

6 p.l., 3–293 p. front. (port.), 7 double-p. plates. 23.5 cm.
Glossary, p. 287–289; bibliography, p. 291–293.
Half title; illus. map on end papers; illus. chapter headings.

906 ———. Lone Star land. Twentieth century Texas in perspective, by Frank Goodwyn. New York, Alfred A. Knopf, 1955. Cloth.

xii p., 2 l., [3]–352, [i]–x p. plates, maps. 22.8 cm.
Appendix, p. [345]–347; acknowledgments p. [348]–352; index, p. [i]–x (at end).
Half title; pub. device; untrimmed.

Published both in a Special Texas Edition with the author's signature, and in a trade edition.

907 GOPLEN, ARNOLD O. The career of Marquis de Mores in the badlands of North Dakota, by Arnold O. Goplen . . . . Reprinted from *North Dakota History*, Vol. XIII, Nos. 1 and 2 (January-April, 1946). Published by the State Historical society of North Dakota. Stiff wrappers. OP.

2 p.l., 5–70 p. plates, port., map, (fold.). 22.9 cm.
Bibliography, p. 66–70.
Device.

908 GORMAN, JOHN ALEXANDER. The western horse; its types and training, by John A. Gorman . . . . [Danville, Ill., the Inter-State], 1939. Pict. cloth. OP.

278 [4] p. front., illus. 21 cm.
"Magazines . . . devoted to horses of different breeds and types," p. [3]–[4] at end.

Revised, enlarged, and republished in 1944.

3 p.l., ₍9₎–365 p. front., ports. 21.6 cm.
Index, p. 359–361.

909 [GOSPER, JOHN J.]. Report of the acting Governor of Arizona made to the Secretary of the Interior for the year 1881. Washington, Government printing office, 1881. Wrappers. Rare.
₍3₎–25 p. tables. 23 cm.

910 GOULD, CHARLES NEWTON. Travels through Oklahoma, by Charles N. Gould . . . . Oklahoma City, Harlow publishing company, 1928. Cloth. Scarce.
5 p.l., 174 p. illus., plates (1 double p.), maps. 19.5 cm.

911 GRACE, JOHN N., and R. B. JONES. A new history of Parker County. By John S. Grace and R. B. Jones, with introductory sketch on early Texas history, entitled "Tableau lights of Texas history." Weatherford, Texas, Democrat publishing co., 1906. Cloth. Scarce.
2 p.l., ₍5₎–206 p. front., plates, ports. 22.3 cm.
20 p. adv. at end.

912 GRADET, ROGER. Images du Far-West. 250 illustrations et textes de Roger Gradet. ₍N. p., achevé d'imprimer—de la Presse Jurassienne à Dole, 1936₎. Stiff pict. wrappers. OP.
5 p.l., 15–172 p. illus. 27.6 cm.
Index, p. 171–172.

A book about cowboys written in French and well illustrated by the author.

913 GRAHAM, CHARLES. Colfax County, New Mexico, brand directory. Compiled by Charles Graham . . . . Cimarron, N. M., printed and published by Whigham & Henderson, ₍1879₎. Boards. Rare.
5–68 p. cattle brands. 19 x 7.7 cm.

One of the early brand books of the cattle country.

914 GRAHAM, ROBERT BONTINE CUNNINGHAME. Rodeo; a collection of the tales and sketches of R. B. Cunninghame Graham, selected and with an introduction by A. F. Tschiffley. Garden City, New York, Doubleday, Doran and company, 1936. Cloth. OP.
xx p., 1 l., 438 p. 21 cm.
Half title; pub. device; untrimmed; "First edition" on copyright p.
English edition published in London same year.

915 GRAND, W. JOSEPH. Illustrated history of the Union Stock Yards; sketch book of familiar faces and places at the yards . . . . By W. Jos. Grand; illustrations from photographs by O. Benson, Jr. Chicago, Thos. Knapp ptg. & bdg. company, ₍1896₎. Pict. cloth. Scarce.

2 p.l., 7–314 [18] p.   front., illus., plates.   20 cm.
Last 18 p. adv.

Republished in 1901 in an enlarged and revised edition.

2 p.l., 7–362 [26] p.   front., illus., ports.   20 cm.
Last 26 p. adv.

916   GRANT, BRUCE.   The cowboy encyclopedia. The old and the new West
from the open range to the dude ranch, by Bruce Grant. Illustrated by
Jackie and Fiore Mastri.   New York, Chicago, San Francisco, Rand,
McNally & company, [1951].   Pict. cloth.

6 p.l., 13–160 [2] p.   front., illus., plates (4 in full-p. col., incl. front.), maps.   26 cm.
Bibliography, last 2 p.
Half title; double column.

917   GRAY, ALFRED.   Population and industries of Kansas. Extracts from the
annual report of the Kansas State Board of Agriculture for 1873. By Alfred
Gray, secretary.   [N.p.], 1873.   Wrappers.   Rare.

[3]–111 p.   tables.   22.7 cm.

918   GRAY, ARTHUR AMOS.   Men who built the West, by Arthur Amos Gray.
Illustrated by photographs.   Caldwell, Idaho, the Caxton printers, ltd.,
1945.   Pict. cloth.

7 p.l., [15]–220 p.   front., plates, ports., facsms., maps.   23.5 cm.
Index, p. [217]–220.
Half title; pub. device.

919   GRAY, FRANK S.   Pioneer adventures, by Frank S. Gray.   [Cherokee,
Texas, privately printed, 1948].   Cloth.   OP.

9 p.l., 19–384 p.   plates, ports.   20.4 cm.

Much on the Chisholm Trail.

920   ———.   Pioneering in southwest Texas. True stories of early day experiences in Edwards and adjoining counties. By Frank S. Gray. Edited
by Marvin Hunter.   [Austin, Texas, the Steck company, 1949].   Cloth.

vii, 247 p.   plates, ports., facsm.   22.8 cm.
Map on front end paper.

921   GREEN, RENA MAVERICK (ED.).   "Mavericks"; authentic account of the
term "maverick" as applied to unbranded cattle.   [San Antonio, Texas,
printed by Guessaz & Ferlet, printers, 1937].   Wrappers.   Scarce.

1 l., 3–13 [1] p.   19.5 cm.

These articles originally appeared in the *St. Louis Republic,* November, 1889.

922   ———.   Samuel Maverick, Texas: 1803–1870. A collection of letters,

journals, and memoirs, edited by Rena Maverick Green. San Antonio, ₁privately printed₁, 1952. Cloth.

xix p., 1 l., 3–430 p. front. (port.), plates, ports., facsms. 23.5 cm.
Appendix, p. 399–421; bibliography, p. 422–423; index, p. 424–430.
Half title.

Through Mr. Maverick's correspondence we learn of his brief experience as a cattleman and the true origin of "maverick" as a cattle term.

923 GREENBURG, DAN W. Sixty years. A brief review. The cattle industry in Wyoming, its organization and present status and data concerning the Wyoming Stock Growers' Association, by Dan W. Greenburg. A souvenir brochure on the occasion of the sixtieth anniversary convention held at Green River, Wyoming, June 7, 8, 9, 1932. Cheyenne, published by Wyoming Stock Growers' association, 1932. Stiff pict. wrappers. Scarce.

4 p.l., 9–73 p. illus., plates, ports., facsms. 22.8 cm.
"First edition" on t.p.

This is the first of three histories written about the Wyoming Stock Growers' Association. Others have followed every ten years.

924 GREER, JAMES KIMMINS. Bois d'arc to barb'd wire; Ken Carey: Southwestern frontier born, by James K. Greer. Dallas, Texas, Dealey and Lowe, 1936. Pict. cloth. OP.

7 p.l., 428 p. plates, maps. 22.5 cm.
Bibliographical notes, p. ₁411₁–423; index, p. ₁425₁–428.
Illus. double t.p.; map on end papers (dif.); double t.p.; vignette.

925 ——. Early in the saddle, by James K. Greer. Dallas, Texas, Dealey and Lowe, 1936. Cloth. OP.

4 p.l., 269 p. front., illus., plates. 20 cm.
Blank pages interspersed.
"Bois d'arc to Barb'd Wire, boy's edition"—2d prelim. leaf.

926 ——. Grand prairie, by James K. Greer. Dallas, Texas, Tardy publishing company, ₁1935₁. Cloth. Scarce.

4 p.l., 284 p. plates, maps. 19.7 cm.
Notes, p. 235–264; index, p. 265–284.

927 ——. A Texas Ranger and frontiersman. The days of Buck Barry in Texas, 1845–1906. Edited by James K. Greer. Dallas, Texas, the Southwest press, 1932. Cloth. Scarce.

xi p., 1 l., 254 p. front., illus., maps. 24 cm.
Index, p. 235–254.

A chapter on stock farming.

928 GREGG, JACOB RAY. Pioneer days in Malheur County. Perpetuating the

memory of prominent pioneers and preserving an authentic history of the county as told to Jacob Ray Gregg.... Los Angeles, privately printed by Lorrin L. Morrison, printing and publishing, 1950. Cloth.

7 p.l., 5–442 p. front. (port.), plates, ports. 23.5 cm.
Half title (recto frontis.); map on end papers.

929 GREW, DAVID. Beyond rope and fence, [by] David Grew. New York, Boni and Liveright, [1922]. Cloth. Scarce.

4 p.l., vii, 240 p. front. (col.). 20 cm.

The story of a cow horse.

930 ———. The sorrel stallion, by David Grew. Illustrated by Paul Brown. New York, Charles Scribner's sons, 1932. Cloth. OP.

xi p., 1 l., 321 p. illus., plates. 21.2 cm.
Half title; map on end papers; vignette; untrimmed.

931 GREY, FREDERICK W. Seeking fortune in America, by F. W. Grey. With a frontispiece. London, Smith Elder & co...., 1912. Cloth. Scarce.

xiv, 307 p. front. (port. with tissue). 20.8 cm.
Half title; 2 l. adv. at end.

932 GRIFFITHS, DAVID. Forage conditions on the northern border of the great basin, being a report upon investigations made during July and August, 1901, in the region between Winnemucca, Nevada, and Ontario, Oregon. By David Griffiths. . . . Washington, Government printing office, 1902. Wrappers. Scarce.

5 p.l., 9–60 p. front. (map), plates. 25 cm.
U. S. Dept. of Agriculture, Bureau of Plant Industry, *Bulletin No. 15.*

933 ———. Range investigations in Arizona, by David Griffiths. Grass and forage plant investigations. Issued October 6, 1904. Washington, Government printing office, 1904. Wrappers. Scarce.

2 p.l., 5–62 p. 10 plates (incl. front.), diagr., tables. 23 cm.

934 GRIGGS, GEORGE. History of Mesilla Valley; or, the Gadsden purchase, known in Mexico as the treaty of Mesilla . . . , by George Griggs. . . . [Las Cruces, N. M., Bronson printing co.], 1930. Stiff wrappers. Rare.

7 pl., [3]–128 p. illus., maps. 22.6 cm.
Index, p. 125–128.
Map on t.p.; double column.

935 GRIMES, W. B., vs. MARY L. WATKINS. Supreme Court case No. 880. Fourth assignment. W. B. Grimes, appellant *vs.* Mary L. Watkins, *et al.,*

appellances. Brief for appellant. ₍N. p., n. d., c.1874₎. Pamphlet. (Caption title). Rare.

17 p. 20.2 cm.

Cattle lawsuit.

936 GRINNELL, JOSIAH BUSHNELL. The cattle industries of the United States, embracing history; lessons in census; great sales of history; experiences of western stockmen; various breeds and characteristics; location of the herds; our stock country geographically. . . . By Hon. J. B. Grinnell. Reprint from the *Agricultural Review* and *Journal of the American Agricultural Association,* Vol. II, No. 2 (1882). New York, Joseph H. Reall, editor and publisher, 1882. Wrappers. Rare.

₍5₎–74 ₍2₎ p. plates, tables. 22.8 cm.

2 p. adv. at end; adv. verso front wrapper; adv. recto and verso back wrapper.

937 ———. Cattle interests of the Mississippi River (in U. S. Dept. of Agriculture, Bureau of Animal Industry, *1st Annual Report,* 1884). Washington, Government printing office, 1885. Wrappers. Scarce.

p. 233–244. 23 cm.

938 GRISWOLD, J. T. From dugout to steeple, by J. T. Griswold. ₍N. p.₎, Parthenon press, ₍1949₎. Cloth. OP.

8 p.l., 19–176 p. plates, ports. 19.2 cm.

Half title.

Has a chapter on cattle and Charles Goodnight.

939 GRISWOLD, WAYNE. Kansas, her resources and developments; or, the Kansas Pilot. Giving a direct road to homes for everybody, also the effect of latitudes on life locations, with important facts for all European emigrants. By Wayne Griswold. Cincinnati, Robert Clarke & co., 1871. Wrappers. Rare.

vi, ₍9₎–95 p. illus. 22.7 cm.

Some head and tail pieces.

940 GUERNSEY, CHARLES ARTHUR. Wyoming cowboy days. An account of the experiences of Charles Arthur Guernsey, in which he tells in his own way of the early territorial cattle days and political strife, and deals with many of the state's and nation's famous characters. . . . True to life, but not autobiographical. Romantic, but not fiction. Facts, but not history. Profusely illustrated. New York, G. P. Putnam's sons, 1936. Cloth. OP.

x p., 1 l., 13–288 p. front., plates, ports., facsms. 24.3 cm.

941 GUYER, JAMES S. Pioneer life in West Texas . . . , by James S. Guyer. . . . Brownwood, Texas . . . , 1938. Pict. cloth. Scarce.

xi p., 1 l., 3–185 ₍2₎ p. illus., plates, ports. 23.4 cm.

Port. of author on t.p.; crudely bound.

942 H., E. M. Ranch life in California. Extracted from the home correspondence of E. M. H. London, W. H. Allen & co., 1886. Cloth.
Scarce.

iv, 171 p. front., illus., plates. 17.5 cm.

943 HADLEY, WALTER C. New Mexico. Pointers for pilgrims to the land
of golden opportunities. How to find a mine and what to do with it
when it is found. By Walter C. Hadley. . . . Las Vegas, published by
the author, 1882. Pict. wrappers. Rare.

24 p. double-p. map in front. 17 cm.

944 HAFEN, LeROY R. Colorado. The story of a western commonwealth.
By LeRoy R. Hafen. Denver, the Peerless publishing co., 1933. Cloth. OP.

5 p.l., [11]–328 p. front., plates, ports., maps. 24.2 cm.
Appendix, p. [315–318]; index, p. [319]–328.
Half title; selected references for reading after each chapter.

945 ———, and ANN W. HAFEN. Colorado. A story of the state and its
people. By LeRoy R. Hafen and Ann W. Hafen. Denver, Colo., the
Old West publishing co., 1943. Pict. cloth. OP.

6 p.l., 13–436 p. front., illus., plates, ports., maps (1 double p.). 20.2 cm.
Appendix, p. 411–[418]; index, p. 419–436.
Half title; illus. end papers; references for further reading at end of each chapter.

946 ———. The Colorado story. A history of your state and mine. By
LeRoy R. Hafen . . . and Ann Hafen. Denver, Colorado, the Old West
publishing company, [1953]. Pict. cloth.

4 p.l., 11–536 [1] p. front. (col.), illus., plates, ports., maps, charts. 22.6 cm.

947 HAFEN, LeROY R., and CARL COKE RISTER. Western America. The
exploration, settlement, and development of the region beyond the Mississippi, by LeRoy R. Hafen . . . and Carl Coke Rister. . . . New York,
Prentice-Hall, inc., 1941. Cloth. OP.

xxiv p., 1 l., 698 p. front. (col. map), illus., facsms., maps. 23.5 cm.
Bibliography after each chapter; index, p. 669–698.
Half title.

948 HAGELL, E. F. When the grass was free, [by] E. F. Hagell. New
York, Boureguy & Curl, inc., [1954]. Cloth.

x p., 1 l., 127 [1] p. illus., plates (4 col.). 20.4 cm.
Pict. half title; illus. double t.p.

A story of the Canadian cow country.

949 HAGENBARTH, FRANK J. Amended constitution of the National Live
Stock Association of the United States. Adopted at Denver, January 13,
1905. Annual address of President Frank J. Hagenbarth; sound advice

of Frank J. Benton; analysis and comparison of old and amended constitution. Denver, 1905. Wrappers. Scarce.

20 p. front. 22.2 cm.
First 4 pages address of President Hagenbarth (double column).

950 HAGER, MRS. ALICE (ROGERS). Big loop and little. The cowboy's story. By Alice Rogers Hager. New York, the Macmillan company, 1937. Cloth. OP.

4 p.l., ₁88₁ p. (no pagination), plates, ports. 26.7 cm.
Half title; illus. t.p.; illus. end papers.

951 HAGEDORN, HERMANN. Roosevelt in the Badlands, by Hermann Hagedorn. With illustrations. Boston and New York, Houghton Mifflin company, 1921. Cloth. OP.

xxvi p., 1 l., ₁3₁–491 p. front. (with tissue), plates, ports., facsms. 25 cm.
Appendix, p. ₁479₁–482; index, p. ₁485₁–491.
Half title: "Publications of the Roosevelt Memorial Association"; map on back end papers; untrimmed.
Colophon: "This large-paper edition consists of three hundred and seventy-five numbered copies, of which three hundred and fifty are for sale. This is No. ——."
Published also in trade edition.

952 HAGERTY, FRANK H. The territory of Dakota, the state of North Dakota, the state of South Dakota; an official statistical, historical, and political abstract. . . . Published by Frank H. Hagerty. . . . Aberdeen, S. D., Daily News print, 1889. Wrappers. Rare.

4 p.l., ₁9₁–119 p. tables. 22 cm.
Index, p. ₁117₁–119.

953 ——. The state of North Dakota, the statistical, historical, and political abstract. Agricultural, mineral, commercial . . . and general statements. Published by Frank H. Hagerty. . . . Aberdeen, S. D., Daily News print, 1889. Wrappers. Rare.

2 p.l., ₁5₁–99 p. tables. 22 cm.

954 ——. The state of South Dakota, the statistical, historical, and political abstract. . . . Published by Frank H. Hagerty. . . . Aberdeen, S. D., Daily News print, 1889. Wrappers. Rare.

2 p.l., ₁5₁–102 p. tables. 22 cm.

955 ——. The year of statehood, 1889. Dakota official guide containing useful information in the handy form for settlers and homeseekers concerning North and South Dakota. Aberdeen, Dakota, published by Frank H. Hagerty, commissioner of immigration, 1889. Wrappers. Rare.

2 p.l., ₁5₁–48 p. 2 maps (col.), tables. 22.3 cm.

956 HAILEY, JOHN. The history of Idaho, by John Hailey. Boise, Idaho, Press of Syms-York company, inc., MCMX. Cloth. Scarce.
5 p.l., 395 [5] p. front. (port. with tissue). 24 cm.
Last 5 (unnumbered) pages contain poetry.

Has several chapters on cattle.

957 HAINES, HELEN. History of New Mexico from the Spanish conquest to the present time, 1530–1890. With portraits and biographical sketches of its prominent people. By Helen Haines. New York, New Mexico Historical publishing co., 1891. Cloth. Scarce.
xix, 631 p. plates, ports. 23.5 cm.

958 HAIRE, FRANCES H. The American costume book, by Frances H. Haire. . . . Illustrations by Gertrude Moser. New York, A. S. Barnes and company, incorporated, 1937. Pict. cloth. OP.
xi p., 1 l., 3–164 p. full-p. plates (all col.). 26 cm.

Contains a chapter on what the cowboy wears.

959 HALEY, J. EVETTS. A bit of bragging about a cow, by J. Evetts Haley. Illustrations by Harold Bugbee. [N. p.], March, 1948. Wrappers.
1 p.l., [5] p. (no pagination). front. 20.4 cm.

960 ———. Charles Goodnight, cowman & plainsman, [by] J. Evetts Haley; with illustrations by Harold Bugbee. Boston, New York, Hougton Mifflin company, 1936. Cloth. Scarce.
xiii p., 1 l., 485 p. front. (port. signed in facsm.), illus. 22 cm.
"A note on bibliography," p. [469]–472; index, p. [475]–485.
Half title; vignette; first edition: "1936" under imprint.
Republished by University of Oklahoma press in 1949 with some changes.
xiii p., 1 l., 485 p. front. (port. signed in facsm.), illus. 23.9 cm.
"A note on bibliography," p. [469]–472; index, p. [475]–485.
Half title.

961 ———. A day with Dan Casement, by J. Evetts Haley. [Kansas City, Mo., 1949]. Stiff wrappers. (Cover title). OP.
[7] p. (no pagination). 22 cm.
Reprinted from the *American Hereford Journal,* September 1, 1949.

962 ———. The heraldry of the range. Some southwestern brands. By J. Evetts Haley. Illustrated by Harold Bugbee. Canyon, Texas, Panhandle Plains Historical society, 1949. Cloth. OP.
2 p.l., 5–35 p. illus., facsms. (in col.). 28 cm.
Illus. chapter headings.
Also issued with "Some Southwester Trails" as a set in an edition of twenty,

specially and separately bound in Hereford red "Homespun" cloth with heavy slip case of the same color, and signed by author, printer, and illustrator.

963 ———. Jim East, trail hand and cowboy, [by] J. Evetts Haley. [Canyon, Texas]. 1931. Wrappers. (Cover title). Scarce.

[23] p. (no pagination). 23.3 cm.
Reprinted from the *Panhandle-Plains Historical Review* for 1931.

964 ———. George W. Littlefield, Texan, by J. Evetts Haley. Drawings by Harold D. Bubgee. Norman, University of Oklahoma press, MCMXLIII. Cloth.

xiv p., 1 l., 3–287 p. illus., ports. 22 cm.
Index, p. 283–287.
Half title; vignette; "First edition" on copyright p.

The biography of an important early-day Texas cattleman.

965 ———. Jeff Milton, a good man with a gun, by J. Evetts Haley, with drawings by Harold D. Bugbee. Norman, University of Oklahoma press, 1948. Cloth.

xiii p., 1 l., 3–430 p. illus., plates, ports., map. 23.8 cm.
Index, p. 417–430.
Half title; illus. t.p.; "First edition" on copyright p.

The first state of this book is distinguished (in the index, p. 421) by the line, "Greenway, John Campbell, 366, 411" being upside down and out of alphabetical order.

966 ———. Life on the Texas range. Photographs by Erwin E. Smith. Text by J. Evetts Haley. Austin, University of Texas press, 1952. Pict. cloth.

7 p.l., 15–112 p. front. (port.), plates, ports. 31 cm.
Half title; illus. end papers (dif.); boxed.

A book of reproductions of pictures taken by Erwin E. Smith on the cattle range in the eighties and nineties for which he became famous.

967 ———. Pastores del Palo Duro, by J. Evetts Haley. Illustrated by Harold Bugbee. Reprinted from *Southwest Review,* Spring, 1934. Pict. wrappers. (Cover title). OP.

16 p. illus. 24 cm.

968 ———. Charles Schriener, general merchandise. The story of a country store, by J. Evetts Haley. Illustrations by Harold Bugbee. Austin, Texas State Historical association, 1944. Cloth. Rare.

x p., 2 l., 73 p. front., illus. 24 cm.
Acknowledgments, p. 72; index, p. 73.

A story of a country merchant and ranchman. Printed in a small edition and now very difficult to come by.

969 ————. The XIT Ranch of Texas, and the early days of the Llano Estacado, by J. Evetts Haley. . . . Chicago, the Lakeside press, 1929. Cloth. Rare.

xvi, 261 p. front. (map), ports., maps (1 fold.), facsms. 23.5 cm.
Appendix, p. 235–250; bibliography, p. 251–255; index, p. 257–261.
Half title; device.

Republished with some changes by the University of Oklahoma press in 1953.

xiv p., 1 l., 3–258 p. plates, ports., fold. map. 23.5 cm.
Appendix, p. 229–245; bibliography, p. 247–252; index, p. 253–258.
Half title; pub. device.

One of the best books about a Texas ranch. Because of a lawsuit most of the edition was recalled and suppressed, making it one of the rarest and most sought after books on cattle. This is the author's first book, and the many books he has written since have enhanced his reputation as a writer.

The University of Oklahoma did readers of Western Americana a great favor when they republished this scarce volume. Their publication gave many persons an opportunity to read this important book who could not financially afford a copy of the original—if they could find one. Some changes were made in the text and the allegedly libelous material deleted. In 1957 a number of copies of the original edition were released, and it is now not so rare.

970 HALL, BERT L. Roundup years, Old Muddy to Black Hills. . . . [Pierre, South Dakota, lithographed from original manuscript by the Reminder, inc., Pierre, South Dakota, and bound by State publishing co., Pierre, South Dakota, 1954]. Pict. cloth.

2 p.l., 1 p., 2–580 [3] p. illus., plates, ports., facsms., cattle brands. 28.2 cm.
Index, p. 573–579; some addresses used by early ranchers, p. 580.
Pict. half title; illus. t.p.
46 blank leaves at end for notes and clippings.

Photo-lithographed, the book deals with the cattle industry as remembered by some old-timers. It is composed of prints of newspaper clippings, and personal reminiscences. A unique book. Reprinted in 1956 with some new material and with maps.

971 HALL, CARROLL DOUGLAS. Heraldry of New Helvetia, with thirty-two cattle brands and ear marks reproduced from the original certificates issued at Sutter's Fort 1845 to 1848. Foreword and biographical sketches by Carroll D. Hall. San Francisco, the Book Club of California, 1945. Half leather. Scarce.

4 p.l., [85] p. (no pagination), facsm. in Spanish, translation on opposite page.
Half title; untrimmed.
Colophon: "This book, hand-set in Bulmer type, was printed on all rag paper at the L. D. Allen Press for members of the Book Club of California. Two hundred fifty copies."

972 HALL, CLAUDE V. The early history of Floyd County, by Claude V. Hall. Canyon, Texas, Panhandle-Plains Historical Society publication, Vol. XX, printed by Russell stationery co., Amarillo, [1947]. Pict. cloth. 3–147 p. 23.6 cm.
Bibliography, p. 139–140; index, p. 141–147.

First issued as Volume XX of the Panhandle-Plains Historical Association's *Review*. Some volumes were bound in cloth in book form. Contains much material on cattle ranches of Floyd County, Texas.

973 HALL, EDWARD H. The great West: emigrants, settlers, & travelers' guide and hand-book to the states of California and Oregon and the territories of Nebraska, Utah, Colorado, Idaho, Montana, Nevada, and Washington, with a full and accurate account of their climate, soil, resources, and products, accompanied by a map showing the several routes to the gold fields. . . . By Edward H. Hall. . . . New York, published and for sale at the Tribune office, 1864. Wrappers. Rare.
3 p.l., [7]–89 p. fold. map in front. 18.2x11.4 cm.

974 HALL, FRANK. History of the state of Colorado, embracing accounts of the prehistoric races and their remains; the earliest Spanish, French, and American explorations . . . the first American settlements founded; the Rocky Mountains, the development of cities and towns, with the various phases of industrial and political transition from 1858 to 1890 . . . , by Frank Hall, for the Rocky Mountain Historical co. Chicago, the Blakely printing co., 1889–95. Pub. in 4 vols. Dec. leather. Scarce.
Vol. I: xvi p., 1 l., 17–564 p. front. (port.), plates, ports. 26.8 cm.
Index, p. 554–564.
Vol. II (pub. in 1890): xiv p., 1 l., 17–574 p. front. (port.), ports., map. 26.8 cm.
Vols. III and IV: biographical.

975 HALL, J. H. Montana. Issued by the department of publicity of the Bureau of Agriculture, Labor, and Industry of the state of Montana. [By] J. H. Hall, commissioner. Edition of 1912. Helena, Mont., Independent publishing co., state printers, 1912. Cloth. OP.
2 p.l., 308 p. front., illus., plates, ports., maps, tables. 26.5 cm.
Index, p. 306–308.

976 HALL, RINALDO M. Oregon, Washington, Idaho, and their resources. The mecca of the homeseeker and investor. A land of promise and opportunity, where the soil, climate, and all conditions are unsurpassable for the successful pursuance of varied industry. . . . By Rinaldo M. Hall. [N. p.], published by the Passenger department of the Oregon Railroad & Navigation company, Southern Pacific company . . . , 1903. Stiff pict. wrappers. Rare.
[3]–88 p. illus., plates, large fold. map at end. 22.8 cm.
Illus. t.p.

[155]

977 HALLIDAY, DICK. The western tradition, by Dick Halliday. . . .
Tucson, Arizona, press of the Betts printing company, 1946. Stiff pict.
wrappers. OP.

5–72 p. front., plates, ports. 25.8 cm.
Double column.

978 HALSELL, H. H. Cowboys and cattleland, by H. H. Halsell. Nashville, Tenn., printed for the author by the Parthenon press, [1937]. Dec.
cloth. OP.

6 p.l., 13–276 p. front., 6 ports. (incl. front.). 20.4 cm.
Half title; pub. device.

979 ———. My autobiography, [by] H. H. Halsell. A thrilling historical
autobiography experienced during the early days of Texas when it was
a primitive wilderness. [Dallas, Texas, printed for the author by Wilkinson printing company, 1948]. Cloth. OP.

5 p.l., 11–253 [2] p. plates, ports., map. 23.3 cm.

980 HAMBLIN, GEORGE W. The Kansas guide. Facts and practical sug-
gestions to those who intend seeking new homes in the "Far West."
Ottawa, Kansas, published by Geo. W. Hamblin, November, 1871.
Wrappers. Rare.

[3]–62 [2] p. 21 cm.
Map issued separately.

981 HAMBRICK, ALMA WARD. The call of the San Saba. A history of San
Saba County, by Alma Ward Hambrick. San Antonio, the Naylor co.,
1941. Cloth. OP.

x, 331 p. plates, ports. 23.5 cm.
Index, p. 319–331.

982 HAMILTON, PATRICK. Arizona for homes, for health, for investments.
By Patrick Hamilton. Phoenix, Arizona, 1886. Wrappers. Scarce.

126 p. front., plates, fold. map at end, tables. 21 cm.

A revision, with alterations, of his *The Resources of Arizona*.

983 ———. The resources of Arizona; its mineral, farming, and grazing
lands, towns and mining camps; its rivers, mountains, plains, and mesas;
with a brief summary of its Indian tribes, early history, ancient ruins,
climate etc. . . . A manual of reliable information concerning the territory. Compiled by Patrick Hamilton, under authority of the Legislature.
[Florence, Ariz., 1881]. Wrappers. Rare.

71 p. 21.2 cm.
Published same year at Prescott, Arizona.

3 p.l., [7]–120 p. tables. 21.2 cm.

[156]

Published same year at Phoenix with same collation. Republished in an enlarged edition by A. L. Bancroft and co., San Francisco, 1883.

275 p. illus., tables, ₁i₁–x p., at end. 22.9 cm.

Greatly enlarged again in 1884 and published by the same publishers.

xii ₁1₁, ₁9₁–414 p., 2 l. fold. illus., fold. map, ₁i₁–xiv p., adv. at end. 19.8 cm.

984 HAMNER, LAURA V. The no gun man of Texas; a century of achievement, 1835–1929. By Laura V. Hamner. Illustrated by Ben Carleton Mead and Terry Stowe. ₁Amarillo, Texas₁, Laura V. Hamner, 1935. Pict. cloth. OP.

viii p., 1 l., 3–256 p. front. (port.), plates, map (front flyleaf). 20 cm.
Appendix, p. 251–254; glossary, p. 255–256.
Half title.

The life of Charles Goodnight written for school reading.

985 ———. Short grass & longhorns, by Laura V. Hamner. Norman, University of Oklahoma press, 1943. Cloth. OP.

5 p.l., 3–269 p. plates, ports., maps. 22 cm.
Index, p. 255–269.

Fifty copies of this book were printed and bound in red cloth, for the purpose of offering it for adoption as a supplementary reader in Texas schools. This printing, published in 1942, contained only 254 pages, as it had no index. These copies have now become collector's items. The trade edition was printed in May, 1943, and reprinted in August of the same year and in January, 1945. The book is a valuble history of the leading ranches of West Texas.

986 HANCHETT, LAFAYETTE. The old sheriff and other true tales, by Lafayette Hanchett. New York, Margent press, 1937. Cloth. OP.

ix p. 1 l., 208 p. front., plates, ports. 23 cm.

987 HANDLY, JAMES. The resources of Madison County, Montana. By James Handly. . . . ₁San Francisco, Francis & Valentine, Steam Book, Job and Poster printing establishment, 1872₁. Wrappers. Rare.

2 p.l., ₁5₁–60 ₁1₁ p. 22.8 cm.
Adv. verso front wrapper and first 3 leaves; adv. recto and verso back wrapper and scattered throughout.

Said to be one of the scarcest of the Montana county histories, it contains material on stock raising.

988 HANSCOM, OTHO ANNE. Parade of the pioneers, by Otho Anne Hanscom. . . . Illustrators Kenneth Hunt, Rudolph Fuchs. Dallas, Texas, Tardy publishing company, inc., ₁1935₁. Cloth. OP.

xi, 266 p. illus., map. 19.6 cm.

[157]

989   HANSFORD LAND AND CATTLE COMPANY, LTD.   Fourth annual report, being for year ending 30th November, 1886. ₁Dundee, Scotland, 1887₁. Pamphlet. Rare.
7 ₁2₁ p.   20.5 cm.

990   ——.   Twenty-ninth annual report, being for year ending 31st December, 1911. ₁Dundee, Scotland, 1912₁. Pamphlet. Scarce.
5 ₁2₁ p.   20.8 cm.

These two pamphlets are examples of the reports of this cattle company that were published each year.

991   HANWAY, J. EDWIN.   The memoirs of J. Edwin Hanway (christened Isreal Edwin). A Wyoming newspaper publisher who traveled various routes and engaged in numerous occupations before achieving his goal in the place of his dreams. With illustrations. ₁Douglas, Wyoming, Douglas Enterprise co., 1942₁.   Cloth.   Scarce.
3 p.l., ₁9₁–246 ₁2₁ p. front. (port.), illus., plates, ports.   23.5 cm.
Half title; "An autobiography."
Date, place of publication, and publisher placed on half title p.
Table of contents and table of illustrations on last 2 p.

Has a chapter on the author's trail herd experiences.

992   HARBER, NORA E.   (PUB.).   Our Fort Benton "the birthplace of Montana." A collection of stories and pictures of early day and modern Fort Benton. Fort Benton, Montana, published by Nora E. Harber, printed by the River press, ₁n. d.₁. Stiff pict. wrappers. Scarce.
₁46₁ p. (no pagination). illus., plates, plan.   22.8 cm.

Has a chapter on the cattle industry.

993   HARKEY, DEE.   Mean as hell, by Dee Harkey. Line drawings by Gene Roberts. ₁Albuquerque₁, the University of New Mexico press, 1948. Cloth.
xvi, 223 p. illus., plates, ports.   20.3 cm.
Index, p. 219–223.
Half title; illus. t.p.; map on end papers.

A most interesting account of lawlessness and cowboys of New Mexico and West Texas. Soon after the book was released, the publisher recalled all unsold copies or requested the dealers to black out with India ink the word "outlaw" after the name Les Dow in the index on page 220. Also, not in the first issues, there was added an errata slip on page xv, correcting the name Ace Christmas to U. R. Christmas on pages 110, 116, and 219. In the next printing, these corrections were made in the text. The first edition may be identified by these errors.

994   HARPER, MINNIE TIMMINS, and GEORGE DEWEY HARPER.   Old ranches,

by Minnie Timmins Harper and George Dewey Harper. . . . Dallas, Texas, Dealey and Lowe, 1936. Stiff pict. wrappers. OP.

5 p.l., [5]-101 p. front., illus., ports. 21.5 cm.

995 HARRIMAN, ALICE. Pacific history stories. Montana edition. By Alice Harriman. . . . San Francisco, the Whitaker & Ray company (incorporated), 1903. Pict. cloth. Scarce.

6 p.l., 11-198 [1] p. front. (col.), illus., plates, ports., facsm. 17.3 cm. Pub. device.

"Western Series of Readers," edited by Hans Wagner.

Has a chapter on cowboys.

996 HARRINGTON, W. P. History of Gove County, Kansas, to the organization of the county in 1886. By W. P. Harrington. . . . Gove City, Kansas, published in the Republican-Gazette office, 1920. Stiff wrappers. (Cover title). Scarce.

[32] p. (no pagination). 22.7 cm. Double column.

Republished in 1930 with illus. and map in an edition of 72 p.

Has a chapter on the Texas cattle trail.

997 HARRIS, BEVERLY DABNEY. Cattle paper, [by] Beverly D. Harris. An address before the Kansas City Live Stock Association, Wichita, Kansas, February 9, 1916. [New York, 1916]. Wrappers. Scarce.

[3]-19 p. 22.8 cm.

998 HARRIS, FRANK. My reminiscences as a cowboy, [by] Frank Harris. Illustrations by William Gropper. New York, Charles Boni . . . , 1930. Stiff pict. wrappers.

7 p.l., 15-217 [2] p. plates. 18.6 cm. Half title; illus. end papers; vignette.

A London edition was published by John Lane, the Bodley Head, ltd., with slight changes in the text and the omission of the last chapter. It was retitled "On the Trail; My Reminiscences as a Cowboy." Cloth. Scarce.

4 p.l., 247 [8] p. 19.2 cm. Half title; last 8 p. adv.

Both editions are full of inaccuracies, wild imagination, and are historically worthless.

999 HARRIS, JUDGE FRANK. History of Washington County and Adams County, by Judge Frank Harris. [N.p., n.d.]. Stiff pict. wrappers. (Cover title). OP.

3 p.l., 7-74 p. front. (port.). 22.2 cm. Pioneer honor roll, p. 71-74; double column.

1000 HARRIS, J. S., and W. A. CLARK. Montana, its climate, industry, and resources. By J. S. Harris and W. A. Clark. Helena, G. E. Boos, print, [1884]. Wrappers. Rare.
74 p. lithographic plates, fold. chart. 20.2 cm.

1001 ———. Montana, its climate, industries, and resources. [Helena, Mont., 1885]. Wrappers. Scarce.
74 p. illus., 1 plate, fold. table. 21.8 cm.

1002 HARRISON, J. M. Book of information and settlers' guide for the Pacific Slope, including the states of California, Oregon, and Nevada, and territories of Washington and Idaho, with a description of and the peculiarities of each. . . . By J. M. Harrison. . . . San Francisco, C. A. Murdock & co., book and job printers, 1875. Wrappers. Rare.
[3]-49 [1] p. 15.8 cm.

1003 HARRISON, R. B. Brand book of the Montana Stock Growers' Association. Fourth issue. Chicago, 1890. Cloth. Scarce.
147 p. plates, cattle brands. 19 cm.

1004 HART, JOHN A. History of pioneer days in Texas and Oklahoma. By John A. Hart and others. [N.p. (? Guthrie), n.d., c.1906]. Cloth. Rare.
249 p. plates, ports. 16.3 cm.
Republished [c.1909] with two chapters added on Arkansas.
271 p. front. (port.), plates, ports. 16.3 cm.

Later there was an enlarged edition (see item No. 892) of 320 pages under the title *Pioneer Days in the Southwest* . . . , which, in turn, was reprinted with the same imprint and collation but with sixteen plates instead of twelve and with a colored frontispiece. Although this edition was labeled "Second edition," it is really the third.

1005 HART, WILLIAM SURREY. My life east and west, by William S. Hart. With illustrations. Boston and New York, Houghton Mifflin company, 1929. Cloth. OP.
vii [1] p., 1 l., 3-362 [1] p. front. (col.), plates, ports. 22 cm.
Index, p. 355-[363].
Half title; pub. device; first edition, "1929" under imprint.

1006 HARTMAN, H. New Mexico lands. Their character and distribution by valleys and counties. Practical observations upon the culture of the soil. Fees and commissions for acquiring land. By H. Hartman. [Las Vegas. J. A. Carruth, printer, binder, and blank book manufacturer, 1889]. Wrappers. (Caption title). Scarce.
48 p. 21.7 cm.

1007 HASKELL, CHARLES W. (ED.). History and business directory of Mesa County, Colorado, containing a description of its valleys, ranges, ditch systems, illustrations and portraits of some of the early settlers and prominent men. . . . Grand Junction, Colorado, edited and published by the Mesa County Democrat, Chas. W. Haskell, editor and proprietor, 1886. Limber cloth. Rare.

2 p.l., 93 p. illus., plates (1 fold.), ports. 21.8 cm.
Double column.

1008 HASKELL, HENRY C., JR., and RICHARD B. FOWLER. City of the future. A narrative history of Kansas City, 1850–1950, by Henry C. Haskell, Jr., [and] Richard B. Fowler. Foreword by Roy A. Roberts. Illustrated by Frank H. Miller. Kansas City, Missouri, Frank Glenn publishing co., inc., [1950]. Cloth.

8 p.l., 15–193 [1] p. illus., full-p. plates. 22.6 cm.
Acknowledgments and bibliography, p. 181–185; index, p. 187–193.
Half title; map on end papers; double t.p.

1009 HASTINGS, FRANK STEWART. A ranchman's recollections; an autobiography in which unfamiliar facts bearing upon the origin of the cattle industry in the Southwest and of the American packing business are stated and characteristic incidents recorded, by Frank S. Hastings. . . . Chicago, Illinois, published by the Breeder's Gazette, 1921. Pict. cloth. Scarce.

xiii, 235 p. front., plates, ports. 19.8 cm.
Half title; untrimmed.

An excellent book, now becoming scarce, written by the manager of the SMS Ranch of Texas. Well-told stories of cowboy life.

1010 [HATCH, RUFUS]. "Uncle Rufus" and "Ma," the story of a summer jaunt with their friends in the Northwest. [N. p.], August, 1882. Cloth. Rare.

[3]–67 p. 17.8 cm.
Gilt edges.

Some information about cattle in Dakota. Consists mainly of letters to the *Chicago Tribune,* signed "Rab," describing an excursion sponsored by Rufus Hatch.

1011 [HAUSER, GOV. S. T.] Report of the Governor of Montana to the Secretary of the Interior, 1886. Washington, Government printing office, 1886. Wrappers. Scarce.
3–9 p. 21.8 cm.

Report on the increase of stock in the territory.

1012 [HAVEMEYER, HENRY, ET AL.]. Prospectus for proposed ranching corporation between Henry and Charles W. Havemeyer, John H. Prentiss,
and Wm. H. Kellogg and H. H. Player. ₁N. p., n. d., c.1879₁. Folder.
Rare.

₁4₁ p. (no pagination). 26.5 cm.

The cattle firm was started by Prentiss, Kellogg, and Player in 1878, and they
were joined by the Havemeyers in 1879 when a stock company was formed.
This rare item seen in the Rollins Collection, Princeton University.

1013 HAWES, ADELAIDE. The valley of tall grass, by Adelaide Hawes. Illustrated with photographs. Bruneau, Idaho, ₁printed by the Caxton printers, ltd.₁, 1950. Cloth.

xii p., 2 l., 244 ₁2₁ p. front. (port.), illus., plates, ports., map at end. 23.6 cm.
Half title; map on end papers.

This privately printed book contains much on cattle and cowboys.

1014 HAWES, CLARENCE. Patches, a Wyoming cow pony, by Clarence
Hawes; illustrated by Griswold Tyng. Springfield, Mass., Milton Bradley company, 1928. Cloth.

9 p.l., 21–268 p. front., illus., plates. 24 cm.
Half title; illus. end papers; vignette.

1015 HAYDON, ARTHUR LINCOLN. The riders of the plains. Adventures and
romance with the North-West Mounted Police, 1873–1910, by A. L. Haydon. Illustrated with photographs, maps, and diagrs. Chicago, A. C.
McClurg & co.; London, Andrew Melrose, 1910. Cloth. OP.

xvi, 385 p. front. (port., with tissue), plates, ports., maps (1 fold.), diagrs.
(1 fold.). 23.3 cm.
Appendices, p. 355–₁380₁; index, p. 381–385.
Half title; pub. device; t.p. in red and black.

1016 HAYES, A. A., JR. New Colorado and the Santa Fe Trail, by A. A.
Hayes, Jr. . . . Illustrated. New York, Harper & brothers . . . , 1880.
Cloth. Scarce.

7 p.l., ₁17₁–200 p. front. (map), illus. 23.3 cm.

1017 HAYSTEAD, LADD. If the prospect pleases; the West the guidebooks
never mention. ₁By₁ Ladd Haystead. Norman, University of Oklahoma
press, 1945. Cloth.

xiii p., 1 l., 3–208 p. 21 cm.
Half title.

1018 HAZARD, LUCY LOCKWOOD. In search of America, by Lucy Lockwood
Hazard. . . . New York, Thomas Y. Crowell co., ₁1930₁. Cloth. OP.

xxv p., 4 l., 7–586 p. 22 cm.
Bibliography after each chapter; index, p. 583–586.

An anthology containing some cowboy material.

1019 HAZELDINE, WILLIAM C. New Mexico. Territorial Bureau of Immigration. Report on Bernalillo County. ₁By₁ William C. Hazeldine, commissioner. New Albuquerque, N. M., printed at the Daily Journal book and job office, 1881. Wrappers. Rare.
₁3₁–31 p. 21.8 cm.

1020 HAZELTON, JOHN M. History and handbook of Hereford cattle and Hereford bull index. Third edition. By John M. Hazelton. Kansas City, Walker publications, inc., 1933. Cloth. OP.
4 p.l., 9–512 p. plates, tables. 23 cm.
Bull index, p. 319–438; general index, p. 508–512.

1021 HEARD, DWIGHT B. Addresses by Dwight B. Heard, president of the American National Live Stock Association at the 19th annual convention of American National Live Stock Association at El Paso, Texas, January 25, 1916. Wrappers. (Cover title). Scarce.
19 p. 23.7 cm.

1022 HEARINGS BEFORE THE COMMITTEE on interstate and foreign commerce of the House of Representatives on H. R. 17721 and 17722 to establish a minimum rate of speed for stock trains. Washington, Government printing office, 1908. Wrappers. Scarce.
35 p. tables. 23 cm.

1023 HEBARD, GRACE RAYMOND. The pathbreakers from river to ocean. The story of the great West from the time of Coronado to the present. ₁By₁ Grace Raymond Hebard, Ph.D. . . . Four maps and numerous illustrations. Chicago, the Lakeside press, 1911. Cloth. Scarce.
x p., 1 l., 263 p. front. plates, ports., maps. 19 cm.
Bibliography, p. 255–257; index, p. 259–263.
Device.

Reprinted by Arthur H. Clark, Glendale, Calif., 1932 and 1940. Pronouncing vocabulary added and different illustrations used.

Chapter VIII on "Cows and Cowboys."

1024 HELLMAN, MRS. WALTER. Blizzard strikes the Rosebud, 1952. Winter of disaster. ₁Compiled and edited by Mrs. Walter Hellman, Millboro, South Dakota, n.d., c.1953₁. Wrappers.
1 p.l., ₁1₁ p., 6–130 p. plates, facsms. 22.8 cm.

1025 HENDERSON, JULIAN, ET AL. Colorado: Short studies of its past and present, by Julian Henderson, E. B. Renaud, Colin B. Goodykoontz, Joe Mills, James F. Willard, H. M. Barrett, Irene Pettit McKeehan, with introduction by George Norlin. Boulder, Colorado, published by the University of Colorado, 1927. Cloth. OP.

x, 202 p. 23.5 cm.

Chapter IV is entitled "Early Range Days," by Joe Mills. This is also published separately. See item No. 1497.

1026 HENRY, STUART OLIVER. Conquering our great American plains. A historical development, by Stuart Henry. . . . Illustrated. New York, E. P. Dutton & co., inc., [1930]. Cloth. OP.

xvi p., 1 l., 3–395 p. front. (map), plates, ports., plan. 21.5 cm.
Appendix, p. 353–381; index, p. 383–395.
Half title; untrimmed.

1027 HENRY, T. C. Addresses by Hon. T. C. Henry of Abilene, Kansas, on "Kansas Stock Interests," and "Kansas Forestry." Abilene, Kansas, Gazette steam printing office, 1882. Wrappers. (Cover title). Rare.

7 p. 24.3 cm.
Double column.

Contains a speech delivered before the Central Kansas Stock Breeders' Association, at Manhattan, February 1, 1882.

1028 HERT, CARL. Tracking the big cats, by Carl Hert, as told to Martha P. McMillin. Illustrated with photographs. Caldwell, Idaho, the Caxton printers, ltd., 1955. Cloth.

8 p.l., [17]–330 p. front., plates, ports. 21.5 cm.
Half title; map on end papers.

1029 HERVEY, GEORGE W. A condensed history of Nebraska for fifty years to date. Profusely and appropriately illustrated. Compiled by Geo. W. Hervey and published by Nebraska Farmer co., Omaha, Neb., 1903. Pict. wrappers. Scarce.

[4]–140 p. front. (map), plates, ports., tables. 20.6 cm.

1030 HICKMAN, GEORGE. History of Marshall County, Dakota. Its topography and natural history and sketches of pioneer settlers, with the names of actual settlers, where they are from, and where they live; also the Military and Sissetin reservations. By George Hickman. Britton, Dakota, J. W. Banbury, publisher, 1886. Wrappers. Rare.

2 p.l., [5]–50 [22] p. illus. 23.2 cm.
Last 20 p. adv.

This copy seen in the Rollins Collection, Princeton University.

1031 HICKMAN, DR. WARREN EDWIN. An echo from the past. A first-hand narration of events of the early history of the Arkansas Valley of Colorado, by Dr. Warren Edwin Hickman. Denver, Colorado, printed by the Western Newspaper Union, 1914. Stiff wrappers. Scarce.

3 p.l., 7–179 p. front. (port.). 19.5 cm.

1032 HIGINBOTHAM, JOHN D. When the West was young. Historical reminiscences of the early Canadian West. By John D. Higinbotham. Toronto, Canada, the Ryerson press, [1933]. Cloth. Scarce.

x, 328 p. front. (port. with tissue), plates, ports., facsms. 21.2 cm.
Appendix, p. 317–321; index, p. 323–328.
Half title; untrimmed.
Colophon: "Author's Edition. Of this edition of When the West Was Young: Historical Reminiscences of the Earl Canadian West, by John D. Higinbotham, five hundred copies only have been printed. This is number —." (Signed).

Also published in trade edition.

1033 HILL, ALEXANDER STAVELEY. From home to home; autumn wanderings in the North-West in the years 1881, 1882, 1883, 1884. By Alex Staveley Hill. Illustrated from sketches by Mrs. Staveley Hill, and photographs by A. S. H. . . . London, Sampson, Low, Marston, Searle & Riverton, 1885. Pict. cloth. Scarce.

vii p., 1 l., 432 [32] p. front. (with tissue), plates, fold. map. 21.8 cm.
Index, p. [427]–432.
Last 32 p. adv.
A second edition issued under the same imprint, collation and date without the 32 p. of adv. at end. Three-quarter leather.

An American edition published in New York by O. Judd Co., 1885.

vii [3], 432 p. front., illus., plates, 2 fold. maps. 22.4 cm.

1034 HILL, EMMA SHEPARD. Foundation stones. Compiled and edited by Emma Shepard Hill. [Denver, Colorado, the Bradford-Robinson printing co., 1926]. Cloth. OP.

5 p.l., [11]–243 p. front. (port.), illus. 19 cm.
Half title: illus. chapter headings.

Some early ranching in Colorado.

1035 HILL, J. L. The end of the cattle trail, by J. L. Hill. Long Beach, Cal., Geo. W. Moyle publishing co., [n. d.]. Wrappers. Scarce.

2 p.l., 5–120 p. front., plates. 22 cm.
Device.

1036 HILL, JOSEPH JOHN. The history of Warner's ranch, and its environs, by Joseph J. Hill, with a preface by Herbert E. Bolton and two etchings by Loren Barton. Los Angeles, California, privately printed, 1927. Cloth and boards. Scarce.

x p., 1 l., 221 p. front. (port. with tissue), plates, ports., facsms., maps. 27.3 cm.
Half title; headpieces; t.p. in red and black; untrimmed.
Colophon: ". . . this edition is limited to three hundred copies for presentation only, of which this is No. —."

Also issued in a trade edition of 1,000 numbered copies.
Colophon: ". . . this edition of one thousand copies have been printed of which this is No. —."

1037 HILL, KATE ADELE. Home builders of West Texas, by Kate Adele Hill. San Antonio, Texas, the Naylor company . . . , 1937. Pict. cloth.

xviii p., 1 l., 108 p. plates, ports., cattle brands. 20 cm.
Half title; map on end papers.

1038 HILL, LUTHER B. A history of the state of Oklahoma, by Luther B. Hill, with the assistance of local authorities. . . . Illustrated. Chicago, New York, the Lewis publishing company, 1909. Leather. Pub. in 2 vols.

Vol. I: xix [1] p., 603 p. plates, ports., maps. 27.5 cm.
Vol. II: xi [1] p., 505 p. plates, ports. (part with tissues). 27.5 cm.
Both volumes double column; seal on t.p.

Reprinted in 1910 with different pagination and fewer pages in Vol. II.

Volume I contains chapters on the cattle industry of the Indian Territory and on the Chisholm Trail and tells of the cattlemen's being forced to vacate the Cherokee Strip (Outlet).

1039 HILZINGER, JOHN GEORGE. Treasure land. A story. Vol. I [the only one published]. Tucson, Arizona, published by the Arizona Advancement company, 1897. Wrappers. Scarce.

2 p.l., [5]–160 [1] p. illus. 23 cm.

1040 HINES, GORDON. True tales of the old 101 Ranch, and other stories. By Gordon Hines. . . . Art by John Selby Metcalf. Oklahoma City, Oklahoma, National printing company, publishers, [1953]. Stiff pict. wrappers.

v, 89 p. illus. 22.8 cm.
Headpieces; marginal drawings.

1041 HINKLE, JAMES FIELDING. Early days of a cowboy on the Pecos, by James F. Hinkle. Roswell, N. M. [privately printed], 1937. Pict. wrappers. Rare.

3–35 p. illus., ports. 17.8 cm.

The experiences of a New Mexico cowboy, written by a man who later became governor of the state. A very rare book, it is said to have been issued in an edition of only thirty-five copies.

1042 HINTON, RICHARD JOSIAH. The hand-book of Arizona; its resources, history, towns, mines, ruins, and scenery. Amply illustrated. Accompanied with a new map of the territory. By Richard J. Hinton. San Francisco, Payot, Upham and co.; New York, American News co., 1878. Cloth. Scarce.

3 p.l., ₁3₁–431 ₁5₁ p. front., illus., maps (1 fold.), tables. 18.9 cm.
Appendix, p. ₁i₁–ci.
43 p. adv. at end.

1043 HOBSON, RICHMOND P., JR. Grass beyond the mountains. Discovering the last great cattle frontier on the North American continent, by Richmond P. Hobson, Jr. Philadelphia, New York, J. B. Lippincott company, ₁1951₁. Cloth.

6 p.l., 13–256 p. 20.8 cm.
Half title; map on end papers; "First edition" on copyright p.

1044 ———. Nothing too good for a cowboy, ₁by₁ Richmond P. Hobson, Jr. Philadelphia and New York, J. B. Lippincott company, ₁1955₁. Boards and cloth.

5 p.l., 11–252 p. 21 cm.
Half title; map on end papers; "First edition" on copyright p.

Ranching and ranch life in British Columbia.

1045 HODGE, HIRAM C. Arizona as it is; or, the coming country. Compiled from notes of travel during the years 1874, 1875, and 1876. By Hiram C. Hodge. New York, published by Hurd and Houghton; Boston, H. O. Houghton and company, 1877. Cloth. Scarce.

xii p., 2 l., ₁13₁–273 p. front. (with tissue), plates, double-p. map. 18 cm.

Chapter on stock raising and grazing lands.

1046 HOGG, Gov. J. S. Proclamation convening the Twenty-second Legislature in special session, and message of Governor J. S. Hogg to the Twenty-second Legislature. ₁Austin₁, Press of Deaf-Mute institute, ₁1892₁. Sewn. Rare.

₁3₁–20 p. 23.5 cm.

Proclamation on livestock quarantining.

1047 HOLBROOK, STEWART H. Far corner, a personal view of the Pacific Northwest. By Stewart H. Holbrook. New York, the Macmillan co., 1952. Cloth.

viii p., 1 l., 3–270 p. 21.6 cm.
Acknowledgments, p. 261–263; index, p. 265–270.
Half title; map on end papers.

1048 HOLCOMBE, A. A. Cattle diseases. Texas fever and pleuro-pneumonia. Symptons and treatment. By A. A. Holcombe. . . . Topeka, Kansas, Kansas publishing house, T. D. Thacker, state printer, 1884. Wrappers. Rare.

10 p. 22.6 cm.

1049 HOLDEN, WILLIAM CURRY. Alkali trails; or social and economic movements of the Texas frontier, 1846–1900, by W. C. Holden. Dallas, Texas, the Southwest press, [1930]. Cloth. Scarce.

ix, 253 p. illus., maps. 24.2 cm.
Biographical footnotes; index, p. 247–253.
Untrimmed.

1050 ———. Rollie Burns; or an account of the ranching industry on the south plains, by William Curry Holden. . . . Dallas, Texas, the Southwest press, [1932]. Pict. cloth. Scarce.

vii, 253 p. front. (port.), 20.5 cm.
Index, p. 237–243.
Untrimmed.

There seems to be some confusion regarding the first state of this book. The publishers first bound 500 copies in tan cloth, with a frontispiece portrait of Rollie Burns. When the publishers went into bankruptcy, they had 500 unbound copies on hand, which were taken over by the author. He had them bound in green cloth by Carl Hertzog, of El Paso, Texas, but as he failed to secure the plates for the cover and the frontispiece, these copies have no frontis. Thus, persons having copies of this book without frontis and bound in green cloth do not have the first state.

1051 ———. The Spur ranch; a study of the inclosed ranch phase of the cattle industry in Texas, by William Curry Holden. . . . Boston, the Christopher publishing house, [1934]. Cloth. OP.

6 p.l., 13–229 p. diagrs. 20.2 cm.
Appendix, p. 209–221; index, p. 223–229.
Half title; map on end papers.

1052 HOLLAND, GUSTAVUS ADOLPHUS. "The double log cabin," being a brief symposium of the early history of Parker County, together with short biographical sketches of early settlers and their trials. . . . Compiled and written by G. A. Holland. [Weatherford, Texas], 1931. Wrappers. Scarce.

1 p.l., [9]–83 p. illus., plates, ports., facsm. 23 cm.

A privately printed little history of a Texas frontier county, which contains, among other material, some information on cattle.

1053 ———. History of Parker County, and the double log cabin; being a brief symposium of the early history of Parker County, together with short biographical sketches of early settlers and their trials, by G. A. Holland, assisted by Violet M. Roberts. Weatherford, Texas, the Herald publishing company, 1937. Cloth. OP.

4 p.l., 11–296 p. plates, ports., facsm. 23.6 cm.
Index, p. 281–296.

This is a greatly expanded edition of the 1931 publication.

1054 ———. The man and his monument. The man was J. R. Couts, his monument the Citizens National Bank. Written and compiled by G. A. Holland.... ₍Weatherford, Texas₎, Press of the Herald publishing co., November, 1924. Wrappers. Scarce.

₍31₎ p. (no pagination), front. (fold. scene). 20.5 cm.
Device.

Has material on the early cattle industry of Parker County.

1055 [HOLLISTER, ORLANDO JAMES]. The resources and attractions of the Territory of Utah. Prepared by the Utah Board of Trade. ₍Omaha₎, printed at the Omaha Republican publishing house, 1879. Wrappers. Rare.

₍3₎–74 p. front., plates, tables, 23.2 cm.

1056 ———. The resources and attractions of Utah. By O. J. Hollister.... Salt Lake City, Tribune printing and publishing co., 1882. Wrappers. Scarce.

₍7₎–93 ₍3₎ p. maps (1 fold.). 22.7 cm.
5 p. adv. in front (incl. verso front wrapper), and adv. on recto and verso back wrapper.

1057 HOLT, O. H. Dakota.... Compiled by O. H. Holt.... Chicago, Rand, McNally & co., printers, 1885. Stiff wrappers. Scarce.

3 p.l., 7–90 ₍6₎ p. illus., large fold. map in front. 22 cm.
Last 6 p. adv.

1058 HOLT, R. D. (ED). Schleicher County; or, Eighty years of development in southwest Texas. Edited by R. D. Holt.... Eldorado, Texas, Eldorado Success, 1930. Pict. wrappers. Scarce.

iv p., 2 l., ₍5₎–110 p. plates, ports. 22.2 cm.

A crudely printed little county history, now becoming scarce, which was written by the pupils of the editor and contains some information on the cattle of that county.

1059 HOLT, WILLIAM F. Memoirs of a Missourian, by William F. Holt, promoter and founder of Imperial Valley, California. Holtville, California, Tribune printing company, ₍c.1944₎. Cloth. OP.

4 p.l., ₍11₎–128 p. 21.7 cm.
Vignette; double column.

1060 HOLTHUSEN, HENRY F.   James W. Wadsworth, Jr., . . . biographical
sketch, by Henry F. Holthusen, with a preface by Hon. Elihu Root. . . .
Illustrated. New York, London, G. P. Putnam's sons, 1926. Cloth.
Scarce.

xi p., 1 l., 3–243 p. front. (port. with tissue), plates, ports. 23.5 cm.
Index, p. 227–243.
Illus. end papers. (dif.).

The subject of this book was the nephew of Mrs. Adair, the co-owner of the
JA Ranch in the Texas Panhandle, and he managed this ranch for five years.
One chapter deals with this phase of his life.

1061 HOPKINS, JOHN A., JR.   Economic history of the production of beef
cattle in Iowa. By John A. Hopkins, Jr.   Iowa City, the State Historical
society, 1928. Cloth. OP.

xii p., 2 l., 248 p. 24.5 cm.
Running title: "Iowa Economic History Series. Edited by Benjamin F. Shambaugh."
Index, p. 241–248.
Half title; untrimmed.

1062 HORAN, JAMES D.   Across the Cimarron, by James D. Horan.   New
York, Crown publishers, inc., [1956]. Cloth and boards.

xvi p., 1 l., 3–301 p. front. (port.), plates, ports., facsms. 21.6 cm.
Half title.

1063 ———, and PAUL SANN.   Pictorial history of the wild West. A true
account of the bad men, desperadoes, rustlers, and outlaws of the old
West—and the men who fought to establish law and order. By James D.
Horan and Paul Sann. New York, Crown publishers, inc., [1954].
Pict. boards and cloth.

4 p.l., [1] p., 10–254 p. front., illus., plates, ports., facsms. 31 cm.
Picture credits, p. 247; bibliography, p. 248–250; index, p. 251–254.
Half title; double column.

Has a section on cowboys and cattle trails.

1064 HORAN, J. W.   On the side of the law. Biography of J. D. Nicholson
. . . , by J. W. Horan. . . . Drawings by James Nicoll. Edmonton, Alberta, published by the Institute of Applied Arts, limited, 1944. Cloth.

7 p.l., 7–275 [4] p. illus., map. 21.8 cm.
Index, last 4 unnumbered pages.

1065 HORGAN, PAUL.   Great River. The Rio Grande in North American
history, by Paul Horgan. New York, Toronto, Rinehart & company, inc.,
1954. Cloth. Pub. in 2 vols. boxed.

Vol. I: xv p., 1 l., 3–447 p. 2 maps (1 double p.). 23.5 cm.
Appendix, p. 443–447.

Vol. II: vii p., 2 l., 453–1020 p.   double-p. map.   23.5 cm.

Appendix, p. 949–953; bibliography, p. 957–977; appendix D, p. 981; index, p. 985–1020.

Half title; double t.p.; first edition, letter "R" in device on copyright p.

Also published in a limited de luxe edition.

1066   HORN, TOM. Life of Tom Horn, government scout and interpreter. Written by himself, together with his letters and statements by his friends. A vindication. Thirteen full page illustrations. Denver, published (for John C. Coble) by the Louthan book company, [1904]. Stiff pict. wrappers. Scarce.

7 p.l., 17[1]–317 p.   front. (port.), plates, ports.   18.8 cm.
Pub. device.

Published also in cloth, but the cloth-bound edition is much rarer than the wrapper-bound copies. Supposedly written by Tom Horn, this book is considered by many people to have been written by Horn's friend and publisher, John C. Coble. Others think it was written by Miss Myrtle Kimmell, Horn's school-teacher friend.

1067   HORNIBROOK, EMMA E. and J. L. Queen of the ranche; or, life in the far West, by Emma E. and J. L. Hornibrook. . . . Illustrated by John Proctor. London, Griffith, Farran, Okeden & Welsh . . . , [c.1890]. Dec. cloth. Scarce.

4 p.l., [11]–317 p.   front. (with tissue), illus.   19.2 cm.
Half title; pub. device; gilt edges.

1068   HORTON, RUFUS LANDON. Philosophy of modern life. An autobiography of a lawyer, by Rufus Landon Horton. Los Angeles, the Times-Mirror press, 1929. Cloth. OP.

xxiv p., 1 l., [27]–303 p.   front. (port.), plates, ports.   20.3 cm.
Half title (with family crest).

Has a chapter on ranching.

1069   HORTON, THOMAS F. History of Jack County. Being accounts of pioneer times, excerpts from county court records, Indian stories, biographical sketches, and interesting events. Written and compiled by Thomas F. Horton. Jacksboro, [Texas], Gazette print, [n.d., c.1932]. Stiff wrappers. Scarce.

2 p.l., 166 p.   23 cm.

This little book is quite scarce because most of the edition was burned. It contains some material on certain notable Texas cattlemen.

1070   HOSMER, HEZEKIAH L. Montana, an address delivered by Chief-Justice H. L. Hosmer before the Traveler's Club, New York City, Jan., 1866.

Published by request. New York, printed by the New York printing co., 1866. Wrappers. (Cover title). Rare.

23 p. 23 cm.

Hosmer was the first chief justice of Montana and brought with him into the territory the first semblance of organized law and order. This work, among the earliest-known books to give authentic information on the region, includes some material on stock raising.

1071 HOUGH, DONALD. Snow above town, by Donald Hough. New York, W. W. Norton & company, inc., [1943]. Cloth. OP.

5 p.l., 11–282 p. 20.5 cm.
Half title; pub. device.
Republished several times.

1072 HOUGH, EMERSON. The passing of the frontier. A chronicle of the old West, by Emerson Hough. New Haven, Yale University press; Toronto, Glascow, Brooks & co.; London, Humphrey Milford, Oxford University press, 1918. Dec. cloth. OP.

x, 181 p. front. (with tissue), plates, ports. (all with tissues), map (fold.). 20.8 cm.
Bibliographical note, p. 175–178; index, p. 179–181.
Half title; vignette; untrimmed.

Has a chapter on cattle trails, one on cattle kings, and another on cowboys.

1073 ———. The story of the cowboy, by E. Hough. . . . Illustrated by William L. Wells and C. M. Russell. New York, D. Appleton and company, 1897. Dec. cloth.

xii, 349 [6] p. front., plates. 19.5 cm.
Addenda, p. 345–349.
Half title; 6 p. adv. at end.

Reprinted many times through the years. Published in 1908 under the title *The Cowboy* in two volumes as a part of a twelve-volume set under the general title of "Builders of a Nation":

Vol. I, Builders of a Nation. The cowboy, I, by E. Hough. . . . Illustrated. New York, the Brampton society, publishers, [1908]. Cloth.

Vol. I: x, 181 p. front. (col. with tissue), plates (all with tissues). 21.3 cm.
Addenda, p. 345–349.
Vol. II: 4 p.l., 182–394 p. front., 6 plates (incl. front., part with tissues). 21.3 cm.
Half title (both volumes): "Builders of the Nation, or From the Indian Trail to the Railroad. National edition complete in twelve volumes"; t.p. in red and black; untrimmed; at head of t.p.: "National Edition, Complete In Twelve Volumes."

1074 HOUSE, BOYCE. City of flaming adventure. The chronicle of San Antonio, by Boyce House. Illustrations by Melvan D. Jordan. San Antonio, the Naylor co., [1949]. Cloth.

ix, 214 p. front. (port.), illus. 21.6 cm.
Acknowledgments and bibliography, p. 201–206; index, p. 209–214.
Half title; illus. end papers.

1075 ———. Texas treasure chest, by Boyce House. San Antonio, Texas, the Naylor company, [1956]. Pict. cloth.
ix p., 1 l., 3–187 p. 28 cm.
Acknowledgments, p. 187.
Half title; vignette.

1076 HOUSEMAN, WILLIAM. Cattle, breeds and management, by William Houseman. With a chapter on diseases of cattle, by Prof. J. Worthley Axe. Illustrated. London, Vinton and co., ltd., 1897. Cloth. Scarce.
270 p. plates. 21.7 cm.
Head of title: "Livestock Hand Book No. 4, edited by James Sinclair."

1077 [HOUSTON, DAVID FRANKLIN]. Marketing of livestock. Address of Hon. David F. Houston, secretary of agriculture; Hon. Walter L. Fisher, attorney, market committee of American National Live Stock Association. Delivered at twentieth annual convention of the American National Live Stock Association held at Cheyenne, Wyoming, January 18 to 20, 1917. Denver, Colo., published by Market Committee of the American National Live Stock association, 1917. Wrappers. (Cover title). Scarce.
18 p. 22.5 cm.

1078 HOWARD, JOSEPH KINSEY. Montana, high, wide, and handsome, by Joseph Kinsey Howard. New Haven, Yale University press . . . , 1943. Cloth. OP.
vi p., 3 l., 1 p., [8]–347 p. 21 cm.
Acknowledgments and bibliography, p. [330]–339; index, p. [341]–347.
Map on end papers.

1079 HOWARD, ROBERT WEST (ED.). This is the West. Edited by Robert West Howard. Illustrated. New York, Chicago, San Francisco, Rand, McNally & company, [1957]. Cloth.
4 p.l., 248 p. illus., plates, map. 24.2 cm.
Appendix, p. 221–248.
Half title.

First published as a Signet book (paper back).
4 p.l., 240 p. 18 cm.
Illus. double t.p.

1080 HOWE, CHARLES WILLIS. Timberleg of the Diamond Tail and other frontier anecdota, by Charles Willis Howe. Illustrated by R. L. McCollister. San Antonio, Texas, the Naylor company, [1949]. Pict. cloth.
ix, 153 p. 21.6 cm.
Half title; illus. chapter headings.

1081 Howe, Evlon L. (ED.). Rocky Mountain empire. Revealing glimpses of the West in transition from old to new, from the pages of the Rocky Mountain Empire Magazine of the Denver Post, edited by Evlon L. Howe. With a foreword by Palmer Hoyt. Garden City, N. Y., Doubleday & company, inc., [1950]. Cloth.

xiv p., 1 l., 272 p. 21 cm.
Half title; map on end papers; illus. chapter headings; pub. device; untrimmed; "First edition" on copyright p.

1082 [Howe, S. Ferdinand]. The commerce of Kansas City in 1886; with a general review of its business progress. Kansas City, Mo., S. Ferd. Howe, publisher, 1886. Dec. cloth. Scarce.

8 p.l., [17]–288 p. front., illus., maps, plan. 20.5 cm.
Index, p. 285–288.

Deals with the cattle trade and Kansas City as a packing center.

1083 Howes, Charles C. This place called Kansas, by Charles C. Howes. Norman, University of Oklahoma press, [1952]. Cloth.

xi p., 1 l., 3–236 p. illus., plates, ports., maps. 22 cm.
Index, p. 225–236.
Half title; double t.p.; "First edition" on copyright p.

Much on Abilene during its cowtown days and the cattle trails which led to it.

1084 Hoyt, Henry Franklin. A frontier doctor, by Henry F. Hoyt; with an introduction by Frank B. Kellogg, and with illustrations. Boston and New York, Houghton Mifflin company, 1929. Cloth. Scarce.

xv, 260 p. front. (port.), plates, ports., facsms. 21.3 cm.
Half title; pub. device; untrimmed; first edition, "1929" under imprint.

1085 [Hoyt, John W.]. Message of Governor Hoyt to the Sixth Legislative Assembly of Wyoming Territory convened at Cheyenne, November 4, 1879. Cheyenne, Wyoming, Leader steam book and job printing house, 1879. Wrappers. Scarce.

[3]–94 p. 22 cm.

1086 ———. Report of the Governor of Wyoming Territory made to the Secretary of the Interior for the year 1878. Washington, Government printing office, 1878. Wrappers. Rare.

2 p.l., [5]–61 p. 23 cm.

1087 Hubbard, Elbert. Little journeys to the homes of great business men, by Elbert Hubbard. John B. Stetson, done into a book by the Roycrofters at their shop, which is in East Aurora, Erie County, New York, MCMXI. Leather.

2 p.l., 7–52 [1] p. front. (port.), plate (double p.), ports. 20.8 cm.
Col. t.p.

Also published in wrappers.

[3]–32 [1] p. front. (port.), 1 plate (double p.). 20.3 cm.
T.p. in red and black.

1088 HUCKABY, IDA LASATER. Ninety-four years in Jack County, 1854–1948. Written and compiled by Ida Lasater Huckaby. [Austin, the Steck company, 1949]. Cloth.

xvi p., 1 l., [3]–513 [1] p. plates, ports., fold. map, tables. 23.7 cm.

1089 HUGHES, DAN DE LARA. South from Tombstone. A life story, by Dan de Lara Hughes. London, Methuen and co., ltd., [1938]. Cloth. Scarce.

v p., 1 l., 311 [1] p. 20.3 cm.

Cowboy experiences in Arizona.

1090 HUGHES, MARION. Oklahoma Charley, by Marion Hughes . . . Oklahoma Charley . . . miner, cowboy, corndoctor, Indian scout, invalid, prospector, polygamist, horsetrader. . . . St. Louis, John P. Wagner & co., [1910]. Pict. wrappers. Scarce.

2 p.l., [7]–159 p. front., illus. 18.8 cm.

1091 HUGHES, THOMAS (ED.). G T T, gone to Texas; letters from our boys, edited by Thomas Hughes. London, Macmillan and co., 1884. Cloth. Scarce.

xiii p., 2 l., [3]–228 p. 19.7 cm.
Half title.

American edition published same year in New York.

1092 HUIDEKOPER, A. C. My experience and investment in the Bad Lands of Dakota and some of the men I met there. By A. C. Huidekoper. Introduction by Usher L. Burdick. Baltimore, Wirth brothers, 1947. Stiff wrappers.

2 p.l., [5]–58 p. front., plates, ports. 22.8 cm.

1093 HUIDEKOPER, WALLIS. The land of the Decotahs, by Wallis Huidekoper. Helena, Montana, published and distributed by the Montana Stockgrowers' association, [n.d.]. Wrappers. (Cover title). OP.

16 p. illus., plates, map on verso of covers. 28.8 cm.
Author's signature in facsm. at end; double column.

1094 ——. Modern beef cattle breeding and ranching methods, by Wallis Huidekoper. . . . Helena, Montana, published and distributed by the

Montana Stockgrowers' association, [1940]. Pict. wrappers. (Cover title). OP.

10 p. illus. 29.6x22 cm.
Double column; blank leaf for notes at end.

Also published in Cheyenne, Wyoming, no date.

16 [1] p. illus. 22.8 cm.

1095 HULTZ, FRED S. Range beef production in the seventeen western states. By Fred S. Hultz. New York, John Wiley and sons, inc.; London, Chapman and Hall, ltd., 1930. Cloth. OP.

xv, 208 p. front., plates, ports., charts, diagrs., tables, maps. 21 cm.
Index, p. 201–208.
Half title.

1096 ———. Wintering range calves. By Fred S. Hultz. University of Wyoming Agricultural Experiment Station, *Bulletin No. 134*, May, 1923. Laramie, Experiment Station, [1923]. Wrappers. (Cover title). OP.

16 p. 1 plate, tables. 22.4 cm.

1097 [HULTZ, FRED S., and S. S. WHEELER]. Type in two-year-old beef steers. [By Fred S. Hultz and S. S. Wheeler]. University of Wyoming Agricultural Experiment Station, *Bulletin No. 155*, June, 1927. Laramie, Experiment Station, [1927]. Wrappers.

147 p. illus., charts, tables. 22.8 cm.

1098 HUM-ISHU-MA. Co-ge-we-a, the half blood. A description of the great Montana cattle range, by Hum-ishu-ma "Mourning Dove". . . . With notes and biographical sketch by Lucullus Virgil McWhorter. Boston, Big Four Seas co., publishers, [1927]. Cloth. OP.

7 p.l., 15–302 p. front. (port.), 19.3 cm.
[Notes on chapters], p. 287–302.
Half title; leaf of errata tipped in.

1099 HUMPHREY, SETH KING. Following the prairie frontier, [by] Seth K. Humphrey. [Minneapolis], the University of Minnesota press, [1931]. Cloth. OP.

5 p.l., 264 [1] p. front. 21.2 cm.
Half title; vignette.

1100 HUNT, FRAZIER. Cap Mossman, last of the great cowmen, by Frazier Hunt. With sixteen illustrations by Ross Santee. New York, Hastings House, publishers, [1951]. Pict. cloth.

5 p.l., 3–277 p. illus. 21 cm.
Half title; illus. end papers (each different); vignette.

1101 ——. The long trail from Texas; the story of Ad Spaugh, cattleman, by Frazier Hunt. New York, Doubleday, Doran & company, Inc.,
1940. Cloth.

5 p.l., 300 p. front. (map). 20.6 cm.
Half title; vignette; untrimmed; "First Edition" on copyright p.
"This story was published serially under the title 'The Last Frontier.'"

1102 HUNT, LENOIR. Bluebonnets and blood. The romance of "Tejas," by
Lenoir Hunt. . . . Illustrated with drawings, photographs, and maps.
Houston, Texas, Texas books, inc., [1938]. Thin boards (imt. cloth.).
Scarce.

xv p., 1 l., 3–433 p. front., plates, ports., maps, facsm. 23.3 cm.
Bibliography, p. 407–409; [notes], p. 413–427; index, p. 431–433.
Vignette.
Colophon (pasted on inside front cover): "Each of five hundred copies of the
Founders' DeLuxe edition of Bluebonnets and Blood is numbered and autographed
by the author."

1103 HUNTER, JOHN MARVIN (ED.). The trail drivers of Texas. Interesting
sketches of early cowboys and their experiences on the range and on
the trail during the days that tried men's souls. True narratives related
by real cow-punchers and men who fathered the cattle industry in Texas.
Published under the direction of George W. Saunders, president of the
Old Trail Drivers' Association. Compiled and edited by J. Marvin Hunter. [San Antonio, Texas, Jackson printing co., 1920–1923]. Pub. in 2
vols. Pict. cloth. Scarce.

Vol. I: [3]–498 p. ports. 23.3 cm.
Index to contents, p. 493–498.
Vol. II: [3]–496 [1] p. plates, ports. 22 cm.
Index to contents, p. 491–496.

Vol. I published in 1920; vol. II in 1923. Both crudely printed and bound.

The first volume was exhausted before the second volume appeared; there-
fore it was reprinted in 1924 with some revisions and additions in an edition
of 500 copies with a "second edition" imprint.

[San Antonio, Globe printing co., 1924]. Pict. cloth. Scarce.

[5]–494 p. plates, ports. 22.8 cm.
Index to contents, p. 488–494.

Both volumes republished in one volume by the Cokesbury press, Nashville, in 1925.

xvi, 1044 p. front., plates, ports. 23.5 cm.

In spite of the crudeness of the two volumes, they are perhaps the most important single contribution to the history of cattle driving on the western trails.

1104 HUNTER, LILLIE MAE. The moving finger, by Lillie Mae Hunter, with illustrations by Bill Hacker. Borger, Texas, Plains printing company, 1956. Cloth.

6 p.l., 171 p. illus. 22.4 cm.

Much on the cattle business of West Texas.

1105 HUNTINGTON, WILLIAM (BILL). Bill Huntington's good men and salty cusses. Illustrated by J. K. Ralston. [Billings, Mont., Western Livestock Reporter press, 1952]. Cloth.

3 p.l., 207 p. illus. 21 cm.
Colophon (pasted on back flyleaf): "This is copy number —— of the limited edition of 2000 imprints."

1106 HUNTON, JOHN. John Hunton's diary. Echoes from 1875 (with glimpses at 1873). [Lingle, Wyoming, printed by Guide-Review, 1956]. Imt. suede.

8 p.l., 15–134 [1] p. illus., ports., fold. map at end. 15.2 cm.
Colophon: "This is number —— of 1500 copies [signed by L. G. Flannery, editor], Fort Laramie, Wyoming."
Marked vol. I.

1107 HURD, C. W. Boggsville, cradle of the Colorado cattle industry, by C. W. Hurd. [Las Animas, published by the Boggsville Committee, 1957]. Pict. wrappers. (Cover title).

2 p.l., 89 [3] p. plates, ports. 23 cm.
Index, p. [90–92].

Chapters on the various ranches of Bent County, Colorado.

1108 HUSON, HOBART. Refugio. A comprehensive history of Refugio County from aboriginal times to 1953. By Hobart Huson, LL.B., Refugio, Texas. . . . Woodsboro, Texas, the Rooke foundation, inc., 1953. Pub. in 2 vols. Cloth.

Vol. I: xvi p., 1 l., 596 [20] p. plates, ports. 23.8 cm.
Half title; last 20 p. plates and ports.
Vol. II: xiii p., 1 l., 633 [1] p. ports., facsms. 23.8 cm.
Appendix, p. 447–499; bibliography, p. 501–536; index (for both volumes): p. 539–633.

Contains a long chapter on the early cattle industry of Refugio County, Texas.

1109 HUTCHINSON, BRUCE. The Frazier, by Bruce Hutchinson. Illustrated by Richard Bennett. New York, Toronto, Rinehart and co., inc., [1950]. Cloth.

8 p.l., 5–368 p. front. (double-p. map), illus. 20.7 cm.
Bibliography, p. 351–355; index, p. 357–368.
Half title, "Rivers of America Series."

1110 HUTCHINSON, CLINTON CARRER. Resources of Kansas. Fifteen years' experience, by C. C. Hutchinson, with a new map and forty illustrations. Topeka, Kansas, published by the author, 1871. Cloth. Scarce.

vii, [9]–287 [1] p. front., illus., fold. map at end, tables. 18.5 cm.
Index, p. [285]–287.
Reprinted with additions in 1886.

1111 HUTCHINSON, W. H. Another notebook of the old West, by W. H. Hutchinson. Companion volume to *A Notebook of the old West*. Chico, designed and printed at Chico, California, by Hurst & Yount, [1954]. Stiff pict. wrappers.

4 p.l., 88 p. illus. 23.3 cm.
Vignette.

A chapter on the Johnson County War.

1112 ———. The life and personal writings of Eugene Manlove Rhodes, a Bar Cross man. [By] W. H. Hutchinson. Norman, University of Oklahoma press, [1956]. Cloth.

xix p., 2 l., 3–432 [1] p. illus., plates, ports., map, facsms. 23.5 cm.
Check list of Eugene Manlove Rhodes' writings, p. 392–407; index, p. 409–432.
Half title; illus. t.p.

1113 HUTTO, JOHN R. Howard County in the making. . . . By John R. Hutto. [N. p., Jordan's print], 1938. Wrappers. (Cover title). OP. [75] p. (no pagination). 22 cm.

A privately printed little county history with chapters on some early Texas ranches and ranchmen.

1114 HYDE, CHARLES LEAVITT. Pioneer days; the story of an adventurous and active life, by Charles L. Hyde. . . . New York, G. P. Putnam's sons, 1939. Cloth. OP.

xv p., 1 l., 19–286 p. front. (port.), plates, ports. 24.2 cm.
An account of the author's family, p. 227–283.
Half title; pub. device.

1115 HYER, JULIEN. The land of beginning again. The romance of the Brazos, by Julien Hyer. Illustrated by Merritt Mauzey. Atlanta, Tupper & Love, inc., [1952]. Pict. cloth. Op.

xi p., 1 l., 3–394 p. illus. 21.5 cm.
Half title; illus. t.p.; map on end papers.

1116 IDAHO. Resources and attractions of Idaho. Facts on farming, stock raising, mining, lumbering, and other industries, and notes on climate, scenery, game, fish, and health and pleasure resorts. . . . Omaha, 1888. Wrappers. Rare.

[3]–72 p. map on verso front wrapper. 21.2 cm.

Another of those promotional books issued by the Union Pacific Railroad.

1117 ———. Idaho. Blaine, Shoshone, Kootenai, Bannock, Bear Lake counties. [N. p., n. d.]. Wrappers. Rare.
16 p. 21.8 cm.

1118 ———. Idaho, a guide in word and picture. Prepared by the Federal
Writers' Project of the Works Progress Administration. The Library edition. Caldwell, Idaho, the Caxton printers, ltd., 1937. Pict. cloth.
8 p.l., [17]–431 p. front., plates, maps. 23.6 cm.
Selected bibliography, p. [415]–418; acknowledgments, p. [419]–421; index, p.
[423]–431.
Half title.

1119 ———. Idaho, its resources and advantages. Facts and statistics concerning farming, stock-raising, mining, lumbering. . . . Omaha, Nebraska, published by the general passenger department, Union Pacific
Ry., 1887. Wrappers. Rare.
3–48 p. map on recto back wrapper. 21.2 cm.

1120 ———. The resources and attractions of Idaho. Facts on farming,
stock-raising, mining, lumbering, and other industries. . . . St. Louis,
Woodward & Tiernan printing co., 1888. Wrappers. Rare.
3 p.l., [7]–128 p. map on verso front wrapper. 20.7 cm.

1121 ILLINGWORTH, S. E. Report on the Rio Arriba Land and Cattle company, limited. [N. p., 1887]. Folder. Rare.
11 p. 32.8 cm.

1122 ILLINOIS. Annual report of the Board of Live Stock Commissioners,
for the state of Illinois, for the fiscal year ending October 31, A.D., 1889.
Springfield, Ill., Springfield printing co., state printers, 1890. Wrappers. Scarce.
2 p.l., [5]–26 p. tables. 22 cm.

1123 ———. Annual report of the Board of Live Stock Commissioners,
for the state of Illinois, for the fiscal year ending October 31, A.D., 1891.
Springfield, Ill., H. W. Rokker, state printer and binder, 1892. Wrappers. Scarce.
2 p.l., [5]–29 p. tables. 22 cm.

1124 INDIAN TERRITORY. Brand book of the Cherokee National Stockman's
Protective and Detective Association. John A. Foreman, secretary Stock
Association. . . . Vinita, I. T., Indian Chieftain, [n.d.]. Wrappers. Rare.
58 p. illus., plates, cattle brands. 16.6 cm.

1125 ———. Cherokee Strip brand book. Authorized by stockmen's convention held at Caldwell, Kansas, March 16, 1881. This strip lies west

of the Arkansas River, north of Cimarron, and south of Kansas line. Kansas City, Sam L. C. Rhodes, printer, 1881. Wrappers. Rare.

66 [2] p. 14.7x9 cm.

Last 10 p. adv.; proceedings of convention and brands of members.

1126 ———. Choctaw Live Stock Protective Association of the Indian Territory, headquarters Lehigh, I. T. . . . [Lehigh, I. T., 1901]. Wrappers. Scarce.

186 [5] p. cattle brands. 12.7 cm.

Brands, constitution, and by-laws of the Choctaw Live Stock Protective Association of the Indian Territory.

1127 ———. Choctaw Protective Association of the Indian Territory, headquarters Lehigh, I. T. Atoka Indian Citizen, 1903. Wrappers. Rare.

167 [1] p. cattle brands. 12.5 cm.

1128 ———. Choctaw Protective Association of the Indian Territory, headquarters Lehigh, I. T. [N. p., 1904]. Wrappers. Rare.

241 p. cattle brands. 12 cm.

1129 ———. Statistics and information concerning the Indian Territory, Oklahoma, and the Cherokee Strip, with its millions of acres of unoccupied lands, for the farmer and stock raiser. Great inducements for the investment of capital. Interesting sights and scenes for the tourist and pleasure-seeker. With compliments of the general passenger department of the Missouri Railway co. [St. Louis, Woodward & Tiernan printing co., 1893]. Wrappers. Rare.

3–85 p. illus., large fold. folio lithographic map (col.), tables. 20.5 cm.

Last 3 p. adv.; adv. verso front wrapper, recto and verso back wrapper.

1130 INFORME de la comisión pesquisdora de la frontera del norte al ejectivo de la unión en cumplimiento del artículo 3° de la ley de 30 de Setiembre de 1872. Monterey, Mayo 15 de 1873. Méjico, imprenta de Diaz de León y White, calle de Lerdo numero 2, 1874. Wrappers. Rare.

[3]–124 p. 28.7 cm.

Device.

1131 INMAN, HENRY. The old Santa Fe Trail. The story of a great highway, by Colonel Henry Inman. New York, London, the Macmillan co., 1897. Pict. cloth. Scarce.

xvi p., 1 l., 493 p. front. (port.), illus., 8 full-page plates, fold. map. 21.5 cm.

"Plates by Frederic Remington." Each plate, except one, accompanied by guard sheet with descriptive letterpress.

Reprinted in 1899 and 1916.

Information on the Maxwell ranch and John Chisum.

1132 ———. The ranche on the Oxhide; a story of boys and girls on the frontier, by Henry Inman. Six full-page illustrations. New York, London, the Macmillan co., 1898. Cloth. Scarce.

xiii, 297 p. front., illus., plates. 19.5 cm.
4 l. adv. at end.
Reprinted in 1923.

1133 INTERIOR DEPARTMENT. The action of the Interior Department in forcing the Standing Rock Indians to lease their lands to cattle syndicates. Philadelphia, 1902. Sewn. (Caption title). Rare.

27 p. 22.9 cm.

1134 INTERNATIONAL CATTLE COMPANY. Memorandum and articles of association of the International Cattle company, ltd. London, Stibbard, Gibson and co., [1886]. Wrappers. Rare.

31 p. 23.3 cm.

1135 INTERNATIONAL COMMISSION. Report of the International Commission on the control of bovine tuberculosis. Reprint from Forty-Seventh Annual Report of the American Veterinary Medical Association. Presented to the American Veterinary Medical Association, September, 1910. Wrappers. Scarce.

31 p. 22.2 cm.

1136 INTERSTATE EXECUTIVE COMMITTEE. Cattle growers' interstate executive committee. The transportation, tax wrongs, and remedy. Denver, Cattle Growers' Interstate Executive Committee, [1904]. Wrappers. (Cover title). Scarce.

48 p. 23 cm.

1137 [IRISH, JOHN P.]. Land leasing. Speech by Col. John P. Irish, of California, before the convention of the American Cattle Growers' Association at Denver, Colorado, March 25, 1902. In support of a resolution to approve Senate Bill 3311, to lease the public lands in the arid states for grazing purposes. Denver, the Smith-Brooks printing co., [n.d., c.1902]. Wrappers. (Cover title). Scarce.

25 p. 22.3 cm.

1138 ISLEY, BLISS. Early days in Kansas. By Bliss Isley. [Wichita], published by the Wichita Board of Education ..., 1927. Pict. wrappers. OP.

3 p.l., [5]–152 p. front., illus., ports. 19 cm.

1139 ———, and W. M. RICHARDS. Four centuries in Kansas. Unit studies, by Bliss Isley and W. M. Richards. Wichita, Kansas, the McCormick-Mathers company, [1936]. Pict. cloth. OP.

viii p., 1 l., 3–344 p. illus., ports., maps. 20 cm.
Bibliography, p. 332–338; index, p. 339–344.
Illus. end papers; suggestions for further study and reference at end of each chapter except Unit XII.

1140 JACKSON, A. P., and E. C. COLE. Oklahoma! Politically and topographically described! History and guide to the Indian Territory. Biographical sketches of Capt. David L. Payne, W. L. Crouch, Wm. H. Osborn, and others. A complete guide to the Indian Territory. Illustrated with map, hunting and fishing grounds. By A. P. Jackson and E. C. Cole. Kansas City, Mo., Publishing House of Ramsey, Millett & Hudson, [1885]. Cloth. Rare.

2 p.l., [5]–150 [2] p. front. (port.), illus., plates, large fold. map in front. 19.5 cm.
2 p. adv. at end.

1141 JACKSON, GEORGE. Sixty years in Texas. . . . [Dallas, Texas, Wilkinson printing co., 1908]. Wrappers. Scarce.

5 p.l., 384 p. front. (port.), illus., plates, ports. 22.5 cm.

1142 JACKSON, W. H., and S. A. LONG. The Texas stock directory; or, book of marks and brands. In a series of volumes designed to embrace the entire state. By W. H. Jackson . . . and S. A. Long. . . . Vol. I [only one published]. San Antonio, printed at the Herald office, 1865. Pict. boards. Exceedingly rare.

402 p. front. (on green paper), cattle brands. 16.5 cm.
Index, p. 373–402.
Calendar of 1866 on verso front cover; 50 numbered pages of adv. at end.

Some copies were bound in salmon pink boards, some in light gray. There were many errors which were corrected by hand, such as on page 127, "W M" corrected to "M W"; on page 210, "Flying Quarter Circle" corrected to "N Bar"; on page 364, "S. Wilson" changed to "S. Wiley" on brand "UP." Page 266 follows page 268, and page 370 has no folio. Later reprinted in facsimile in a limited edition by The Book Farm, New Braunfels, Texas. As stated in the text, this work was intended to cover each county in the state, but aside from the supplement (see item No. 1143 below) the work fell through.

1143 ———. Supplement to Volume I, Texas stock directory, [by] W. H. Jackson and S. A. Long. San Antonio, 1866. Victoria County. Wrappers. Exceedingly rare.

61 p. cattle brands. 16 cm.

1144 JACKSON, W. TURRENTINE. The Wyoming Stock Growers' Association: political power in Wyoming Territory, 1873–1890. By W. Turrentine Jackson. Reprinted from the *Mississippi Valley Historical Review,* Vol. XXXIII, No. 4 (March, 1947). Stiff wrappers. (Cover title). OP.

p. 571–594. 24.5 cm.

1145 ——. The Wyoming Stock Growers' Association, its years of temporary decline, 1886–1890. [By] W. Turrentine Jackson. Reprinted from *Agricultural History,* Vol. XXII (October, 1948). Wrappers. (Cover title). OP.

p. 260–270. 25 cm.
Double column.

1146 JAHNS, PAT. The frontier world of Doc Holliday, faro dealer from Dallas to Deadwood, by Pat Jahns. New York, Hastings House, publishers, [1957]. Cloth and boards.

xii p., 1 l., 3–305 p. 21.6 cm.
Bibliography, p. 287–293; index, p. 295–305; footnotes after each chapter.
Half title.

Has some information on Dodge City during the days of the trail drives and on cowboys.

1147 JAMES, GEORGE WHARTON. Arizona, the wonderland. The history of its ancient cliff and cave dwellers, ruined pueblos, conquest by the Spaniards, Jesuit and Franciscan missions, trail makers and Indians; a survey of its climate, scenic marvels, topography, deserts, mountains, rivers, and valleys; a review of its industries; an account of its influence on art, literature, and science; and some references to what it offers of delight to the automobilist, sportsman, pleasure and health seeker. By George Wharton James. . . . With a map and sixty plates of which twelve are in colour. Boston, the Page company, MDCCCCXVII. Pict. cloth. OP.

xxiv, 478 p. front. (col. with tissue), plates (part col.), ports., fold. map. 24.6 cm.
Bibliography, p. 467–468; index, p. 469–478.
Half title; illus. end papers (dif.); untrimmed; on verso of t.p., "See America First Series."
Each colored plate accompanied by guard tissue with descriptive letterpress.

1148 JAMES, JASON W. Memories and viewpoints. By Capt. Jason W. James. Roswell, N. M., 1928. Cloth. Scarce.

7 p.l., [15]–183 p. 18.8 cm.

Ranching on the Río Grande in 1883.

1149 JAMES, VINTON LEE. Frontier and pioneer recollections of early days in San Antonio and west Texas, by Vinton Lee James, San Antonio, Texas, published by the author, Artes Graficas press, 1938. Cloth. Scarce.

7 p.l., 15–210 p. plates, ports. 23.8 cm.
Half title.

1150 JAMES, WILLIAM RODERICK. All in the day's riding, by Will James;

illustrated by the author. New York, London, Charles Scribner's sons, 1933. Pict. cloth.

xiv p., 1 l., 251 ₁1₁ p. illus. 24 cm.

Half title; illus. t.p.; untrimmed; first edition, letter "A" on copyright p.

1151 ———. American cowboy, by Will James. Illustrated by the author. New York, Charles Scribner's sons, 1942. Cloth.

6 p.l., 273 p. illus., plates. 21.5 cm.

Half title; vignette; untrimmed; first edition, letter "A" on copyright p.

1152 ———. Cow country, by Will James; illustrated by the author. New York, London, Charles Scribner's sons, 1927. Pict cloth.

xii p., 1 l., 3–242 p. front., illus., plates. 24 cm.

Half title; vignette; untrimmed; first edition, letter "A" on copyright p.

1153 ———. Cowboys north and south, by Will James; illustrated by the author. New York and London, Charles Scribner's sons, 1924. Pict. cloth.

xvii p., 1 l., 3–217 p. front., illus., plates. 24 cm.

Half title; vignette; untrimmed; first edition, letter "A" on copyright p.

1154 ———. The drifting cowboy, by Will James; illustrated by the author. New York, London, Charles Scribner's sons, 1925. Cloth and pict. boards.

xii p., 1 l., 3–241 p. illus., plates. 24.2 cm.

Half title; vignette; first edition, letter "A" on copyright p.

1155 ———. Home ranch, by Will James; illustrated by the author. New York, Charles Scribner's sons; London, Charles Scribner's sons, ltd., 1935. Cloth.

xvii p., 1 l., 3–346 p. front., illus., plates. 21.4 cm.

Half title; vignette; untrimmed; first edition, letter "A" on copyright p.

1156 ———. Horses I have known, by Will James. New York, Charles Scribner's sons, 1940. Cloth.

xv p., 1 l., 280 ₁1₁ p. front. (col.), illus., plates. 21.5 cm.

Half title; vignette; untrimmed; first edition, letter "A" on copyright p.

1157 ———. Lone cowboy; my life story, by Will James; illustrated by the author. New York, London, Charles Scribner's sons, 1930. Pict. cloth.

x p., 1 l., 431 ₁2₁ p. front. (port.), illus., plates, facsms. 21.5 cm.

Half title; vignette; untrimmed; first edition, letter "A" on copyright p.

1158 ———. Sun up; tales of the cow camps, by Will James. New York, London, Charles Scribner's sons, 1931. Cloth. Col. illus. pasted on.

4 p.l., 342 p.   front., illus., facsm.   23 cm.
Half title; vignette; untrimmed; first edition, letter "A" on copyright p.

Will James wrote some fourteen other books, but since they are either juvenile or fiction, they have no place in this work.

1159   JAMES, W. S.   Cow-boy life in Texas; or, 27 years a mavrick [*sic*]. A realistic and true recital of wild life on the boundless plains of Texas, being the actual experience of twenty-seven years in the exciting life of a genuine cow-boy among the roughs and toughs of Texas. Over fifty illustrations taken from life. By W. S. James.   Chicago, Donohue, Henneberry & co., publishers, [1893].   Pict. cloth.   Scarce.
7 p.l., 21–213 p.   front. (port.), 34 plates (incl. front.).   19.7 cm.
Reprinted in Chicago without date under title, *Twenty-seven Years a Mavrick; or, Life on a Texas Range.*
Reprinted in 1898 under the imprint of M. A. Donohue with seven fewer plates.

I have never seen a copy of this book with fifty illustrations as stated in the title. Both editions of this scarce book are crudely printed on cheap paper, but are much sought by collectors of cattle books.

1160   JANIVER, THOMAS A.   Santa Fe's partner. Being some memorials of events in a New Mexico track-end town, by Thomas A. Janiver.   New York, London, Harper and brothers, publishers, 1907.   Pict. cloth.   Scarce.
6 p.l., 237 p.   front., illus.   19 cm.

1161   JAQUES, MARY J.   Texan ranch life; with three months through Mexico in a "prairie schooner." By Mary J. Jaques.   London, Horace Cox . . . , 1894.   Pict. cloth.   Scarce.
x p., 1 l., 363 p.   front. (with tissue), illus., plates.   25.5 cm.
Half title.

1162   JARDINE, JAMES TERTIUS, and CLARENCE L. FORSLING.   Range and cattle management during drought. By James T. Jardine . . . and Clarence L. Forsling. . . .   Washington, Government printing office, 1922.   Wrappers.   (Cover title).   OP.
83 p.   plates, charts, tables.   23.2 cm.
U. S. Dept. of Agriculture *Bulletin No. 1031.*

1163   JARDINE, JAMES TERTIUS, and C. L. HURTT.   Increased cattle production on southwest ranges. By James T. Jardine and C. L. Hurtt. . . .   Washington, Government printing office, 1917.   Wrappers.   (Cover title).   OP.
32 p.   incl. double-p. map, 2 diagrs., xii plates on 6 p.   23 cm.
"List of publications relating to this subject . . . ," p. 32.
Contribution from the Forest Service.

1164   [JARVIS, JUDSON].   Grass is king. [By Judson Jarvis].   [New York, 1883].   Stiff wrappers.   Rare.

24 p. 2 fold. maps (col.), tables. 24.4 cm.
"For private circulation only."

Extracts from reports on cattle raising in New Mexico.

1165 JASTROM, H. A. Annual address of H. A. Jastrom, president of the American National Live Stock Association, delivered at the 17th annual convention at Denver, Colorado, January 20, 1914. ₍Denver, 1914₎. Wrappers. (Cover title). Scarce.

16 p. 22.7 cm.

1166 JEFFREY, J. K. The territory of Wyoming; its history, soil, climate, resources etc. Published by authority of the Board of Immigration. Laramie City, Daily Sentinel print, December, 1874. Wrappers. Rare.

3–83 ₍1₎ p. tables. 22 cm.

An early Laramie imprint and one of the earliest descriptions of Wyoming Territory. Said to be the first book printed in Laramie. A rare and much sought item of early Wyoming with information relating to the first days of stock raising and mining. The "Journal of Travels in the Territory" (p. 45–83) is from the pen of E. A. Curley, who explored the region in 1873 and 1874.

1167 JELINEK, GEORGE. Ellsworth, Kansas, 1867–1947, by George Jelinek. Salina, published by Consolidated, ₍1947₎. Stiff wrappers. OP.

2 p.l., 5–32 p. plates, ports., facsm. 21.5 cm.

1168 ———. 90 years of Ellsworth and Ellsworth County history, by George Jelinek. Published in conjunction with Ellsworth's 90th anniversary ob-servance—August, 1957. ₍Ellsworth, Kan.₎, the Messenger press, ₍1957₎. Stiff pict. wrappers.

₍70₎ p. (no pagination). 17.2 cm.
Double column.

1169 JENKINS, A. O. Olive's last roundup, by A. O. Jenkins. ₍Loup City, Nebr., the Sherman County Times, n.d.₎. Wrappers. Rare.

₍98₎ p. (no pagination). plates, ports. 16.8 cm.
Last 17 p. adv.

Tells of the high-handed way I. P. Olive tried to control the cattle business in his section of Nebraska.

1170 JENNY, WALTER P. The mineral wealth, climate, and rain fall and natural resources of the Black Hills of Dakota. By Walter P. Jenny. . . . Department of the Interior. Office of Indian Affairs, 1876. . . . Wash-ington, Government printing office, 1876. Wrappers. Scarce.

71 p. 23 cm.
44 Cong., 1st sess., *Senate Ex. Doc. No. 51.*

Has a section on stock raising.

1171 JENSEN, ANN (ED.). Texas Ranger's diary and scrapbook. Edited by Ann Jensen. Dallas, Texas, the Kaleidograph press, [1936]. Cloth. Scarce.

6 p.l., 13–81 p. front., illus. 19.8 cm.

1172 JERNIGAN, REV. C. B. From prairie schooner to a city flat. By Rev. C. B. Jernigan. . . . [Brooklyn, N. Y., privately printed, 1926]. Cloth. Pict. label pasted on. Scarce.

6 p.l., 13–140 p. front. (port.), illus., plates, ports. 20.3 cm.

1173 JOCKNICK, SIDNEY. Early days on the western slope of Colorado, and campfire chats with Otto Mears, the pathfinder, from 1870 to 1883, inclusive, by Sidney Jocknick. Denver, Colo., the Carson-Harper co., MCMXIII. Cloth. Scarce.

4 p.l., [9]–384 p. front. (port., signature in facsm.), plates, ports, map. 20.2 cm. Appendix, p. [341]–384.

1174 JOHNSON, BURGES. As much as I dare. A personal recollection, by Burges Johnson. . . . New York, N. Y., Ives Washburn, inc., [1944]. Cloth. OP.

x p., 1 l., 3–346 p. front. (port.). 22.3 cm.
Half title; untrimmed.

The last third of this book deals with the author's experiences in the cattle country.

1175 JOHNSON COUNTY WAR. The cattle barons' rebellion against law and order. A true history of the Johnson County invasion by an armed band of assassins. As published in the Buffalo Bulletin. Dedicated to the "Rustlers" of Johnson and other counties who rustled at the risk of their lives to defend their homes, their lives and their constitutional rights. [N.p., n.d., Buffalo (?), c.1892]. Folder. (Cover title). Excessively rare.

[5] p. (no pagination). 30 cm.
Triple column.

This rare pamphlet makes many serious accusations and calls names, listing some of Wyoming's most prominent cattlemen. Efforts made to destroy all copies were so successful that only a very few survive. It originally appeared in the *Buffalo Bulletin* and ten days later was issued in pamphlet form.

In 1955 the Branding Iron Press, of Evanston, Illinois, reprinted it in a limited edition of 1,000 copies. The text is placed in a part-pocket on the inside of a stiff pictorial wrapper. Printed on the inside of this wrapper is an introduction giving some of the facts relative to the pamphlet and the history of the war.

Colophon: "Of this limited edition, designed by Philip Reed, this is Number ——." Decorations by David T. Vernon.

The editors of this reprint claim that it was reprinted from the only known copy, but the copy I examined was in the library of the American Antiquarian Society at Worcester, Mass.

1176 JOHNSON, (MRS.) GROVER C. Wagon yard, by Mrs. Grover C. Johnson. Illustrated by Jerry Bywaters. Dallas, William T. Tardy, [1938]. Cloth. Scarce.

3 p.l., 201 p. front., illus. 23.5 cm.

1177 JOHNSON, HARRISON. Johnson's history of Nebraska, by Harrison Johnson. . . . Omaha, Neb., published by Henry Gibson, Herald printing house, 1880. Pict. cloth. Rare.

xvi, [33]–591 p. front., illus., large fold. map, tables. 22.8 cm.

Section on stock raising. Copy examined in the Rollins Collection, Princeton University.

1178 JOHNSON, M. B., and R. D. JENNINGS. Cattle ranching and range utilization in western North Dakota. Special report to co-operators. By M. B. Johnson and R. D. Jennings. . . . Washington, D. C., February, 1937. Wrappers. Scarce.

96 p. maps, tables. 26.4 cm.
U. S. Dept. Agriculture, Bureau of Agricultural Economics and Bureau of Animal Industry in co-operation with the North Dakota Agricultural Experiment Station and Extension Service.

1179 JOHNSON, M. L. Intensely interesting little volume of true history of the struggles with hostile Indians on the frontier of Texas in the early days never before published in book form. A real cowboy's experience with Indians and the cow trail. Written by M. L. Johnson. . . . [Dallas, Texas, 1923]. Stiff wrappers. (Cover title). Scarce.

30 p. front. (port.). 16 cm.
Later republished in a second edition with 8 pages added.

1180 JOHNSON, OLGA WEYDEMEYER (MRS. PETE) (ED.). The story of the Tobacco Plains country. The autobiography of a community. . . . [Caldwell, Idaho, the Caxton printers, ltd.], 1950. Cloth.

x. p, 1 l., 273 p. plates, ports. 23.5 cm.
Half title; map on end papers.

1181 [JOHNSON, PHIL]. Phil Johnson's life on the plains. Chicago, Rhodes & McClure publishing company, 1888. Cloth. Rare.

4 p.l., (plates in front), 17–358 [2] p. 19 cm.
2 p. adv. at end.

This book is word for word the same as *Ten Years a Cowboy,* by C. C. Post, published two years earlier. For further details on this book, see item No. 1819.

1182 JOHNSON, VANCE. Heaven's tableland, the dust bowl story, by Vance Johnson. New York, Farrar, Straus and company, 1947. Cloth.

4 p.l., 11–288 p. 21 cm.

Some West Texas cattle material.

1183 JOHNSON, W. F. History of Cooper County, Missouri. ₁By₁ W. F. Johnson. Illustrated. Topeka, Cleveland, Historical publishing company, 1919. Three-quarter leather. Scarce.

10 p.l., ₁33₁–1166 p. front. (port.), plates, ports. 27.7 cm.

1184 JOHNSTON, HARRY V. My home on the range. Frontier life in the Bad Lands, by Harry V. Johnston. St. Paul, Minn., printed by the Webb publishing co., ₁1942₁. Pict. cloth. OP.

6 p.l., 313 p. front. (port.), plates, ports, cattle brands. 23.5 cm.
Vignette.

1185 ———. The last roundup. By H. V. Johnston. ₁Minneapolis, published by H. V. Johnston publishing co., n.d., c.1949₁. Cloth.

6 p.l., 336 p. front. (port.), illus., ports. 22.4 cm.
Half title.

1186 JOHNSTON, LUKIN. Beyond the Rockies. Three thousand miles by trail and canoe through little-known British Columbia. By Lukin Johnston. With fifty-two illustrations and a map. London and Toronto, J. M. Dent and sons, ltd., ₁1929₁. Cloth. OP.

xii, 212 p. front., plates, ports., map (double p.). 20.9 cm.
Half title.

1187 JOHNSTON, WINIFRED. Cow country theatre, by Winifred Johnston. Reprinted from *The Southwest Review,* Vol. XVIII, pp. 10–27. ₁N. p., n. d.₁. Wrappers. (Cover title). Scarce.

₁18₁ p. (no pagination). 23 cm.

Deals with the rodeo as a show.

1188 JONES, C. N. Early days in Cooke County, 1848–1873. Compiled by C. N. Jones. ₁Gainesville, Texas, n.d., c.1936₁. Stiff wrappers. Rare.

3 p.l., 5–88 p. front., ports. 23.8 cm.

1189 JONES, HORACE. The story of early Rice County. By Horace Jones. ₁Wichita, Kansas, Wichita Eagle₁, 1928. Cloth. OP.

5 p.l., 9–135 p. illus. 19.5 cm.

1190 JONES, J. O. A cowman's memoirs, by J. O. Jones. Ft. Worth, Texas, Texas Christian University press, 1953. Cloth.

xvii p., 1 l., 204, ccviii p. front., plates, ports., cattle brands. 22.5 cm.
Index, p. ccv–ccviii.
Half title; map on end papers; pub. device.

1191 JONES, J. W. C. The Elkhorn Valley; its climate, soil, surface . . . and industrial resources. . . . By J. W. C. Jones. West Point, Nebraska, Republican job office print, 1880. Wrappers. Rare.

[54] p. (no pagination). large fold. map in front. 20.4 cm.
Adv. verso front wrapper; adv. recto and verso back wrapper.

1192 KALFUS, JOSEPH H. Dr. Kalfus' book. A sportsman's experiences and impressions in east and west, by Dr. Joseph H. Kalfus. . . . With a preface by his friend and successor, Seth E. Gordon. . . . [Altoona, Pa., the Times Tribune co., 1926]. Cloth. Scarce.

4 p.l., 342 p. front. (port.), port. 21.4 cm.

1193 KANSAS. The Big Four brand book containing nearly all the brands west of the 100th meridian to the foothills on all four rivers: Arkansas, Cimarron, Beaver, and Canadian rivers and their tributaries, covering the parts of five states: Kansas, Colorado, Oklahoma Territory, Texas, and New Mexico. . . . Kansas City, published by C. V. Shepler, 1897. Calf. Scarce.

117 [1] p. cattle brands. 16.5 cm.

1194 ———. Brand book containing the brands of the western Kansas Cattle Growers' Association. Authorized by the Stockmen's Convention held at Dodge City, Kansas, April 2d, 1884. Kansas City, Mo., Isaac P. Moore, steam printer and binder, 1884. Wrappers. Rare.

vi (index to brands), 3–75 p. cattle brands. 17x9 cm.
Proceedings of the convention, p. 3–33; brands, p. 35–75.

1195 ———. Marks and brands used by the members of the Greenwood County Stock Association. . . . Eureka, Kansas, Herald book and job printing establishment, 1881. Wrappers. Rare.

[3]–21 p. cattle brands. 21 cm.

1196 ———. 1941 brand book of the state of Kansas, showing all state recorded brands of cattle, horses, mules, and sheep. This book contains all the livestock brands on record in the state office at Topeka, Kansas, up to the close of business on July 15, 1941, as provided for in the act of March 29, 1939. Topeka, Kansas, issued by the State Brand Commissioner. Topeka, printed by Kansas state printing plant, W. C. Austin, state printer, 1941. Cloth. OP.

6 p.l., 214 p. cattle brands. 20.3 cm.
Index, p. 152–214.

1197 ———. 1943 brand book of the state of Kansas, showing all state recorded brands of cattle, horses, mules, and sheep. . . . Topeka, printed by Kansas state printing plant, W. C. Austin, state printer, 1943. Cloth. OP.

6 p.l., 421 p. cattle brands. 20.3 cm.
Index, p. 307–421.

1198 ———. 1950 brand book of the state of Kansas, showing all state recorded brands of cattle, horses, mules, and sheep. . . . This book contains all the livestock brands of record in the state office at Topeka, Kansas, up to the close of business January 23, 1950. . . . Topeka, Kansas, issued by the State Brand Commissioner. Topeka, printed by the Kansas state printing plant, W. C. Austin, state printer, 1950. Cloth.

10 p.l., 365 [23] p. cattle brands. 20.2 cm.
Index, p. 326–365.
Last 23 p. supplements.

1199 ———. Chase County historical sketches. Volume I. Published by the Chase County Historical Society, 1940. [Emporia, Kansas, printed by Emporia Gazette]. Cloth. OP.

3 p.l., 9–448 p. front., plates, cattle brands, fold. map. 23.6 cm.

1200 ———. The citizens circular upon the interest of Franklin County as promoted by the stock law. Ottawa, Western Home Journal print, 1866. Wrappers. Excessively rare.

[5]–20 p. 20.5 cm.

Ottawa's first imprint. The only known copy of this little book is in the Rollins Collection, Princeton University.

1201 ———. Compendious history of Ellsworth County, Kansas, from its early settlement to the present time. Embracing the executive and educational departments, population, sketches of prominent men, general character of the land, and condition of the people. . . . Ellsworth, Kan., printed at the Reporter office, 1879. Wrappers. Rare.

2 p.l., 5–59 p. 17.7 cm.
3 p. business cards at end:; "First edition" on t.p.

1202 ———. Concerning protection of domestic animals. Livestock Commissioner. [N. p., 1907]. Wrappers. (Caption title). Scarce.

16 p. 15.3x8.6 cm.

1203 ———. The emigrant's guide. A history and description of northwestern Kansas, with a full synopsis of the government land laws. . . . Kirwin, Kansas, W. W. & L. L. Gray, publishers, 1880. Wrappers. (Cover title). Rare.

[34] p. (no pagination). 17.5 cm.
Adv. scattered throughout, including verso front wrapper, recto and verso back wrapper.

1204 ———. Facts about Kansas. A book for home-seekers and home-builders. Statistics from state and national reports. . . . ₁St. Louis, Woodward & Tiernan printing co., 1891₁. Wrappers. Rare.

₁3₁–82 ₁2₁ p. illus., fold. map at end. 19 cm.

Issued by the Missouri Pacific Railway Company, this book appeared in many editions, though all are now rare.

1205 ———. Facts and figures about Kansas. An emigrants' and settlers' guide; containing reliable information as to the advantage of the state of Kansas, the finest fruit, grain, stock, and farming country in America. With a correct map of the state of Kansas. . . . Lawrence, Kansas, Blackburn & co., publishers, 1870. Wrappers. Rare.

₁3₁–64 p. fold. map. 21.5 cm.

1206 ———. Farming and irrigation. Map and description of the irrigable and grazing lands of the Atchison, Topeka and Santa Fe Railroad Company in western Kansas showing sold and unsold tracts in Finney, formerly Sequoyah, and Hamilton counties, together with the location of the famous irrigating canals. Chicago, Poole brothers, printers and engravers, ₁1884₁. Wrappers. Rare.

₁10₁ p. (no pagination). fold. broadside, map on reverse side. 22.6 cm.

1207 ———. First biennial report of the Live Stock Sanitary Commission of the state of Kansas, 1887–1888. Topeka, Kansas publishing house, 1888. Wrappers. Scarce.

₁3₁–p. (no pagination). 23.3 cm.

These reports were published every year down to the present time, with different commissioners and different publishers as the years passed. To give them all would be monotonous.

1208 ———. A glimpse of Garden City and Finney County, Kansas. Garden City, Kansas, Morris bros., printers and binders, 1905. Wrappers. (Cover title). OP.

1 p.l., 3–32 p. illus. 23 cm.

1209 ———. Hand book of Scott County, Kansas. . . . Chicago, C. S. Burch publishing co., 1887. Pict. wrappers. (Cover title). Scarce.
18 p. illus. 39.3 cm.
Triple column; last 2 p. adv.

1210 ———. How and where to get a living. A sketch of "The Garden of the West," presenting facts worth knowing concerning the lands of the Atchison, Topeka & Santa Fe Railroad Co., in southwestern Kansas. Boston, published by the company, 1876. Wrappers. Rare.

2 p.l., ₁3₁–46 p. large fold. map in front, tables. 22.5 cm.

Republished in 1878 with illustrations.

1211 ——. An illustrated sketch book of Riley County, Kansas, the "Blue Ribbon County". . . . Manhattan, Kansas, published by the Nationalist, a weekly Republican newspaper, 1881. Wrappers. Rare.

[7]–149 p. illus., tables. 23.4 cm.
Double column; last 5 p. adv.

1212 ——. Impartial testimony as to the profit of sheep and cattle raising in southwest Kansas, together with official reports on the condition and number of live stock in the state, and an estimate of the profits and expenses of a ranch in the Arkansas Valley of Kansas. Topeka, Kansas, Hamilton, Woodruff & co., printers, 1884. Wrappers. Scarce.

[3]–39 p. diagrs., tables. 21.6 cm.

1213 ——. Impartial testimony as to the profit of sheep and cattle raising in southwest Kansas, together with official reports on the condition and number of live stock in the state, and an estimate of the profits and expenses of a ranch in the Arkansas Valley of Kansas. Topeka, Kansas, A. S. Johnson, land commissioner, 1885. Wrappers. Scarce.

[3]–40 p. diagrs., tables. 21.6 cm.

1214 ——. Information in connection with Kansas brand law. Topeka, Kansas, issued by State Brand Commissioner, [n. d., c.1940]. Single sheet.

[2] p. (no pagination). 21.4 cm.

1215 ——. Kansas, the bountiful. With special reference to that part of Kansas on the Rock Island Lines. Chicago, Passenger Department Rock Island Lines, 1907. Pict. wrappers. Scarce.

5–47 [1] p. front., illus., plates, fold. map at end, facsm. 22.7 cm.

1216 ——. Kansas: The golden belt lands along the line of the Kansas division of the U. P. R'y. Kansas City, Mo., B. McAllaster, land commissioner, [n. d.]. Pict. wrappers. Rare.

48 [8] p. illus., map on recto back wrapper, tables. 22.5 cm.
Last 8 p. adv.

1217 ——. Kansas: its history, resources, and prospects. Wichita, Kansas, Eagle printing house, 1890. Wrappers. Scarce.

[3]–77 p. illus. 21 cm.

1218 ——. Kansas and her resources. . . . [N. p.], Passenger Department, the Atchison, Topeka & Santa Fe Railway company, 1902. Pict. wrappers. Rare.

[5]–69 p. illus., plates, map, tables. 15.5 cm.

1219 ——. Kansas, its resources and capabilities, its position, dimensions and topography. Information relating to vacant lands, agriculture, horticulture and livestock. . . . Prepared by the State Board of Agriculture, William Sims, secretary. Topeka, Kan., Kansas publishing co., 1883. Wrappers. Scarce.

60 p. illus., diagrs., fold. map at end, tables. 22.4 cm.

1220 ———. Marketing feeder cattle and calves in Kansas. Manhattan, Kansas, Agricultural Experiment Station, Kansas State College of Agricultural and Applied Science, October, 1953. Pict. wrappers.

3–55 p. graphs, maps, tables. 22.2 cm.

1221 ———. Office of Livestock Sanitary Commissioner. Biennial report for fiscal years, 1943 and 1944. ₁Topeka, Kansas, 1944₁. Wrappers. (Cover title).

23 p. tables. 23 cm.

1222 ———. Office of State Brand Commissioner. Biennial report for fiscal years 1947 and 1948. ₁Topeka, Kansas, printed by Ferd Voiland, Jr., 1948₁. Stiff wrappers.

14 p. 22.8 cm.

1223 ———. Office of State Brand Commissioner. Biennial report for fiscal years 1949 and 1950. ₁Topeka, Kansas, printed by Ferd Voiland, Jr., 1950₁. Stiff wrappers.

11 p. 22.8 cm.

1224 ———. Office of State Brand Commissioner. Biennial report for fiscal years 1951 and 1952. ₁Topeka, Kansas, printed by Ferd Voiland, Jr., 1952₁. Stiff wrappers.

12 p. 22.8 cm.

1225 ———. Office of State Brand Commissioner. Biennial report for fiscal years 1953 and 1954. ₁Topeka, Kansas, printed by Ferd Voiland, Jr., state printers, 1955₁. Wrappers. (Cover title).

2 p.l., 5–16 p. illus., tables. 23 cm.

1226 ———. The resources and attractions of Kansas for the home seeker, capitalist, and tourist. Facts on climate, soil, farming, stock raising. . . . St. Louis, Woodward & Tiernan printing co., 1894. Wrappers. Rare.

3 p.l., ₁5₁–59 p. map, tables. 19.5 cm.
Map on verso front wrapper.

Issued by the Union Pacific Railway Company.

1227 ———. Some general practical information in regard to the "Great State of Kansas," the greatest fruit, stock, and grain country in the world. . . . Lawrence, Kansas, published by the Kansas publishing company, 1870. Wrappers. Rare.

2 p.l., ₁5₁–64 p. plate (fold.), fold. map at end. 21 cm.

1228 ———. The state of Kansas, a home for immigrants. Agricultural, mineral and commercial resources of the state. Great inducements offered to persons desiring homes in a new country. The homestead law. Topeka, Kansas, MacDonald & Baker, printers, 1865. Pict. wrappers. Rare.

₁3₁–24 p. 22 cm.

1229 ———. Third annual report of the Livestock Sanitary Commission and State Veterinarian of the state of Kansas. Published by the State Board of Agriculture. Topeka, Kansas publishing house, 1887. Wrappers. Rare.

₁3₁–39 p. 23 cm.

1230 ———. Trends in livestock and meat industry in Kansas. Manhattan, Kansas, Agricultural Experiment Station, Kansas State College of Agriculture and Applied Science, November, 1952. Pict. wrappers.

3–34 p. graphs, tables. 22.2 cm.
Bulletin No. 355.

1231 KANSAS CITY. 75 years of Kansas City livestock market history with which is combined the 75th annual livestock report for year ending December 31, 1945. ₁Kansas City₁, the Kansas City Stock Yards company, 1946. Pict. wrappers. OP.

3–40 p. plates (1 double p.), ports., tables. 26.6 cm.
Double column.

1232 KANSAS LAWS. House Bill No. 290. An act relating to livestock, creating the state brand board and brand commissioner. . . . ₁Topeka, Kansas, 1919₁. Folder.

₁3₁ p. (no pagination). 23 cm.

1233 ———. House Bill No. 579. An act to prevent the spread of infestious and contagious diseases of livestock. . . . ₁N. p., n. d.₁. Stapled. (Caption title). Rare.

5 p. 22.8 cm.

1234 ———. The Kansas livestock remedy law as amended by the Legislature of 1945. ₁Topeka, printed by Kansas State printing plant, Leonard McCall, state printer, 1945₁. Stapled. (Caption title).

7 p. 22.8 cm.

1235 ———. Kansas regulations concerning cattle transportation. Proclamation quarantining certain localities on account of Texas fever. ₁Topeka, Kansas, 1899₁. Folder. (Caption title).

4 p. 35.4 cm.

1236 ———. Kansas regulations concerning cattle transportation. Proclamation quarantining certain localities on account of Texas fever. ₁Topeka, Kansas, 1900₁. Folder. (Caption title).

4 p. 25.4 cm.

1237 ———. Kansas regulations concerning cattle transportation. Proclamation quarantining certain localities on account of Texas fever and itch, or mange. ₁Topeka, Kansas, 1904₁. Folder. (Caption title).

4 p. map on verso back wrapper. 25.4 cm.

1238 ———. Laws and statutes of Kansas. Protection of cattle from disease. Extracts from the laws of the state of Kansas. ₁N. p., 1885₁. Wrappers. (Cover title). Rare.

13 p. 23 cm.

1239 ———. Livestock laws of Kansas. Issued by the State Livestock Sanitary Commissioner. . . . ₁Topeka, printed by Kansas State printing plant, W. C. Austin, state printer, 1941₁. Stiff wrappers. (Cover title).

74 p. 23x10 cm.

1240 ———. Livestock laws of Kansas. Issued by the State Livestock Sanitary Commissioner. . . . ₁Topeka, printed by Ferd Voiland, Jr., state printer, 1948₁. Stiff wrappers. (Cover title).

86 p. 22.8x9.8 cm.

1241 ———. Protection of cattle from disease. Extracts from the laws of the state of Kansas. ₁N.p., n.d.₁. Wrappers. (Caption title).

13 p. 22.7 cm.

1242 ———. Regulations in connection with administration of community sales law. ₁Topeka, Kansas, 1937₁. Folder. (Caption title).

₁3₁ p. (no pagination). 22.8 cm.

1243 ———. Regulations and inspection requirements issued in connection with the administration of the community sales law. ₁Topeka, printed by Kansas State printing plant, W. C. Austin, state printer, 1942₁. Stapled. (Caption title).

8 p. 22.2 cm.

1244 ———. Regulations and inspection requirements issued in connection with the administration of the community sales law. Chapter 224, Ses-

sion Laws 1939, as amended. ₍Topeka, Kansas, printed by Ferd Voiland, Jr., state printer, 1946₎. Stapled. (Caption title).
10 p.   21.6x10.2 cm.

1245 ———. Regulations and inspection requirements issued in connection with the administration of the community sales law, chapter 224, session laws 1939, as amended July 1, 1949. Topeka, state of Kansas, Office of Livestock Sanitation Commissioner. ₍Topeka, Kansas, printed by Ferd Voiland, Jr., state printer, 1949₎. Stiff wrappers. (Cover title).
13 p.   22.8x10.2 cm.

1246 ———. Rules and regulations of the State Livestock Sanitary Commissioner governing the movement of livestock into and/or through Kansas. . . . ₍Topeka, Kansas, printed by Ferd Voiland, Jr., state printer, 1946₎. Wrappers. (Cover title).
6 p.   21.6 cm.

1247 ———. Rules and regulations governing the movement of livestock into and/or through Kansas. Topeka, state of Kansas, State Livestock Sanitary Commissioner. ₍Topeka, printed by Ferd Voiland, Jr., state printer, 1950₎. Stiff wrappers. (Cover title).
5 ₍1₎ p.   21.5x10.2 cm.

1248 ———. State of Kansas, session laws 1939, passed at the forty-eighth regular session—the same being the thirty-first biennial session of the Legislature of the state of Kansas. . . . Topeka, printed by Kansas State printing plant, W. C. Austin, state printer, 1939. Cloth.
xvii, 738 p.   23.2 cm.
Index to bills, p. 668–670; index to chapters, p. 671–697; statutes repealed or amended, p. 698–702; general index, p. 703–738.

1249 ———. State of Kansas, session laws 1947, passed at the fifty-second regular session, the same being the thirty-fifth biennial session of the Legislature of the state of Kansas. . . . Topeka, Kansas, printed by Ferd Voiland, Jr., state printer, 1947. Cloth.
xvi, 946 p.   23.3 cm.
Index to chapters, p. 877–906; index to bills, p. 907–910; statutes repealed or amended, p. 911–920; general index, p. 921–946.

1250 ———. Western Kansas Cattle Growers' Association brand book containing the brands of the Western Kansas Cattle Growers' Association. Authorized by the stockmen's convention held at Dodge City, Kansas, April 10, 1883. Kansas City, Isaac P. Moore, printer and binder, 1883. Wrappers. Rare.
43 ₍1₎ p.   cattle brands.   17x9.5 cm.

Proceedings and brands of members.

1251 KANSAS AND NEW MEXICO CATTLE AND LAND CO. Memorandum and articles of association. London, Eardley, Holt and Richardson, 1883. Wrappers. Rare.

32 p.   25 cm.

1252 KANSAS PACIFIC RAILWAY CO. Emigrant's guide to the Kansas Pacific Railway lands. Best and cheapest farming and grazing lands in America. 6,000,000 acres for sale by the Kansas Pacific Railway co. . . . Lawrence, Kansas, Land Department, Kansas Pacific Railway co., 1871. Wrappers. Rare.

[3]–32 p.   22.5 cm.

Also published in St. Louis, by R. P. Studley co., without date.

1253 ———. Kansas Pacific gold loan. $6,500,000 first mortgage seven per cent. Gold bonds, 30 years to run. A railroad and land-grant sinking fund bond (registered or coupon), principal and interest payable in gold, free from government tax, secured by mortgage of three million acres of land in Kansas and Colorado adjoining this road and 663 miles of railway and telegraph, of which 437 miles are now in successful operation, and on 236 miles of the line, with the land, it is a first and only mortgage. Secured also by a sinking fund, being an unusually safe investment, yielding nearly 10 per cent per annum in currency free from tax. . . . [New York, 1869]. Wrappers. Rare.

2 p.l., [5]–48 p.   large fold. map in front, tables.   21.5 cm.

Contains some material describing the cattle trade of the plains.

1254 ———. Hand book for the Kansas Pacific Railway containing a description of the country, cities, towns &c., lying along the line of the road and its branches. Extracted from "Tracy's Guide to the Great West". . . . St. Louis, Mo., Aug. Weibusch & son, printers, 1870. Wrappers. (Cover title). Rare.

[55]–80 [1] p.   large fold. map in front.   18 cm.
3 p. adv. in front; 1 p. adv. at end.

1255 ———. Map of the best and shortest cattle route from Texas to the Kansas Pacific Railway. Published by the Kansas Pacific Railway company, 1871. The great stock route. Brooksville, Salina, Solomon, Abilene, and Ellsworth. . . . [N. p.], 1871. Excessively rare.

1-sheet folder.   tables of distances, map on verso.

1256 ———. Guide map to the best and shortest cattle trail to the Kansas Pacific Railway; with a concise and accurate description of the route; showing the distances, streams, crossings, camping grounds, wood and water, supply stores, etc., from the Red River Crossing to Ellis, Ellsworth, Brookville, Saline, Solomon, and Abilene. St. Louis, Mo., Levin-son & Blythe, printers and stationers . . . , 1873.

15 p. fold. map. 16.5 cm.
Text starts on verso front wrapper; adv. on verso back wrapper.

This copy seen in the private collection of Thomas W. Streeter.

1257 ———. Guide map and the best and shortest cattle trail to the Kansas Pacific Railway with a concise and accurate description of the route; showing distances, streams, crossings, camping grounds, wood and water, supply stores, etc., from the Red River Crossing to Ellis, Russell, Ells-worth, Brookville, Saline, Solomon, and Abilene. With illustrations. . . . ₁Kansas City, Millett and Hudson, steam printers, book binders and engravers, 1874₁. Wrappers. Very rare.

₁3₁–21 ₁1₁ p. 6 fold. illus. (incl. front.), fold. map at end. 17.5x10.6 cm.

These little guidebooks showing the best route to the Kansas market were issued for the benefit of the trail drivers. The 1874 edition is the most common, though it, too, is exceedingly rare. It is the first illustrated edition, and its illustrations were taken from Joseph McCoy's *Historic Sketches of the Cattle Trade,* published the same year, the illustrations being tipped in.

1258 KEATING, DAVID T. Land of the Flatheads to be opened to settlement soon. . . . Columbus, Ohio, 1907. Pict. limber cloth. Scarce.

₁5₁–116 p. plates. 22.2 cm.

1259 KEELER, B. C. Where to go and become rich. Farmers', miners', and tourists' guide to Kansas, New Mexico, Arizona, and Colorado. By B. C. Keeler, with complete text of the mining laws, glossary of mining terms, and maps of New Mexico, Arizona, and Colorado. Illustrated. Chicago, Belford, Clarke & co., publishers, ₁1880₁. Pict. wrappers. Rare.

5 p.l., 17–180 p. illus., 5 maps (4 fold.), tables. 19.8 cm.
8 p. adv. in front; 7 p. adv. at end.

Also bound in cloth.

1260 KEGLEY, MAX. Rodeo, the sport of the cow country, by Max Kegley. New York, Hastings House, publishers, ₁1942₁. Cloth. OP.

3 p.l., 7–64 p. front. (group port.), illus. 21 cm.
Half title.

The frontispiece and 55 pages of illustrations are reproductions from photographs by the author.

1261 KEITH, NOEL L. The Brites of Capote. ₁By₁ Noel L. Keith. . . . Ft. Worth, Texas, the Texas Christian University press, 1950. Cloth.

xlvi p., 1 l., 272 p. 29 plates in front. 23.5 cm.
Chronology, p. ₁xli₁–xlvi; appendix, p. ₁201₁–266; index, p. ₁267₁–272.
Illus. end papers; pub. device; "First printing" on copyright p.

1262 KELEHER, WILLIAM A. The fabulous frontier; twelve New Mexico items, by William A. Keleher. Santa Fe, New Mexico, the Rydal press, [1945]. Cloth. Scarce.

ix p., 3 l., 3–317 p. illus., plates, ports. 23.5 cm.
Some sources of reference, p. 283–286; index, p. 287–317.
Half title; map on end papers.
Originally printed in a limited edition of 500 copies, but has since been reprinted.

1263 ———. Maxwell land grant, a New Mexico item, by William A. Keleher. Santa Fe, the Rydal press, [1942]. Pict. cloth. Scarce.

xiii p., 1 l., 3–168 p. front. (port.), plates, port. 23.5 cm.
Sources, p. 155–156; index, p. 157–168.
Half title.

1264 ———. Violence in Lincoln County, 1869–1881. A New Mexico item, by William A. Keleher. Frontispiece by Ernest L. Blumenschein. Albuquerque, University of New Mexico press, [1957]. Cloth.

xvi p., 1 l., 3–390 p. front., plates, ports., facsms. 23.8 cm.
Index, p. 373–390.
Half title; map on end papers; "First edition" on copyright p.

1265 KELLY, FLORENCE FINCH. Flowing stream. The story of fifty-six years in American newspaper life. By Florence Finch Kelly. . . . New York, E. P. Dutton & co., inc., 1939. Pict. cloth. OP.

xvi p., 1 l., 3–571 p. front. (port.). 24.3 cm.
Index, p. 561–571.
Half title; untrimmed.

Has a chapter on life on a cattle ranch in New Mexico.

1266 KELLY, GEORGE BENSON. The biography of George Benson Kelly. [N. p., n. d.]. Stiff wrappers. (Cover title). OP.

4–58 p. front., plates, ports. 23 cm.

1267 KELLY, LEROY VICTOR. The range men. The story of the ranches and Indians of Alberta, by L. V. Kelly. Toronto, William Briggs, 1913. Pict. cloth. Very scarce.

6 p.l., 11–468 p. front. (port. with tissue), plates, ports. 23.5 cm.
Gilt top; untrimmed.

1268 KELLY, ROBIN A. The sky was their roof. [By] Robin A. Kelly, with many rare photographs, drawings and four maps. London, Stratford Place, Andrew Melrose, [1955]. Cloth.

xii, 252 p. illus., plates, ports., maps. 21.8 cm.
Notes, p. 217–228; bibliography, p. 229–231; glossary, p. 233–235; main Plains Indian tribes, p. 237–239; index, p. 243–252.
Half title; vignette.

1269 KELSEY, ANNA MARIETTA. Through the years. Reminiscences of pioneer days of the Texas border, by Anna Marietta Kelsey. San Antonio, Texas, the Naylor company, [1952]. Cloth.

xii p., 4 l., 179 p. front., plates, ports. 21.6 cm.
Index, p. 177–179.
Half title; device.

Has a chapter on the large cattle ranches of Texas.

1270 [KENDRICK, JOHN B.]. An address by the Honorable John B. Kendrick, first vice-president of the American National Live Stock Association, at the 30th annual convention of the National Live Stock Exchange at New York, May 17, 1918. Pamphlet. (Cover title). Scarce.

[6] p. (no pagination). 22.7 cm.

1271 ———. Address of the Honorable John B. Kendrick, president of the American National Live Stock Association, at the 23rd annual convention of the American National Live Stock Association held in the Davenport Hotel, Spokane, Wash., January 27th, 28th, and 29th, 1920. Spokane, Wash., Moore's printcraft shop, [1920]. Wrappers. (Cover title). Scarce.

[12] p. (no pagination). 22.6 cm.

1272 KENNEDY, MARGUERITE WALLACE. My home on the range, by Marguerite Wallace Kennedy. Drawings by Lorence F. Bjorklund. Boston, Little, Brown and company, 1951. Cloth.

5 p.l., 3–341 p. illus. 21 cm.
Half title; illus. end papers; illus. chapter headings; vignette.

A most interesting book on the experiences of a ranch woman in Arizona.

1273 KENT, WILLIAM. Reminiscences of outdoor life, by William Kent, with a foreword by Stewart Edward White. Illustrated. San Francisco, California, A. M. Robertson, MCMXXIX. Boards and cloth. OP.

xii p., 1 l., 3–304 [1] p. front. (tissue with letterpress), plates. 20.7 cm.
Title label on spine pasted on; untrimmed.

1274 KING, FRANK M. Longhorn trail drivers; being a true story of the cattle drives of long ago, [by] Frank M. King. Illustrated. This first edition privately published for his friends by the author. [Los Angeles, printed by Haynes corp.]. Fabricoid. Scarce.

xiii, 15–272 p. front. (port.), plates, ports. 23.6 cm.
Illus. front end papers; map on back end papers.
Colophon: "This autographed first edition is limited to 400 copies to be sold at five dollars the copy, of which this is No. ———."

1275 ———. Mavericks. The salty comments of an old-time cowpuncher, by Frank M. King. Illustrations by Charles M. Russell. Introduction by Ramon F. Adams. Pasadena, Calif., the Trail's End publishing co., inc., [1947]. Cloth. OP.

xii p., 2 l., [5]–275 p. front. (col.), illus. 21.5 cm.
Index, p. [273]–275.
Illus. end papers; illus. chapter divisions; pub. device.

Also published in a de luxe edition of 350 copies, numbered, signed, and bound in morocco.

Colophon: "De luxe edition limited to 350 copies, numbered and signed by the author. This is copy No. ——."

The material in this book was selected from the author's column "Mavericks," which ran for many years in the *Western Livestock Journal* of Los Angeles.

1276 ——. Pioneer western empire builders. A true story of the men and women of pioneer days, by Frank M. King. Profusely illustrated, including an original illustration by Charles M. Russell. . . . [Pasadena, Calif., the Trail's End publishing co., inc., 1946]. Cloth. OP.

8 p.l., [21]–383 p. front., plates, ports., map, facsm. 22 cm.

Also published in a de luxe edition, bound in morocco.

Colophon: "De luxe edition, numbered and signed by the author. This is No. ——."

1277 ——. Wranglin' the past; being the reminiscences of Frank M. King. Illustrated. [Los Angeles], this first edition privately published for his friends by the author [printed by Haynes corp.], 1935. Fabricoid. Scarce.

xi [1] p., 13–244 p. front. (port.), illus., plates, ports. 23.5 cm.
Illus. t.p.
Colophon: "This autograph first edition is limited to 300 copies to be sold at five dollars the copy, of which this is No. ——."

Five hundred copies of this book were printed, 300 copies having the above colophon, the other 200 without colophon. The former was an autographed edition; the other 200 carried on the title page the same statement as did the autographed edition: "This first edition privately published for his friends by the author, 1936."

Republished in 1946 by the Trail's End publishing co., Pasadena, with a preface by H. E. Britzman, and an illustration by Charles M. Russell.

"First revised edition" appears on the title page; this edition contains 248 pages.

1278 KING, LEONARD. From cattle rustler to pulpit, by Leonard King. San Antonio, Texas, the Naylor company, 1943. Cloth.

x, 216 p. front. (port.), illus. 21 cm.
Index, p. [215]–216.
Half title.

1279 KINGSBURY, GEORGE W. History of Dakota Territory, by George W. Kingsbury. South Dakota, its history and its people, edited by George Martin Smith. . . . Illustrated. Chicago, the S. J. Clarke publishing company, 1915. Cloth. Scarce. Pub. in 5 vols.

Vol. I: xxv, 983 p. front. (port.), plates, ports. 26 cm.
Vol. II: xiv, 985–1953 p. front., plates, ports. 26 cm.
Vol. III: v, 982 p. front. (port.), plates, ports. 26 cm.
Vol. IV: 5–126 p. front. (port.), plates, ports. 26 cm.
Vol. V: 5–273, i–viii p. front. (port.), ports. 26 cm.
Index, V, i–viii.

Vols. I and II paged continuously.
Vol. II contains a section on Roosevelt as a cattleman; Vol. III has a chapter on livestock; Vols. IV and V, biographical.

1280 KINGSBURY, WILLIAM GILLIAM. A description of the belt of country in south-western Texas as traveled by the San Antonio & Aransas Pass Railways. . . . Kendall County as a health resort and location for settlers. By W. G. Kingsbury. San Antonio, Johnson bros., print, [n. d.]. Wrappers. Rare.

36 [12] p. 18.6 cm.
Last 12 p. adv.

1281 ———. A description of south-western and middle Texas (United States), the soil, climate and productions, together with prospective sources of wealth, the great inducements offered to all classes of European emigrants. By W. G. Kingsbury. . . . London, printed by Waterlow and sons, ltd., 1883. Wrappers. (Cover title). Rare.

2 p.l., 48 p. fold. map. 21.5 cm.
Illus. on verso of map.

1282 KINO, EUSEBIO FRANCISCO. Kino's historical memoir of Pimeria Alta; a contemporary account of the beginning of California, Sonora, and Arizona, by Father Eusebio Francisco Kino, pioneer missionary, explorer, cartographer, and ranchman, 1683–1711. Published for the first time from the original manuscript in the archives of Mexico; translated into English, edited, and annotated by Herbert Eugene Bolton. . . . Cleveland, the Arthur H. Clark co., 1919. Pub. in 2 vols. Cloth. Scarce.

Vol. I: 2 l., 7–379 p. front. (map), map, plan. 24 cm.
Vol. II: 2 l., 7–329 p. front., map, facsm. 24 cm.

A scholarly work dealing with, among other things, the early cattle soon after their introduction into this country.

1283 KNIGHT, ELLA. The live stock industry in Nebraska. Educational pamphlet No. 1. . . . Bureau of Publicity, Chamber of Commerce, Omaha, Neb., [n. d.]. Wrappers. Scarce.

[3]–11 p. front., plates. 23.2 cm.

1284 KNIGHT, OLIVER. Fort Worth, outpost on the Trinity. By Oliver Knight. Norman, University of Oklahoma press, [1952]. Pict. cloth.

xiii p., 1 l., 3–302 p. plates, ports., plan, map. 22 cm.
Appendices, p. 231–277; bibliography, p. 279–282; index, p. 283–302.
Half title; "First edition" on copyright p.

1285 KOCH, FELIX J. A little journey through the great Southwest. . . . By Felix J. Koch. . . . Chicago, A. Flanagan co., [1907]. Dec. cloth. Scarce.

3–123 p. front., illus. 19.3 cm.

The author tells of his travels, including those through the cattle country of the Southwest.

1286 KRAENZEL, CARL FREDERICK. The great plains in transition, by Carl Frederick Kraenzel. Norman, University of Oklahoma press, [1955]. Cloth.

xiv p., 1 l., 3–428 [1] p. front., maps (1 col. fold.), tables. 24.2 cm.
Bibliographical notes, p. 391–418; index, p. 419–428.
Half title; "First edition" on copyright p.

1287 KRAKEL, DEAN F. The saga of Tom Horn. The story of a cattleman's war, with personal narratives, newspaper accounts, and official documents and testimonials. Illustrated with the pageant of personalities. By Dean F. Krakel. [Laramie, Wyoming, manufactured . . . by the Laramie printing co., Laramie, Wyoming, for the Powder River publishers, 1954]. Cloth.

ix p., 1 l., [3]–277 p. illus., plates, ports. 23.6 cm.
Bibliography, p. 268–269; index, p. 272–277.

This book was not released for some time after it was printed on account of a threatened lawsuit—until the pictures on pages 25, 27, 28, 37, and 240, and the text on pages 13 and 54 were deleted and changes tipped in. The book deals mostly with the trial of Tom Horn for the killing of Willie Nickels.

1288 ———. South Platte country. "A history of Old Weld County, Colorado, 1739–1900," by Dean K. Krakel. . . . Laramie, Wyoming, published by the Powder River publishers, 1954. Pict. wrappers.

vi, 268 [49] p. front., plates, ports., maps, facsms. 27.5 cm.
Chronology, p. [271]–[275]; [notes], p. [376]–[305]; "List of Members," p. [307]–[317].
Photo-lithograph process.

1289 KRUEGER, MAX. Pioneer life in Texas; an autobiography, by M. Krueger. [San Antonio, press of the Glegg co., 1930]. Leather. Rare.

3 p.l., 13–225 p., 1 l. 20.8 cm.

1290 KUPPER, WINIFRED. The golden hoof; the story of the sheep of the Southwest. [By] Winifred Kupper. New York, Alfred A. Knopf, 1945. Cloth.

xi p., 1 l., 3–203 [1] p. front. 22 cm.
Notes, p. 199–203.
At head of title, "Winifred Kupper"; pub. device.
Printed on yellow paper.

Has a chapter on the war between sheepmen and cattlemen.

1291 ———. (ED.). Texas sheepman. The reminiscences of Robert Maudslay. Edited by Winifred Kupper. Illustrations by Hilda Wilcox Phelps. Austin, University of Texas press, 1951. Pict. cloth.

xi p., 1 l., 138 p. front., illus., plates, port., facsms. 24.2 cm.
Notes, p. 127–134; index, p. 135–138.
Half title.

1292 KUYKENDALL, IVAN LEE. Ghost riders of the Mogollon, by Ivan Lee Kuykendall. San Antonio, Texas, the Naylor company, [1954]. Cloth. Exceedingly rare.

viii, 158 p. 19.7 cm.
Half title.

Because of a threatened lawsuit this book was withdrawn after only about 200 copies were released.

1293 LACY, CHARLES DE LACY. The history of the spur, by Charles De Lacy Lacy. [London], published by the Connoisseur (Otto limited), [n.d.]. Pict. cloth. Scarce.

vi p., 1 l., 81 p. front., illus., 47 plates. 28.6 cm.
Half title; t.p. in red and black; device.

1294 LAFONT, DON. Rugged life in the Rockies, by Don LaFont. With illustrations by the author and family. Casper, Wyoming, Prairie publishing company, 1951. Cloth.

3 p.l., 9–207 p. illus., plates, ports. 23.6 cm.
Vignette; copyright notice on preface p.

1295 LAFRENTZ, FERDINAND WILLIAM. Cowboy stuff, poems by F. W. LaFrentz; introduction by John Wesley Hill. . . . Publisher's foreword by George Haven Putnam; illustrations by Henry Zeigler. New York, G. P. Putnam's sons, 1927. Boards. Title pasted on. Rare.

[117] p. (no pagination). front. (port.), illus., 49 plates. 31.4 cm.
Half title; marginal decorations; untrimmed.
Colophon: "Author's autograph edition. . . . Five hundred copies of this edition have been printed on Whitechurch, English hand-made, antique laid paper. Each copy numbered has been signed by the author, the illustrator, and the publisher. No. ——."

Republished same year:

₍119₎ p. front. (port.), illus., 50 plates. 21.4 cm.

Although it is against my policy to include poetry in this work, the above item is such a collector's item that it deserves a place here. For many years the author was the secretary of the Swan Land and Cattle Company of Wyoming.

1296 LAKE, CHARLES R. Brand laws, regulations, and pertinent facts on brands, branding, and livestock inspection. . . . Topeka, Kansas, Charles R. Lake, brand commissioner, ₍printed by Ferd Voiland, Jr., printer, 1948₎. Wrappers.
3–21 p. 22.8 cm.

1297 ———. Brand laws, regulations, and pertinent facts on brands, branding, and livestock inspection. . . . Topeka, Kansas, Charles R. Lake, brand commissioner, ₍printed by Ferd Voiland, Jr., printer, 1949₎. Wrappers.
19 p. 22.8 cm.

1298 ———. Brand laws, regulations, and pertinent facts on brands, branding, and livestock inspection. . . . Topeka, Kansas, Charles R. Lake, brand commissioner, ₍printed by Ferd Voiland, Jr., printer, 1951₎. Stiff wrappers.
19 ₍1₎ p. 22.8 cm.

1299 ———. State of Kansas brand laws, regulations, and pertinent facts on brands, branding, and livestock brand inspection. . . . Topeka, Kansas, Charles R. Lake, brand inspector, 1953. Wrappers. (Cover title).
19 ₍1₎ p. 22.8 cm.

1300 LAKE, STUART N. Wyatt Earp, frontier marshal, by Stuart N. Lake. With illustrations. Boston and New York, Houghton Mifflin company, 1931. Cloth.
xiv p., 1 l., ₍3₎–392 p. front., plates, ports., facsm. 22.2 cm.
Index, p. ₍377₎–392.
Half title; pub. device; first edition, "1931" under imprint.

Republished many times. Also published in England under the title:

He carried a six-shooter. The biography of Wyatt Earp, by Stuart N. Lake, with an introduction by Philip Lindsay. London and New York, Peter Nevill, limited, ₍MCMLII₎. Cloth.
xi p., 3 l., ₍3₎–392 p. front. (port.), plates, ports. 20.5 cm.
Index, p. ₍377₎–392.
Half title.

Often a typographical error will identify the first printing, for the error is usually corrected in the second printing. But the error "senventy-five" (page

25) in the first American edition appears in all editions of this book, even in the "paper shortage" editions of World War II and the reprint of 1955. The error "ellby" for "belly" on page 54 was corrected in the second printing, but the editors seem never to have discovered the error on page 25.

1301 LAMB, GENE. R-O-D-E-O back of the chutes, by Gene Lamb. . . . Denver, Colorado, the Bell press, 1956. Cloth.

8 p.l., 9–279 p. illus., plates. 20.8 cm.
Rodeo rules, p. 260–272; glossary of rodeo terms, p. 273–279.
Illus. chapter headings.

1302 LAMPMAN, CLIFTON PARKS. The great western trail, by Clifton Parks Lampman. Illustrated. [New York], G. P. Putnam's sons, 1939. Cloth. OP.

xi p., 2 l., 17–280 p. front., plates, port. 22.2 cm.
Half title.

1303 LANG, H. O. (ED.). History of the Willamette Valley, being a description of the valley and its resources, with an account of its discovery and settlement by white men, and its subsequent history; together with personal reminiscences of its early pioneers. Edited by H. O. Lang. . . . Portland, Ore., Geo. H. Hines, book and job printers, 1885. Calf. Scarce.

xv, [17]–902, i–xiii p. front. (port.), plate. 25.2 cm.
Index, p. i–xiii.
Leaf of errata tipped in.

1304 LANG, LINCOLN ALEXANDER. Ranching with Roosevelt, by a companion rancher, Lincoln A. Lang. With 24 illustrations. Philadelphia & London, J. B. Lippincott company, 1926. Pict. cloth. OP.

6 p.l., 13–267 p. front. plates, ports., facsms., 22 cm.
Half title; "First edition" on copyright p.

1305 LANG, COLONEL WILLIAM W. A paper on the resources and capabilities of Texas, read by Col. William W. Lang before the Farmers' Club of the American Institute, Cooper Union, New York, March 8th, 1881. . . . To which is appended a paper on the social and economic condition of the state. [N. p.], 1881. Wrappers. Rare.

[3]–19 p. 22.7 cm.

Reprinted same year, New York, Wm. H. Thomas, mercantile printer, with 31 pages. It was later enlarged and reissued by the South-Western Immigration Company, Austin, Texas, in an edition of 62 pages and with a frontis. Double column.

1306 LANGSTON, ARTHUR EUGENE. Brief sketches from the life of Texas Jack, Jr., by Arthur Eugene Langston. New York, Robert Andrews, general job printer, [n. d.]. Pict. wrappers. Exceedingly rare.

v, [7]–27 p. front., illus., 2 ports. (incl. front.). 14.7 cm.

This rare little book was written as an introductory sample of a larger work to follow, but the latter was never published.

1307 LANGSTON, MRS. GEORGE. History of Eastland County, Texas. By Mrs. George Langston. Dallas, Texas, A. D. Allridge & co., stationers, printers, and book binders, 1904. Cloth. Scarce.

x, [11]–220 p. front. (port.), plates, ports. 19.8 cm.

1308 LARMER, FORREST M. Financing the livestock industry. By Forrest M. Larmer, with the aid of the council and staff of the Institute of Economics. New York, the Macmillan company, 1926. Cloth. OP.

xvi p., 1 l., 327 p. 19.2 cm.
Appendices, p. 305–321; index, p. 323–327.
Half title, "The Institute of Economics. Investigations in Agricultural Economics."

1309 LATHAM, DR. H. Trans-Missouri stock raising; the pasture lands of North America; winter grazing; the sources of the future beef and wool supply of the United States. . . . By Dr. H. Latham. . . . Written originally as letters to the Omaha Daily Herald. Omaha, Nebraska, Daily Herald steam printing house, 1871. Wrappers. Very rare.

[3]–88 p. fold. col. map in front, map on verso back wrapper. 22 cm.
Adv. verso front wrapper; adv. recto back wrapper.

1310 LAUDE, G. A. Kansas shorthorns; a history of the breed in the state from 1857 to 1920. By G. A. Laude. . . . Compiled and published under the direction of the committee on publication of the Kansas Shorthorn Breeders' Association. . . . Iola, Kansas, the Laude printing company, 1920. Cloth. OP.

[5]–647 p. front., plates. 20.2 cm.
Index, p. [635]–647.
Republished same year.

1311 LAUDERDALE, ROBERT JASPER (BOB), and JOHN M. DOAK. Life on the range and the trail, as told by R. J. (Bob) Lauderdale and John M. Doak. Edited by Lela Neal Prittle, pen and ink sketches by Arrie Neal Fricke. San Antonio, Texas, the Naylor company, 1936. Pict. cloth.

xiii p., 1 l., 227 p. front., illus., ports., cattle brands. 23.5 cm.
Glossary, p. 214–219; cattle brands, p. 220–227.

Experiences of two real old-time cowboys.

1312 LAUGHLIN, EDWARD DOUGLAS. The Yaqui gold, by Edward Douglas Laughlin. San Antonio, Texas, the Naylor company, 1943. Pict. cloth.

3 p.l., 80 p. plates. 21 cm.

Has some information on ranching.

1313 LAUGHLIN, RUTH (BARKER). Caballeros, by Ruth Laughlin Barker; illustrations by Norma van Sweringen. New York, Toronto, D. Appleton and co., inc., 1931. Cloth. Scarce.

4 p.l., 379 ₁1₁ p. front., illus. 22 cm.
Index, p. 373–₁380₁.
Half title; vignette; first edition, figure "(1)" at end of index.
Republished in 1937.

Published again in 1945 by the Caxton printers, ltd., Caldwell, Idaho, with the addition of a glossary.

4 p.l., 418 p. front., illus. 22 cm.
Map on end papers.

1314 LAVENDER, DAVID. The big divide, ₁by₁ David Lavender. Garden City, N. Y., Doubleday & company, inc., 1948. Cloth. OP.

x p., 1 l., 321 p. plates, ports. 22 cm.
Acknowledgments, p. ₁295₁–297; bibliography, p. ₁301₁–307; index, p. ₁311₁–321.
Half title; map on end papers; device; untrimmed; "First edition" on copyright p.

1315 ———. One man's West, by David Lavender; line drawings by William Arthur Smith. Garden City, New York, Doubleday, Doran & co., inc., 1943. Cloth. OP.

vi p., 1 l., 3–298 p. front., illus. 20.6 cm.
Half title; pub. device; untrimmed; "First edition" on copyright p.

Part II deals with stock trails and has some good stories about cowboy life.

1316 LAWRENCE, W. H. New Mexico. Territorial Bureau of Immigration. Report of Grant County. This report was prepared by W. H. Lawrence, commissioner, Silver City, Grant County. Silver City, N. M., W. Cardnell, printer, Southwest office, 1881. Wrappers. Scarce.

₁3₁–31 p. 21.8 cm.

1317 LEA, TOM. Randado. ₁El Paso, Texas, Carl Hertzog, 1941₁. Stiff wrappers. Pict. label pasted on.

₁7₁ p. (no pagination). illus. 29.5 cm.
Illus. t.p.
Colophon: "100 numbered and signed copies, of which 25 are for sale, have been printed by Carl Hertzog at El Paso, Texas,—February, 1941. This is number ———."

1318 ———. Volume One. The King Ranch, by Tom Lea. Maps and drawings by the author. Research Holland McCombs, annotation Francis L. Fugate. Boston, Toronto, Little, Brown and company, ₁1957₁. Two-toned buckram. Boxed. Pub. in 2 vols.

6 p.l., 467 ₁1₁ p. illus., plates (part col.), 6 maps (part col., 3 double-p.), facsms. 24 cm.
Appendices, p. 375–₁419₁; notes and sources, p. 421–467.
Half title; illus. chapter headings.

Volume Two.

6 p.l., [469]–838 [1] p. illus., plates (part col., 1 double-p.), map (col. double-p.), facsms. 24 cm.

Appendices, p. 707–773; notes and sources, p. 777–801; index, p. 805–838 [1].
Half title; illus. chapter headings.

1319 ———. Volume One. The King Ranch, by Tom Lea. Drawings by the author. Research Holland McCombs, annotation Francis L. Fugate. Kingsville, Texas, printed for the King Ranch, MCMLVII. Dec. crash linen. Boxed. Pub. in 2 vols.

5 p.l., 467 [1] p. illus., plates (part col.), 6 maps (all col., 3 double-p.), facsms. 24 cm.

Appendices, p. 375–[419]; notes and sources, p. 421–467.
Half title; illus. chapter headings; untrimmed.

Volume Two.

5 p.l., [469]–838 [1] p. illus., plates (part col., 1 double-p.), map (col. double-p.), facsms. 24 cm.

Appendices, p. 707–773; notes and sources, p. 777–801; index, p. 805–838 [1].
Half title; illus. chapter headings; untrimmed.

The binding of this special limited edition is of crash linen in facsimile of the saddle blankets woven and used on the King Ranch, having a running "W" in the center. Both volumes in a box covered with like material. On the front fly leaf of volume I, fastened with Scotch tape, is a card reading: "This is your copy of the Private Edition of 'The King Ranch' by Tom Lea. To be published in 1957. This book is not for public distribution."
  Not a single volume of this edition was sold, for all were given to friends and relatives. The main difference in the two editions is the paper and the binding. An all-rag paper, made especially for this book by the Curtis Paper Company, and watermarked with the running "W" brand, was used in the special edition. This edition is also untrimmed and is somewhat thicker than the trade edition.

1320 LECKENBY, CHARLES H. The tread of pioneers. . . . Some highlights in the dramatic and colorful history of northwestern Colorado, compiled by Charles H. Leckenby. Steamboat Springs, Colo., from the Pilot press, [1945]. Cloth. OP.

1 p.l., [1] p., 6–206 [1] p. plates, ports. 23.6 cm.
Table of contents labeled "Index" at end; vignette; copyright notice on verso of flyleaf before t.p.

Privately printed and issued in a small edition, thus quite scarce.

1321 LECKY, PETER. Peter Lecky, by himself. New York, Charles Scribner's sons, 1936. Cloth. OP.

5 p.l., 13–349 p. 21 cm.
Half title; pub. device; untrimmed; first edition, letter "A" on copyright p.

1322 [LEESON, MICHAEL A]. History of Montana, 1739–1885. A history of
its discovery and settlement, social and commercial progress, mines and
miners, agriculture and stock growing, churches, schools, and societies,
Indians and Indian war, vigilantes, court of justice. . . . Illustrated.
Chicago, Warner, Beers & company, 1885. Three-quarter leather.
Scarce.

7 p.l., 15–1367 p. large fold. map (col.) in front., plates, ports. 27.7 cm.

Has a chapter on cattle and cowboys.

1323 LeFORS, JOE. Wyoming peace officer. By Joe LeFors. An autobiography. Laramie, Wyoming, Laramie printing company, [1953].
Cloth.

xiii [1] p., 1 l., 200 p. plates, ports. 24.2 cm.
Appendix, p. 187–192; index, p. 195–200.
Tailpieces.

Published by the author's wife after his death, this book reveals heretofore
unwritten information about Tom Horn and the Johnson County War.

1324 LEFTWICH, BILL. Tracks along the Pecos, by Bill Leftwich. [Pecos,
Texas, Pecos press, 1957]. Pict. wrappers. (Cover title).

4 p.l., 70 p. illus., plates, ports., maps, plans, facsms. 25 cm.

1325 LEIGH, WILLIAM ROBERTSON. The western pony, written and illustrated by William R. Leigh; foreword by James L. Clark. New York,
Huntington press, [1933]. Pict. cloth. Scarce.

9 p.l., 21–116 [1] p. illus. (col. part mounted, with tissues). 31.8 cm.
Half title; illus. t.p.; col. plate laid in; tailpieces; untrimmed; gilt top; "First edition" on copyright p.

Republished in 1935 by Harper and Brothers, with same collation and format.

1326 LEMMON, GEORGE E. Developing the West, by G. E. Lemmon . . . ,
well-known early day cattle man. Taken from Belle Fourche Bee, Belle
Fourche, S. D., [n. d.] Rare.

145 p. 1 port. 20.4x15.3 cm.
Double column.

This appears to be bound galley sheets of the various articles which appeared
in the *Belle Fourche Bee*. The few copies of which I know are bound in
various ways, my personal copy being bound in leather with five buckskin
ties. Gives much important information by this well-known cattleman.

1327 LEWIS, ALFRED HENRY. The sunset trail, by Alfred Henry Lewis. . . .
Illustrated. New York, A. S. Barnes & co., 1905. Pict. cloth. Scarce.

x p., 3 l., 393 [6] p. front., plates. 19 cm.
Half title; device.
Last 6 p. adv.
Republished by A. L. Burt in 1906.

1328 LEWIS, GEORGE McCOY. A market analysis of the cattle industry of
Texas, by George McCoy Lewis. Austin, Texas, the University, [1928].
Wrappers. OP.

7 p.l., [13]–171 p. 1 illus., fold. map, 2 fold. tables, diagrs. (1 fold.). 22 cm.
(*University of Texas Bulletin No. 2836,* September 22, 1928).
Bureau of Business Research; *Research Monograph No. 2.*

1329 LEWIS, WILLIAM S. The story of early days in the Big Bend country;
breaking trails, rush of miners, coming of cattlemen, making homes, pioneer hardships in the Big Bend country, as told by William S. Lewis. . . .
Spokane, Wash., W. D. Allen, publisher, 1926. Stiff wrappers. Scarce.

[3]–35 [1] p. front., plates. 24.6 cm.

Issued in an edition limited to 105 copies "Big Bend Edition" and 100 autographed numbered copies.

1330 LEWIS, WILLIE NEWBURY. Between sun and sod, by Willie Newbury
Lewis; with illustrations by H. D. Bugbee. Clarendon, Texas, Clarendon press, [1938]. Pict. cloth. OP.

xv p., 1 l., 244 p. illus. 23.5 cm.
Appendix, p. 229–244.
Half-title; vignette.

The first printing of this book was quickly withdrawn by the publishers on
account of typographical errors and omissions. This first printing differs from
the commonly accepted "first" finally issued in that it does not contain the
introduction by John McCarty, the "contents" precedes the "foreword," it
does not include the "list of illustrations," and it does not have the Roman
numerals. It also has a different binding and the name "Newbury" was spelled
"Newberry." About 25 copies were issued before errors were discovered. This
edition was destroyed, and the book was reprinted in an edition of 1,000 copies,
followed later by another printing of 2,000.

1331 LILLIE, GORDON WILLIAM (PAWNEE BILL). Life story of Pawnee Bill.
[By Gordon William Lillie. . . . N.p., n.d.]. Pamphlet. Scarce.

22 p. illus. 21.3 cm.
Double column.

1332 ———. Life of G. W. Lillie, "Pawnee Bill," hero of Oklahoma, school
teacher, Indian interpreter, town founder, banker, and sole owner of
Pawnee Bill's Historic Wild West and Great Far East Combined. [N.p.,
n.d.]. Pict. wrappers. (Cover title). Scarce.

5–38 p. illus., plates, ports. 24.3 cm.
Adv. scattered throughout.

1333 LINDERMAN, FRANK BIRD. Bunch-grass and blue-joint, by Frank B.
Linderman. C. Scribner's sons, 1921. Cloth. Scarce.

ix p., 1 l., 115 p. front. 17.5 cm.

1334 ——. On a passing frontier; sketches from the Northwest, by Frank B. Linderman. New York, Charles Scribner's sons, 1920. Cloth. Scarce.

5 p.l., 3–214 p. 19.4 cm.
Half title; untrimmed.

1335 LINDSAY, CHARLES. Big Horn Basin, by Charles Lindsay. ₁Lincoln, Nebr., 1932₁. Stiff wrappers. (Cover title). OP.

6 p.l., 11–274 p. illus., maps (part fold.). 23 cm.
Bibliography, p. 261–274.
Thesis (Ph. D.), University of Nebraska, 1930.
Also issued as *University of Nebraska Studies,* Vol. XXVIII–XXIX.

Contains a long chapter on the cattle industry.

1336 LINFORD, VELMA. Wyoming, frontier state, by Velma Linford. Drawings by Ramona Bowman. Denver, Colorado, the Old West publishing co., 1947. Pict. cloth. OP.

xii p., 1 l., ₁3₁–428 p. front., illus., plates, ports., maps. 23.2 cm.
Bibliography at end of each chapter; appendix, p. 407–414; full bibliography, p. 415–418; pronouncing index, p. 419–428.
Illus. end papers.

Written as a school history, this book contains much material on the cattle industry of Wyoming and the cattle war in Johnson County.

1337 LINTHICUM, RICHARD. A book of Rocky Mountain tales (souvenir edition), by Richard Linthicum. ₁Denver, Colorado, W. F. Robinson & co., printers, 1892₁. Pict. cloth. Scarce.

4 p.l., ₁9₁–158 p. front. (port.), illus. 20.3 cm.
Author's roll of honor, p. ₁151₁–158.

1338 LINZEE, E. H. Development of Oklahoma Territory, by E. H. Linzee, 1940. ₁Oklahoma City, 1941₁. Cloth. Scarce.

₁49₁ p. (no pagination). front., plates, ports. 28.6 cm.

1339 LISTER, JOHN HAROLD, and C. G. RANDELL. Analysis of the operation of a co-operative livestock concentration point. By John H. Lister . . . and C. G. Randell. . . . Washington, ₁Government printing office₁, 1931. Wrappers. OP.

32 p. illus., maps, diagrs. 23.4 cm.
(U. S. Dept. of Agriculture *Circular No. 142*).
A contribution from the Bureau of Agricultural Economics.

1340 LOCKARD, FRANK MARION. Black Kettle, by Frank M. Lockard. . . . Goodland, Kansas, R. G. Wolfe, publisher, ₁n. d.₁. Wrappers. Scarce.

1 p.l., 3–40 p. illus., ports. 18.8 cm.
Seal on t.p. and cover.

1341 LOCKWOOD, FRANK CUMMINS. Arizona characters, by Frank C. Lockwood. . . . Los Angeles, the Times-Mirror press, 1928. Pict. cloth. OP.
xiv p., 1 l., 230 p. front., illus., plates, ports. 20.2 cm.
Half title.

1342 ———. Life in old Tucson, 1854–1864, as remembered by the little maid Atanacia Santa Cruz, by Frank C. Lockwood. . . . Los Angeles, the Ward Ritchie press, published by the Tucson Civic Committee, MCMXLIII.
xx p., 1 l., 3–255 p. front. (port.), plates, ports. 21.5 cm.
Half title; t.p. in red and black.

1343 ———. Pioneer days in Arizona, from the Spanish occupation to statehood, by Frank C. Lockwood. . . . New York, the Macmillan company, 1932. Cloth. OP.
xiv p., 5 l., 9–387 p. front. (port.), illus., plates, ports., maps. 24 cm.
Index, p. 379–387.
Half title; untrimmed.

1344 LOGAN, HERSCHEL C. Buckskin and satin. The life of Texas Jack (J. B. Omohundro), buckskin clad scout, Indian fighter, plainsman, cowboy, hunter, guide, and actor, and his wife Mlle. Morlacchi, première danseuse in satin slippers, by Herschel C. Logan, with a foreword by Paul I. Wellman. Harrisburg, Pennsylvania, published by the Stackpole company, [1954]. Pict. cloth.
xiv, 218 p. front. (port.)., illus., plates, ports., facsms., maps. 22.6 cm.
Chronology, p. 205–207; bibliography, p. 208–211; acknowledgments, p. 212–213; index, p. 214–218.
Illus. half title; illus. end papers; "First edition" on copyright p.

Has a chapter on the Texas cattle days and the Chisholm Trail.

1345 [LOGAN, WALTER S., ET AL.]. Arizona and some of her friends. The toasts and responses at a complimentary dinner given by Walter S. Logan, at the Marine and Field Club, Bath Beach, N. Y., Tuesday, July 28, 1891, to Hon. John N. Irwin, governor of Arizona, and Herbert H. Logan, of Phoenix, Arizona. [N. p.], 1891. Stiff wrappers. Scarce.
[3]–48 p. 21.5 cm.
Headpieces; tailpieces.

Has some information on stock raising.

1346 LOGUE, ROSCOE. Tumbleweeds and barb wire fences, by Roscoe Logue. Amarillo, Texas, printed by Russell stationery co., 1936. Stiff pict. wrappers.
5 p.l., 11–110 p. illus., plates, ports. 23.6 cm.
Vignette; copyright notice on t.p.

1347 ———. Under Texas and border skies, by Roscoe Logue. Amarillo, Texas, printed by Russell stationery co., 1935. Stiff pict. wrappers.
4 p.l., 5–111 p. illus., plates, facsm. 23.6 cm.
Vignette; copyright notice on t.p.

1348 Lomax, E. L. (ed.). The resources and attractions of Wyoming for the home seeker, capitalist, and tourist. Facts on farming, stock raising, mining, lumbering, and other industries. . . . Battle Creek, Mich., Wm. C. Gage & sons, printers, 1890. Wrappers. Scarce.
3 p.l., ₁7₁–88 p. 20.8 cm.
Map on verso front wrapper.

Information on stock raising throughout. Issued by the Union Pacific Railway and reprinted many times.

1349 ———. Oregon: a complete and comprehensive description of the agriculture, stock raising, and mineral resources. St. Louis, 1892. Wrappers. Scarce.
98 p. 21.5 cm.

1350 Lomax, John Avery. Adventures of a ballad hunter, by John A. Lomax. Sketches by Ken Chamberlain. New York, the Macmillan co., 1947. Cloth. OP.
xi ₁1₁ p., 302 p. illus. 21 cm.
Half title; illus. chapter headings; vignette; "First printing" on copyright p.

Chapter III, "Hunting Cowboy Songs," deals with the cowboy and the author's experiences in gathering songs in the cow country.

1351 Long, E. Hudson. O. Henry, the man and his work, by E. Hudson Long. Philadelphia, University of Pennsylvania press, 1949. Cloth.
xi ₁1₁ p., 1 l., 158 p. front. (port.). 22.2 cm.
Notes, p. 138–148; selected bibliography, p. 149–152; index, p. 153–158.
Half title; pub. device.

Has a chapter on O. Henry's life on a Texas ranch.

1352 Long, Margaret. The Smoky Hill Trail; following the old historic pioneer trails on the modern highways, ₁by₁ Margaret Long. . . . ₁Denver, the W. H. Kistler stationery company, 1943₁. Cloth. OP.
xi p., 1 l., 336 ₁38₁ p. front., plates, ports., 10 maps (8 fold.). 24.3 cm.
Map on end papers; leaf of errata tipped in after viii; 36 unnumbered pages of plates at end.

1353 Long, Richard M. "Dick" (ed.). Wichita, 1866–1883. Cradle days of a midwestern city. Wichita, Kansas, ₁McCormick-Armstrong co.₁, 1945. Cloth. OP.

₍79₎ p. (no pagination).   plates, ports. 28.6 cm.
Map on front end paper; facsm. on back end paper.
Colophon: ". . . three hundred copies have been printed, of which this is No. ⸺."

1354 LORD, JOHN. Frontier dust, by John Lord. Edited, with an introduction, by Natalie Shipman. Hartford, Connecticut, Edwin Valentine Mitchell, 1926. Cloth. Title label pasted on. OP.

x p., 1 l., 198 ₍1₎ p. 22.2 cm.
Half title.
Colophon: "This book has been designed by Robert S. Josephy and a thousand copies have been printed under his supervision at the shop of Douglas C. McMurtrie, N. Y., in December, MCMXXVI."

A very unreliable book.

1355 LOVE, NAT. The life and adventures of Nat Love, better known in the cattle country as "Deadwood Dick," by himself. A true history of slavery days, life on the great cattle ranges and on the plains of the "wild and woolly" West, based on facts, and personal experiences of the author. Los Angeles, California, ₍Wayside press₎, 1907. Pict. cloth. Scarce.

3 p. l., ₍7₎–162 p. front. (port.), illus., plates, ports. 23.3 cm.

Although this Negro author is supposed to have been writing of his own experiences, he either had a bad memory or a good imagination.

1356 LOVING, GEORGE B. Stock manual containing the name, post office address, ranch location, marks, and brands of all the principal stockmen of western and northwestern Texas, showing marks and brands on electrotype cuts as they appear on the animal. . . . Ft. Worth, Texas, George B. Loving, publisher, 1881. Cloth. Exceedingly rare.

274 p. cattle brands. 18.3 cm.
Index, 10 unnumbered pages; index to advertisements, 3 unnumbered pages; index to brands, 9 unnumbered pages.
Adv. scattered throughout.

1357 LOWE, PAUL EMILIUS (HARRY HAWKEYE, PSEUD.). Cowboys of the wild West. A graphic portrayal of cowboy life on the boundless plains of the wild West with its attending realistic and exciting incidents and adventures, by Harry Hawkeye. New York, L. Lipkind, 1908. Pict. wrappers. Scarce.

4 p.l., 9–189 p. illus. 18.5 cm.
Reprinted by I. and M. Ottenheimer, Baltimore, ₍n.d.₎.

Both editions crudely printed on pulp paper.

1358 LOWTHER, CHARLES C. Dodge City, Kansas, by Charles C. Lowther. . . . Illustrated. Philadelphia, Dorrance and company, publishers, ₍1940₎. Cloth. OP.

4 p.l., 9–213 p. front., illus., plates. 19.3 cm.
Pub. device.

1359 ———. Panhandle parson. By Charles C. Lowther. Nashville, Tenn., the Parthenon press, [1942]. Fabricoid. OP.

5 p.l., 11–253 p. illus. 19.4 cm.
Half title; device.

1360 LUDLOW, FITZ HUGH. The heart of the continent; a record of travel across the plains and in Oregon, with an examination of the Mormon principle. By Fitz Hugh Ludlow. With illustrations. New York, published by Hurd and Houghton, 1870. Cloth. Rare.

vi, 568 p. front. (with tissue), plates. 21.8 cm.

1361 LUMMIS, CHARLES FLETCHER. The king of bronchos and other stories of New Mexico, by Charles F. Lummis. New York, Charles Scribner's sons, 1897. Cloth. Scarce.

ix, 254 p. front. (port.), plates. 19 cm.

1362 ———. A New Mexico David and other stories and sketches of the Southwest, by Charles F. Lummis. New York, Charles Scribner's sons, 1891. Pict. cloth. OP.

ix, 217 p. front. (port., with tissue), illus., plates. 19 cm.
Half title.

1363 ———. A tramp across the continent, by Charles F. Lummis. New York, Charles Scribner's sons, 1892. Cloth. OP.

xiii, 270 p. 19 cm.

1364 LYMAN, CLARENCE A. The fertile lands of Colorado and northern New Mexico. A concise description of the vast area of agricultural, horticultural, and grazing lands located on the line of the Denver & Rio Grande Railroad in the state of Colorado and the territory of New Mexico. . . . Compiled by Clarence A. Lyman. . . . [N.p.], published by the Passenger Department, the Denver & Rio Grande Railroad, 1908. Stiff pict. wrappers. Scarce.

2 p.l., [5]–72 [7] p. front., illus., plates, large fold. map at end. 22.5 cm.

1365 MABRY, W. S. Some memories of W. S. Mabry, XIT. [Bandera, Texas, Frontier Times print, 1927]. Wrappers. (Cover title). Scarce.

32 p. 18.5 cm.

1366 MCALLASTER, B. (COMPILER). Kansas, the golden belt lands along the line of the Kansas division of the U. P. R'y. Kansas City, Mo., [n. d.]. Pict. wrappers. Rare.

48 p. illus., maps (1 col. i fold.). 22.6 cm.

1367 MCATEE, JOHN L. Brief for the Cherokee Strip Live Stock Association. The Cherokee Live Stock Association *vs.* the McClellan Cattle Company, Case Land and Cattle Co., Head and Lawrence, Jot Gunter, Tom Green Cattle Co., Hall Brothers, Smith, Tuttle and Holecraft, Winfield Cattle Co., George W. Miller, J. R. Stroller . . . and others. Statement, points, and authorities for the plaintiff. John L. McAtee, attorney for plaintiff. Kansas City, press of Lawton and Burnap, ₁1890₁. Stiff wrappers. (Cover title). Very rare.

78 p. 22.2 cm.

This important cattle-trade trial concerns the right of the Cherokee Nation to charge rental for the use of its Oklahoma lands for grazing, when, in 1890, President Harrison issued a proclamation denying the right of the Cherokees to lease their lands and demanded the removal of cattle from these lands. This brief is in behalf of the Indians and vigorously attacks the President's action.

1368 McCARTHY, DONALD (ED.). "Language of the longhorn"; a glossary of cowboy lingo, rodeo terms, dude ranch jargon, range profanity, and other western expressions. Compiled by native authorities, edited by Don McCarthy; illustrations by Will James and Dale Petit. ₁Billings, Mont., the Gazette printing co., 1936₁. Pict. wrappers. Scarce.

3 p.l., ₁12₁ p. (no pagination). illus., plates (1 double p.). 27 cm.
Double column; "First printing" on verso fly leaf.

1369 McCARTY, JOHN L. Adobe Walls bride. The story of Billy and Olive King Dixon, by John L. McCarty. San Antonio, Texas, the Naylor company, ₁1955₁. Cloth.

xi p., 281 p. illus., plates, ports. 21.7 cm.
Notes, p. 261–264; bibliography, p. 265–273; index, p. 275–281.
Half title; illus. end papers; illus. t.p.

1370 ———. The enchanted West. ₁Illustrated by Ignatz Sahula-Dycke₁. ₁Dallas, Texas, Dr. Pepper co., 1944.₁ Stiff col. pict. wrappers. OP.

₁40₁ p. (no pagination). illus., (in col.). 22.8 cm.
Double column.

1371 ———. Maverick town, the story of old Tascosa, by John L. McCarty, with chapter decorations by Harold Bugbee. Norman, University of Oklahoma press, 1946. Pict. cloth.

xiii p., 1 l., 3–277 p. plates, ports. 21 cm.
Bibliography, p. 261–266; index, p. 267–277.
Half title; map on end papers; illus. chapter headings; illus. double t.p.

1372 ———. Some experiences of Boss Neff in the Texas and Oklahoma Panhandle, ₁by John L. McCarty. Chapter decorations by Harold D. Bugbee₁. ₁Amarillo, Texas, Globe-News publishing co., 1941₁. Stiff pict. wrappers. (Cover title). OP.

₁28₁ p. (no pagination). front. (port.), illus. 27 cm.
Triple column.

1373 McCAULEY, JAMES EMMITT. A stove-up cowboy's story, by James Emmitt McCauley. Introduction by John A. Lomax. Drawings by Tom Lea. ₍Dallas, Texas₎, published by the Texas Folklore Society, Austin, Texas, and the University press in Dallas, 1943. Pict. cloth. OP.

xxii p., 1 l., 73 p. front., illus. 22.2 cm.
Illus. end papers.
Colophon: "700 copies of this book have been printed and the type melted."

1374 McCLINTOCK, JAMES H. Arizona, with particular attention to its imperial county of Maricopa. A land of plenty, under smiling skies. Written by James H. McClintock. . . . Phoenix, Arizona, press of the Arizona Republican, 1901. Wrappers. Scarce.

₍5₎-64 ₍4₎ p. front., illus., plates, fold. map at end. 19.5 cm.

1375 ———. Arizona, prehistoric, aboriginal, pioneer, modern. The nation's youngest commonwealth within a land of ancient culture. By James H. McClintock. Chicago, the S. J. Clarke publishing co., 1916. Three-quarter leather. Pub. in 3 vols. Scarce.

Vol. I: x, 312 p. front. (port. with tissue), plates, ports., maps. 26.2 cm.
Vol. II: vii, 313–633 p. plates, ports. 26.6 cm.
Index, p. 623–633.
Vol. III: 2 p.l., 5–961 p. front., ports. 26.6 cm.
Index, p. 955–961.
Vols. I and II paged continuously; Vol. III, biographical; title on spine; "Arizona, the Youngest State."

1376 McCLINTOCK, JOHN S. Pioneer days in the Black Hills. Accurate history and facts related by one of the early day pioneers. Author John S. McClintock, Deadwood, S. D., edited by Edward L. Senn, Deadwood, S. D. Deadwood, South Dakota, published by John S. McClintock. Cloth. Scarce.

x p., 2 l., 336 p. front. (port.), plates, ports. 23.5 cm.
Half title; device.

1377 McCLURE, ALEXANDER KELLY. Three thousand miles through the Rocky Mountains, by A. K. McClure. Philadelphia, J. B. Lippincott & co., 1869. Cloth. Scarce.

8 p.l., 17–456 p. front. (with tissue), plates. 19.5 cm.
Appendix, p. 453–456.
Pub. device.

1378 McCLURE, MEADE L. Major Andrew Drumm, 1828–1919. A sketch prepared and read by Meade L. McClure before the Missouri Valley Historical Society, May 31, 1919. ₍N.p., n.d., c.1919₎. Suede binding. Scarce.

2 p.l., 5–41 p. front. (port. with tissue), plates, ports. (with tissues). 24 cm. Untrimmed.

Material on the Cherokee Strip Live Stock Association, of which Mr. Drumm was at one time president.

1379 McCOMBS, R. V. "Watch the chutes! The story of a roundup, by R. V. McCombs, with over seventy illustrations from photographs. Boston, Richard C. Badger, the Gorman press, [1930]. Cloth. OP.

7 p.l., 15–128 [1] p. front., plates, ports. 20.9 cm.
Half title; pub. device.

A story of the rodeo, not the roundup.

1380 McCONNELL, H. H. Five years a cavalryman; or, sketches of regular army life on the Texas frontier, twenty odd years ago. By H. H. McConnell. . . . Jacksboro, Texas, J. H. Rogers & co., printers, 1889. Cloth. Scarce.

viii p., 1 l., [11]–319 p. 19.6 cm.
Appendix, p. [301]–313; table of contents, p. [315]–319.
Printed on pink paper.

The appendix concerns cowboys and cattle thieves.

1381 McCORMICK, RICHARD CUNNINGHAM. Arizona: its resources and prospects. A letter to the editor of the New York Tribune (reprinted from that journal of June 26th, 1865). By the Hon. Richard C. McCormick. New York, D. van Nostrand, 1865. Wrappers. Rare.

22 p. front. (fold. map). 23.5 cm.

1382 ———. Message of Hon. R. C. McCormick, acting governor of the territory of Arizona, to the second legislative assembly at Prescott, December 11, 1865. Prescott, Office of the *Arizona Miner,* official paper of the territory, 1865. Sewn. Rare.

13 p. 19.5 cm.

Two copies located: in the Library of Congress and the Bancroft Library. Among other subjects, it describes ranching in the Territory's second year of civil government.

1383 McCORMICK, S. D. An address delivered before the annual convention of the Butcher's National Protective Association, May 28th, 1890. Being a review of the cattle industry, and showing the compilation of the cattle pool. By S. D. McCormick. [N. p., n. d.]. Wrappers. (Cover title). Rare.

20 p. 22.2 cm.

1384 McCOY, JOSEPH GEITING. Address of invitation to a mass-meeting of live stock men, provision dealers, and packers at Kansas City, Mo., Sep-

Courteously Yours

Jos. G. McCoy

HISTORIC SKETCHES

OF THE

CATTLE TRADE

OF THE

WEST AND SOUTHWEST.

By JOSEPH G. McCOY,

THE PIONEER WESTERN CATTLE SHIPPER.

ILLUSTRATED BY PROF. HENRY WORRALL, TOPEKA, KAS.
ENGRAVED BY BAKER & CO., CHICAGO, ILL.
ELECTROTYPED BY J. T. RETON & CO., KANSAS CITY, MO.

PUBLISHED BY
RAMSEY, MILLETT & HUDSON, KANSAS CITY, MO.,
PRINTERS, BINDERS, ENGRAVERS, LITHOGRAPHERS & STATIONERS.
1874.

tember 17th, 1873. ₁Kansas City₁, Daily News steam book and job printing house, 1873. Folder. (Cover title). Excessively rare.
₁4₁ p. (no pagination). 20x13.3 cm.

Originally published for free circulation, this item is now excessively rare.
It is an address of invitation for the organization of cattlemen, provision men,
and packers for their mutual benefit. It was perhaps the first attempt to
organize the cattle trade. It was instrumental in bringing together nearly
2,000 cattlemen for a banquet, and the following day the association was
organized. This copy seen in the library of Thomas W. Streeter, though a
photostat copy has been in my own library for many years.

1385 ———. Historic sketches of the cattle trade of the West and Southwest, by Joseph G. McCoy, the pioneer western cattle shipper. Illustrated
by Prof. Henry Worrall . . . , engraved by Baker and co. . . . , electrotyped
by J. T. Reton and co. . . . , Kansas City, Mo., published by Ramsey,
Millett & Hudson, 1874. Pict. cloth. Rare.
3 p.l., 427 ₁22₁ p. front., illus., ports. 22.8 cm.
22 p. adv. at end.

One of the "big four" cattle books, written by a man who opened the market
for Texas cattle. This is one of the first and most important books on the
cattle trade. Some copies were published with full-page advertisements on
inside of front and back covers, some without.

Reprinted in facsimile, Washington, D. C., Rare Book shop, 1932.
3 p.l., 427 ₁20₁ p. front. (port.), illus., plates, ports. 23.6 cm.
20 p. adv. at end (last 2 l. of the original edition being omitted).

Reprinted in 1940 by Arthur H. Clark, Glendale, Calif., edited by Ralph
P. Bieber, with biographical notes. Includes reproduction of title page of
original edition.
6 p.l., ₁13₁–435 p., 1 l. front. (port.), plates, ports. 24.2 cm.
Half title, "The Southwest Historical Series, ed. by Ralph P. Bieber."

Because of the valuable footnotes, this is easily the best edition.

Reprinted again in facsimile by Long's College Book shop, Columbus,
Ohio, in 1951.

1386 McCRACKEN, HAROLD. Frederic Remington, artist of the old West,
with a bibliographical check list of Remington pictures and books, by
Harold McCracken. Introduction by James Chillman, Jr. . . . . Philadelphia, and New York, J. B. Lippincott company, ₁1947₁. Cloth.
11 p.l., 21–157 ₁79₁ p. illus., plates (part col.). 21.2 cm.
Bibliographical check list, p. 123–157 (triple column).
Half title; last 79 p. plates (last 32 col. with letterpress on opposite p.); device on t.p.

1387 ———. The Charles M. Russell book. The life and work of the cowboy artist. By Harold McCracken. Garden City, N. Y., Doubleday & company, inc., 1957. Dec. cloth.

9 p.l., 13–326 p. front., illus., plates (all col., 12 double p.), port., facsms. 34.2 cm.
Notes, p. 232–233; index, p. 234–236.
Half title; vignette; gilt top.

Also published in a de luxe edition with better paper and different binding. Also published in a limited edition, bound in leather and cased. This edition has an extra plate (col.) tipped in before the title page of a picture entitled "The Free Trappers."

Colophon: "This edition of *The Charles M. Russell Book* is limited to two hundred and fifty copies and signed, of which this is number ———."

This edition was oversubscribed and is very difficult to secure.

1388 McCRARY, G. W., and WALLACE PRATT. Does the territorial law of New Mexico, requiring the inspection of live animals for human food, conflict with the constitution? Opinion by Hon. C. W. McCrary and Wallace Pratt. . . . ₍N. p., n. d.₎. Wrappers.

16 p. 21.4 cm.

1389 McCULLOCH, BRUCE. Molly Whiteface, the tale of a cow, by Bruce McCulloch. ₍Omaha, Nebr., Journal-Stockman co., printers₎, 1935. Stiff pict. wrappers. OP.

32 p., illus. 18 cm.
Illus. chapter headings.

1390 McDEARMON, RAY. Without the shedding of blood. The story of Dr. U. D. Ezell and of pioneer life at Old Kimball. ₍By₎ Ray McDearmon. San Antonio, Texas, the Naylor company, ₍1953₎. Cloth.

xii, 81 p. 21.6 cm.
Half title.

1391 McDERMOTT, EDITH SWAIN. The pioneer history of Greeley County, Nebraska. ₍By₎ Edith Swain McDermott. ₍Greeley, Nebraska, printed by Citizen printing company, 1939₎. Cloth. OP.

3 p.l., ₍7₎–174 p. map. 19.6 cm.

1392 McDERMOTT-STEVENSON, MYRA E. Lariat letters, by Myra E. McDermott-Stevenson. Illustrated by Zella Bey Maine. ₍N. p., privately printed, 1907₎. Limp leather. Rare.

2 p.l., 5–42 p. illus. 18.9 cm.
Illus. half title.

Some humorous cowboy letters.

1393 MacDONALD, JAMES. Food from the far West; or, American agriculture with special reference to beef production and importation of dead meat from America to Great Britain, by James MacDonald. . . . London and Edinburgh, William P. Nimmo, 1878. Dec. cloth. Scarce.

xvi, 331 [4] p. 19.5 cm.
Half title; 4 unnumbered p. adv. at end.

1394 MacDonald, James, and James Sinclair. History of Aberdeen-Angus cattle, by James MacDonald . . . and James Sinclair. . . . Revised edition by James Sinclair. . . . London, Vinton and co., ltd., 1910. Cloth. OP.

xxviii, 682 p. front., plates, ports. 22 cm.

1395 ———. History of Hereford cattle, by James MacDonald . . . and James Sinclair. . . . London, Vinton and co., ltd., 1909. Cloth. OP.

xvi, 501 p., 1 l. front., plates, ports. 22.4 cm.

1396 McDougall, John. Saddle, sled, and snowshoe. Pioneering on the Saskatchewann in the sixties. By John McDougall . . . , with illustrations by J. E. Laughlin. Cincinnati, Jennings and Graham; New York, Eaton and Mains, [n.d., c.1896]. Pict. cloth. Scarce.

ix, [11]–282 p. front., plates. 19. cm.

Contains some material on ranching in Canada.

1397 McElrath, Thompson P. The Yellowstone Valley, what it is, where it is, and how to get to it. A hand-book for tourists and settlers. Illustrated. By Thompson P. McElrath. St. Paul, the Pioneer press Co., 1880. Cloth. Rare.

3 p.l., [7]–138 [6] p. illus., large fold. map in front. 18.8 cm.
Index, p. [134]–138.
Last 6 p. adv.

Has a long chapter on stock raising and Montana ranches.

1398 MacEwan, Grant. Between the Red and the Rockies, by Grant MacEwan. [Toronto], University of Toronto press, 1952. Pict. cloth.

x p., 1 l., 8–300 p. illus., maps. 21.8 cm.
Index, p. 297–300.
Half title; headpieces; illus. t.p.
Reprinted in 1953.

A history of the cattle industry in Canada.

1399 McEwen, Inez Puckett. So this is ranching, By Inez Puckett McEwen. Illustrated with photographs. Limited edition. Caldwell, Idaho, the Caxton printers, ltd., 1948. Cloth.

6 p.l., [11]–270 p. front., plates. 24 cm.
Half title; map on end papers; untrimmed.
Colophon: "The limited edition of So This Is Ranching is 1,000 numbered copies signed by the author, of which this is number ———. First edition."
Also published in a trade edition.

1400 McGEE, TOM. An incident on the Chisholm Trail, by Tom McGee. Oklahoma City, Okla., Times-Journal publishing co., 1933. Stiff wrappers. Scarce.

vi, ₍7₎–55 p. diagrs. 21.5 cm.
"First edition" on wrapper.

1401 McGILLYCUDDY, JULIA B. McGillycuddy agent; a biography of Dr. Valentine T. McGillycuddy, by Julia B. McGillycuddy. Stanford, University press . . . , ₍1941₎. Pict. cloth. OP.

xi p., 1 l., 3–291 p. front. (port.), ports. 23.5 cm.
Half title.

1402 McGINTY, BILLY. The old West as written in the words of Billy McGinty, ₍as told to Glenn L. Eyler₎. ₍N. p., 1937₎. Stiff pict. wrappers. (Cover title). Scarce.

1 p.l., 108 ₍2₎ p. front. illus. 22 cm.
Half title.

1403 McGONNIGLE, ROBERT D. When I went West. From the Bad Lands to California. With illustrations made from photographs taken by the author. By Robt. D. McGonnigle. Pittsburg [*sic*], Pa. ₍press of Edward F. Anderson co., ltd.₎, 1901. Pict. cloth. Rare.

6 p.l., 17–167 ₍1₎ p. front. (port. with tissue), illus., plates. 20.5 cm.
"Two hundred and fifty copies printed."

1404 MacINNES, C. M. In the shadow of the Rockies, by C. M. MacInnes. London, Riverton's, 1930. Pict. cloth. Scarce.

viii, 347 p. plates (with tissues), 2 large fold. maps at end. 22.6 cm.
Index, p. 341–347.
Half title.

1405 McINTIRE, JAMES. Early days in Texas; a trip to hell and heaven. By Jim McIntire. Kansas City, Mo., McIntire publishing company, ₍1902₎. Pict. cloth. Rare.

4 p.l., 9–229 p. front., 12 plates (incl. front.), ports. 20.2 cm.
Preface signed "James McIntire."

Although the author was better known as a gunman, he tells some of his experiences as a cowboy.

1406 M'KEAN, CAPT. G. B. Making good. A story of northwest Canada, 1920. By Capt. G. B. M'Kean. . . . New York, the Macmillan company, 1920. Cloth. OP.

3 p.l., 3–230 p. front. 19.6 cm.

Chapters on ranching, cattle rustlers, roundups, bronc riding, and stampedes.

1407 McKENNA, JAMES A. Black Range tales, chronicling sixty years of life

[227]

and adventures in the Southwest, by James A. McKenna ("Uncle Jimmie"). Introduction by Shane Leslie; illustrated with numerous woodcuts by Howard Simon. New York, Wilson-Erickson, inc., 1936. Cloth.
OP.

xiv p., 1 l., 300 [1] p. front., illus., plates. 23.5 cm.
Half title.
Colophon: "Of this autographed edition of *Black Range Tales,* five hundred copies
have been printed and all have been autographed by the author ———. This copy
is No. ———."

1408 McKINNEY, JOHN LAWRENCE. Influence of the Platte River upon the
history of the valley, by John L. McKinney. Minneapolis, Minn., Bur-
gess publishing co., mimeoprint and photo offset, publishers, [1938]. Stiff
wrappers. OP.

2 p.l., iii, 138 p. maps, diagrs. 27.3 cm.
Bibliography, p. 132–138.
Thesis (Ph. D.), University of Nebraska, 1935.
Printed on one side of paper only in photo-offset.

1409 MACK, EFFIE MONA, and BYRD WALL SAWYER. Our state, Nevada, by
Effie Mona Mack and Byrd Wall Sawyer. Illustrated. Caldwell, Idaho,
the Caxton printers, ltd., 1946. Cloth.

7 p.l., [15]–323 p. front., illus., plates, ports., maps. 21.5 cm.
Appendices, p. [305]–309; reading list, p. [311]–314; index, p. [313]–323.
Half title.

1410 MACK, H. C. Texas. Information for emigrants, comprising a general
view of the state . . . its natural resources. . . . By H. C. Mack.
Franklin, Tenn., Haynes & Figuers, publishers, 1869. Wrappers. Scarce.
iv, [5]–207 p. 20.7 cm.

1411 MACKAY, MALCOLM SUTHERLAND. Cow range and hunting trail, by
Malcolm S. Mackay; with 38 illustrations. New York & London, G. P.
Putnam's sons, 1925. Cloth. OP.
xv p., 1 l., 3–243 p. front. (with tissue), plates, ports. 22.2 cm.
Untrimmed.

1412 MACKEY, GORDON. Tall talin' and oratin', by Gordon Mackey. . . .
Illustrated by Anthony Stanush. San Antonio, Texas, the Naylor company, 1939. Cloth.
xi, 145 p. front., illus. 21 cm.

1413 MACLANE, JOHN F. A sagebrush lawyer, [by] John F. MacLane. . . .
[New York, Pandic press, inc., 1953]. Cloth.
viii p., 1 l., 177 p. plates, ports. 23.8 cm.
Half title.

1414 McLeod, George A. History of Alturas and Blaine counties, Idaho. By George A. McLeod. Hailey, Idaho, the *Hailey Times,* 1930. Cloth. OP.

7 p.l., 15–119 p. 17 cm.

1415 McMechen, Edgar Carlisle. The Shining Mountains, Colorado, by Edgar C. McMechen. Denver, Colorado, Denver Public Library, 1935. Stiff pict. wrappers. OP.

2 p.l., 7–56 p. front., illus., maps, facsm. 23.5 cm.
Bibliography, p. 54–56.

Chapter VIII is on cattle kings.

1416 McMurray, Floyd I. Westbound. ₁By₁ Floyd I. McMurray. . . . New York, Chicago, Boston, Atlanta, San Francisco, Dallas, Charles Scribner's sons, ₁1943₁. Pict. cloth. OP.

2 p.l., 394 p. plates, ports., map. 20.7 cm.
Bibliography after each chapter; index, p. 389–394.
Half title; double illus. t.p.; map on end papers.

Much on cattle and cowboys.

1417 McNeal, Thomas Allen. When Kansas was young, by T. A. McNeal. New York, the Macmillan company, 1922. Cloth. Scarce.

ix p., 1 l., 287 p. 19.5 cm.
Half title.
"The stories contained in this book have been written at odd times and published in the Daily Capital of Topeka, Kansas."—Foreword.

1418 McNitt, Frank. Richard Wetherill: Anasazi, by Frank McNitt, with maps and drawings by the author. Albuquerque, University of New Mexico press, ₁1957₁. Pict. cloth.

xii p., 3 l., 5–362 p. illus., plates, ports., maps. 26.3 cm.
Appendices, p. 322–344; bibliography, p. 345–349; index, p. 350–362.
Half title; map on end papers; "First edition" on copyright p.

1419 McPherren, Ida (Mrs. Geneva Gibson). Empire builders, by Ida McPherren. A history of the founding of Sheridan. Dedicated to the memory of John D. Loucks, the founder of the town. ₁Sheridan, Wyoming, printed by Star publishing co., 1942₁. Pict. wrappers. OP.

₁6₁–72 p. 20.6 cm.

1420 ———. Imprints on frontier trails, by Ida McPherren. Boston, the Christopher publishing co., ₁1950₁. Cloth. OP.

xi p., 2 l., 17–380 ₁1₁ p. 3 plates (incl. front.). 20.3 cm.
Half title; pub. device.

1421 ———. Trail's end, by Ida McPherren. [Casper, Wyoming, printed by Prairie publishing co., 1938]. Pict. cloth. Scarce.

4 p.l., [9]–322 p. front. 20.3 cm.
Bibliography, p. [5].
Half title.

1422 McReynolds, Edwin C. Oklahoma. A history of the Sooner State, by Edwin C. McReynolds. Norman, University of Oklahoma press, [1945]. Cloth.

xii p., 1 l., 3–461 p. plates, ports., maps. 24.2 cm.
Bibliography, p. 434–445; index, p. 446–461.
Half title; pub. device; "First edition" on copyright p.

1423 McReynolds, Robert. Thirty years on the frontier, by Robert Mc-Reynolds. . . . Colorado Springs, Colo., El Paso publishing co., 1906. Pict. cloth. Scarce.

4 p.l., 256 p. front., plates, ports. 19.5 cm.

1424 Maddox, William Allen. Historical carvings in leather; a lost art reclaimed. [By] Dr. William Allen Maddox. San Antonio, the Naylor company, publishers, 1940. Cloth. OP.

xv, 325 p. front. (port.), plates. 21 cm.
At head of title: Dr. William Allen Maddox.
Half title.

Has a chapter on the cowboys of the Southwest.

1425 Madison, Virginia. The Big Bend country of Texas, [by] Virginia Madison. [Albuquerque, N. M.], the University of New Mexico press, [1955]. Boards.

xv, 263 p. illus., plates, ports. 23.6 cm.
Bibliography, p. 249–256; index, p. 257–263.
Half title; map on t.p.

1426 Maerdian, Otto. Pioneer ranching in central Montana, from the letters of Otto Maerdian, written in 1882–1883. Edited by Lucia B. Mirrielees. . . . Missoula, State University of Montana, 1930. Wrappers. (Cover title).

3–17 p. 24 cm.
Double column.
("Historical reprint . . . Sources of Northwest History No. 10") . . .
"Reprinted from the historical section of *Frontier,* a magazine of the Northwest, published at the State University of Montana, Missoula, Vol. X, No. 3 (March, 1930)."

1427 Maguire, H. N. The Black Hills of Dakota. A miniature history of their settlement, resources, population, and prospects, with accurate tables of local distances and a general business directory of the principal towns. Edited and compiled by H. N. Maguire and published by Jacob S. Gantz. Chicago, 1879. Wrappers. Rare.

[2]–19 p. tables. 16.7 cm.

1428 ———. The coming empire. A complete and reliable treatise on the Black Hills, Yellowstone and Big Horn regions. By H. N. Maguire. . . . Sioux City, Iowa, Watkins & Smead, publishers and stereotypers, 1878. Cloth. Rare.

2 p.l., [6]–177 [12] p. illus., plates, large fold. map in front. 17 cm. Last 12 p. adv.

1429 ———. Historical sketch and essay on the resources of Montana, including a business directory of the metropolis. . . . Helena, Herald book and job printing office, 1868. Wrappers. Rare.

2 p.l., [3]–168 p. 22.5 cm. 2 p. adv. in front; adv. on verso of most pages of text.

1430 ———. The pioneer directory of the metropolis of Montana. [Helena, Montana, Allen & co., 1869]. Wrappers. Exceedingly rare.

[3]–168 p. 20.8 cm. Adv. on verso text pages.

1431 MAHOOD, MRS. R. F. Texas cowboy reunion, Stamford, Texas, by Mrs. R. F. Mahood. . . . [N. p., c.1956]. Pict. wrappers.

3–32 p. plates, port. 22.8 cm.

1432 MAINE, FLOYD SHUSTER. Lone Eagle, the white Sioux, by Floyd Shuster Maine. Albuquerque, the University of New Mexico press, 1956. Pict. cloth.

6 p.l., 208 p. plates, port. 23.7 cm. Illus. t.p.; headpieces.

Chapters on roundup days and the cattle industry of Montana.

1433 MAJORS, MABEL, and REBECCA W. SMITH, (EDS.). The Southwest in literature. An anthology for high schools. Edited by Mabel Majors and Rebecca W. Smith. New York, the Macmillan co., 1929. Cloth. OP.

xvii p., 1 l., 3–370 p. front., illus. 20.5 cm.

1434 MALIN, JAMES C. The grassland of North America. Prolegomena to its history, by James C. Malin. Lawrence, Kansas, [lithoprinted from the author's typescript by Edwards brothers, inc., Ann Arbor, Michigan], James C. Malin, 1947. Stiff wrappers. OP.

vii, 398 p. tables. 21.6 cm. Bibliography, p. 336–397; appendix, p. 398.

1435 MANDAT-GRANCEY, EDMOND, BARON DE. Dans les Montagnes Rocheuses, par le Baron E. de Mandat-Grancey, dessins de Crafty et Carte spéciale; couronné par l'Académie française, prix Montyon. Paris, E. Plon, Nourrit et cie., 1884. Wrappers. Scarce.
2 p.l., 314 p. front., plates, fold. map. 18.5 cm.
Reprinted in 1889 and 1894.

1436 ———. La brèche aux buffles par le Baron E. de Mandat-Grancey. Dessins de R. J. De Boisvray. Paris, E. Plon, Nourrit et cie., imprimeurs-éditeurs . . . 1889. Wrappers. Rare.
xvi, 292 p. front. (double p. with tissue), illus., (double p.). 18.5 cm.
Half title; pub. device; untrimmed; table of contents at end.
Reprinted in 1894 with same collation.

1437 MANN, L. B. Co-operative marketing on range livestock. Farm Credit Administration, Bulletin No. 7. Washington, Government printing office, 1936. Wrappers. OP.
133 p. illus. 23.5 cm.

1438 ———. Western cattle and sheep areas. Farm Credit Administration Circular No. C–103. Washington, Government printing office, 1936. Wrappers. OP.
101 p. illus. 23.5 cm.

1439 MANNY, MRS. H. J. (ED.). Kinney County, Bracketville, Spofford, Ft. Clark. [Bracketville, Texas, 1947]. Stiff wrappers. (Cover title). OP.
80 p. plates. 27 cm.
Triple column; adv. at end, p. 55–80.

1440 MARCHANT, SYLVIE (ED.). Pioneering on the Cheyenne River, compiled by the Historical Committee of the Robber's Roost Historical Society. The stories of pioneers and early settlers. . . . [Lusk, (Wyo.), published by the Lusk Herald], 1947. Stiff pict. wrappers. OP.
2 p.l., 5–94 p. 24 cm.
Index, p. 93–94.

1441 MARKET FOR RANGE HORSES, THE. What to ship, how to ship them, where and how to sell them. Chicago, published by T. H. Spaulding and co., 1890. Wrappers. (Cover title). Scarce.
24 p. 20.4 cm.
2 l. adv. at end; 1 l. adv. in front.

1442 MARKETING LIVESTOCK. Statement prepared by market committee appointed at the convention of the American National Live Stock Association at El Paso, Texas, January 26, 1916. [N. p., c.1916]. Wrappers. Scarce.
33 p. 22.5 cm.

1443 MARRIOTT, ALICE. Hell on horses and women, with drawings by Margaret LeFranc. ₍By₎ Alice Marriott. Norman, University of Oklahoma press, ₍1953₎. Cloth.

viii p., 2 l., 3–290 ₍1₎ p. 23.5 cm.
Bibliography, p. 281–283; acknowledgments, p. 285–290.
Half title; illus. double t.p.; headpieces.

1444 MARRS, W. P. An Arkansas boy in Texas, by W. P. Marrs, Christian evangelist. ₍Gainesville, Texas, Smythe printing co., n.d.₎. Wrappers. Scarce.

₍3₎–87 p. port. 17 cm.

The author tells some of his experiences as a cowboy before he became an evangelist.

1445 MARRYAT, FRANCIS SAMUEL. Mountains and molehills; or, recollections of a burnt journal, by Frank Marryat, with illustrations by the author. New York, Harper and brothers, 1855. Cloth. Rare.

x p., 1 l., ₍13₎–393 p. illus., plates, ports. 20 cm.

1446 MARSH, CHARLES DWIGHT, and GLENWOOD C. ROW. The "alkali disease" of livestock in the Pecos Valley. ₍By₎ C. Dwight Marsh . . . and Glenwood C. Row. . . . Washington, Government printing office, 1921. Wrappers. OP.

8 p. illus. 23 cm.
U. S. Dept. of Agriculture, Department *Circular 180*. A contribution from the Bureau of Animal Husbandry.

1447 MARSH, FRANK. Official brand book of the state of Nebraska, and a compilation of the brand and mark laws in effect June 1, 1928. Issued by Frank Marsh. . . . Aurora, Nebr., Burr publishing co., 1928. Stiff wrappers. OP.

307 p. cattle brands. 21 cm.

1448 MARSTON, E. Frank's ranche; or, my holiday in the Rockies. Being a contribution to the inquiry into what we are to do with our boys, ₍by E. Marston₎. Boston and New York, Houghton Mifflin company, 1886. Cloth. Scarce.

xvi, 214 p. front. (double-p. map), illus. 17.5 cm.

A narrative in the form of letters about ranch life in Wyoming and Montana.

1449 MARTIN, DOUGLAS D. Tombstone's epitaph, ₍by₎ Douglas D. Martin. ₍Albuquerque, the University of New Mexico press, 1951₎. Pict. cloth.

xii, 272 p. illus. 23.5 cm.
Half title; illus. front end papers; plan on back end papers; vignette.

1450 MARTIN, J. L. It happened in West Texas, by J. L. Martin, with illus-

trations by Jimmie Martin. Dallas, Mathis, van Nort and co., [1945].
Pict. cloth. OP.

3 p.l., 136 p. front., illus. 19.8 cm.
Half title.

1451 MASTERSON, VINCENT VICTOR. The Katy railroad and the last frontier,
by V. V. Masterson. Norman, University of Oklahoma press, [1952].
Cloth.

xvi p., 1 l., 3–312 p. illus., plates, ports., maps, facsms., tables. 23.5 cm.
Bibliography, p. 291–297; index, p. 298–312.
Half title; "First edition" on copyright p.

1452 MATADOR CATTLE COMPANY. Memorandum of association of the Matador Land and Cattle Company, ltd. . . . Dundee [Scotland], Hendry
and Pollock, [1882]. Wrappers. Scarce.

27 p. 23.2 cm.

1453 ———. Report of the proceedings at the first general statutory meeting of the shareholders of the Matador Land and Cattle Company, Ltd.,
held at Dundee, 3rd April, 1883. Dundee [Scotland], printed by John
Land and co., 1883. Pamphlet. Rare.

10 p. 21.5 cm.

1454 MATTHEWS, SALLIE REYNOLDS. Interwoven, a pioneer chronicle, by
Sallie Reynolds Matthews. Houston, Texas, the Anson Jones press, 1936.
Cloth. Scarce.

x p., 2 l., 3–234 p. front. (port.). 19.8 cm.
Addenda, p. 213–234; letter of introduction by Will James.
Half title; untrimmed.

This scarce, privately printed little book gives a good picture of early Texas
ranch life and trail driving, related by a woman whose father and husband
were well-known ranchmen.

1455 MATTHEWS, W. B. The settlers' map and guide book. Oklahoma. A
brief review of the history, government, soil, and resources of the Indian
Territory, Oklahoma proper, the public land strip, and Cherokee Outlet.
. . . Published by W. B. Matthews. . . . Washington, D. C., Wm. H.
Lepley, electric power printer, 1889. Wrappers. Rare.

[3]–66 p. large fold. map in front. 23.7 cm.

1456 MATTISON, RAY H. Roosevelt's Dakota ranches, by Ray H. Mattison.
[Bismarck, S. D., Bismarck Tribune, c.1957]. Wrappers. (Caption title).

15 p. plates. 22.9 cm.

1457 ———. Roosevelt and the stockmen's association, by Ray H. Mattison.
Reprinted from the *North Dakota History,* Vol. XVII, No. 2 (April,

1950); Vol. XVII, No. 3 (July, 1950). Bismarck, North Dakota, published by the State Historical Society of North Dakota, [1950]. Stiff wrappers.

[3]-59 [2] p. front. (port.), 3 plates at end. 22.8 cm.
Appendices, p. [52]-57; bibliography, p. [58]-59.

Contains the by-laws of the Little Missouri Stockmen's Association and the by-laws of the Montana Stock Growers' Association.

1458 MAULSBY, O. W. Rolling stone. The autobiography of O. W. Maulsby. Los Angeles, privately printed, MCMXXXI. Cloth. Scarce.

3 p.l., 130 [1] p. front. (port. signed in facsm.). 24.2 cm.
Vignette.
Colophon: "150 copies printed by Young & McCallister, Los Angeles, California, March, 1931."

1459 [MAVERICK, GEORGE]. Ye maverick. Authentic account of the term "maverick" as applied to unbranded cattle. Two extracts from the *St. Louis Republic* of November, 1889. Preserved in the interest of Mr. Maverick's descendants and in the interest of truth. San Antonio, Guessaz & Ferlet, printers, [n. d., c.1905]. Wrappers. (Cover title). Scarce.

[7] p. (no pagination). 16 x 8.6 cm.

1460 MAVERICK, MARY ANN (ADAMS). Memoirs of Mary A. Maverick, arranged by Mary A. Maverick and her son George Madison Maverick; edited by Rena Maverick Green.... San Antonio, Texas, Alamo printing co., 1921. Stiff pict. wrappers. Scarce.

3 p.l., [7]-136 p., 2 l. front., ports., facsms. 23.3 cm.

An appendix gives the history of her husband's experiences in his cattle venture, and the true origin of the term "maverick" as applied to unbranded cattle. The first state can be recognized by printer's errors such as misplaced lines, e.g., page 63, line 5, continues on line 24, page 69; page 69 continues on page 72, line 25; and page 72, line 24, continues on page 63, line 6.

1461 MAYFIELD, EUGENE O. The backbone of Nebraska. Wherein is contained many interesting matters pertaining to pioneer and more modern days. By Eugene O. Mayfield. [Omaha, Neb.], 1916. Wrappers. Scarce.

2 p.l., [9]-21 p. plate, ports., map. 22.2 cm.

1462 ———. Fairy tales of the western range and other tales. By Eugene O. Mayfield. Lincoln, Jacob North & co., printers, [1902]. Dec. cloth. Scarce.

4 p.l., [9]-165 p. front. 19.9 cm.

1463 MAYNARD, E. J. Hints to western stockmen on growing and fattening live stock. [By] E. J. Maynard. . . . Denver, Record Stockman publishing co., 1924. Stiff pict. wrappers. (Cover title). OP.

32 p. 19 cm.

1464 MAZZANOVICH, ANTON. Trailing Geronimo, by Anton Mazzanovich. . . . Edited and arranged by E. A. Brininstool. . . . Some hitherto unrecorded incidents bearing upon the outbreak of the White Mountain Apaches and Geronimo's band in Arizona, 1881–1886. The experiences of a private soldier in the ranks; chief of pack-train service, and scout at Ft. Grant; also with the New Mexican rangers. Los Angeles, California, Gem publishing company, 1926. Pict. cloth. OP.

10 p.l., 23–277 p. front. (col. with tissue), illus., plates, ports. 19.7 cm. Half title; tailpieces.

Some stories about cowboys around Willcox, Arizona.

1465 MEADOR, DOUGLAS. Trail dust; friendly heart-warming, star-dusted philosophy by the sage of Matador. By Douglas Meador. San Antonio, Texas, the Naylor co., 1940. Pict. cloth. OP.

xv [1], 134 p. front. (port.). 21 cm.

Originally published in the author's column, "Trail Dust," in the *Amarillo* (Texas) *Globe-News* and other papers.

1466 MECHEN, KIRKE. The story of Home on the Range, by Kirke Mechen. [Topeka, Kan., published by the Kansas State Historical Society, 1949]. Stiff wrappers. OP.

p. 313–339. 2 ports., facsm., music. 22.8 cm. Reprinted from the *Kansas Historical Quarterly,* November, 1949.

The true story of the famous cowboy song and its origin.

1467 MECKLENBURG, GEORGE. The last of the old West, by George Mecklenburg. Washington, D. C., the Capital book company, [1927]. Cloth. OP.

11 p.l., 21–149 p. plates, ports. 19.6 cm.

1468 MELLON, JOHN S. Hog-cholera and Texas cattle disease. . . . Cause, prevention, and cure, by John S. Mellon. St. Louis, Pierce bros., 1878. Pict. boards. Rare.

2 p.l., 32 p. 16.7 cm.

1469 MELTON, A. B. Seventy years in the saddle, by A. B. Melton. . . . Kansas City, printed by Warden printing service, 1948. Pict. wrappers.

3 p.l., 3–104 [1] p. front. (port.), illus. 21 cm. Reprinted in 1950 with added material.

A little-known and crudely illustrated book dealing with the life of a cowboy in West Texas.

1470 MELTON, W. W. Stories from life, by W. W. Melton. . . . Dallas, Texas, Helms printing company, 1943. Cloth. OP.

5 p.l., 13–222 p. front. (port. with tissue). 19.8 cm.

Contains a long chapter on ranching.

1471 MEMORIAL TO CONGRESS praying for the establishment of a Bureau of Information and statistics on live stock with an explanation of the proposed system, and letters of endorsement from over thirty states. San Angelo, Texas, Murphy and Guthrie printers, [1890]. Wrappers. Scarce.

21 p. tables. 23.5 cm.

At head of title: "Interstate Convention of Cattlemen."

1472 [MENDENHALL, E.]. Western Texas, the Australia of America; or, the place to live. . . . By a Six Years' Resident. Cincinnati . . . , 1860. Wrappers. Rare.

vii, 9–235 p. 18.6 cm.

Sections on stock raising, stock driving, and catching wild cattle.

1473 MENEFEE, EUGENE L., and FRED A. DODGE. History of Tulare and Kings counties, California, with biographical sketches of the leading men and women of the counties who have been identified with their growth and development from the early days to the present. History by Eugene L. Menefee and Fred A. Dodge. Illustrated. . . . Los Angeles, Calif., Historic record co., 1913. Three-quarter leather. Scarce.

xiv, [5]–890 p. plates, ports. 27.8 cm.

Gilt edges.

1474 MERCER, ASA SHINN. The banditti of the plains; or, the cattlemen's invasion of Wyoming in 1892. [The crowning infamy of the ages]. By A. S. Mercer. [Cheyenne, Wyo., 1894]. Cloth. Exceedingly rare.

5 p.l., [1] p., [12]–139 p. illus., map. 21.3 cm.

Appendix (confession of George Dunning), p. [107]–139.

This rare book has had a tempestuous history. Although purporting to have been copyrighted in 1894, this book was never published, but printed. Immediately after it made its appearance in Cheyenne, Wyoming, the entire issue was impounded by a local court in the course of a libel suit and ordered to be destroyed. While the edition was in custody of the court, a number of copies were stolen and smuggled to Denver, which city lay outside the court's jurisdiction. It is claimed that the books were unbound at the time and later bound in Denver. The scarcity of the book is due not only to the impounding, but also to the fact that for many years members of the Wyoming Stock Growers' Association and their sympathizers would destroy any copy discovered. The author's print shop was burned and he was ordered to leave the state.

Rewritten and republished under the title "Powder River Invasion. War on the Rustlers in 1892," by John Mercer Boots. ₍Los Angeles, 1923₎. Cloth. Scarce.

7 p.l., ₍15₎–146 p.   19.8 cm.

Republished: "The Banditti of the Plains," I. G. McPherren, Sheridan, Wyo., 1930. Wrappers. Scarce.

₍80₎ p. (no pagination).   20.5 cm.

Also published in a new edition by the Grabhorn press, with a foreword by James Mitchell Clarke and illustrations by Arville Parker. San Francisco, printed for George Fields by the Grabhorn press, MCMXXXV. Cloth and boards. Scarce.

xiv p., 1 l., 3–136 p.   illus.   24.8 cm.
Appendix, p. 111–136.
Illus. t.p.; illus. chapter headings; untrimmed.

This edition, too, has become quite scarce and expensive.

Again it was republished by the University of Oklahoma Press as item No. 2 in their Western Frontier Library, with a long introduction by William H. Kittrell.

1 p., 8 l., 17–195 p.   19.6 cm.
Half title.

1475 ――――. Big Horn County, Wyoming, the gem of the Rockies, by A. S. Mercer. Hyattville, Wyoming, ₍privately printed, 1906₎. Cloth. Scarce.

3 p.l., 7–115 ₍1₎ p.   front., plates, ports., tables.   18.4 cm.

1476 ――――. The cattle industry of California (in U. S. Dept. of Agriculture, Bureau of Animal Husbandry, Annual Report, 3rd, 1886). Washington, 1887. Sewn. Scarce.

p. 239–253.   23 cm.

1477 ――――. The material resources of Marion County, Oregon, with a complete business directory. By A. S. Mercer. Salem, Oregon, E. M. White, book and job printers, 1876. Wrappers. Rare.

₍3₎–78 ₍1₎ p.   fold. map in front.   20.7 cm.
Advertisements scattered throughout and on both wrappers.

1478 ――――. Washington Territory. The great North West, her natural resources and claims to emigration. A plain statement of things as they exist. By A. S. Mercer, a resident of the Territory. Utica, N. Y., L. C. Childs, book and job printer, 1865. Wrappers. Rare.

2 p.l., ₍5₎–38 p.   tables.   22.9 cm.

1479 MERCER, J. H. Farmers' Bulletin No. 2, of interest to Kansas livestock

THE

Banditti of the Plains

— OR THE —

Cattlemen's Invasion of Wyoming in 1892

[THE CROWNING INFAMY OF THE AGES.]

By A. S. MERCER.

producers. . . . By J. H. Mercer. . . . Topeka, Kansas, State printing plant, W. R. Smith, state printer, 1918. Stapled. (Cover title).

11 p. 22.8 cm.

1480 MERSFELDER, L. C. (LARRY). Cowboy—fisherman—hunter. True stories of the great Southwest. [By] L. C. (Larry) Mersfelder. Kansas City, Missouri, Brown-White-Lowell press, 1941. Pict. cloth. OP.

xiv p., 1 l., 3–246 p. front., plates, fold. map. 22.3 cm.
Half title.

1481 METHUIN, REV. J. J. In the limelight; or history of Anadarko [Caddo County] and vicinity, from the earliest days. By Rev. J. J. Methuin. . . . [Oklahoma City, Walker, Wilson title co., n.d.]. Cloth. Scarce.

iii [1] p., 1 l., 137 p. front. (port.), plates, ports. 19 cm.
Last 11 p. adv.; vignette.

1482 MILES, W. H., and JOHN BRATT. Early history and reminiscences of Frontier County, Neb. By W. H. Miles and John Bratt. . . . Maywood, Nebraska, published by N. H. Bogue, editor of the Eagle, 1894. Stiff wrappers. Rare.

39 p. 19.5 cm.

1483 MILLARD, F. S. A cowpuncher of the Pecos, by F. S. Millard. [Introduction by J. Marvin Hunter, n.p., n.d.]. Wrappers. (Cover title). Scarce.

2 p.l., 5–47 p. illus., plates, port. 20.6 cm.

Crudely printed and full of typographical errors, but a story of and by a genuine old cowboy.

1484 MILLBROOK, MINNIE DUBBS. Ness, Western County, Kansas, by Minnie Dubbs Millbrook. Pen and ink drawings Cecilia Benwell. Detroit, Michigan, Millbrook printing company, [1955]. Cloth.

8 p.l., 319 [11] p. illus., plates, ports., facsms., graphs, maps. 28.5 cm.
Errata, p. [321]; index, p. [323–331].
Half title; facsm. on end papers; seal on t.p.; double column.

1485 MILLER, BENJAMIN S. Ranch life in southern Kansas and the Indian Territory, as told by a novice. How a fortune was made in cattle, by Benjamin S. Miller. New York, Fless & Ridge printing company, 1896. Wrappers. Rare.

2 p.l., [7]–163 [1] p. port. 20.4 cm.

The author was one of the early presidents of the Cherokee Strip Live Stock Association and held that office for three years, when he resigned. His book deals with the cattlemen of that section in the 1870's.

1486 MILLER, JOAQUIN. An illustrated history of the state of Montana, containing a history of the state of Montana from the earliest period of its discovery to the present time, together with glimpses of its auspicious future. . . . By Joaquin Miller. . . . Chicago, the Lewis publishing co., 1894. Cloth. Pub. in 2 vols. Scarce.

Vol. I: xv, 9–292 p. front., ports. (incl. front., all with tissues). 29.2 cm.
Vol. II: 292 [repeated from vol. I]–822 p. front., plates, ports. (part with tissues). 29.2 cm.

Vol. II has some information on cattle.

1487 MILLER, JOSEPH. Arizona: the last frontier, by Joseph Miller, with drawings by Ross Santee. New York, Hastings house, publishers, [1956]. Pict. cloth.

x, 350 p. illus. 21 cm.
Index, p. [343]–350.
Illus. half title; illus. double t.p.; map on end papers.

1488 MILLER, JOSEPH (ED.). The Arizona story, compiled and edited from original newspaper sources, by Joseph Miller, with drawings by Ross Santee. New York, Hastings house, publishers, [1952]. Cloth.

xvii p., 1 l., 3–345 p. illus. 20.8 cm.
Half title; map on end papers; illus. double t.p.

1489 MILLER, LEWIS B. A crooked trail; the story of a thousand-mile saddle trip up and down the Texas frontier in pursuit of a runaway ox, with adventures by the way, by Lewis B. Miller. Pittsburgh, Pennsylvania, the Axtell-Rush publishing company, [1908]. Cloth. Scarce.

[3]–184 p. 23.5 cm.
"Published originally as a serial story in the *National Stockman and Farmer*, Pittsburgh."
On cover: "Stockman's Series, No. 1."

Republished by Dana Estes and co., Boston, [1911]. Pict. cloth.

vi p., 2 l., 11–413 p. front. (with tissue), illus. 21.4 cm.
Illustrated by J. W. F. Kennedy.

1490 ———. Saddles and lariats. The largely true story of the Bar-Circle outfit and their attempt to take a big drove of longhorns from Texas to California in the days when the gold fever raged. By Lewis B. Miller. . . . Boston, Dana Estes & company, publishers, [1912]. Pict. cloth. Scarce.

6 p.l., 11–285 [2] p. front. (with tissue), illus. 21.3 cm.
Half title; 2 p. adv. at end.
Reprinted in 1917.

1491 MILLER, MRS. S. G. Sixty years in the Nueces Valley, 1870 to 1930.

By Mrs. S. G. Miller. . . . San Antonio, the Naylor printing company, [1930]. Pict. cloth. Label pasted on. OP.

viii p., 1 l., 374 p. plates, ports., maps. 22.8 cm.

Published with "Autobiography of a Revolutionary Soldier," by John M. Roberts, first published in 1859.

1492 MILLER, T. B. New Mexico, San Miguel County. Illustrated. Its health, wealth, resources, and advantages. . . . Las Vegas, N. M., J. A. Carruth, printer and binder, 1885. Wrappers. Rare.

[3]–52 p. illus., large fold. map in front. 22 cm.

1493 MILLER, T. L. History of Hereford cattle, proven exclusively the oldest improved breeds. By T. L. Miller, with which is incorporated a history of the Herefords of America by William H. Sotham. Chillicothe, Mo., T. E. B. Sotham, publisher, 1902. Pict. cloth. Scarce.

3–592 p. front. (port.), plates, ports. (4 col.), tables. 27 cm.
Index, p. 583–592.
Double column.

1494 MILLER, WILLIAM ALEXANDER. Early days in the wild West. By William Alexander Miller. . . . [N. p., press of Franc. E. Shiery], 1943. Stiff wrappers. OP.

3–15 p. front., plates, ports. 23 cm.

1495 MILLER, W. H. The history of Kansas City, together with a sketch of the commercial resources of the country with which it is surrounded. By W. H. Miller. . . . Illustrated. Kansas City, Birdsall & Miller, 1881. Dec. cloth. Rare.

vi, [5]–264 p. illus., large fold. map (col.) in front. 25 cm.

Has a chapter on the cattle trade and the stock yards.

1496 MILLER, W. HENRY. Pioneering north Texas, by W. Henry Miller. San Antonio, Texas, the Naylor company, [1953]. Cloth.

xi p., 4 l., 303 p. plates, cattle brands, map, facsm. 21.6 cm.
Bibliography, p. 295–297; index, p. 299–303.
Half title; map on end papers.

1497 MILLS, JOE. Colorado: short studies of its past and present. Early range days, [by] Joe Mills. Wrappers. [1927]. (Cover title). Rare.

p. 91–100. 23 cm.

A separate reprint of Chapter 4 from item No. 1025.

1498 MISSOURI. The history of Henry and St. Clair counties, Missouri, containing a history of these counties, their cities, towns, etc. . . . Illustrated.

St. Joseph, Mo., National Historical company, 1883. Dec. leath. Scarce. xii, [9]–1224 p. plates, 2 fold. maps (col.). 26.6 cm.

Has a section on stock raising.

1499 ———. The history of Jackson, Missouri, containing a history of the county, its cities, towns, etc. Biographical sketches of its citizens, Jackson County in the late war, general and local statistics, portraits of early settlers and prominent men, history of Missouri, map of Jackson County, miscellaneous matters etc., etc. . . . Illustrated. Kansas City, Mo., Union Historical company, Birdsall, Williams & co., 1881. Cloth. Scarce.

x p., 1 l., [9]–1006 p. front. (with tissue), illus., plates, ports. (with tissues), large fold. map. 25.5 cm.

Has a chapter devoted to the cattle trail, Abilene as a cattle market, and Kansas City as a packing house center.

1500 ———. History of Vernon County, Missouri, written and compiled from the most authentic official and private sources, including a history of its townships, towns, and villages. . . . Illustrated. St. Louis, Brown & co., 1887. Cloth. Scarce.

xiii, 903 p. 26.3 cm.

1501 ———. Map and description of Barton County, Missouri, her situation, climate, soil, resources, population, products &c., &c. Hannibal, Mo., Hannibal printing co., [n. d.]. Wrappers. Rare.

[3]–8 p. fold. plat in front. 23.4 cm.

1502 ———. The Ozark region, its history and its people. Illustrated. Springfield, Missouri, Interstate Historical Society, 1917. Three-quarter leather. Scarce.

4 p. l., [3]–353 p. plates, ports. 27.4 cm.

Has a chapter on cattle raising.

1503 MISSOURI LAND AND LIVE STOCK COMPANY, LTD. Incorporated 21st March, 1882. Memorandum and articles of association. Edinburgh, printed by W. Burness, printer to Her Majesty, 1882. Wrappers. Rare. 27 p. 24.6 cm.

1504 MITCHELL, WILLIAM ANSEL. Linn County, Kansas. A history by William Ansel Mitchell. . . . Kansas City, [Mo.], Campbell-Gates, 1928. Cloth. OP.

[5]–404 p. front. (port.), plate, map. 23.2 cm.

1505 MIX, OLIVE STOKES. The fabulous Tom Mix, by Olive Stokes Mix

with Eric Heath. Englewood Cliffs, N. J., Prentice-Hall, inc., [1957].
Pict. cloth.

5 p.l., 177 p. plates, ports. 22 cm.
Half title.

1506 MIX, TOM. The West of yesterday, by Tom Mix, and Tony's story
by himself. Compiled and edited by J. B. M. Clark from interviews with
the author. Los Angeles, the Times-Mirror press, [1923]. Pict. cloth.
OP.

5 p.l., [11]-162 p. front. (port.), plates. 19.5 cm.
Half title.

1507 MOCK, H. J. Kalispell and the famous Flathead Valley in northwest
Montana. . . . Written by H. J. Mock. . . . Kalispell, Montana, 1892.
Wrappers. (Cover title). Rare.

16 p. large fold. map at end. 23 cm.

1508 MOHLER, J. C. Report of the Kansas State Board of Agriculture for
the quarter ending Sept. 1934. Beef cattle in Kansas. [By] J. C. Mohler.
Topeka, printed by Kansas State printing plant, 1935. Stiff pict. wrappers. OP.

289 p. plates, ports., tables. 22.9 cm.
Index, p. 287–289.

1509 MOKLER, ALFRED JAMES. History of Natrona County, Wyoming, 1888–
1922. True portrayal of the yesterdays of a new county and a typical frontier town in the middle west. Fortunes and misfortunes, tragedies and
comedies, struggles and triumphs of the pioneers. Map and illustrations,
by Alfred James Mokler. . . . Chicago, R. R. Donnelley & sons company,
1923. Cloth. OP.

xiv p. 1 l., 477 p. front. (port. with tissue), plates, ports., map, facsm. 23.5 cm.
Index, p. 475–477.
Half title.

Privately printed in a small edition and very scarce, this book has some
excellent material on this county and its livestock interests.

1510 MOLLIN, F. E. If and when it rains. The stockman's view of the range
question. [Denver, Colo.], published by American National Live Stock
association, [1938]. Wrappers. (Cover title). Scarce.

iv, 57 p. plates, graphs, map. 23 cm.

Public land policy and range control.

1511 MONAGHAN, JAY. The legend of Tom Horn, last of the bad men, by
Jay Monaghan. Indianapolis, New York, the Bobbs-Merrill company,
publishers, [1946]. Cloth. OP.

9 p.l., 19–293 p. front. (port.), illus., plates, ports. 22 cm.
Acknowledgments, p. 271–274; list of sources, p. 275–284; index, p. 287–293.
Half title; untrimmed; "First edition" on copyright p.

1512 MONROE, ANNE SHANNON. Feelin' fine! Bill Hanley's book put together by Anne Shannon Monroe. . . . Photographic illustrations by William L. Finley and others. Garden City, N. Y., Doubleday, Doran &
company, 1930. Cloth. OP.

xv p., 1 l., 304 p. plates, port. 21.3 cm.
Half title; map on end papers; illus. t.p.; untrimmed; "First edition" on copyright p.

1513 MONROE, ARTHUR WORLEY. San Juan silver, by Arthur W. Monroe.
. . . Historical tales of the silvery San Juan and western Colorado. ₁Grand
Junction, Colo., printed by Grand Junction Sentinel₁, 1940. Pict. cloth.
OP.

ix, 3–250 ₁1₁ p. 23.5 cm.

1514 MONTANA. Annual report of the Auditor and Treasurer of the territory of Montana for the fiscal year 1879. Together with an appendix
containing a record of marks and brands. Helena, M. T., Independent
steam power print, 1880. Wrappers. Rare.

79 p. cattle brands. 20x13.5 cm.

1515 ——. Annual report of the Auditor and Treasurer of the territory
of Montana for the fiscal year 1883. Together with an appendix containing a record of marks and brands. Helena, M. T., Fisk bros., printers
and binders, 1884. Wrappers. Scarce.

2 p.l., ₁5₁–98 p. cattle brands, tables. 21.2 cm.
Index, p. ₁93₁–98.

1516 ——. Annual report of the Auditor and Treasurer of the territory
of Montana for the fiscal year 1885, together with an appendix containing a record of marks and brands. Helena, M. T., Fisk bros., printers and
binders, 1886. Wrappers. Scarce.

217 p. cattle brands. 20.8 cm.
Appendix (marks and brands), p. ₁71₁–206; index to appendix, p. ₁207₁–217.

1517 ——. Annual report of the Board of Stock Commissioners of Montana territory. Report of the veterinary surgeon of Montana territory.
Report of the Recorder of Marks and Brands of Montana territory for
the year 1888. Helena, M. T., Journal publishing co., 1889. Wrappers.
Rare.

₁3₁–106 p. cattle brands. 22.2 cm.
Index, p. ₁101₁–106.

1518 ——. Annual reports of the Board of Stock Commissioners and the Recorder of Marks and Brands of the state of Montana for the year 1894. Helena, Mont., Independent pub. co., 1895. Wrappers. Scarce.

[3]–88 p. cattle brands. 22.4 cm.
Index, p. [84]–88.

1519 ——. Annual reports of the Board of Stock Commissioners, the state Veterinarian, and the Recorder of Marks and Brands of the state of Montana for the year 1897. Helena, Independent publishing company, 1898. Wrappers. Scarce.

[3]–104 p. cattle brands. 23.3 cm.
Index, p. [98]–104.

1520 ——. Annual reports of the Board of Stock Commissioners, the state Veterinarian and the Recorder of Marks and Brands of the state of Montana for the year 1898. Helena, Montana, Independent publishing co. . . , 1899. Wrappers. Scarce.

[3]–113 p. cattle brands. 22.5 cm.
Index, p. [105]–113.

1521 ——. Annual reports of the Board of Stock Commissioners, the state Veterinarian and the Recorder of Marks and Brands of the state of Montana for the year 1900. Helena, Montana, Independent publishing company, 1901. Wrappers. Scarce.

[3]–160 p. cattle brands. 22.5 cm.
Index, p. 148–160.

1522 ——. Annual reports of the Board of Commissioners, the state Veterinarian, and the Recorder of Marks and Brands of the state of Montana for the year 1901. Helena, Montana, Independent publishing company, 1902. Wrappers. Scarce.

[3]–191 p. cattle brands. 22.2 cm.
Index, p. 177–191.

1523 ——. Annual reports of the Board of Stock Commissioners, the state Veterinarian and the Recorder of Marks and Brands of the state of Montana for the year 1902. Helena, Montana, Independent publishing company, 1903. Wrappers. Scarce.

[3]–213 p. cattle brands. 22.2 cm.
Index, p. 198–213.

1524 ——. Annual reports of the Board of Stock Commissioners, the state Veterinarian and the Recorder of Marks and Brands of the state of Montana for the year 1903. Helena, Montana, Independent publishing company, [1904]. Wrappers. Scarce.

[3]–193 p. cattle brands. 22.2 cm.
Index, [181]–193.

1525 ———. Annual reports of the Board of Stock Commissioners, the state Veterinarian and the Recorder of Marks and Brands of the state of Montana for the year 1904. Helena, Montana, Independent publishing company, [1905]. Wrappers. Scarce.

[3]–152 p. cattle brands. 22.2 cm.
Index, p. 141–152.

1526 ———. Annual reports of the Board of Commissioners, the state Veterinarian and the Recorder of Marks and Brands of the state of Montana for the year 1905. Helena, Montana, Independent publishing company, [1906]. Wrappers. Scarce.

[3]–169 p. cattle brands. 22.2 cm.
Index, p. 161–169.

1527 ———. Annual reports of the Board of Stock Commissioners and the Recorder of Marks and Brands of the state of Montana for the year 1908. Helena, Montana, Independent publishing co., [1908]. Wrappers. Scarce.

204 p. cattle brands. 22.8 cm.
Index, p. 191–204.

1528 ———. Annual reports of the Livestock Commission of the state of Montana for the year 1919. Helena, Montana, Independent publishing co., [1920]. Wrappers. Scarce.

5–15 p. 22.8 cm.

1529 ———. Annual report of the Livestock Commission of the state of Montana for the year 1920. Helena, Montana, Independent publishing company, [1921]. Wrappers. Scarce.

[5]–19 p. 22.8 cm.

1530 ———. Annual report of the Livestock Commission of the state of Montana for the year 1921. [Helena, Montana, Independent publishing company, 1922]. Wrappers. Scarce.

[5]–14 p. 22.8 cm.

1531 ———. Annual report of the Livestock Commission of the state of Montana, 1928. [Great Falls, Montana, the Tribune printing co., 1928]. Wrappers. Scarce.

2 p.l., [5]–16 p. 22.8 cm.

1532 ———. Brand book Montana Stock Growers' Association. [Helena, Mont., 1885]. Leather. Rare.

3 p.l., [7]–147 p. cattle brands. 19 cm.
16 blank memoranda pages at end.

1533 ———. Brand book of the Montana Stock Growers' Association for 1890. Fourth issue. Published by the Montana Stock Growers' Association. Chicago, Ill., the J. M. W. Jones stationery & printing co., 1890. Leather. Rare.

3 p.l., [7]–147 p. cattle brands. 19 cm.
16 blank memoranda pages at end.

1534 ———. Brand book of the Montana Stock Growers' Association for 1899. Sixth publication. Helena, Mont., Independent publishing co., 1899. Leather. Rare.

3 p.l., [6]–207 p. cattle brands. 19.5 cm.
16 blank memoranda pages at end.

1535 ———. Climate, soil, and resources of Yellowstone Valley, with accurate maps of the Yellowstone country, the transcontinental route and connections of the Northern Pacific Railroad, and a plat and description of the town of Glendive at the junction of this railroad, with the steamboat navigation of the Yellowstone and upper Missouri rivers. Compiled from official maps and reports and other authentic sources. St. Paul, the Frontier press co., 1882. Wrappers. Rare.

3 p.l., [7]–100 p. 2 fold. maps (1 col.), fold. plat. 23.2 cm.
10 p. adv. in front (incl. verso of wrapper); 10 p. adv. at end and verso of back wrapper.

1536 ———. A concise description of the climate, soil, grazing lands, agricultural and mineral productions of the country adjacent and tributary to the Northern Pacific Railroad. . . . Helena, Montana, Fisk bros., book & job printers, 1882. Wrappers. (Cover title). Rare.

16 p. fold. map (col.). 19.3 cm.

1537 ———. Exhibit at the World's Fair and a description of the various resources of the state. Mining, agriculture, and stock growing. Presented with the compliments of the State Board of World's Fair Managers. Butte, Mont., Butte Inter-Mountain print, 1893. Pict. wrappers. Scarce.

64 p. tables. 17.5 cm.

1538 ———. "The heart of the continent," Montana. Its climate, soil, scenery, resources, and industries. Its advantages for general farming, stock raising, wood growing, mining, and other occupations. New York, published at the office of "The Northwest," 1883. Wrappers. Rare.

[3]–32 p. large fold. map at end. 23 cm.
Adv. verso front wrapper; adv. recto and verso back wrapper.

1539 ———. History of Montana, 1739–1885. A history of its discovery and agriculture, social and commercial progress, mines and miners, agri-

culture and stock raising . . . Indians and Indian wars, vigilantes, courts
of justice. . . . Illustrated. Chicago, Warner, Beers & co., 1885. Three-
quarter leather. Rare.

7 p.l., 15–1397 p. plates, ports., map. 27.8 cm.
Large fold. map in front.

1540 ——. An illustrated history of the Yellowstone Valley, embracing
the counties of Part Sweet Grass, Carbon, Yellowstone, Rosebud, Custer,
and Dawson. State of Montana. Spokane, Wash., Western Historical
publishing co., ₁n. d.₁. Full leather. Scarce.

xxi, 669 p. front. (port. with tissue), plates, ports. (part with tissues). 29.7 cm.
Double column; gilt edges.

1541 ——. Kalispell and the famous Flathead Valley, northwest Montana. Interesting reading for capitalists, manufacturers, investors, & home-
seekers. ₁Kalispell, Montana, Mock & Conner, printers, n.d.₁. Stiff
pict. wrappers. Rare.

₁3₁–23 ₁1₁ p. illus. 23.2 cm.

1542 ——. Live stock sanitary laws of Montana; also rules and regulations and orders of the Montana Sanitary Board, May 1, 1907. Governor's proclamation. Helena, Independent publishing co., ₁1907₁.
Wrappers. Scarce.

23 p. 23.5 cm.

1543 ——. Live stock sanitary laws of Montana; also rules and regulations and orders of the Montana Livestock Sanitary Board, Jan. 1, 1910.
₁Helena, 1910₁. Wrappers. Scarce.

23 p. 23 cm.

1544 ——. Live stock sanitary laws of Montana; also rules and regulations and orders of the Montana Sanitary Board, Oct. 1, 1917. ₁Helena,
1917₁. Wrappers. Scarce.

136 p. 23 cm.

1545 ——. Live stock sanitary laws of Montana; also rules and regulations and orders of the Montana Sanitary Board, Nov. 1, 1919. ₁Helena,
1919₁. Wrappers. Scarce.

4 p.l., ₁9₁–160 p. 23 cm.

1546 ——. Live stock sanitary laws of Montana; also rules and regulations
and orders of the Montana Livestock Sanitary Board, April 1, 1921.
₁Helena, 1921₁. Wrappers. Scarce.

73 ₁2₁ p. 23.6 cm.

1547 ———. Live stock sanitary laws of Montana; also rules and regulations and orders of the Montana Livestock Sanitary Board, July 1, 1927.
[Helena, 1927]. Wrappers. Scarce.

89 [4] p. 23.6 cm.

1548 ———. Local community history of Valley County, Montana, by
Montana Federation of Women's Clubs, with illustrations by H. Irvin
Shope. Glascow, Montana, printed by the Glascow Courier, 1925. Stiff
pict. wrappers. Scarce.

4 p.l., [9]–78 [1] p. illus. 26.8 cm.

A chapter on the history of the ranches of the county.

1549 ———. Montana and the northwest territory. Review of the mercantile, manufacturing, mining, milling, agricultural, stock raising, and
general pursuits of her citizens. . . . Chicago, Ill., Blakeley, Brown &
Marsh, printers, 1879. Wrappers. Rare.

3 p.l., [7]–85 [11] p. illus., tables. 22.8 cm.
3 p. adv. (incl. verso front wrapper) and 11 p. adv. at end.

1550 ———. Montana, resources and opportunities edition. Published by
the Department of Agriculture, Labor, and Industry. . . . Helena, Montana, 1928. Stiff wrappers. Scarce.

[3]–320 p. front. (map), plates (3 fold. col.), maps (1 large fold. at end). 23 cm.
Index, p. [317]–320.

1551 ———. Official report of the auditor and treasurer of the territory
of Montana for the fiscal year 1878, together with an appendix containing
a record of marks and brands. Helena, M. T., "Independent" steam
power print, 1879. Wrappers. Rare.

52 p. cattle brands. 21x13.5 cm.

1552 ———. Proceedings of the first annual session of the Territory Grange
of Montana, of the Order of Patrons of Husbandry, held in Gallatin City,
June 2–6, 1875. Diamond City, Montana, Rocky Mountain Husbandman printing establishment, 1875. Wrappers. Rare.

38 p. 14.5x10 cm.

1553 ———. Progressive men of the state of Montana. Illustrated. . . .
Chicago, A. W. Bowen & co., engravers and publishers, [n.d.]. Leather.
Scarce.

xv, 1886 p. front., ports. (part with tissues). 29.4 cm.

1554 ———. A record of the stock brands and marks of Montana Territory. Ordered published by the Eighth Legislative Assembly of the ter-

ritory of Montana. ₁Virginia City₁, "Montanian" steam print, ₁1872₁. Wrappers. Rare.

44 p.   cattle brands.   20.5x14 cm.

1555 ――――. A record of the stock brands and marks of Montana Territory. Published by authority. Helena, Montana, Fisk bros., printers, 1876. Wrappers. Rare.

45 p.   cattle brands.   19x12.5 cm.

1556 ――――. A record of stock brands and marks of Montana Territory. Published by authority of an act passed at the Eleventh Session of the Legislative Assembly of Montana Territory. Helena, Montana, Helena "Independent," 1879. Wrappers. Rare.

166 p.   cattle brands.   20.5x13.5 cm.

1557 ――――. Report of the Board of Stock Commissioners of the state of Montana. Report of the state Veterinarian. Annual report of the state Recorder of Marks and Brands for the year 1889. Helena, Mont., Journal publishing co., 1890. Wrappers. Scarce.

₁3₁–157 p.   cattle brands.   22 cm.
Index, p. ₁151₁–157.

1558 ――――. Report of the Board of Stock Commissioners of the state of Montana. Annual report of the state Recorder of Marks and Brands for the year 1891. Helena, Montana, Independent publishing co., 1892. Wrappers. Scarce.

₁3₁–90 ₁7₁ p.   cattle brands.   22.4 cm.
Index, last 7 unnumbered pages.

1559 ――――. Report of the Secretary of the Helena Board of Trade for the year 1878. Territory of Montana. ₁Helena₁, Fisk bros., Daily and Weekly Herald. 1879. Wrappers. Rare.

2 p.l., ₁5₁–32 p.   fold. map in front.   22.4 cm.

1560 ――――. Resources of Montana. Chicago, Rand, McNally and co., printers, 1889. Wrappers. Rare.

68 p.   tables, map on verso of front wrapper.   21.2 cm.

1561 ――――. Second annual report of the Secretary of the Helena Board of Trade for the year 1879. Territory of Montana. ₁Helena₁, Woolfolk, Macquaid & La Croix, Daily and Weekly Independent, 1880. Wrappers. Rare.

2 p.l., ₁5₁–40 p.   fold. map in front.   22 cm.

In a dialog between a "pilgrim" and a "pioneer," by questions and answers, some information is given about cattle raising in Montana.

1562 ———. Stock laws of Montana Territory, passed or amended by the 15th Legislative Assembly. Helena, Montana, Montana Live Stock Journal print, 1887. Wrappers. (Cover title). Rare.

9 p. 22.9 cm.
Double column.

1563 ———. Stock laws of Montana. Published by the Montana Stock Growers' association. Helena, Independent publishing co., [1911]. Wrappers. Scarce.

125 p., 1 l. 23 cm.

Laws compiled by W. S. Towner, assistant attorney general.

1564 ———. The Yellowstone Valley in the territory of Montana, with accurate map; climate, resources, principal towns, and the country between. Bismarck, Dakota, and Glendive, Montana. St. Paul, Pioneer press, 1882. Wrappers. Scarce.

80 p. large fold. map. 22 cm.

1565 ———. The Yellowstone Valley and the town of Glendive. St. Paul, Pioneer press, 1882. Wrappers. Scarce.

108 p. fold. lithographic map and town plat. 22 cm.

1566 Moody, Ralph. Man of the family, by Ralph Moody. Illustrated by Edward Shenton. New York, W. W. Norton & company, [1951]. Cloth.

5 p.l., 11–272 p. illus. 21.9 cm.
Half title; illus. t.p.; "First edition" on copyright p.

1567 Mooney, Booth. 75 years in Victoria, by Booth Mooney. Victoria, Texas, published by Victoria bank & trust company, [1950]. Pict. col. boards.

3 p.l., 51 p. front., plates, ports. 26 cm.

1568 Moore, John M. (Tex). Hell raising for pastime, by Tex Moore, old time Texas cowpuncher and trail driver. . . . [Riverside, Calif., 1935]. Pict. wrappers. (Cover title). Scarce.

3 p.l., 9–66 p. 6 plates. 15.4 cm.
At head of title: "Tex Moore, Texas' Official Cowboy Artist."

In his own unique fashion the author tells of some of his experiences as a cowboy.

1569 ———. The West, [by] Tex Moore, the official cowboy artist of Texas, and old time cowpuncher. [Wichita Falls, Texas, Wichita printing company, 1935]. Pict. cloth. (Cover title). Scarce.

4 p.l., 147 [1] p. front., plates, facsm. 24 cm.
Half title; no t.p.

1570 Mora, Jo. Californios. The saga of the hard-riding vaqueros. America's first cowboys, written and illustrated by Jo Mora. Garden City, New York, Doubleday & company, inc., 1949. Pict. cloth. OP.
7 p.l., 17–175 p. illus. 24.8 cm.
Half title; illus. end papers.

1571 ———. Trail dust and saddle leather, by Jo Mora. ₁Illustrated by the author₁. New York, Charles Scribner's sons, 1946. Pict. cloth. OP.
viii p., 1 l., 246 p. front., illus. 24 cm.
Half title; illus. end papers; vignette; first edition, letter "A" on copyright p.

1572 Morecamp, Arthur (pseud.) [Thomas Pilgrim]. The live boys; or, Charlie and Nasho in Texas. A narrative relating to two boys, one a Texan, the other a Mexican. Showing their life on the great Texas cattle trail, and their adventures in the Indian Territory, Kansas, and northern Texas; embracing many thrilling adventures. Taken down from Charley's narrative by Arthur Morecamp. Boston, Lee and Shepard, publishers, ₁1878₁. Cloth. Scarce.
6 p.l., ₁11₁–308 p. front., plates. 19 cm.

This scarce book is fiction, but important because it is said to be the first to use the cattle trail as a theme.

1573 ———. Live boys in the Black Hills; or, the young Texas gold hunters. A narrative of adventure during a second trip over the great Texas cattle trail; life among the miners and experiences with the Indians. Boston, Lee and Shepard, publishers; New York, Charles T. Dillingham, 1880. Cloth. Scarce.
x, ₁11₁–363 p. front., plates. 18 cm.

A sequel to the preceding book, and perhaps even scarcer.

1574 Morgan, Dale L. The Humboldt, highroad of the West, by Dale L. Morgan. Illustrated by Arnold Blanch. New York, Toronto, Farrar & Rinehart, incorporated, ₁1943₁. Cloth. OP.
x p., 1 l., 3–374 p. illus., 1 double-p. plate, map. 20.8 cm.
Acknowledgments, p. 351–353; bibliography, p. 355–365; index, p. 367–374.
Half title; illus. end papers; illus. t.p.; illus. chapter headings; first edition, "FR" in device on copyright p.

1575 Morgan, Learah Cooper (ed.). Echoes of the past. Tales of Old Yavapai. ₁By various authors₁. ₁Prescott, Arizona, Prescott Courier, inc., 1955₁. Published by The Yavapai Cow Belles of Arizona. Pict. cloth.
viii, 160 p. plates, ports. 23.6 cm.
Half title; map on end papers.

Contains chapters on cattle, life on the range, cowboys, and rodeos.

1576 MORGAN, WALLACE M. History of Kern County, California, with biographical sketches of the leading men and women of the county who
have been identified with its growth and development from the early
days to the present. History by Wallace M. Morgan. Illustrated. . . . Los
Angeles, Calif., Historic Record co., 1914. Three-quarter leather. Scarce.
xvi p., 1 l., ₍17₎–1556 p. plates, ports. (part with tissues). 28 cm.

Contains a chapter on the Miller and Lux ranches and the cattle industry of
Kern County, California.

1577 MORRIS, LEOPOLD. Pictorial history of Victoria and Victoria County.
"Where the history of Texas began." By Leopold Morris. ₍San Antonio,
printed by Clements printing co., 1953₎. Cloth.
3 p.l., ₍86₎ p. (no pagination). plates, ports., facsms., maps, cattle brands. 31.3 cm.
Photo-litho process.

1578 MORRIS, LERONA ROSEMOND (ED.). Oklahoma yesterday—today—tomorrow, edited by Lerona Rosemond Morris. Guthrie, Oklahoma, published by Co-operative publishing co., December, 1930. Cloth. Scarce.
viii p., 9 l., 15–922 ₍10₎ p. illus., ports., maps. 26 cm.
Index, p. ₍923–932₎.
Illus. end papers.

1579 MORRIS, ROBERT C. Cheyenne illustrated. Report of the Cheyenne
Board of Trade issued March, 1888, showing the advantages of the Magic
City of the plains as a manufacturing and business center with reliable
statistics and information. Compiled by Robert C. Morris. . . . Cheyenne, Wyoming, the Daily Sun steam printing house, 1888. Pict. wrappers. Rare.
₍28₎ p. (no pagination). illus., map. 33.5 cm.
Last 2 p. adv.

1580 MORRISEY, RICHARD J. The early range cattle industry in Arizona.
₍By₎ Richard J. Morrisey. . . . ₍N.p., c.1950₎. Wrappers.
p. ₍151₎–156. 25.3 cm.
Double column.
Reprinted from *Agricultural History,* July, 1950.

1581 MORTON, CYRUS. Autobiography of Cyrus Morton. Omaha, Neb.,
the Douglas printing co., 1895. Wrappers. Rare.
₍3₎–46 p. front. (port.). 23 cm.

An account of the author's driving cattle to Helena, Montana.

1582 MOSELEY, H. N. Oregon; its resources, climate, people, and productions. By H. N. Moseley. London, Edward Stanford, 1878. Cloth. Rare.
₍3₎–125 p. fold. map in front (col.), tables. 17 cm.

1583 Moss, William Paul. Rough and tumble. The autobiography of a West Texas judge. By William Paul Moss. New York, Vantage press, inc., [1954]. Cloth.

1 p.l., 177 [19] p. plates, ports., map, cattle brands. 22 cm.
Pub. device; last 19 p. plates and ports.

1584 Muller, Dan. Chico of the Cross Up, by Dan Muller. Illustrated by the author. Chicago, Reilly and Lee, [1938]. Pict. cloth. OP.

5 p.l., 15–249 p. front., illus. 23.7 cm.

1585 ———. Horses, by Dan Muller. Chicago, the Reilly & Lee co., publishers, [1936]. Cloth. OP.

6 p.l., 14–204 [2] p. front., illus. 20.5 cm.
Half title.
First printing before the trade edition limited to 100 copies. Boxed.

1586 ———. My life with Buffalo Bill, by Dan Muller, with illustrations by the author. Chicago, Reilly & Lee, [1948]. Cloth. OP.

4 p.l., 11–303 p. front., illus. 22.3 cm.
Half title; illus. end papers.

1587 Mumford, Herbert Winsor. Beef production, by Herbert Winsor Mumford. . . . Urbana, Ill., the author, 1907. Cloth. Scarce.

209 p. front., illus., tables. 20.5 cm.

1588 Munk, Joseph Amasa. Activities of a lifetime, by Joseph Amasa Munk. Los Angeles, the Times-Mirror press, 1924. Cloth. Scarce.

4 p.l., [9]–221 p. front. (port.), plates, ports. 20.2 cm.
Half title.

1589 ———. Arizona sketches, by Joseph A. Munk, M.D. Illustrated. New York, the Grafton press, publishers, [1905]. Pict. cloth. OP.

ix p., 1 l., [11]–230 p. front., plates. 24 cm.
Half title; device.

1590 Murphy, N.O. Biennial message of N.O. Murphy, governor of Arizona, to the Seventeenth Legislative Assembly, February 14th, 1893. Phoenix, Arizona, the Republican book printers, 1893. Wrappers. Scarce.

[3]–34 p. tables. 23.9 cm.

1591 ———. Biennial message of Governor N.O. Murphy to the Twenty-first Legislative Assembly of the territory of Arizona. Session of 1901. [N.p., 1901]. Wrappers. Scarce.

39 p. 21.6 cm.

1592 Mutz, Otto. Stockman's brand book. Brown and Cherry counties

[Nebraska]. By Otto Mutz. Ainsworth, Nebraska, Herald print, 1902.
Limber cloth folder. Scarce.

8 p.l., [17]–135 [18] p. cattle brands. 17 cm.
Index, 13 unnumbered pages at end.

1593 ———. Stockmen's brand book. Holt, Rock, and Boyd counties [Nebraska]. By Otto Mutz. Ainsworth, Nebraska, Western Rancher print, 1904. Limber cloth folder. Scarce.

8 p.l., 17–72 [28] p. cattle brands. 16.5 cm.
Last 28 p. index and blanks for notes.

1594 ———. Stockman's brand book. Keya Paha County. By Otto Mutz. Lincoln, Nebraska, George brothers, printers, 1902. Limber cloth folder. Scarce.

9 p.l., 17–106 [17] p. cattle brands. 16.5 cm.
Last 17 p. index and blanks for notes.

1595 MYERS, JOHN MYERS. The last chance. Tombstone's early years, by John Myers Myers. New York, E. P. Dutton & co., inc., publisher, 1950. Cloth.

4 p.l., 13–260 p. front., plates, ports., maps, plan. 22.2 cm.
Bibliography, p. 244–246; index, p. 247–260.
Half title; map on front end papers; vignette; untrimmed; "First edition" on copyright p.

Republished by Grossett and Dunlap under the title "The Tombstone Story" in 1951.

1596 MYRICK, HERBERT. Cache la Poudre; the romance of a tenderfoot in the days of Custer, by Herbert Myrick. Illustrated from paintings by Charles Schreyvogel, Edward W. Deming, and Henry Fangel, also with many photographs and numerous human documents. New York, Chicago, Orange Judd company . . . , 1905. Bound in fringed, smoked buckskin. Rare.

7 p.l., [19]–202 p. front., illus., plates (6 col.), ports., map, 10 illus. tipped in. 29 cm.
Addenda, p. [187]–202.
Half title; double column.
Colophon: "Edition limited to five hundred copies. This is number ———."

Also published in a trade edition bound in pict. cloth.

7 p.l., [19]–202 p. front., illus., plates (1 col.), ports., map. 23.8 cm.

1597 NATIONAL LIVE STOCK GROWERS. The National Cattle Growers' Association of America. . . . Chicago, 1885. Wrappers. Rare.

[3]–20 p. 14.5 cm.

Gives the constitution of this, at that time, newly organized association.

[256]

1598 ———. Proceedings of the first National Convention of cattle growers of the United States. Held in St. Louis, Mo., 17th to 22nd Nov., 1884. St. Louis, R. P. Studley and co., printers and binders, 1884. Wrappers. Rare.

3 p.l., 3–126 ₁11₁ p.   23.2 cm.
Seal on t.p.

Last 11 p. proceedings of the first annual meeting of the National Cattle and Horse Growers' Association of the U. S. held in St. Louis, Nov. 22, 1884.

1599 ———. Proceedings of the National Convention of Cattle Growers held at the Call Board Hall of the Chicago Board of Trade, Tuesday, Wednesday and Thursday, November 16, 17, and 18, 1886, under the auspices of the Consolidated Cattle Growers' Association of the United States. Together with the constitution, board of officers, and other particulars concerning the latter organization. Chicago, John Morris printing co., 1887. Wrappers. Rare.

116 p.   23.2 cm.

1600 ———. Proceedings of the National Live Stock Sanitary convention held in Washington City, D. C., on Tuesday, Wednesday and Thursday, June 19, 20, and 21, 1894. ₁N.p., c.1894₁. Wrappers. Scarce.

38 p.   21 cm.

1601 ———. Proceedings of the National Live Stock Growers' convention and organization of the National Live Stock Association in the United States. Denver, Colo., January 25, 26, 27. . . . Officially compiled by Charles F. Martin, recording secretary. Denver, News job printing co., 1898. Cloth. Scarce.

4 p.l., 395 ₁1₁ p.   front. (port.), plates, ports., maps.   23 cm.

1602 ———. Proceedings of the second annual convention of the National Live Stock Association, Denver, Colorado, January 24, 25, 26, and 27. Published by and presented to the National Live Stock Association by the Denver Chamber of Commerce, with an appendix on the city of Denver and its resources. Officially compiled by Charles F. Martin. Denver, Colo., News job printing co., 1899. Cloth. Scarce.

5 p.l., 13–453 p.   front. (port.), illus., ports., tables.   23 cm.

1603 ———. Proceedings of the third annual convention of the National Live Stock Association, Ft. Worth, Texas, January 16, 17, 18, and 19, with an appendix on the great resources of Denver and Colorado. Presented to the National Live Stock Association by the Denver Chamber of Commerce. Officially compiled by Charles F. Martin, 1900. Denver, Colorado, the Smith-Brooks printing company, 1900. Cloth. Scarce.

5 p.l., ₁13₁–528 p.   front. (port.), plates, ports.   23.2 cm.

1604 ———. Proceedings of the fourth annual convention of the National Live Stock Association, Salt Lake, Utah, January 15, 16, 17, and 18, 1901. Officially compiled by Charles F. Martin. Denver, Colorado, the Smith-Brooks printing company, 1901. Cloth. Scarce.

8 p.l., ₁19₁–509 p. front. (port.), plates, ports. 23.5 cm.

1605 ———. Proceedings of the fifth annual convention of the National Live Stock Association, Chicago, Illinois, December 3, 4, 5, 6, 1902. Officially compiled by Charles F. Martin. Chicago, Ill., Pettibone and co., ₁1902₁. Cloth. Scarce.

601 p. front. (port.), ports., tables. 23.3 cm.

1606 ———. Proceedings of the sixth annual convention and annual report of the National Live Stock Association, Kansas City, Mo., January 13, 14, 15, 16, 1903. ₁N.p., 1903₁. Cloth. Scarce.

11 p.l., ₁23₁–462 p. front. (port.), ports., tables. 23.3 cm.

1607 ———. Proceedings of the seventh annual convention of the National Live Stock Association with report of business transacted during 1903. Portland, Ore., January 11, 12, 13, 14, 15, 1904. Officially compiled by Charles F. Martin. ₁N.p., 1904₁. Wrappers. Scarce.

454 p. front., (port.), ports., tables. 22.8 cm.
24 p. adv. at end.

1608 ———. Proceedings of the eighth annual convention of the National Live Stock Association. ₁Denver, Colo., January 10, 1905₁. Cloth. Scarce.

400 p. ports., tables. 23 cm.
21 p. adv. at end.

1609 ———. Proceedings of the tenth annual convention of the National Live Stock Association, held at Denver, January 22 and 23, 1907. Denver, Colo., the Smith-Brooks printing co., 1907. Wrappers. Scarce.

125 p. front. (port.), ports. 22.2 cm.

1610 NEBRASKA. The Broken Bow country in central and western Nebraska and how to get there. With a sectional map of Nebraska showing towns and railway lines, completed and in course of construction on August 1st, 1886. Published by "Burlington Route," August, 1886. Omaha, Nebraska, Lincoln, Neb., Journal company, state printers, 1886. Wrappers. Rare.

₁3₁–15 ₁1₁ p. large fold. map at end. 22 cm.
Adv. verso front wrapper; railroad map verso back wrapper.

1611 ———. Great opportunities for farmers, business men, and investors in Nebraska, northwestern Kansas, and eastern Colorado. . . . Chicago, Ill., 1893. Wrappers. Rare.

32 p. map on verso of front wrapper, recto of back wrapper; fold. map at end. 19.2 cm.

1612 ———. Great opportunities for farmers, business men, and investors in Nebraska and northwestern Kansas. Omaha, Neb., 1895. Wrappers. Rare.

32 p. map on verso of front wrapper, recto of back wrapper; large fold. map at end. 18.2 cm.

1613 ———. Nebraska. ₁N.p., n.d., c.1876₁. Wrappers. Rare.

16 p. front., 4 full-p. plates (incl. front.). 16.7 cm.

1614 ———. Official brand book of the state of Nebraska. This book is intended as a complete transcript of all the live stock brands and marks of record in the office of the Secretary of State at Lincoln, January 1, 1934. Lincoln, Nebraska, ₁1934₁. Limber cloth. OP.

2 p.l., 307 p. cattle brands. 20.8x11 cm.

1615 ———. Pioneer stories of Custer County, Nebraska, contributed by more than one hundred present and former residents of Custer County. Broken Bow, Nebraska, published by E. R. Purcell, publisher Custer County Chief, 1936. Stiff wrappers. Scarce.

4 p.l., 193 p. 23.5 cm.
Index, p. 186–193.
Double column.

1616 ———. Pioneer stories of Furnas County, Nebraska. Compiled from the files of the Beaver City Times-Tribune. University Place, Nebraska, Clafin printing company, 1914. Cloth. OP.

2 p.l., ₁7₁–212 p. plates, ports. 22.4 cm.

Each chapter written by a different person, telling of his experiences in the early days of the county's settlement, with some of the chapters concerning ranching and the cattle industry.

1617 ———. The resources and attractions of Nebraska. Facts on farming, stock raising, and other industries and notes on climate. . . . St. Louis, Woodward & Tiernan printing co., 1893. Wrappers. Rare.

3 p.l., ₁7₁–74 ₁1₁ p. map on verso of front wrapper. 20.2 cm.

1618 ———. A sketch of the history, resources, and advantages it offers to settlers. By the authority of the State Board of Immigration. Nebraska City, Morning Chronicle print, 1870. Wrappers. Rare.

₁3₁–32 p. tables. 22.3 cm.
Last 6 p. adv.

1619 ——. South Omaha Union Stock Yards directory and statistical review. Devoted exclusively to the stock interests of South Omaha. Compiled from the records of the Union Stock Yards Company. Omaha, published by Bert Anderson, A. F. Stryker, printed by Ackermann brothers and Heintz, ₍n.d.₎. Imt. leather. Scarce.
56 ₍1₎ p. tables. 24.8 cm.
Advertisements scattered throughout.

1620 ——. The South Platte country and the advantages it offers to home seekers in the new West. Lincoln, Nebraska, published by the immigration bureau of the Burlington & Missouri River Railroad co., 1883. Wrappers. (Cover title). Rare.
24 p. map on verso of back wrapper, tables. 20.7 cm.

1621 ——. Southwestern Nebraska and Northwestern Kansas. A brief description of the country, its products and resources, together with a synopsis of the homestead, pre-emption and timber culture laws. . . . Lincoln, Neb., Journal company, state printers, 1887. Wrappers. Rare.
16 p. map, tables. 22.2 cm.

1622 ——. The state of Nebraska and its resources. A pamphlet for general circulation, showing how lands and homes may be acquired in the state, and the prospects of settlers therein. Issued by the state. Lincoln, Journal company, state printers, 1875. Wrappers. Rare.
2 p.l., ₍5₎–32 p. fold. map in front. 23 cm.

1623 ——. West Nebraska grazing country. ₍N.p., issued by the Burlington Railway co., n.d.₎. Fold. pamphlet. Rare.
32 p. plates, ports., fold. map at end. 19.5 cm.

1624 NEFF, PAT M. The battles of peace, ₍by₎ Pat M. Neff. . . . Ft. Worth, Texas, Pioneer publishing company, 1925. Cloth. Scarce.
3 p.l., 7–324 p. front. (port.). 23.2 cm.
Vignette; device.

Has a chapter on the Texas cowboy.

1625 NEIL, Gov. JOHN B. Report of the Governor of Idaho made to the Secretary of the Interior for the year 1880. Washington, Government printing office, 1880. Wrappers. Rare.
3–15 p. 23.2 cm.

1626 NELSON, BRUCE. Land of the Dacotahs, by Bruce Nelson. Minneapolis, University of Minnesota press . . . , ₍1946₎. Cloth. OP.
6 p.l., 3–354 p. plates, ports., map (double p.). 23.5 cm.
Acknowledgments and bibliography, p. 339–343; index, p. 344–354.
Half title; vignette.

"Brief sections of this book were first published elsewhere . . ."—verso title page. Republished with same format and collation in 1947 with "Second printing" on copyright p.

1627 NELSON, DICK J. Only a cow country at one time. Wyoming counties Crook, Weston, and Campbell, 1875 to 1951. Facts not fiction. [By Dick Nelson]. [San Diego, Pioneer printers]. Pict. wrappers. OP.

6 p.l., 13–104 p. front. (map), plates, ports. 22.9 cm.

1628 ——. Wyoming has a distinguished heritage and its Big Horn Basin of merit whose nextdoor neighbor on the West is the fascinating, fabulous Yellowstone National Park. Glimpsing the past 1806–1957. [By] Dick J. Nelson. Privately printed, n.d. Stiff wrappers.

6 p.l., 13–76 [1] p. front., plates, map. 23 cm.

1629 NEVADA. Description of the Humboldt Valley as a stock growing country. Central Pacific Railroad lands. [N.p., n.d.]. Wrappers. (Cover title). Scarce.

[3]–31 p. 22.4 cm.

1630 ——. History of Nevada with illustrations and biographical sketches of its prominent men and pioneers. Oakland, Cal., Thompson & West, 1881. Cloth. Scarce.

xiv p., 2 l., [17]–680 p. plates, ports. (part with tissues), tables. 30.8 cm.

1631 ——. Nevada and her resources. A brief sketch of the advantages and possibilities of the state and the opportunities and inducements offered to capitalists and home seekers. Compiled under the direction of the State Bureau of Immigration. Carson City, Nevada, State printing office, 1894. Pict. wrappers. Scarce.

2 p.l., [82] p. (no pagination). plates, 2 fold. maps, 1 fold. panoramic scene. 22 cm.

1632 ——. Pioneer Nevada. Reno, Nevada, lithographed in the United States of America, copyright by Harolds Club, 1951. Stiff pict. wrappers.

204 [2] p. illus. 35 cm.
Index, p. [205]; appendix, p. [206].

Reprints of advertisements published once a week in the newspapers of Nevada during the years 1946 through 1951. Each page is a separate advertisement, and each concerns some phase of history or folklore of Nevada.

1633 ——. Report on the Clover Valley cattle range, controlling 1,400,000 acres of grazing land, located in Humboldt and Elko counties, Nevada. [N.p., n.d.]. Wrappers. (Cover title). Rare.

12 p. double-p. map. 23.3 cm.

1634 NEVILLE, ALEXANDER WHITE. The history of Lamar County (Texas), by A. W. Neville. . . . Paris, Texas, published by the North Texas publishing co., [1937]. Cloth.

2 p.l., 5–246 p. 1 port. 23.5 cm.
Map on end papers.
"Edition limited to 700 copies."

Contains material on John Chisum and his early cattle drives.

1635 NEWELL, DAVID M. Cougars & cowboys, by David M. Newell. New York, London, the Century co., [1927]. Pict. cloth. OP.

xi p., 1 l., 3–222 p. front., illus. 19.3 cm.
Half title; vignette.

1636 NEW HAMPSHIRE CATTLE COMPANY. Location of range: Wyoming. . . . Concord, N. H., printed by the Republican press association, 1885. Wrappers. Rare.

[3]–10 p. 18.3 cm.

1637 NEW HOMES; or where to settle in America. Being a guide for the use of intending settlers, for purchasers of land for investment, and for those in search of health and recreation. . . . New York, the American and Foreign publications co., 1875. Pict. cloth. Rare.

4 p.l., 153 [3] p. 17.5 cm.
Last 3 p. tables.

1638 NEWMARK, HARRIS. Sixty years in southern California, 1853–1913, containing the reminiscences of Harris Newmark. Edited by Maurice H. Newmark [and] Marco R. Newmark. . . . With 150 illustrations. New York, the Knickerbocker press, 1916. Leather and boards. Scarce.

xxviii p., 1 l., 688 p. front. (port. with tissue), plates, ports., facsm. 23.2 cm.
Index, p. 653–688.
T.p. in red and black.
Colophon: "Memorial edition limited to fifty copies. This is No. ——."

Republished by the same publishers in a revised edition and augmented to 732 pages with 172 illustrations in 1926. Published again in 1930 by Houghton Mifflin in an edition of 744 pages with 182 illustrations.

1639 NEW MEXICO. Agriculture and horticulture. New Mexico, Territorial Bureau of Immigration. Santa Fe, New Mexican printing co., 1898. Wrappers. Scarce.

47 p. 14.5 cm.

1640 ——. Bernalillo County, New Mexico, the richest and most populous county in the sunshine territory. Its resources include agriculture, horticulture, sheep and wool, gold, coal, and other minerals. Manufacturers,

[262]

railroads, etc., by the Bureau of Immigration of the territory of New Mexico. Santa Fe, New Mexican printing co., 1901. Wrappers. Rare.
24 p. 5 plates (incl. front.). 14.5x8.5 cm.

1641 ———. Chaves County, New Mexico, an imperial domain with a magnificent stock range; a wonderful artesian belt; splendid irrigation facilities; the best soil and climate for horticulture and agriculture. Most rapidly growing county in the territory. By the Bureau of Immigration of the territory of New Mexico. Santa Fe, N. M., New Mexican printing co., 1901. Wrappers. Rare.
24 p. illus., 5 plates. 14.5x8.5 cm.

1642 ———. Colfax County, New Mexico; its resources and opportunities. ₁Denver, 1892₁. Wrappers. Scarce.
15 p. plates, map. 22.5 cm.

The plates are from photographs and the map is one of the Maxwell Land Grant.

1643 ———. Colfax County, its resources and opportunities, compiled by the Women's Columbian Committee of Colfax County. For distribution at the World's Fair. Denver, Colo., press of M. A. Tully, ₁n.d.₁. Wrappers. Scarce.
15 p. illus., 6 full-p. plates. 22.5 cm.

1644 ———. Colfax County, New Mexico, one of the richest counties in the territory. Principal resources: stock raising, agriculture, coal, precious metals, and horticulture. By the Bureau of Immigration of the territory of New Mexico. Santa Fe, N. M., New Mexican printing co., 1901. Pamphlet. Scarce.
15 p. 14.5x8.5 cm.

1645 ———. Doña Ana County, New Mexico. The Mesilla Valley—the garden of New Mexico. Mineral wealth in picturesque mountain ranges. Cattle, sheep and goats by the thousands. An ideal winter climate. By the Bureau of Immigration of the territory of New Mexico. Santa Fe, New Mexican printing co., 1901. Wrappers. Scarce.
27 p. 9 plates. 14.5x8.5 cm.

1646 ———. Grant County, New Mexico, rich in gold, silver, copper, iron, zinc, turquoise, and other minerals. Thousands of cattle on a thousand hills. Enterprising, prosperous. By the Bureau of Immigration of the territory of New Mexico. Santa Fe, N. M., New Mexican printing co., 1901. Wrappers. Scarce.
40 p. 8 plates (incl. front.). 14.5x8.5 cm.

1647 ———. History of New Mexico, its resources and people. Illustrated. Los Angeles, Chicago, New York, Pacific States publishing co., 1907. Cloth. Pub. in 2 vols. Scarce.

Vol. I: xxvii, 522 p. plates, ports. (part with tissues). 25 cm.
Vol. II: [523]–1047 p. plates, ports. (part with tissues). 25 cm.
Paged continuously.

1648 ———. Inventory and description of the La Cueva Ranch, Mora County, New Mexico. Las Vegas, J. A. Carruth, printer and binder, 1885. Wrappers. Rare.

9 p. fold. map. 17.4 cm.

1649 ———. The Maxwell Land Grant Co., comprising 1,714,765 acres in Colorado and New Mexico is offering its lands for sale. . . . [N.p., n.d.]. Wrappers. Rare.

8 p. plates (verso front wrapper, recto back wrapper), fold. map in front. 23.3 cm.

1650 ———. Memorandum and articles of the Scottish Mortgage and Land Investment Company of New Mexico (ltd.). Incorporated under the company's acts 1862–1882. Glascow, 1882. Wrappers. Rare.

35 p. 21.3x14.2 cm.

1651 ———. New Mexico; its advantages for stock raising, mining, and agricultural pursuits, with a correct map of the territory. Chicago, published by the New Mexico Stock and Agricultural association, 1876. Wrappers. Very rare.

32 p. map. 17.4 cm.
3 p. adv. at end.

1652 ———. New Mexico: its attractions and resources, with its rich deposits of gold, silver, copper, coal, and other minerals; its extensive grazing districts, rich farming lands, and delightful climate. . . . St. Louis, Slawson & Pierrot, 1880. Wrappers. Rare.

15 [2]–p. 21 cm.

1653 ———. New Mexico's Land and Cattle Company. President's report. [N.p., May 12, 1884]. Wrappers. Rare.

14 p. 23 cm.
(Cover title: "Report of the New Mexico Land and Cattle Company").

1654 ———. New Mexico, the land of opportunity. Official data on the resources and industries of New Mexico—the sunshine state. Albuquerque, N. M., press of the Albuquerque Morning Journal, [1915]. Stiff col. wrappers. OP.

5–240, i–v [11] p. plates, ports., maps. 29.5 cm.
Index, p. i–v.

[264]

Last 11 p. adv.; 2 p. adv. in front (incl. verso front wrapper); adv. recto and verso back wrapper.

1655 ———. New Mexico: its resources in public lands, agriculture, horticulture, stock raising, coal, copper, gold, and other minerals. Its attractions for tourists, homeseekers, investor, sportsman, health-seeker and archaeologist. Santa Fe, New Mexico, published by the bureau of publicity of the State Land office, 1916. Stiff wrappers. OP.

2 p.l., [5]–84 p. 19.4x8.5 cm.

1656 ———. New Mexico Stock and Agricultural Association. Incorporated under the laws of Illinois for the purpose of colonizing, developing and improving lands in the territory of New Mexico for stock raising, agricultural and mining purposes. Chicago, 1876. Wrappers. Rare.

16 p. 19 cm.

1657 ———. The Pecos Valley, New Mexico. [N.p.], 1902. Pict. wrappers. Scarce.

[5]–63 [1] p. illus., plates, map at end. 18 cm.

Issued by the Santa Fe Railroad, this booklet contains a section on stock raising.

1658 ———. The resources of New Mexico. Prepared under the auspices of the Bureau of Immigration for the Territorial Fair to be held at Albuquerque, N. M., October 3d to 8th, 1881. Santa Fe, N. M., New Mexican book and job printing department, 1881. Wrappers. Rare.

3–64 p. 22.6 cm.
Errata leaf tipped in.
Adv. scattered throughout; adv. verso front wrapper, recto and verso back wrapper.

1659 ———. Report of the acting Governor to the Secretary of the Interior, 1889. Washington, Government printing office, 1889. Wrappers. Rare.

25 p. 23 cm.

1660 ———. Report of the New Mexico Land and Cattle Company. [N.p.], 1884. Wrappers. Rare.

14 p. 22.7 cm.

1661 ———. San Juan County, New Mexico. A section of sunshine territory that is gaining world wide fame. . . . [Aztec, New Mexico, J. S. Duncan, public printer, n.d.]. Pict. wrappers. Rare.

[3]–31 p. front. (port.), plates. 29.8 cm.
Leaf of errata tipped in.

1662 ———. San Juan County, New Mexico, the great fruit belt of the Rocky Mountain region, and the finest agricultural country in the Southwest. By the Bureau of Immigration of the territory of New Mexico. Santa Fe, N. M., New Mexican printing co., 1901. Pamphlet. Scarce.

11 p. 14.5x8.5 cm.

1663 ———. San Miguel County, New Mexico, an empire in itself. One of the greatest wool growing and agricultural sections in the territory. Offers excellent opportunities and advantages for investment. By the Bureau of Immigration of the territory of New Mexico. Santa Fe, N. M., New Mexican printing co., 1901. Pamphlet. Scarce.

39 p. 10 plates. 14.5x8.5 cm.

1664 ———. Santa Fe County, New Mexico, magnificent and health giving climate. A fine agricultural and fruit section. Stock raising; mining of precious metals and coal among its leading industries. By the Bureau of Immigration of the territory of New Mexico. Santa Fe, N. M., New Mexican printing co., 1901. Wrappers. Scarce.

41 p. 10 plates. 14.5x8.5 cm.

1665 ———. Second annual report of the Cattle Sanitary Board of the territory of New Mexico. . . . Las Vegas, N. M., printed by the Stock Growers' co., 1888. Wrappers. Rare.

15 p. tables. 21 cm.

1666 ———. Socorro County, New Mexico, the largest county in the territory. Possesses great mineral riches. Stock ranges as large as a European kingdom. Fertile valleys and canyons. Mild and equitable climate. By the Bureau of Immigration of the territory of New Mexico. Santa Fe, N. M., New Mexican printing co., 1901. Wrappers. Scarce.

24 p. front., 9 plates (incl. front.). 14.5x8.5 cm.

1667 ———. Supplement number 1 to the brand book of the territory of New Mexico, showing all the brands on cattle, horses, mules, and asses recorded and re-recorded since July 1st, 1900, to January 1st, 1902. Issued by the Cattle Sanitary Board of New Mexico. . . . Santa Fe, New Mexican printing co., 1902. Wrappers. Scarce.

133 p. cattle brands. 22.6 cm.

1668 ———. Supplement number two to the brand book of the territory of New Mexico, showing all the brands on cattle, horses, mules, and asses recorded and re-recorded since January 1st, 1902, to January 1st, 1903. Issued by the Cattle Sanitary Board of New Mexico. . . . Santa Fe, New Mexican printing co., 1903. Wrappers. Scarce.

91 p. cattle brands. 23 cm.

1669 ———. Supplement number three to the brand book of the territory of New Mexico, showing all the brands on cattle, horses, mules, and asses recorded and re-recorded since January 1st, 1903, to January 1st, 1904. Santa Fe, New Mexican printing co., 1904. Wrappers. Scarce.

91 p. cattle brands. 22.8 cm.

1670 ———. Transcript of record in the Supreme Court of the territory of New Mexico, July term, A.D., 1892. Maxwell Land Grant Co. *vs.* John B. Dawson. Las Vegas, N. M., printed at Office of the Stock Grower, 1892. Wrappers. Rare.

464 p. 23.2 cm.

1671 NEWTON, LEWIS W., and HERBERT P. GAMBRELL. A social and political history of Texas, by Lewis W. Newton and Herbert P. Gambrell. Dallas, Turner co., [1935]. Cloth. OP.

xvi p., 2 l., 422 p. front. (port.), plates, ports., maps. 22.5 cm.

1672 NICHOLL, EDITH M. (MRS. EDITH M. BOYER). Observations of a ranch woman in New Mexico, by Edith M. Nicholl. London, Macmillan and co., limited; New York, the Macmillan company, 1898. Dec. cloth. Scarce.

4 p.l., 271 p. front. (with tissue), plates. 19.4 cm.
Half title; illus. t.p.

Republished, Cincinnati, the Editor publishing co., 1901.

3 p.l., 260 p. 19 cm.

1673 NIMMO, JOSEPH, JR. Range and cattle traffic. Letter from the Secretary of the Treasury, transmitting a report from the Chief of the Bureau of Statistics, in response to a resolution of the House calling for information in regard to the range and ranch cattle traffic in the western states and territories. House of Representatives, 48th Congress, 2nd Session, *Ex. Doc. No. 267.* [Washington, 1885]. Wrappers. Scarce.

200 p., 4 large fold. maps at end. 23 cm.
Appendices, p. 73–200.
No title page.

1674 ———. Treasury Department. Report on the Internal commerce of the United States, by Joseph Nimmo, Jr. . . . Submitted May 6, 1885. Commerce and navigation. Washington, Government printing office, 1885. Boards. Rare.

8 p.l., 17–562 p. 5 large fold. maps at end, tables. 23.4 cm.
Appendices, p. 167–562.

This edition, beginning with Part 3 (p. 95), is the same as item No. 1673 above. There are several other editions, all of the same year, one by the Senate and another with only one map, though four were called for. This book is

LETTER

FROM

THE SECRETARY OF THE TREASURY,

TRANSMITTING

A report from the Chief of the Bureau of Statistics, in response to a resolution of the House calling for information in regard to the range and ranch cattle traffic in the Western States and Territories.

MARCH 2, 1885.—Referred to the Committee on Agriculture and ordered to be printed.

TREASURY DEPARTMENT,
OFFICE OF THE SECRETARY,
Washington, D. C., March 2, 1885.

SIR: I have the honor to transmit, herewith, to the House of Representatives, a report prepared under my direction, by the Chief of the Bureau of Statistics of this Department, in reply to a resolution of the House of Representatives of February 17, 1885, requesting the Secretary of the Treasury to submit to the House such information as he may be able to communicate at an early day in regard to the range and ranch cattle traffic of the Western, Southwestern, and Northwestern States and Territories, with special reference to the bearings of that traffic upon the internal and foreign commerce of the United States.

Very respectfully,

H. McCULLOCH,
Secretary.

Hon. JOHN G. CARLISLE,
Speaker of the House of Representatives.

held to be among the most important of the "big four" cattle books, and its contents were compiled by experts on the subject.

1675 NOLEN, OREN WARDER. Galloping down the Texas trail, by Oren Warder Nolen. Anecdotes and sketches of the Texas cowboys, rangers, sheriffs, wild cattle, wild horses, and guns and game. Written by a native Texan from the experiences of fifty years in the Lone Star State. ₁Odem, Texas, privately printed, 1947₁. Cloth. Scarce.

3 p.l., 7–181 p. 23.3 cm.

1676 NORDHOFF, CHARLES. California: for health, pleasure and residence. A book for travelers and settlers. By Charles Nordhoff. New York, Harper and brothers, publishers, 1872. Cloth. Scarce.

2 p.l., ₁11₁–255 p. front. (map), illus., plates, maps. 23 cm.

Republished in 1873 and 1878.

6 p.l., ₁17₁–255 p. front. (map), illus., maps. 23 cm.
Appendix, p. ₁247₁–255.
Illus. chapter headings; 4 p. adv. at end.

Completely revised in 1882.

1 p.l., ₁9₁–206 p. illus., plates, maps. 23.4 cm.

1677 NORDYKE, LEWIS. Cattle empire. The fabulous story of the 3,000,000 acre XIT. By Lewis Nordyke. New York, William Morrow and company, 1949. Pict. cloth. OP.

xiii p., 1 l., 3–273 p. plates, ports., facsms. 21.8 cm.
Acknowledgments, p. 253–254; appendix, p. 255–273.
Half title; pub. device.

1678 ———. Great roundup, the story of Texas and Southwestern cowmen, by Lewis Nordyke. . . . Special edition for the Texas and Southwestern Cattle Raisers Association. New York, William Morrow & company, 1955. Pict. boards and cloth.

8 p.l., 17–316 p. front. (col.), illus., plates, ports., maps. 22 cm.
Acknowledgments, p. 277–280; index, p. 280–288; appendix, p. 291–316.
Half title; illus. end papers.

A history of the Texas and Southwestern Cattle Raisers' Association and the cattle industry of that state. The trade edition is the same as the special edition, except that it ends with the index and does not contain the appendix listing the officers, board of directors, inspectors, and members.

1679 ———. John Wesley Hardin, Texas gunman. By Lewis Nordyke. New York, William Morrow & company, 1957. Boards.

6 p.l., ₁3₁–278 p. 21.6 cm.
Acknowledgments, p. ₁271₁–272; index, p. ₁273₁–278.
Half title.

1680 ———. The truth about Texas, ₍by₎ Lewis Nordyke. New York, Thomas Y. Crowell company, ₍1957₎. Cloth.

x p., 1 l., 276 p. 20.9 cm.
Index, p. 267–276.
Half title; map on end papers.

1681 NORTH DAKOTA. Brand book of the North Dakota Stock Growers' Association for 1893. Second issue. Published by the North Dakota Stock Growers' Association. Bismarck, N. D., Tribune printers and binders, 1893. Boards and cloth. Scarce.

4 p.l., ₍7₎–219 p. cattle brands. 17.5 cm.

1682 ———. Green pastures and vast wheat fields. A sketch, historical, descriptive, and statistical. . . . The county of Cass and the city of Fargo, the county seat, territory of Dakota. Prepared and compiled under the supervision of the Board of Trade of the city of Fargo by the Secretary. Fargo, Dak., Republican steam printing house, 1888. Wrappers. Rare.

₍3₎–48 p. illus., large fold. map in front. 20.7 cm.
Last 5 p. adv.; adv. recto and verso back wrapper.

Seen in the Coe Collection, Yale University.

1683 ———. Mouse River cattle raising, ₍St. Paul, Minn., published by the St. Paul, Minneapolis and Manitoba Railway company, 1885₎. Wrappers. (Caption title). Scarce.

12 p. map on verso back wrapper. 22 cm.
(Cover title: "Mouse River, North Dakota").

Deals with the pioneer history and conditions of the cattle industry in the Red River and Mouse River regions of North Dakota from 1870.

1684 ———. State of North Dakota. Information on livestock marks and brands, brand inspectors, and estray laws. Compiled by Department of Agriculture and Labor. Joseph A. Kitchen, commissioner. Bismarck, N. D. . . . ₍Grand Forks, N. D., Normanden publishing co., n.d.₎. Pamphlet. (Cover title). Scarce.

₍9₎ p. (no pagination). 23.3 cm.

1685 ———. The state of North Dakota, the state of South Dakota; an official statistical, historical, and political abstract. Agricultural, mineral, commercial, manufacturing, educational, social, and general statements. Published by Frank H. Hagerty. . . . Aberdeen, S. D., Daily News print, 1889. Cloth. Scarce.

4 p.l., ₍9₎–102 p. fold. map at end (col.), tables. 23 cm.
Index, p. ₍101₎–102.

1686 NORTH, ESCOTT. The saga of the cowboy. All about the cattleman, and the part he played in the great drama of the West, by Escott North. . . . London . . . Jarolds, publishers, limited, [1942]. Cloth. OP.

xii, 13–192 p. front. (port.), plates, ports., cattle brands. 21.8 cm.
Index, p. 189–192.
Half title.

1687 NORTHERN PACIFIC RAILWAY. The great Northwest. A guide-book and itinerary for the use of tourists and travelers over the lines of the Northern Pacific Railroad, the Oregon Railway and Navigation Company and the Oregon and California Railroad. . . . With maps and many illustrations. . . . St. Paul, Northern News co., 1888. Cloth. Scarce.

5 p.l., 13–390 p. front., illus., plates. 17.5 cm.

Although the title page mentions maps, there are none listed in the table of illustrations and none in the book.

1688 ———. The official Northern Pacific Railway guide for the use of tourists and travelers over the lines of the Northern Pacific Railroad and its branches. . . . Profusely illustrated. St. Paul, W. C. Riley, publisher, [1897]. Limp cloth. Rare.

8 p.l., 20–442 p. illus., plates. 17.2 cm.

1689 NOTEWARE, J. H. The state of Nebraska, illustrated by a new and authentic map, accompanied by some statements in answer to the following questions: Where is it? What is it? What is it to become? When shall these things be? Approved by the Commissioners and published by J. H. Noteware. . . . Lincoln, Neb., State Journal company print, 1873. Wrappers. Rare.

[3]–23 p. large fold. map at end. 22.2 cm.

1690 NOYES, ALVA JOSIAH. In the land of Chinook; or, the story of Blaine County, by A. J. Noyes (Ajax). Helena, Mont., State publishing co., [1917]. Cloth. Scarce.

3 p.l., [7]–152 p. plates, ports., facsms. 24 cm.
Index, p. 148–152.
Device.
The first page marked "index" is really the table of contents.

1691 ———. The story of Ajax; life in the Big Hole Basin, by Alva J. Noyes. Helena, Montana, State publishing company, 1914. Cloth. Scarce.

4 p.l., 158 p. front., plates, ports. 24 cm.
Index, p. [153]–158.
Errata, 4th prelim. page.

Said to be the first autobiography published in Montana.

1692 NUTTING, LUCIUS A. Raw country. Recollections of the West during ninety years. By L. A. Nutting, with contributions by two old friends, B. F. Lamb and Mrs. Mary Lamb. Laurel, Montana, 1948. Cloth. Scarce.

5 p.l., 41 p. front. (port.), plates, ports. 23.4 cm.
Half title, preface, introduction, and second half title precede the title page.

This privately printed little book was given to the Billings (Mont.) Orthopedic Foundation to be sold for the benefit of crippled children.

1693 NYE, W. S. Carbine and lance, the story of old Fort Sill. By Captain W. S. Nye. Norman, University of Oklahoma press, 1937. Cloth.

xviii p., 1 l., 3–441 p. front., plates, ports., map, plan. 23.7 cm.
Index, p. 423–441.
Half title; "First edition" on copyright p.

Contains a chapter on cattle in the Indian Territory.

1694 OCAIN, E. H. The trail of the buffalo wolves, with short stories and poems. By E. H. Ocain. . . . Santa Monica, California, printed by Steward and Flood printing co., inc., [1952]. Cloth.

4 p.l., 9–143 p. illus. 22.3 cm.
Pub. device.

1695 O'DELL, SCOTT. Country of the sun. Southern California, an informal history and guide, by Scott O'Dell. New York, Thomas Y. Crowell company, [1957]. Cloth.

viii p., 1 l., 310 p. 21 cm.
Glossary, p. 297–298; pronunciation guide, p. 299–300; index, p. 301–310.
Half title; map on end papers.

Much material on the California vaqueros and cattle ranching.

1696 O'KEEFE, RUFE. Cowboy life; reminiscences of an early life, early boyhood, and experiences as a cowboy on the range, on the trail, as manager of a ranch, and then owner and operator in cattle. By Rufe O'Keefe. San Antonio, Texas, the Naylor company, 1936. Cloth.

3 p.l., 244 p. front. (port.), illus. 21 cm.
Half title; device.

1697 OKLAHOMA. First biennial report of the Secretary of the Oklahoma Live Stock Sanitary Commission, 1897–8. [Guthrie, Oklahoma, State Capital printing company, 1899]. Wrappers. Scarce.

[3]–11 p. 23.2 cm.

1698 ———. Fourth biennial report of the Secretary of the Oklahoma Live Stock Sanitary Commission of Oklahoma Territory, 1904. Okeene, Okla., Eagle power print, 1904. Wrappers. Scarce.

[3]–5 p. 21.6 cm.

[272]

1699 ———. Kay County, Oklahoma. Ponca City, Oklahoma, published by Kay County gas co., [1919]. Cloth. Scarce.

2 p.l., 7–75 [1] p. illus., plates (9 fold. 8 double p.), maps (2 double p.), graphs (1 double p.). 22.2 cm.
Copyright notice on verso of flyleaf.

1700 ———. Oklahoma. St. Louis, press of Woodward & Tiernan, [n.d.]. Pict. wrappers. Rare.

[60] p. (no pagination), plates, fold. col. maps in front and back. 19 cm.

Promotional pamphlet issued by the Frisco Railroad.

1701 ———. Oklahoma, the beautiful land, by the 89ers. Oklahoma City, Oklahoma, published by the Times-Journal publishing company, [1943]. Pict. cloth. OP.

3 p.l., 352 p. plates, ports., map, cattle brands. 24 cm.

Contains some information about the early cattle ranches of Oklahoma.

1702 ———. Oklahoma, its history and growth officially detailed. Its finances, agriculture, and industries. . . . [N.p., n.d.]. Wrappers. Rare.
64 p. tables. 21.6 cm.

1703 ———. Oklahoma, past and present. Brief sketches of men and events in Oklahoma history—from Coronado to the present. Oklahoma City, Frontier publishing co., [c.1907]. Stiff wrappers. Scarce.

4–86 p. front. (port.), plates, port., map. 24.2 cm.

1704 ———. The romance of Oklahoma, Oklahoma Authors' Club [by various members]. Oklahoma City, 1920. Pict. cloth. Scarce.

3 p.l., 86 p. plates, ports. 23 cm.

A chapter on ranching and one on the Chisholm Trail.

1705 ———. Second biennial report of the Secretary of the Oklahoma Live Stock Sanitary Commission of the territory of Oklahoma, for the years 1899 and 1900. [Guthrie, O. T., State Capital printing co., 1900]. Wrappers. Rare.

[3]–6 p. 22.2 cm.

1706 ———. Statistics and information concerning the Indian Territory, Oklahoma, and the Cherokee Strip with its millions of acres of unoccupied lands for the farmer and stock raiser. . . . [St. Louis, Woodward & Tiernan printing co., n.d., 1894]. Wrappers. Rare.

3–85 p. plates, large fold. map at end, tables. 19.2 cm.
3 p. adv. at end.

1707 ———. The truth about Oklahoma. Pen-and-ink drawings by C. M.

Tuttle and Jas. McCracken. Half tone from special photographs. ₁N.p.₁, passenger department Santa Fe, 1903. Stiff wrappers. Rare.

2 p.l., 5–127 ₁1₁ p. illus., plates, large fold. map at end. 16x8.5 cm.

1708 OLD COWHAND. Horse sense ain't common, as told by an old cow-hand from the Rio Grande. San Antonio, Texas, the Naylor company, 1938. Stiff pict. wrappers. OP.

xiii, 53 p. illus. 16.5 cm.
Half title; vignette.

1709 OLIPHANT, J. ORIN. The cattle herds and ranches of the Oregon coun-try, 1860–1890. ₁By₁ J. Orin Oliphant. . . . ₁N.p.₁, 1947. Wrappers. OP.

p. ₁217₁–238. 24 cm.
Reprinted from *Agricultural History*, Vol. XX, No. 4, (October, 1946).

1710 ———. The cattle trade from the far Northwest to Montana, by J. Orin Oliphant. Reprinted from *Agricultural History*, Vol. VI, No. 2 (April, 1932). Stiff wrappers. (Cover title). Scarce.

p. 69–83 25.2 cm.

1711 ———. The cattle trade through the Snoqualmie Pass. ₁By₁ J. Orin Oliphant. ₁N.p.₁, 1947. Stapled. (Caption title). Scarce.

p. 193–213 22.8 cm.
Reprinted from *Pacific Northwest Quarterly*, Vol. XXXVIII, No. 3 (July, 1947).

1712 ———. The eastward movement of cattle from the Oregon country. ₁By₁ J. Orin Oliphant. . . . ₁N.p.₁, 1946. Wrappers. (Cover title). Scarce.

p. 19–43. 25.4 cm.
Double column.
Reprinted from *Agricultural History*, Vol. XX (January, 1946).

1713 ———. William Emsley Jackson's diary of a cattle drive from La Grand, Oregon, to Cheyenne, Wyoming, in 1876. ₁Washington₁, 1949. Wrappers.

p. 260–273. 24.3 cm.
Double column.
Republished from *Agricultural History*, Vol. XXIII, No. 4 (1949).

1714 OLSON, JAMES C. History of Nebraska, by James C. Olson. Line draw-ings by Franz Altschuler. Lincoln, University of Nebraska press, 1955. Pict. cloth.

xii p., 1 l., 3–372 p. illus., plates, ports., maps. 23.6 cm.
Index, p. 361–372.
Half title; map on end papers; illus. double t.p.; illus. headpieces; "suggested read-ing" after each chapter.

1715 OLSSON, ANNA. "I'm scairt." Childhood days on the prairie, by Anna Olsson. . . . Rock Island, Illinois, Augustana book concern, [1927]. Boards. OP.

4 p.l., 9–155 p. 19.3 cm.

1716 ON THE PLAINS. The Companion Library, Number thirteen. Selections from the *Youth's Companion*. . . . Boston, Mass., Perry Mason company, 1897. Pict. wrappers. Scarce.

[3]–64 p., illus., plates, cattle brands. 20.3 cm.

Chapters on ranch life, cowboys, the great cattle trails, the language of brands, breaking a bronc, and a chase for wild horses.

1717 ONDERDONK, JAMES LAWRENCE. Idaho: facts and statistics concerning its mining, farming, stock-raising, lumbering, and other resources and industries. Together with notes on the climate, scenery, game, and mineral springs. Information for the home-seeker, capitalist, prospector, and traveler. By James L. Onderdonk. . . . San Francisco, Cal., A. L. Bancroft & co., book and job printers, 1885. Pict. wrappers. Rare.

4 p.l., 9–150 p. tables. 22.3 cm.
Index, p. 149–150.

1718 O'NEIL, JAMES BRADAS. They die but once, the story of a Tejano, by James B. O'Neil. New York, Knight publications, inc., 1935. Cloth. OP.

viii p., 2 l., 228 p. 23.5 cm.
Half title.

1719 O'NEILL, JOHN. Northern Nebraska as a home for immigrants. Containing a general description of the state, sketches of northern Nebraska counties, and answers to correspondence of intending immigrants. By John O'Neill. . . . Sioux City, Iowa, Sioux City Times print, 1875. Wrappers. Rare.

2 p.l., [5]–108 p. large fold. map in front. 21.5 cm.
Double column.
Last 13 p. adv.; adv. verso front wrapper, recto and verso back wrapper.

1720 O'NEILL, WILLIAM O. Central Arizona for homes, for health, for wealth. By Wm. O. O'Neill. Prescott, Ariz., Hoofs and Horns print, 1887. Wrappers. Scarce.

[5]–130 p. illus., plates, fold. panoramic view in front. 19.3 cm.
Last 7 p., business cards.

1721 O'REILLY, HARRINGTON. Fifty years on the trail. A true story of western life, by Harrington O'Reilly, with over one hundred illustrations by Paul Frenzeny. London, Chatto & Windus, Piccadilly, 1889. Pict. cloth. Scarce.

xvi, 381 p. front. (with tissue), illus. 19.9 cm.
Device; 32 numbered pages of adv. at end.

Reprinted in 1890 and 1891 with same imprint and collation; an American
edition was made from the same plates as the London edition in New York
in 1889. Also there was a French translation with 348 pages published in Paris
the same year.

1722 OREGON. A brief history of the resources of the Willamette, Umpqua,
and Rogue River valleys, being three of the most fertile and highly pro-
ductive valleys on the Pacific Coast. . . . Washington City, M'Gill &
Witherow, printers and stereotypers, 1869. Wrappers. Rare.
[3]–24 p. 21 cm.

1723 ———. Facts regarding its climate, soil, mineral and agricultural resources, means of communication, commerce and industry, laws, &c.,
&c. . . . For use of immigrants. With maps. . . . Portland, Oregon, Boston, Mass. . . . , 1875. Wrappers. Rare.
[3]–42 p. fold. map in front, fold. map at end. 22.8 cm.
Adv. verso front wrapper; adv. recto and verso back wrapper.

1724 ———. Facts regarding its climate, soil, mineral and agricultural resources, means of communication, commerce and industry, laws, &c., &c.
For use of immigrants. With map. . . . Boston, Mass., 1876. Wrappers.
Rare.
[3]–13 [1] p. map at end. 17 cm.

1725 ———. Facts regarding its climate, soil, mineral and agricultural
resources, means of communication, commerce and industry, laws, &c.,
&c. For use of immigrants. With maps. . . . Portland, Oregon, Boston,
Mass., 1876. Wrappers. Rare.
3–44 [2] p. fold. map in front, fold. map at end. 23 cm.
Last 2 p. adv.; adv. verso front wrapper; adv. recto and verso back wrapper.

1726 ———. Facts regarding its climate, soil, mineral and agricultural resources, means of communication, commerce and industry, laws, etc. For
general information. With maps. . . . New York, Boston . . . , 1877.
Wrappers. Rare.
3–48 p. fold. map in front; fold. map at end. 23 cm.

1727 ———. Facts regarding its climate, soil, mineral and agricultural resources, means of communication, commerce and industry, laws, etc.
For general information. . . . New York and Boston . . . , 1878. Wrappers. Rare.
3–48 p. fold. map in front, fold. map at end. 23.3 cm.

1728 ———. Facts regarding its climate, soil, mineral and agricultural resources, means of communication, commerce and industry, laws, etc. For general information. With maps. . . . New York and Boston . . . , 1880. Wrappers. Rare.

3–48 p. fold. map in front, fold. map at end. 22 cm.

1729 ———. Facts regarding its climate, soil, mineral and agricultural resources, means of communication, commerce and industry, laws, etc. For general information. With map and appendix. . . . Issued from eastern office Oregon Railway and Navigation co., New York City, 1880. Pict. wrappers. Scarce.

3–59 p. large fold. map at end, tables. 22.5 cm.
Adv. recto and verso of back wrapper.

1730 ———. The new empire, Oregon, Washington, Idaho. Its resources, climate, present development, and its advantages as a place of residence and field for investment. . . . Portland, Oregon, issued by the Oregon Immigration Board, ₁n.d.₁. Pict. wrappers. Rare.

₁3₁–89 ₁7₁ p. 25.8 cm.
Illus. verso front wrapper, recto and verso back wrapper.

1731 ———. Oregon as it is. Published for gratuitous distribution by the state Board of Immigration. A brief description of the state, containing accurate and trustworthy information for those seeking new homes in a mild and healthful climate. . . . Portland, Oregon, R. H. Shaw & Bro. . . . , 1887. Wrappers. Rare.

₁3₁–112 p. large fold. map in front. 21.3 cm.

1732 ———. The resources of the state of Oregon. A book of statistical information treating upon Oregon as a whole, and by counties. Collated and prepared by the state Board of Agriculture. Salem, Oregon, W. H. Leeds, state printer, 1898. Wrappers. Scarce.

2 p.l., ₁5₁–203 p. 22.2 cm.

1733 ———. Settlers' guide to Oregon and Washington Territory and to the lands of the Northern Pacific Railroad on the Pacific Slope. . . . ₁N.p., c.1872₁. Wrappers. Rare.

32 ₁1₁ p. maps verso front and back wrappers. 23.5 cm.

1734 ORMEROD, LEONARD. The curving shore. The Gulf Coast from Brownsville to Key West. By Leonard Ormerod. New York, Harper & brothers, publishers, ₁1957₁. Pict. cloth.

xii p., 1 l., 331 p. plates, maps. 21.7 cm.
Index, p. 323–331.
Half title; map on end papers; untrimmed.
Errata slip laid in.

Chapter III deals with the King Ranch of Texas.

1735 ORNDUFF, DONALD R. The Hereford in America. A compilation of historic facts about the breed's background and bloodlines. By Donald R. Ornduff. . . . Kansas City, Missouri, published privately by the author, [1957]. Cloth.

xii p., 1 l., 3–500 p. illus., maps, tables. 23.6 cm.
Appendix, p. 423–491 [1]; index, p. 493–500.
Half title; illus. double t.p.; "First edition" on copyright p.

1736 ORTEGA, LUIS. California hackamore (La Jaquima). An authentic story of the use of the hackamore, by Luis Ortega. [Sacramento, California, printed by News publishing co., 1948]. Pict. leather. Scarce.

8 p.l., 133 p. illus., plates, ports. 21.6 cm.
Glossary, p. 133.
Half title; illus. end papers; illus. t.p.; 4 blank leaves at end.

1737 ———. California stock horse . . . , by Luis Ortega. . . . [Sacramento, California, printed by News publishing company, 1949]. Pict. leather. Scarce.

3 p.l., 169 [1] p. illus., plates, ports. 21.6 cm.
Glossary, p. [170].
Illus. end papers; illus. t.p.; copyright p. precedes t.p.; "First edition" on copyright p.

1738 OSBORN, CAMPBELL. Let freedom ring, [by] Campbell Osborn. Tokyo, the Inter-Nation company, [1954]. Cloth.

ii p., 2 l., 211 p. map. 17.5 cm.
Half title.

Chapters on cattle and cowboys.

1739 OSGOOD, ERNEST STAPLES. The day of the cattleman, by Ernest Staples Osgood. Minneapolis, the University of Minnesota press, 1929. Cloth. OP.

x p., 2 l., 283 p. front., plates, maps (part double p.), diagrs., facsms. 24.6 cm.
Bibliography, p. 259–268; index, p. 269–283.
Half title; illus. end papers; untrimmed.
Thesis (Ph.D.), University of Wisconsin, 1927. (Without thesis note).
Republished in 1954.

1740 O'SHEA, ELENE ZAMORA. El mesquite. A story of the early Spanish settlements between the Nueces and the Rio Grande as told by "La Poata del Palo Alto." By Elena Zamora O'Shea, with an introduction by L. B. Russell. Dallas, Mathis publishing co., [1935]. Cloth. OP.

8 p.l., 80 p. 19.6 cm.
Half title; pub. device.

1741 OTIS, JAMES. Philip of Texas. A story of sheep raising in Texas. By James Otis. New York, American book co., [1913]. Pict. cloth. Scarce.

5 p.l., 9–155 p. front. (map), illus. 18.7 cm.

[278]

THE DAY OF THE
CATTLEMAN

BY
ERNEST STAPLES OSGOOD

MINNEAPOLIS
THE UNIVERSITY OF MINNESOTA PRESS
1929

1742 OUTCALT, JOHN. History of Merced County, California, with a bio-graphical review of the leading men and women of the county who have been identified with its growth and development from the early days to the present. History by John Outcalt. Illustrated. . . . Los Angeles, Calif., Historic Record co., 1925. Three-quarter leather. Scarce.

7 p.l., ₍33₎–913 p. plates. 27.6 cm.
Index, p. ₍907₎–913.

Has a chapter on the cattle industry of Merced County.

1743 PABOR, WILLIAM E. Colorado as an agricultural state. Its farms, fields, and garden lands. By William E. Pabor. . . . Illustrated. New York, Orange Judd company, 1883. Dec. cloth. Scarce.

4 p.l., 9–213 ₍1₎ p. illus., tables. 19 cm.
Pub. device; 1 p. adv. at end.

1744 PACIFIC NORTHWEST. The Pacific Northwest, a guide for settlers and travelers. Oregon and Washington Territory, with a map and illustrations. New York, E. Wells Sackett & Rankin, 1882. Wrappers. (Cover title). Rare.

81 p. front. (double p.), plates, large fold. map (col.) at end. 22.6 cm.

1745 ———. The Pacific Northwest. Information for settlers and others. Oregon and Washington Territory. With map. New York . . . , 1883. Wrappers. (Cover title). Rare.

32 p. double-p. map at end. 22.7 cm.

1746 ———. The Pacific Northwest, its wealth and resources. Oregon, Washington, Idaho. The city of Portland. Portland, Oregon, issued by the Oregon Immigration Board, ₍1891₎. Wrappers. Scarce.

₍3₎–158 p. front., illus., plates. 20.2 cm.

1747 PADDOCK, CAPT. B. B. (ED.). History of Texas. Fort Worth and the Texas Northwest edition. Edited by Capt. B. B. Paddock. Chicago and New York, the Lewis publishing company, 1922. Cloth. Pub. in 4 vols. Scarce.

Vol. I: xxxv ₍1₎, 439 p. front. (port.), plates, ports. 27.5 cm.
Vol. II: 441–886 p. front., plates. 27.5 cm.
Vol. III: 3–368 p. front., ports. (incl. front.). 27.5 cm.
Vol. IV: 369–752 p. front. ports. (incl. front.). 27.5 cm.

Volume II contains a chapter on livestock.

1748 ———. A twentieth century history and biographical record of north and west Texas. Capt. B. B. Paddock, editor. Illustrated. Chicago, New York, the Lewis publishing co., 1906. Cloth. Pub. in 2 vols. Scarce.

Vol. I: 5 p.l., 704 p. front., ports. (incl. front.). 26.5 cm.

Vol. II: 3 p.l., 714 p. ports. 26.5 cm.

Both volumes double column.

Volume I contains a chapter on the range cattle industry; volume II is biographical.

1749 PAGE, ELIZABETH. Wild horses and gold; from Wyoming to the Yukon, by Elizabeth Page; illustrated by Paul Brown. New York, Farrar & Rinehart, inc., [1932]. Cloth. OP.

xiii p., 1 l., 3–362 p. front., illus., fold. map. 23.2 cm.

"Notes on historical sources," p. 350–357; "list of Klondikers passed," p. 359–362.

Half title; illus. end papers (col.); pub. device; untrimmed.

A narrative of the journey of "Kansas" Gilbert and his party driving a band of wild horses to the Klondike, 1897–98, based on Gilbert's diary and other contemporary sources.

1750 PAINE, BAYARD H. Pioneers, Indians, and buffaloes, by Bayard H. Paine. With foreword by Addison E. Sheldon. Curtis, Nebr., the Curtis Enterprises, 1935. Cloth. OP.

4 p.l., 9–192 p. front. (port.)., illus., plates, ports. 21.6 cm.

Index, p. 185–192.

Contains some minor cattle material and tells the story of Samuel A. Maverick, although the author gets some details wrong, such as Maverick's living near El Paso, Texas, and having about four million acres of land.

1751 PALOMARES, JOSÉ FRANCISCO. Memoirs of José Francisco Palomares. Translated from the manuscript in the Bancroft Library by Thomas Workman Temple II. Los Angeles, Glen Dawson, 1955. Pict. white boards. Scarce.

4 p.l., 69 [1] p. illus., 1 plate (col.), map. 18.8 cm.

Half title; maps on end papers.

Colophon: "205 copies printed and bound by George Yamada, 1955. The end sheet maps are from Emory, *Notes of a Military Reconnaissance, 1848.* The color plate of Los Angeles in 1857 courtesy of Title Insurance and Trust Company. Drawings by Janice Pettee."

1752 PALOUSE COUNTRY. The Palouse country. An attractive region for general farming and stock raising. [N.p., n.d.]. Stapled. (Cover title). Rare.

32 p. illus., plates. 13.5x20 cm.

Double column.

1753 PANGBORN, J. G. The new Rocky Mountain tourist's Arkansas Valley and San Juan guide. The tour through the grain districts of the Arkansas Valley, the sheep and cattle ranges and hunting grounds of southwestern Kansas, to the pleasure resorts of the Rocky Mountains. . . . By J. G.

Pangborn. Third edition. Chicago, Knight & Leonard, 1878. Pict. wrappers. Rare.

2 p.l., [5]–64 p. illus., plates, maps (1 large fold. at end). 29 cm.

I was unable to locate a first edition of this work.

1754 PANNELL, WALTER. Civil war on the range, by Walter Pannell. Los Angeles, published by Welcome News, [1943]. Pict. wrappers. (Cover title). OP.

2 p.l., 5–45 p. 15 cm.
[Published with "The Empire of the Big Bend," p. 37–45].
Cover title: "Civil War On the Range. An Historic Acount of the Battle for the Prairies, the Lincoln County War and Subsequent Events."
3 p. adv. at end.

1755 PARKE, ADELIA. Memoirs of an old timer, by Adelia Parke. Weiser, Idaho, Signal-American printers, [1955]. Stiff pict. wrappers.

5 p.l., [3]–65 p. plates. 22.9 cm.
Double column.

1756 PARKER, FRANK J. Washington Territory. The present and prospective future of the upper Columbia country, embracing the counties of Walla Walla, Whitman, Spokane, and Stevens. With a detailed description of northern Idaho. Compiled and edited by Frank J. Parker. . . . Walla Walla, W. T. Statesman book and job office, 1881. Wrappers. (Cover title). Rare.

17 p. 23 cm.

1757 PARKER, J. M. An aged wanderer; a life sketch of J. M. Parker, a cowboy on the western plains in the early days. San Angelo, Texas, headquarters Elkhorn Wagon Yard, [n.d.]. Pict. wrappers. (Cover title). Rare.

32 p. front. (port. on verso front wrapper). 21.3 cm.

Also published under the title: "The poor orphan boy, a life sketch of a western cowboy." [n.p., n.d.]. Wrappers. Very rare.

2 p.l., [5]–39 [1] p. front. 16.6 cm.

1758 PARR, VIRGIL VERSER. Beef cattle production in the range area. [By Virgil V. Parr, Washington, Government printing office, 1925]. Wrappers. OP.

ii, 44 p. illus., maps. 21 cm.
U. S. Dept. of Agriculture *Farmer's Bulletin No. 1395.*

1759 ——. Brahman (Zebu) cattle. [By Virgil V. Parr]. [Washington, Government printing office, 1923]. Wrappers. OP.

ii, 21 p. illus., map. 23 cm.
U. S. Dept. of Agriculture, *Farmer's Bulletin No. 1361.*

[282]

1760 PARRISH, RANDALL. The great plains. The romance of western American exploration, warfare, and settlement, 1527–1870. By Randall Parrish. . . . Chicago, A. C. McClurg & co., 1907. Pict. cloth. OP.

xiv p., 1 l., 17–399 p. front., illus. 21.5 cm.
Index, p. 385–399.
Half title; pub. device; untrimmed.

1761 PARRY, DR. C. C. Preliminary report on the physical geography and natural resources of the country along the route of the Kansas Pacific Railway on the thirty-fifth parallel. . . . By Dr. C. C. Parry. Philadelphia, Review printing house, 1868. Wrappers. Rare.

[3]–20 p. large fold. map in front. 22.8 cm.

1762 PATTERSON, PAUL. Sam McGoo and Texas too, by Paul Patterson. Illustrations by Elmer Kelton. Dallas, Mathis, Van Nort and co., [1947]. Cloth. OP.

5 p.l., 183 p. front., illus. 19.8 cm.
Half title; illus. end papers.

A frivolous tall tale of the cow country.

1763 PAUL, ELLIOTT. A ghost town on the Yellowstone, by Elliott Paul. New York, Random house, [1948]. Cloth. OP.

5 p. l., 3–341 p. 20.8 cm.
Half title.

A collection of stories dealing with Montana and cowboys.

1764 PAXSON, FREDERIC LOGAN. The cow country, by Frederic L. Paxson. Reprinted from the *American Historical Review,* Vol. XXII, No. 1 (October, 1916). [N.p., 1916]. Wrappers. (Cover title). OP.

p. 65–82. 27 cm.

1765 ———. History of the American frontier, 1763–1893, by Frederic L. Paxson. Boston, Houghton Mifflin company, 1924. Cloth. OP.

xvii p., 1 l., 598 p. maps (2 double p. and col.). 23.8 cm.
Index, p. 575–598.
Half title; pub. device.
Republished same year.

1766 PAYNE, E. W. South-western brand-book containing marks and brands of the cattle and horse raisers of southwestern Kansas, the Indian Territory, and the Panhandle of Texas for the round-up of 1884. By E. W. Payne. Medicine Lodge, Ks., Barber County Index, 1884. Calf. Rare.

[3]–88 p. cattle brands. 15.5 cm.

1767 PAYNE, J. E. The plains of Colorado. Bulletins by J. E. Payne. Fort

Collins, Colorado, published by the Experiment Station, 1904. Wrappers. Scarce.

2 p.l., [7]–17 p. 21 cm.
Agricultural Experiment Station *Bulletin 87.*

1768 PAYNE, J. J. From saddle to pulpit; or, from cow-puncher to preacher. The life story of Rev. J. J. ("Cowboy Joe") Payne. . . . Dayton, O., John J. Scruby, printer, [1928]. Stiff wrappers. Scarce.

2 p.l., [5]–56 p. front. (port.). 19.4 cm.

1769 PAYTON, WILLIAM. The last man over the trail, by Col. Wm. Payton. [N.p., 1939]. Stiff pict. wrappers. OP.

60 p. front., illus., plates, map (double p.). 22.8 cm.

1770 PEAK, HOWARD W. A ranger of commerce; or, 52 years on the road. By Howard W. Peak. San Antonio, Naylor printing company, [1929]. Pict. cloth. OP.

5 p.l., 262 p. front. (port.). 22 cm.

Has a chapter on the cattle trails.

1771 PEAKE, ORA BROOKS. The Colorado range cattle industry, by Ora Brooks Peake. . . . Glendale, California, the Arthur H. Clark company, 1937. Cloth. OP.

9 p.l., [21]–357 p. front. (with tissue), port., 2 fold. maps, facsms. (1 fold.). 24.5 cm. Bibliography, p. [325]–341; index, p. [345]–357.
Half title; untrimmed; gilt top.

1772 PEARCE, WILLIAM M. The establishment and early development of the Matador ranch, 1882–1890. [By] William M. Pearce. Abilene, Texas, reprinted from *Bulletin* of the West Texas Historical Association, Vol. XXVII (October, 1951). Stiff wrappers.

[3]–31 p. 22.8 cm.

1773 PEARSON, HARRY W. The early history and development of the range livestock industry, by Harry W. Pearson. Thesis submitted to the Department of Agronomy and Agricultural Economics and the Committee on Graduate Work of the University of Wyoming, in partial fulfillment of the requirements for the degree of Master of Science. Laramie, Wyoming, 1931. Boards.

4 p.l., 88 [11] p. 28 cm.
Last 11 p. bibliography; photo-lithoprint on one side of paper only.

1774 PEATTIE, RODERICK (ED.). The Black Hills. Edited by Roderick Peattie. The contributors: Leland D. Case, Badger Clark, Paul Friggens, R. V.

Hunkins, Clarence S. Paine, Elmo Scott Watson. New York, the Vanguard press, inc., [1952]. Pict. cloth.

8 p.l., 17–320 p. plates, ports., map. 24.2 cm.
Index, p. 311–320.
Half title; illus. double t.p.

1775 PECK, ANNE MERRIMAN. Southwest roundup, by Anne Merriman Peck. Illustrated by the author. New York, Dodd-Mead & company, 1950. Cloth.

4 p.l., 248 p. illus., map (double p.). 20.8 cm.
Half title; illus. t.p.; illus. chapter headings; untrimmed.
Reprinted in 1954.

1776 PECK, LEIGH. Pecos Bill and lightning. By Leigh Peck. Illustrated by Burt Wiese. Boston, Houghton Mifflin company, 1940. Cloth. OP.

67 p. illus. (col.). 25 cm.
Illus. col. t.p.

1777 PEFFER, E. LOUISE. The closing of the public domain. Disposal and reservation policies, 1900–'50. By E. Louise Peffer. Stanford, Calif., Stanford, University press, [1951]. Cloth.

xi p., 1 l., 3–372 p. tables. 23.5 cm.
Appendix, p. 345–360; index, p. 361–372.
Half title.

1778 PELZER, LOUIS. The cattlemen's frontier; a record of the trans-Mississippi cattle industry from ox trains to pooling companies, 1850–1890, by Louis Pelzer. . . . Glendale, California, the Arthur H. Clark company, 1936. Cloth.

11 pl., [25]–351 p. front. (with tissue), illus., plates. 24.5 cm.
Appendix, p. [251]–[312]; bibliography, p. [315]–323; index, p. [327]–351.
Half title; untrimmed; gilt top.

The appendix is a reprint of "Cattle brands owned by members of the Wyoming Stock Growers' Association. Chicago, the J. M. Jones Stationery and Printing Co., 1882."

1779 ———. A cattleman's commonwealth on the western range. By Louis Pelzer. Reprinted from the *Mississippi Valley Historical Review,* Vol. XIII, No. 1 (June, 1926). Wrappers. OP.

p. [30]–49. 25.6 cm.

1780 ———. Financial management of the cattle ranges. [By] Louis Pelzer. Reprinted from the *Journal of Economic and Business History,* Vol. II, No. 4 (August, 1930). Stiff wrappers. (Cover title). OP.

p. [723]–741 [1]. 23.6 cm.

1781 ———. The shifting cow towns of Kansas, by Louis Pelzer. Reprinted from *Transaction of the Illinois State Historical Society,* 1926. Wrappers. OP.

[3]-13 p. 23 cm.

1782 PENCE, MARY LOU, and LOLA M. HOMSHER. The ghost towns of Wyoming, by Mary Lou Pence and Lola M. Homsher. New York, Hastings house, publishers, [1956]. Boards.

xii p., 1 l., 242 p. illus., plates (1 double p.), ports., facsms., map (double p). 26 cm. Acknowledgments, p. 236; index, p. 237-242.

Half title; map on end papers; illus. double t.p.

1783 PENDER, ROSE. A lady's experiences in the wild West in 1883, by Rose Pender. . . . London, George Tucker, [1888]. Cloth. Scarce.

vii, 80 p. 21.7 cm.

Top of each page given the title, "In Search of a Roundup."

An English lady's impression of the West and the cattle country, unflattering to say the least.

1784 PENDLETON, GRANVILLE. San Juan County, New Mexico. An ideal agricultural section with plenty of water for irrigation and land for homeseekers. Written by Granville Pendleton. Published by authority of the Bureau of Immigration of New Mexico. [N.p], 1906. Wrappers. Scarce.

69 p. front., plates, ports. 23.3 cm.

1785 PENROSE, CHARLES BINGHAM. The Johnson County War. The papers of Charles Bingham Penrose in the library of the University of Wyoming with introduction and notes by Lois Van Valkenburgh. Thesis submitted to the Department of History and the Committee on Graduate Study at the University of Wyoming, in partial fulfillment of the requirements for the degree of Master of Arts. Laramie, Wyoming, 1939. Cloth.

xxxvi p., 1 l., 108, lxxvii p. 28.3 cm.

Bibliography, p. [lxxv]-lxxvii.

Photo-lithographed on one side of paper.

There are errors in pagination, some pages being unnumbered though included in the pagination. Also error in binding, pages i-xxi of 3d Series bound between lxi and [lxii].

1786 PEPLOW, BONNIE, and ED PEPLOW. Pioneer stories of Arizona's Verde Valley. . . . Supervised by and with preface and introduction by Bonnie Peplow and Ed Peplow. [N.p.], Verde Valley Pioneers, 1954. Stiff pict. wrappers.

xvi p., 2 l., ₁5₁–219 p. plates, ports. 21.8 cm.
Index, p. 213–219.

1787 ———. Roundup recipes, ₁by₁ Bonnie & Ed Peplow, with the help of the Arizona Cowbelles. Cleveland and New York, the World publishing company, ₁1951₁. Cloth.
ix p., 1 l., 3–278 p. 22 cm.
Glossary, p. 263–271; index, p. 273–278.
Half title; cattle brands on end papers; device; untrimmed; "First edition" on copyright p.

1788 PERKINS, CHARLES ELLIOTT. The phantom bull, by Charles E. Perkins; with illustrations by Edward Borein. Boston and New York, Houghton Mifflin company, 1932. Pict. cloth. OP.
2 p.l., 70 p. front., illus. 26 cm.
Half title; untrimmed; first edition, "1932" under imprint.

1789 ———. The pinto horse, by Charles Elliott Perkins; illustrations by Edward Borein and a foreword by Owen Wister. Santa Barbara, California, Wallace Hebberd, 1927. Pict. boards. Scarce.
2 p.l., 76 p. front. (col.), illus., facsm. 28.2 cm.
Republished, Santa Barbara, Fisher and Skofield, 1937.
2 p.l., 76 p. front. (col.), illus., facsm. 28.2 cm.

1790 [PERKY, H. D.]. Homes in Saunders County and state of Nebraska. Published by the Wahoo Merchant's and Business Men's Club, Wahoo, Saunders County, Neb. Omaha, Neb., E. H. Mortimer & co., printers, 1879. Wrappers. Rare.
₁3₁–40 p. illus., fold. map in front. 23. cm.

1791 PERRINE, HENRY E. The true story of some eventful years in Grandpa's life; containing the journal of the trip to California in 1849; life at the diggings; the southern mines; the great fire of '51; the vigilance committee and its doings. . . . Buffalo, 1885. Cloth. Rare.
303 p. plates, map. 20 cm.
"Privately printed for relatives and a few friends—not for general circulation."

1792 PERRY, GEORGE SESSIONS. Texas, a world in itself, by George Sessions Perry. Illustrated by Arthur Fuller. New York, London, Whittlesey house, McGraw-Hill book company, ₁1942₁. Cloth. OP.
xi p., 1 l., 3–293 p. 23.4 cm.
Index, p. 287–293.
Half title; illus. map on end papers; illus. chapter headings; 6 blank leaves at end.
Republished in 1952 by Grossett and Dunlap.

1793 PETERSON, P. D. Through the Black Hills and Bad Lands of South

Dakota, by P. D. Peterson. Pierre, S. D., J. Fred Olander co., ₁1929₁.
Cloth. OP.

4 p.l., 9–189 p. front., illus., plates, ports., map. 21.8 cm.

1794 PEYTON, GREEN (pseud. of Green Peyton Wertenbaker). America's
heartland, the Southwest, by Green Peyton. Norman, University of Oklahoma press, 1948. Cloth.

xvii p., 1 l., 3–285 ₁1₁ p. plates, ports., map. 22 cm.
Index, p. 278–₁286₁.
Half title.

1795 ——. San Antonio, city in the sun, by Green Peyton. New York,
London, Whittlesey house, McGraw-Hill book company, ₁1946₁. Cloth.
OP.

ix, 292 p. plates, ports., maps (1 fold.). 20.8 cm.
Index, p. 277–292.
Half title.

Chapters I and II deal with cattle and the Maverick family.

1796 PHARES, ROSS. Texas tradition, ₁by₁ Ross Phares, with line drawings
by Nick Eggenhofer. New York, Henry Holt and company, ₁1954₁.
Pict. two-tone cloth.

xi p., 1 l., 239 p. illus. 21.6 cm.
Notes, p. 214–230; index, p. 231–239.
Half title; "First edition" on copyright p.

Little stories of customs, traditions, and folklore of the cattle range, most of
them familiar.

1797 PHILIPS, SHINE. Big Spring, the casual biography of a prairie town,
by Shine Philips. Drawings by Jerry Bywaters. New York, Prentice-
Hall, inc., 1942. Cloth.

vi p., 1 l., 231 p. illus. 23.5 cm.
Half title.
Reprinted many times.

A humorous story of a cow town of West Texas in its early days.

1798 PHILLIPS, EDWARD HAKE. The Texas norther, by Edward Hake Phillips. . . . The Rice Institute Pamphlet, Vol. XLI, No. 4 (January, 1955).
Wrappers.

3 p.l., 158 p. 23.6 cm.
Notes, p. 143–158.

Has a chapter entitled "Cattle, Cowmen, and the Norther."

1799 PHILLIPS, RUFUS. Colorado's first industry. Early days of cattle business

in the Arkansas Valley of Colorado, by Rufus Phillips. La Junta, Colo., ₍n.d.₎. Wrappers. (Cover title). Scarce.
17 p. 24.7 cm.
Double column.

1800 PHILLIPS-WOLLEY, CLIVE. A sportsman's Eden, by Clive Phillips-Wolley. London, Richard Bentley and son, 1886. Pict. cloth in col. Scarce.
xv, 266 ₍1₎ p. 22.8 cm.
Half title; 2 p. adv. at end.

1801 PIERCE, Gov. GILBERT A. Report of the Governor of Dakota to the Secretary of the Interior, 1885. Washington, Government printing office, 1885. Wrappers. Rare.
3–53 p. tables. 23 cm.

1802 PIERCE, N. H., and NUGENT E. BROWN. The free state of Menard. A history of the county. Compiled by N. H. Pierce, assisted by Nugent E. Brown. Menard, Texas, Menard News press, 1946. Pict. cloth. OP.
3 p.l., 9–213 p. illus., plates, ports. 23.5 cm.
Index, p. 206–213.

1803 PINE, GEORGE W. Beyond the West; containing an account of two years' travel in that other half of our great continent far beyond the old West, on the plains, in the Rocky Mountains. . . . By George W. Pine. Utica, N. Y., published and printed by T. J. Griffiths, 1870. Cloth. Rare.
xii, ₍13₎–444 p. front., plates. 19.4 cm.

1804 PLEASANTS, MRS. J. E. History of Orange County, California, by Mrs. J. E. Pleasants. . . . Los Angeles, J. H. Finnell & sons publishing co.; Phoenix, Ariz., Record publishing co., 1931. Pub. in 3 vols. Scarce.
Vol. I: 3 p.l., 7–567 p. front., plates, ports., map. 26 cm.
Index, p. 553–567.
Vols. II and III: biographical.

1805 PLENN, J. H. Saddle in the sky. The Lone Star State, by J. H. Plenn. Illustrated by Agnes Lilienberg Muench. Indianapolis, New York, the Bobbs-Merrill company, publishers, ₍1940₎. Cloth. OP.
6 p.l., 11–287 p. illus., plates. 22.2 cm.
Half title; map on end papers; untrimmed; "First edition" on copyright p.

Contains some information on the King Ranch and also the cattle ranches of West Texas.

1806 PLUMB, CHARLES S. Little sketches of famous beef cattle. By Charles S. Plumb. . . . Columbus, Ohio, published by the author, 1904. Cloth. Scarce.
3 p.l., 5–99 p. 21.5 cm.

1807 ———. Marketing farm animals. By Charles S. Plumb. Boston . . . , Ginn and co., [1927]. Cloth. OP.

vii, 366 p. front., illus., ports., maps, tables. 21.2 cm.
Appendix, p. 343–354; index, p. 355–366.

1808 [PLUMB, J. B.]. Cattle ranching, [by J. B. Plumb]. [Hamilton, Ohio, 1885]. Sewn. Rare.

12 p. 21 cm.

A paper read before the Wentworth Farmers' Institute at Hamilton.

1809 [PLYMOUTH ROCK CATTLE COMPANY]. Schedule of the ranches, live stock, and personal property owned by the Plymouth Rock Cattle Company, January 1st, 1885. [Bennington, Vt., Banner print, 1885]. Wrappers. (Caption title). Rare.

[3]–18 p. 13.7x8 cm.

Contains a certificate of incorporation and by-laws of the company. Although it was organized in Wyoming, with offices in Cheyenne, the company's principal ranches were located in Beaverhead County, Montana, in the vicinity of Red Rock and Horse Prairie.

1810 POCOCK, ROGER S. Curly, a tale of the Arizona desert, by Roger S. Pocock, with illustrations from drawings by Stanley L. Wood. Boston, Little, Brown and co., 1905. Pict. cloth. Scarce.

4 p.l., 320 p., 1 l. 9 plates. 19.5 cm.
Half title; 2 l. adv. at end.

1811 ———. Following the frontier, by Roger Pocock. New York, McClure, Phillips & co., MCMIII. Pict. cloth. Scarce.

4 p.l., 3–338 [8] p. 20 cm.
Half title; device; untrimmed; last 8 p. adv.

1812 ———. Horses, by Roger S. Pocock, with an introduction by Prof. J. Cossar Ewart, F.R.S. . . . London, J. Murray, 1917. Cloth. Scarce.

x, 252 p. 19 cm.

1813 POE, SOPHIE (ALBERDING). Buckboard days, by Sophie A. Poe; edited by Eugene Cunningham. Illustrated with many photographs from the famous Rose Collection of San Antonio and from private collections. Caldwell, Idaho, the Caxton printers, ltd., 1936. Cloth. OP.

8 p.l., [17]–292 p. front., plates, ports., facsm. 23.5 cm.
Notes, p. [269]–287; index, p. [289]–292.
Half title; map on end papers; pub. device; vignette.
At head of title: "The Thrilling Experiences on Our Southwestern Frontier of John William Poe, as Buffalo Hunter, U. S. Marshal. . . ."

1814 POLLOCK, J. M. The unvarnished West; ranching as I found it, by

J. M. Pollock. . . . London, Simpkin, Marshall, Hamilton, Kent & co., ltd. . . , [1911]. Pict. cloth. Very scarce.

4 p.l., 252 [1] p., 1 l. front. (port. with tissue), illus., plates. 18.7 cm. 1 p. adv. at end.

1815 [PONTING, TOM CANDY]. Life of Tom Candy Ponting. [By Tom Candy Ponting]. [Decatur, Ill., the Review press, 1907]. Wrappers. Excessively rare.

[3]–102 p. 2 ports. 19 cm.
Half title only.

Privately printed in an edition of twenty-five paper-bound copies for private circulation. In 1908 another twenty-five copies identical to the first were issued, of which twelve were bound in black cloth.

Republished by the Branding Iron Press, Evanston, Ill., 1952, with introduction and notes by Herbert O. Brayer, and illustrations by David T. Vernon. Pict. boards. OP.

x p., 1 l., 132 [1] p. front. (port.), illus., ports., map. 19.7 cm.
Notes, p. 111–118; index, p. 119–132.
Vignette.
Colophon: "This book was designed at the printing office of Philip Reed, Chicago, Illinois, and five hundred copies printed in January, 1952. Binding by Elizabeth Kner. This is number ——."

This book tells of one of the first cattle drives north from Texas.

1816 PORTER, HENRY M. Pencilings of an early western pioneer, [by] Henry M. Porter. Denver, Colorado, the World press, inc., 1929. Cloth. Scarce.

vi p., 1 l., 198 p. 22.3 cm.
Device.

1817 PORTER, MILLIE JONES (MRS. J. M.). Memory cups of Panhandle pioneers, by Millie Jones Porter. A belated attempt at Panhandle history with special emphasis on Wheeler County and her relations to the other counties in the long ago as told by the few remaining old times [*sic*] and the records. Clarendon, Texas, Clarendon press, 1945. Cloth. OP.

xv, 648 p. illus., plates, ports., maps. 23.2 cm.
Index, p. [617]–648.

1818 ———. Put up or shut up, by Millie Jones Porter. In memory of my husband, the straight-from-the-shoulder old timer who said what he meant and meant what he said and others like him. . . . [Dallas, Wilkinson publishing co., 1950]. Cloth.

6 p.l., 13–350 p. plates. 23.2 cm.
Index, p. 341–350.
Copyright date stamped on with rubber stamp.

1819 POST, CHARLES CLEMENT. Ten years a cowboy, ₁by C. C. Post₁. Chicago, Rhodes & McClure publishing company, 1886. Pict. cloth. Scarce.
6 p.l., 17–358 p. front., illus., plates. 20.3 cm.

Republished in the same year with same collation, but with the author identified as Tex Bender. Another edition issued under the same date and collation has Post as the author. There are eighteen plates here instead of the original fourteen, but four are duplicates. This edition has 113 pages with an addenda by Bender. This book was reissued in 1887 with 471 pages. In 1888 it was published under the name of Phil Johnson, with the changed title, *Phil Johnson's Life on the Plains.* . . . (See Item No. 1181). For the next ten or eleven years this book was issued at intervals of two or three years under the names of various authors, such as Post, Bender, and Johnson in the years 1890, 1893, 1896, 1897, and 1899. This is probably the second book written about the cowboy and evidently made the publishers some money, although they were unscrupulous about authorship.

1820 POTTER, ERMINE L. (ED.). Western live-stock management. Edited by Ermine L. Potter. . . . New York, the Macmillan co., 1917. Cloth. OP.
xiv p., 1 l., 3–462 p. illus., plates, maps. 19.5 cm.
Glossary, p. 437–446; index, p. 447–462.
Half title; 4 p. adv. at end.
Republished in 1921.

1821 POTTER, JACK M. Cattle trails of the old West, by Colonel Jack Potter. Clayton, N. M., the Leader publishing co., 1935. Pict. wrappers. Scarce.
40 p. illus., ports., fold. map. 22.5 cm.
Republished with changes and additions, edited by Laura R. Krehbiel. Clayton, N. M., Laura R. Krehbiel, ₁1939₁. Pict. wrappers. Scarce.
87 p. illus., fold. map. 20.3 cm.

1822 ———. Lead steer and other tales, by Pack Potter. Foreword by J. Frank Dobie. . . . Clayton, N. M., printed . . . by the Leader press, 1939. Stiff pict. wrappers. Scarce.
9 p.l., ₁13₁–116 ₁1₁ p. illus., plates, ports. 23 cm.
Copyright notice and dedication on t.p.

1823 POTTER, THEODORE EDGAR. The autobiography of Theodore Edgar Potter. ₁Concord, N. H., the Rumford press, 1913₁. Cloth. Scarce.
ix p., 1 l., 228 p. front. (port.), ports. 21.5 cm.
Published with half title only.

The manuscript of this book was found after the author's death and published for his children at his written request.

1824 [POTTER, MRS. W. R.]. History of Montague County. ₁By Mrs. W. R. Potter₁. . . . Austin, E. L. Steck, ₁n.d.₁. Cloth. Rare.
viii, 191 p. 18.3 cm.

Reprinted, ₁IPTA printers, Saint Jo, Texas₁, 1957.

4 p.l., 184 p.   18.6 cm.

1825 POWDER RIVER CATTLE COMPANY. In the High Court of Justice, Chancery Division, 1885, F. No. 3073, Folios 10. Between Moreton Frewen, plaintiff, and the Powder River Cattle Company, limited, and His Grace the Duke of Manchester, K. P. The Right Honorable the Earl of Wharncliffe, Lord Henry Nevill, Sir Frederick Milner, Baronet W. Tipping, and Andrew Whittin, directors of said company, defendants. Reply. ₁London, Veale, Chifferiel & co., 1885₁. Folder. (Caption title). Rare.

2 p.   34 cm.

1826 ——. Memorandum and articles of association of the Powder River Cattle Company, ltd. London, Witherby and co., printers, ₁1882₁. Wrappers. Rare.

34 ₁1₁ p.   33 cm.

1827 POWELL, CUTHBERT. Twenty years of Kansas City's live stock trade and traders. By Cuthbert Powell. Illustrated. ₁Kansas City, Mo., Pearl printing company, 1893₁. Cloth. Scarce.

1 l., 1 p., 4–345 p.   illus., plates, ports., tables. 20.4 cm.

Last 5 p. adv.

A history of the Kansas City Stock Yards with many biographies of its traders. First issue does not have the author's name on spine.

1828 POWER, JOHN. Missouri and Mouse River brand book. North Dakota. ₁By₁ John Power. Donnybrook, N. D., 1898. Stiff pict. wrappers. Rare.

3 p.l., 5–45 p.   cattle brands. 15 cm.

1829 PRAIRIE CATTLE COMPANY, LTD. Memorandum and articles of association. Edinburgh [Scotland], Muir, Paterson and Brodie, printers, 1880. Wrappers. Rare.

24 ₁3₁ p.   24.3x16 cm.

1830 ——. Eighth annual report, 1888. ₁Edinburgh, 1889₁. Pamphlet. Rare.

16 ₁2₁ p.   24.5 cm.

1831 ——. Report of the company's officers in America. . . . ₁N.p.₁, 1886. Pamphlet. Rare.

7 p.   24.7 cm.

1832 PRATT, ALICE DAY. A homesteader's portfolio, by Alice Day Pratt. New York, the Macmillan company, 1922. Pict. cloth. OP.

vi p., 2 l., 181 p.   front., plates. 19.5 cm.

Half title.

Deals with cowboys and rodeos.   [293]

1833 [PRATT, C. N.]. Kansas and Colorado. [N.p., n.d.]. Pict. wrappers. Rare.

[3]–14 p. fold. map. 23.2 cm.
Double column; adv. verso front wrapper; adv. recto and verso back wrapper.

1834 PREECE, HAROLD. Living pioneers. The epic of the West by those who lived it, [by] Harold Preece. Cleveland, New York, the World publishing company, [1952]. Pict. cloth. OP.

9 p.l., 19–317 p. 21.8 cm.
Half title; vignette; "First edition" on copyright p.

1835 PRENTIS, NOBLE L. South-western letters. By Noble L. Prentis. Topeka, Kansas, Kansas publishing house, 1882. Wrappers. Scarce.

3 p.l., [5]–133 p. 19 cm.

1836 PRESENT CONDITION OF THE live cattle and beef markets of the United States and the causes therefor. Statement of Philip D. Armour before the special committee of the U. S. Senate. Presented at Washington, November 30, 1889. Chicago, Chicago Legal News company, printers, 1889. Wrappers. Rare.

23 p. tables. 22 cm.

1837 PRETTYMAN, W. S. Indian Territory. A frontier photographic record, by W. S. Prettyman. Selected and edited by Robert E. Cunningham. Norman, University of Oklahoma press, [1957]. Cloth.

xi p., 1 l., 3–174 p. front. (port.), plates, ports. 24.8 cm.
Index, p. 171–174.
Half title; "First edition" on copyright p.

Chapter 4 deals with the cattleman.

1838 PREUITT, W. G. Brand book of the Montana Stock Growers' Association. Sixth publication. . . . Helena, Independent print, 1899. Cloth. Scarce.

207 p. plates, cattle brands. 19 cm.

1839 PRICE, CON. Memories of old Montana, by Con Price (Masachele Opa Barusha). Hollywood, California, the Highland press, [1945]. Cloth. OP.

4 p.l., 9–154 p. plates, ports. 22.8 cm.
"First edition" on copyright p.

Also published in a de luxe edition of 125 copies, numbered and signed by the author and bound in pigskin.

1840 ——. Trails I rode, by Con Price. Illustrations by Charles M. Russell. Pasadena, California, Trail's End publishing co., inc., [1947]. Cloth.

7 p.l., [17]–262 p. front. (col.), plates, ports. 21.7 cm.
Index, p. [259]–262.

Half title; illus. chapter headings; cattle brands on end papers.

Published also in a de luxe edition of 350 copies, numbered and signed by the author and bound in morocco.

1841 PRICE, SIR ROSE LAMBART. A summer on the Rockies, by Major Sir Rose Lambart Price . . . with map and illustrations. London, Sampson Low, Marston & company, ltd., 1898. Cloth. Scarce.

x, 279 p. front. (port. with tissue), plates, fold. map (col.), tables. 19.8 cm. Half title; device; untrimmed.

An Englishman's story of his travels in the American West, telling, among other things, of the Johnson County War.

1842 PRICHARD, G. W. Bureau of Immigration of the territory of New Mexico. Report of San Miguel County. By G. W. Prichard, commissioner. Santa Fe, New Mexican print, 1882. Wrappers. Scarce.

[3]–16 p. tables. 21.5 cm.

1843 ———. Bureau of Immigration of the territory of New Mexico. Report of San Miguel County. By G. W. Prichard, commissioner. Las Vegas, New Mexico, Carruth & Layton, printers and binders, 1882. Wrappers. Rare.

[3]–30 p. illus., fold. plates in front. 23.4 cm.

1844 PUCKETT, J. L., and ELLEN PUCKET. History of Oklahoma and Indian Territory and homeseeker's guide. By J. L. Puckett and Ellen Puckett. Vinita, Okla., Chieftain publishing co., 1906. Cloth. Scarce.

2 p.l., [7]–149 [2] p. front., plates, ports. 22.2 cm.

Some experiences of an old cowboy in the Indian Territory.

1845 PURCELL, MAE FISHER. History of Contra Costa County, by Mae Fisher Purcell. . . . Illustrated. Berkeley, Calif., the Gillick press, 1940. Cloth. OP.

8 p.l., [17]–742 p. front. (col.), illus., plates, ports., maps. 24.5 cm. Bibliography, p. 740–742.

1846 QUAIL, JOSEPH N. Brockman's maverick, by Joseph N. Quail, with illustrations by D. F. Thompson. New York, Quail and Warner, 1901. Pict. cloth. OP.

5 p.l., 11–256 p. front., plates. 19.2 cm. Half title.

1847 QUICKFALL, BOB GRANTHAM. Western life and how I became a bronco buster. By Bob Grantham Quickfall. London, F. Charles & co.; Windsor, J. W. Wright, [n.d.]. Pict. col. wrappers. (Cover title). Exceedingly rare.

2 p.l., [7]–96 p. front. (port.). 18 cm.

1848 QUIGG, LEMUEL ELY. New empires in the Northwest. . . . ₍by Lemuel E. Quigg₎. New York, the Tribune association, 1889. Wrappers. (Cover title). Scarce.

84 p. tables. 26 cm.
Double column.
Cover title: "Library of Tribune Extras, Vol. I, No. 8, August, 1889."

A collection of thirty-seven letters on the Dakotas, Montana, and Washington, signed "L. E. Q." These letters concern travels and observations in the Northwest, including the cowboys of Wyoming.

1849 RAFTERY, JOHN H. The truth about Texas. By John H. Raftery. ₍Chicago, the Henry O. Shepard company₎, 1904. Stiff pict. wrappers. Rare.

5–104 p. plates, 3 maps at end (1 fold.). 17.4 cm.

1850 RAHT, CARLISLE GRAHAM. The romance of Davis Mountains and Big Bend country. A history by Carlisle Graham Raht. Drawings by Waldo Williams. El Paso, the Rahtbooks company, ₍1919₎. Pict. cloth. Scarce.

3 p.l., 381 p. front. (port.), plates, ports., map (double p.). 20 cm.

1851 RAINE, WILLIAM MACLEOD. Guns of the frontier. The story of how law came to the West, by William MacLeod Raine. Illustrated. Boston, Houghton Mifflin company, 1940. Pict. cloth. OP.

x p., 2 l., 282 p. front. (port.), plates, ports., facsm. 21.2 cm.
Bibliography, p. ₍272₎–274; index, p. ₍277₎–282.
Half title.

Chapters on Abilene, Kansas, and the Johnson County War.

1852 ——, and WILL CROFT BARNES. Cattle, by William MacLeod Raine and Will C. Barnes. Garden City, New York, Doubleday, Doran & company, MCMXXX. Pict. cloth. OP.

xii p., 1 l., 340 p. front., illus., plates, facsms. 21.2 cm.
Appendix, p. 309–324; index, p. 327–340.
Half title; illus. end papers; illus. t.p.; untrimmed; "First edition" on copyright p.
Republished by Grossett and Dunlap in 1930 under the title *Cattle, Cowboys, and Rangers.*

1853 RAINEY, GEORGE. The Cherokee Strip, its history, by George Rainey. Illustrated. ₍Enid, Oklahoma, 1925₎. Wrappers. Scarce.

₍30₎ p. (no pagination). illus. 17 cm.

1854 ——. The Cherokee Strip, by George Rainey. Guthrie, Okla., Co-Operative publishing co., 1933. Pict. cloth. OP.

x, 504 p. plates, ports. 22 cm.
Index, p. 503–504.
Vignette.

[296]

1855 ———. No man's land. The historic story of a landed orphan, by George Rainey. [Guthrie, Okla., Co-Operative publishing co.], 1937. Pict. cloth. Scarce.

5 p.l., 245 p. front. (port.), plates, ports., maps, diagrs. 21.8 cm.
Acknowledgments, p. 241–242; index, p. 243–245.
Half title; copyright notice on t.p.

Has some information about the 101 Ranch, Dodge City, and the cow town of Tascosa.

1856 RAK, MRS. MARY KIDDER. A cowman's wife, by Mary Kidder Rak; with illustrations by Charles Owens. Boston and New York, Houghton Mifflin company, 1934. Cloth. OP.

vi p., 1 l., 292 p. front., illus., plates. 21 cm.
Pict. map on end papers; device; first edition, "1934" under imprint.

1857 ———. Mountain cattle, [by] Mary Kidder Rak; with illustrations by Charles Owens. Boston & New York, Houghton Mifflin company, 1936. Cloth. OP.

viii p., 1 l., [3]–275 p. illus. 21 cm.
Half title; illus. map on end papers; headpieces; first edition, "1936" under imprint.

1858 RALPH, JULIAN. Our great West. A study of the present conditions and future possibilities of the new commonwealth and capitals of the United States, by Julian Ralph. . . . New York, Harper & brothers, publishers, 1893. Dec. cloth. OP.

xi [1], 477 [1] p. front., illus., plates, maps. 23 cm.
Pub. device; 4 p. adv. at end.

Chapters on Montana and Wyoming, with information on cattle raising in these states. Much of this material first appeared in *Harper's Magazine* and *Harper's Weekly*.

1859 RALSTON, HARRY M. Cowpokes tales from a roundup campfire, by Harry M. Ralston. Illustrated by J. K. Ralston. New York, N. Y., the Hobson book press, [1945]. Pict. wrappers. OP.

x p., 2 l., 39 p. front., illus. 20.8 cm.
Lithoprint.

1860 R[ANDALL], I[SABELLA]. A lady's ranche life in Montana. By I. R. London, W. H. Allen & co., 1887. Cloth. Scarce.

viii, 170 [2] p. 17.4 cm.
2 p. adv. at end.

There is a seeming error on page 59. I believe the date should be March 16, which was when the solar eclipse occurred.

1861 RANDOLPH, EDMUND. Hell among the yearlings, by Edmund Randolph. Drawings by James Ryan. New York, W. W. Norton & company, inc., ₁1955₁. Pict. boards and cloth.

5 p.l., 13–308 p. illus. 21.8 cm.
Half title; illus. double t.p.; pub. device; headpieces.
Published in England under the title *Don't Fence Me In*.

1862 RANKIN, M. WILSON. Reminiscences of frontier days, including an authentic account of the Thornburg and Meeker massacre, by M. Wilson Rankin. . . . Denver, photo-lithographed by Smith-Brooks, ₁1938₁. Fabricoid. Scarce.

5 p.l., 140 p. front., illus., plates, maps. 28 cm.

This privately printed book was issued in a very small edition and has crude illustrations. There is much material on cattle and cowboys.

1863 RAREY, J. S. The modern art of taming wild horses. By J. S. Rarey. Portland, Oregon, printed at the Democratic Standard office, 1858. Wrappers. Rare.

27 p. 18 cm.

1864 RAULSTON, MARION CHURCHILL. Memories of Owen Humphrey Churchill and his family. ₁By₁ Marion Churchill Raulston. ₁N.p.₁, 1950. Boards. Scarce.

4 p.l., ₁91₁ p. (no pagination). plates, ports., facsm., 1 col. plate tipped in, coat-of-arms. 23.4 cm.

A privately printed history of the Churchill family, published in a small edition and now scarce. A mimeographed supplement accompanies a few copies, but only a few supplements were printed.

1865 RAY, WORTH S. Down in the Cross Timber, by Worth S. Ray (illustrated by the author). Austin, Texas, published by Worth S. Ray, ₁1947₁. Cloth. OP.

4 p.l., 160 p. illus. 23.5 cm.
"First edition, 500 copies" on t.p.
Photolithography, with crude illustrations.

1866 RAYMER, ROBERT GEORGE. Montana, the land and the people. By Robert George Raymer. Montana biography by special staff of writers. Issued in three volumes. . . . Illustrated. Chicago and New York, the Lewis publishing company, 1930. Cloth. Scarce.

Vol. I: xlvi, 3–634 p. plates, ports. 25.7 cm.
Vol. II: 3–842 p. plates, ports. 25.7 cm.
Vol. III: 3–863 p. ports. 25.7 cm.

Volume I has chapters on the open-range cattle days; volumes II and III, biographical.

1867 REAUGH, FRANK. Paintings of the Southwest, by Frank Reaugh. Notes by the painter. [Dallas, printed by Wilkinson printing company, n.d.]. Stiff wrappers. Scarce.

3–45 p. front., 11 plates (incl. front.), facsm. 24 cm.

Descriptions of the artist's paintings of the cattle country.

1868 RECEIPTS AND SHIPMENTS of live stock at Kansas City Stock Yards, Kansas City, for the year 1914. . . . Kansas City, Mo., Tiernan-Dart printing company, 1914. Wrappers. Scarce.

28 p. tables. 19x11.5 cm.

1869 ——— of live stock at Kansas City Stock Yards, Kansas City, for the year 1916. . . . Kansas City, Mo., Stockyards printing company, 1916. Wrappers. Scarce.

27 p. tables. 19x11.5 cm.

1870 REECE, CHARLES S. A history of Cherry County, Nebraska. The story of its organization, development, and people. By Charles S. Reece. . . . [N.p., 1945]. Cloth. OP.

6 p.l., 13–173 p. plates, ports. 23.5 cm.

1871 [REED, H. W.] Arizona cowman, [by H. W. Reed], drawings by Richard H. Reed. Tucson, Arizona, published by Reed publications. Printed by Commercial printers, Tucson, Arizona, [n.d.]. Pict. cloth. OP.

5 p.l., 200 p. illus., plates. 23 cm.
Half title.

1872 REED, SILAS. Report of Silas Reed, surveyor general of Wyoming Territory for the year 1871. Washington, Government printing office, 1871. Wrappers. Scarce.

[3]–46 p. tables. 22.2 cm.

One of the earliest detailed descriptions of the Territory. From personal observation, he tells of the resources of Wyoming, including stock raising and its possibilities.

1873 REEVES, FRANK. A century of Texas cattle brands. Foreword by Amon Carter. A brief outline of Texas history by Peter Molynneaux and a sketch of the Texas cattle industry and story of cattle brands by Frank Reeves, Sr. . . . Ft. Worth, Texas, published by the Fair publishing company. . . . [1936]. Stiff pict. wrappers.

2 p.l., 7–80 p. illus., cattle brands. 23.6 cm.

Reprinted several years later by Russell stationery co., of Amarillo, Texas.

1874 ———. Hacienda de Atotonilco, compiled and written by Frank Reeves, November, 1936. Illustrations are from unretouched photographs

that were made on the ranch while gathering the data. Front cover drawings by Mary Aubrey Keating. . . . Yerbanis, Durango, Mexico, published by the Atotonilco livestock co., [1936]. Pict. wrappers. OP.

3 p.l., 7–87 p. front., plates, map. 25.2 cm.
Pages 7 to 64 full-p. plates.

1875 ———. The story of the Highlands. Compiled and written by Frank
Reeves. Cover design and decorations by Warren Hunter. . . . Marfa,
Texas, published by the Highlands Hereford Breeders' association, 1936.
Stiff wrappers. OP.

88 p. plates, decorations, map, cattle brands. 26 cm.

1876 REGULATIONS GOVERNING the admission of southern cattle into Colorado, Wyoming, and Montana for 1889. [N.p., n.d., 1889]. Large folder.
(Caption title). Rare.

[4] p. (no pagination). map. 27.8 cm.
Map on verso last p.; signed by Charles G. Lamb, state veterinarian of Colorado,
A. A. Holcomb, of Wyoming, and Herbert Holloway, of Montana.

1877 REMINGTON, FREDERIC. Crooked trails, written and illustrated by
Frederic Remington. New York and London, Harper & brothers, publishers, 1898. Pict. cloth. Scarce.

[vi] 1 l., 150 [1] p. front., illus., plates. 22 cm.
T.p. in red and black; pub. device.

Reprinted with same imprint and collation in 1899, and many times since.

1878 ———. Pony tracks, written and illustrated by Frederic Remington.
New York, Harper & brothers, publishers, 1895. Pict. cloth. Scarce.

viii p., 1 l., 269 p. front. (with tissue), illus., plates. 22 cm.

Reprinted many times, including one by the Long college book co., Columbus,
Ohio, in 1951.

1879 RENICK, WILLIAM. Memoirs, correspondence, and reminiscences of
William Renick. Circleville, Ohio, Union-Herald book and job printing house, 1880. Cloth. Scarce.

3 p.l., 115 p. front. (port. with tissue). 23.5 cm.
Errata slip tipped in.

Most of the text, written from 1848 to 1879, first appeared as contributions
to newspapers and as articles furnished for public reports. Part of it appeared
in *Nimmo's Report of 1860.* Reminiscences of an Ohio cattle drover in and
after 1820; earliest importation of Texas cattle into the North and East.

1880 RHOAD, ALBERT O. (ED.). Breeding beef cattle for unfavorable environ-
ments. A symposium presented at the King Ranch centennial conference. Edited by Albert O. Rhoad. Austin, University of Texas press,
1955. Cloth.

xiv p., 1 l., 3–248 p. plates (2 col.), diagrs., map, tables. 23.8 cm.
Appendix, p. 235–242; index, p. 245–248.
Half title; pub. device on t.p.

1881 RHODES, EDWIN (ED.). The break of day in Chino. A collection of incidents and impressions marking the early life of Chino, as recorded by various reliable authors. Compiled and edited by Edwin Rhodes. ₁N.p., printed by Progress-Bulletin press, inc.₁, 1951. Stiff pict. wrappers.
6 p.l., 15–95 ₁1₁ p. ports. 22.8 cm.

1882 RHODES, FULLER. Where the trail divides. By Fuller Rhodes, the cowboy preacher. ₁N.p., n.d.₁. Pict. wrappers. Scarce.
₁5₁ p. (no pagination). 22 cm.

1883 RHODES, MRS. MAY (DAVISON). The hired man on horseback; my story of Eugene Manlove Rhodes, by May Davison Rhodes. Illustrated. Boston, Houghton Mifflin company, 1938. Cloth. OP.
xliii ₁1₁ p., 1 l., 263 ₁1₁ p. front. (port.), plates, ports. 21.4 cm.
"The novelist of the cattle kingdom, by Bernard DeVoto," p. xix–₁xliv₁.
Half title; pub. device; first edition, "1938" under imprint.

Contains a chapter on Gene Rhodes' cowboy years.

1884 RICE, J. M. Idaho. How to make money in Idaho Territory. Farming, stock-raising, mining, merchandising, and other branches of business and labor. The yield of precious metals since the first discovery in 1862. With sketches of the principal towns, settlements. . . . From personal observation. Omaha, the Republican print, 1886. Wrappers. Rare.
₁3₁–32 p. map (recto back wrapper). 22.7 cm.

1885 RICHARDS, MRS. CLARICE (EASTABROOK). A tenderfoot bride; tales from an old ranch, by Clarice E. Richards. New York, Chicago. . . , Fleming H. Revell company, ₁1920₁. Pict. cloth. OP.
4 p.l., 11–226 p. front., plates. 19.4 cm.
Half title.

In these recollections of life at her husband's ranch on Bijou Creek, Colorado, the author, for reasons of her own, has altered the names of various persons, even to calling her husband "Owen Brook" instead of Jarvis Richards. She states that there is no other intentional fictional element. The description of "Courtney Drake's" death, if this Drake was in fact Robert Ray Hamilton, as told to her and repeated in her book, is not accurate. Hamilton was not murdered by his partner, John Sargent, but was accidentally drowned when fording the Snake River a short distance below Jackson Lake. He had not been shot.

1886 RICHARDSON, E. E. Receipts and shipments of live stock at Kansas City Stock Yards, Kansas City, for the year 1893, with a summary of receipts and shipments of all livestock for a term of twenty-three years, ending

December 31, 1893. By E. E. Richardson, secretary. Kansas City, Tiernan-Havens printing co., 1894. Wrappers. Scarce.

51 p. tables. 17.8 cm.

Contains statistics and tables of cattle brought into the stock yards by the various railroads.

1887 ———. Receipts and shipments of livestock at Kansas City Stock Yards for the year 1908. . . . By E. E. Richardson. Kansas City, Mo., Tiernan-Dart printing company, 1909. Wrappers. Scarce.

60 p. tables. 19x11.5 cm.

1888 RICHARDSON, RUPERT NORVAL. Adventuring with a purpose. Life story of Arthur Lee Wasson, by Rupert Norval Richardson. San Antonio, Texas, the Naylor company . . . , [1951]. Cloth.

xiii p., 4 l. (plates, ports, double-p. map), 114 p. 21.6 cm.
Half title.

1889 ———. Texas, the Lone Star State, by Rupert Norval Richardson, with illustrations, maps, and charts. New York, Prentice-Hall, inc., 1943. Cloth. OP.

xix p., 1 l., 590 p. front. (col. map), plates, maps, charts. 23.5 cm.

1890 ———, and CARL COKE RISTER. The greater Southwest. The economic, social, and cultural development of Kansas, Oklahoma, Texas, Utah, Colorado, Nevada, New Mexico, Arizona, and California from the Spanish conquest to the twentieth century, by Rupert Norval Richardson . . . and Carl Coke Rister. . . . Glendale, California, the Arthur H. Clark company, 1934. Cloth. OP.

6 pl., [13]–506 p. 6 maps (all double p. except one). 24.8 cm.
Index, p. [489]–506.
Half title; references for additional reading at end of each chapter; pub. device; untrimmed; gilt top.

1891 RICHARDSON, SULLIVAN CALVIN. In desert Arizona, by S. C. Richardson. . . . Independence, Mo., Press of Zion's printing and publishing company, [1938]. Cloth. OP.

4 p.l., [11]–182 p., 2 l. front., plates, ports. 20.2 cm.
Illus. t.p.

1892 RICHTHOFEN, WALTER, BARON VON. Cattle-raising on the plains of North America, by Walter Baron von Richthofen. New York, D. Appleton and company . . . , 1885. Cloth. Scarce.

4 p.l., [9]–102 [6] p. 18 cm.
6 p. adv. at end.

A scarce little book dealing with the business side of cattle raising, giving tables of profits to be made. This, with several other books of its kind, helped to create the cattle boom of the eighties.

[302]

CATTLE-RAISING

ON THE

PLAINS OF NORTH AMERICA

BY

WALTER BARON VON RICHTHOFEN.

NEW YORK:
D. APPLETON AND COMPANY,
1, 8, AND 5 BOND STREET.
1885.

1893 RICKETTS, WILLIAM PENDLETON. 50 years in the saddle, by W. P. Ricketts. Sheridan, Wyoming, Star publishing company, publishers, 1942. Cloth. Scarce.

6 p.l., 198 p. front. (port.), plates, map. 23.2 cm.
Half title; device; "First edition" on copyright p.

1894 RIDDELL, C. L. Immigrants' guide to Texas. A complete review of Texas of today showing her great fertility of soil, and wonderful salubrity of climate. . . . Profits of farming, stock raising, and sheep husbandry. . . . By C. L. Riddell. ₁Louisville, Ky.₁, Courier-Journal book rooms, 1875. Pict. wrappers. Rare.

3 p.l., ₁3₁–76 ₁20₁ p. fold. map in front, tables. 19 cm.
Vignette; last 20 p. adv.

1895 RIDEING, WILLIAM HENRY. A-saddle in the wild West. A glimpse of travel among the mountains, lava beds, sand deserts, adobe towns, Indian reservations, and ancient pueblos of southern Colorado, New Mexico, and Arizona. By William H. Rideing. . . . London, J. C. Nimmo and Bain, ₁1879₁. Cloth. Scarce.

4 p.l., ₁9₁–165 p. 16.3 cm.
American edition published same year by D. Appleton and co., N. Y.

Some of the material in this book first appeared in various newspapers and periodicals.

1896 RIDEOUT, HENRY MILNER. William Jones, Indian, cowboy, American scholar, and anthropologist in the field, by Henry Milner Rideout. New York, Frederick A. Stokes company, MCMXII. Cloth. Scarce.

4 p.l., 212 ₁1₁ p. 2 ports. (incl. front., both with tissues). 21.2 cm.
Half title.
"Writings of William Jones," 1 p. at end.

1897 RIDINGS, SAM P. The Chisholm Trail. A history of the world's greatest cattle trail, together with a description of the persons, a narrative of the events, and reminiscences associated with the same, by Sam P. Ridings. Illustrated. Guthrie, Oklahoma, Co-Operative publishing company, publishers, ₁1936₁. Pict. cloth. OP.

6 p.l., 591 p. front. (port.), plates, ports., fold. map at end. 23.2 cm.
Index, p. 587–591.
Half title.

1898 RIEGEL, ROBERT E. America moves west, by Robert E. Riegel. . . . New York, Henry Holt and company, ₁1930₁. Cloth. OP.

x p., 1 l., 3–595 p. maps. 22.2 cm.
Supplementary readings, p. 567–585; index, p. 587–595.
Half title; pub. device.

1899 RINGGOLD, JENNIE PARKS. Frontier days in the Southwest. Pioneer days in old Arizona, by Jennie Parks Ringgold. San Antonio, Texas, the Naylor company, [1952]. Cloth.
ix, 197 p. plates, ports., facsms. 21.5 cm.
Index, p. 189–197.
Half title; map on end papers (dif.).

1900 RIO ARRIBA LAND AND CATTLE COMPANY. An agreement between John Gerald Potter and Valentine Walbran Chapman for the sale of land to the Rio Arriba Land and Cattle co., [N.p., n.d.].
[5] p. (no pagination). large fold. map. 33.8 cm.

1901 ——. Memorandum and articles of association of the Rio Arriba Land and Cattle company, ltd. Articles of incorporation. [N.p., n.d., c.1888]. Wrappers. Rare.
34 [1] p. 26x16 cm.

1902 ——. The Rio Arriba Land and Cattle company, limited. Prospectus. [With] memorandum of association of the Rio Arriba Land and Cattle company, limited. [N.p., c.1886]. Folder. Rare.
3 [1] p. 24.5 cm.

Forms for shares with extracts from reports laid in.

1903 RIPLEY, HENRY and MARTHA. Hand-clasp of the East and West. A story of pioneer life on the Western Slope of Colorado. By Henry and Martha Ripley. [Denver, Colorado, Press of the Williamson-Haffner engraving & printing co., 1914]. Cloth. Scarce.
5 p.l., 14–471 p. plates. 19.3 cm.

1904 RIPLEY, THOMAS. They died with their boots on, by Thomas Ripley. Garden City, N. Y., Doubleday, Doran & co., inc., MCMXXXV. Cloth. OP.
5 p.l., ix–xx p., 1 l., 285 p. front., plates, ports. 21.3 cm.
Bibliography included in "Foreword and Acknowledgments."
Half title; illus. end papers; 8 ports. before t.p.; 1 p. adv. at end; pub. device; untrimmed; "First edition" on copyright p.

1905 RISTER, CARL COKE. Fort Griffin on the Texas frontier, by Carl Coke Rister. Norman, University of Oklahoma press, [1956]. Cloth.
xv p., 1 l., 3–216 p. plates, ports., plan. 21 cm.
Index, p. 209–216.
Half title; "First edition" on copyright p.

This is the author's last book, published after his death.

1906 ——. Land hunger; David L. Payne and the Oklahoma boomers.

By Carl Coke Rister. Norman, University of Oklahoma press, 1942. Cloth.

xiii p., 1 l., 3–245 ₁1₁ p. front. (port.), plates, ports., map, facsms. 23.5 cm.
Bibliography, p. 215–233; index, p. 235–245.
Half title; map on end papers.

1907 ———. No man's land, by Carl Coke Rister. Norman, University of Oklahoma press, 1948. Cloth.

xi p., 1 l., 3–210 p. plates, ports., map. 21 cm.
Bibliography, p. 193–199; index, p. 201–210.
Half title; "First edition" on copyright p.

1908 ———. Southern plainsman, ₁by₁ Carl Coke Rister. Norman, University of Oklahoma press, 1938. Cloth. OP.

xviii p., 1 l., 3–289 ₁1₁ p. plates, fold. map, facsms. 23.5 cm.
Bibliography, p. 263–279; index, p. 283–289.
Half title; "First edition" on copyright p.

1909 ———. The Southwestern frontier, 1865–1881. A history of the coming of the settlers, Indian depredations and massacres, ranching activities, operations of white desperadoes and thieves, government protection, building of railways, and the disappearance of the frontier, by Carl Coke Rister.... Cleveland, the Arthur H. Clark company, 1928. Cloth. OP.

10 p.l., ₁25₁–336 p. front. (double-p. col. map), plates, 2 fold. maps. 24.5 cm.
Bibliography, p. ₁311₁–320; index, p. ₁323₁–336.
Half title; pub. device; untrimmed; gilt top.

1910 RITCH, WILLIAM G. Illustrated New Mexico. By Hon. William G. Ritch. Third edition, eleven thousand, revised and enlarged. Published by the Bureau of Immigration. Santa Fe, N. M., New Mexican printing and publishing co., 1883. Wrappers. Scarce.

xvii, ₁19₁–140 ₁1₁ p. front., illus., 2 fold. maps, fold. panorama scene. 21.5 cm.
Errata leaf.

I have failed to find a copy of the first edition.

1911 ———. New Mexico, wealth, health, home. The tourists' shrine. Published by the Bureau of Immigration. Santa Fe, New Mexican print, ₁n.d.₁. Stapled. Scarce.

3–32 p. illus. 28.8 cm.

1912 RITZ, PHILIP. Letter to Hon. John W. Forney upon the agricultural and mineral resources of the North-Western territories, north of the 45th parallel. By Philip Ritz. . . . ₁Washington, D. C., Chronicle print, 1867₁. Wrappers. (Cover title). Rare.

8 p. 23 cm.
Double column.
Republished in 1868.

1913 RIVER FALLS LIVE STOCK COMPANY. By-laws of the River Falls and Tickilwa Live Stock company. ₍N.p., c.1884₎. Wrappers. Rare. 8 p. 15x9 cm.

1914 ROBB, HARRY. Poddy, the story of a rangeland orphan, by Harry Robb. Illustrations by Wauneta Wyoming Robb. Pasadena, Calif., Trail's End publishing co., inc., ₍1947₎. Cloth. OP.

xv p., 1 l., 237 ₍1₎ p. front. (col.), illus. 21.5 cm.
Also published in a de luxe edition of 200 copies bound in morocco.

1915 ROBERTS, BRUCE. Springs from the parched ground, by Bruce Roberts. ... Drawings on jacket by Emille Topperwein. Uvalde, Texas, printed by the Hornsby press. Binding by Highland press, Boerne, Texas, ₍1950₎. Cloth.

5 p.l., 177 p. front. (port.), plates, ports., map. 20.6 cm.
Index, p. ₍167₎–177.

1916 ROBERTS, CECIL. Adrift in America; or, work and adventure in the States. By Cecil Roberts, with an appendix by Morley Roberts. London, Lawrence and Bullen, 1891. Pict. cloth. Scarce.

2 p.l., ₍5₎–254 p. 23 cm.
Untrimmed.

1917 ROBERTS, EDWARD. With the invader; glimpses of the Southwest. By Edward Roberts. San Francisco, Samuel Carson & co., publishers, 1885. Wrappers. Rare.

3 p.l., ₍5₎–156 ₍18₎ p. front., illus., plates. 17.3 cm.
Last 18 p. and wrappers adv.

1918 ROBERTS, MORLEY. Painted Rock. Tales and narratives of Painted Rock, south Panhandle, Texas, told by Charlie Baker, late of that city and also of Snyder, Scurry County. By Morley Roberts. ... Philadelphia, J. B. Lippincott company, 1907. Dec. cloth. Scarce.

3 p.l., 273 ₍1₎ p. 19.5 cm.
Half title; untrimmed.

1919 ———. The western avernus; or, toil and travel in further North America, by Morley Roberts. London, Smith, Elder and co., 1887. Pict. cloth. Scarce.

4 p.l., 307 p. front. (fold. map). 21 cm.
Republished in 1896 with 277 pages.

1920 ROBINSON, CLARENCE C. Ranching in the gay '90s. ₍By₎ Clarence C. Robinson. ₍Marysville, California, 1951₎. Pict. cloth.

4 p.l., 199 p. illus., plates, 1 port. 21.6 cm.
Acknowledgments and bibliography, p. 198–199.

1921 ROBINSON, SARA T. L. Kansas: its interior and exterior life. Including a full view of its settlement, political history, social life, climate, soil, productions, scenery, etc., by Sara T. L. Robinson. Boston, Crosby, Nichols and co.; Cincinnati, George S. Blanchard; London, Sampson Low, son and co., 1856. Cloth. Scarce.

ix [1] p., 266 p. front., plates. 19.8 cm.
6 l. adv. at end.

1922 ROBINSON, WILLIAM HENRY. The story of Arizona, by Will H. Robinson. . . . Illustrated. Phoenix, Arizona, the Berryhill company, publishers, [1919]. Cloth. Scarce.

6 p.l., 13–458 p. front., plates, map. 20 cm.
Bibliography, p. 457–458.

1923 ———. Under turquoise skies. Outstanding features of the story of America's Southwest from the days of ancient cliff-dwellers to modern times. By Will H. Robinson. New York, the Macmillan co., MCMXXVIII. Cloth. OP.

xvi p., 1 l., 3–538 p. front., plates, ports. 21 cm.
Index, p. 533–538.
Half title.

1924 ROBINSON, WILLIAM WILCOX. The old Spanish and Mexican ranchos of Orange County. By W. W. Robinson. Los Angeles, Title Insurance and Trust co., 1950. Stiff pict. wrappers. OP.

18 [1] p. fold. map at end. 17.3 cm.

1925 ———. Panorama, a picture history of southern California. Issued on the 60th anniversary of Title Insurance and Trust company. Compiled and written by W. W. Robinson. Los Angeles, Title Insurance and Trust company, 1953. Pict. wrappers.

[160] p. (no pagination). front. (col.), plates, ports., facsms., maps. 25.3 cm.

1926 ———. Ranchos become cities, by W. W. Robinson. With illustrations by Irene Robinson. Pasadena, California, San Pasqual press, 1939. Pict. cloth. OP.

4 p.l., 9–243 p. illus. 23.2 cm.
Appendix, p. 219–234; index, p. 235–243.
Half title; map on end papers; vignette; illus. chapter headings; "First edition" on copyright p.

1927 ROCK, JAMES L., and W. I. SMITH. Southern and western Texas guide for 1878. James L. Rock and W. I. Smith, authors. St. Louis, Mo., A. H. Granger, publisher, 1878. Stiff pict. wrappers. Rare.

3 p.l., 7–282 p. front. (port. with tissue), illus., plates, large fold. map (col.) at end, tables. 21.5 cm.
Index, p. [279]–282.

1928 ROCKFELLOW, JOHN ALEXANDER. Log of an Arizona trail blazer, by John A. Rockfellow. Tucson, Arizona, printed by Acme Printing co., [1933]. Cloth. Scarce.

xv, 201 p. front., plates, ports. 21.6 cm.

1929 ROCKWELL, WILSON. New frontier. Saga of the North Fork, by Wilson Rockwell. Illustrations by Josephine McKittrick. Denver, Colorado, the World press, inc., 1938. Pict. cloth. OP.

xvi p., 1 l., 3–215 p. front., illus., plates, ports. 20.7 cm.
Appendix, p. 197–207; bibliography, p. 211–215.
Half title; illus. map on end papers.

1930 RODRÍGUEZ, JOSÉ POLICARPO. José Policarpo Rodríguez, "the Old Guide." Surveyor, scout, hunter, Indian fighter, ranchman, preacher. His life in his own words. Nashville, Tenn., Dallas, Texas, publishing house of the Methodist Episcopal Church South . . . , [n.d.]. Stiff wrappers. Rare.

3 p.l., 7–121 p. front. (port.). 18.3 cm.

1931 ROEDEL, A. E. Brands. Published by A. E. Roedel. Cheyenne, Wyoming, [Pioneer, n.d.]. Pict. wrappers. Scarce.

[19] p. (no pagination). plates, cattle brands. 23.8x10.2 cm.

1932 ROENIGK, ADOLPH. Pioneer history of Kansas. [By Adolph Roenigk]. [Lincoln, Kan.], published by Adolph Roenigk, [1933]. Pict. cloth. Scarce.

6 p.l., 365 [7] p. front. (port.), plates, ports. 24 cm.
Appendix and index, 7 unnumbered pages at end.
Vignette.
"The material for the first part was collected and written by John C. Baird."

1933 ROFF, JOE T. A brief history of early days in north Texas and the Indian Territory, by Joe T. Roff. [Allen, Okla., Pontotoc County Democrat], MCMXXX. Wrappers. Scarce.

2 p.l., 5–40 p. 17.5 cm.
Device.

1934 ROGERS, FRED B. Bear Flag lieutenant. The life story of Henry L. Ford [1822–1860], together with some reproductions of related and contemporary paintings by Alexander Edouart. By Fred B. Rogers. San Francisco, California, Historical society, 1951. Cloth.

4 p.l., 87 p. front., plates. 27 cm.
Notes, p. 69–79; index, p. 81–87.
Colophon: "Two hundred and fifty numbered copies printed by the Westgate Press, Oakland, California. No. ——."

1935 ROGERS, VIRGINIA. The Giles chronicle. Vignette of Panhandle history, 1887–1956, by Virginia Rogers. ₁Clarendon, Texas₁, printed by the Clarendon press, author's edition, 1956. Stiff pict. wrappers.

vii, 98 p. plates, ports., map. 22.6 cm.

1936 ROJAS, ARNOLD R. California vaquero, by A. R. Rojas. Fresno, California, Academy Literary Guild, 1953. Cloth.

3 p.l., 11–125 ₁1₁ p., 6 l. front. (port.), illus., plates, ports. 22 cm.
Half title; illus. end papers (dif.), last 6 l. plates and ports.

1937 ROLFSRUD, ERLING NICOLAI. Extraordinary North Dakotans, by Erling Nicolai Rolfsrud. Alexandria, Minnesota, published by Lantern books, ₁1954₁. Cloth.

x p., 1 l., 228 p. illus., plates, ports., facsms. 21 cm.
"First printing" on copyright p.

1938 ROLLINS, PHILIP ASHTON. The cowboy; his characteristics, his equipment, and his part in the development of the West, by Philip Ashton Rollins. New York, C. Scribner's sons, 1922. Cloth.

xiv p., 1 l., 353 p. 21.2 cm.
Half title.
Republished in August of the same year with illustrations.

1939 ———. The cowboy. An unconventional history of civilization on the old-time cattle range, by Philip Ashton Rollins. Revised and enlarged edition. New York, Charles Scribner's sons, 1936. Cloth.

xx p., 1 l., 402 p. front., illus., plates, double-p. map, facsms. 22.3 cm.
Appendix (notes on various statements in text), p. 387–393; index, p. 397–402.
Half title; illus. end papers.

This is a completely revised edition of the previous book, with a new chapter and illustrations added.

1940 ———. Gone haywire. Two tenderfoots on the Montana cattle range in 1886, by Philip Ashton Rollins. Pictures by Peter Hurd. New York, Charles Scribner's sons, 1939. Pict. cloth.

ix p., 1 l., 269 p. 2 plates (both double p.). 21.3 cm.
Half title; illus. end papers; illus. t.p.; first edition, letter "A" on copyright p.

1941 ———. Jinglebob. A true story of a real cowboy, by Philip Ashton Rollins. . . . New York, London, Charles Scribner's sons, 1927. Cloth.

ix p., 3 l., 262 ₁1₁ p. front., illus. 21 cm.
Half title; illus. end papers; vignette; first edition, letter "A" on copyright p.

1942 ROLLINSON, JOHN K. Hoofprints of a cowboy and U. S. ranger; pony trails in Wyoming, by John K. Rollinson; edited and arranged by E. A.

Brininstool; illustrated with photographs. Caldwell, Idaho, the Caxton printers, ltd., 1941. Cloth.

7 p.l., ₁15₁–410 ₁1₁ p. front., plates, ports., map. 23.6 cm.
Cover title and half title: "Pony Trails in Wyoming"; headpieces; pub. device.

1943 ———. History of the migration of Oregon-raised herds to midwestern markets. Wyoming cattle trails, by John K. Rollinson . . . ; edited and arranged by E. A. Brininstool; illustrated with photographs and maps. Caldwell, Idaho, the Caxton printers, ltd., 1948. Cloth.

9 p.l., ₁19₁–366 p. front. (col.), plates, ports., facsms., map. 24.2 cm.
Appendices, p. ₁301₁–348; bibliography, p. ₁349₁–351; index, p. ₁353₁–366.
Half title: "Wyoming Cattle Trails"; headpieces. pub. device; untrimmed.
Also published in a de luxe edition limited to a 1,000 signed and numbered copies.
Colophon: "The limited edition of Wyoming Cattle Trails is 1,000 numbered copies,
signed by the author, of which this is No. ———. First edition."

The author, who was a personal friend of mine, died about the time the book was published. He had signed the signatures of the de luxe edition, but died before its release.

1944 ROLT-WHEELER, FRANCIS WILLIAM. The book of cowboys, by Francis Rolt-Wheeler, with 33 illustrations from photographs, sketches, and early prints. Boston, Lothrop, Lee & Shepard co., ₁1921₁. Pict. cloth. OP.

7 p.l., 13–394 p. front., plates. 20.5 cm.
Half title; pub. device.

1945 ROMSPERT, GEORGE W. The western echo; a description of the western states and territories of the United States as gathered in a tour by wagon. By George W. Romspert. Dayton, Ohio, United Brethren publishing house, 1881. Dec. cloth. Scarce.

7 p.l., ₁17₁–406 p. front. (port.), illus. 18.5 cm.
Title on cover: "We Went West."

The author, who started from Dayton, Ohio, on a tour of the West by wagon, describes the country as he saw it. Contains a discussion of cowboys, their work, and their history.

1946 ROOSEVELT, THEODORE. By-laws of the Little Missouri River Stockmen's Association. Theodore Roosevelt, chairman, Henry S. Boice, vice-chairman. New York, Press of G. P. Putnam's sons, 1885. Wrappers. (Cover title). Excessively rare.

₁3₁–6 p. 16.7 cm.
List of members on last page.

The copy I examined is in the Roosevelt Collection, Harvard University, Cambridge, Mass., and it is said that there is only one other known copy.

1947 ———. Cowboys and kings. Three great letters by Theodore Roosevelt, with an introduction by Elting E. Morison. Cambridge, Harvard University press, 1954. Cloth.

xii p., 1 l., 128 p. 21.7 cm.
Index, p. 121–128.
Half title.

In his letter to John Hay, Roosevelt tells much of his ranch experiences.

1948 ———. Good hunting in pursuit of big game in the West. By Theodore Roosevelt. Illustrated. . . . New York and London, Harper & brothers, publishers, 1907. Pict. cloth. Pict. label pasted on. OP.

vi p., 3 l., 13–106 [1] p. front. (with tissue), illus., plates. 19.3 cm.
Half title.

Has a chapter on ranching.

1949 ———. Hunting trips of a ranchman; sketches of a sport on the northern cattle plains, by Theodore Roosevelt. Illustrated by A. B. Frost, R. Swain Gifford, J. C. Beard, Fannie E. Gifford, Henry Dandham. New York & London, G. P. Putnam's sons, 1885. Pict. cloth. Scarce.

xvi, 318 p. front. (port. with tissue), plates. 29.3 cm.
Half title; initials, head and tail pieces; each plate accompanied by leaf with descriptive letterpress not included in pagination; t.p. in red and black; vignette; untrimmed.
"The Medora Edition. 500 copies only printed."
Trade edition published in 1886 and republished many times.

1950 ———. Letters from Theodore Roosevelt to Anna Roosevelt Cowles, 1870–1918. New York, London, Charles Scribner's sons, MCMXXIV. Cloth. Scarce.

viii p., 1 l., 323 p. front. (with tissue). 22.3 cm.
Index, p. 319–323.
Half title; untrimmed.

1951 ———. Ranch life and hunting-trail, by Theodore Roosevelt . . . illustrated by Frederic Remington. New York, the Century co., [1888]. Pict. cloth. OP.

4 p.l., 186 [1] p. front., illus. 31x25 cm.
Half title; gilt edges.
Reprinted with 12 additional illustrations in 1896. Published again in 1899 and 1901.

The first issue was bound in tan buckram stamped in green and gold; the second issue was bound in smooth brown linen stamped in brown and gold.

1952 ———. Stories of the great West, by Theodore Roosevelt; illustrated [by Frederic Remington]. New York, the Century co., [1909]. Dec. cloth. OP.

6 p.l., 3–254 p. front., illus. 19.3 cm.
Half title; device.

The last half of this book is a reprint of the author's *Ranch Life and Hunting-Trail*.

1953 ———. Who should go West? [By] Theodore Roosevelt. New York, privately printed, 1927. Boards. Rare.

2 p.l., 9 [1] p. 21 cm.
Title label pasted on.
Colophon: "Seventy three copies of this book have been printed."

1954 ———. The wilderness hunter. An account of the big game of the United States and its chase with horse, hound, and rifle. By Theodore Roosevelt. . . . Illustrated. New York, London, G. P. Putnam's sons, [1893]. Pict. cloth. OP.

xvi, 472 p. front. (with tissue), illus., plates. 23.8 cm.
Index, p. 469–472.
Illus. chapter headings.

1955 ROSE, DAN. Prehistoric and historic Gila County. By Dan Rose. . . . Phoenix, Republic and Gazette printery, [n.d.], Wrappers. Rare.

1 p.l., [3]–37 p. 23 cm.

1956 [Ross, C. P., and T. L. ROUSE]. Early-day history of Wilbarger County. Vernon, Texas, published by the Vernon Times, 1933. Stiff pict. wrappers. Scarce.

5 p.l., 208 p. plates, ports. 24.5 cm.

Some cattle material on the trail and Doan's Crossing.

1957 [Ross, Gov. EDMUND G.]. Report of the Governor of New Mexico to the Secretary of the Interior, 1886. Washington, Government printing office, 1886. Wrappers. Rare.

3–12 p. 23 cm.

1958 ———. Report of the Governor of New Mexico to the Secretary of the Interior, 1888. Washington, Government printing office, 1888. Wrappers. Rare.

3–18 p. 20.8 cm.

1959 ROUSIERS, PAUL DE. American life. [By] Paul de Rousiers. Translated from the French by A. J. Herbertson. Paris, New York, Firmin-Didot & co., publishers, 1891. Cloth. Scarce.

8 p.l., [19]–437 p. 25.8 cm.
At head of title: "Paul de Rousiers."

The author, a Frenchman, visited the United States in 1890. He analyzes American civilization and gives his impression of the people and customs encountered on the western ranches and in the western towns and cities.

1960 RUCKER, MAUD A. The Oregon Trail and some of its blazers, by Maud A. Rucker.... New York, Walker Neale, publisher, 1930. Cloth. OP.
10 p.l., 19–293 p. front. (port.), plates, ports. 20 cm.
Half title; pub. device.

Much about Jesse Applegate and his recollections. It repeats his *A Day with the Cow Column.*

1961 RULE and COLE (given names unknown). Caldwell, "the magic city." In the Boise Valley, Idaho. Facts pertaining to the magic city and its great tributary resources; also statistics as to climate, health, agriculture, stock raising, mining etc. . . . Presented by Rule and Cole. Caldwell, Idaho, Tribune job print, 1891. Wrappers. Rare.
23 [9] p. 23 cm.
Last 9 p. adv.; adv. verso front wrapper; adv. recto and verso back wrapper.

1962 RUSH, OSCAR. The open range, and bunk house philosophy, by Oscar Rush. [Denver, Colorado Herald printing co.], 1930. Stiff pict. wrappers. OP.
2 p.l., 7–110 p. front., illus., plates. 20.4 cm.

1963 ——. The open range, by Oscar Rush. Illustrated with authentic photographs and pen-and-ink drawings by R. H. Hall. Caldwell, Idaho, the Caxton printers, ltd., 1936. Leather.
5 p.l., [13]–263 p. front. (col. with tissue), plates. 19.5 cm.
Half title; illus. end papers; illus. t.p.
Colophon: "The De Luxe Edition of The Open Range is limited to ten signed and numbered copies of which this is number ——." (*Signed*).
Also published in a trade edition. This edition contains some chapters not in the original edition.

My friend Jeff Dykes owns one of these ten copies, and I was privileged to examine it in his home at College Park, Maryland.

1964 RUSLING, JAMES F. Across America; or, the great West and Pacific coast, by James F. Rusling. . . . New York, Sheldon & company, 1875. Pict. cloth. Scarce.
9 p.l., [21]–503 p. front. (with tissue), illus., plates. 20 cm.
Appendix, p. [481]–492; index, p. [493]–503.

1965 RUSSELL, AUSTIN. C. M. R., Charles M. Russell. A biography, by Austin Russell. New York, Twayne publishers, [1957]. Cloth.
4 p.l., 9–247 p. front. (port.), plates, ports. 22.2 cm.
Sources, p. 246–247.
Half title.

1966 RUSSELL, CHARLES EDWARD. The greatest trust in the world, by Charles

Edward Russell. New York, the Ridgeway-Thayer company, publishers, 1905. Pict. cloth. Scarce.

viii, 252 p. facsm. 21 cm.

Half title; pub. device.

1967 RUSSELL, CHARLES MARION. Back-trailing on old frontiers. Illustrated by Charles M. Russell. Great Falls, Montana, published by Cheely-Raban syndicate, 1922. Pict. wrappers. Rare.

2 p.l., 56 p. 14 full-p. plates. 28.6 cm.

Has a chapter on the Texas cattle trail.

1968 ———. Good medicine; the illustrated letters of Charles M. Russell; with an introduction by Will Rogers and a biographical note by Nancy C. Russell. Garden City, New York, Doubleday, Doran & company, inc., 1929. Bound in three-quarter blue buckram, vellum sides. Enclosed in case. Exceedingly rare.

xii, 13–162 p., 1 l. front. (col. with tissue), illus. (part col.). 31.5 cm.

Half title; part of letters in facsimile; "First edition" on copyright p.

Colophon: "This edition of Good Medicine is limited to one hundred thirty-four copies. It was produced from lithographic plates on antique laid paper made particularly for this printing. The text was hand-set in old style Caslon type and the volume designed under the supervision of Walter Dorwin Teague. The editorial arrangement was by Harry E. Maule. The edition was produced by Doubleday, Doran and Company, Incorporated, by William C. D. Glasser of New York City, and completed this sixteenth day of December, Nineteen Hundred Twenty Nine, this copy being number ———."

This de luxe edition is practically unprocurable, and I count myself fortunate in possessing one. The trade edition has the same title page, except that it bears the date 1930. The end papers in this edition are illustrated in color with the author's painting "Where Tracks Spell War or Meat," and the volume is bound in brown buckram, gold stamped. "First edition after printing 134 de luxe copies" on copyright page. Fifty-nine copies of this edition were bound in blue buckram for presentation. All were cased. There are many later reprints.

1969 ———. More rawhides, by C. M. Russell . . . , with illustrations by the author. Great Falls, Montana, printed by the Montana Newspaper association, 1925. Pict. wrappers. Scarce.

3 p.l., [5]–59 [1] p. illus. 28 cm.

Republished in 1946 by Trail's End publishing co., Pasadena, Calif., bound both in cloth and in leather.

1970 ———. Pen sketches, by Chas. M. Russell, the cowboy artist. Great Falls, Mont., W. T. Ridgley printing co., [1899]. Wrappers. Rare.

12 plates. 29x36 cm.

Title and imprint on cover; each plate accompanied by leaf with descriptive letter-press.

The second issue is the same except that the vignette of the scene above the publisher's imprint on the fly leaf has been replaced by a buffalo skull. The next issue has same collation, but has no titles on plates, and the following issue has the same collation, but the publisher's name is stamped in gold on cover. Some of the first editions were issued in limp black morocco stamped in gold.

1971 ———. Pen and ink sketches, by Charles M. Russell. ₁Great Falls, Montana, Glazier printing co., 1945₁. Wrappers. (Cover title). Scarce.
50 p. plates. 32.5x26 cm.
Three-hole tie.

Later republished by Trail's End publishing co., Pasadena, Calif., 1946, in two volumes, bound in boards, with title label pasted on.

1972 ———. Rawhide Rawlins stories, by C. M. Russell; with illustrations by the author. Great Falls, Montana, printed by the Montana News-paper association, 1921. Pict. wrappers. Very rare.
2 p.l., 60 p. illus. 28 cm.

This is Russell's first book of stories. Four editions followed; the fourth edition is fairly common, but the first is rarely found. It was reprinted with biography added in 1946 by Trail's End Publishing Company, bound in cloth and in leather.

1973 ———. Rawhide Rawlins rides again; or, behind the swinging doors. A collection of Charlie Russell's favorite stories. Illustrations by Charles M. Russell and others. Pasadena, Calif., published by Trail's End publishing co., inc., ₁1948₁. Gold-stamped saddle leather. Scarce.
6 p.l., 13–61 ₁1₁ p. illus. 16.3 cm.
Illus. end papers; vignette; pub. device; untrimmed.
Colophon: "300 copies lithographed and plates destroyed. Copy No. ———. C. M. Russell's personal stamping die, hand-cut from Russell's design used to gold-stamp the back cover of this book." Each book numbered and boxed.

This little book is a collection of Russell's favorite saloon stories and could not be sent through the mails when it was published.

1974 ———. Studies of western life. By Charles M. Russell, the cowboy artist, with descriptions by Granville Stuart. New York, the Albertype co., 1890. Cloth. Three-hole tie. Rare.
₁47₁ p. (no pagination). 12 plates. 18x24.5 cm.
Letterpress describing each plate on separate sheet except plate No. 1. Second issue same, with letterpress relating to plate No. 1 added to verso of title page. Each plate, except the first, is on a separate sheet, printed on the recto, with verso blank; the first plate is on the verso of the title page.
Another edition was published by J. L. Robbins, in Spokane, ₁c.1919₁, with 26

pages, letterpress for each plate on verso of preceding page. Reprinted in Helena, Montana, 1929.

This little book of Russell's early art is the first book published under his name.

1975 ——. Trails plowed under, by Charles M. Russell; with illustrations in color and line by the author. Garden City, New York, Doubleday, Page & company, 1927. Cloth.

xx p., 1 l., 211 p. illus., plates (part double-p. col.). 26.3 cm.
Half title; illus. t.p.; t.p. in red and black; "First edition" on copyright p.

This book is composed of the stories which originally appeared in the author's two little books *Rawhide Rawlins Stories* and *More Rawhides,* with the exception of one from the first book, "Johnny Sees the Big Show." The popularity of these stories has kept this book in print continuously. Russell, both as an author and as an illustrator, is an authority on ranching techniques and various forms of western life. Philip Rollins said that "his writings are in part patently fictional, but it does not lessen their value as infallible mirrors." For this reason they are included in this bibliography.

1976 RUSSELL, MRS. HAL. Land of enchantment. Memoirs of Marian Russell along the Santa Fe Trail as dictated to Mrs. Hal Russell. Edited by Garnet M. Brayer. Decorations by David T. Vernon. Evanston, Illinois, the Branding Iron press, 1954. Pict. cloth.

x, 155 [1] p. front., 2 ports. (incl. front.). 23.7 cm.
Notes, p. 145–148; index, p. 149–155.
Half title; "Memoirs of Marian Russell"; map on end papers; illus. t.p.
Colophon: "This book was designed and printed by Philip Reed, Chicago, Illinois in the summer of 1954. Of seven hundred fifty copies, this is number ——."

1977 ——. Settler Mac and the charmed quarter-section. [By] Mrs. Hal Russell. Denver, Sage books, [1956]. Cloth.

5 p.l., 11–159 p. 21 cm.
Half title.

Some material on early ranching in Colorado.

1978 RUSSELL, J. H. Cattle on the Conejo, by J. H. Russell. [Los Angeles], the Ward Ritchie press, 1957. Decorated boards.

vii p., 1 l., 3–135 p. plates. 23.5 cm.
Half title; map on end papers; illus. t.p.

1979 RUTH, KENT. Oklahoma, a guide to the Sooner State. Compiled by Kent Ruth and the staff of the University of Oklahoma Press, with articles by leading authorities and photographic section arranged by J. Eldon Peek. Norman, University of Oklahoma press, [1957]. Cloth.

xxxv p., 1 l., 3–532 p. plates, maps (5 double p., 1 fold.). 21 cm.
Chronology, p. 495–503; selected reading list, p. 504–511; picture sources, p. 512–513; index, p. 515–532.
Half title.

1980 RUTHERFORD, J. G. The cattle trade of western Canada. Special report, by J. G. Rutherford. . . . Ottawa, Ont., published by direction of the Hon. Sydney A. Fisher, minister of agriculture, August, 1909. Wrappers. Scarce.

2 p.l., 5–23 p. 24.9 cm.
At head of title: "Dominion of Canada, Department of Agriculture, Branch of Live Stock Commissioner."

1981 RYAN, J. C. A skeptic dude in Arizona, by J. C. Ryan. Illustrated by Sid Stone. San Antonio, the Naylor company, [1952]. Cloth.

xi, 176 p. front. (map), illus. 21.6 cm.
Appendix, p. 175–176.
Half title; vignette.

1982 RYE, EDGAR. The quirt and the spur; vanishing shadows of the Texas frontier, by Edgar Rye. Chicago, W. B. Conkey company, publishers, [1909]. Dec. cloth. Scarce.

4 p.l., 9–363 p. front. (port.), 10 plates. 19.8 cm.

Wild days of the cowboy and buffalo hunter around Fort Griffin, Texas.

1983 RYNNING, CAPTAIN THOMAS H. Gun notches. The life story of a cowboy-soldier, by Captain Thomas H. Rynning as told to Al Cohn and Joe Chisholm. With a foreword by Rupert Hughes. New York, Frederick A. Stokes company, MCMXXXI. Cloth. OP.

xvii p., 1 l., 332 p. 21.2 cm.
Half title; pub. device; untrimmed.

1984 RYUS, WILLIAM H. The second William Penn. A true account of incidents that happened along the old Santa Fe Trail in the sixties, by W. H. Ryus. Kansas City, Press of Frank T. Riley publishing co., [1913]. Pict. wrappers. Scarce.

176 p. front. (port.), illus. 19.5 cm.

Contains some information on Lucien B. Maxwell as a ranchman.

1985 SAFFORD, Gov. A. P. K. Fourth biennial message of Gov. A. P. K. Safford to the Legislative Assembly of Arizona at the session commencing January 1, 1877. Tucson, Arizona Citizen print, 1877. Wrappers. Rare.

[3]–14 p. 21.3 cm.
Double column.

1986 ———. The territory of Arizona; a history of the territory's acquisition, organization, and mineral, agricultural, and grazing resources; a review of its Indian tribes, their depredations and subjugation; and showing the present condition and prospects of the territory. Tucson, Citizen office print, 1874. Wrappers. (Cover title). Rare.

[3]–38 p. tables. 22.3 cm.

One of the first examples of printing in Arizona.

1987 ———. Third biennial message of Governor A. P. K. Safford to the Legislative Assembly of Arizona Territory at the session commencing January 4, 1875. Tucson, Arizona Citizen print, 1875. Wrappers. Rare.

[3]–11 p. 21 cm.
Double column.

1988 SAGE, LEE. Gopher Dick, the story of a northern cowpuncher, by Lee Sage. New York, W. Morrow and co., 1932. Cloth. OP.

4 p.l., 296 p. 19.5 cm.

1989 ———. The last rustler. The autobiography of Lee Sage, with illustrations by Paul Clowes. Boston, Little, Brown and company, 1930. Pict. cloth. OP.

x p., 1 l., [3]–303 p. illus. 21.6 cm.
Half title; headpieces; tailpieces; vignette.

1990 ST. CLEMENT, DOROTHY (BERRY) DE. White gumbo, by Dorothy De St. Clement [Countess Dorotea de Sauteiron de St. Clement]. New York, Vantage press, inc., [1951]. Cloth.

5 p.l., 186 p. 22.2 cm.
Half title.

1991 ST. MAUR, MRS. ALGERNON (SUSAN MARGARET MCKINNON, DUCHESS OF SOMERSET). Impressions of a tenderfoot during a journey in search of sport in the far West, by Mrs. Algernon St. Maur. London, J. Murray, 1890. Pict. cloth. OP.

xv, 279 p. front., plates, fold. map. 21 cm.
16 l. adv. at end.

Some ranch experiences of an English lady told in the form of a diary.

1992 SALMON, ROSS. Ross Salmon's cowboy book. London, Edinburgh, Paris, Melbourne, Toronto, New York, Thomas Nelson and sons, ltd., [1955]. Pict. col. boards.

4 p.l., 112 p. front. (col.), plates (3 col., 3 double p.). 24 cm.

The story of an Englishman who came to the American West and became a cowboy.

1993 SAMPSON, ARTHUR W. Livestock husbandry on range and pasture. By

Arthur W. Sampson. . . . New York, John Wiley & sons, inc.; London, Chapman & Hall, ltd., 1928. Cloth. OP.

xxi p., 1 l., 3–411 p. front., illus., graphs, tables. 23.3 cm.
Questions and bibliography after each chapter; index, p. 405–411.

1994 ———. Range management, principles and practices. ɪByɪ Arthur W. Sampson. . . . New York, John Wiley & sons, inc.; London, Chapman & Hall, ltd., ɪ1952ɪ. Cloth.

xiv p., 1 l., 3–570 p. plates, charts, maps. 28.2 cm.
"Literature cited" after each chapter; index, p. 551–570.
Half title.

1995 SAMUELS, CHARLES. The magnificent rube. The life and gaudy times of Tex Rickard, by Charles Samuels. New York, Toronto, London, McGraw-Hill book company, inc., ɪ1957ɪ. Cloth.

5 p.l., 301 ɪ1ɪ p. plates, ports. 21 cm.
Bibliography, p. 297–301.
Half title.

Contains material on Rickard's years as a cowboy and trail driver in Texas as well as his ranching experiences in Paraguay.

1996 SANDERS, ALVIN HOWARD. At the sign of the Stock Yard Inn; the same being a true account of how certain great achievements of the past have been commemorated and cleverly linked with the present; together with sundry recollections inspired by the portraits at the Saddle and Sirloin Club, by Alvin Howard Sanders. . . . Chicago, Breeder's Gazette print, 1915. Three-quarter leather. Scarce.

2 p.l., 3–322 p. front. (col.), plates, ports. 20 cm.
Vignette; t.p. in red and black; each p. of text enclosed in red lines.

1997 ———. The black swans, and other friends indoors and out. By Alvin Howard Sanders. . . . Chicago, Breeder's Gazette print, 1918. Cloth. OP.

4 p.l., 205 ɪ1ɪ p. front., illus., plates. 18.5 cm.
Half title; pub. device; headpieces; untrimmed.

1998 ———. The cattle of the world. Their place in the human scheme— wild types and modern breeds in many lands, by Alvin Howard Sanders. . . . Paintings by Edward Herbert Miner, with 114 illustrations, including 20 pages in color. Washington, D. C., published by the National Geographic society, 1926. Morocco. OP.

3 p.l., 142 ɪ1ɪ p. front., illus. (part col.), plates, ports. 25.4 cm.
Index, p. 138–142.
Half title; double column.

A separate publication of an article from *The National Geographic* magazine.

AT THE SIGN OF
THE STOCK YARD INN

THE SAME BEING A TRUE ACCOUNT OF
HOW CERTAIN GREAT ACHIEVEMENTS OF
THE PAST HAVE BEEN COMMEMORATED
AND CLEVERLY LINKED WITH THE PRESENT;
TOGETHER WITH SUNDRY RECOLLEC-
TIONS INSPIRED BY THE PORTRAITS
AT THE SADDLE AND SIRLOIN CLUB

By ALVIN HOWARD SANDERS, D. AGR., LL. D.

EDITOR "THE BREEDER'S GAZETTE,"
AUTHOR OF "SHORTHORN CATTLE"
AND "THE STORY OF THE HEREFORDS"

CHICAGO
BREEDER'S GAZETTE PRINT
1915

1999 ———. A history of Aberdeen-Angus cattle, with particular reference to their introduction, distribution, and rise to popularity in the field of beef production in North America, by Alvin Howard Sanders. . . . Chicago, Ill., the New Breeder's Gazette, [1928]. Cloth. OP.

xx, 1042 p. front., plates, ports. 23.6 cm.

2000 ———. Short-horn cattle; a series of historical sketches, memoirs, and records of the breed and its development in the United States and Canada, by Alvin H. Sanders. Chicago, Sanders publishing co., 1900. Three-quarter leather. OP.

xiii [1] p., 9–872 p. front. (col.), plates, ports., map. 20.3 cm.
Republished in 1916, greatly enlarged, and published again in 1918.

2001 ———. The story of Herefords. An account of the origin and development of the breed in Herefordshire, a sketch of its early introduction into the United States and Canada, and subsequent rise to popularity in the western cattle trade, with sundry notes on the management of breeding herds. By Alvin H. Sanders. Chicago, the Breeder's Gazette, 1914. Cloth. Pict. label (col.) pasted on. OP.

11 p.l., 23–1087 p. front., plates, ports., tables. 19.9 cm.

2002 SANDERS, HELEN FITZGERALD. A history of Montana, by Helen Fitz-gerald Sanders. Illustrated. Chicago and New York, the Lewis publishing company, 1913. Leather. Scarce. Pub. in 3 vols.

Vol. I: xxxv, 19–847 p. front. (port. with tissue), plates, ports., facsm., tables. 27.6 cm.
Vols. II and III: biographical.
Double column: gilt top.

2003 SANDERS, WILLIAM PERRY. Days that are gone, by William Perry Sanders. . . . Los Angeles, Grafton publishing corporation, 1918. Stiff pict. wrappers. OP.

7 p.l., [13]–134 p. front. (port.), illus., plates, facsm. 17.2 cm.
Half title.

2004 SANDOZ, MARI. The cattlemen, from the Rio Grande across the far Marias, by Mari Sandoz. New York, Hastings house, publishers, [1958]. Cloth.

xiv p., 1 l., 3–527 p. plates, ports. 21 cm.
Notes, p. 499–501; bibliography, p. 503–509; index, p. 511–527.
Half title; map on end papers; "American Procession Series."

Also published in a de luxe edition.

Colophon: "This copy is number —— of a special edition of The Cattlemen, limited to 199 copies." (Signed).

Bound in cloth and boards, with a colored folding plate by Nick Eggenhofer in front.

2005 ———. Old Jules, by Mari Sandoz. With illustrations. Boston, Little, Brown and company, 1935. Cloth.

x p., 3 l., [3]–424 p. front. (port.), plates, ports., facsms. 22.2 cm.
Half title; illus. end papers; pub. device.
Republished in 1955.

This is the story of the author's father, a cattleman of the Nebraska Sand Hills.

2006 SANDS, FRANK. A pastoral prince. The history and reminiscences of J. W. Cooper, by Frank Sands. Santa Barbara, Cal., 1893. Pict. cloth. Scarce.

xiv p., 1 l., 190 p. front. (port.), ports. 20 cm.

2007 SANTEE, ROSS. Apache land, written and illustrated by Ross Santee. New York, Charles Scribner's sons; London, Charles Scribner's sons, ltd., 1947. Pict. cloth.

vii p., 1 l., 216 p. illus. 23.6 cm.
Illus. double t.p.; first editions, letter "A" on copyright p.

2008 ———. Cowboy, by Ross Santee. Illustrated by the author. New York, Cosmopolitan book corporation, 1928. Pict. cloth. OP.

5 p.l., 257 p. front., illus. 20.7 cm.
Half title; vignette; untrimmed.

2009 ———. Lost pony tracks, by Ross Santee. New York, Charles Scribner's sons, 1953. Pict. cloth.

3 p.l., 303 p. illus. (part double p.). 21.6 cm.
Half title; illus. t.p.

2010 ———. Men and horses, by Ross Santee, with more than one hundred original drawings by the author. New York and London, the Century co., [1926]. Pict. cloth. OP.

5 p.l., 3–268 p. front., illus. 24.3 cm.
Half title; illus. t.p.; untrimmed.

Ross Santee wrote several other books not included here because they are fiction.

2011 SAUNDERS, ARTHUR C. The history of Bannock County, Idaho. By Arthur C. Saunders. Pocatello, Idaho, the Tribune co., ltd., 1915. Cloth. OP.

4 p.l., 11–143 p. 19.5 cm.
Half title; vignette.

2012 SAUNDERSON, MONT. H. Montana stock ranches and ranching opportunities. By Mont. H. Saunderson. Lincoln, Nebr., reproduced by U. S.

Department of Agriculture Soil Conservation Service . . . , 1950. Wrappers.

[10] p. (no pagination). 2 maps, tables. 26.6 cm.
Double column; printed on one side of paper only.

A reprint of an article appearing in the February and March issues of *"The Montana Stockgrower*. Reproduction permission granted April 17, 1950, by Montana Stockgrowers' Association on May 5, 1950, by the author."

2013 ———. Western land and water use. By Mont. H. Saunderson. Norman, University of Oklahoma press, [1950]. Cloth.

xi p., 1 l., 3–217 [1] p. plates, tables, relief map. 22 cm.
Bibliography, p. 208–212; index, p. 213–217.
Half title.

2014 ———. Western stock ranching, by Mont. H. Saunderson. . . . Minneapolis, University of Minnesota press, [1950]. Cloth.

xiii, p., 1 l., 3–247 p. plates, tables, charts, maps. 23.5 cm.
Bibliography, p. 241–243; index, p. 244–247.
Half title; "First edition" on copyright p.

2015 ———, and D. W. CHITTENDEN. Cattle ranching in Montana. An analysis of operating methods, costs, and returns in western, central, and eastern areas of the state. By M. H. Saunderson and D. W. Chittenden. Bozeman, Montana, State College Agricultural Experiment Station, *Bulletin No. 341,* May, 1937. Pamphlet. (Cover title). OP.

32 p. maps, tables. 22.2 cm.

2016 SAVAGE, JAMES WOODRUFF, JOHN T. BELL, ET AL. History of the city of Omaha, Nebraska, by James W. Savage and John T. Bell; and South Omaha, by Consul W. Butterfield. New York, and Chicago, Munsell & company, 1894. Three-quarter leather. OP.

xvi, 699 p. front. (port. with tissue), plates, ports. 27.8 cm.
Index, p. 673–699.
State seal on t.p.; gilt edges.

2017 SCHATZ, AUGUST HERMAN. Opening a cow country. A history of the pioneer's struggle in conquering the prairies south of the Black Hills, by A. H. Schatz. Ann Arbor, Michigan, Edwards brothers, inc., 1939. Stiff wrappers. Very scarce.

x, 141 p. front., illus., plates, ports., maps, plan. 21 cm.
Appendix, p. 109–141.
Lithoprinted and privately published by the author in a small edition and now scarce.

A letter from the author states that he had only a very small number printed, selling them to friends at just what they cost him, and the edition was soon exhausted.

2018 SCHELL, HERBERT SAMUEL. South Dakota, its beginning and growth, by Herbert Samuel Schell. New York, American book co., [1942]. Cloth. OP.

x p., 1 l., 359 p. front. (double-p. map), plates, ports., maps, charts. 20.5 cm. Appendix, p. 335–344; index, p. 345–359.
Questions and bibliography at end of each chapter.

2019 [SCHENCK, DR. J. H.]. The wild ranger of Santa Fe, [by Dr. J. H. Schenck]. [N.p. (? Philadelphia), n.d.] Pict. wrappers. (Cover title). Very rare.

3–31 p. illus. 18.5 cm.
Last 14 p. testimonials.

Historically, this is a worthless little pamphlet, but it is a collector's item because of its rarity. Written as fact, it is no doubt fiction and an original means of advertising by a doctor who made pills and cough syrup.

2020 SCHLESINGER, ARTHUR MEIER. The rise of the city, 1878–1898, by Arthur Meier Schlesinger. . . . New York, the Macmillan company, 1933. Cloth. OP.

xvi p., 1 l., 494 p. illus., plates, map (col.), facsms. 22 cm.
Index, p. 475–494.
Half title; illus. end papers.

This is volume X of the twelve-volume set entitled "A History of American Life," and has a chapter on cattle.

2021 SCHMEDDING, JOSEPH. Cowboy and Indian trader, by Joseph Schmedding. Caldwell, Idaho, the Caxton printers, ltd., 1951. Pict. cloth.

8 p.l., [17]–364 p. front., plates, facsm. 23.5 cm.
Half title; map on end papers; headpieces; pub. device; vignette.

2022 SCHMIDT, HEINIE. Ashes of my campfire. Historical anecdotes of old Dodge City as told and retold, by Heinie Schmidt. . . . Vol. I [only one published]. Dodge City, Kansas, Journal, inc., publishers, [1952]. Stiff pict. wrappers.

3 p.l., 9–72 p. plates, ports. 19.7 cm.
Double column; "First edition" on copyright p.

Little stories of people and events in Dodge City.

2023 SCHMITT, MARTIN F. (ED.). The cattle drives of David Shirk from Texas to the Idaho mines, 1871 and 1873. Reminiscences of David L. Shirk, wherein are described his two successful cattle drives from Texas, in company with George T. Miller. His later experiences as a cattleman in eastern Oregon during the terrible depredations of hostile Indians, and the range warfare with Pete French, from the original manuscript and related papers, now in the University of Oregon Library. Edited by

Martin F. Schmitt. ₁Portland, Oregon₁, published by the Champoeg press, MCMLVI. Pict. cloth.

ix, 148 p. front. (port. tipped in). 22.8 cm.
Half title; vignette; untrimmed.
Published in an ediiton of 750 copies.

2024 ———, and DEE BROWN. The settlers' West, by Martin F. Schmitt and Dee Brown. New York, Charles Scribner's sons, 1955. Pict. cloth.

xxviii p., 1 l., 258 p. plates, ports., maps, facsms. 30.5 cm.
Bibliography, p. 253–258.
Half title; vignette; first edition, letter "A" on copyright p.

2025 SCOBEE, BARRY. Old Fort Davis. San Antonio, Texas, the Naylor company, ₁1947₁. Cloth.

ix, 101 p. plates, ports., map. 21 cm.

2026 ———. The steer branded murder, by Barry Scobee. The true and authentic account of a frontier tragedy. Documented by eye witnesses, it presents the story of cattlemen, cowboys, and the cattle country of far western Texas. . . . ₁Houston, Texas, Frontier press of Texas, 1952₁. Stiff pict. wrappers.

5–56 ₁2₁ p. front., port. 17 cm.
Index tipped in (last 2 p.).
Vignette.

A crudely printed and bound little book, but the author seems to have made an honest effort to dig up the facts concerning this well-known Texas incident, which has become legendary.

2027 ———. The story of Fort Davis, Jeff Davis County, and the Davis Mountains, by Barry Scobee. Illustrated by Warren Hunter. . . . Fort Davis, Texas, Marvin Hunter, Jr., publisher and editor of the Dispatch, 1936. Pict. wrappers. OP.

38 p. illus. 18.8 cm.

2028 SCOGGINS, J. ARTHUR. From saddle to pulpit. By J. Arthur Scoggins. Dallas, Texas, Wilkinson publishing company, ₁1952₁. Cloth.

5 p.l., 11–232 ₁1₁ p. plates, ports. 19.8 cm.
Vignette.

2029 SCOTT, HUGH LENOX. Some memories of a soldier, by Hugh Lenox Scott, major-general U. S. Army, retired. Illustrated. New York, London, the Century co., ₁1928₁. Cloth. Scarce.

xvii p., 1 l., 3–673 p. front. (port.), plates, ports. 22.8 cm.
Appendix, p. 629–635; index, p. 637–673.
Half title; pub. device; "First printing" on copyright p.

2030 SCOTT, Z. T. Robert Benjamin Masterson, pioneer ranchman of the

Texas Panhandle. A character sketch, by Z. T. Scott. ₁Austin, 1930₁. Privately printed. Wrappers. Scarce.

₁3₁–24 p. front., 1 plate, 4 ports. (incl. front., all with tissues). 24.2 cm. Vignette.

2031 SEARS, R. W. (BERT). A survey of the cycle of the sod and the live-stock industries here and abroad, by R. W. (Bert) Sears. Los Angeles, California, Wetzel publishing co., inc., ₁1941₁. Cloth. OP.

9 p.l., 1 p., 22–306 p. front., plates. 23.6 cm.

2032 SEARS, GEN. W. H. Notes from a cowboy's diary, by Gen. W. H. Sears. Lawrence, Kansas, ₁n.d.₁. Wrappers. Scarce.

₁6₁ p. (no pagination). 20.3 cm.

2033 SEELY, HOWARD. A ranchman's stories . . . , by Howard Seely. New York, Dodd, Mead & company, ₁1885₁. Cloth. Scarce.

3 p.l., 356 p. 17.8 cm.

2034 SEMPLE, GOV. EUGENE. Biennial message of Eugene Semple, governor of Washington Territory, to the Legislative Assembly, session of 1887–8. Published by authority. Olympia, Thos. H. Cavanaugh, public printer, 1887. Wrappers. Rare.

₁3₁–16 p. 23 cm.

Has a section on cattle quarantine.

2035 SEWALL, WILLIAM WINGATE. Bill Sewall's story of T. R., by William Wingate Sewall, with an introduction by Hermann Hagedorn. Illustrated. . . . New York and London, Harper & brothers, publishers, ₁1919₁. Pict. cloth. Port. pasted on. OP.

7 p.l., 115 ₁1₁ p. front. (port.), plates, port., facsms. 19.4 cm. Half title.

Story of Roosevelt's cowboy days.

2036 SHANNON, FRED ALBERT. Economic history of the people of the United States. By Fred Albert Shannon. . . . New York, the Macmillan company, 1934. Cloth. OP.

xi, 942 p. maps (part col., 2 double p.), tables. 22.2 cm. Index, p. 913–942. Half title.

2037 SHANNON, S. D. Resources of Wyoming. The soil, climate, production, advantages, and development. . . . The vacant public lands and how to obtain them. . . . Cheyenne, the Daily Sun electric print, 1889. Wrappers. Rare.

77 p. illus., plates, maps. 22 cm.

2038 SHARP, PAUL F. Whoop-up country. The Canadian-American West, 1865–1885, by Paul F. Sharp. Minneapolis, University of Minnesota press, [1955]. Pict. cloth.

xiii p., 1 l., 3–347 p. plates, ports., maps. 22.5 cm.
Notes, p. 319–336; index, p. 337–347.
Half title; vignette.

2039 SHAW, F. E. King of the cowboys; or, wild life on the border, by the publisher. Garrettsville, O., F. E. Shaw, publisher, [n.d.]. Pict. wrappers. Rare.

[9]–35 p. 14.7 cm.

2040 SHAW, JAMES C. Pioneering in Texas and Wyoming. Incidents in the life of James C. Shaw. Orin, Wyo., [1931]. Wrappers. Exceedingly rare.

43 p. 20.3 cm.

The edition of this privately printed little book was soon exhausted because the author took the books home and let his visiting friends carry them off. It is now a much sought collector's item.

2041 ——. North from Texas. Incidents in the early life of a range cowman in Texas, Dakota, and Wyoming, 1852–1883, by James C. Shaw. Edited by Herbert O. Brayer; illustrated by David T. Vernon. Evanston, Illinois, the Branding Iron press, 1952. Boards. OP.

xiii, 109 [2] p. front. (port.), illus., port., map. 23.5 cm.
Notes, p. 89–98; index, p. 99–109.
Half title; cattle brands on end papers; vignette.
Colophon: "This book was designed at the printing office of Philip Reed, Chicago, Illinois, and seven hundred fifty copies printed in July, 1952. Binding by Elizabeth Kner. This is number ——."

A reprint of the original edition described above, with notes and introduction. This, too, is becoming scarce.

2042 SHAW, THOMAS. Animal breeding, by Thomas Shaw. . . . New York and Chicago, O. Judd co., 1916. Cloth. OP.

ix [1] p., 1 l., 406 p. front., illus. 19 cm.

2043 SHAWVER, LONA. Chuckwagon windies, by Lona Shawver, and the range poems of Walt Cousins, compiled by Lona Shawver. San Antonio, Texas, the Naylor company, 1934. Cloth. OP.

6 p.l., 3–192 p. front., plates, port. 20.2 cm.
Half title.

2044 ——. Chuckwagon windies and true stories, by Lona Shawver. San Antonio, Texas, the Naylor company, publishers, [1950]. Cloth.

xv, 139 p. front., illus. 21.7 cm.
Half title; vignette.

A rewrite of the preceding book, with some new material.

2045 SHAY, JOHN C. Twenty years in the backwoods of California, by John
 C. Shay. Being the actual experiences and observations of a native son
 of California, covering a period of twenty years in one locality, while
 engaged in prospecting, gold mining, homesteading, stock raising, and
 the roadside smithy. Boston, the Roxburgh publishing co., inc., [1923].
 Cloth. Scarce.

4 p.l., [9]–142 p. 20 cm.
Half title.

2046 SHEEDY, DENNIS. Autobiography of Dennis Sheedy. [N.p., n.d.,
 c.1922]. Limp leather. (Cover title). Exceedingly rare.

60 [1] p. 23 cm.

Printed for a few friends in a very small edition. Mr. Sheedy was one of the
important cattlemen of Colorado and also became one of Denver's leading
merchants.

2047 SHEETS, EARL WOODALL. The beef calf; its growth and development,
 [by Earl W. Sheets, Washington, Government printing office, 1920].
 Wrappers. OP.

32 p. illus. 23 cm.
U. S. Dept. of Agriculture *Farmer's Bulletin 1135.*

2048 ——. Breeds of beef cattle. [By Earl W. Sheets. Issued Jan., 1915;
 revised Nov., 1921]. [Washington, Government printing office, 1921].
 Wrappers. OP.

31 [1] p. illus. 23 cm.
U. S. Dept. of Agriculture *Farmer's Bulletin 612.*

2049 ——. Influence of winter rations on the growth of steers on pasture.
 By E. W. Sheets. . . . Washington, Government printing office, 1921.
 Wrappers. OP.

11 p. diagrs. 23 cm.
U. S. Dept. of Agriculture *Department Circular 166.*

2050 ——. Our beef supply, by E. W. Sheets. . . . [Washington, separate from *Year Book* of Department of Agriculture, 1921]. Cloth. OP.

227–322 [1] p. illus., graphs, maps. 21 cm.
Bulletin 874.

2051 SHEFFY, L. F. The life and times of Timothy Dwight Hobart, 1855–
 1935, by L. F. Sheffy. Canyon, Texas, the Panhandle-Plains Historical

society, 1950. [Typography of Carl Hertzog; printed by Russell stationery co., Amarillo]. Cloth.

6 p.l., 322 p. front. (port.), 8 full-p. plates (incl. front.). 24 cm.
Bibliography, p. [310]–314; index, p. [315]–322.
Half title; map on end papers.

Chapters on the Texas cattle industry and the JA Ranch.

2052 ———. The Spanish horse on the great plains. By L. F. Sheffy. [N.p., n.d.]. Pict. wrappers. (Cover title). OP.

[22] p. (no pagination). 22.4 cm.
Reprinted from *The Panhandle-Plains Historical Review.*

2053 SHELDON, ADDISON ERWIN. History and stories of Nebraska. By Addison Erwin Sheldon, with maps and illustrations. Chicago and Lincoln, the University publishing co., 1913. Cloth. OP.

xvi, 306 p. front., illus., maps, facsms. 19.7 cm.
Glossary, p. 297; index, p. 299–306.
Questions after each chapter.
Republished in 1919 and 1926.

2054 ———. Nebraska old and new. History, stories, folklore, by Addison Erwin Sheldon. . . . Lincoln . . . , the University publishing company, [1937]. Pict. cloth. OP.

x, 470 p. front. (map), illus., ports., maps, facsms., plan. 20.8 cm.
Index, p. 465–470.
Half title; vignette.

2055 [SHELDON, GOV. LIONEL A.]. Report of the Governor of New Mexico made to the Secretary of the Interior for the year 1884. Washington, Government printing office, 1884. Wrappers. Rare.

3–11 p. 23 cm.

2056 SHELLER, ROSCOE. Ben Snipes, northwest cattle king, by Roscoe Sheller. Portland, Ore., Binfords & Mort, publishers, [1957]. Pict. cloth.

4 p.l., 205 p. plates, ports. 22.3 cm.
Appendix, p. 203–205.
"First edition" on copyright p.

2057 SHEPHERD, MAJOR WILLIAM. Prairie experiences in handling cattle and sheep, by Major W. Shepherd; with illustrations from sketches by the author. London, Chapman and Hall, ltd., 1884. Pict. cloth. Scarce.

3 p.l., 266 [1–32] p. front. (with tissue), plates, fold. map. 22.8 cm.
Half title; 32 numbered p. of adv. at end; untrimmed.

American edition published in New York by O. Judd co., 1885.

2058 SHEPLER, C. V. Little gem brand book (continuation of Big Four

Book) for the spring work of 1900. . . . Kansas City, Mo., Little Gem Brand Book co., [printed by the Ackermann-Quigley co.], 1900. Calf. Scarce.

xlviii, 155 p. cattle brands. 17 cm.
Advertisements scattered throughout.

Contains brands of North and South Dakota, Montana, northeastern Colorado, Wyoming, and Nebraska.

2059 SHIEL, ROGER R. "Early to bed and early to rise." "Twenty years in hell with the beef trust." "Facts, not fiction," by Roger R. Shiel. Indianapolis, Indiana, 1909. Cloth. Scarce.

3 p.l., 7–288 p. ports. 19 cm.
Index, p. 287–288.

Letters and speeches protesting the monopoly of the beef trust.

2060 SHIELDS, GEORGE O. Cruising in the Cascades. A narrative of travel, exploration, amateur photography, hunting, and fishing, with special chapters on hunting the grizzly bear, the buffalo, elk, antelope, Rocky Mountain goat, and deer; also on trouting in the Rocky Mountains; on a Montana roundup; life among the cowboys, etc., by G. O. Shields ("Conquina"). . . . Chicago and New York, Rand, McNally & company, publishers, 1889. Pict. cloth. Scarce.

7 p.l., 17–339 [12] p. front., illus. 22 cm.
12 p. adv. at end.

2061 SHINN, CAPT. JONATHAN. Memoirs of Capt. Jonathan Shinn. Greeley, Colo., Weld County, 1890. Wrappers. Rare.

[3]–88 p. 18.3 cm.

2062 SHIPMAN, MRS. O. L. Letters, past and present. . . . By Mrs. O. L. Shipman. [N.p., n.d.]. Stiff wrappers. Scarce.

5 p.l., 9–137 p. ports. 22.8 cm.
Index, p. 131–137.

A series of letters to the author's nieces and nephews containing some material on the cattle ranges of West Texas.

2063 ———. Taming the Big Bend. A history of the extreme western portion of Texas from Ft. Clark to El Paso, by Mrs. O. L. Shipman. [Marfa, Texas, 1926]. Cloth. Scarce.

viii, p. 1 l., [3]–215 p. front. (port. with tissue), plates, ports., large fold. map at end. 23.7 cm.
Index, p. [209]–215.

2064 SHREWDER, DOROTHY BERRYMAN, and MELVILLE CAMPBELL HARPER. Note on early Clark County, Kansas, by the Clark County chapter of the Kansas State Historical Society. Editorial staff Dorothy Berryman Shrewder, Melville Campbell Harper. Volume I, number 1, July, 1939–August, 1940. Reprinted from the Clark County Historical Society column in the Clark County Clipper. Ashland, Kansas, [1941]. Stiff wrappers. Scarce.

4 p.l., 97 p. illus. 21.6 cm.
Index, p. 85–97.

Volume II, August, 1940–September, 1941.

4 p.l., 9–99 p. 21.6 cm.
Index, p. 85–99.

Much on cattle and the cattle trails.

2065 SILLOWAY, PERLEY MILTON. Silloway's history of central Montana. A review of the development of Montana's inland empire. Compiled and edited by P. M. Silloway. Lewistown, Montana, Fergus County Democrat, inc., [1935]. Stiff wrappers. Scarce.

[3]–59 [1] p. port. 23 cm.

Section on open-range cattle.

2066 SILVERSMITH, JULIUS. The new Northwest. Its immense mineral, metallic, and agricultural resources, commerce. . . . The territory of Wyoming. . . . Cheyenne, the "Magic City," &c. by Julius Silversmith. . . . Cheyenne, I. B. Joseph, publisher and bookseller, 1869. Wrappers. (Cover title). Very rare.

72 p. large fold. map in front. 23.3 cm.
5 p. adv. in front, incl. verso front wrapper; last 54 p. adv.; adv. on recto and verso of back wrapper.
Published same year at Omaha, Barkolow bros. and co., in a 32-p. edition.

2067 SIMMONS, FRANK E. History of Coryell County, by Frank E. Simmons. [N.p.], published by Coryell County News, 1936. Stiff wrappers. OP.

3 p.l., [1] p., 2–102 p. 20.2 cm.
Page of errata 3d prelim. leaf.

2068 SIMPSON, CHARLES. El rodeo, one hundred sketches made in the arena during the great international contest (1924). By Charles Simpson. . . . Reproduced in colour and black and white. With an introduction by R. B. Cunninghame Graham and descriptive letterpress by the artist. London, John Lane, the Bodley Head, limited, [1925]. Cloth. Scarce.

x p., 1 l., [3]–174 p. front. (col.), illus. (part col.). 29.6 cm.
Half title; untrimmed.

2069 SIMPSON, S. R. Llano Estacado; or, the plains of West Texas, by S. R.

Simpson. San Antonio, Texas, the Naylor company . . . , [1957].
Pict. cloth.

7 p.l., 41 p. plates, ports. 21.7 cm.
Index, p. 39–41.
Half title.

2070 SIMS, WILLIAM. Kansas: its resources and capabilities, its position, dimensions, and topography. Information relating to vacant lands, agriculture, horticulture, and live stock. . . . Topeka, Kansas, prepared by the State Board of Agriculture, Wm. Sims, secretary. Topeka, Kansas, Kansas publishing house, 1883. Wrappers. Scarce.

60 p. illus., tables. 22.8 cm.

2071 ———. Special report of the Kansas State Board of Agriculture for the information of home-seekers . . . Wm. Sims, secretary. . . . Topeka, Kansas publishing house, 1886. Wrappers. Scarce.

[3]–33 p. tables. 22.8 cm.

2072 SIRINGO, CHARLES A. A cowboy detective. A true story of twenty-two years with a world-famous detective agency; giving the inside facts of the bloody Coeur d'Alene labor riots, and the many ups and downs of the author throughout the United States, Alaska, British Columbia, and Old Mexico. Also exciting scenes among the moonshiners of Kentucky and Virginia, by Charles A. Siringo. . . . Chicago, W. B. Conkey company, 1912. Pict. cloth. Scarce.

5 p.l., 11–519 p. front. (port.), plates (2 double p.), ports. 19.7 cm.
Published same year by J. S. Ogilvie.

Siringo's original title was *Pinkerton's Cowboy Detective,* but the Pinkerton Agency held up publication of the book through court action until he changed the title to *Cowboy Detective,* changed the name of Pinkerton to Dickinson, and substituted other fictitious names. Later, when he sold many of the books himself, he took his pen and wrote in many of the actual names.

2073 ———. Further adventures of a cowboy detective. A true story of twenty-two years with a world-famous detective agency. Giving the inside facts of the bloody Coeur d'Alene labor riots, and the many ups and downs of the author throughout the United States, Alaska, British Columbia, and Old Mexico . . . , by Charles A. Siringo. New York, J. S. Ogilvie publishing co., [1912]. Col. pict. wrappers. Rare.

3 p.l., [247]–519 p. 17.4 cm.
3 p. adv. at end.

When Ogilvie published *Cowboy Detective,* the company retained the title and issued the work in two volumes, this being the second. The two books were paper bound, being numbered 127 and 128 in the Railroad Series. Both of these paper-bound books are exceedingly scarce, though at one time every news-butch carried a plentiful supply.

2074 ———. A Lone Star cowboy, being fifty years' experience in the saddle as cowboy, detective, and New Mexico ranger, on every cow trail in the wooly old West. Also the doings of some "bad" cowboys, such as "Billy the Kid," Wess Harding [*sic*] and "Kid Curry," by Chas. A. Siringo. . . . Santa Fe, New Mexico, 1919. Pict. cloth. OP.

4 p.l., 291 ₁l₁ p.   plates, ports., facsm.   20.5 cm.
1 p. adv. at end.

Like many of the author's books, this one contains many repetitions from his previous volumes. Here the author recalls some incidents not related in his first book. He states in his preface, "This volume is to take the place of *A Texas Cowboy*."

2075 ———. Riata and spurs. The story of a lifetime spent in the saddle as cowboy and detective, by Charles A. Siringo, with an introduction by Gifford Pinchot, and with illustrations.   Boston and New York, Houghton Mifflin company, 1927.   Pict. cloth.   OP.

xiv p., 1 l., 276 p.   front., plates, ports., facsm.   21.2 cm.
Vignette; first edition, "1927" under imprint.
"Certain parts of this book were reprinted, in revised form, from the author's privately printed narratives *Lone Star Cowboy* and *Cowboy Detective*."

The last half of this book was taken from the author's *Cowboy Detective*, with real names used. Again the Pinkertons threatened a lawsuit, so this edition was recalled after release and pages 120 to 268 were removed and other material substituted. All references to the author's experiences with the Pinkerton Agency were deleted and material on bad men substituted. Only a few copies of this edition got out; hence its scarcity.

2076 ———. Riata and spurs. The story of a lifetime spent in the saddle as cowboy and ranger, by Charles A. Siringo, with an introduction by Gifford Pinchot, and with illustrations. Revised edition.   Boston and New York, Houghton Mifflin company, ₁1927₁.   Pict. cloth.   OP.

xiv p., 1 l., 261 p.   front., plates, ports., facsm.   21.2 cm.
Half title; vignette.
"Letters from Gifford Pinchot and Emerson Hough to the author" (1 l. inserted between pages 260 and 261).
Reprinted in 1913 under the imprint of "Riverside Library."

In this edition, issued after the first printing was recalled, the entire last half of the book was changed, but no explanation was made. The author used material on bad men he had intended for another book. Note that the word "ranger" was substituted for "detective" in the title. Also, the first edition has no half title.

2077 ———. A Texas cowboy; or, fifteen years on the hurricane deck of a Spanish pony. Taken from real life, by Charles A. Siringo, an old stove up "cowpuncher," who has spent nearly twenty years on the great western cattle ranges. Chicago, Illinois, M. Umbdenstock & co., publishers, 1885. Pict. cloth. Exceedingly rare.

2 p.l., ₍ix₎–xii, ₍13₎–316 p.   double front. (col.), illus., ports.   20 cm.
Added t.p. illus. in col.; decorated end papers.

Republished in 1886 under the imprint of Siringo and Dobson, with the same title page and with an addendum (p. 317–347), an index to the addendum, and a dedication. The second frontispiece of the first edition is the only frontis in this second printing. This frontispiece was later used as the cover for the paper-back editions of the news-butchers.

This book was reprinted many times between 1914 and 1926 by various publishers, such as the Eagle Publishing Company and Rand, McNally and Company; and finally in a cheap pulp edition by J. S. Ogilvie Publishing Company. It was the first autobiography written by a cowboy and perhaps received wider circulation than any published since; yet it is now next to impossible to locate a copy of the first printing.

It was republished again in 1950:

A Texas cowboy; or, fifteen years on the hurricane deck of a Spanish pony—taken from real life, by Charles A. Siringo. With bibliographical study & introduction by J. Frank Dobie and drawings by Tom Lea. Typography by Carl Hertzog. New York, William Sloane Associates, ₍1950₎. Cloth.

xl p., 1 l., 3–198 p.   illus., facsm.   22 cm.
Half title; illus. double t.p.; headpieces; first edition, pub. device with "WSA" on copyright p.

2078 SKETCHES OF THE Inter-mountain states, together with biographies of many prominent and progressive citizens who have helped in the development and history making of this marvelous region, 1847–1909. Utah, Idaho, Nevada. Illustrated. Salt Lake City, Utah, published by the Salt Lake Tribune, 1909. Limp leather. Rare.

2 p.l., 5–376 p.   front., plates, ports.   28.4 cm.
Index, p. 371–376.
Gilt edges.

2079 SKINNER, C. W. The livestock industry for Wyoming, an industrial study, by C. W. Skinner. Cheyenne, Wyoming, Federal Security Agency . . . , 1939. Pict. wrappers. OP.

9 p.l., 2–115 p.   illus., maps, tables.   26.8 cm.
Bibliography, p. ₍111₎–115.
Mimeoprinted on one side of paper only.

2080 SLOAN, RICHARD E. Memories of an Arizona judge, by Richard E.

Sloan. . . . Stanford University, California, Stanford University press; London, Humphrey Milford, Oxford University press, 1932. Cloth. OP.

xii, 250 p.   20 cm.
Index, p. 247–250.
Half title.

2081 ———. History of Arizona. Hon. Richard E. Sloan, supervising editor, Ward R. Adams, author, assisted by an advisory council. Issued in four volumes, profusely illustrated. Arizona biography by special staff of writers.   Phoenix, Record publishing co., publishers, 1930.   Full leather.   Scarce.

Vol. I: 9 p.l., 21–525 p.   front. (port.), plates, ports., maps, plan.   27.5 cm.
Index, p. 521–525.
Vol. II: 2 p.l., 7–530 p.   front., plates, map, plan.   27.5 cm.
Index, p. 519–523; chronological history, p. 525–530.
Vols. III and IV: biographical.
Device; gilt top.

2082 SLOAN, ROBERT W.   Utah gazetteer and directory of Logan, Ogden, and Salt Lake cities for 1884. Edited and compiled by Robert W. Sloan. Containing a history of Utah, her resources, attractions, statistics, etc. . . . Salt Lake City, Utah, printed for Sloan & Dunbar by the Herald printing and publishing company, 1884.   Cloth.   Rare.

8 p.l., [17]–634 p.   plates, large fold. map (col.) in front, tables (1 fold.).   26.3 cm.
Advertisements scattered throughout.
Errata on last p.

2083 SMALL, FLOYD B.   Autobiography of a pioneer, by Floyd B. Small; being an account of the personal experiences of the author from 1867 to 1916. . . . Seattle, Wash., F. B. Small, 1916.   Stiff pict. wrappers. Scarce.

2 p.l., 7–106 p.   illus.   23.4 cm.

2084 SMART, GEORGE.   Original facts, no fiction. This book a complete story. By George Smart.   Kansas City, Mo., Tiernan-Havers printers, binders, 1892.   Stiff pict. wrappers.   Scarce.

2 p.l., [5]–165 p.   front. (port.).   25.3 cm.

A cowboy's ride to Argentina and back.

2085 SMEAD, WILLIAM HENRY.   Land of the Flatheads. A sketch of the Flathead reservation, Montana, its past and present, its hopes and possibilities for the future. By W. H. Smead. . . .   St. Paul, Minn., Pioneer press, mfg. dept., 1905.   Pict. cloth.   Scarce.

2 p.l., [5]–142 p.   front. (port.), plates, ports., tables.   23 cm.
Last 10 p. adv.

[336]

Also published in 1905 at Missoula, Montana, by the Press of the Daily Missoulian.

144 p. illus., fold. map. 23.5 cm.
Advertising matter, p. 129–144.

2086 SMITH, A. MORTON. The first 100 years in Cooke County, by A. Morton Smith. San Antonio, Texas, the Naylor company, publishers, [1955]. Cloth.

vii p., 8 l., 290 p. illus., plates, ports. 21.6 cm.
Appendix, p. [236]–[247]; bibliography, p. 248–249; index, p. 251–290.
Half title; map on end papers.

Has a chapter on "Cattle Boom Days."

2087 SMITH, ALSON JESSE. Brother Van, a biography of Rev. William Wesley Van Orsdel, by Alson Jesse Smith. New York, Nashville, Abingdon-Cokesbury press, [MCMXLVIII]. Cloth. OP.

6 p.l., 13–240 p. front. (port.), illus., plates, ports. 20.3 cm.
Index, p. 237–240.
Decorative half title; map on end papers; illus. t.p.

2088 SMITH, C. ALPHONSO. O. Henry biography, by C. Alphonso Smith. . . . Illustrated. Garden City, New York, Doubleday, Page & company, 1916. Cloth. OP.

v [1] p., 3 l., 3–258 p. front. (port.), plates, ports., facsm. 24 cm.
Index, p. 253–258.
Half title; pub. device; untrimmed.

Contains a chapter on O. Henry's ranch life in Texas.

2089 SMITH, C. C. Nebraska; a sketch of its history, resources and advantages. Nebraska City, Morning Chronicle print, 1870. Wrappers. Rare.

32 p. 21.6 cm.

2090 SMITH, CLARETA OLMSTEAD. The trail leads west, by Clareta Olmstead Smith. Sketches by Leta May Smith. Philadelphia, Dorrance & company, [1946]. Cloth. OP.

vi, 7–174 p. illus. 19.5 cm.
Pub. device; illus. chapter headings.

Has a chapter on the cattle trails.

2091 [SMITH, ERWIN E.] Pictures of the West which reflect the very spirit of ranch and range life. . . . [Issued by Erwin E. Smith, Bonham, Texas, n.d.]. Pamphlet. (Cover title). Rare.

26 p. plates. 19 cm.

A descriptive catalog of photographs of ranch life taken by Erwin E. Smith, noted for his early-day photographs of ranch life.

2092 SMITH, EUGENE. Pioneer epic, [by] Eugene Smith. Boulder, Colorado, Johnson publishing company, 1951. Pict. boards.

4 p.l., 9–106 p. 21.4 cm.
Half title.

This privately printed little book is about the experiences of Sarah Ann Smith and her family in Colorado during the early days, as told to her son, Eugene Smith. It contains some material on ranching.

2093 SMITH, HARRY H. Beef production in Colorado. [By Harry H. Smith]. Fort Collins, Extension Service Colorado Agricultural and Mechanical College. *Bulletin 389–A,* September, 1946. Pict. wrappers. (Cover title).

38 p. ports. 22.8 cm.
References for further reading, p. 28.

2094 SMITH, HOWARD R. Cattle for the Northwest, by Howard R. Smith. . . . Saint Paul, compliments of the First National Bank, 1916. Limp leather. 3-hole tie.

[58] p. (no pagination). illus. 17 cm.

2095 SMITH, JOSEPH R. Observations on Texas cattle. Age, weight, temperature, liver, and spleen. By Joseph R. Smith. . . . Reprinted from American Health Association reports, 1882. Boston, Press of Rockwell and Churchill, 1883. Wrappers. Scarce.

[3]–14 p. tables. 23.2 cm.
Republished at Concord, N. H., in 1884, printed by the Republican Press association.

2096 SMITH, L. WALDEN. Saddles up, by L. Walden Smith. . . . San Antonio, Texas, the Naylor company, 1937. Pict. cloth.

4 p.l., 276 p. front., plates. 23.5 cm.
Half title; cattle brands at end of each chapter.

2097 SMITH, LAWRENCE BREESE. Dude ranches and ponies, [by] Lawrence B. Smith (Lon Smith). Illustrated with photographs; foreword by Phillip Ashton Rollins. New York, Coward-McCann, 1936. Cloth. OP.

xxvi p., 1 l., 29–288 p. front., illus., plates. 24.2 cm.
Appendix, p. 246–286.
Half title; illus. t.p.

2098 SMITH, MORRIS M. General science of livestock. [By] Morris M. Smith. Boerne, Texas, published by Boerne Star, [1941]. Cloth. OP.

4 p.l., [1] p., 2–381 p. plates. 22.4 cm.
Index, p. 378–381.

2099 SMITH, TEVIS CLYDE, JR. From the memories of men, by T. C. Smith,

Jr., . . . Brownwood, Texas, published by T. C. Smith, Jr., [1954].
Wrappers.

3 p.l., [7]–66 p. 22.7 cm.
Business cards scattered throughout.

2100 ———. Frontier's generation. The pioneer history of Brown County
with sidelights on the surrounding territory, by Tevis Clyde Smith.
Brownwood, Texas, published by the author, [1931]. Stiff wrappers.

4 p.l., [5]–63 p. front. (port.), plates, ports. 22.2 cm.
Adv. scattered throughout.

2101 SMITH, WALLACE. Garden of the sun, by Wallace Smith. A history
of the San Joaquin Valley, 1772–1939. Los Angeles, Calif., Lymanhouse,
[1939]. Cloth. Scarce.

v, 555 p., [i]–iii p. plates, maps, plan. 23.4 cm.
Appendix, p. 541–558; index, p. [i]–iii (at end).
Half title.

2102 SMITH, WALLACE. Oregon sketches, by Wallace Smith. New York
and London, G. P. Putnam's sons, 1925. Cloth. OP.

xii p., 1 l., 3–247 p. front. (with tissue), illus. 22 cm.
Illus. end papers.

This is another Wallace Smith, *not* the author of item No. 2101.

2103 SMYTHE, HENRY. Historical sketch of Parker County and Weatherford, Texas. By H. Smythe. St. Louis, Louis C. Lavat book and job
printer, 1877. Cloth. Rare.

xvi p., (adv.), vii, 476 p. tables. 19.4 cm.
Directory of Weatherford, p. [443]–459; index, p. [461]–476.

2104 SMYTHE, WILLIAM E. The conquest of arid America. (New and revised edition). Illustrated. By William E. Smythe. . . . New York, the
Macmillan company; London, Macmillan & co., ltd., 1905. Cloth. OP.

xxv [1] p. 2 l., 3–360 [1] p. front. (port. with tissue), plates, ports. 21 cm.
Appendix, p. 333–349; index, p. 351–360.
Half title; untrimmed.

Contains some material on the Johnson County War of Wyoming.

2105 SNEDDER, GENEVIA (SISSON). Mountain cattle and frontier people, by
Genevia (Sisson) Snedder, assisted by many of the family group. Stories
of the Snedder family, 1867 to 1947. [Stanford, Stanford University press,
1947]. Pict. cloth. OP.

xiii p., 1 l., 3–158 p. plates, ports., cattle brands. 22.2 cm.
Map on end papers.

2106 [SNELL, JESSIE KENNEDY]. Lore of the great plains, [by Jessie Kennedy

Snell]. Colby Kansas, Colby Free Press-Tribune, publishers, MCMXXXVII]. Stiff wrappers. OP.

2 p.l., 78 [3] p.   21.7 cm.

Has a chapter on the cattle trails from Texas.

2107 SNYDER, A. B., and NELLIE SNYDER YOST. Pinnacle Jake, as told by A. B. Snyder to Nellie Snyder Yost. Illustrated from photographs. Caldwell, Idaho, the Caxton printers, ltd., 1951. Pict. cloth.

8 p.l., [1] p., [18]–252 [1] p.   front. (port.), plates, ports., cattle brands.   23.5 cm.
Half title; map on end papers; vignette.

2108 SONNICHSEN, C. L. Cowboys and cattle kings. Life on the range today, by C. L. Sonnichsen. Norman, University of Oklahoma press, [1950]. Cloth.

xviii p., 2 l., 5–316 p.   plates, ports.   23.5 cm.
"Not in books" (acknowledgments), p. 296–304; index, p. 305–316.
Half title; vignette; "First edition" on copyright p.

2109 ———. I'll die before I'll run. A story of the great feuds of Texas, by C. L. Sonnichsen. New York, Harper & brothers, publishers, [1951]. Cloth.

xviii p., 1 l., 3–294 p.   plates, ports.   21.8 cm.
Resources and notes, p. 267–294.
Half title; illus. map on end papers.

2110 ———. Ten Texas feuds, by C. L. Sonnichsen. Albuquerque, University of New Mexico press, 1957. Pict. cloth.

5 p.l., 3–248 p.   23.7 cm.
Notes and bibliography, p. 217–243; index, p. 244–248.
Half title.

2111 SOUTH DAKOTA. Dakota: how to go and what to do when you get there. Milwaukee, Sentinel co., printers, 1882. Wrappers. Rare.

32 p.   map on back wrapper, tables.   21.5 cm.

The last ten pages are letters from actual settlers. The map shows routes to Deadwood and the Black Hills. There is some information on stock raising.

2112 ———. Development and resources of Beadle County in the state of South Dakota. Its opportunities for investment. . . . [N.p.], published and endorsed by the County Commissioners, 1889. Wrappers. Rare.

2 p.l., [5]–47 p.   illus., map on verso of both front and back wrappers, plat at end.   21.8 cm.

2113 ———. Facts about South Dakota; an official encyclopedia containing useful information in handy form for settlers, homeseekers, and in-

[340]

vestors. . . . Published by the Commissioner of Immigration under authority granted by the State Legislature. . . . Aberdeen, S. D., Aberdeen News company, 1890. Wrappers. Scarce.

2 p.l., [7]–64 p. 21.9 cm.

2114 ——. The fifty-ninth annual stock growers' convention . . . Thursday, Friday, and Saturday, June 1, 2, 3, 1950. Fort Pierre, South Dakota, 1950. Stiff pict. wrappers. Scarce.

3 p.l., 1 p., 8–200 p. plates, ports. 21.6 cm.
Adv. scattered throughout.

2115 ——. Guide to the Black Hills and Centennial mines, by Harte & co., Laramie City, Wyoming. [Laramie Sentinel job print, n.d.]. Wrappers. Rare.

[3]–16 p. 14.6x8.4 cm.

2116 ——. History of the resources and advantages of Hanson County, South Dakota. . . . Alexandria, S. D., Herald printing house, 1893. Wrappers. Rare.

[3]–24 p. illus., fold. map at end. 21.7 cm.

2117 ——. More facts about South Dakota regarding agriculture, sheep raising, climate, soil, and its other resources. Milwaukee, Burdick, Armitage & Allen, printers, [1892]. Wrappers. (Cover title). Rare.

48 p. illus., plates, map on verso of back wrapper, tables. 22.6 cm.
Plate on verso of front wrapper.

2118 ——. Reliable information concerning Hughes County and Pierre, South Dakota, and the great Sioux Reservation. Pierre, 1889. Wrappers. Rare.

[3]–17 [2] p. illus. 21 cm.
Adv. verso both wrappers; adv. verso all pages of text except the last.

2119 ——. Resources of Dakota. An official publication compiled by the Commissioner of Immigration, under authority granted by the Territorial Legislature. . . . Sioux Falls, Dakota, Argus-Leader company, printers, 1887. Wrappers. Scarce.

2 p.l., [7]–498 p. front., illus., plates, map (col.), tables, charts. 21.3 cm.
Index, p. [492]–498.

2120 ——. The southern districts of the Black Hills and their varied resources. Omaha, Nebraska, the Herald job printing rooms, 1889. Wrappers. (Cover title). Scarce.

32 p. illus. 22.3 cm.
Double column.

2121 ——. Southern Dakota, its great opportunities for settlers and in-

vestors. ₁Sioux Falls, Minnehaha Trust company, c.1886₁. Folder.
Exceedingly rare.

4 p. illus. 21 cm.

Only known copy in the Coe Collection, Yale University.

2122 ———. Southern Dakota, the Black Hills, Big Horn and Yellowstone
countries, the richest mineral regions of America. . . . With an appendix
containing the mining laws of the United States and Dakota. Compiled
by an early pioneer. . . . Chicago, Rand, McNally & co., printers, 1875.
Wrappers. (Cover title). Rare.

31 p. illus., maps. 17.4 cm.
Text starts on verso of cover title; adv. recto and verso of back wrapper.

2123 ———. Woonsocket, the gem of the prairie, Sanborn County, the
husbandman's paradise, Dakota. . . . Woonsocket, Dakota, "News" job
printing house, ₁1885₁. Wrappers. Scarce.

₁26₁ p. (no pagination). fold. map. 19.5 cm.
1 p. adv. in front; adv. verso front wrapper; adv. recto and verso back wrapper.

2124 SOUTHWESTERN BRAND BOOK containing the marks and brands of the
cattle and horse raisers of south-western Kansas, the Indian Territory,
and the Panhandle of Texas for the roundup of 1883. Medicine Lodge,
published by Medicine Lodge Cresset, Barbour County Index, 1883.
Calf. Rare.

3–84 p. cattle brands. 15.8 cm.

2125 SOUTHWESTERN TRAILS. Some Southwestern trails ₁by various authors.
Illustrated by Harold Bugbee₁. El Paso, Texas, ₁designed and printed
by₁ Carl Hertzog, 1948. Pict. cloth in slip case. Scarce.

₁25₁ p. (no pagination). 22x28.6 cm.
Maps on margins; illus. t.p.; full-p. illustrations opposite pages of text.

Published in a limited edition, this little book contains short descriptions of
the various trails of the Southwest. Also issued with "Heraldry of the Range"
in sets of twenty specially separately bound in Hereford red "homespun"
cloth with heavy slip case of the same cloth, and autographed by printer and
illustrator.

2126 SPAIGHT, A. W. (COMPILER). The resources, soil, and climate of Texas.
Report of the Commissioner of Insurance, Statistics, and History. A. W.
Spaight, commissioner. Galveston, A. H. Belo & co., printers, 1882.
Cloth. Rare.

x, 360 p. 23.4 cm.

2127 SPARKS, BUREN. Riding herd for the Lord; or, the life story of R. W.

Smith, in two parts. By Buren Sparks. . . . San Antonio, the Naylor co., publishers, 1942. Cloth. OP.

x p., 4 l., 3–130 p. front., plates, ports. 20.8 cm.

2128 SPEER, MARION A. Western trails, [by Marion A. Speer]. [Huntington Beach, Calif., printed by the Huntington Beach News, 1931]. Cloth. OP.

4 p.l., [11]–377 [2] p. plates, ports. 23.6 cm.
Half title only.
Colophon: "This particular volume is one of a limited edition, and is personally inscribed and numbered by the author."

2129 SPENCER, DICK, III. Cow tails and cattle trails, by Dick Spencer, III. Iowa City, Iowa, published by Mercer printing co., [n.d.]. Pict. wrappers.

[20] p. (no pagination). illus. 21.5 cm.
Illus. t.p.
"Cartoons reprinted by permission of *The Cattleman,* Ft. Worth, Texas."

2130 SPENCER, FRANK CLARENCE. Colorado's story, by Frank C. Spencer. . . . Denver, Colorado, the World press, incorporated, [1930]. Cloth. OP.

3 p.l., 249 p. front. (col. flag), illus., plates, ports., map. 20 cm.

Two chapters on ranch and range.

2131 ———. The story of the San Luis Valley, by Frank C. Spencer. Alamosa, Colorado, [printed by Alamosa Journal, 1925]. Stiff pict. wrappers. Pict. label pasted on. OP.

3 p.l., [7]–83 [1] p. 8 plates. 24 cm.

2132 SPIKES, NELLIE WITT. The early days of the south plains, by Nellie Witt Spikes. [N.p., n.d.]. Pict. wrappers. (Cover title). Scarce.

[36] p. (no pagination). 22.7 cm.

2133 ———, and TEMPLE ANN ELLIS. Through the years. A history of Crosby County, Texas, by Nellie Witt Spikes and Temple Ann Ellis. San Antonio, Texas, the Naylor company, [1952]. Cloth.

xxix p., 8 l., 493 p. plates, ports., cattle brands. 23.4 cm.
Index, p. 491–493.
Half title; facsm. of early newspaper on end papers; leaf of errata tipped in.

2134 SPINDLER, WILL HENRY. Bad Lands trails. Range stories of the South Dakota Bad Lands, and an authentic handbook to the Bad Lands. By Will Henry Spindler. . . . Mitchell, South Dakota, published by the Educator Supply company, [1948]. Stiff wrappers. OP.

xxiv, 96 p. plates, ports. 19.2 cm.
The Roman numerals include the first two chapters. Four blank leaves at end.

[343]

2135 ———. Rim of the Sandhills. A true picture of the old Holt County horsethief-vigilante days, by Will Henry Spindler. . . . Mitchell, South Dakota, published by the Educator Supply company, [1941]. Cloth.

7 p.l., [15]–346 p. plates, ports. 19.8 cm.

2136 SPLAWN, ANDREW JACKSON. Ka-Mi-Akin, the last hero of the Yakimas, by A. J. Splawn. [Portland, Oregon, press of Kilham stationery & printing co., 1917]. Cloth. Scarce.

5 p.l., 436 [6] p. front., plates. ports. 23.5 cm.
Last 6 p. biography and eulogy.

Reprinted in 1914 in an edition of 500 pages.

2137 SPLENIC FEVER or black water of Texas. Report of Commissioners on the Texas cattle disease to the Pork Packers' Association of Chicago, October, 1868. Chicago, Prairie Farmer company print, 1868. Sewn. (Cover title). Rare.

[3]–39 p. 23.7 cm.

2138 SPRATT, JOHN S. The road to Spindletop. Economic change in Texas, 1875–1901, by John S. Spratt. Drawings by Ed Beardon. Dallas, Southern Methodist University press, [1955]. Cloth.

xxix p., 1 l., 3–337 p. 23.7 cm.
Appendix, p. 287–302; notes, p. 303–316; bibliography, p. 317–324; index, p. 325–337.
Half title; pub. device.

A chapter entitled "Fencing the Range" deals with the cattle industry and trail drives.

2139 SPRING, AGNES WRIGHT. William Chapin Deming, of Wyoming, pioneer publisher, and state and federal official. A biography, by Agnes Wright Spring. . . . Glendale, Calif., privately printed in a limited edition, by the Arthur H. Clark co., 1944. Cloth. OP.

9 p.l., [21]–531 p. front. (port.), plates, ports., facsms. 24.5 cm.
Appendix, p. [495–511]; index, p. [513]–531.
Half title; device.

2140 ———. The Plains Hotel, Cheyenne, Wyoming. [Compiled by Agnes Wright Spring. Casper, Prairie publishing co., n.d.]. Pict wrappers. Scarce.

[14] p. (no pagination). illus., cattle brands. 20.6x9.6 cm.

This is a collection of cattle brands on display in the lobby of the Plains Hotel, of Cheyenne, Wyoming.

2141 ———. Seventy years, a panoramic history of the Wyoming Stock Growers' Association; interwoven with data relative to the cattle industry in Wyoming, by Agnes Wright Spring. . . . Cheyenne, Wyo., published by Wyoming Stock Growers' association, 1942. Pict. wrappers. Scarce.

4 p.l., 9–273 p. front., plates, ports., facsm., fold. facsm. of page from *Northwestern Livestock Journal,* giving cattle brands at end. 23 cm.
Appendix, p. 239–273.
"First edition" on t.p.

A history of the Wyoming Stock Growers' Association written by an able historian. One hundred copies bound in cloth for libraries. The history of this association has been written every ten years for the past thirty years.

2142 STAHL, F. A. Rolling stones, by F. A. Stahl. Glendale, California, ₁printed by Wetzel publishing co., Los Angeles₁, 1928. Cloth. Scarce.

3 p.l., 9–231 p. 20.5 cm.
Device on t.p.

2143 STALKER, BEN. Life and adventures of "Buckskin Ben" (Ben Stalker), twenty years a cowboy, thirty years a showman, ₁by Ben Stalker₁. ₁Columbus, Ohio, Schmitt printing company, 1906₁. Pict. wrappers. Scarce.

5–31 ₁1₁ p. 2 ports. 20.7 cm.
Vignette.

2144 STAMBAUGH, J. LEE, and LILLIAN J. STAMBAUGH. The lower Rio Grande Valley of Texas, by J. Lee Stambaugh and Lillian J. Stambaugh. . . . San Antonio, the Naylor company, ₁1954₁. Cloth.

xiv p., 6 l., 344 p. plates, ports., maps. 21.5 cm.
Bibliography, p. 320–327; index, p. 329–344.
Half title; map on end papers; double t.p. in red and black; vignette.

Has a chapter on cattle and one on the King Ranch.

2145 STANART, S. H. Colorado brand book and stockgrowers' and breeders' ready reference with index of brands and index of owners, containing all stock brands on record in the office of Secretary of State of Colorado. Denver, Colo., S. H. Stanart, publisher and proprietor, ₁1887₁. Limber cloth. Rare.

3 p.l., 313 ₁7₁ p. 18.6 cm.

2146 STANBERY, LON R. The passing of 3D Ranch, by Lon R. Stanbery. ₁Tulsa, Okla., printed for the author by Geo. W. Henry printing company, n.d., c.1930₁. Pict. cloth. (Cover title). Rare.

92 p. illus., plates, ports. 19.4 cm.

2147 STANLEY, CLARK. The life and adventures of the American cow-boy; life in the far West, by Clark Stanley, better known as the Rattlesnake

King. ₁N.p.₁, published by Clark Stanley, 1897. Pict. wrappers. Scarce.
3 p.l., ₁7₁–39 p. illus., ports. 23.5 cm.
"History of snakes" and "Antidotes for snake bite," p. 32–39; index, 2d prelim. p.
10 p. adv. at end.

Another edition same title, ₁n.p., n.d.₁.
₁78₁ p. (no pagination). illus., plates. 22.2 cm.

2148 ——. True life in the far West, by the American cowboy, Clark
Stanley. Worcester, Mass., published by Clark Stanley by Messenger
printing co., ₁n.d. c.1898₁. Pict. wrappers. Scarce.
2 p.l., ₁5₁–78 ₁2₁ p. front., illus. 22.2 cm.
Vignette.

There is some difference in the illustrations in this and the other printings.
Another edition of this work, with additions, bound with "Something Interesting to Read," ₁by₁ Clark Stanley, the Texas cowboy, 8 numbered pages
plus 23 p. adv. at end.

2149 STANLEY, F. (pseud. of Father Stanley Crocchiola). The grant that
Maxwell bought, by F. Stanley. ₁Denver, Colorado, printed by the
World press, 1952₁. Cloth. Rare.
4 p.l., 236 p. 15 p. plates and ports. at end, fold. map in pocket at end. 28.7 cm.
Bibliography, p. 254–256.
Half title; double column.
Colophon: "Limited edition of The Grant That Maxwell Bought. This book num-
ber —— of an edition limited to two hundred and fifty volumes." (Signed).

This limited edition was immediately sold out and is now very hard to
come by.

2150 Rodeo town (Canadian, Texas). By F. Stanley. ₁Denver, Colo.,
printed by the World press, inc., 1953₁. Cloth.
xii, 418 p. plates, ports. 22.3 cm.
Bibliography, p. 415–418.
Half title.
Colophon: "Only 500 copies of this book being printed, of which this is number ——."

2151 STANTON, GERRITT SMITH. "When the wildwood was in flower." A
narrative covering the fifteen years' experiences of a stockman on the
western plains and his vacation days in the open. By G. Smith Stanton.
. . . New York, J. S. Ogilvie publishing company, ₁1909₁. Cloth.
Scarce.
2 p.l., ₁7₁–130 p. illus., plates, ports. 20 cm.

Republished in 1910 with same imprint.
5 p.l., ₁11₁–123 ₁2₁ p. illus., plates, ports. 20 cm.
2 p. adv. at end.

2152 STEAD, ROBERT JAMES CAMPBELL. The cowpuncher, by Robert J. C. Stead. New York and London, Harper & brothers, [1918]. Cloth. Scarce.

4 p.l., 331 p. front., plates. 19.5 cm.

2153 STEEDMAN, CHARLES JOHN. Bucking the sagebrush; or, the Oregon Trail in the seventies, by Charles J. Steedman. Illustrated by Charles M. Russell. New York and London, G. P. Putnam's sons, 1904. Pict. cloth. Scarce.

ix, 270 p. front. (col. with tissue), illus., plates, ports., large fold. map at end. 21.4 cm.
Untrimmed.

2154 STEELE, JAMES W. Rand, McNally and Company's new overland guide to the Pacific coast, California, Arizona, New Mexico, Colorado, and Kansas, by James W. Steele. Chicago, Rand, McNally and co., publishers, 1888. Cloth. Scarce.

2 p.l., 3–212 p., 1 l. illus., maps (1 fold.). 22 cm.

Contains a chapter on the Texas cowboy.

2155 STEELE, RUFUS. Mustangs of the mesas. A saga of the wild horse, by Rufus Steele. . . . Illustrated. Los Angeles, Calif., published by Mabel Walden Steele (Mrs. Rufus Steele) . . . , [1914]. Cloth. Scarce.

6 p.l., 13–220 p. front. (port.), plates. 21.7 cm.
Half title; illus. end papers.

2156 ———. Scar neck, the adventurous story of a great Nevada mustang, by Rufus Steele; with illustrations by Herbert Stoops. New York and London, Harper & brothers, publishers, 1930. Pict. cloth. OP.

3 p.l., 92 p. front., plates. 17.3 cm.
Half title; illus. end papers.

2157 STEEN, RALPH W. The Texas story, by Ralph W. Steen. Austin, Texas, the Steck co., publishers, [1948]. Cloth. OP.

ix, 451 p. front. (port.), plates, ports., maps. 21.6 cm.
Index, p. 445–451.
Half title.

2158 STEGNER, WALLACE. Mormon country, by Wallace Stegner. Edited by Erskine Caldwell. New York, Duell, Sloan & Pearce, [1942]. Cloth. OP.

x p., 1 l., 3–362 p. 22 cm.
Half title; map on end papers; "First printing" on copyright p.

2159 STEINEL, ALVIN T. History of agriculture in Colorado. A chronological record of progress in the development of general farming, livestock production, and agricultural education and investigation, on the western border of the Great Plains and in the mountains of Colorado, 1858 to 1926. By Alvin T. Steinel. Ft. Collins, published in honor of the 50th anniversary of the admission of Colorado to the Union, by the State Agricultural College, Ft. Collins, August 1, 1926. Cloth. OP.

5 p.l., [11]–659 p. front., plates, ports., tables, facsm. 23.4 cm.
"Books by Faculty Members," p. 646–647; index, p. [649]–659.

Contains a long chapter on the range livestock industry.

2160 STEPHENS, L. Dow. Life sketches of a Jayhawker. By L. Dow Stephens. Actual experiences of a pioneer told by himself in his own way. [N.p.], 1916. Stiff wrappers. Scarce.

2 p.l., [7]–68 p. plates, ports. 23.6 cm.

Some information on driving cattle in California.

2161 STEVANS, CHARLES McCLELLAN. Lucky Ten Bar of Paradise Valley; his humorous, pathetic, and tragic adventures, by C. M. Stevans. The story copiously illustrated by H. S. LeMay. His travels by reproductions from photographs constituting almost a pictorial America. Chicago, Rhodes and McClure publishing co., [1900]. Cloth Scarce.

13 p.l., 17–279 p. front., illus., plates, ports. 20 cm.
Last 34 unnumbered pages plates and advertising matter.

2162 STEVENS, JOHN AUSTIN, JR. The valley of the Rio Grande; its topography and resources. By John Austin Stevens, Jr. . . . . New York, Wm. C. Bryant & co., printers, 1864. Wrappers. Rare.

[3]–33 p. 22.8 cm.

2163 STEVENS, MONTAGUE. Meet Mr. Grizzly. A saga on the passing of the grizzly, by Montague Stevens. Albuquerque, the University of New Mexico press, 1943. Cloth. OP.

x, 281 p. front., plates, ports. 23 cm.
Half title; device.

2164 STEVENS, ROBERT CONWAY. A history of Chandler, Arizona, 1912–1953, by Robert Conway Stevens. Tucson, Arizona, published by University of Arizona press, [1955]. Stiff wrappers.

3 p.l., 7–106 p. plates, facsm., tables. 22.8 cm.
Bibliography, p. 102–106.
University of Arizona *Social Science Bulletin No. 25.*

2165 STEVENS, WALTER BARLOW. Through Texas. A series of interesting letters, by Walter B. Stevens, special correspondent of the St. Louis Globe-

Democrat. Illustrated by Armand Walker. ₁St. Louis₁, 1892. Wrappers. Scarce.

₁5₁–108 p. illus. 21.5 cm.
Double column.
Republished in 1893.

2166 [STEVENSON, GOV. EDWARD A.]. Report of the Governor of Idaho to the Secretary of the Interior, 1886. Washington, Government printing office, 1886. Wrappers. Rare.

3–22 p. 23.2 cm.

2167 [STICKNEY, V. H.]. Theodore Roosevelt, ranchman. An address by Doctor V. H. Stickney, of Dickinson, North Dakota, at the laying of the foundation for the Roosevelt Memorial, at Medora, North Dakota, by the National Editorial Association, July 11, 1922. ₁Pasadena, Calif., Post printing & binding co., 1922₁. Stiff wrappers. (Cover title). OP.

2 p.l., 9–22 p. front. (port.). 22 cm.

2168 STIEL, HENRY (SHORTY). "The life of a frontier builder." Autobiography of Henry (Shorty) Stiel. ₁Salt Lake City, Utah, Utah printing co., 1941₁. Cloth. OP.

3 p.l., ₁7₁–417 p. front. (port.), plates. 20 cm.
Cattle brands on end papers; copyright and publisher's imprint on first flyleaf before title page.

2169 STILGEBOUER, F. G. Nebraska pioneers. The story of sixty-five years of pioneering in southwest Nebraska, 1875–1940, by F. G. Stilgebouer. Grand Rapids, Michigan, Wm. B. Werdmans publishing company, 1944. Cloth. OP.

9 p.l., 21–414 p. plates, ports. 22 cm.

2170 STOCK, A. B. Ranching in the Canadian West. A few hints to would-be stock raisers on the care of cattle, horses, and sheep. By A. B. Stock. London, Adam and Charles Black, 1912. Cloth. Scarce.

x, 84 p. 19.2 cm.
Index, p. 83–84.
Half title.

2171 STOCK, RALPH. The confessions of a tenderfoot, being a true and unvarnished account of his world-wanderings, by Ralph Stock, with illustrations reproduced from photographs by the author. London, Grant Richards, ltd., MDCCCCXIII. Cloth. OP.

6 p.l., 13–260 p. front. (with tissue), plates, ports. 22.8 cm.
Half title; untrimmed.
"Reprinted in part from *The Captain and the Wide World.*"

2172 STOCKER, JOSEPH. Arizona, a guide to easier living, by Joseph Stocker. New York, Harper & brothers, [1955]. Cloth.

vii, 216 p. fold. map. 21.2 cm.
Appendix (bibliography), p. 206–208; index, p. 209–216.
Half title; "First edition" on copyright p.; untrimmed.

2173 STOCK OWNER'S GUIDE Appliances and improvements. Sydney, Melbourne, London, published by the Pastoralist's Review proprietary, ltd., 1912. Cloth. Scarce.

viii, 252 p. plates, diagrs. (2 fold.), tables. 24.3 cm.
22 p. adv. at end.

2174 STOKES, WILL E. Episodes of early days in central and western Kansas. By Will E. Stokes. Illustrated by Charles Allen. Vol. I [only volume published]. Great Bend, Kansas, published by Will E. Stokes, [Printed by the McCormick-Armstrong press, Wichita, Kansas, 1926]. Pict. cloth. OP.

4 p.l., [9]–197 p. front. (port.), illus. 20 cm.
Half title; illus. chapter headings.

2175 STONE, WILLIAM HALE. Twenty-four years a cowboy and ranchman in southern Texas and Old Mexico; desperate fights with the Indians and Mexicans, by Will Hale [pseud.]. Illustrated. Hedrick, O. T., published by W. H. Stone, [1905]. Stiff wrappers. Extremely rare.

1 p.l., 5–268 p. illus. 19 cm.
Reprinted 1959 by the University of Oklahoma press.

A copy of this book in the Phillips Collection of the University of Oklahoma Library has a full-page advertisement on the back leaf stating that the book was printed and bound by the Henneberry Company of Chicago. This advertisement reads as follows: "We will send this book prepaid on the receipt of 75¢. We want someone to sell our books in every small town. Write at once for our offer. W. H. Stone, Agent, Southwestern Branch, Hedrick, O.T. Printed and Bound by The Henneberry Co., Chicago."

2176 STONG, PHILIP DUFFIELD. Horses and Americans, by Phil Stong; with frontispiece in color and one hundred and three illustrations from old prints and photographs. End paper and chapter heads by Kurt Wiese. New York, Frederick A. Stokes company, MCMXXXIX. Cloth. OP.

xx p., 1 l., 3–333 p. front. (col. with tissue), illus., plates, ports. 26.4 cm.
Bibliography, p. 317–328; index, p. 329–333.
Half title; illus. end papers; illus. chapter headings; illus. title label pasted on; signature of author in facsm.; vignette.
Colophon: "Author's autograph edition . . . printed on all rag paper and . . . limited to 500 copies. . . ."
Published also in trade edition same year and later reprinted.

Twenty-four Years a Cowboy and Ranchman

In Southern Texas and Old Mexico

Desperate Fights with the Indians and Mexicans

By
WILL HALE

ILLUSTRATED

Published by
W. H. STONE, · HEDRICK, O. T.

2177 STORK, B. C. Pioneer days in Montana, by B. C. Stork.... New York, Pageant press, [1952]. Cloth.

vi p., 4 l., 67 p. illus., plates. 21 cm.
Half title; "First edition" on copyright p.

2178 STOUT, TOM (ED.). Montana, its story and biography. A history of aboriginal and territorial Montana and three decades of statehood. Under the editorial supervision of Tom Stout. Chicago and New York, the American Historical society, 1921. Full leather. Pub. in 3 vols. Scarce.

Vol. I: xlix, 894 p. front. (port.), plates, ports. 27 cm.
Vols. II and III: biographical.

2179 STOVER, ELIZABETH MATCHETT (ED.). Son-of-a-gun stew; a sampling of the Southwest, edited by Elizabeth Matchett Stover; foreword by John William Rogers; illustrations by Harold D. Bugbee. [Dallas], University Press at Dallas, Southern Methodist University, 1945. Cloth. OP.

x p., 1 l., 216 p. illus. 21.5 cm.
Half title; illus. double t.p.
Also published in wrappers; later reprinted by Grossett and Dunlap.

This is an anthology of the best articles published in *The Southwest Review* up to 1945, representing a thirty years' file. It was published to commemorate the first Southwest Book Fair held in Dallas in 1945.

2180 STRAHORN, CARRIE ADELL. Fifteen thousand miles by stage. A woman's unique experience during thirty years of path finding and pioneering from the Missouri to the Pacific and from Alaska to Mexico, by Carrie Adell Strahorn. With 350 illustrations from drawings by Charles M. Russell and others, and from photographs. New York, London, G. P. Putnam's sons, 1911. Cloth. Pict. label pasted on. Scarce.

xxv p., 1 l., 673 p. front. (port. with tissue), illus., plates (4 col. with tissues), ports. 23.2 cm.
Title page in red and black.
Reprinted with same collation in 1915.

2181 STRAHORN, ROBERT E. ("ALTER EGO"). The hand-book of Wyoming and guide to the Black Hills and Big Horn regions for citizen, emigrant, and tourist. By Robert E. Strahorn. Cheyenne, Wyoming, [press of Knight and Leonard, Chicago], 1877. Cloth. Scarce.

vi p., 1 l., [9]–272 p. illus., plates, tables. 23.5 cm.
Last 22 p. adv.; published in both cloth and wrappers.

2182 ———. Montana and Yellowstone National Park. Facts and experiences on the farming, stock raising, mining, lumbering, and other industries of Montana. . . . By Robert E. Strahorn. Kansas City, Ramsey, Millet & Hudson, 1881. Cloth. Scarce.

2 p.l., ₁₅₁–191 ₁13₁ p. front., plates, tables. 22.2 cm.
13 p. adv. at end.

2183 ———. The resources and attractions of Idaho Territory. Facts regarding climate, soil, minerals, agricultural and grazing lands. . . . By Robert E. Strahorn. . . . Published and circulated by direction of the Idaho Legislature. Special act of the Eleventh Session. Boise City, Idaho, 1881. Stiff pict. wrappers. Scarce.

1 p.l., ₁3₁–88 ₁8₁ p. illus., plates, fold. map in front, tables. 23.3 cm.
Last 8 p. adv.

2184 ———. The resources of Montana Territory and attractions of Yellowstone National Park. Facts and experiences on the farming, stock raising, mining, lumbering, and other industries of Montana, and notes on the climate, scenery, game, fish, and mineral springs, with full and reliable data on routes, distances, rates of fare, expenses of living, wages, school and church privileges, society, means of acquiring homes, and other valuable and reliable information applicable to the wants of the capitalist, homeseeker, or tourist. By Robert E. Strahorn. Published and circulated by direction of the Montana Legislature. Special act of the Eleventh Session. Helena, Montana, 1879. Stiff wrappers. Scarce.

₁3₁–77₁3₁ p. front. (map), illus., plates. 22.8 cm.
3 p. adv. at end and recto back wrapper.

2185 ———. To the Rockies and beyond; or, a summer on the Union Pacific Railway and branches. Saunterings in the popular health, pleasure, and hunting resorts of Nebraska, Dakota, Wyoming, Colorado, New Mexico, Utah, Idaho, Oregon, Washington, and Montana. . . . By Robert E. Strahorn. Omaha, the New West publishing co., Omaha Republican print, 1878. Pict. wrappers. Scarce.

3 p.l., ₁5₁–141 ₁2₁ p. illus., plates, large fold. map in front, tables. 22.2 cm.
Adv. scattered throughout; in some copies the map is placed at the end.

Revised and enlarged in 1879, and republished same year with different arrangement of illustrations, lacking the plates and having but one map.

2186 STRALEY, W. Pioneer sketches of Nebraska and Texas, ₁by W. Straley₁. Hico, Texas, Hico printing co., 1915. Wrappers. OP.

3 p.l., 58 p. front., illus., plates, ports. 21.8 cm.

The first part (p. ₁1₁–21) includes sketches of pioneer life in Nebraska County, Nebraska.

2187 STREET, GEORGE G. Che! Wah! Wah! or the modern Montezuma in Mexico. By George G. Street. . . . Illustrated with photographs taken during the trip by C. D. Cleveland and woodcuts from the sketches made by the author. Rochester, N. Y., E. R. Andrews, printer and bookbinder, 1883. Pict. cloth. Scarce.

2 p.l., [5]–115 p. front. (with tissue), illus. (photographs tipped in), fold. map. 26.2 cm.

Has a chapter on cowboys.

2188 STREETER, FLOYD BENJAMIN. The Kaw; the heart of a nation, by Floyd Benjamin Streeter; illustrated by Isabel Bate and Harold Black. New York, Toronto, Farrar & Rinehart, inc., [1941]. Cloth. OP.

ix [1] p., 1 l., 3–371 p. illus., map. 21 cm.
Acknowledgments, p. 351–352; bibliography, p. 353–359; index, p. 261–371.
Half title; illus. t.p.; illus. end papers; first edition, letter "FR" in device on copyright p.
Rivers of America Series.

2189 ———. Prairie trails & cow towns, [by] Floyd Benjamin Streeter; with illustrations from old prints. Boston, Chapman & Grimes, [1936]. Cloth. OP.

5 p.l., 11–236 p. front., plates, ports. 20.8 cm.
Notes (bibliographical), p. 219–225; index, p. 227–232.
Vignette; untrimmed.

2190 ———. Tragedies of a Kansas cow town, by F. B. Streeter. Reprint from *The Aerend,* Vol. V, Nos. 2 and 3 (Spring and Summer, 1934), published quarterly by the faculty of the Fort Hays Kansas State College, [n.d., c.1934]. Wrappers. (Cover title). Scarce.

p. 81–162. 23 cm.

2191 STRONG, HENRY W. My frontier days & Indian fights on the plains of Texas. By Henry W. Strong. [N.p., n.d., c.1926]. Pict. wrappers. (Cover title). Scarce.

122 p. 1 l. port. 22 cm.

2192 STRONG, JOHN KENDRICK. Sagebrush circuit. [By] Kendrick Strong. New York, the Macmillan company, 1950. Pict. cloth.

ix, 194 p. 20.8 cm.
Half title.

2193 STROUD, JOSEPH G. Memories of old western trails in Texas longhorn days, by Joseph G. Stroud; a tale of the West that was in the days when the trail herds came from the Panhandle to the Little Missouri country through the West's great pasture in the days of the open range. . . . [Williston, N. D., printed by the Interstate press, 1932]. Stiff pict. wrappers. OP.

3 p.l., 93 [3] p. illus., plates. 22.7 cm.

2194 STUART, MRS. A. H. H. Washington Territory; its soil, climate, productions, and general resources, compiled by Mrs. A. H. H. Stuart. . . . Published by authority of the Legislature. Olympia, printed at the office of the Washington Standard, 1875. Wrappers. Rare.

iv, [5]–61 p. 21.8 cm.

2195 STUART, GRANVILLE. Forty years on the frontier as seen in the journals and reminiscences of Granville Stuart, gold-miner, trader, merchant, rancher and politician; edited by Paul C. Phillips. Cleveland, the Arthur H. Clark company, 1925. Cloth. Pub. in 2 vols.

Vol. I: 10 p.l., [23]–272 p. front. (port. with tissue), plates. 24.4 cm.
Vol. II: 5 p.l., [13]–265 p. front. (with tissue), plates. 24.4 cm.
Index, p. [243]–265 (Vol. II).
Half title: "Northwest Historical Series II"; pub. device; untrimmed; gilt top.

Written by a well-educated and influential pioneer of early Montana, this work contains much valuable history and tells many of the author's experiences in the cattle business.

2196 SULLIVAN, FRANK S. A history of Meade County, Kansas. By Frank S. Sullivan. Topeka, Kansas, Crane & company, printers, binders, publishers, 1916. Cloth. OP.

6 p.l., 13–184 p. plates, ports., tables. 23.2 cm.

2197 SULLIVAN, JOHN H. Broncho John writes a letter of his first trip up the trail and sends copies of war credentials to Theodore Roosevelt, president of all the United States. [N.p. (? Valparaiso, Ind.), 1905]. Wrappers. (Cover title). Rare.

31 [1] p. port. 21.5 cm.

2198 ———. First trip up the trails, by Broncho John. . . . [Valparaiso, Ind., 1900]. Pict. wrappers. Rare.

[3]–24 p. illus. 19 cm.
Cover title: "Life and Adventures of Broncho John. His First Trip Up the Trail."

2199 ———. Life and adventures of Broncho John. His second trip up the trail, by himself. [N.p., n.d.]. Pict. wrappers. (Cover title). Scarce.

[3]–32 p. illus. 19.4 cm.

2200 ———. Life and adventures of a genuine cowboy, by Broncho John. . . . [N.p., 1900]. Wrappers. (Cover title). Rare.

36 p. illus. 18 cm.
Republished in an edition of 24 pages in 1908.

These emphemeral little tracts were originally intended to be the basis of a larger work never written.

2201   SULLIVAN, W. JOHN L.   Twelve years in the saddle for law and order on the frontiers of Texas, by Sergeant W. J. L. Sullivan, Texas Ranger, Co. B, Frontier Battalion.   Austin, von Boeckmann-Jones co., printers, 1909.   Cloth.   Port. pasted on.   Rare.

4 p.l., [3]–284 p.   front., plates, ports.   21 cm.
Errata on verso of 3d prelim. leaf.

2202   SUNDAY, EDWARD.   A line rider in the Cherokee Nation, by Edward Sunday. Edited and introduction by Ellsworth Collings.   [Tulsa, Standard printing company, c.1942].   Stiff pict. wrappers.   Scarce.

4 p.l., [1] p., [12]–87 p.   front. (port.), illus., plates, ports.   21.8 cm.
Table of contents precedes t.p.

2203   [SUNDAY, WILLIAM E.].   Gah dah gwa stee [by W. E. Sunday]. [Pryor, Okla., printed by Byron Smith, 1953].   Cloth.   Scarce.

4 p.l., 172 p.   plates, ports., map, cattle brands.   24 cm.

2204   SUTLEY, ZACHARY TAYLOR.   The last frontier, by Zach T. Sutley.   New York, the Macmillan company, MCMXXX.   Cloth.   Scarce.

vi p., 2 l., 350 p.   fold. map.   22.5 cm.
Half title; untrimmed.

Contains a chapter on the trail, but is a most unreliable book.

2205   SWAN, OLIVER G. (ED.).   Frontier days, edited by Oliver G. Swan. Philadelphia, Macrae-Smith company, publishers, [1928].   Pict. cloth. OP.

6 p.l., 13–512 p.   front. (col.), illus., 12 col. plates (incl. front.).   24.8 cm.
Illus. end papers (col.); illus. t.p.
On spine, "The Romance of American History."
Also published in a de luxe edition and boxed. Reprinted by Grossett and Dunlap under the title *Covered Wagon Days*.

2206   SWAN LAND AND CATTLE COMPANY, LTD.   First general meeting 30th July, 1883.   [Edinburgh, (Scotland), 1883].   Pamphlet.   (Cover title).   Rare.

15 p.   21.5 cm.

2207   ——.   Incorporated 30th March, 1883.   Memorandum and articles of association.   Edinburgh, printed by Burmess and co., printers to Her Majesty, [1883].   Wrappers.   Rare.

28 p.   24.7 cm.

2208   ——.   Joint report to the directors by George Prentice and Finlay Dun.   [N.p.], 1884.   Wrappers.   Cover title).   Rare.

31 p.   21.5 cm.
Appendix, p. 3–31.

2209 ———. List of shareholders as at 18th April, 1883. ₁N.p.₁, 1883.
Wrappers. Rare.
19 p. 22.2 cm.
Double column.

2210 ———. Report of the directors by the chairman, Mr. Colin J. Mac-
kenzie, of Portmore. ₁N.p.₁, 1883. Wrappers. (Cover title). Rare.
31 ₁1₁ p. 21.5 cm.

2211 ———. Report to the directors by the chairman, Mr. Colin J. Mac-
kenzie, of Portmore, ₁N.p.₁, 1884. Wrappers. (Cover title). Rare.
30 p. 21.5 cm.

2212 ———. Report to the directors by the secretary, Mr. Finlay Dun.
₁N.p.₁, 1884. Wrappers. (Cover title). Rare.
24 p. 21.5 cm.

2213 ———. Report of the first annual meeting, 2nd April, 1884. ₁Edinburgh, 1884₁. Wrappers. (Cover title). Rare.
15 p. 21.5 cm.

2214 ———. Report of the fourth annual meeting, 17th March, 1887.
₁Edinburgh, printed by Charles Gibson, 1887₁. Wrappers. (Cover
title). Rare.
20 p. 21.5 cm.

2215 ———. Supreme court of the United States, October term, A.D. 1892,
No. 150. The Swan Land and Cattle Company versus Joseph Frank,
et al. Brief and argument for appellant. Chicago, Barnard and Gun-
throp, law printers, 1892. Wrappers. Rare.
57 p. 21.7 cm.

2216 SWANSON, HARRY R. Official brand book of the state of Nebraska.
This book is intended as a complete transcript of all the live stock
brands and marks of record in the office of the Secretary of State at
Lincoln, January 1st, 1934. Lincoln, Nebraska, Harry S. Swanson, 1934.
Cloth. Scarce.
2 p.l., 308 p. cattle brands. 20.8 cm.
Index, p. 218–283; last 7 p. blank for memoranda.

2217 SWEET, ALEXANDER ESWIN, and J. ARMORY KNOX. On a Mexican mustang through Texas, from the Gulf to the Rio Grande. By Alex E. Sweet
and J. Armory Knox. . . . Illustrated. Hartford, Conn., S. S. Scranton
& company . . . , 1883. Pict. cloth. Scarce.
7 p.l., 15–672 p. front., illus., plates, facsms. 22.8 cm.
Headpieces; tailpieces.
Republished in London by Chatto and Windus, 1884, and reprinted in 1905.

2218 ———. Sketches from "Texas siftings," by Sweet and Knox. Illustrated by W. H. Caskie. New York and Chicago, J. S. Ogilvie, publisher, [1882]. Cloth. Scarce.

viii, [9]–228 p. illus. 19 cm.

2219 SWEET, GEORGE H. Texas: her early history, climate, soil, and material resources, with sketches of eastern, central, and western Texas, principal counties and cities. . . . By George H. Sweet, of Texas. New York, E. O'Keefe, printer and stationer, 1871. Wrappers. Rare.

[3]–160 p. 19.2 cm.
Last 7 p. adv.; adv. verso front wrapper; adv. recto and verso back wrapper.

2220 SWEETMAN, LUKE D. Back trailing on open range. By Luke D. Sweetman. Illustrated by L. D. Cram. Caldwell, Idaho, the Caxton printers, ltd., 1951. Pict. cloth.

6 p.l., 13–248 p. front. (col.), illus., map. 23.5 cm.
Half title; illus. end papers; illus. t.p.; illus. chapter headings.

2221 ———. A story of a cow horse, Gotch, [by] Luke D. Sweetman; illustrated by L. D. Cram. Caldwell, Idaho, the Caxton printers, ltd., 1936. Pict. cloth. OP.

6 p.l., 11–318 p. front. (col. with tissue), illus., plates. 19.5 cm.
Half title; cattle brands on end papers.
Cover title: "Gotch, the Story of a Horse."

2222 SWIFT, HELEN. My father and my mother, by Helen Swift. Chicago, privately printed, 1937. Morocco in slip case. Scarce.

xii, p., 1 l., 167 p. front. (port., col., with tissue), plates, ports. 23.8 cm.
Half title; untrimmed.

Has some cattle material.

2223 SWIFT, KAY. Who could ask for anything more? By Kay Swift. Illustrated by Julian Brazelton. New York, Simon and Schuster, 1943. Pict. cloth. Scarce.

2 p.l., 211 p. illus. 20.8 cm.
Illus. t.p.; untrimmed.

2224 SWIFT, LOUIS F. The Yankee of the Yards. The biography of Gustavus Franklin Swift. By Louis F. Swift in collaboration with Arthur van Vlissingen, Jr. Chicago and New York, A. W. Shaw and co. . . . , 1927. Pict. cloth. OP.

viii p., 2 l., 3–218 p. illus., plates, ports. 23.5 cm.
Index, p. 213–218.

2225 SWISHER, JAMES. How I know; or, sixteen years' eventful experience. An authentic narrative, embracing a brief record of serious and severe service on the battle fields of the South; a detailed account of hazardous enterprises . . . on the western frontier. . . . By James Swisher. Illustrated. Cincinnati, Ohio, published by the author, 1880. Dec. cloth. Scarce.

x, [11]-384 p. front. (port. with tissue), illus., ports. 21.5 cm.

Contains a chapter on stock raising and the cowboy.

2226 SYKES, GODFREY. A westerly trend, being a veracious chronicle of more than sixty years of joyous wanderings, mainly in search of space and sunshine, by Godfrey Sykes, F.R.G.S. Tucson, Arizona Pioneers Historical society, 1944. Pict. cloth. OP.

xiv p., 1 l., 325 [1] p. illus., plates, ports. 23.5 cm.
Half title; illus. double t.p.

2227 TAIT, J. L. A six-months exploration of the state of Texas; giving an account of its climate, productions, and mineral resources. By J. L. Tait. . . . London, published at the "Anglo-American Times" press, 1878. Wrappers. (Cover title). Rare.

31 p. 21 cm.

2228 TAIT, JAMES SELWICK. The cattle-fields of the far West; their present and future. By J. S. Tait. . . . Edinburgh & London, William Blackwood & sons, MDCCCLXXXIV. Stiff pict. wrappers. Scarce.

4 p.l., [9]-71 [2] p. 21.8 cm.
2 p. adv., at end.

The cattle business from an investor's point of view.

2229 TALBOT, ETHELBERT. My people of the plains, by the Right Reverend Ethelbert Talbot . . . Bishop of Central Pennsylvania. . . . Illustrated. New York and London, Harper & brothers, publishers, MCMVI. Cloth. Scarce.

x [1] p., 1 l., 264 [1] p. front. (port. with tissue), plates, ports. 21.2 cm.
Pub. device; untrimmed.

2230 TALBOT, MURRELL WILLIAMS. Indications of southwestern range conditions. [By M. W. Talbot . . .]. Washington, U. S. Government printing office, 1937. Wrappers. OP.

ii, 35 p. illus. 23 cm.
U. S. Dept. of Agriculture *Farmer's Bulletin No. 1783.*

2231 ———. Range watering places in the Southwest, by M. W. Talbot. U. S. Department of Agriculture *Bulletin 1358.* Washington, Government printing office, 1926. Wrappers. (Cover title). OP.

44 p. 23 cm.

2232 TALLENT, ANNIE D. The Black Hills; or, the last hunting ground of the Dakotahs. A complete history of the Black Hills of Dakota from their first invasion in 1874 to the present time, comprising a comprehensive account of how they lost them; of numerous adventures of the early settlers; their heroic struggles for supremacy against the hostile Dakotah tribes, and their final victory; the opening of the country to white settlement, and its subsequent development, by Annie D. Tallent. St. Louis, Nixon-Jones printing co., 1899. Cloth. Scarce.

xxii, 713 p. front. (port. with tissue), illus., plates, ports. 23.6 cm. Tailpieces.

2233 TARG, WILLIAM (ED.). The great American West. A treasury of stories, legends, narratives, songs, and ballads of western America, edited with an introduction by William Targ. Cleveland and New York, the World publishing company, [1946]. Pict. cloth. OP.

xii p., 1 l., 3–595 p. 21.8 cm.
Glossary of western words, p. 587–591; acknowledgments, p. 593–595.
Half title: "Tales and Legends"; vignette.

2234 TAYLOR, DREW KIRKSEY. Taylor's thrilling tales of Texas, being the experiences of Drew Kirksey Taylor, ex-Texas Ranger and peace officer on the border of Texas. Written by himself and narrating true incidents of frontier life. [San Antonio, Guaranty Bond printing co.], 1926. Stiff wrappers. OP.

2 p.l., 7–93 p. front. (port. with tissue), illus. 22 cm.

2235 TAYLOR, NAT M. A brief history of Roger Mills County, By Nat M. Taylor. [N.p., n.d.]. Cloth. (Cover title). Scarce.

2 p.l., 5–64 p. front. (port.), plates. 21.7 cm.

2236 TAYLOR, THOMAS ULVAN. The Chisholm Trail and other routes, by T. U. Taylor. San Antonio, Texas, printed for Frontier Times by the Naylor company, 1936. Cloth. Scarce.

xi, 222 p. front. (map), ports., maps. 19.7 cm.
Index, p. 189–194; appendix, p. 195–222.
Half title.

2237 ———. Jesse Chisholm, by T. U. Taylor. . . . Bandera, Texas, Frontier Times, [1939]. Cloth. Scarce.

xix p., 1 l., 217 p. front. (port.), plates, ports., maps, facsm. 19.5 cm.
Index, p. 203–217.
Half title.

The story of the man who blazed the Chisholm Trail; also information on John Chisum and his antecedents.

2238 TEICHERT, MINERVA KOHLHEPP. Drowned memories, by Minerva

Kohlhepp Teighert. ₍Salt Lake City, Deseret News, 1926₎. Stiff pict. wrappers. 2-hole ribbon tie. Scarce.

2 p.l., ₍7₎-37 ₍2₎ p. illus., plates. 22.8 cm.

2239 [TELLER, H. M.]. Letter from the Secretary of the Interior transmitting, in compliance with Senate resolution of December 4, 1883, copies of documents and correspondence relating to leases of lands in the Indian Territory to citizens of the United States for cattle grazing and other purposes. ₍Washington, Government printing office, 1884₎. Sewn. (Caption title). Rare.

160 p. fold. diagr., 2 fold. maps. 23x14.5 cm.
48 Cong., 1 sess., *Senate Ex. Doc. No. 54.*

Seen in the Rollins Collection, Princeton University.

2240 TERRELL, A. W. Speech of Hon. A. W. Terrell delivered in the Senate of Texas, January 21, 1884, on Senate Bill No. 2, entitled "An act to regulate the grazing of stock in Texas, and to prescribe and provide penalties for its violation." Reported by Thos. H. Wheless. Austin, E. W. Swindells, state printer, 1884. Wrappers. Rare.

₍3₎-24 p. 23.2 cm.

Also deals with fence cutting.

2241 TERRELL, CHARLES VERNON. The Terrells. Eighty-five years Texas from Indians to atomic bomb . . . , ₍by₎ C. V. Terrell. Austin, Texas, ₍privately printed, 1948₎. Fabricoid. OP.

6 p.l., 13-336 p. plates, ports. 23.3 cm.
Vignette.

2242 TERRY, CLEO TOM, and OSIE WILSON. The rawhide tree. The story of Florence Reynolds in rodeo, by Cleo Tom Terry and Osie Wilson. ₍Clarendon, Texas₎, Clarendon press, 1957. Cloth.

xiii, 259 p. illus., plates, port. 22.3 cm.
Half title; illus. t.p.; "First edition" on copyright p.
Also published in wrappers.

2243 TEWKSBURY, G. E. The Kansas picture book. By G. E. Tewksbury. Topeka, Kan., A. S. Johnson, ₍Press of Knight and Leonard, Chicago₎, 1883. Pict. col. wrappers. Scarce.

3 p.l., 7-111 p. illus., plates, map, tables. 24.2 cm.

2244 TEXAS. Agricultural resources of the Texas Pan Handle country on the line of the Texas Pan Handle route. ₍N.p., n.d.₎. Pict. wrappers. Rare.

₍3₎-44 ₍1₎ p. fold. map (col.), in front. 18.2 cm.

2245 ———. Brief description of western Texas, together with a report of the third annual fair of the Agricultural, Stockraising, and Industrial Association, held at San Antonio. San Antonio, Texas, Herald steam job printing house and book bindery, 1872. Wrappers. Rare.
60 p. 22.7 cm.

2246 ———. Brief No. 466. Cattle Raisers' Association of Texas, complainant, and the Chicago Livestock Exchange, Intervener vs. Chicago, Burlington & Quincy Railroad Company, et al. Stapled. (Caption title). Rare.
2 p. 24 cm.

2247 ———. Brief No. 732. The Cattle Raisers' Association of Texas vs. Missouri, Kansas and Texas Railway Company, et al. . . . . ₁N.p., n.d.₁.
4 p. 23.5 cm.

2248 ———. Bulletin of the Agricultural and Mechanical College of Texas. Dedication of the animal industries building as a memorial to the pioneer livestock men of Texas. College Station, Texas . . . Feb. 1, 1937. Wrappers. OP.
2 p.l., 5–30 p. front. 23 cm.
Fourth Series, Vol. VIII, No. 2.

2249 ———. Charter and by-laws of the Pecos Land and Cattle Company of Texas. Exeter, N. H., printed by William B. Morrill, 1886. Pict. wrappers. Rare.
₁3₁–14 p., 1 l. 19.9 cm.
Illus. t.p.

2250 ———. The city and county of El Paso, Texas, containing useful and reliable information concerning the future great metropolis of the Southwest. Its resources and advantages for the agriculturist, artisan, and capitalist. El Paso, Texas, Times publishing co., 1886. Wrappers. Scarce.
2 p.l., 5–84 p. large fold. map at end. 21.7 cm.

Has a section on cattle raising.

2251 ———. Constitution of the Central Wire Fence Protective Association. Organized April the 28th, 1888, at Meridian, Texas. Meridian, Texas, Bosque Citizen printing house, ₁1888₁. Pamphlet. Rare.
4 ₁1₁ p. 19.5 cm.

2252 ———. Four score years in Jack County. ₁N.p., n.d., c.1940₁. Stiff pict. wrappers. (Cover title). Scarce.
3–34 p. illus., ports. 28.6 cm.
Double and triple column; advertisements scattered throughout.

2253 ———. Hand-book of northern Texas. Chicago, G. S. Burch publishing co., 1886. Wrappers. Scarce.

28 ₍2₎ p. illus., map on verso of back wrapper. 23.5 cm.
Triple column.

2254 ———. History of the cattlemen of Texas. A brief résumé of the livestock industry of the Southwest and a biographical sketch of the important characters whose lives are interwoven therein. Illustrated. Dallas, compiled and published by the Johnson printing and advertising co., 1914. Imt. leather. Exceedingly rare.

6 p.l., 15–327 p., 1 l. front. (col.), plates, ports. 27 cm.
Half title.

2255 ———. A history of Collingsworth County and other stories, by the staff of the Wellington Leader. Wellington, Leader printing co., inc., 1925. Cloth. Scarce.

xxii p., 1 l., 3–234 p. front., illus., plates, ports. 18.3 cm.
Half title; 4 p. adv. in front; last 36 p. adv. and adv. scattered throughout.
Also published in stiff pict. wrappers.

2256 ———. History of Winkler County, by Wink Wednesday Study Club. Wink, Texas, printed at the Wink Bulletin, 1942. Stiff wrappers. Scarce.

52 p. illus., plates, ports. 22.2 cm.

2257 ———. The home for the emigrant, Texas; her vast extent of territory, fertility of soil, diversity of productions, geniality of climate, and the facilities she affords emigrants for acquiring homes. . . . Austin, Institution for Deaf and Dumb, 1877. Wrappers. Rare.

₍5₎–36 p. 22.8 cm.

2258 ———. Inter-state convention of cattlemen. Papers relating to a proposed system of bureaus for information and statistics in live stock, together with an argument showing that there has been no overproduction in cattle, but every indication points to an alarming shortage. ₍San Angelo, Texas₎, San Angelo Standard print, ₍1892₎. Wrappers. Scarce.

14 p. tables. 23.5 cm.

2259 ———. Notes on Texas and the Texas and Pacific Railway. Compiled from official and other authentic data. Philadelphia, ₍Ringwalt & Brown, prs.₎, 1873. Wrappers. Rare.

3–48 p. large fold. map (col.) in front. 23 cm.
Adv. verso front wrapper; adv. recto and verso back wrapper.

2260 ———. 100 years of ranching. King Ranch, sponsored and published by Corpus Christi Caller-Times, 1953. ₍Corpus Christi, 1953₎. Pict. cloth.

7 p.l., 15–143 p.   plates, ports., maps.   27.5 cm.
Double column.

2261 ———. The Panhandle of Texas. Chicago, issued by the passenger department of the Santa Fe, 1903. Stiff pict. wrappers. Rare.

₍3₎–48 p.   plates, 2 maps (1 double p.), tables.   18 cm.
Illus. t.p.

2262 ———. Pan-Handle Stock Association. Brand book containing the constitution, by-laws, and brands of the members of the Pan-Handle Stock Association of Mobeetie, Texas. Incorporated under the laws of Texas, 1886. Kansas City, Press of Ramsey, Millett and Hudson, ₍N.d.₎. Wrappers. Rare.

v (index to brands), 40 p.   17x8.5 cm.

2263 ———. Prospectus Texas Agricultural and Live Stock Company. Incorporated under the laws of Texas, 1878. ... Chicago, Ill., the J. M. W. Jones stationery and printing co., ₍1878₎. Wrappers. Rare.

₍3₎–32 p.   22.4 cm.

2264 ———. Reports of the committee of investigation. Sent in 1873 by the Mexican government to the frontier of Texas. Translated from the official edition made in Mexico.   New York, Barker and Godwin, printers, 1875. Leather. Rare.

viii, 443 p.   2 maps (col.).   23.3 cm.

Translated from the Spanish.

2265 ———. Resources and attractions of the Texas Panhandle for the home-seeker, capitalist, and tourist. Facts on climate, soil, farming, stock raising. ... Battle Creek, Mich., William C. Gage & son, printers, 1890. Wrappers. Rare.

2 p.l., ₍7₎–100 p.   map on verso front wrapper; fold. map at end, tables.   21 cm.

2266 ———. The resources and attractions of the Texas Panhandle for the home seeker, capitalist, and tourist. Facts on climate, soil, farming, stock raising. ... St. Louis, Woodward & Tiernan printing co., 1892. Wrappers. Rare.

3 p.l., ₍7₎–107 ₍1₎ p.   fold. map at end, tables.   19.8 cm.

2267 ———. Resources and attractions of the Texas Panhandle for the home seeker, capitalist, and tourist. Facts on climate, soil, farming, and stock raising, fruit growing, game, and fish. ... St. Louis, Woodward & Tiernan printing co., 1893. Wrappers. Rare.

3 p.l., ₍7₎–127 ₍1₎ p.   fold. map at end, tables.   20 cm.

2268 ———. Statistics and information concerning the state of Texas with its millions of acres of unoccupied lands, for the farmer and stock raiser. . . . ₁St. Louis, Woodward & Tiernan printing co., 1884₁. Wrappers. Rare.

₁3₁–93 ₁3₁ p.   illus., fold. map at end.   19.2 cm.
3 p. adv. at end.

Reprinted 1889 and 1890 with same imprint and collation.

2269 ———. Story of the SMS Ranch, together with "Some glimpses into ranch life," ₁by Frank S. Hastings. N.p., n.d.₁. Pict. wrappers. (Cover title). Scarce.
106 p.   91 plates.   15.2x23 cm.

These booklets were issued from time to time as an advertisement.

2270 ———. The Texarkana gateway to Texas and the Southwest. . . . St. Louis, Press of Woodward & Tiernan printing co., 1896. Pict. wrappers. Rare.
3–224 p.   illus., plates, maps.   23.2 cm.

2271 ———. Texas along the line of the Texas and Pacific Ry. To people seeking new homes, good health, an enjoyable climate, a fruitful soil, and new opportunities, this book is specially dedicated. Dallas, Texas, published by the passenger department of the Texas and Pacific Railway, ₁1908₁. Pict. wrappers. Rare.
3–144 p.   front., plates, 8 maps (col.).   14.4x22.5 cm.

2272 ———. Texas as it is; or, the main facts in a nut-shell. Containing more common sense and practical information about Texas for twenty-five cents than ordinarily gained for the same amount of dollars. . . . ₁Weatherford, Parker co., Texas, Donoho, Milliken & co., 1876₁. Wrappers. Rare.
₁3₁–41 p.   large fold. map in front.   21.6 cm.
Adv. verso front wrapper; adv. recto and verso back wrapper.

2273 ———. Texas frontier troubles. House of Representatives, 44th Congress, 1st Session, *Report No. 343*, 1876. Sewn. (Caption title). Rare.
xxi, 180 p.   22.8 cm.

Testimony taken by the special committee on the Texas frontier trouble with cattle thefts.

2274 ———. Texas, her resources and capabilities. . . . New York, 1881. Wrappers. Scarce.
255 p.   plates, large fold. map.   22.5 cm.

Published by the Southwestern Immigration Company of Austin, this book gives much information on the cattle industry of West Texas and the Pan-handle.

2275 ———. Texas the home for the emigrant from everywhere. Published by authority of the Legislature and under the auspices of the Super-intendent of Immigration of the state of Texas. . . . Houston, A. C. Gray, state printer, 1875. Wrappers. Rare.

[3]–43 p. fold. map in front. 21.6 cm.

2276 ———. Texas in 1840. Emigrants' guide to the new republic; being the result of observation, enquiry, and travel in that beautiful country. By an Emigrant, late of the United States . . . with an introduction by the Rev. A. B. Lawrence, of New Orleans. New York, published by William W. Allen . . . , 1840. Cloth. Rare.

xxii, [23]–275 p. front. (col.). 19.7 cm.

2277 ———. The Texas Pan-Handle. [N.p.], issued under the auspices of the Colonization Agency Southwestern Lines, [N.d.]. Folder. Pict. wrapper. Rare.

44 p. plates; map on verso of back wrapper. 19.5 cm.

Much on cattle.

2278 ———. Texas stock laws, containing all the laws of the state of Texas which apply to, or in any manner the stock interests; Federal laws rela-tive to the responsibility of common carriers; state inspectors, also officers and by-laws of the Cattle Raisers' Association of Texas. [N.p., (?Den-ver)], S. H. Calhoun, Jr., compiler. Denver, November 20, 1893. Wrap-pers. Rare.

40 p. 19.5 cm.
Advertisements scattered throughout.

2279 ———. Texas, a world of plenty. Chicago, passenger department, Rock Island Lines, 1907. Pict. wrappers. Rare.

69 p. front., illus. 22.5 cm.

2280 ———. A twentieth century history of southwest Texas. Illustrated Chicago, New York, Los Angeles, the Lewis publishing company, 1907. Three-quarter leather. Pub. in 2 vols. Scarce.

Vol. I: x p., 2 l., 504 p. plates, ports., maps. 26 cm.
Vol. II: biographical.

Volume I has a chapter on the history of the livestock industry.

2281 ———. Twice-told tales of Texas. [Houston], published by Humble Oil & Refining company, [1936]. Wrappers. (Cover title). OP.

5–46 p. illus. 22.8 cm.
Double column.

[366]

2282 ——. Western Texas, the Australia of America; or, the place to live. . . . By a six years' resident. Cincinnati, E. Mendenhall, 1860. Wrappers. Rare.

vii, [9]–235 p. 19 cm.

Much information on cattle raising in the early days of Texas.

2283 TEXAS LAND AND CATTLE COMPANY, LTD. Fifth annual report and accounts, year 1886. Dundee [Scotland], [1887]. Wrappers. Rare.

18 p. tables. 21 cm.

2284 ——. List of shareholders as at 23rd February, 1900. Dundee, John Lang and co., [1900]. Wrappers. Scarce.

13 p. 21 cm.

Lists the shareholders in this company and the number of shares each held.

2285 ——. Memorandum and articles of association of the Texas Land and Cattle Company, ltd. [N.p., 1881]. Wrappers. Scarce.

26 p. 33 cm.

2286 ——. Twenty-fifth annual report and accounts. Year 1906. Dundee, [1907]. Wrappers. Scarce.

9 p. 21 cm.

2287 THANE, ERIC (pseud. of Ralph Chester Henry). High border country, by Eric Thane. Edited by Erskine Caldwell. New York, Duell, Sloan & Pearce, [1942]. Cloth. OP.

ix p., 1 l., 3–335 p. 22 cm.

Index, p. 333–335.

Half title; map on end papers; "First edition" on copyright p.

2288 ——. The majestic land. Peaks, parks, & prevaricators of the Rockies & highlands of the Northwest, by Eric Thane. Illustrated. Indianapolis, New York, the Bobbs-Merrill company, inc., publishers, [1950]. Cloth.

5 p.l., 11–347 p. plates. 22.2 cm.

Index, p. 333–347.

Half title; map on end papers; untrimmed; "First edition" on copyright p.

2289 [THAYER, Gov. JOHN M.]. Message of Governor Thayer to the Fourth Legislative Assembly of Wyoming Territory, convened at Cheyenne, November 22nd, 1875. Cheyenne, Wyoming Territory, H. Glafcke, printer, Daily Leader office, 1875. Wrappers. Rare.

[3]–25 p. 22.6 cm.

2290 ——. Message of Governor Thayer to the Fifth Legislative Assembly of Wyoming Territory convened at Cheyenne, November 6, 1877.

Cheyenne, H. Glafche, printer, Daily Leader office, 1877. Wrappers. Rare.

[3]-15 p. 21.8 cm.

2291 THAYER, WILLIAM MAKEPEACE. Marvels of the new West. A vivid portrayal of the stupendous marvels in the vast wonderland west of the Missouri River. Six books in one volume, comprising marvels of nature, marvels of race, marvels of enterprises, marvels of mining, marvels of stock-raising, and marvels of agriculture . . . , by William M. Thayer. Illustrated with over 350 engravings and maps. Norwich, Conn., the Henry Bill publishing co., 1887. . . . Cloth. Scarce.

2 p.l., xxvi, 715 p. illus., ports., maps. 25 cm.

A second edition was published in 1890.

Part V devoted to cattle raising.

2292 THOBURN, JOSEPH B., and ISAAC M. HOLCOMB. A history of Oklahoma. By Joseph B. Thoburn and Isaac M. Holcomb. San Francisco, Doub & co., 1908. Pict. cloth. Scarce.

xi [1] p., 270, i–xiii p. front., plates, ports., 5 maps (col., 1 double p.). 20 cm.
Appendix, p. 219–270; index, p. i–xiii.

2293 ———, and MURIEL H. WRIGHT. Oklahoma, a history of the state and its people. By Joseph B. Thoburn and Muriel H. Wright. New York, Lewis Historical publishing co., inc., 1929. Three-quarter leather. Pub. in 4 vols. Scarce.

Vol. I: viii p., 2 l., [3]–471 p. front., plates, ports., maps. 26.2 cm.
Vol. II: 2 p.l., [475]–941 p. front., plates, ports., facsms., maps. 26.2 cm.
Appendix, p. [783]–928; index, p. [931]–941.
Vol. III: 450 p. front., ports. 26.2 cm.
Vol. IV: 451–856 p. front., ports. 26.2 cm.
Index, p. [821]–856.
Vols. I and II paged continuously; vols. III and IV paged continuously and biographical; double column.

Chapters on the Chisholm Trail and the range cattle industry in Vol. II.

2294 THOMAS, CYRUS. The agricultural & pastoral resources of southern Colorado and northern New Mexico, condensed from the official report of Professor Cyrus Thomas, forming part of the report of geological survey made to the Secretary of the Interior of the United States in 1871. London, John King & co. . . . , 1872. Wrappers. Scarce.

[3]-23 p. 21.7 cm.

2295 THOMAS, R. L. How and where to earn a living. The lands of the A. T. & S. F. Railroad in southwestern Kansas. Boston, 1878. Wrappers. Rare.

64 p. plates, maps. 23 cm.

2296 THOMPSON, ALBERT W. The story of early Clayton, New Mexico, [by] Albert W. Thompson. [Clayton, printed by the Clayton News, 1933]. Wrappers. (Cover title). Scarce.

95 p. plates, ports. 21.5 cm.
Last 6 p. plates.

2297 ———. They were open range days; annals of a western frontier, by Albert W. Thompson. Denver, Colorado, the World press, inc., 1946. Cloth. OP.

viii p., 1 l., 3–193 [1] p. plates, ports., map, plan. 21.5 cm.
Half title; untrimmed; copyright notice on t.p.

Only 500 copies of this book were printed.

2298 THOMPSON, CLIFF J. Born a cowboy, by Cliff J. Thompson. . . . This book contains twenty poems, one cowboy story, and one article entitled "When do horses sleep." This article contains valuable information regarding breeding, breaking, and racing of horses. The low down on picking a winner. [Stockton, California, published by John Muldowney printing co., 1944]. Stiff pict. wrappers. Scarce.

3 p.l., 7–78 p. illus. 22.8 cm.
Vignette; "First edition" on first p. after t.p.

2299 THOMPSON, GEORGE G. Bat Masterson; the Dodge City years, by George G. Thompson. Topeka, printed by Kansas State printing plant . . . , 1943. Wrappers. OP.

3–55 p. 22.8 cm.
Appendix, p. 47–54; bibliography, p. 55.
(*Fort Hays Kansas State College Studies, Language and Literature Series, No. 1,* F. B. Streeter, editor. *General Series, No. 6*).

2300 THOMPSON, I. OWEN. Adventures and day dreams, by I. Owen Thompson. Illustrated. Long Beach, California, 1913. Cloth. Scarce.

[5]–100 p. plates. 17.3 cm.

2301 THOMPSON, JAMES WESTFALL. A history of livestock raising in the United States, 1607–1860, by James Westfall Thompson. United States Department of Agriculture. [N.p.], November, 1942. Wrappers. (Cover title). OP.

viii, 182 [1] p. 26.7 cm.
Bibliography, p. 147–182.
At head of title, "Agricultural History Series No. 5."
Printed by offset.

2302 THOMPSON, SAMUEL HOLLISTON. Economic trends in livestock marketing. ₁By₁ Sam H. Thompson, Ph. D.   St. Louis, Chicago, New York, Cincinnati, planographed by John S. Swift co., inc., ₁1940₁.   Boards.   OP.

vii, 174 p.   graphs, maps, tables.   28 cm.
Appendix, p. 144–168; bibliography, p. 170–174.
Double column.

2303   THOMSON, EDITH CAMPBELL.   Pages from the Southwest. Compiled by Edith Campbell Thomson.   ₁N.p., n.d.₁.   Cloth.   OP.

3 p.l., 7–56 p.   front., illus., plates, cattle brands.   22.5 cm.

2304   THORNBER, J. J.   The grazing ranges of Arizona. By J. J. Thornber. Tucson, Ariz., Sept. 12, 1910.   University of Arizona Agricultural Experiment Station *Bulletin No. 65*. Pict. wrappers.   OP.

4 p.l., ₁245₁–360 p.   illus., plates, fold. map, graphs, tables.   22.2 cm.
Index, p. ₁357₁–360.
Illus. t.p.

2305   THORP, NATHAN HOWARD (JACK).   Story of the southwestern cowboy, pardner of the wind, by N. Howard (Jack) Thorp . . . in collaboration with Neill M. Clark. Illustrated. . . .   Caldwell, Idaho, the Caxton printers, ltd., 1945.   Cloth.

10 p.l., ₁21₁–309 p.   front., plates, ports., music.   23.6 cm.
Appendix, p. ₁285₁–301; index, p. ₁303₁–309.
Half title; "Pardner of the Wind"; pub. device.

An outstanding book about the life of an interesting character.

2306   ——.   Tales of the chuck wagon, by N. H. (Jack) Thorp.   ₁Santa Fe, N. M., 1926₁.   Stiff pict. wrappers.   OP.

3 p.l., ₁7₁–123 p.   front.   23 cm.

2307   THURMAN, VIOLET BIERMAN.   "Old Town" Indianola, cattle folks in Texas. ₁By₁ Violet Bierman Thurman.   San Antonio, Texas, Standard printing company, 1952.   Cloth.

5 p.l., 55 ₁1₁ p.   illus., plates, ports.   20.4 cm.
Half title; map on front end papers; cattle brands on back end papers; vignette.

2308   TILGHMAN, ZOE A.   Marshal of the last frontier. Life and services of William Matthew (Bill) Tilghman, for 50 years one of the greatest peace officers of the West, by his wife Zoe A. Tilghman.   Glendale, California, the Arthur H. Clark company, 1949.   Cloth.

8 p.l., ₁19₁–406 p.   front. (port.), plates, ports., facsm., large fold. map at end. 24 cm.
Index, p. ₁397₁–406.
Half title: "Western Frontier Series III"; pub. device.

2309   TINKER, EDWARD LAROCQUE.   A bond between men, ₁by₁ Edward Larocque Tinker. A lecture at the Argentine Embassy, Washington, 1956. Stiff pict. wrappers. (Cover title).

12 p. illus. (1 double p.). 24.6 cm.

A lecture on the history of the South American *gaucho* and his cattle.

2310 ———. Los Jinetes de las Américas y la literatura por ellos inspirada, con una bibliografia. ₁By₁ Edward Larocque Tinker. Buenos Aires, Editorial Guillermo Kraft limitada . . . , ₁1949₁. Stiff pict. wrappers.

8 p.l., 19–147 ₁1₁ p. front. (col.), illus. (part col.), plates (col.). 29.6 cm. Notes, p. 113–117; bibliography, p. 119–147. Half title.

Also published in an American edition bound in boards.

2311 TONGE, THOMAS. All about Colorado for the home-seekers, tourists, investors, health-seekers. Written and compiled by Thomas Tonge. . . . Denver, Press of the Smith-Brooks printing co., 1913. Stiff pict. wrappers. OP.

7–112 p. plates. 22.8 cm.

2312 TOPPING, E. S. The chronicles of the Yellowstone. An accurate, comprehensive history of the country drained by the Yellowstone River—its Indian inhabitants—its first explorers—the early fur traders and trappers —the coming and trial of the emigrants. A full account of all expeditions military and civil—the discovery of the geysers and wonders of the national park—fights with the Sioux by wolfers, trappers, and gold seekers. . . . By E. S. Topping. St. Paul, Pioneer press co., 1883. Cloth. Scarce.

2 p.l., 245 ₁1₁ p. illus., plates, large fold. map at end. 20 cm. Reprinted with same collation and imprint in 1888.

2313 TORCHIANA, HENRY ALBERT WILLIAM VAN COENEN. California gringos, by H. A. van Coenen Torchiana. . . . San Francisco, California, Paul Elder and company, ₁1930₁. Cloth. OP.

5 p.l., 281 p. front. (port.), plates. 19.6 cm.

2314 ———. Story of the mission Santa Cruz, by H. A. van Coenen Torchiana. . . . San Francisco, California, Paul Elder and company, 1933. Pict. cloth. Scarce.

xix p., 2 l., 5–460 p. plates, maps, facsms. 24.3 cm. Appendix, p. 403–447; index, p. 449–460.

2315 TORREY, EDWIN C. Early days in Dakota, by Edwin C. Torrey. Minneapolis, Farnham printing and stationery co., ₁1925₁. Cloth. Scarce.

4 p.l., ₁11₁–289 p. 19.7 cm. Half title.

Contains a chapter on Roosevelt's ranching days.

2316 TOWNE, ARTHUR E. Old prairie days, by Arthur E. Towne. . . . A historic narrative of the stirring pioneer days in Dakota Territory in the eighties. . . . Otsego, Michigan, published by the Otsego Union press, [1941]. Cloth. OP.

6 p.l., [1] p., 10–415 p. 19.5 cm.

2317 TOWNE, CHARLES WAYLAND. "Her Majesty Montana." The pioneer period: 1743–1877; the industrial period: 1878–1938. Text by Charles W. Towne. Illustrated by Frank Ward and Bob Hall. [N.p., c.1939]. Wrappers. OP.

150 p. illus. 22.5 cm.

Has a chapter on cattle and the Texas trail.

2318 ——, and EDWARD NORRIS WENTWORTH. Cattle & men. By Charles Wayland Towne & Edward Norris Wentworth. Norman, University of Oklahoma press, [1955]. Cloth.

xiii p., 1 l., 3–384 p. plates, map, facsm. 22 cm.
Bibliography, p. 341–353; index, p. 355–384.
Half title; "First edition" on copyright p.

2319 ——. Shepherd's empire, by Charles Wayland Towne and Edward Norris Wentworth, with drawings by Harold D. Bugbee. Norman, University of Oklahoma press, 1945. Cloth.

xii p., 1 l., 3–364 p. illus., maps (2 double p.). 22 cm.
Bibliography, p. 335–347; index, p. 349–364.
Half title; illus. double t.p.

2320 TOWNER, W. S. (COMPILER). Stock laws of Montana. Published by the Montana Stockgrowers' Association. Helena, Montana, Independent publishing company, [n.d.]. Stiff wrappers. Rare.

[3]–125 p. 22.5 cm.

2321 TOWNSHEND, RICHARD BAXTER. A tenderfoot in Colorado, by R. B. Townshend. London, John Lane, the Bodley Head, limited, 1923. Cloth. OP.

xiii p., 1 l., 282 p. front., plates. 22.5 cm.
Half title.
Published same year in New York by Dodd, Mead and co.

2322 ——. The tenderfoot in New Mexico, by R. B. Townshend. London, John Lane, the Bodley Head, limited, [1923]. Cloth. OP.
ix p., 1 l., 257 p. front., plates, ports. 22.5 cm.
Half title; untrimmed.
American edition, New York, Dodd, Mead and Co., 1924.

2323 ——. Last memories of a tenderfoot, by R. B. Townshend. With

illustrations. London, John Lane, the Bodley Head, limited, [1926].
Cloth.

xi p., 1 l., 270 [2] p. front., plates. 22.2 cm.
Half title; last 2 p. adv.

2324 TOWNSHEND, SAMUEL NUGENT. Colorado: its agriculture, stockfeed-
ing, scenery, and shooting. By S. Nugent Townshend. London, "The
Field" office, 1879. Limp cloth. Scarce.

viii, 122 [6] p. 19 cm.
Index, p. [121]–122.
Last 6 p. adv.

2325 ———. Our Indian summer in the far West. An autumn tour of
15,000 miles in Kansas, Texas, New Mexico, Colorado, and Indian Territory, by S. Nugent Townshend. Illustrated by J. G. Hyde. London,
printed by Charles Whittingham, 1880. Cloth. Rare.

2 p.l., 123 p. front., plates. 28.2 cm.
Plates are mounted photographs.

2326 TRACY, J. L. Guide to the great West; being a brief, but carefully
written description of the country bordering upon all the principal railroads of the West, with maps and illustrations. By J. L. Tracy. St. Louis,
published by Tracy & Eaton, 1870. Cloth. Very rare.

3 p.l., [9]–261 [9] p. front., 2 large fold. maps. 18.4 cm.
Index, p. [263–267].
Double column.
Last 3 p. adv.; 4 p. adv. before t.p.; adv. on verso both front and back wrappers;
adv. scattered throughout.

This copy examined in the Rollins Collection, Princeton University.

2327 TRAVIS, HELGA ANDERSON. The Umatilla trail. Pioneer days in the
Washington Territory, by Helga Anderson Travis. New York, Exposition press, [1951]. Cloth.

6 p.l., 13–243 p. front. (facsm.), plates, ports. 22.2 cm.
Half title; pub. device.

2328 TREADWELL, EDWARD FRANCIS. The cattle king, a dramatized biography, by Edward F. Treadwell. New York, the Macmillan company,
1931. Cloth. OP.

x p., 1 l., 3–367 p. front. (port.), ports. 22.4 cm.
Half title; map on end papers; untrimmed.
Republished in Boston, 1950, with 286 pages.

Life of Henry Miller of the Miller and Lux Ranch.

2329 TRENHOLM, VIRGINIA COLE. Footprints on the frontier. Saga of the

La Ramie region of Wyoming, by Virginia Cole Trenholm. [Douglas, Wyo., printed by Douglas Enterprise co., 1945]. Cloth. Scarce.

10 p.l., [21]–384 p. front., plates, ports. 23.5 cm.
Bibliography, p. [362]–365; index, p. [366]–384.
Half title; vignette.
Colophon: "Edition limited to one thousand copies of which this is No. ——."

2330 ——, and MAURINE CARLEY. Wyoming pageant, by Virginia Cole Trenholm . . . and Maurine Carley. . . . Casper, Wyoming, Prairie publishing company, [1946]. Pict. cloth. OP.

4 p.l., [9]–272 p. front. (port.), illus., plates (2 col.), ports., maps, tables. 20.2 cm.
Bibliography, p. 256–262; index, p. 263–272.
Map on end papers.

2331 TRIGGS, J. H. History of Cheyenne and northern Wyoming, embracing the gold fields of the Black Hills, Powder River, and Big Horn countries. . . . By J. H. Triggs. Omaha, Neb., printed at the Herald steam book and job printing house, 1876. Wrappers. Very rare.

3 p.l., 7–144 p. front. (fold. map). 22.5 cm.
Adv. p. 132–144 and front and back wrappers.

2332 ——. History and directory of Laramie City, Wyoming Territory, comprising a brief history of Laramie City from its first settlement to the present time, together with sketches of the characteristics and resources of the surrounding country; including a minute description of a portion of the mining region of the Black Hills. Also a general and business directory of Laramie City, by J. H. Triggs. Laramie City, Daily Sentinel print, 1875. Wrappers. Very rare.

[3]–91 p. 22.3 cm.
Official directory, p. 62–63; general directory, p. 64–91.
Full-p. adv. on verso of first 23 pages and back wrapper.
Reprinted (both volumes) in facsimile and boxed as a two-volume set by the Powder River publishers, Laramie, Wyoming, in 1955.

2333 ——. A reliable and correct guide to the Black Hills, Powder River, and Big Horn gold fields. Full description of the country, how to get to it, including a correct map of the gold regions . . . , by J. H. Triggs. Omaha, Neb., printed at the Herald steam book and job printing house, 1876. Wrappers. Very rare.

1 p.l., [3]–144 p. front. (fold. map). 22.2 cm.
Adv. on verso of front wrapper and last 13 pages.
Another edition, Omaha, 1878.

With the exception of the first sixteen pages, this is identical with the author's *History of Cheyenne and Northern Wyoming*. Only three or four copies are known to exist.

2334 TRINKA, ZENA IRMA. Medora, by Zena Irma Trinka. . . . New York, Paris, London, First Award Books, 1940. Cloth. Scarce.

6 p.l., 9–261 p. 21 cm.
Bibliography, p. 261.

A history of the Marquis de Mores, including his experiences in the cattle business in Dakota.

2335 ———. Out where the West begins, being the early and romantic history of North Dakota, by Zena Irma Trinka. . . . Illustrated from photographs by D. F. Barry, the noted Indian photographer. Map and 74 illustrations. St. Paul, the Pioneer company, 1920. Pict. leather. Scarce.

xvi p., 1 l., 432 p. front. (port. with tissue), plates (1 col.), ports., fold. map. 22 cm.
Index, p. 427–432.

2336 [TRITLE, Gov. F. A.]. Report of the Governor of Arizona made to the Secretary of the Interior for the year 1883. Washington, Government printing office, 1883. Wrappers. Rare.

[3]–14 p. tables. 23 cm.

2337 ———. Report of the Governor of Arizona made to the Secretary of the Interior for the year 1884. Washington, Government printing office, 1884. Wrappers. Rare.

[3]–13 p. 23 cm.

2338 [TRUE, LEWIS C.]. Decision of Hon. C. L. [*sic*] [Lewis C.] True, judge of the District Court Wyandotte County, Kansas, declaring the Traders' Live Stock Exchange, at the Kansas City market, to be a trust, and dissolving said exchange and permanently enjoining its members. Opinion rendered Dec. 30, 1909. [N.p., n.d., c.1909]. Stapled. (Caption title). Rare.

24 p. 22.8 cm.

2339 [TRUETT, VELMA STEVENS]. Hot iron history of Elko County. Elko, Nevada, [1947]. Pict. wrappers. OP.

[16] p. (no pagination). illus., cattle brands. 22.7 cm.

This is a brief account of cattle brands, giving the brands and their owners on a margin of each page. The brands are reproduced in color. It was issued by the Crumley Hotels as a souvenir.

2340 ———. On the hoof in Nevada, [by] Velma Stevens Truett. Los Angeles, Gehrett-Truett-Hall, 1950. Pict. cloth.

7 p.l., 17–613 p. illus., plates, ports., cattle brands, ear-marks, facsm. 17.6x26 cm. (oblong).
Index, p. 549–613.
Half title; illus. end papers. vignette.

2341 TRUITT, BESS. Range rhymes and recollections. Compiled and edited by Bess Truitt. Poems, ballads, stories of Oklahoma cowboys. Enid, Oklahoma, Commercial press, [1939]. Stiff pict. wrappers. OP.

4 p.l., 9-86 [5] p. illus. 16.8 cm.
Vignette.

Tells of the roundup on the 101 Ranch.

2342 TUCKER, PATRICK T. Riding the high country, by Patrick T. Tucker; edited by Grace Stone Coates. Caldwell, Idaho, the Caxton printers, ltd., 1933. leather. OP.

7 p.l., [15]-210 p. front. (col. with facsm. letter and tissue with letterpress), plates, ports. 19.5 cm.
Half title; pub. device; illus. end papers.
Colophon: "The De Luxe Edition of Riding the High Country is limited to 25 signed and numbered copies of which this is number ——." (Signed by both author and editor).

Published in trade edition in cloth with same imprint and collation.

2343 [TUFTS, JAMES]. A tract description of Montana Territory; with a sketch of its mineral and agricultural resources. New York, R. Craighead, printer, 1865. Wrappers. Extremely rare.

15 p. map. 23 cm.
Signed, "James Tufts."
"24 copies and fine paper, with map."

The copy examined in the Thomas W. Streeter Library, Morristown, N. J.

2344 TURNER, JOHN PETER. The North-West mounted police, 1873-1893, by John Peter Turner. Volume I. Inclusive of the great transition period in the Canadian West, 1873-1893, when law and order was introduced and established. Ottawa, Edmund Cloutier . . . , King's printer and controller of stationery, 1950. Stiff wrappers.

Vol. I: xiii, 686 p. plates, ports., fold. map at end, tables. 24.8 cm.
Half title; pub. device.
Vol. II: vii, 610 p. plates, ports. 24.8 cm.
Index, p. 577-610.
Half title; errata at end; pub. device.

Vol. II contains a chapter on the cattle industry of Canada.

2345 TURNER, MARY HONEYMAN TEN EYCK (MRS. AVERY TURNER). Into the West, by Mary Honeyman Ten Eyck Turner, Mrs. Avery Turner. Amarillo, Texas, [privately printed by Russell stationery co.], 1938. Cloth. Pict. label pasted on. Scarce.

4 p.l., 11-61 p. front. (port.), plates, ports. 24 cm.
Half title; vignette.

2346 ———. These high plains, by Mary Honeyman Ten Eyck Turner

(Mrs. Avery Turner). Amarillo, Texas, ⌜privately printed by Russell stationery co.⌝, 1941. Cloth. Pict. label pasted on. Scarce.

4 p.l., 11–94 p. front. (port.), plates. 24 cm.
Half title; device.
"Limited to 150 books."

2347 TUTTLE, REV. E. B. Six months on the plains; or, the travelers' guide to Cheyenne and the Rocky Mountains. By Rev. E. B. Tuttle. . . . Chicago, Horton & Leonard, book and job printers, 1868. Wrappers. Rare.

3 p.l., ⌜7⌝–31 ⌜21⌝ p. map on verso back wrapper. 27.5 cm.
Last 20 p. adv.; adv. verso front wrapper and recto back wrapper.

2348 TYLER, GEORGE W. The history of Bell County, by George W. Tyler; edited by Charles W. Ramsdell. San Antonio, the Naylor co., 1936. Cloth.

xxiii p., 1 l., 425 p. front. (port.), plates, ports., 2 fold. maps. 23.4 cm.
Index, p. 405–425.
Half title.
Some copies were issued without the maps.

"At ⌜the author's death⌝ the writing was incomplete and some was in the form of rough notes. It was left to the editor . . . to revise and condense the manuscript, and, in a few instances, to fill out the narrative."—p. ix.

2349 "UNCLE JOHN" (pseud.). Life in the wild West. ⌜N.p., n.d.⌝. Pict. wrappers. Rare.

2 p.l., 76 p. 16 cm.
Illus. t.p.

2350 UNION LAND AND CATTLE COMPANY, LTD. Memorandum and articles of association. London, Neish and Howell, 1883. Wrappers. Rare.

21 p. 32.5 cm.

2351 UNION PACIFIC RAILWAY COMPANY. Guide to the Union Pacific Railroad lands. 12,000,000 acres best farming, grazing and mineral lands in America, in the states of Nebraska, and the territories of Colorado, Wyoming, and Utah for sale by the Union Pacific Railroad Company in tracts to suit purchasers and at low prices. . . . Omaha, Nebr., Omaha Herald book and job office, 1872. Boards. Rare.

iv, ⌜5⌝–48 p. 2 fold. maps (1 col.). 22.2 cm.
Republished in 1873.

2352 UNION STOCK YARDS. Communication received Feb. 12, 1878, from the Union Stock Yards at Chicago and the National Stock Yards at East St. Louis, Ill. ⌜Chicago, 1879⌝. Sewn. Rare.

4 p. 21.8 cm.

2353 ———. Report of sub-committee on Union Stock Yards at Chicago and East St. Louis. ₁Washington₁, 1877. Sewn. Rare.

₁3₁–15 p. 21.8 cm.

2354 U. S. BUREAU OF ANIMAL INDUSTRY. Annual report, 16th, 1899. Washington, 1900. Wrappers. OP.

p. 514. plates xx–xxii. 23 cm.

2355 UNITED STATES CATTLE RAISING COMPANY. United States Cattle Raising Company. ₁N.p., c.1878₁. Cloth. (Caption title). Rare.

24 p. 2 maps, 3 illus., on one fold. sheet. 17.2 cm.
"For private circulation only," and trade-mark of the company stamped in gilt on front cover.

There are many indications that this company was a successor to the Fort Bascom Cattle Raising Company of Connecticut, also entered here under 1878. Wilson Waddington was president of both companies, much of the text of the two prospectuses is identical, and the large map included in each is from the same original, though with one or two changes, indicating a later issue. From the plat map it appears that the holdings of the Fort Bascom Company now belonged to the United States Company, with much adjoining property added.

This is an early record for a New Mexico cattle company. The copy described was seen in the library of Thomas W. Streeter, of Morristown, N. J.

2356 U. S. CLAIMS COMMISSION. Texas cattle claims. General memorandum opinion of the American Mexican Claims Commission, established pursuant to the settlement of Mexican claims act of 1912. ₁Washington, U. S. Government printing office, 1944₁. Stapled. (Caption title). OP.

21 p. 22.3 cm.

2357 U. S. COMMISSIONER OF AGRICULTURE. On the diseases of cattle in the United States. Washington, Government printing office, 1871. Wrappers. Scarce.

205 p. illus., plates (7 col. with tissues), tables. 29.6 cm.

2358 ———. U. S. report of the Commissioner of Agriculture for the year 1866. Washington, Government printing office, 1867. Cloth. Scarce.

2 p.l., ₁5₁–565 p. front., illus., charts, tables. 22.5 cm.

Chapter on "Improvement of Native Cattle," by Lewis F. Allen, on p. 294–321.

2359 ———. U. S. report of the Commissioner of Agriculture for the year 1870. Washington, Government printing office, 1871. Cloth. Scarce.

p. 346–352. plate VIII. 23 cm.

Texas cattle trade.

2360 ――――. U. S. report of the Commissioner of Agriculture for the year 1870. Washington, Government printing office, 1871. Cloth. Scarce.
2 p.l., ₁3₁–688 p. front., illus., fold. map, tables. 22.5 cm.

P. 548–569 on grazing lands and cattle.

2361 ――――. U. S. Report of the Commissioner of Agriculture on the diseases of cattle in the United States. Washington, Government printing office, 1871. Cloth. Scarce.
2 p.l., 205 p. illus., plates (part col. with tissues), tables. 30 cm.
Index, p. ₁203₁–205.

2362 ――――. U. S. report of the Commissioner of Agriculture. Special report No. 50. The dissemination of Texas fever of cattle and how to control it. Washington, Government printing office, 1882. Pamphlet. OP.
14 p. 22.8 cm.

2363 U. S. Congress. U. S. Secretary of Agriculture, 74th Congress, 2d Session, *Doc. 199*. The western range. Letters from the Secretary of Agriculture transmitting in response to Senate resolution No. 289 a report on the western range—a great but neglected natural resource. Washington, government printing office, 1936. Wrappers. OP.
xvi, 620 p. maps, tables. 23.2 cm.

2364 ――――. U. S. Thirty-Sixth Congress, 2d Session, *House of Rep. Doc. No. 48*. Report of the Commissioner of Patents for the year 1860. Washington, Government printing office, 1861. Wrappers. Rare.
p. 239–267. 22.5 cm.

2365 U. S. Department of Agriculture. First annual report of the Bureau of Animal Industry for the year 1884. Washington, Government printing office, 1885. Wrappers. Scarce.
3 p.l., 7–512 p. plates (part with tissues), fold. map, tables. 23.5 cm.
Index, p. 503–512.

2366 ――――. Proceedings of an interstate convention of cattlemen held at Ft. Worth, Texas . . . March 11, 12, 13, 1890. . . . Washington, Government printing office, 1890. Wrappers. Scarce.
1 p.l., 102 p. 23 cm.
U. S. Dept. of Agriculture, Bureau of Animal Industry, *Special Bulletin*.

2367 ――――. Second annual report of the Bureau of Animal Industry for the year 1885. Washington, Government printing office, 1886. Cloth. Scarce.
4 p.l., 9–662 p. plates (col.), tables. 23.5 cm.
Index, p. 655–662.

2368 ———. Third annual report of the Bureau of Animal Industry for the year 1886. Washington, Government printing office, 1887. Cloth. Scarce.

4 p.l., 9–456 p. plates (12 col. 1 fold.), tables. 23.4 cm. Index, p. 453–456.

Contains a report on the condition of the range cattle industry by H. M. Taylor, on calf-raising on the plains, by George W. Rust, and on the cattle industry in California, by A. S. Mercer.

2369 ———. Fourth and fifth annual reports of the Bureau of Animal Industry for the years 1887 and 1888. Washington, Government printing office, 1889. Cloth. Scarce.

p. 306–338. 22 cm.

2370 ———. Eighth and ninth reports of the Bureau of Animal Industry for the years 1891 and 1892. Washington, Government printing office, 1893. Cloth. Scarce.

p. 177–304. 10 p. col. plates. 22 cm.

2371 ———. Eighteenth annual report of the Bureau of Animal Industry for the year 1901. Washington, Government printing office, 1902. Wrappers. Scarce.

p. 267–274. 22 cm.

2372 ———. Year book for the year 1906. Washington, Government printing office, 1907. Cloth. OP.

4 p.l., 9–720 p. front. (port.), plates (10 col.), maps, charts, tables. 23.2 cm. Index, p. 695–720.

Contains a chapter on range management and cattle, by J. S. Cotton.

2373 U. S. DEPARTMENT OF THE INTERIOR, CENSUS OFFICE. Report of the productions of agriculture as returned at the tenth census (June 1, 1880). . . . Washington, Government printing office, 1883. Cloth. Scarce.

xxxiii p., 1 l., 3–1149 p. 29.3 cm.

2374 U. S. HOUSE OF REPRESENTATIVES. Depredations on the Texas frontier. U. S. House of Representatives, 43d Congress, 1st Session, *Report No. 395,* [1874]. Folder. Very rare.

3 p. 22.8 cm.

Much on cattle stealing.

2375 U. S. REPORT on cattle, sheep, and swine supplementary to enumeration of live stock on the farm in 1880. Washington, Government printing office, 1880. Wrappers. Rare.

p. 60–162. tables. 29.3 cm.
Index, p. ₍157₎–162.

2376 U. S. SENATE. Administration and use of public lands. Hearing before a subcommittee of the committee on public lands and surveys. U. S. Senate, 78th Congress, 1st Session . . . Part 6, February 16 and 17, 1943, Vernal, Utah. Washington, U. S. government printing office, 1943. Wrappers. OP.

p. 2137–2404. tables (2 fold.). 23.2 cm.

2377 ———. Administration and use of public lands. Hearings before a subcommittee of the committee on lands and surveys. U. S. Senate, 77th Congress, 1st Session . . . Part 3, October 2, 3, and 4, Salt Lake, Utah, October 8, 9 and 10, 1941, Reno, Nevada. Washington, U. S. Government printing office, 1941. Wrappers. OP.

p. iv, 897–1335. tables. 23.2 cm.

2378 ———. Administration and use of public lands. Hearings before a subcommittee of the committee on public lands and surveys. U. S. Senate, 77th Congress, 1st Session . . . Part 4, November 25 and 26, 1941, Las Vegas, Nevada; November 28, Kingman, Arizona; December 1 and 2, 1941, Phoenix, Arizona. Washington, U. S. government printing office, 1942. Wrappers. OP.

Part V, p. 1337–1766. 23 cm.

2379 ———. Administration and use of public lands. Hearings before a subcommittee of the committee on public lands and surveys, U. S. Senate, 77th Congress, Second Session . . . Part V, October 28, 1942, Tonapah, Nevada; November 19 and 20, 1942, Glenwood Springs, Colorado. Washington, U. S. Government printing office, 1943. Wrappers. OP.

Part IV, p. 1767–2135. 23 cm.

2380 ———. Present conditions of the live cattle and beef markets of the United States and the causes therefor. Statement of Philip D. Armour before the special committee of the U. S. Senate. Presented at Washington, November 30, 1889. Chicago, Chicago Legal News co., printers, 1889. Wrappers. Rare.

23 p. tables. 22 cm.

2381 U. S. TARIFF COMMISSION. Cattle and beef in the U. S. The tariff problem involved. Washington, Government printing office, 1922. Sewn. (Cover title). Scarce.

vi, 125 p. diagrs. (2 fold.), tables. 23 cm.
Tariff information series No. 30; at head of title; "United States Tariff Commission, Washington"; running title, "Cattle and Beef Production in the U. S."

2382 ———. The cattle industry in the United States and Canada. Washington, Government printing office, 1925. Wrappers. OP.

iv, 51 p. diagrs., graphs, tables. 22.5 cm.
At head of title, "U. S. Tariff Commissioner, Washington."

2383 UTAH. Book of recorded marks and brands, embracing all the marks and brands recorded from the first organization of the territory to December 9th, 1874. . . . Compiled with great care and published by authority of the Legislative Assembly. Salt Lake City, printed at the Deseret News steam printing and publishing establishment, [1874]. Cloth. Rare.

168 p. cattle brands. 27 cm.

A record giving the brand, place of brand, date recorded, owner, and residence of owner.

2384 ———. Brand directory comprising Davis, Weber, Summit, Morgan, Wasatch, part of Utah, and part of Uintah counties. Arranged alphabetically. Wanship, Summit County, Utah, published by H. F. Peterson, 1913. Cloth. Scarce.

185 p. cattle brands. 21x11.7 cm.

2385 ———. Complete and comprehensive description of the agricultural, stock raising and mineral resources of Utah . . . Battle Creek, Mich., William C. Gage and son, printers, 1890. Wrappers. Rare.

68 p. front. (map), tables. 21 cm.

2386 ———. Complete and comprehensive description of the agricultural, stock raising, and mineral resources of Utah. St. Louis, Woodward & Tiernan printing co., 1894. Wrappers. Rare.

124 p. tables. 20 cm.
Map on verso of front wrapper.

2387 ———. History of Sanpete and Emery counties, Utah, with sketches of cities, towns, villages, chronology of important events. . . . Illustrated. Ogden, W. H. Lever, 1898. Three-quarter leather. Scarce.

4 p.l., [11]–81 [2] p. front., plates, ports. 24 cm.

2388 ———. Ordinances passed by the Legislative Council of Great Salt Lake, and ordered to be printed. Great Salt Lake City, 1850. Wrappers. Very rare.

4 p. 12x22.2 cm.

An ordinance creating an office for the recording of marks and brands on horses, mules, cattle, and other stock. One of the earliest examples of printing in Utah.

[382]

2389 ———. The resources and attractions of the territory of Utah. Prepared by the Utah Board of Trade. ₍Omaha₎, printed at the Omaha Republican publishing house, 1879. Wrappers. Rare.

₍3₎–74 p. front., illus., tables. 22.7 cm.

2390 ———. Resources and attractions of Utah. . . . Second edition, revised and enlarged. Chicago, Rand, McNally and co., printers, 1889. Wrappers. Scarce.

80 p. map on verso of front wrapper, tables. 21.2 cm.

2391 ———. Utah, the inland empire. Illustrated. The story of the pioneers. Resources and industries of the state. Attractions of Salt Lake City. Leading men of the community. Salt Lake City, Utah, the Deseret News, 1902. Stiff pict. wrappers. Scarce.

110 p. front., illus., plates, ports. 29.4 cm.

Chapter entitled "Life On the Range" on the cattle industry of the state.

2392 VACHELL, HORACE ANNESLEY. Life and sport on the Pacific Slope. By Horace Annesley Vachell. . . . New York, Dodd, Mead and company, 1901. Cloth. OP.

x p., 1 l., ₍3₎–393 p. front. (with tissue), plates. 19.5 cm.
Appendices, p. ₍347₎–393.
Half title.

Two chapters on ranching.

2393 VANDEGRIFT, F. L. Panhandle and South Plains, Texas. ₍By F. L. Vandegrift₎. Chicago, issued by colonization department, Atchison, Topeka & Santa Fe Ry., ₍n.d.₎ Folder. Rare.

3–18 p. plates, map on recto of back wrapper. 23 cm.

2394 VAN DERSAL, SAMUEL. Van Dersal's stock growers' directory of marks and brands for the State of North Dakota, 1902. . . . St. Paul, Minn., McGill-Warner co., 1902. Cloth. Scarce.

3–213 ₍34₎ p. cattle brands. 22.7 cm.
Last 34 p. adv. and adv. scattered throughout.

2395 VAN DER VEER, JUDY. The river pasture. ₍By₎ Judy Van Der Veer. Illustrations by Dorothy Waugh. New York, Toronto, Longmans, Green and co., 1936. Cloth. Scarce.

4 p.l., 5–213 p. illus. 19.5 cm.

Ranch life in southern California. Memoirs of a ranch girl.

2396 VAN DYKE, JOHN CHARLES. The open spaces. Incidents of nights and days under the blue sky, by John C. Dyke. . . . New York, Charles Scribner's sons, 1922. Cloth. OP.

vii p., 1 l., 272 p.   front. (with tissue).   19.2 cm.
Half title.

Has a chapter on cowboys.

2397   VAN SICKEL, CAPT. S. S.   A story of real life on the plains, written by Capt. S. S. Van Sickel, during a short period of his life on the plains, giving an account of some of his experiences with the Indians and his narrow escape from death. . . .   ₍N.p. (pref. dated Bull City, Kan., 1875), 1875₎. Wrappers. Rare.

50 p.   19.4 cm.

Republished in 1876 in Chicago, under the title *Thrilling Adventures with the Indians* . . . ; with 36 p. Reprinted again in Harper, Kan., in 1885; again reprinted, in Cedar Rapids, Iowa, by the T. S. Metcalf book and job printer, in 1892, 1895, and 1896.

2398   VASS, A. F.   Control and value of western grazing lands. A comprehensive statement that should be read by every live stock rancher in the range states. By A. F. Vass. ₍N.p.₎, published by American National Live Stock association, Wyoming Stock Growers' association, Wyoming Wool Growers' association, 1941. Wrappers. (Cover title). OP.

19 p.   front. (port.), charts, tables.   22 cm.

2399   ———.   Ranch and range studies in Wyoming. *Bulletin No. 147,* June, 1926. ₍By A. F. Vass₎. Laramie, University of Wyoming Experiment station, ₍1926₎. Wrappers. (Cover title). OP.

151 ₍1₎ p.   illus., charts, tables.   22.6 cm.

2400   ———.   Research investigations on the livestock ranches of the United States, by A. F. Vass. Reprinted from *Proceedings of the International Conference of Agricultural Economics,* Vol. II. ₍N.p., n.d.₎. Wrappers. (Cover title). Scarce.

p. ₍864₎–884.   tables.   23 cm.

2401   ———, and HARRY PEARSON.   Cattle production in Wyoming's mountain valley ranches. By A. F. Vass and Harry Pearson. University of Wyoming Agricultural Experiment Station, *Bulletin No. 197,* July, 1933. Laramie, Experiment Station, ₍1933₎. Pict. wrappers. (Cover title). OP.

125 p.   illus., charts (1 fold.), tables.   22.6 cm.

2402   VAUGHN, H. W.   Types and market classes of live stock. By H. W. Vaughn. . . .   Columbus, Ohio, R. G. Adams & co., 1915. Cloth. OP.

7 p.l., 19–448 p.   front., illus., plates, tables.   23.5 cm.

2403 VAUGHN, ROBERT. Then and now; or, thirty-six years in the Rockies. Personal reminiscences of some of the first pioneers of the state of Montana. Indians and Indian wars. The past and present of the Rocky Mountain country, 1864–1900, by Robert Vaughn. Minneapolis, Tribune printing company, 1900. Pict. cloth. Scarce.

5 p.l., ₁17₁–461 p. front. (port., signed in facsm.), plates, ports. 22.5 cm.

2404 VERNON, ARTHUR. History and romance of the horse, by Arthur Vernon; illustrated by Ernest John Donnelly. Boston, Waverly house, ₁1939₁. Pict. cloth. OP.

xiii p., 2 l., 525 p. front., illus., diagrs. 23.8 cm.
Index, p. 521–525.
Half title; vignette; "First edition" on copyright p.

2405 VERNON, JOSEPH S., and CAPT. HENRY BOOTH. Along the old trail. A history of the old and a story of the new Santa Fe Trail. Cimarron, Kan., Larned, Kan., Tucker-Vernon company, publishers, ₁1910₁. Cloth. Scarce.

190 p. front. (col.), plates (2 col., incl. front.), ports. 21.7 cm.
Vignette; published in three parts.

2406 VESTAL, STANLEY (pseud. of WALTER STANLEY CAMPBELL). Queen of cowtowns, Dodge City. "The wickedest little city in America," 1872–1886, by Stanley Vestal. New York, Harper & brothers, ₁1952₁. Cloth.

viii p., 2 l., 285 p. plates, ports. 21.5 cm.
Notes, p. 271–279; bibliography, p. 281–282; acknowledgments, p. 283–285.
Half title; pub. device; untrimmed; "First edition" on copyright p.

2407 ———. Short grass country, by Stanley Vestal. New York, Duell, Sloan & Pearce, ₁1942₁. Cloth. OP.

x p., 1 l., 3–304 p. 22 cm.
Index, p. 299–304.
Half title; map on end papers; "First edition" on copyright p.

2408 VICKERS, C. L. (ED.). History of the Arkansas Valley, Colorado. Illustrated. Chicago, O. L. Baskin and co., 1881. Morocco. Scarce.

vii p., 1 l., ₁11₁–889 p. front., plates, ports. 25.3 cm.
Double column.

2409 [VICKERS, W. B.]. History of Clear Creek and Boulder valleys, Colorado. Containing a brief history of the state of Colorado from its earliest settlement to the present time, embracing its geological, physical, and climatic features; its agricultural, stockgrowing, and mining interests. . . . Illustrated. Chicago, O. L. Baskin & co., historical publishers, 1880. Three-quarter leather. Scarce.

vi p., 3 l., ₁17₁–713 p. illus., plates, ports. (all signed in facsm.). 25.4 cm.
Double column; gilt edges.

2410 VINCENT, JOSEPH J. Streak o' lean and a streak o' fat. Illustrations and story by Joseph J. Vincent. Edited and published by Southern Historical Associates, publishers, Tampa, Florida. [Printed by the Steck company, Austin, Texas, 1953]. Pict. cloth.

ix, 109 p. illus. 23.6 cm.
Map on front end papers; back end papers illus.
Chapters on cattle, branding, marking, and calf roping.

2411 VINKE, LOUIS, and C. N. ARNETT. Beef cattle in Montana, by Louis Vinke and C. N. Arnett. Bozeman, Montana, University of Montana Agricultural Experiment station, 1927. Pict. wrappers. OP.

[3]–67 p. plates, tables. 20.8 cm.
Bulletin No. 132.

2412 VISHER, STEPHEN SARGENT. The geography of South Dakota. A dissertation submitted to the faculty of the Ogden Graduate School of Science in candidacy for the degree of Doctor of Philosophy. Department of Geography. By Stephen Sargent Visher. Chicago, Illinois, private edition distributed by the University of Chicago Libraries . . . , 1918. Wrappers. Scarce.

3 p.l., [7]–189 p. illus., map. 21.5 cm.
Head of title, "University of Chicago."
Reprinted from South Dakota State Geological Survey, *Bulletin No. 8,* July, 1918.

2413 VIVIAN, SIR ARTHUR PENDARVES. Wanderings in the western land, by A. Pendarves Vivian, with illustrations from original sketches by Mr. Albert Bierstadt and the author. London, Sampson Low, Marston, Searle and Rivington, 1879. Pict. cloth. Scarce.

xvi, 426 p. front. (with tissue), 3 maps (2 fold., 1 col.), 8 full-p. engravings (incl. front.), illus., plates. 22.6 cm.

2414 VIVIAN, H. HUSSEY. Notes of a tour of America from August 7th to November 17th, 1877. By H. Hussey Vivian. . . . London, Edward Stanford, 1878. Dec. cloth. Rare.

5 p.l., 260 p. front. (large fold. map with tissue). 22.7 cm.
Half title.

2415 VOLLWEILER, ALBERT TANGEMAN. Roosevelt's ranch life in North Dakota. [By] Albert Tangeman Vollweiler. Reprint from the *Quarterly Journal of the University of North Dakota,* Vol. IX, No. 1 (October, 1918). Wrappers. Scarce.

p. [31]–49. plates, ports., facsm., cattle brands. 24 cm.

2416 WAGGONER, GEORGE ANDREW. Stories of old Oregon, by George A. Waggoner. Salem, Ore., Statesman publishing co., 1905. Cloth. Scarce.

5 p.l., [7]–292 p. plates. 19.5 cm.

2417 WAGONER, JUNIOR JEAN. History of the cattle industry in southern Arizona, 1540–1940. By J. J. Wagoner. Originally submitted in 1949 in partial fulfillment of the requirements for the degree of Master of Arts in the Graduate College, University of Arizona. . . . Tucson, Arizona, published by University of Arizona, 1952. Wrappers.

2 p.l., 5–132 p. cattle brands, maps, tables. 22.8 cm.
Bibliography, p. 125–132.
University of Arizona *Bulletin*, Vol. XXIII, No. 2, *Social Science Bulletin No. 20.*

2418 WALGAMOTT, CHARLES SHIRLEY. Reminiscences of early days. A series of historical sketches and happenings in the early days of Snake River Valley, by C. S. Walgamott. Cloth. Scarce. Pub. in 2 vols.

Vol. I: 3 p.l., 127 ₁1₁ p. front., ports. 23.3 cm. ₁N.p., 1926₁.
Double column.
Vol. II: 4 p.l., 9–127 ₁1₁ p. illus., plates (1 tipped in). 23.5 cm. ₁Twin Falls, Idaho, the Idaho Citizen, 1927₁.

2419 ———. A series of historical sketches of early days in Idaho. Six decades back, ₁by₁ Charles Shirley Walgamott. Illustrated by R. H. Hall. Caldwell, Idaho, the Caxton printers, ltd., 1936. Cloth.

8 p.l., ₁17₁–358 p. front. (col. with tissue), illus., plates. 23.5 cm.
Half title; illus. end papers (dif.); pub. device.

This book has the same text as the two volumes in the preceding entry, now published under one cover.

2420 WALKER, FRED. Destination unknown. Running away to danger, by Fred Walker. Philadelphia & London, J. B. Lippincott company, 1935. Cloth. OP.

3 p.l., 7–284 ₁1₁ p. front. (port.). 20.6 cm.
Half title; map on end papers; pub. device; untrimmed.

2421 WALKER, STANLEY. Home to Texas, by Stanley Walker. New York, Harper & brothers, ₁1956₁. Cloth.

v p., 1 l., 307 p. 21.5 cm.
Half title; untrimmed; "First edition" on copyright p.

2422 WALKER, TACETTA B. Stories of early days in Wyoming; Big Horn Basin, by Tacetta Walker. Casper, Wyoming, Prairie publishing company, ₁1936₁. Cloth. OP.

iv p., 1 l., 271 p. plates, ports., maps. 23.5 cm.
Bibliography, p. 268; index, p. ₁269₁–271.
Maps on end papers (dif.).

2423 WALLACE, CHARLES (COMPILER). The cattle queen of Montana. A story of the personal experience of Mrs. Nat Collins, familiarly known to western people as "The Cattle Queen of Montana," or "The Cowboy's Mother," in which is included narratives of thrilling adventures . . . and descriptions of the plains, the mines, cattle raising industry, and other features of western life, learned during forty years' residence in the far West; compiled by Charles Wallace. Illustrations from special photographs. St. James, Minn., C. W. Foote ₁printed in Chicago by Donohue and Henneberry₁, 1894. Stiff wrappers. Rare.

xiii, ₁15₁–249 p. front., illus., plates. 19 cm.

The editor states that he prepared this book while attending the University of Washington. Of the one thousand copies which were printed, he sold about twelve and gave away a few. The remaining copies he burned, an act he regretted later. Because he did so, it is now almost impossible to find a copy of this edition.

Revised and edited by Alvin E. Dyer and republished in Spokane, Wash., by Press of Dyer printing co., ₁1902₁.

5–260 p. front. (port.), illus., plates, ports. 20 cm.

This edition is also becoming scarce.

2424 WALLACE, EDWARD R. Parson Hanks, fourteen years in the West. A story of the author's frontier life in the Panhandle of Texas, by Ed. R. Wallace. . . . Arlington, Texas, ₁Journal print, 1906₁. Wrappers. Rare.

14 p.l., ₁1₁ p. 30–162 p. 21.8 cm.

Republished in 1950 with six more pages than the original edition, bringing the story up to 1950.

2425 WALLIS, GEORGE A. Cattle kings of the Staked Plains, by George A. Wallis. Dallas, Texas, American Guild press, ₁1957₁. Cloth.

5 p.l., 11–180 p. plates, ports. 19.6 cm.

Map on front end papers; cattle brands on back end papers; "First edition" on copyright p.

Much on the ranches of West Texas and New Mexico.

2426 WALTHER, C. F. The state of Nebraska, its resources and advantages. Where to emigrate and why. Written by order of the Board of Immigration of the state of Nebraska, by C. F. Walther. . . . Nebraska City, Morning Chronicle book and job office, 1871. Wrappers. Rare.

₁3₁–22 p. large fold. map at end. 20.5 cm.

2427 ——, and I. N. TAYLOR. The resources and advantages of the state of Nebraska. Where to emigrate and why. Written by C. F. Walther and I. N. Taylor, and published by order of the Board. . . . ₁N.p., n.d.₁. Wrappers. (Cover title). Scarce.

₁3₁–26 ₁1₁ p. large fold. map at end. 19.5 ₂m.

2428 WARD, HORTENSE WARNER. Cattle brands and cow hides, by Hortense Warner Ward. Dallas, Texas, the Story Book press, [1953]. Pict. cloth.

ix, 218 p. cattle brands. 19.8 cm.
Bibliography, p. 204–215; glossary, p. 216–218.

2429 WARD, WILLIAM FRANCIS. Breeds of beef cattle. By W. F. Ward. [Washington, Government printing office], 1915. Wrappers. OP.

23 p. illus. 23 cm.
"Standard books on breeds and breeding," p. 23.
U. S. Dept. of Agriculture *Farmer's Bulletin 612.*

2430 WARING, GUY. My pioneer past, by Guy Waring, with an introduction by Owen Wister. Boston, Bruce Humphries, inc., publishers, [1936]. Cloth. OP.

12 p.l., 25–256 p. front., plates, ports., plan. 23.3 cm.
Index, p. 254–256.
Half title; map on end papers; pub. device; untrimmed.

2431 WARMAN, CY. Frontier stories, by Cy Warman. New York, Charles Scribner's sons, 1898. Pict. cloth. Scarce.

4 p.l., [3]–246 p. 18.2 cm.
Half title.

2432 ———. The story of the railroad, by Cy Warman. . . . Illustrated. New York, and London, D. Appleton and company, [1898]. Pict. cloth. Scarce.

xix, 280 p. front., plates, fold. map. 19.3 cm.

Has a chapter on the cowboys and the fight at Newton, Kansas.

2433 WARNER, C. A. San Juan, its past and present. Ways of getting there, developments and prospects, gold and silver mines, water power, timber and agricultural lands . . . Denver, Colorado, published by C. A. Warner & co., 1878. Wrappers. Rare.

[3]–93 p. 16.3 cm.
Last 20 p. adv.; adv. recto and verso back wrapper.

2434 WARNER, CAPT. C. C. Products, resources, opportunities for capital and advantages to emigrants of Nevada. . . . Compiled by Capt C. C. Warner. Reno, Nevada, Gazette book and job print, 1889. Wrappers. Rare.

2 p.l., [3]–26 [8] p. 23.3 cm.
Last 8 p. adv.; adv. verso front wrapper; adv. recto and verso back wrapper.

2435 [WARREN, GOV. FRANCIS E.]. Biennial message of Francis E. Warner, governor, to the Legislature of Wyoming, Ninth Assembly, 1886. Cheyenne, Wyo., Press of the Daily Sun, 1886. Wrappers. Rare.

[3]–23 p. 21 cm.

2436 ——. Report of the Governor of Wyoming to the Secretary of the Interior, 1886. Washington, Government printing office, 1886. Wrappers. Rare.

3–60 p. tables. 23 cm.

2437 ——. Report of the Governor of Wyoming to the Secretary of the Interior, 1889. Washington, Government printing office, 1889. Wrappers. Rare.

p. 561–705. 22.7 cm.

2438 WARREN, HENRY MATHER. To and fro, by Henry Mather Warren. Philadelphia, Wm. F. Fell company, [1908]. Pict. cloth. Scarce.

4 p.l., 106 p. plates. 23.9 cm.
Half title; untrimmed.

2439 WARREN, JOHN, and COLQUET WARREN. The Matadors, 1879–1951, by John Warren [and] Colquet Warren. Drawings by John L. Koonsman, maps by John Warren. . . . [N.p.], 1952. Wrappers.

2 p.l., 35 p. illus., maps. 28 cm.
Mimeographed on one side of paper only; 1-p. supplement laid in.

2440 WASHINGTON (territory and state). Brand book of the Eastern Washington Protective Stock Association for 1901. Helena, Montana, Independent publishing company, 1901. Leather. Rare.

62 p. blank leaf, 8 leaves, cattle brands. 19.3 cm.

This rare book examined in the library of Thomas W. Streeter, Morristown, N. J.

2441 ——. Appendix to the brand book of Eastern Washington Protective Stock Association for 1901. Helena, Montana, Independent publishing company, 1902. Wrappers. Rare.

32 p. cattle brands. 18.7 cm.

This item seen in the library of Thomas W. Streeter, Morristown, N. J.

2442 ——. The county of Clarke in Washington Territory, its climate, soil, production, and general resources. Information for emigrants. Published by the Board of Trade of the city of Vancouver. Vancouver, Beeson, printer, [n.d.]. Sewn. (Cover title). Rare.

10 [14] p. 18.6 cm.
Last 14 p. adv.

2443 ——. Eastern Washington Territory; or, the Walla Walla country. A general description of its climate, soil, productions, and advantages. Walla Walla, W. T., "Walla Walla Union" job printing establishment, 1875. Wrappers. (Cover title). Rare.

16 p.   23 cm.
Double column; adv. verso front wrapper; adv. recto and verso back wrapper.

2444 ———. Glimpses of pioneer life. A series of biographies, experiences, and events intimately concerned with the settlement of Okanogan County, Washington. . . . ₁Okanogan, Washington, published by Okanogan Independent, 1924₁. Wrappers. Scarce.

2 p.l., ₁5₁–143 p.   18 cm.
Double column.

2445 ———. The resources and attractions of Washington Territory for the home seeker, capitalist, and tourist. Facts on climate, soil, farming, stock raising. . . . Omaha, 1888. Wrappers. Scarce.

₁4₁–76 p.   front. (map on verso of front wrapper).   21 cm.

2446 ———. The resources and attractions of Washington for the home seeker, capitalist, and tourist. Facts on climate, soil, farming, stock raising. . . . Chicago, Rand McNally & co., printers, 1889. Wrappers. Rare.

3 p.l., 7–80 p.   front. (map on verso of front wrapper).   21.2 cm.

2447 ———. Settler's guide to Washington Territory and to the lands of the Northern Pacific Railroad on the Pacific Slope. . . . New York, Van Vleeck, Clark & co., printers & stationers, ₁1876₁. Wrappers. (Cover title). Rare.

28 p.   front. (double-p. col. map).   22.8 cm.

2448 ———. Settler's guide to Washington Territory and to the lands of the Northern Pacific Railroad. . . . ₁Portland, Himes, the printer, 1880₁. Wrappers. Rare.

₁3₁–30 p.   large fold. map in front.   22.6 cm.

2449 WATERHOUSE, S. Address of S. Waterhouse (of Washington University) before the first national convention of American cattlemen, St. Louis, November 18th, 1884. St. Louis, Mo., R. P. Studley & co., printers and general stationers, 1885. Pamphlet. (Cover title). Rare.

8 p.   22.5 cm.

2450 WATERS, L. L. Steel tracks to Santa Fe, by L. L. Waters. Lawrence, Kan., University of Kansas press, 1950. Cloth.

11 p.l., ₁9₁–500 p.   plates, ports., maps, graphs, tables.   23.6 cm.
Appendix, p. ₁484₁–491; references, p. ₁492₁–493; index, p. ₁495₁–500.
Half title; map on end papers.

2451 WATROUS, ANSEL. History of Larimer County, Colorado. Collated and compiled from historical authorities, public reports, official records, and other reliable sources . . . , by Ansel Watrous. Illustrated. Ft. Collins, Colorado, the Courier printing & publishing company, 1911. Leather. OP.

4 p.l., 7–513 p. front. (port. with tissue), plates, ports. (full p., with tissues). 29 cm. Index, p. 505–513.
Double column; gilt edges.

2452 WATSON, MAY M. GREEN. Taft Ranch, a history of the fifty years of development sponsored by Coleman-Fulton Pasture Company with sketches of Gregory and Taft, the two towns it created, by Mrs. May M. Green Watson [and] Alex Lillico. [N.p., n.d.]. Stiff wrappers. (Cover title). Scarce.

[52] p. (no pagination). illus., plates, ports. 23 cm.
Double column; last 16 p. adv.

2453 WATTS, GEORGE C. The long trail, by George C. Watts. [Oakdale, California, printed and bound by Stevens & Wallis, inc., 1949]. Cloth. OP.

vii, 180 p. front. (port.). 21 cm.
Illus. t.p.

2454 WEADOCK, JACK. Dust of the desert. Plain tales of the desert and the border, by Jack Weadock. Illustrated by Jack Van Ryder, with an introduction by George H. Doran. New York, London, D. Appleton-Century company, incorporated, 1936. Pict. cloth. OP.

xx p., 1 l., 3–306 p. front., illus. 24.5 cm.
Half title; illus. end papers; pub. device; untrimmed; first edition, figure "(1)" at end of text.

2455 WEBB, WALTER PRESCOTT. The great plains, by Walter Prescott Webb. . . . [Boston], Ginn and company, [1931]. Pict. cloth. OP.

xv p., 1 l., 3–525 p. illus., plates, ports., double-p. maps, diagrs. 21.8 cm.
Bibliography at end of each chapter except the first; index, p. 517–525.

Later republished by Houghton Mifflin company, and again by the original publishers, Ginn and company.

A well-written book with a long chapter on the cattle industry. The first state may be identified by the typographical errors in the chapter heading on p. 10—"poo" for "poor" and "oil" for "soil."

2456 ———(ED.). The handbook of Texas. Walter Prescott Webb, editor-in-chief. H. Bailey Carroll, managing editor. . . . In two volumes. . . . Austin, the Texas State Historical association, 1952. Pict. cloth.

Vol. I: xv p., 1 l., 977 p. 25 cm.
Vol. II: ix p., 1 l., 953 p. 25 cm.
Both volumes double column.

2457 WEIS, G. Stock raising in the Northwest, 1884. "Notes recueillies sur les élevages d'animaux dans des états de l'Ouest de l'Amérique du Nord," by G. Weis. San Francisco, 1884. Translated with historical note by Herbert O. Brayer. Decorations by David T. Vernon. Evanston, Ill., the Branding Iron press, 1951. Pict. boards. Scarce.

xii p., 1 l., 24 p. illus. 19 cm.
Vignette.
Colophon: "This book was designed at the printing office of Philip Reed, Chicago, Illinois, and five hundred copies printed in June, 1951. This is number ——."

2458 WELCH, CHARLES A. History of the Big Horn Basin, with stories of early days, sketches of pioneers, and writings of the author, by Charles A. Welch. [Salt Lake], printed by . . . the Deseret News press, 1940. Cloth. OP.

3 p.l., [7]–276 p. illus., plates, ports. 23.5 cm.
Index, p. [275]–276.

2459 WELLES, ALONZO MERRITT. Reminiscent ramblings, by A. M. Welles. Illustrations by the author. Denver, Colo., the W. F. Robinson printing co., 1905. Cloth. Scarce.

459 p. illus. 19.5 cm.

2460 WELLMAN, PAUL ISELIN. The Callaghan, yesterday and today, by Paul I. Wellman. . . . Encinal, Texas, published by the Callaghan land and pastoral co., [n.d.]. Stiff pict. wrappers. OP.

3 p.l., 7–82 p. illus., 56 plates, ports., map. 25 cm.

A story of the Callaghan Ranch in Texas with many scenes of the ranch, cattle, and cowboys.

2461 ——. Glory, God, and gold, a narrative history. By Paul Wellman. Garden City, N. Y., Doubleday & company, inc., 1954. Cloth.

xii p., 1 l., [3]–402 p. 7 maps. 24 cm.
Some books to read, p. [389]–390; index, p. [391]–402.
Half title; map on end papers.

2462 ——. The trampling herd, [by] Paul I. Wellman; illustrations by F. Miller. New York, Carrick & Evans, inc., [1939]. Cloth. OP.

6 p.l., 13–433 p. illus. 21.8 cm.
"Some books to read," p. 417–419; index, p. 421–433.
Half title; map on end papers; illus. t.p.
At head of title: "The Story of the Cattle Range of America."
Republished in 1951 by Doubleday and co., inc.

2463 WELLS, ROLLA. Episodes of my life, [by] Rolla Wells. [St. Louis, printed in St. Louis, Missouri, 1933]. Leather and boards. Privately printed and scarce. Boxed.

6 p.l., 510 p. front. (port. with tissue), plates, ports., facsms. 26.3 cm.
Index, p. 499–510.
Half title; untrimmed.

Has a chapter on cattle ranching on the Cheyenne-Arapahoe reservation in the Indian Territory in which the author tells of driving cattle up the Chism [*sic*] Trail and of life in Caldwell and Dodge City, Kansas.

2464 WELSH, DONALD H. Pierre Wibaux, cattle king, by Donald H. Welsh. Bismarck, North Dakota, published by the State Historical society of North Dakota. Reprinted from Vol. XX, No. 1 (January, 1953). Wrappers. (Cover title).

20 p. map. 22.8 cm.

2465 WENDLING CATTLE AND LAND COMPANY. Certificate of incorporation and by-laws of the Wendling Cattle and Land Company of Colorado and New Mexico. Capital stock $500,000, stock non-assessable. Denver, News printing company, 1887. Wrappers. Rare.

[3]–16 [4] p. fold. map in front. 22.8 cm.
Last 4 p. (praising beef production) laid in.

2466 WENDT, LLOYD, and HERMAN KOGAN. Bet a million! The story of John W. Gates, by Lloyd Wendt and Herman Kogan. Indianapolis, New York, the Bobbs-Merrill company, publishers, [1948]. Cloth. OP.

4 p.l., 9–357 p. front., plates, ports. 22.2 cm.
Bibliography, p. 335–342; index, p. 345–357.
Half title; untrimmed.

Gives a story of the introduction of barbed wire into Texas which revolutionized the cattle business.

2467 WENTWORTH, EDWARD NORRIS. America's sheep trails, history, personalities, by Edward Norris Wentworth. Ames, Iowa, the Iowa State College press, 1948. Pict. cloth.

xxii p., 1 l., 3–667 p. front. (double p.), illus., plates, ports., maps, facsms., tables. 26.5 cm.
Appendix, p. 591–604; bibliographical appendix, p. 605–621; references cited, p. 622–632; index, p. 633–667.
Half title; pub. device; double column.

Contains a chapter on the wars between the cattlemen and sheepmen.

2468 ———. A biographical catalog of the portrait gallery of the Saddle and Sirloin Club, by Edward N. Wentworth. Chicago, Illinois, Union Stock Yards, 1920. Three-quarter leather. Scarce.

3 p.l., [7]–343 [2] p. front., ports. 20 cm.

2469 ———. Historical phases of the sheep industry in Wyoming. Address by Col. Edward N. Wentworth, director Armour's Livestock Bureau, Chicago, Illinois, before Wyoming Wool Growers' Association convention, Worland, Wyo., August 2, 1940. Wrappers. (Cover title). Scarce.
3–46 p. 24.7x8.8 cm.

Contains some information on the cattle-sheep wars of Wyoming.

2470 ———. Southwest cattle empires, by Colonel Edward N. Wentworth. ₍An address before the Society of Westerners at the Saddle and Sirloin Club. . . . Reprinted from the March, 1948, issue of *The Cattleman*₎. Wrappers. (Cover title).
₍6₎ p. (no pagination). ports. 27.8 cm.

Deals with many of the prominent early cattlemen, such as Goodnight, Kleberg, Murdo McKenzie, and others, as well as with the Chisholm Trail and the Loving-Goodnight Trail.

2471 WENTWORTH, M. P. (ED.). Forged in strong fires; the early life and experiences of John Edward Dalton. As told by John Edward Dalton, looking back over the years, and taken down and edited by M. P. Wentworth. Illustrated by Cecil Smith. Limited edition. Caldwell, Idaho, the Caxton printers, ltd., 1948. Cloth. OP.
5 p.l., 11–373 p. front. (col.), illus. 24.2 cm.
Half title; illus. end papers; untrimmed.
Colophon: "The limited edition Forged in Strong Fires is 1,000 numbered copies, signed by the author, of which this is No. ———. First edition."
Also published in a trade edition.

2472 [WEST, GOV. CALEB W.]. Report of the Governor of Utah to the Secretary of the Interior, 1886. Washington, Government printing office, 1886. Wrappers. Rare.
3–17 p. 23 cm.

2473 WEST, RAY B., JR., (ED.). Rocky Mountain cities, edited by Ray B. West, Jr., with an introduction by Carey McWilliams. New York, Norton & company, inc., ₍1949₎. Cloth. OP.
14 p. 29–320 p. 21.8 cm.
Notes on contributors, p. 318–320.
Half title; pub. device; "First edition" on copyright p.

One chapter deals with Cheyenne as a cow town and the Johnson County War.

2474 WESTERMEIER, CLIFFORD P. Man, beast, dust. The story of rodeo, by Clifford P. Westermeier. . . . ₍Denver, Colo., the World press, inc., 1947₎. Pict. cloth. OP.

[395]

xviii p., 2 l., 23–450 p. front., plates, ports. 21 cm.
Bibliography, p. 419–440; index, p. 441–450.
Half title; signatures in facsm. on end papers.
Colophon: "This is number —— of a limited edition" (on t.p.).
Also published in a trade edition.

2475 ——. Trailing the cowboy. His life and lore as told by frontier journalists. Compiled and edited by Clifford P. Westermeier. Caldwell, Idaho, the Caxton printers, ltd., 1955. Pict. cloth.

8 p.l., [17]–414 p. illus. 21.7 cm.
Bibliography, p. [399]–404; index, p. [405]–414.
Half title; illus. end papers; headpieces; pub. device; note references after each chapter.

2476 WESTERNERS' BRAND BOOK (CHICAGO CORRAL). The Westerners' brand book, 1945–46. Being the papers presented during the second year of the Westerners (1945–46), together with some original papers rescued from manuscripts and ephemera. Chicago, Illinois, [1947]. Cloth. OP.

5 p.l., 9–166 [4] p. illus. 23.5 cm.
Index, p. [169–170].
Half title; illus. end papers.

Some material on the cattle rustler and the range war of Wyoming. This is the second and final volume issued by the Chicago Corral in this form. The first volume is not listed here because it contains nothing relative to the cattle industry.

2477 WESTERNERS' BRAND BOOK (DENVER CORRAL). 1945 brand book, containing twelve original papers relating to western and Rocky Mountain history. Edited by Herbert O. Brayer. The Westerners, Denver, Colorado, [Bradford-Robinson printing co.], 1946. Pict. cloth. OP.

xiii, 251 p. illus., map. 23.6 cm.
Appendix, p. [219]–237; index, p. [241]–251.
Half title.
Colophon: "Three hundred and fifty copies of which this is No. ——."

2478 ——. 1946 brand book. Twelve original papers pertaining to the history of the West. Edited by Virgil V. Peterson. Denver, Colorado, [the Artcraft press], 1947. Pict. cloth. OP.

xii p., 1 l., 242 p. plates, ports., maps, facsms., fold. col. panorama. 23.6 cm.
Index, p. 232–242.
Half title.
Colophon: "Five hundred copies of which this is No. ——."

2479 ——. Denver Posse the Westerners' brand book. Twelve original studies in western and Rocky Mountain history. Vol. III. Edited by

Herbert O. Brayer; illustrations by Herndon Davis; photographs by William Henry Jackson. Denver, Colorado, ₍the Artcraft press₎, 1949. Pict. cloth. OP.

xiv p., 1 l., 294 p. illus., plates, ports., map. 23.6 cm.
Index, p. 281–294.
Half title; illus., end papers; errata slip tipped in.
Colophon: "Five hundred copies printed from type of which this is No. ——."

2480 ——. 1948 brand book. Twelve original papers pertaining to the history of the West. Edited by Dabney Otis Collins. Denver, Colorado, the Westerners, ₍printed by the Artcraft press, 1949₎. Pict. cloth. OP.

xx p., 2 l., 271 p. illus., plates, ports. 23.6 cm.
Index, p. 265–271.
Colophon: "Limited edition of 500 copies of which this is No. ——."

2481 ——. 1949 brand book. A baker's dozen of essays of the West; its history, places, and people. Written by members and guests of the Denver Posse of the Westerners. Edited by Don Bloch, registrar of marks and brands, 1949. Denver, Colorado, ₍the Golden press₎, 1950. Pict. cloth. OP.

xix p., 1 l., 3–309 ₍1₎ p. plates, ports., maps, facsms. 23.3 cm.
Index, p. 301–309.
Half title; illus. end papers; illus. double t.p.
Colophon: "Limited edition of 500 copies of which this is ——."

2482 ——. 1950 brand book. Volume VI. Edited by Harold H. Dunham. Denver, Colorado, the University of Denver press, ₍1951₎. Pict. cloth. OP.

ix ₍1₎ p., 5 l., 5–312 p. front., plates, ports., map, facsm. 23.6 cm.
Index, p. ₍307₎–312.
Half title; illus. end papers.
Colophon: "Regular edition of seven hundred copies of which this is number ——."

2483 ——. Original contributions to western history, edited by Nolie Mumey. Illustrated by Inez Tatum. Denver, Colorado, the Westerners, the Artcraft press, 1952. Pict. cloth. OP.

11 p.l., 25–579 p. front. (fold. port.), plates (part col.), ports., maps (4 fold.), facsms. (2 fold.), cattle brands. 26.3 cm.
Index, p. 571–579.
Half title; illus. end papers; illus. t.p. (col.); illus. chapter headings (col.); untrimmed.
Colophon: "This is No. —— of the regular edition limited to 500 copies."

2484 ——. 1952 brand book. Sixteen original studies in western history. Edited by Elvon L. Howe, with special sketches by H. D. Bugbee. Denver, Colorado, the Westerners, ₍1953₎. Pict. cloth. OP.

xxi p., 2 l., 297 p. plates, ports. 23.6 cm.
Index, p. 279–297.
Half title; copyright notice on 2d p. after t.p.
Colophon: "Regular edition of five hundred copies. This is copy No. ——."

2485 ——. The Denver Westerners' 1953 brand book: IX. Maurice Frink
—editor, Francis B. Rizzari—associate editor, Nick Eggenhofer—illustrator. Denver, the Westerners, 1954. Pict. cloth. OP.
11 p.l., ₃₃₁–331 ₁₁ p. illus., plates, facsms. 23.5 cm.
Appendix, p. ₃₀₉₁–315; index, p. ₃₁₇₁–331.
Half title; cattle brands on end papers; illus. double t.p.
Colophon: "Regular edition of five hundred copies."

2486 ——. 1954 brand book. Edited by Earl H. Ellis with assistance from
Alan Swallow and sketches by Jeannie Pear as volume ten of the Denver
Posse of the Westerners. ₁Boulder, Colorado, printed by the Johnson
printing company, 1955₁. Pict. cloth.
xxii p., 1 l., ₃₃₁–368 ₁₁ p. plates (1 fold.), ports., map. 23.5 cm.
Index, p. 346–368.
Half title; illus. end papers.
Colophon: "This is No. —— of the regular edition which is limited to 500 copies."

2487 ——. 1955 brand book, being volume eleven of the Denver Posse
of the Westerners, edited by Alan Swallow with original sketches by
Muriel Sibell Wolle. ₁Boulder, Colorado, Johnson publishing company,
1956₁. Pict. cloth.
10 p.l., 21–454 p. plates, ports., facsms., 2 fold. maps. 24 cm.
Index, p. 449–454.
Half title; map on end papers.
Colophon: "This is No. —— of the regular edition limited to five hundred copies."

2488 WESTERNERS' BRAND BOOK (LOS ANGELES CORRAL). The Westerners'
brand book, Los Angeles Corral, 1947. ₁Los Angeles, 1948₁. Cloth and
leather. OP.
8 p.l., 19–176 p. front., illus., plates, ports. 26 cm.
Bibliography, p. 161–168; page of errata, 169; index, p. 170–173.
Half title; illus. end papers.
Colophon: "The Westerners' Brand Book Los Angeles Corral 1947 is limited to
600 copies."

2489 ——. The Westerners' brand book, Los Angeles Corral, 1948. ₁Los
Angeles, 1949₁. Pict. cloth. OP.
7 p.l., 17–175 ₁₁ p. illus., plates, (1 double p. col.), ports., facsms., 2 fold. maps.
26 cm.
Bibliography, p. 163–169; index, p. 170–173.
Half title; illus. end papers.
Colophon: "The Westerners' Brand Book, Los Angeles Corral, 1948, is limited
to 400 copies."

[398]

2490 ——. The Westerners' brand book, Los Angeles Corral, 1949. ₁Los Angeles, 1950₁. Cloth and leather. OP.

7 p.l., 17–263 ₁1₁ p. front., illus. (84 in col.), plates, ports., large fold. map, fold. facsm. 26 cm.
Bibliography, p. 251–254; index, p. 257–262.
Half title; illus. end papers.
Colophon: "The Westerners' Brand Book, Los Angeles Corral, 1949, is limited to 400 copies."

2491 ——. The Westerners' brand book 1950, Los Angeles Corral. ₁Los Angeles, 1951₁. Cloth and leather. OP.

8 p.l., 17–232 p. plates (part col.), ports., facsms., cattle brands. 26 cm.
Contributors, p. 211–214; bibliography, p. 215–226; index, p. 227–230.
Half title; illus. end papers; illus. t.p.
Colophon: "The Westerners' Brand Book, Los Angeles Corral, 1950, is limited to 400 copies."

2492 ——. Westerners' brand book, Los Angeles Corral. Book Five. ₁Los Angeles, 1953₁. Cloth. OP.

7 p.l., 17–180 p. illus. (1 col. double p.), plates, ports., maps, facsms. 26 cm.
Contributors, p. 165–168; bibliography, p. 169–172; index, p. 173–178.
Half title; illus. end papers; illus. t.p.
Colophon: "The Westerners' Brand Book of Los Angeles Corral, Book V . . . limited edition."

2493 ——. The Westerners' brand book, Los Angeles Corral, Book 6. Los Angeles, California, 1956. Cloth and leather.

7 p.l., 17–163 ₁1₁ p. illus., plates, ports., maps, facsms. 26 cm.
Contributors, p. 147–151; bibliography, p. 153–158; index, p. 159–162.
Half title; map on end papers; illus. t.p.
Colophon: "The Westerners' Brand Book of Los Angeles Corral is limited to 400 copies."

2494 WESTON, A. H. Territorial report for 1877; together with an appendix containing a record of marks and brands. Helena, Independent steam print, 1878. Wrappers. Very rare.

32 p. cattle brands. 20 cm.

McMurtie could locate but one copy, that in the Montana Historical Society, Helena.

2495 WESTON, D. H. A record of marks and brands, by D. H. Weston. Helena, Independent steam print, 1881. Wrappers. Very rare.

43 p. cattle brands. 20 cm.

Lists some three hundred Montana marks and brands, their owners and range.

2496 WESTON, W. (ED.). Weston's guide to the Kansas Pacific Railway, containing full and reliable description of the cities and towns, lands, minerals, climate, hunting grounds, etc., along the line of this great national highway, from Kansas City, Mo., and Leavenworth, Kansas, to Denver, Colorado. . . . Map of the railway and its connecting lines. Also a map of lands belonging to the company. . . . "Land map of the Kansas Pacific Railroad Company" and "the best and shortest cattle route from Texas to Abilene." W. Weston, editor. . . . Kansas City, Mo., Bulletin steam printing and engraving house, 1872. Wrappers. Exceedingly rare.

2 p.l., [5]–208 [26] p. plates, ports., 2 fold. maps. 17.2 cm.
Six blank leaves inserted between p. 96 and 97 for memoranda.

There are two later issues with different pagination, one of 204 pages and the other of 216 pages.

2497 ———. Guide map of the best and shortest cattle trail to the Kansas Pacific Railway. Kansas City, 1874. Wrappers. Rare.

21 p. 4 fold. plates, fold. map. 18 cm.

Reprinted with same imprint, same collation but with no plates and with title altered in 1875. These were a separately printed portion of the preceding item.

2498 WHEELER, B. CLARK. Western Colorado and her resources, mineral, agricultural, horticultural, stock raising, manufacturing, and other industries accurately enumerated by reliable and painstaking historians. . . . [By B. Clark Wheeler]. Aspen, Aspen Times print, [1891]. Wrappers. Scarce.

73 p. fold. map at end. 23 cm.
5 p. adv. at end.

2499 WHEELER, HOMER WEBSTER. Buffalo days; forty years in the old West; the personal narrative of a cattleman, Indian fighter, and army officer, by Colonel Homer W. Wheeler . . . with an introduction by Major-General James G. Harbord. Indianapolis, the Bobbs-Merrill co., [1925]. Cloth. OP.

12 p.l., 369 p. front., plates, ports. 22 cm.
Index, p. 365–369.
Half title; vignette.

Rewritten from the author's *The Frontier Trail,* published in 1923; see item No. 2500.

2500 ———. The frontier trail; or, from cowboy to colonel; an authentic narrative of forty-three years in the old West as cattleman, Indian fighter, and army officer, by Colonel Homer W. Wheeler . . . with an introduction by Major-General James Harbord. . . . Los Angeles, published by Times-Mirror press, 1923. Pict. cloth. Scarce.

9 p.l., [15]–334 p. front., illus., plates, ports., facsms. 23.3 cm.

The author is in error when he writes that Samuel Maverick was the "largest land owner in Texas, if not the United States," and that he "owned more cattle on the free public range than any other man in the Lone Star state."

2501 WHETSTONE, DANIEL W. Frontier editor, by Daniel W. Whetstone. New York, Hastings house, publishers, [1956]. Cloth.
viii, 287 p. 2 double-p. maps. 21 cm.
Half title.

A story of Cut Bank, Montana.

2502 WHILLDIN, M. A description of western Texas published by the Galveston, Harrisburg & San Antonio Railroad company. . . . Compiled by M. Whilldin. Galveston, Texas, printed at the "News" steam book & job office, 1876. Stiff pict. wrappers. Rare.
2 p.l., [3]–120 p. front. plates (1 double p.), map (col., verso front wrapper). 18.8 cm.

2503 [WHITE, GOV. BENJAMIN F.]. Report of the Governor of Montana to the Secretary of the Interior, 1889. Washington, Government printing office, 1889. Wrappers. Rare.
3–16 p. tables. 23 cm.

2504 WHITE, JAMES C. The promised land. A history of Brown County, Texas. By James C. White, publisher of the Brownwood Banner. . . . Brownwood, published by Brownwood Banner, 1941. Pict. wrappers. Scarce.
2 p.l., 5–123 p. 19.2 cm.
Index, p. 119–123.
Double column.

2505 WHITE, JOHN. Sketches from America. Part I, Canada; Part II, a picnic to the Rocky Mountains; Part III, the Irish of America, by John White. . . . London, Sampson Low and Marston, 1870. Cloth. Scarce.
viii p., 1 l., 3–373 [16] p. 22.8 cm.
Untrimmed; last 16 p. adv.

2506 WHITE, OWEN PAYNE. The autobiography of a durable sinner. [By] Owen P. White. New York, G. P. Putnam's sons, [1942]. Cloth. OP.
vi p., 1 l., 3–344 p. 22 cm.
Index, p. 339–344.
Half title.
At head of title, "Owen P. White."

Because of a threatened lawsuit, the first printing of this book was recalled before release date for certain deletions. Only a few copies got into private hands; thus copies of the first printing are quite scarce. Pages 239–244 were deleted and new material tipped in.

2507 ———. A frontier mother, by Owen P. White. New York, Minton, Balch & company, 1929. Cloth. Title label pasted on. Scarce.

5 p.l., 11–101 p. 18.3 cm.
Half title.
First published serially in the issues of *Collier's Weekly* for October 12, 19, and 26, 1929.

2508 ———. My Texas 'tis of thee, by Owen P. White. New York, G. P. Putnam's sons, 1936. Cloth. OP.

6 p.l., 274 p. 19.6 cm.
Half title; pub. device; untrimmed.

2509 ———. Texas, an informal biography, by Owen P. White. New York, G. P. Putnam's sons, [1945]. Cloth. OP.

ix p., 1 l., 3–268 p. front. (port.), illus., plates, ports., facsm. 20.5 cm.
Index, p. 265–268.
Half title; map on end papers.

2510 ———. Them was the days; from El Paso to prohibition, by Owen P. White, with drawings by Ross Santee. New York, Minton, Balch & company, 1925. Cloth. OP.

6 p.l., 3–235 p. front., illus. 21.4 cm.
Half title; pub. device; untrimmed.

2511 WHITE, STEWART EDWARD. Arizona nights, by Stewart Edward White; illustrations by N. C. Wyeth. New York, the McClure company, MCMVII. Cloth. Col. pict. label pasted on. OP.

viii p., 3 l., [3]–351 [4] p. front. (with tissue), 7 plates (incl. front., all col.). 19.7 cm.
Half title; device.
Last 4 p. adv.

2512 ———. The mountains, by Stewart Edward White. . . . Illustrated by Fernand Lungren. New York, McClure, Phillips & company, 1904. Pict. cloth. OP.

5 p.l., 3–282 p. front. (col.), 16 plates (incl. front.). 21.8 cm.
Pub. device; untrimmed.

2513 WHITING, PERRY. Autobiography of Perry Whiting, pioneer building material merchant of Los Angeles. Compiled and published by Perry Whiting. . . . Los Angeles, printed by Smith-Barnes corporation, [1930]. Pict. fabricoid. OP.

7 p.l., 17–334 p. front. (port.), illus., plates, ports., map. 23.5 cm.

2514 WHITSON, DON. Cowhand, by Don Whitson. [Monrovia, California, Donlen company, 1946]. Col. pict. boards. OP.

3 p.l., [87] p. (no pagination). illus. 21 cm.

Cartoons and text on cowboy life. Printed on one side of paper only.

[402]

2515 WIDMER, JACK. Practical beef production, by Jack Widmer, with photographs by Barney Seligman and Jack Widmer. New York, Charles Scribner's sons, [1946]. Cloth. OP.

xvii, 93 p. 8 p. plates, tables. 24 cm.

2516 WILCOX, E. V. The grazing industry, by E. V. Wilcox. Hawaii Agricultural Experiment Station.... Honolulu, Paradise of the Pacific print, 1911. Wrappers. Scarce.

[5]–91 p. 22 cm.

Though published in Hawaii, this book deals with the cattle industry of the American West.

2517 WILDER, D. W. The annals of Kansas City. By D. W. Wilder.... Topeka, Kan., T. Dwight Thacker, Kansas publishing house, 1886. Boards and cloth. Scarce.

2 p.l., [5]–1196 p. front. (port. with tissue), tables. 23.2 cm.
Index, p. [1171]–1196.

Abilene, Dodge City, cattle, and cattle trails.

2518 WILHELM, STEPHEN R. Texas, yesterday and tomorrow, by Steve Wilhelm. Houston, Texas, Gulf publishing company, [1947]. Cloth. Scarce.

4 p.l., 134 p. 20.7 cm.
Index, p. 132–134.

2519 WILLARD, JAMES F., and COLLIN B. GOODYKOONTZ (EDS.). The trans-Mississippi West. Papers read at a conference held at the University of Colorado June 18–June 21, 1929. Edited by James F. Willard and Collin B. Goodykoontz. Boulder, University of Colorado, 1930. Cloth. OP.

xi, 366 p. 20.4 cm.
Index, p. 343–366.
Half title.

2520 WILLCOX, R. N. Reminiscences of California life, being an abridged description of scenes which the author passed through in California and other lands . . . , by R. N. Willcox. Avery, Ohio, Willcox print, 1897. Cloth. Scarce.

3 p.l., 5–290 p. 21.5 cm.

It is said that only seventy-five copies of this work were issued.

2521 WILLIAMS, D. W. Beef cattle production in the South, by D. W. Williams. [Danville, Ill., the Interstate printers and publishers], 1941. Pict. cloth.

5 p.l., 11–442 p. front., plates, maps, graphs, tables. 22 cm.
Appendix, p. 420–437; index, p. 438–442.
Illus. end papers.

2522 WILLIAMS, HARRY. Texas trails; legends of the great Southwest, by Harry Williams. . . . Pen and ink sketches by Hans Reuter. . . . San Antonio, Texas, Naylor printing company, [1932]. Pict. cloth. OP.

vii p., 2 l., 269 p. illus. 24 cm.
Index, p. 263–269.
Half title; illus. end papers; tailpieces; vignette; "First edition" on t.p.

"These stories, some now revised and altered, appeared in the 'Texas Trail' column of the *San Antonio Light* between the years 1927 and 1931."—Foreword.

2523 WILLIAMS, J. E. (JIM). Fifty-eight years in the Panhandle of Texas, by J. E. (Jim) Williams. Austin, Texas, Firm Foundation publishing house, [1944]. Cloth. Scarce.

2 p.l., [5]–137 p. plates, ports., cattle brands. 23.6 cm.

2524 WILLIAMS, J. R. Cowboys out our way, [by] J. R. Williams, with an introduction by J. Frank Dobie. New York, Charles Scribner's sons, 1951. Cloth.

4 p.l., 103 p. illus., plates. 19x27.6 cm.
Illus. t.p.; first edition: letter "A" on copyright p.

A book of cartoons about the cowboy.

2525 ———. Out our way, [by] J. R. Williams. New York, Charles Scribner's sons, 1943. Pict. boards. OP.

[126] p. (no pagination). plates. 20.5 cm.

2526 ———. Twenty years of out our way, by J. R. Williams. [N.p., n.d.]. Stiff wrappers. (Cover title). OP.

[16] p. (no pagination). front. (port.), plates. 24 cm.

All these books contain splendid cartoons of cowboy life created by a man who knows his subject thoroughly.

2527 WILLIAMS, J. W. The big ranch country, by J. W. Williams. Illustrations by Stephen D. Thorpe. Wichita Falls, Texas, Terry brothers, printers, 1954. Cloth.

6 p.l., [13]–307 p. illus., plates, map. 23.6 cm.
Index, p. [285]–307.
Half title; illus. chapter headings.

2528 WILLIAMS, R. H. With the border ruffians. Memories of the far West, 1852–1868, by R. H. Williams, sometime lieutenant in the Kansas Rangers, and afterward captain in the Texas Rangers. Edited by E. W. Williams. With portraits. London, 1907. Cloth. Scarce.

xviii p., 1 l., 3–476 p. front. (port. with tissue), plates, ports. 22.3 cm.
Index, p. 473–478.

[404]

Half title.

Reprinted with same collation in 1908; American edition, New York, E. P. Dutton and Co., 1907, with same collation; another edition printed in Toronto in 1919.

2529 WILLIAMSON, CHARLES OWEN. Breaking and training the stock horse, by Charles O. Williamson. Silhouettes by James Wallis, sketches by Carl Hoobing. ₁Caldwell, Idaho, the Caxton printers, ltd., 1950₁. Cloth.
x, 89 p. illus. 26 cm.
Illus. t.p.

2530 WILLIS, JACK. Roosevelt in the rough, by Jack Willis, as told to Horace Smith. Illustrated. New York, Ives Washburn, 1931. Cloth. Scarce.
xiv p., 1 l., 3–246 p. front., plates, letters in facsm. 22.3 cm.
Half title; pub. device; untrimmed.

2531 WILLIS, W. S. A story of the big western ranches. W. S. Willis, author. . . . Ft. Worth, Texas, ₁1955₁. Stiff pict. wrappers. (Cover title).
4 p.l., ₁1₁ p., 6–67 p. illus., 1 port. 23.7 cm.
Privately printed in an edition of 400 copies.

2532 WILLSON, MRS. EUGENE B. Cabin days in Wyoming, by Mrs. E. B. Willson. A historical romance of the Running Water range. ₁Lusk₁, privately printed by Mrs. E. B. Willson, 1939. Cloth. OP.
₁3₁–64 p. front., illus., plates, port. 23.5 cm.

2533 WILLSON, ROSCOE G. Pioneer cattlemen of Arizona, by Roscoe G. Willson. Phoenix, Arizona, printed by McGrew commercial printery, ₁1951₁. Stiff pict. wrappers.
3 p.l., 7–48 p. illus., ports. 23 cm.
Vignette.

2534 WILSHIRE, W. W. Leases of land in the Indian Territory for cattle grazing purposes. Washington, Milans, 1890. Wrappers. Rare.
18 p. 19 cm.

"Set forth to prove the right of the cattlemen to occupy the lands of the Indian Nation because of their direct lease from the Indians."

2535 WILSON, MRS. AUGUSTA. Memorial sketch of the first national convention of cattlemen held November 17–22, 1884, at St. Louis, Mo., with appendix of official report of convention. St. Louis, Mo., Joseph G. McCoy, 1885. Stiff wrappers. Very rare.
95 p. illus., plate (2 col., 1 double p.), ports., fold. map at end. 23 cm.
Appendix, p. 73–95.

2536 ———. Parson's memorial and historical library magazine. History of the memorial and historical library at Parsons, Kansas, and other libraries in the state and elsewhere . . . , edited and compiled by Mrs. Augusta Wilson, January, 1885. Illustrated. St. Louis, Mo., published by Becktold & co., 1885. Pict. cloth. Scarce.

xiii, 409 p. front. (port. with tissue), illus., ports. 26.7 cm.
75 p. adv. at end; double column.

Contains the "Opening session of the First National Cattle Growers' Convention . . . of ten thousand cattlemen . . . biographical sketches and portraits of prominent men attending the convention."

2537 WILSON, EDWARD. An unwritten history. A record from the exciting days of early Arizona, by Edward Wilson. Cover design by O. D. Brown. [Phoenix, Ariz., the McNeil co., 1915]. Pict. cloth. Rare.

3 p.l., 7–77 [1] p. 17.3 cm.

2538 WILSON, GOODRIDGE. Roosevelts and ranches, by Goodridge Wilson. [N.p.], Texas Centennial edition, [1936]. Wrappers. Scarce.

2 p.l., [7]–67 p. illus. 23.8 cm.

2539 WILSON, H. T. Historical sketch of Santa Fe, by H. T. Wilson. Chicago, 1880. Wrappers. Rare.

86 p. illus., photographic view of Santa Fe. 20.2 cm.

This rare little volume gives a general history of the territory, biographical sketches of some of its inhabitants, and accounts of stock raising and mining; and has appended the mining laws, a table of distances, and a business directory.

2540 WILSON, ROBERT R., and ETHEL M. SEARS. History of Grant County, Kansas, by R. R. Wilson and Ethel M. Sears. [Wichita, Kansas, printed by Wichita Press, 1950]. Cloth.

4 p.l., 13–278 p. front. (port.), maps. 20.5 cm.

2541 WILSON, RUFUS ROCKWELL. A noble company of adventurers, by Rufus Rockwell Wilson. . . . Illustrated from drawings by May Fratz and from photographs. New York, B. W. Dodge and company, 1908. Pict. cloth. Scarce.

2 p.l., 219 p. front., plates. 19.2 cm.
Device.

Chapter III is on the cowboy.

2542 ———. Out of the West, by Rufus Rockwell Wilson. . . . Illustrations by Sidney E. Fletcher. New York, the Press of the Pioneers, 1933. Cloth. OP.

7 p.l., 452 p. illus. 24.5 cm.

Republished in a revised and enlarged edition, New York, Wilson-Erickson, inc., 1936.

xvii, 480 p. front., illus. 24.2 cm.
Bibliography, p. 461–468; index, p. 469–480.
Half title.
Colophon: "Of this edition Out of the West, three hundred copies have been signed by the author. This is copy No. ——."

2543 WING, JACK. The great Union Stock Yards of Chicago. Their railroad connections, bank and exchange, the Hough House, the water supply, and general features. Also a sketch of the live stock trade and the old yards. By Jack Wing. Chicago, published by the Religio-Philosophical publishing associates, 1865. Wrappers. Rare.
2 p.l., [3]–32 [10] p. front. (map). 22.2 cm.
Adv. recto back wrapper.

This rare book examined in the library of Thomas W. Streeter, Morristown, N. J.

2544 WINN, MARY DAY. The macadam trail. Ten thousand miles by motor coach, by Mary Day Winn. Illustrated by E. H. Suydam. New York, Alfred A. Knopf, MCMXXXI. Cloth. OP.
xiv p., 1 l., 3–319, i–xii p. front. (col.), full-p. plates. 23 cm.
Index, p. i–xii.
Half title; illus. end papers; illus. chapter headings; vignette; "First edition" on copyright p.

Contains some information on the Johnson County War of Wyoming.

2545 WINSER, HENRY J. The great Northwest. A guide-book and itinerary for the use of tourists and travellers over the lines of the Northern Pacific Railroad.... With map and many illustrations. By Henry J. Winser.... New York, G. P. Putnam's sons, 1883. Cloth. Scarce.
6 p.l., 13–276 [8] p. front. (with tissue), illus., plates, large fold. map in pocket at end. 17.5 cm.

Has a chapter on ranching and cowboys.

2546 WINSLOW, EDITH (BLACK). In those days, by Edith (Black) Winslow. Memoirs of Edwards Plateau. San Antonio, Texas, the Naylor company, [1950]. Cloth.
ix p., 2 l., 184 p. plates, ports. 21.5 cm.

2547 WINTER, NEVIN OTTO. Texas, the marvelous. The state of six flags. ... By Nevin O. Winter.... With a map and fifty-four plates, of which six are in colour. Boston, the Page company, MDCCCCXVI. Pict. cloth. Scarce.
xii, 343 p. front. (col. with tissue), plates (part col.), ports. (1 col.), fold. map. 25 cm.
Bibliography, p. 337; index, p. 339–343.
Half title; illus. end papers (dif.); untrimmed.

Republished, New York, Garden City publishing co., inc., [1936].

[407]

2548 WISE, EMMA CLEMENT. Pioneering days in Oregon. ₁By₁ Emma Clement Wise. New York, Vantage press, ₁1955₁. Cloth.

3 p.l., 7–104 p. 20.8 cm.
"First edition" on copyright p.

2549 WISTER, FANNY KEMBLE (ED.). Owen Wister out West. His journals and letters. Edited by Fanny Kemble Wister. ₁Chicago₁, the University of Chicago press, ₁1958₁. Pict. cloth and boards.

xix ₁2₁ p., 2–269 p. illus., plates, port. 22.8 cm.
A Wister bibliography, p. 262–264; acknowledgments, p. 265–266; index, p. 267–269.
Half title; pub. device.

Some of Wister's recollections of ranch life and cowboys.

2550 WOOD, ASA BUTLER. Fifty years of yesterdays, ₁by₁ A. B. Wood. An autobiographical history of a western Nebraska region from its initial settlement, its half century of progress and final development into the most fertile, prosperous, and populous section of the state. Gering, Nebr., Courier press, 1945. Cloth. OP.

5 p.l., 9–204 p. front. (port.), plates, ports., facsms., tables. 23.5 cm.
Half title; foreword precedes t.p.

2551 ———. Pioneer tales of the North Platte Valley and Nebraska Panhandle. A miscellaneous collection of historical reference material, anecdotal and reminiscent, as written or compiled by A. B. Woods. . . . Gering, Nebraska, Courier press, 1938. Pict. cloth. OP.

5 ₁1₁ p., 1 l., 10–288 p. port. 23.4 cm.
Double column.

2552 WOOD, ELIZABETH (LAMBERT). Pete French, cattle king. A biographical novel. ₁By₁ Elizabeth (Lambert) Wood. Portland, Oregon, Binfords & Mort, publishers, ₁1951₁. Pict. cloth.

3 p.l., 7–229 ₁1₁ p. 22.2 cm.
Half title; pict. map front end papers only.

Although written as a novel, the book follows closely the life of this well-known cattleman.

2553 WOOTEN, ELMER OTIS. Carrying capacity of grazing ranges in southern Arizona. By E. O. Wooten. Washington, Government printing office, 1918. Wrappers. (Cover title). OP.

40 p. plates on 6 leaves, maps, diagrs., tables. 23 cm.
U. S. Dept. of Agriculture *Bulletin No. 367*.

2554 ———. Certain desert plants as emergency stock feed. By E. O. Wooten. Washington, Government printing office, 1918. Wrappers. (Cover title).

31 ₁1₁ p. map, viii plates on 4 l. 23 cm.
U. S. Dept. of Agriculture *Bulletin No. 728.*

2555 ———. Factors affecting range management in New Mexico. By E. O. Wooten. Washington, Government printing office, 1915. Wrappers. (Cover title).

39 p. ix plates on 5 l., maps, tables. 23 cm.
U. S. Dept. of Agriculture *Bulletin No. 211.*

2556 ———. The range problem in New Mexico, by E. O. Wooten. *Bulletin 66,* April, 1908, New Mexico College of Agriculture and Mechanical Arts. Agricultural Experiment Station. Albuquerque, Albuquerque Morning Journal, 1908. Wrappers. Scarce.

46 p. ports., map, tables. 22 cm.

2557 ———. The relation of land tenure to the use of arid grazing lands of the southwestern states. By E. O. Wooten. Washington, Government printing office, 1922. Wrappers. (Cover title). OP.

72 p. maps (1 fold.), diagr. 23 cm.
U. S. Dept. of Agriculture *Bulletin No. 1001.*

2558 WOOTEN, MATTIE LLOYD (ED.). Women tell the story of the Southwest. Compiled and edited by Mattie Lloyd Wooten. . . . San Antonio, Texas, the Naylor company, 1940. Cloth. OP.

xvii, 394 p. front. 23.5 cm.
Glossary, p. 375–376; index, p. 379–394.
Half title; device.

Has several chapters on cattle and cowboys.

2559 WORKMAN, BOYLE. Boyle Workman's The city that grew, as told to Caroline Walker. Illustrations, a series of original pen drawings by Harriet Morton Holmes; with additional drawings by Orpha Klinker Carpenter; drawings from old photographs by Daniel S. MacManus. Los Angeles, the Southland publishing co., 1935. Cloth. Scarce.

xiv p., 2 l., ₁5₁–430 p. front. (port.), illus. 25 cm.
Index, p. 393–430.
Illus. half title; untrimmed.
Colophon: "This copy of the de luxe edition was prepared for ———."

2560 WREN, THOMAS (ED.). A history of the state of Nevada, its resources and people. ₁By₁ the late Hon. Thomas Wren, of Reno, editor-in-chief. . . . Illustrated. Complete in one volume. New York, Chicago, the Lewis publishing company, 1904. Cloth. Scarce.

5 p.l., ₁11₁–760 p. front. (port. with tissue), plates, ports. (part with tissues).
26.7 cm.

2561 WRIGHT, EDGAR. The representative old cowboy, Ed Wright, by Edgar Wright. An autobiography. Illustrated by Don Whiston. . . . Proofed and typed by Edith Ballow. ₍N.p., n.d.₎. Pict. boards.

viii, 216 p. illus., plates, ports. 22.2 cm.
"Five hundred copies of this book have been printed and paid for by author for charity, two hundred copies have been given to St. Joseph's Orphanage of Torrington, Wyoming. This book has not been published for sale. . . ."—t.p.

2562 WRIGHT, MURIEL HAZEL. The story of Oklahoma, by Muriel H. Wright. Editorially assisted by Joseph B. Thoburn. Oklahoma City, Oklahoma, Webb publishing company, ₍1930₎. Cloth. OP.

xix, 342 p. front., plates, ports., maps. 19.6 cm.
Bibliography, p. 320–325; vocabulary, p. 327–330; index, p. 331–342.
"Points to be remembered" (summary) after each chapter.

2563 WRIGHT, PETER. A three-foot stool, by Peter Wright. . . . London, Smith, Elder & co., 1909. Cloth. Scarce.

3 p.l., 256 ₍8₎ p. 20.6 cm.
Half title; last 8 p. adv.
American edition, New York, E. P. Dutton and co., same year.

2564 WRIGHT, ROBERT MARR. Dodge City, the cowboy capital, and the great Southwest in the days of the wild Indian, the buffalo, the cowboy, dance halls, gambling halls, and bad men, by Robert M. Wright. . . . ₍Wichita, Kan., Wichita Eagle press, 1913₎. Pict. cloth. Scarce.

4 p.l., 9–344 p. front. (col.), plates, ports. 20.3 cm.
Copyright notice on recto of frontispiece.

It is said that most of the edition was destroyed by the printer, hence its scarcity. A later edition without date or colored frontispiece is sometimes confused with the first edition. The first edition may be identified by the colored frontispiece with copyright date on recto. The reprint has a portrait of the author in black and white instead of the colored frontispiece.

2565 WRIGHT, SOLOMON ALEXANDER. My rambles as East Texas cowboy, hunter, fisherman, tie-cutter, by Solomon Alexander Wright. Arranged with introduction by J. Frank Dobie. Illustrations by B. E. Lewis. Austin, Texas, Texas Folklore society, 1942. Pict. cloth. OP.

xiii p., 1 l., 159 p. front. (double p.), illus. 22.2 cm.
(Range Life Series).

2566 WYATT, FRANK S., and GEORGE RAINEY. Brief history of Oklahoma, by Frank S. Wyatt . . . and George Rainey. . . . Oklahoma City, Okla., published by Webb publishing company, ₍1919₎. Cloth. Scarce.

3 p.l., 13–135 p. ports., map. 20.2 cm.

A chapter on the Chisholm Trail and the overland cattle trade, and one on cattle ranches of Oklahoma with information on Jesse Chisholm.

2567 WYLLYS, RUFUS KAY. Arizona, the history of a frontier state, by Rufus Kay Wyllys. Phoenix, Arizona, Hobson & Herr, [1950]. Cloth.

xiii p., 1 l., 408 p. illus., plates, ports., 9 maps, facsm. 22 cm.

Guide to references, p. 365–384; index, p. 387–408.

Half title ("Frontier" misspelled "Frintier"); illus. end papers; t.p. in red and black; vignette; "First edition" on copyright p.

Also published in a de luxe edition limited to 406 copies and signed by the artist, cartographer, designer, and author.

2568 WYMAN, WALKER D. Nothing but prairie and sky. Life on the Dakota range in the early days. Recorded by Walker D. Wyman from the original notes of Bruce Siberts. Norman, University of Oklahoma press, [1953]. Cloth.

xiii p., 1 l., 2–217 p. plates, ports., pict. map. 22 cm.

Index, p. 209–217.

Half title; double t.p.; "First edition" on copyright p.

2569 ———. The wild horse of the West, by Walker D. Wyman. Illustrated by Harold Bryant. Caldwell, Idaho, the Caxton printers, ltd., 1945. Pict. cloth. OP.

8 p.l., [17]–348 p. front. (col.), illus. 23.5 cm.

Bibliography, p. [329]–342; index, p. [343]–348.

Half title; map on end papers; vignette.

2570 WYOMING. Abstracts from the Wyoming stock laws. [N.p.], 1926. Pamphlet. (Cover title). OP.

[21] p. (no pagination). 13.5x10.6 cm.

2571 ———. Albany County, Wyoming; its climate and educational advantages, accessible to the open market, has won most important recognition at the great expositions; room for settlement and development. . . . Agricultural resources, livestock, and mixed husbandry. [N.p., n.d.]. Wrappers. Scarce.

80 p. front., plates, ports., tables. 23 cm.

2572 ———. An act providing for a board of live stock commissioners of the state of Wyoming and regulating the number, duties, and compensations of such commission and its officers and employees. Cheyenne, the Daily Sun publishing house, 1891. Wrappers. (Cover title). Scarce.

7 p. 25.4 cm.

2573 ———. Annual report of the Wyoming Agricultural College and Experiment Station for the year 1893. Laramie, Wyo., the Republican book and job printers, 1894. Wrappers. Scarce.

2 p.l., [5]–248 p. tables. 22 cm.

2574 ———. Biennial report of the state veterinarian of the state of Wyoming for the years 1913 and 1914, ending September 30, 1914. . . . Sheridan, Wyo., Miller printing co., [1914]. Wrappers. Scarce.
120 p. tables. 23.3 cm.

2575 ———. Biennial report of the Board of Live Stock Commissioners of Wyoming to the acting Governor of Wyoming, 1917–1918. [Cheyenne, Wyo., Labor Journal co., 1919]. Wrappers. Scarce.
23 [1] p. tables, reports. 22.8 cm.

2576 ———. Biennial report of the Board of Live Stock Commissioners of Wyoming, 1920–1922. [Cheyenne, Wyoming, 1922]. Wrappers. Scarce.
8 p. 22.8 cm.

2577 ———. Biennial report of the Board of Live Stock Commissioners of Wyoming to the Governor of Wyoming, 1922–1924. Cheyenne, Wyo., Labor Journal publishing co., 1924. Wrappers. Scarce.
8 [1] p. 22.6 cm.

2578 ———. Brands and notes concerning them in Albany County. [N.p., n.d.]. Boards. Rare.
105 p. cattle brands. 26.7 cm.
Photo-lithoprinted on one side of paper only.

2579 ———. Brands owned by members of the Wyoming Stock Growers' Association. Chicago, the J. M. W. Jones stationery & printing co., 1882. Leather. Rare.
2 p.l., [5]–57 [2] p. cattle brands. 16.8 cm.
Last 2 p. index.

2580 ———. Brands published by the Wyoming Stock Growers' Association. Second edition. Chicago, the J. M. W. Jones stationery & printing co., 1883. Leather. Rare.
2 p.l., [5]–81 [2] p. cattle brands. 16.8 cm.
Last 2 p. index.

Both the above brand books seen in the library of Thomas W. Streeter, Morristown, N. J.

2581 ———. Brand book for 1884. Published by the Wyoming Stock Growers' Association. Third edition. Cheyenne, Northwestern Live Stock Journal, [1884]. Leather. Rare.
2 p.l., [128] p. (no pagination). cattle brands. 19 cm.

2582 ———. Brand book for 1885. Published by the Wyoming Stock Growers' Association. Fourth edition. Cheyenne, Northwestern Live Stock Journal, 1885. Cloth. Rare.
2 p.l., [118] p. (no pagination). cattle brands. 18.6 cm.

[412]

2583 ———. Brand book published by the Wyoming Stock Growers' Association, 1887. Fifth edition. Cheyenne, the Northwestern Live Stock Journal, 1887. Cloth. Rare.

3 p.l., ₍9₎–125 p. cattle brands. 20 cm.

2584 ———. By-laws of the Wyoming Stock Growers' Association. ₍Cheyenne, Wyo., Gereke quick job printing, n.d.₎. Pamphlet. (Cover title). Rare.

8 p. 21.5 cm.

2585 ———. By-laws of the Wyoming Stock Growers' Association amended and adopted April 4, 1881, and the laws of Wyoming for protection of stock growers. Compiled May 3, 1881, by Wyoming Stock Growers' Association. Cheyenne, Wyo., Daily Sun steam printing house, ₍1881₎. Wrappers. Rare.

31 ₍1₎ p. 20.8 cm.

2586 ———. By-laws and reports of the Wyoming Stock Growers' Association amended and adopted April 4, 1882, and the laws of Wyoming for the protection of stock growers, as amended by the Seventh Assembly. Compiled October 15, 1882 by Wyoming Stock Growers' Association. Cheyenne, Wyo., Bristol and Knabe, printers and bookbinders, 1883. Wrappers. Rare.

78 ₍1₎ p. 20.5 cm.

2587 ———. By-laws and reports of the Wyoming Stock Growers' Association and the laws of Wyoming for the protection of stock growers, as amended by the Eighth Assembly. Cheyenne, Wyo., Bristol and Knabe, printers and bookbinders, 1884. Limber cloth. Scarce.

120 p. 22.9 cm.
Instructions to foremen, stock laws, and list of members, p. ₍66₎–103.
Leaf of adv. preceding t.p. and leaf of adv. follows p. 96.

2588 ———. By-laws and reports of the Wyoming Stock Growers' Association and the laws of Wyoming for the protection of stock growers, as amended by the Eighth Assembly. Cheyenne, Wyo., Bristol and Knabe, printers and bookbinders, 1885. Limber cloth. Scarce.

179 p. 22.5 cm.

2589 ———. By-laws of the Wyoming Stock Growers' Association, adopted at Laramie, Wyoming, June 6, 1946. Seventy-fourth annual convention. ₍N.p., n.d.₎. Pamphlet. (Cover title). OP.

8 p. 15.6x8.5 cm.

2590 ———. By-laws, resolutions, and list of members of the Wyoming

Stock Growers' Association and the laws of Wyoming to protect stock growers. Compiled May 3, 1881, by Wyoming Stock Growers' Association. Cheyenne, Wyo., Daily Sun steam printing house, ₁1881₁. Wrappers. Rare.

31 ₁2₁ p.   20.4 cm.

2591 ——. By-laws, secretary's report, resolutions, and list of members of the Wyoming Stock Growers' Association, amended and adopted April 4, 1882, and the laws of Wyoming to protect stock growers as amended by the Seventh Assembly. Compiled October 15, 1882, by Wyoming Stock Growers' Association. Cheyenne, Wyo., Bristol and Knabe, printers and bookbinders, 1882. Wrappers. Rare.

59 ₁2₁ p.   20.5 cm.
2 p. adv. at end.

2592 ——. Cattle production on Wyoming's valley ranches. ₁Laramie, Wyo.₁. *Bulletin No. 197,* July, 1933. ₁University of Wyoming Agricultural Experiment Station₁. Wrappers. (Cover title). Scarce.

125 p.   plates charts (1 fold.), tables.   22.6 cm.

2593 ——. Constitution and by-laws of the International Range Association with list of permanent officers and circular by the executive committee. Cheyenne, Wyo., Northwestern Live Stock Journal, 1886. Pamphlet. (Cover title). Rare.

14 p.   22.6 cm.

2594 ——. Constitution of the proposed state of Wyoming. Adopted in convention at Cheyenne, Wyoming, September 30, 1889. Cheyenne, Wyo., the Cheyenne Leader printing co., 1889. Wrappers. Rare.

60 p.   21.2 cm.

Has a section on stock raising.

2595 ——. Description and map of lands for sale belonging to the Swan Land and Cattle Company, Chugwater, Wyoming. ₁N.p., n.d.₁. Stiff wrappers. (Cover title). Rare.

13 p.   fold. map.   26 cm.

2596 ——. Fifth biennial report of the Live Stock and Sanitary Board, state of Wyoming. For the period October 1, 1940 to October 1, 1942. Wrappers. (Cover title). OP.

2 p.l., 2–15 p.   tables.   28 cm.
Mimeographed on one side of paper only.

2597 ——. First biennial report of the Live Stock and Sanitary Board of the state of Wyoming. Covering the period April 1, 1933 to October 1, 1934. Wrappers. (Cover title). OP.

2 p.l., 13 p.   28.2 cm.
Mimeographed on one side of paper only.

2598 ———. Fourth biennial report of the Live Stock and Sanitary Board of the state of Wyoming. For the period October 1, 1938 to October 1, 1940. Wrappers. (Cover title). OP.

2 p.l., 2–18 p.   tables.   28 cm.
Mimeographed on one side of paper only.

2599 ———. Laws and regulations of the Stock Association of Laramie County, Wyoming Territory. Adopted February 23, 1874. Cheyenne, Leader job and book print, 1874. Wrappers. Rare.

7 p.   15 cm.

2600 ———. Laws of Wyoming passed for the protection of the live stock growers. Published under the direction of the Stock Growers' Association of Laramie County, Wyoming. Cheyenne, Daily Sun book and job printing house, 1876. Wrappers. Rare.

7 p.   20.5 cm.

2601 ———. Letters from old friends and members of the Wyoming Stock Growers' Association. Cheyenne, Wyo., the S. A. Bristol co., [1923]. Stiff wrappers. Rare.

2 p.l., 5–55 p.   23.4 cm.

2602 ———. List of members, by-laws and reports of the Wyoming Stock Growers' Association and the laws of Wyoming for the protection of stock growers, as amended by the Ninth Assembly. Cheyenne, Wyo., Bristol and Knabe printing co., 1886. Wrappers. Rare.

129 p.   21.8 cm.

2603 ———. List of members, by-laws, and reports of the Wyoming Stock Growers' Association. Cheyenne, Wyo., Bristol and Knabe printing co., printers and bookbinders, 1887. Wrappers. Rare.

79 p.   21.8 cm.

2604 ———. Live stock laws and regulations of Wyoming. [Cheyenne], 1921. Wrappers. (Cover title). Scarce.

54 p.   22.6 cm.
12 p. adv. at end.

2605 ———. Maverick bill passed by the Wyoming Legislature at its session of 1888. Cheyenne, Wyoming, published by the Stock Journal, [n.d., c.1888]. Wrappers. Rare.

24 p.   14.5x8.2 cm.

2606 ———. New Hampshire Cattle Company. Location of range: Wyoming Territory. . . . Concord, N. H., printed by the Republican press association, 1885. Wrappers. Rare.

[3]–10 p. 18.3 cm.

First annual report, issued January 10, 1885.

2607 ———. Official brand book of the state of Wyoming. Showing all the brands on cattle, horses, mules, asses, and sheep recorded under the provisions of the act approved February 18th, 1909, and other brands recorded up to October 11th, 1912. Issued by the State Board of Live Stock Commissioners of Wyoming. Laramie, Wyoming, the Laramie Republican company, printers and binders, 1913. Leather. Scarce.

2 p.l., 252 p. cattle brands. 20 cm.
Index, p. [207]–252.

2608 ———. Official brand book of the state of Wyoming and a compilation of laws affecting live stock. This book is intended as a complete transcript of all the live stock brands and marks of record in the office of the State Board of Live Stock Commissioners at Cheyenne, June 30, 1916. Cheyenne, issued by the State Board of Live Stock Commissioners of Wyoming, [1916]. Leather. Scarce.

2 p.l., 450 p. cattle brands. 19.4 cm.

2609 ———. Official brand book of the state of Wyoming and a compilation of laws affecting live stock. This book is intended as a complete transcript of all the live stock brands and marks of record in the office of the State Board of Live Stock Commissioners at Cheyenne, July 1, 1919. Issued by the State Board of Live Stock Commissioners of Wyoming at Cheyenne. Laramie, Wyoming, the Laramie Republican company, printers and binders, 1919. Leather. Scarce.

2 p.l., 5–639 p. cattle brands. 20.5 cm.

2610 ———. Official brand book of the state of Wyoming. This book is intended as a complete transcript of all the live stock brands and marks of record in the office of the State Board of Live Stock Commissioners at Cheyenne, July 1, 1927. . . . Casper, Wyoming, published by S. E. Boyer and company, 1927. Leather. Scarce.

2 p.l., 446 p. cattle brands. 20.7 cm.

2611 ———. Official brand book of the state of Wyoming. This book is a complete transcript of all the live stock brands and marks of record in the office of the Live Stock & Sanitary Board at Cheyenne, June 30, 1936. . . . Sheridan, Wyoming, published by the Mills company, printers . . . 1936. Leather. Scarce.

3 p.l., 446 p. cattle brands. 20.4 cm.

2612 ———. Official report of the state examiner of the financial condition of the Wyoming Stock Growers' Association, covering the period from April 1, 1886, to March 1, 1915. Report of the auditing committee appointed by the executive committee of the association. Cheyenne, Wyo., the S. A. Bristol co., 1916. Wrappers. Scarce.

24 p. tables. 23 cm.

2613 ———. Poisonous plants and livestock poisoning. ₍Laramie, Wyo.₎, *Bulletin No. 231,* May, 1939. ₍University of Wyoming Agricultural Experiment Station₎. Wrappers. OP.

104 p. plates, ports. 23 cm.

2614 ———. Report of the Board of Live Stock Commissioners of Wyoming. ₍Cheyenne, Wyo., 1892₎. Wrappers. Rare.

10 p. 23.2 cm.

2615 ———. Report of the Board of Live Stock Commissioners of Wyoming to the Governor of Wyoming, 1919–1920. Sheridan, Wyo., the Mills co., ₍1920₎. Wrappers. Scarce.

10 p. 22.2 cm.

2616 ———. Report of the acting Governor of Wyoming Territory, made to the Secretary of the Interior for the year 1878. Washington, Government printing office, 1878. Wrappers. Rare.

2 p.l., ₍5₎–61 p. tables. 23 cm.

2617 ———. Report of the acting Governor of Wyoming Territory made to the Secretary of the Interior for the year 1880. Washington, Government printing office, 1880. Wrappers. Rare.

12 p. 23 cm.

2618 ———. Report of the acting Governor of Wyoming Territory made to the Secretary of the Interior for the year 1881. Washington, Government printing office, 1882. Wrappers. Scarce.

79 p. tables. 23 cm.

2619 ———. Report of the acting Governor of Wyoming Territory made to the Secretary of the Interior for the year 1883. Washington, Government printing office, 1883. Wrappers. Scarce.

69 p. tables, fold. map at end. 23 cm.

2620 ———. Report of the acting Governor of Wyoming Territory made to the Secretary of the Interior, 1885. Washington, Government printing office, 1885. Wrappers. Scarce.

118 p. tables, fold. map at end. 23 cm.

2621 ———. Report of the acting Governor of Wyoming Territory made to the Secretary of the Interior for the year 1886. Washington, Government printing office, 1886. Wrappers. Scarce.

60 p.   tables.   23 cm.

2622 ———. Report of the acting Governor of Wyoming Territory made to the Secretary of the Interior for the year 1887. Washington, Government printing office, 1887. Wrappers. Scarce.

63 p.   tables.   23 cm.

2623 ———. Report of the acting Governor of Wyoming Territory made to the Secretary of the Interior for the year 1888. Washington, Government printing office, 1888. Wrappers. Scarce.

32 p.   tables.   23 cm.

2624 ———. Report of the acting Governor of Wyoming Territory made to the Secretary of the Interior, 1889. Washington, Government printing office, 1889. Wrappers. Scarce.

151 p.   col. map at end, tables.   23 cm.

2625 ———. Report of the acting Governor of Wyoming Territory made to the Secretary of the Interior for the year 1890. Washington, Government printing office, 1890. Wrappers. Scarce.

19 p.   23 cm.

2626 ———. Report of the secretary and treasurer of the Wyoming Stock Growers' Association for the year ending March 31, 1894. Cheyenne, S. A. Bristol co., printers and binders, [1894]. Wrappers. Rare.

15 [1] p.   fold. financial statement.   13x9 cm.

2627 ———. Report of the secretary and treasurer of the Wyoming Stock Growers' Association for the year ending March 31, 1895. Cheyenne, the S. A. Bristol co., printers and bookbinders, [1895]. Wrappers. Rare.

22 [1] p.   12.5x10 cm.

2628 ———. Resources of Wyoming, 1889. An official publication compiled by the Secretary of the Territory, under authority granted by the Territorial Legislature. Containing descriptive statements and general information relating to the soil, climate, productions, advantages, and development. . . . Cheyenne, Wyoming, the Daily Sun electric print, 1889. Pict. wrappers. Rare.

2 p.l., [5]–77 [1] p.   illus., map.   23 cm.
Map on verso of title page.

2629 ———. Resources and attractions of Wyoming for the home seeker, capitalist, and tourist. Facts on farming, stock raising, mining, lumbering, and other industries, and notes on climate, scenery, game, fish, and health and pleasure resorts. . . . St. Louis, Woodward & Tiernan printing co., 1891. Wrappers. Scarce.

3 p.l., ₍7₎–90 p.   map on verso of front wrapper.   20.2 cm.

2630 ———. The resources and attractions of Wyoming for the home seeker, capitalist, and tourist. Facts on farming, stock raising, mining. . . . St. Louis, Woodward & Tiernan printing co., 1893. Wrappers. Scarce.

3 p.l., ₍7₎–119 ₍1₎ p.   map (verso front wrapper), tables.   20 cm.
1 p. adv. and adv. recto and verso back wrapper.

2631 ———. Resources of Albany County. Laramie, Wyo., 1913. Wrappers. Scarce.

3 p.l., ₍7₎–104 p.   front., plates, ports.   22.7 cm.

2632 ———. Resources of Johnson County, Wyoming, with a sketch of the city of Buffalo. ₍Buffalo, Buffalo Echo print₎, published under the direction of the Citizen's Business Club of Buffalo, 1889. Wrappers. Exceedingly rare.

63 p.   illus., fold. map in front.   14.4x9.5 cm.

2633 ———. Second biennial report of the Live Stock and Sanitary Board of the state of Wyoming. Covering the period October 1, 1934 to October 1, 1936. ₍N.p., 1936₎. Wrappers. (Cover title). OP.

4 p.l., 2–23 p.   tables.   28 cm.

2634 ———. Special report of J. D. Hopkins, territorial veterinarian, to Governor Thomas Moonlight, September 12, 1887. With paper on glanders and farcy, Wyoming Territory. Cheyenne, Northwestern Live Stock Journal publishing co., ₍1887₎. Wrappers. Rare.

25 p.   22.7 cm.

2635 ———. Star Valley and its communities. Material collected and written by University of Wyoming extension class in Education 603, School and Community Relations, in August and September, 1951. Art and map work by Mrs. Beatrice Murray. . . . ₍N.p., c.1951₎. Stiff pict. wrappers.

4 p.l., 2–129 p.   illus., plates, maps.   27.5 cm.
Crudely mimeographed on one side of gray paper.

2636 ———. State of Wyoming. An official publication containing reliable information concerning the resources of the state. Edited and published by Fenimore Chatterton, secretary of state, 1904. Laramie, Wyo., Chaplin, Spafford and Mathison, printers, 1904. Wrappers. Scarce.

3 p.l., ₍7₎–144 p.   front., plates, ports., tables, col. map on back wrapper.   23.4 cm.
Another edition issued in 1908.

2637 ———. State of Wyoming. A book of reliable information published by authority of the Eighth Legislature. Edited and published under the direction of Bryant B. Brooks, governor, 1905. Sheridan, Wyo., Sheridan Post co., printers, 1905. Stiff wrappers. Scarce.

5 p.l., ₁9₁–144 ₁1₁ p. plates, col. map on back wrapper, tables. 22.5 cm.

2638 ———. Territory of Wyoming, its history, soil, climate, resources, etc. . . . Published by authority of the Board of Immigration. Laramie City, Daily Sentinel print, December, 1874. Wrappers. Rare.

3–83 ₁1₁ p. 22.3 cm.

2639 ———. Wyoming, a complete and comprehensive description of the agricultural and mineral resources and stock raising interests. . . . ₁Omaha, Nebraska, 1903₁. Wrappers. Scarce.

2 p.l., ₁7₁–114 p. map on verso back wrapper, tables. 20.7 cm.

Another of those promotional books issued by the Union Pacific Railway Company.

2640 YATES, HAYDIE. 70 miles from a lemon, by Haydie Yates. Illustrated by John O'Hara Cosgrove II. Boston, Houghton Mifflin company, 1947. Pict. cloth. OP.

4 p.l., 234 ₁1₁ p. front. (col.). 21.3 cm.
Half title; illus. end papers (col.); first edition, "1947" under imprint.

2641 YEIGH, FRANK. Through the heart of Canada, by Frank Yeigh. . . . With thirty-eight illustrations. Toronto, Henry Frowde, 1911. Pict. cloth. OP.

4 p.l., 9–319 p. front. (with tissue), plates. 22.7 cm.
Index, p. 313–319.
Half title.

2642 YODER, SANFORD C. Horse trails along the desert. ₁By₁ Sanford C. Yoder. Illustrated by Ezra Hershberger. Scottdale, Pennsylvania, Herald press, ₁1954₁. Cloth.

vii, 181 ₁1₁ p. front., illus. 20 cm.
Half title; headpieces.

2643 YOKLEY, ANN. Grass and water, by Ann Yokley. Pierre, South Dakota, State publishing company, first edition, ₁1955₁. Cloth.

7 p.l., 280 ₁42₁ p. plates, ports. 23.6 cm.
Index, p. 275–280.
42 blank pages at end for "memorandum."

2644 YOUATT, W., and W. C. L. MARTIN. Cattle, by W. Youatt and W. C. L. Martin, being a treatise on their breeds, management, and diseases, comprising a full history of the various races . . . the whole forming a complete guide . . . with 100 illustrations. Edited by A. Stevens. New York, C. M. Saxton, Agricultural book publishers, 1851. Cloth. Rare.

viii, 469 p. front., illus. 19.5 cm.
Index, p. ₍461₎–469.
10 p. adv. at end.

2645 YOUNG, ERNEST. West of the Rockies, by Ernest Young. London, Edward Stanford, limited, 1949. Cloth.

xi, 235 ₍1₎ p. front., plates, maps, plan. 21.8 cm.
Appendix, p. 225–229; index, p. 230–₍236₎.
Half title; pub. device.

2646 YOUNG, LEIGH, ET AL. Our country: West. Boston, Mass., Perry Mason & company, 1897. Pict. cloth. Scarce.

2 p.l., ₍3₎–256 ₍4₎ p. front., illus., plates. 20.8 cm.

2647 YOUNGBLOOD, B. and A. B. COX. Division of farm and ranch economics. An economic study of a typical ranching area on the Edwards Plateau of Texas. By B. Youngblood and A. B. Cox. College Station, Texas, July, 1922. Wrappers. OP.

11 p.l., 23–437 p. plates, maps, diagrs., tables. 23 cm.
Bibliography, p. 426–437.
Bulletin No. 297.

2648 ZAHM, REV. J. A. The great Southwest, its attractions, resources, and people. A lecture by Rev. J. A. Zahm. . . . Delivered before the students of Notre Dame University, May 25, 1883. Notre Dame, Indiana, University press, 1883. Pict. wrappers. Rare.

₍3₎–39 p. illus., plates. 23.4 cm.
Vignette.

2649 ZORNOW, WILLIAM FRANK. Kansas. A history of the Jayhawk State, by William Frank Zornow. Norman, University of Oklahoma press, ₍1957₎. Cloth.

xii p., 1 l., 3–417 p. illus., plates, ports., maps. 24.2 cm.
Bibliography, p. 379–400; index, p. 401–417.
Half title; device; "First edition" on copyright p.

2650 [ZULICK, GOV. C. MEYER]. Governor's message to the Fourteenth Legislative Assembly of Arizona, 1887. Prescott, Arizona, Courier print, 1887. Wrappers. (Cover title). Rare.

30 p. 21.7 cm.

2651 ———. Report of the Governor of Arizona to the Secretary of the Interior, 1888. Washington, Government printing office, 1888. Wrappers. Rare.

3–17 p. 23 cm.

Index

(All index numbers refer to items, not to pages. Names of authors are arranged alphabetically in the text and are not repeated in the index.)

THE RAMPAGING HERD

BY RAMON F. ADAMS

HAS BEEN COMPOSED ON THE

LINOTYPE IN SEVERAL SIZES OF GRANJON.

THE PAPER IS ANTIQUE WOVE.

THE UNIVERSITY OF OKLAHOMA PRESS
NORMAN